The Palgrave Handbook of Macrophenomenology and Social Theory

Carlos Belvedere • Alexis Gros
Editors

The Palgrave Handbook of Macrophenomenology and Social Theory

palgrave
macmillan

Editors
Carlos Belvedere
Instituto de Investigaciones
Gino Germani
CONICET – Universidad de
Buenos Aires
Buenos Aires, Argentina

Alexis Gros
Institut für Soziologie
Friedrich Schiller University Jena
Jena, Germany

CONICET – Universidad de
Buenos Aires
Buenos Aires, Argentina

ISBN 978-3-031-34711-5   ISBN 978-3-031-34712-2   (eBook)
https://doi.org/10.1007/978-3-031-34712-2

CONTENTS

Notes on Contributors

Michael D. Barber (Yale, 1985), Professor of Philosophy at Saint Louis University, is the author of seven books, including *The Participating Citizen: A Biography of Alfred Schutz* (2004), and over a hundred articles on the phenomenology of the social world. He has held office in many different phenomenological organizations.

Carlos Belvedere Principal Researcher at the National Council for Technical and Scientific Research of Argentina (CONICET). Associate Professor of Sociology at the Universidad de Buenos Aires. Associate Professor and former Chair of the Department of Philosophy at Instituto de Ciencias, Universidad Nacional de General Sarmiento.

George Bondor is a professor at the "Alexandru Ioan Cuza" University of Iasi, Romania. He is the author of *The Dance of the Masks: Nietzsche and the Philosophy of Interpretation* (2008, 2nd edition 2020) and *Metaphysical Files: Hermeneutical Reconstruction and Critical History* (2013). He is a fellow of the Alexander von Humboldt Foundation.

Evandro Camara Professor of Sociology at the Emporia State University, the US.

Maximiliano Cladakis Researcher at the National Council for Technical and Scientific Research of Argentina (CONICET).

Javier Cristiano Researcher at the National Council for Technical and Scientific Research of Argentina (CONICET).

Jochen Dreher Executive Director of the Social Science Archive Konstanz, University of Konstanz, Germany.

Thomas S. Eberle Emeritus Professor of Sociology at the University of St. Gallen, Switzerland.

Alexis Gros Researcher at the Friedrich Schiller University Jena, Germany, and the National Council for Technical and Scientific Research of Argentina (CONICET). Lecturer at the University of Buenos Aires and the Friedrich Schiller University Jena.

Mercedes Krause holds a PhD in Social Sciences from the University of Buenos Aires (UBA), Argentina. She is a researcher at Instituto de Investigaciones Gino Germani (IIGG-UBA) and at Centro de Estudios de Estado y Sociedad (CEDES). She is also Assistant Professor of Research Methods. Her areas of interest include social phenomenology, class analysis, intersectionality and health inequalities.

Daniela López Associate Professor of Sociology at the National University of General Sarmiento and Researcher of Sociology at the National Council for Technical and Scientific Research of Argentina.

Esteban Marín-Ávila Professor of Philosophy at the Universidad Michoacana de San Nicolás de Hidalgo, Mexico.

Rosana Déborah Motta Assistant Professor of Sociology at the Universidad de Buenos Aires, Argentina.

Charlotte Nell Lecturer in Sociology at the University of Jena, Germany.

Ossi I. Ollinaho Lecturer and Postdoctoral Researcher of Sociology at the University of Helsinki, Finland.

Graciela Ralón Associate Professor of Philosophy at the Universidad Nacional de San Martín (UNSAM), Argentina.

Hartmut Rosa Professor of Sociology at the University of Jena and Director of the Max Weber Centre for Advanced Cultural and Social Studies at the University of Erfurt, Germany.

Nicolai Ruh In his dissertation project at the "Center of Excellence: Cultural Foundations of Social Inegration", Nicolai Ruh examined the perspective of a politicized expert culture on the invisible ontological foundations of a digitalized life-world. He is a long-term fellow at the Social Science Archive Konstanz. Currently he is working as a research associate at the Lucerne School of Computer Science and Information Technology.

Roberto Walton Emeritus Professor of Philosophy at the Universidad de Buenos Aires, Argentina.

Jerry Williams Professor of Sociology at the Stephen F. Austin State University, the US.

Chung-Chi YU Professor of Philosophy at the National Sun Yat-sen University, Taiwan.

Introduction

Carlos Belvedere and Alexis Gros

Perhaps the title of this Handbook may seem a little odd to the reader. Not only because the notion of "macrophenomenology" is far from being an established concept but also because it appears to contradict the way in which the phenomenological paradigm is commonly regarded in philosophy and the social sciences.

To our best knowledge, until the publication of the present book, the word "macrophenomenology" was never systematically used. However, the practice of macrophenomenology has been well-established for some time. We just needed to coin a new term for this long-held investigative practice. For this reason, it was not difficult to find a wide range of studies in this field conducted by well-respected scholars, who, by the way, were sympathetic to the idea of this Handbook and kindly agreed to contribute.

Nonetheless, at first sight the combination of the prefix "macro-" with the term phenomenology seems to be as an impossible amalgam as that of water

C. Belvedere
Instituto de Investigaciones Gino Germani, CONICET – Universidad de Buenos Aires, Buenos Aires, Argentina

Universidad Nacional de General Sarmiento, Los Polvorines, Argentina
e-mail: cbelvedere@campus.ungs.edu.ar

A. Gros (✉)
Friedrich Schiller University Jena, Jena, Germany

Universidad de Buenos Aires, Buenos Aires, Argentina

CONICET, Buenos Aires, Argentina
e-mail: alexis.gros@uni-jena.de

© The Author(s), under exclusive license to Springer Nature Switzerland AG 2023
C. Belvedere, A. Gros (eds.), *The Palgrave Handbook of Macrophenomenology and Social Theory*,
https://doi.org/10.1007/978-3-031-34712-2_1

and oil, given that the method and tradition founded by Edmund Husserl are traditionally associated with the "microscopic" analysis of lived experience (see, e.g., Loch, 2019, p. 400). Perhaps it is for this reason that there is currently a relatively established "discipline" called "micro-phenomenology," dedicated to the infinitesimal study of experiential life through qualitative interviews (see Petitmengin, 2021; Microphenomenology, 2023), whereas the idea of a "macrophenomenology" has not yet been utilized or developed in any systematic way.

Things get even more difficult in the research field where this Handbook aims to situate itself, namely, social theory.[1] For it is widely believed that the phenomenological perspective in social sciences, so-called social phenomenology (see Waldenfels, 1992; Belvedere, 2011) or phenomenological sociology (see Eberle, 2021; Belvedere, 2022), belongs to the "microtraditions" of social-theoretical thinking (see, e.g., Benzecry & Winchester, 2017, p. 43). Along with paradigms such as symbolic interactionism, rational action theory, or ethnomethodology, the phenomenological theory of the life-world, developed by Alfred Schutz, Thomas Luckmann, and others, tends to be categorized as a "micro social theory" (Roberts, 2019, pp. 80–86; see Schützeichel, 2020, p. 228), positioned at the antipodes of "macro-sociological" schools like structural-functionalism, systems theory, or Marxism in its different variants (Scott, 2014, p. 622; Münch & Smelser, 1987, pp. 367–368).

As is well known, since the 1980s many theoretical attempts have been made to bridge the micro-macro polarization (Manzo, 2015, p. 419).[2] Unfortunately, many of these attempts were based on the subjectivism-objectivism divide. In this light, phenomenology was seen as a one-sided subjectivist approach (see, e.g., Bourdieu, 1989, p. 15). This is neither totally false nor entirely true. Phenomenology indisputably stands for the subjective point of view. However, social theory has often confused this emphasis on subjective experience with so-called subjectivism. True, the sociologist must always remember that every social phenomenon starts with, and must be retrieved to, the subjectivity of the actor(s) whose product it is, but this does not mean that the social world consists only of subjective experiences of individuals. There exists—and this book provides eloquent illustrations of that—an objective dimension of social experience, consisting partly in anonymous types to which we cannot ascribe any subjective dimension at all, being this objectivity its distinctive feature.

Returning to the micro-macro divide, a glance at the most widely read sociology and social theory handbooks today (e.g., Giddens & Sutton, 2021; Ritzer & Smart, 2003, pp. 339–353), and at the current curricula of social

---

[1] We use here the term "social theory" in the wide and interdisciplinary sense classically given to it by Giddens (1982, p. 5).

[2] These include, among others, Alexander et al.'s (1987) effort to establish a "micro-macro link," Giddens's (1984) structuration theory, Bourdieu's (1989) practice theory, Habermas's (1981) communicative action theory, and Archer's (1995) realist social theory.

sciences programs worldwide,[3]shows that this antinomy is more alive than ever, continuing to influence how social theories are perceived, classified, and used. The present Handbook aims to challenge the place traditionally assigned to phenomenology within the micro-macro polarization in the social sciences by showing its vast potential to address issues usually associated with macrosociology.

To fully comprehend what this entails, it is crucial to clarify the precise meaning of the distinction between micro and macrosociological approaches. As the terms suggest, this distinction essentially refers to the spatiotemporal "size" or "scope" of the units of social-scientific analysis. While macrotraditions study "big" social phenomena like large-scale organizations or institutions, nation states, or whole societies, microtraditions deal with "small" ones such as everyday experiences, (inter-)actions, or conversations (see Giddens & Sutton, 2021, p. 53; Maiwald & Sürig, 2018, p. 3; Boatcă, 2007, p. 363). As Randall Collins (1981, p. 984) puts it in a now-classical 1981 paper, if microsociology "is the detailed analysis of what people do, say, and think in the actual flow of momentary experience," macrosociology focuses on "the analysis of large-scale and long-term social processes, often treated as self-subsistent entities such as 'state,' 'organization,' 'class,' 'economy,' 'culture' and 'society'."[4]

Against this background, phenomenology has been generally seen as a paradigm that provides thorough accounts of small-scale social phenomena but has not much to say about large-scale ones. The argument goes that phenomenological analysis can help us understand everyday experiences, actions, or face-to-face interactions, but when it comes to analyzing wide-reaching social institutions, processes, or structures, we would be better off resorting to perspectives such as Marxism, systems theory, (post-)structuralism, or Critical Theory. This is precisely the assumption our Handbook comes to contest.

As the texts gathered in this volume amply demonstrate, social phenomenology, especially but not only in the Schutzian tradition, makes vital and unique contributions to the theoretical analysis of macro-social phenomena. The authors assembled in this volume address a variety of subjects, starting with the fundamental concepts of macrophenomenology and the study of collective entities. They also deal with crucial issues for empirical and theoretical social research, such as social organizations and institutions, and the large

---

[3] Both in universities of the Global South and North, it is still a common practice to have separate chairs for micro and macrosociology at sociology and social sciences departments.

[4] The distinction between micro and macrosociology becomes established from the 1970s onward (Maiwald & Sürig, 2018, p. 2). Although it is used worldwide, it originated and has the most significant impact in the U.S., while in Europe the distinction between action and structure appears to be more prevalent (Archer, 1995, p. 7). The idea of a "meso" level, mediating between the "micro" and the "macro," is also introduced in some cases (see Maiwald & Sürig, 2018, p. 4; Weymann, 2020). However, there is no such thing as a "mesosociology" as an established research field or sociological subdiscipline. Importantly, the distinction between the micro and the macro levels is never sharp and absolute but rather relative to the viewpoint (see Collins, 1981, p. 984). For an in-depth treatment of the micro-macro divide in social theory, see Greve et al. (2008) and Alexander et al. (1987).

dimensions of politics, culture, history, economy, class structure, and the state. Likewise, contemporary topics such as the current state of public opinion and climate change, the datafication of the life-world, and the depragmatization of common-sense are considered.

More specifically, the contributed papers to this volume address the following topics: history (Chaps. 12, 13, and 14), the state (Chaps. 2 and 12), culture and interculturality (Chaps. 10 and 11), social classes (Chaps. 2 and 20), institutions (Chaps. 2, 8, and 9), organizations (Chap. 7), public opinion (Chap. 6), collective agency (Chaps. 15, 16, and 17), democracy (Chap. 4), power structures (Chap. 5), digitalization processes (Chaps. 18 and 19), sociomaterial structures (Chap. 21), and the workings of modern societies (Chaps. 2 and 3). The Handbook attempts to show that phenomenological analysis provides something that other social-theoretical perspectives cannot: an exhaustive account of the inextricable link between these large-scale phenomena and (inter)subjective experience, including the ways in which they are lived, constituted, encountered, and transformed within the everyday life-world.

It is true that phenomenology shows a certain affinity toward microsociological approaches, as it seeks to offer a "reflective analysis" (see Embree, 2011) of the morphological features of (inter)subjective lived experience. However, contrary to what the mainstream of social theory suggests (see, e.g., Bourdieu, 1989, p. 15; Reckwitz in Reckwitz & Rosa, 2021, p. 288), phenomenological analysis was never associated with an "extremist" microsociological position (see Manzo, 2015, p. 415). Even though phenomenologists have always focused on the description of the life-world, they have never neglected the existence and powers of macro-social structures and processes, such as institutional arrangements, states, technological apparatuses, long-term historical developments, or economic systems. And they have consistently called attention to the inescapable embeddedness of everyday experience within these large-scale conditions, as well as on the significant impacts of the latter on the former.

Importantly, this holds true both for phenomenological philosophers (see, e.g., Husserl, 1973, pp. 106–107; Heidegger, 2000; Merleau-Ponty, 1945, pp. 416–417; Henry, 2012) and phenomenological social theorists (see, for instance, Schutz, 1964, p. 129; Luckmann, 1980, p. 206; Srubar, 2007, pp. 317–355; Knoblauch, 2016, pp. 381–399). After all, when it comes to structure, size is not important. As Richard Hilbert keenly noted a couple of decades ago, ethnomethodology—and, we would like to say, phenomenological sociology at large—is indifferent to the size of structures; its aim "is not to legitimize one level of structure at the expense of the others, but rather to examine social practices whereby structure is made to happen, made to appear" (Hilbert, 1990, p. 795).

To put it phenomenologically, macrosociological issues have always been present in phenomenologists' "field of consciousness," but they tended to remain in the "horizon" or "margin" of attention (see Gurwitsch, 2012). Much of the effort of the contributions contained in the present Handbook is related to thematizing and explicating these marginal "macrophenomenological" insights, always implicitly present in the tradition, and to further developing them by means of a dialogue with other classical and contemporary perspectives in social theory.

Further, and this is crucial, our Handbook aims to rehabilitate the genuinely *sociological* or *social-theoretical* way of "doing phenomenology" founded by Schutz and his disciples, even though it also addresses macrophenomenological contributions from other classical and contemporary phenomenologists such as Edmund Husserl, Maurice Merleau-Ponty, and Bernhard Waldenfels. Nowadays, much of the phenomenological research on issues related to sociality and social reality is conducted by philosophers within the thriving field of what might be called "non-sociological" social phenomenology. There are many valuable phenomenological investigations today on topics such as empathy, intersubjectivity, social cognition, collective intentionality, we-ness, community, and the political, among many other (social) things (e.g., Moran & Szanto, 2015; Salice & Schmid, 2016; Bedorf & Hermann, 2020; Zahavi, 2021). What is missing, however, is a truly sociological-phenomenological analysis of macro-social structures and processes, which can only be done from a perspective informed by current theoretical and empirical research in the social sciences. Despite their interdisciplinary openness, "non-sociological" social phenomenologists have, at most, superficial contact with social-scientific work.

This is problematic because macrophenomenology, as we see it, is a subdiscipline of phenomenological sociology, a science dealing with the constitution of the natural attitude of groups (Belvedere, 2022). In this sense, when its core issues are addressed from a non-sociological lens, its intrinsic meaning may be overlooked. The research object of macrophenomenological research is the macro strata of objective, anonymous, big-scale social phenomena, which play a key role in the constitution and articulation of large social groups.

Fortunately, novel developments in the field of social theory, such as Hartmut Rosa's "phenomenological critical theory of society" (Gros, 2019; see Rosa, 2016) and Martin Endreß and Gesa Lindemann's (2021) effort to establish a link between "phenomenologies and theories of society," suggest that it is indeed possible to think macrosociological phenomena from a sociological-phenomenological perspective. Moreover, the recent attempts to (re-)combine Marxism with phenomenology also point in a similar direction, albeit from a philosophical standpoint (see Angus, 2021; Smyth & Westerman, 2021). Although it proceeds from a perspective primarily influenced by Schutzian phenomenology, our Handbook takes inspiration from these new developments.

From its earliest up to these latest developments, macrophenomenology has proved itself a reality. As the things themselves do, it first started by existing. Only with the work on and the publication of this Handbook did it come to be thought of as a collective endeavor. This is why the studies herein collected display a family resemblance. Long before the term was coined, the doing of macrophenomenology ran in the family. However, it is not its fully fledged idea but its practice that has come to exist. We may say, then, that macrophenomenology is, in its present state, an "intellectual movement," just as the wider field of phenomenological sociology was at the beginning, as described by Hisashi Nasu (2012). Let us hope it ends up proving itself a paradigm in its full right, as it happened so many years ago with the latter (Psathas, 1973). We are honored to be a part of such a promising movement and thank every author for their trust and generosity. Hopefully, the years to come will keep us working together for the sake of macrophenomenology.

References

Alexander, J. C., et al. (Eds.). (1987). *The micro-macro link*. University of California Press.

Angus, I. (2021). *Groundwork of phenomenological marxism: Crisis, body, world*. Lexington.

Archer, M. (1995). *Realist social theory. The morphogenetic approach*. Cambridge University Press.

Bedorf, T., & Hermann, S. (2020). *Political phenomenology. Experience, ontology, episteme*. Routledge.

Belvedere, C. (2011). *Problemas de fenomenología social*. Prometeo.

Belvedere, C. (2022). *A treatise in phenomenological sociology: Object, method, findings, and applications*. Lexington.

Benzecry, C., & Winchester, D. (2017). Varieties of microsociology. In C. Benzecry et al. (Eds.), *Social theory now* (pp. 42–75). University of Chicago Press.

Boatcă, M. (2007). Macrosociology. In G. Ritzer (Ed.), *Blackwell encyclopedia of sociology* (pp. 362–363). Blackwell.

Bourdieu, P. (1989). Social space and symbolic power. *Sociological Theory, 7*(1), 14–25.

Collins, R. (1981). On the microfoundations of macrosociology. *American Journal of Sociology, 86*(5), 984–1014.

Eberle, T. (2021). Spielarten phänomenologischer Soziologie. In J. Dreher (Ed.), *Mathesis universalis—Die aktuelle Relevanz der "Strukturen der Lebenswelt"* (pp. 15–49). Springer.

Embree, L. (2011). *Reflective analysis. A first introduction into phenomenology*. Zeta Books.

Endreß, M., & Lindemann, G. (2021). Phänomenologien und Gesellschaftstheorien, Call for Papers der Interdisziplinären Arbeitskreis Phänomenologie und Soziologie, Sommertagung der DGS-Sektion Soziologische Theorien. https://soziologie.de/fileadmin/sektionen/iaps/6._Tagung_des_IAPS_-_Gesellschaftstheorien__Delmenhorst_2022_.pdf

Giddens, A. (1982). *Profiles and critiques in social theory*. The Macmillan Press.

Giddens, A. (1984). *The constitution of society: Outline of the theory of structuration*. University of California Press.

Giddens, A., & Sutton, P. W. (2021). *Sociology*. Polity.

Greve, J., et al. (Eds.). (2008). *Das Mikro-Makro-Modell der soziologischen Erklärung: Zur Ontologie, Methodologie und Metatheorie eines Forschungsprogramms*. Springer.

Gros, A. (2019). Towards a phenomenological critical theory: Hartmut Rosa's sociology of the relationship to the world. *Revista Científica Foz, 3*(1), 9–46.

Gurwitsch, A. (2012). *The Collected Works of Aron Gurwitsch (1901–1973): Volume III: The Field of Consciousness: Theme, Thematic Field, and Margin.* New York: Springer.

Habermas, J. (1981). *Theorie des kommunikativen Handelns, Bd. 2.* Suhrkamp.

Heidegger, M. (2000). Die Frage nach der Technik. In M. Heidegger (Ed.), *Gesamtausgabe, Bd. 7, Vorträge und Aufsätze* (pp. 1–53). Vittorio Klostermann.

Henry, M. (2012). *Barbarism.* London: Continuum.

Hilbert, R. A. (1990). Ethnomethodology and the micro-macro order. *American Sociological Review, 55*(6), 794–808.

Husserl, E. (1973). *Zur Phänomenologie der Intersubjektivität. Erster Teil: 1905–1920.* Martinus Nijhoff.

Knoblauch, H. (2016). *Die kommunikative Konstruktion der Wirklichkeit.* Springer.

Loch, W. (2019). Die allgemeine Pädagogik in phänomenologischer Hinsicht (1998). In M. Brinkmann (Ed.), *Phänomenologische Erziehungswissenschaft von ihren Anfängen bis heute* (pp. 393–423). Springer.

Luckmann, T. (1980). *Lebenswelt und Gesellschaft: Grundstrukturen und geschichtliche Wandlungen.* Schöningh.

Maiwald, K. O., & Sürig, I. (2018). *Mikrosoziologie.* Springer.

Manzo, G. (2015). Macrosociology-Microsociology. In J. D. Wright (Ed.), *International encyclopedia of the social & behavioral sciences, Vol. 14* (pp. 414–421). Elsevier.

Merleau-Ponty, M. (1945). *Phénoménologie de la perception.* Gallimard.

Microphenomenology. (2023, March 17). What is micro-phenomenology? https://www.microphenomenology.com/home

Moran, D., & Szanto, T. (2015). *Phenomenology of sociality: Discovering the 'we'.* Routledge.

Münch, R., & Smelser, N. (1987). Conclusion: Relating the micro and the macro. In J. Alexander et al. (Eds.), *The micro-macro link* (pp. 356–389). University of California Press.

Nasu, H. (2012). Phenomenological sociology in the United States: The developmental process of an intellectual movement. In H. Nasu & F. C. Waksler (Eds.), *Interaction and everyday life. Phenomenological and ethnomethodological essays in honor of George Psathas* (pp. 3–21). Lexington.

Petitmengin, C. (2021). On the veiling and unveiling of experience: A comparison between the micro-phenomenological method and the practice of meditation. *Journal of Phenomenological Psychology, 52,* 36–77.

Psathas, G. (1973). Introduction. In G. Psathas (Ed.), *Phenomenological sociology: Issues and applications* (pp. 1–21). Wiley.

Reckwitz, A., & Rosa, H. (2021). *Spätmoderne in der Krise. Was leistet die Gesellschaftstheorie?* Suhrkamp.

Ritzer, G., & Smart, B. (Eds.). (2003). *Handbook of social theory.* Sage.

Roberts, B. (2019). *Micro social theory.* Bloomsbury.

Rosa, H. (2016). *Resonanz: Eine Soziologie der Weltbeziehung.* Suhrkamp.

Salice, A., & Schmid, H. B. (Eds.). (2016). *The phenomenological approach to social reality: History, concepts, problems.* Springer.

Schutz, A. (1964). *Collected papers II: Studies in social theory.* Martinus Nijhoff.

Schützeichel, R. (2020). Microsociology. In B. Hollstein et al. (Eds.), *Soziologie—Sociology in the German-speaking world* (pp. 227–244). De Gruyter.

Scott, J. (2014). *Oxford dictionary of sociology.* Oxford University Press.

Smyth, B., & Westerman, R. (Eds.). (2021). *Marxism and phenomenology: The dialectical horizons of critique.* Lexington.

Srubar, I. (2007). *Phänomenologie und soziologische Theorie*. UVK.
Waldenfels, B. (1992). *Einführung in die Phänomenologie*. UTB.
Weymann A. (2020). Interaktion, Institution und Gesellschaft. In H. Joas & S. Mau, *Lehrbuch der Soziologie* (pp. 107–135). Frankfurt am Main: Campus.
Zahavi, D. (2021). We in me or me in we? Collective intentionality and selfhood. *Journal of Social Ontology, 7*(1), 1–20.

PART I

General Considerations on Macrophenomenology

Macro Strata of the Social World: Institutions, Social Classes, and the State

Carlos Belvedere

1 THE OBLIVION OF MACRO PHENOMENOLOGY IN CONTEMPORARY SOCIAL THEORY

Phenomenology is deemed to be a microsociological approach focused on face-to-face relationships, everyday life, and subjective processes. In this view, the current literature neglects the important insights that can be found in the phenomenological tradition, in line with prominent thinkers such as Pierre Bourdieu (1980, 1989) and Anthony Giddens (1983, 1984):

> Broadly speaking, Bourdieu and Giddens consider Schutzian phenomenology as a *subjectivist* social theory. That is, it is a one-sided social-theoretical approach that merely focuses on the voluntary, everyday (inter)subjective (inter)actions taking place at the microsociological level, thereby systematically neglecting the constraining, objective, and macro aspects of social reality. (Belvedere & Gros, 2019, p. 45)

I will not simply contest this idea. Rather, I will turn this argument against its champions by claiming that it is not phenomenological sociologists but contemporary social theorists who are one-sided. It is not that phenomenology

C. Belvedere (✉)
Instituto de Investigaciones Gino Germani, CONICET – Universidad de Buenos Aires, Buenos Aires, Argentina

Universidad Nacional de General Sarmiento, Los Polvorines, Argentina
e-mail: cbelvedere@campus.ungs.edu.ar

© The Author(s), under exclusive license to Springer Nature Switzerland AG 2023
C. Belvedere, A. Gros (eds.), *The Palgrave Handbook of Macrophenomenology and Social Theory*,
https://doi.org/10.1007/978-3-031-34712-2_2

11

neglects the objective macro strata of the social world but that the abovemen-
tioned authors fail to grasp the phenomenological view on these issues. With
that aim, I will address Schutz's notion of collective entities since the subject
matters of our chapter are considered by him as entities of that kind.

2   COLLECTIVE ENTITIES AS ANONYMOUS IDEAL TYPES

Collective entities such as the state and social classes belong to the "more
remote and anonymous" (Schutz, 1962, p. 180) strata of our experience of
others. They are some of the most anonymous inhabitants of the social world,
which is stratified in gradients going from familiarity to anonymity.

The concept of anonymity refers to "the *relative scope* of the typifying
scheme," which is:

> determined by the relative completeness and generality of that segment of the
> stock of knowledge which guided my selection of the trait to be typified as an
> invariant attribute within the typifying scheme. If the scheme is derived from
> previous experiences of a particular fellow-man, the typification is relatively con-
> crete; if it is derived from personal ideal types available in my stock of general
> knowledge concerning social reality, it is relatively anonymous. (Schutz,
> 1976, p. 49)

In other words, the generality of the typifying scheme is in opposition to its
concreteness (Schutz, 1962, p. 195). Schutz expresses this in the form of a rule
of proportionality: "We may say that *the degree of concreteness of the typifying
scheme* is *inversely proportionate to the level of generality of those experiences sedimented in the stock of knowledge from which the scheme* is *derived*" (Schutz,
1976, p. 49; Schutz's emphasis). Another way to put it is saying that "[t]he
relative degree of concreteness or anonymity of an ideal type" is related to:

> the facility with which a They-relation—of which a given type is a constituent—
> can be transformed into a We-relation. The likelier I am to apprehend directly the
> ideal-typical traits of 'someone' as elements of the ongoing conscious life of a
> concrete individual, the less anonymous are these traits. (Schutz, 1976, p. 49)

Schutz considers that this rule of proportionality is based on

> the fact that, as the interpreter falls back on lower- and lower-level ideal types, he
> must take more and more for granted. He can hardly examine all these more
> general ideal types in detail but must take them in at a glance, being content with
> a vague picture. The more dependent he is on such ready-made types in the
> construction of his own ideal type, the vaguer will be his account of the latter.
> (Schutz, 1967, p. 195)

Accordingly, "each typification involves other typifications. The more substrata of typifying schemes are involved in a given ideal type, the more

anonymous it is, and the larger is the region of things simply taken for granted in the application of the ideal type" (Schutz, 1976, p. 49).

This rule applies, for instance, to the world of contemporaries: the farther out we get into it, "the more anonymous its inhabitants become, starting with the innermost region, where they can almost be seen, and ending with the region where they are by definition forever inaccessible to experience" (Schutz, 1962, p. 181). Relatively concrete ideal types, such as the United States Senate, presuppose a quite limited number of other ideal types, while ideal types such as the state or the working class are not "real persons known in direct social experience" but absolutely anonymous types (Schutz, 1962, pp. 198–199).

Consequently, "[a]ny attribution of behavior we make to the type permits no inference whatever as to a corresponding subjective meaning-context in the mind of a contemporary actor" (Schutz, 1962, p. 199). Indeed, "whereas the conscious experiences of typical individuals are quite conceivable, the conscious experiences of a collective are not" because they lack "this subjective meaning-context as something that is even conceivable" (Schutz, 1962, pp. 199–200).

As social constructs, their analysis is one of the most important tasks of sociology. A sociological theory of construct formation "will have as its primary task the description of the stratification of social collectivities in terms of their relative anonymity or concreteness" (Schutz, 1962, p. 200). In Schutz's view, it is an unfulfilled task.

The analysis of the structures of ideal typifications which form the substrata of social collectivities is an important task which sociology still has to accomplish. It will be necessary to describe the stratification of social collectivities in terms of relative anonymity and, according to their origin, in direct or indirect experiences of social reality. (Schutz, 1976, p. 51)

This discipline addresses issues such as (a) "whether a social collectivity is essentially based on a direct or an indirect social relationship, or possibly on a relationship of both kinds"; (b) in what sense and to what extent "a subjective meaning-context can be ascribed to a social collectivity"; and (c) "whether and to what extent the concept of social collectivity can serve as a scheme of interpretation for the actions of contemporaries, since it is itself a function of certain objective standards common to a certain group [...] and they may be not only taken for granted but obeyed" (Schutz, 1962, p. 200).

Even though Schutz admits that the obeyance of a social order "is one legitimate sense in which one can speak of the subjective meaning of a social collectivity" (Schutz, 1962, p. 200), with regard to social constructs (let aside the individuals' attitudes toward them):

there corresponds no subjective meaning-context in the mind of a real individual whom we could meet face to face. Rather, corresponding to the objective meaning-context of the culture object we always find an abstract and anonymous personal ideal type of its producer toward which we characteristically assume a They-orientation. (Schutz, 1962, p. 201)

From this perspective, macro phenomena are the result of objectifying processes of abstraction, depersonalization, and generalization of meaning structures. These processes start with the institutionalization of social behavior.

3   SOCIAL INSTITUTIONS AS REIFIED PATTERNS OF SOCIAL BEHAVIOR

According to Schutz, social institutions are "Pragmatic (praxeological) techniques of mastering life in forms of organization of sub- and super-ordination, of cooperation and conflict" (Schutz and Luckmann, 1989, p. 202). It is interesting to note that, in this view, institutions involve not only social integration but also social conflict.

The phenomenology of social institutions has been elaborated in the Schutzian tradition by Berger and Luckmann (1967), Berger and Pullberg (1965), and Thomason (1982). Synthesizing some of their utmost contributions, we may say that institutions are a kind of cultural pattern of group life, consisting of typifications and relevances that define objective meanings that are constructs of common-sense thinking that can only be apprehended by symbols and are a part of the social world naively accepted in the natural attitude (Belvedere & Gros, 2019, pp. 70–71).

Even if they are intersubjectively produced, once they exist, they tend to "harden" and solidify, being experienced by the individual as objective, as "possessing a reality of their own, as if they were rock–solid, external and unalterable things" (Belvedere & Gros, 2019, p. 71). In other words, social institutions are reifications.

As Thomason (1982) notes, "reification is a cognitive process whereby experience comes to acquire an inappropriate ontological fixedness. [...] To reify something means to ignore that experienced objectivities are constituted and therefore dependent upon subjective processes" (Belvedere & Gros, 2019, p. 71). However, there are good reasons for this ignorance, since—as seen in the previous section—once types of behavior acquire a certain degree of objectivity, they become anonymous and, consequently, no subjective meaning context can be assigned to them.

4   THE STATE AND SOCIAL CLASSES AS INSTANTIATIONS OF COLLECTIVE ENTITIES

That types of behavior may acquire some objectivity and anonymity "becomes immediately obvious when we try to analyze such culture objects as the state" (Schutz, 1962, p. 195) and—I would add—social classes because they are types of the greatest degree of anonymity consisting of "constructs referring to the world of contemporaries" (Schutz, 1962, p. 198). However, these substrata "are not explicitly grasped in clear and distinct acts of thought," as can be appreciated "if one takes social realities such as the state or the economic system or art and begins to explicate all the substrata of typifications upon which they are based" (Schutz, 1976, p. 49).

Indeed, social collectivities are typifications that cannot be grasped in direct experience: "even if they retain personal character, [they] are highly anonymous since the collectivities cannot ever be experienced directly and by their very nature belong to the transcendent social world of mere contemporaries and predecessors. The large class of such typifications also contains different strata of anonymity" (Schutz, 1976, p. 51). In comparison to typifications of lower level (e.g., the Congress), "which are still *relatively* concrete, since they are based on a limited number of substrata of personal ideal types," larger-scale typifications such as the state and the social classes are "a completely anonymous context" (Schutz, 1976, p. 51).

Let us take a closer look at this by considering the world of contemporaries to which the constructs of the state and of social classes belong. Schutz describes it as structured in different levels of anonymity, "[b]eginning with the transitions from direct experience of fellowmen in face-to-face situations to indirect experience of former fellow-men" as a process of "progressively more anonymous typifications which mediate the experience of transcendent social realities," going "from the relatively concrete characterological personal ideal type and the relatively more anonymous functional type to the typifying schemes for highly anonymous social collectivities, cultural objects, sign systems, and artifacts" (Schutz, 1976, p. 53).

More specifically, the world of contemporaries is structured in eight different regions, starting with that of those whom I can encounter face to face, up to the region of artifacts, which "bear witness to the subjective meaning-context of some unknown person" (Schutz, 1962, p. 181). Of particular interest for our purpose is region six, which Schutz characterizes as the region of "collective entities which are by their very nature anonymous and of which I could never in principle have direct experience, such as 'state' and 'nation' " (Schutz, 1962, p. 181). In this view, the state is "a highly anonymous institution of the contemporary world" (Schutz, 2013, pp. 254–255). It is a concrete cultural formation. As such, it is an object of a higher order essentially founded on communities of humans (Schutz, 2010a, p. 14).

As a social construct, the state is "an abbreviated designation for a highly complex system of interdependent personal ideal types" that the man on the street naively takes for granted and whose "complex structure of typifications" and "objective matrices of meaning which manifest themselves in the anonymous action patterns of functionaries" cannot be ascribed to any personal type, unlike the individual action, that is coordinated with a typical actor. In this case, "no individual consciousness can be construed from which the 'activities' of a social collectivity constitute a *subjective* configuration of meaning" (Schutz, 1976, p. 51). In other words, "there can be no typical 'individual' for whom the objective structure is a subjective meaning configuration" (Schutz, 1976, p. 51).

Likewise, social classes are typifications imposed by the social conditionedness of relevance systems that are socioculturally codetermined by the "social (cultural) structuring of the distribution of knowledge (secret knowledge, shared knowledge, etc.)" based on political and economic organization (among other kinds of organization) (Schutz, 1989, p. 202). Schutz mentions "the priestly class" (Schutz, 2010b, p. 94), "the middle and upper classes" (for instance, when a nation conquers another and annexes it as a territory and the "merchants and colonists become the middle and upper classes") (Schutz, 2010b, p. 95), and "upper" and "lower" classes" (Schutz, 2010b, pp. 96–97). However, his favorite example is "the working class."

Some meaningful differences must be stressed regarding the state. Social classes and social stratification are specifically based on the distribution of wealth and the disposal of leisure time among groups (Schutz, 2010b, p. 92). Consequently, they are not just typifications but groups interrelated to each other, in the first place. Additionally, "social barriers among classes" can be created (Schutz, 2010b, p. 94).

5   How Can Social Collectives Be Dealt With? Some Methodological Issues

The peculiar nature of social collectives also demands a peculiar methodological approach. Because they lack a veritable subjective meaning context, understanding sociology cannot properly address them since it focuses on the subjective interpretation of meanings. That is why it never claimed that "its assertions about the state or other social formations can or should comprehend the full content of these formations" (Schutz, 1996, p. 206).

However, social collectives are, to some extent, relevant for understanding sociology, insofar as "these contents of objective meaning enter into the contents of objective meaning of the actor or actors" (Schutz, 1996, p. 206). In other words, "inasmuch as social actors and social groups take them as a part of their actions and worldviews" (Schutz, 1976, p. 52), and to the extent that the concept of social collectivity serves them as a scheme for interpretation and is subsumed to value judgments "accepted as valid and 'lived by' in a given society or social group" (Schutz, 1976, p. 52), it can be said that social collectives hold a subjective meaning.

The way in which understanding sociology addressed the subjective aspect of social collectives was by dissolving them into subjective concatenations of meaning, with the aim of showing "how social organization (for instance, the state) constitutes itself in and on the basis of these concatenations of subjective meaning" (Schutz, 1996, p. 207). No matter how precious this contribution might be, to the eyes of Schutz it does not suffice. In his opinion, only a constructivist approach would help address abstract collectives such as social classes (for instance, the "proletariat"): "Type <construction> of specifically abstract collectives <reveals that> they cannot be grasped otherwise" (Schutz, 1996, p. 78) because there is only "*[s]ymbolic experience of social collectivities*" (Schutz and Luckmann, 1989, pp. 291–292). In accordance, macro phenomenology should be conceived as a constructivist approach to the highest symbolic strata of our social experience. This leads us to consider what symbols are.

According to Schutz, symbols are "vehicles for the *conception* of objects; it is the conception and not the things that symbols directly 'mean.' [And it is] not the act of conceiving but what is conceived [that] enters into the meaning pattern" (Schutz, 1962, p. 289).

Symbols can be defined as appresentational references of a higher order "in which the appresenting member of the pair is an object, fact, or event within the reality of our daily life, whereas the other appresented member of the pair refers to an idea which transcends our experience of everyday life" (Schutz, 1962, p. 331) that, in turn, is "based on preformed appresentational references, such as marks, indications, signs, or even symbol" (Schutz, 1962, p. 337).

All appresentational references "are characterized by a specific transcendence of the appresented object in relation to the actual 'Here and Now' of the interpreter" (Schutz, 1962, p. 343). Symbolic references, in particular, transcend "the finite province of meaning of everyday life so that only the appresenting member of the related pair pertains to it, whereas the appresented member has its reality in another finite province of meaning" (Schutz, 1962, p. 343). Accordingly, it can be defined "as an appresentational relationship between entities belonging to at least two finite provinces of meaning so that the appresenting symbol is an element of the paramount reality of everyday life" (Schutz, 1962, p. 343).

Therefore, macro phenomenology must deal with symbolic objects pertaining to the highest strata of our social experience by finding marks, indications, and signs in everyday life that refer to ideal objects that transcend its concrete, familiar environment toward a different province of meaning.[1] This means that social collectives such as institutions, social classes, and the state are anchored in, but strictly do not belong to, everyday life. They belong to another finite province of meaning that transcends our ordinary experience, which itself bears a meaning of its own.

6   The Symbolic Nature of Social Collectives

Any social group experiences itself under a system of types, which involves "an existing typification of social relations, of social forms of intercommunication, of social stratification taken for granted by the group, and therefore socially

---

[1] On the relation of everyday life with different transcendent provinces of meaning, see Barber's (2017) excellent book on religion and humor.

approved by it [... that] has to be learned by a process of acculturation" (Schutz, 1962, p. 350).

This kind of system includes "various marks and indications for the position, status, role, and prestige each individual occupies or has within the stratification of the group" (Schutz, 1962, p. 350), with which every member must be familiar:

> In order to find my bearings within the social group, I have to know the different ways of dressing and behaving, the manifold insignia, emblems, tools, etc., which are considered by the group as indicating social status and are therefore socially approved as relevant. They indicate also the typical behavior, actions, and motives which I may expect from a chief, a medicine man, a priest, a hunter, a married woman, a young girl, etc. In a word, I have to learn the typical social roles and the typical expectations of the behavior of the incumbents of such roles, in order to assume the appropriate corresponding role and the appropriate corresponding behavior expected to be approved by the social group. (Schutz, 1962, pp. 350–351)

Additionally, every member must learn the typical, socially derived "knowledge of the appresentational, referential, and interpretive schemes which each of the subgroups takes for granted and applies to its respective appresentational reference" (Schutz, 1962, p. 351).

Social situations of everyday life are usually intertwined with the anonymous dimensions of contemporaries, predecessors, and successors, where "a fellowman is not experienced in his individual uniqueness but in terms of his typical behavior-patterns, typical motives, and typical attitudes" (Schutz, 1962, p. 352).

Accordingly, two different levels of appresentational references can be distinguished in the way we experience the social world in common-sense thinking. On the one hand, "[w]e apprehend *individual* fellow-men and their cogitations as realities within the world of everyday life" (Schutz, 1962, p. 352). On the other hand, we apprehend social collectivities and institutionalized relations as constructs of common-sense thinking that have their reality in the subuniverse of ideal relations, which therefore can be apprehended only symbolically, even if the symbols appresenting them themselves pertain to the paramount reality of everyday life and motivate our actions within it (Schutz, 1962, p. 353).

However, in common-sense thinking, we experience social collectivities as if they were represented by individuals; for example, "To us government is represented by individuals: Congressmen, judges, tax collectors, soldiers, policemen, public servants, perhaps the President or the Queen or the Fuehrer" (Schutz, 1962, p. 353). Notwithstanding, social relationships are not concrete experiences of individuals but abstract types that can only be appresented symbolically. For instance, "the We-relation as such transcends the existence of either consociate within the paramount reality and can be appresented only by symbolization" (Schutz, 1962, p. 353). It is a purely formal relationship that refers face-to-face situations to the symbols by which such relationships are appresented. This can be clearly appreciated in the case of friendship[2]: "My friend is to me and I am to him an element of the reality of everyday life. However, our friendship surpasses our individual situation within the finite province of meaning of the paramount reality" (Schutz, 1962, p. 353).

7   Institutions, Social Classes, and the State as Ideal Relations

Symbols and social institutions are tied together. On the one hand, institutions are stabilized systems of symbolic apprehensions of entities pertaining to the realm of ideal relations. On the other hand, "symbols become more discernible the more the social relationship is stabilized and institutionalized" (Schutz, 1962, p. 354).

In addition, for being socially constructed, symbolic appresentations are the work of a group: they are means "by which the in-group interprets itself," which, in turn, "have their counterpart in the interpretations of the same symbols by the out-group or out-groups" (Schutz, 1962, p. 355). For the same reason, those interpretations will necessarily differ from one group to another because their respective system of relevances "(and the respective apperceptual, appresentational, and referential schemes taken as systems of reference for interpreting the 'order' so created) cannot coincide" (Schutz, 1962, pp. 355–356).

If we follow this line of argument, it is possible to outline the macro strata of the social world as the region of ideal relations that arrange and rule our relationships with others who are not experienced in direct perception (as in face-to-face relationships) but indirectly appresented through indications, signs, and symbols.

Symbolic appresentation not only gives us the concrete, familiar other but also the abstract, anonymous one who does not belong to the finite province of everyday life but to that of ideal relations. It gives us both of them intertwined by the pairing of elements pertaining to the lifeworld with elements pertaining to the realm of idealities. In other words, it opens the lifeworld to the transcendence of ideality.

By means of this kind of transcendence, our everyday life is symbolically structured in such a way that various aspects of our concrete experiences in it are arranged and reshaped in a higher, ideal order. This allows our practices to be rationalized. This happens when marks and indications are socially constructed, interpreted, and sanctioned as paired with ideas about what they mean for any of us and about what they should be like.

In Western modern societies, the symbolic arrangement of collective experience is strongly structured on three bases that make up the ribbing of their

---

[2] On the phenomenology of friendship, see Dreher (2009).

macro strata: institutions, social classes, and the state. These are ways of tran-scending—and therefore of transforming—concrete, personal experiences into abstract, collective ways of being-together.

Within this framework, institutions are the symbolic structuration of human behavior pertaining to the lower range of the macro strata of the social world. They consist of typical patterns of behavior derived, sanctioned, and stocked socially that embody typical social actors, roles, and relationships that any member of an in-group must know and take into account to become a member and have meaningful interactions with other members. In other words, institu-tions are a basic, and a major, aspect of the cultural background of groups.

For being a cultural feature, institutions are symbolic structures. They emerge from individual actors and actions and interpersonal interactions in which typical and nontypical features are distinguished, the former being elab-orated as signs and indications of nonindividual but social behaviors. In this way, a pairing is established by correlating observable, tangible, ordinary ele-ments from everyday life (such as ways of dressing, modes of talking and walk-ing, and the like) with invisible, ideal forms of behavior available to anyone, which are not distinctive to anyone in concrete. These forms of behavior will not tell you much about someone you actually know, in particular, but will tell you a lot about what everyone in the group should be and how they should behave, in general. Those forms of behavior do not belong to anyone but to everyone. They are impersonal, transferable, and reiterable forms that tran-scend individual conduct toward the establishment of impersonal, social man-ners that are strictly ideal and thus collective. Institutions, then, are the first step in the emergence of collective entities.

Social classes, in turn, do not address individuals as typical actors or as incumbents of typical social roles; instead, they address typical actors and typi-fied ways of acting as marks and indications of the social groups to which they allegedly belong. In other words, marks and indications are not taken from individuals but from typical actions, actors, interactions, and relationships.

These typified forms of behavior—that have been symbolically structured previously—are now taken to a higher level of symbolization. We may say that they are symbols of symbols. Of course, lower-level symbols are still pairings including elements taken from the lifeworld (in our case, from individuals and face-to-face interactions). Therefore, Schutz's dictum that symbols are pairings that correlate elements pertaining to the lifeworld with elements pertaining to a different province of meaning is still respected, although they are now related not immediately but mediately. In this way, a chain of pairings is started whose first link correlates elements pertaining to the lifeworld and elements pertain-ing to the subuniverse of ideal relations (such as typical ways of being, of act-ing, of relating) and whose second link correlates ideal entities pertaining to different levels of ideation among them. Thus, social classes are pairings of symbols—that is, pairings of a second order directly correlating two ideal ele-ments and indirectly correlating, through symbolic mediation, elements pertaining to actual, concrete, tangible experiences in the lifeworld with at least two different levels of ideal relations.

Specifically, social classes are a form of ideal relation that gathers a number of similar, typical ways of being, of acting, and of relating that are considered peculiar to a group of people. They immediately group up these typical ways and mediately group up the individuals who embody them. All this requires sophisticated hermeneutic work.

As quoted before, Schutz claims that any group experiences itself under a system of socially approved typifications of social relations, social forms of intercommunication, and social stratification that includes marks and indications for the position, status, role, and prestige each individual occupies within the stratification of the group, with which all its members have to be acquainted. This involves getting to know "the different ways of dressing and behaving, the manifold insignia, emblems, tools, etc., which are considered by the group as indicating social status" (Schutz, 1962, pp. 350–351). In other words, this involves the hermeneutic work of interpreting what clothing, manners, tools, and so on *truly* mean—that is, what they mean *socially*. A dress is not just a dress, talking with an accent is not just talking, and the like. All of these, and many other, ways of acting, of being, of relating are marks and indications of social positions.

In this view, elements pertaining to the lifeworld, which are experienced in actuality, can be referred to elements pertaining to the subuniverse of ideal relations, which are experienced in virtuality, by means of a two-step process of social hermeneutics. First, they are interpreted as typical ways of dressing, talking, and the like. Here, "typical" means peculiar to a kind of person. It constitutes what Schutz calls "a personal type." Then, typical manners can be marked and classified as distinctive (or not) to a particular group. As long as wearing a peculiar outfit (let us say, an overall) can be seen not as a personal choice but as a group outfit (for instance, as working-class clothing), not only a reference to a social group but also the very existence of that group is instituted. A pair of jeans, a hat, a way of walking, anything can be seen as something else: it can be interpreted as a sign or an indication of belonging to a given social group.

However, social classes are not just any group. They are in-groups whose subjective collective meanings[3] are defined in opposition to objective meanings attributed to an outgroup or outgroups. However, this meaning is not just subjective: it is a subjective meaning grounded on material conditions that, at the same time, work as their substratum and as an object in dispute. That is why conflict is the most frequent and typical kind of relation among social classes.

Regarding the state, instead, subjective meaning is out of the question. As seen previously, Schutz claims that the state is a highly anonymous institution of the contemporary world. Therefore, it is a kind of typification that cannot be grasped in direct experience. Unlike individual action, which is coordinated

---

[3] On collective subjects and subjective meanings, see Embree (2010, 2011, 2015).

with a typical actor, no individual consciousness can be construed for "activities" of the state because it is not a typical "individual" for whom the objective structures would be subjective meaning configurations.

As a concrete cultural formation, the state is an object of higher order. It is a cultural object consisting of a social construct having one of the greatest degrees of objectivity and anonymity. It refers to the world of contemporaries, which is based on several substrata of typifications of lower level. In comparison to lower-level typifications, levels such as the Congress (which is still a relatively concrete type), larger-scale typifications such as the state are completely anonymous contexts of meaning.

The state is essentially founded on communities of humans. Indeed, as a social construct, it is an abbreviated designation for a highly complex system of interdependent personal ideal types that the man on the street naively takes for granted. It is a complex structure of typifications and objective matrices of meaning that manifest themselves in the anonymous action patterns of functionaries and cannot be ascribed to any personal type.

In this view, the state is a typification that works in the opposite direction than social classes. Instead of going from individuals to personal types and then to general types, it goes from the most general, abstract types (from the idea of the state) to personal types (functionaries, officials, and the like) and then to the individuals who incarnate those types (who perform those functions). The state, then, is a normative idea, not a heuristic one (like social classes are).

For this reason, much of what the state "does" has the mode of an imposition. For example, Schutz mentions "administrative and legislative measures" that place "individuals under imposed social categories" such as tax laws, income classes, draft laws, and rent laws (Schutz, 1976, pp. 255–256). For being imposed, this kind of relevance and typification "will hardly achieve the effect that those subjected to it consider themselves members of a We-group" (Schutz, 1976, p. 256). They are meant to be "imposed group membership and imposed systems of relevances" (Schutz, 1976, p. 228).

8   Society as an Appresentational Apperception

Viewed as a whole, institutions, social classes, and the state are three structuring factors of modern society. Then, at least a few words about what society is must be said.

According to Schutz, society is the outcome of an appresentational apperception (Schutz, 1962, p. 318). In this perspective, society is a representation belonging to the common-sense thinking of everyday life whereby we simply take for granted the existence of an unspecified kind of order. In common-sense thinking, society represents "some kind of order; yet the essence of this order as such is unknowable to us. It reveals itself merely in images by analogical apprehending. However, the images, once constituted, are taken for granted, and so are the transcendences to which they refer" (Schutz, 1962, p. 331).

Consequently, from the individual's perspective, society is experienced as a form of transcendence: "From the outset I know [...] that any human being experiences the same imposed" transcendence of society, although he experiences it "with individual adumbrations" (Schutz, 1962, p. 331). However, the order of society "is common to all mankind" (Schutz, 1962, p. 331).

The imposition of society is experienced by the individual in a double sense. On the one hand, he finds himself at any moment of his existence as being "within society." In this way, society is permanently a coconstitutive element of his biographical situation and is, therefore, "experienced as inescapably belonging to it" (Schutz, 1962, p. 330). On the other hand, it constitutes the framework within which alone he has the freedom of his potentialities, and this means that it prescribes "the scope of all possibilities" for defining his situation. In this sense, it is not an element of his situation but a determination of it. In the first sense, he has to take it for granted; in the second sense, he has to come to terms with it; in either sense, he has to understand the social world in spite of its transcendence, "in terms of an order of things and events" (Schutz, 1962, p. 330). In other words, for being an unfulfilled apperception, we cannot assign society as such any specific content. Society is an unfulfilled anticipation. What we anticipate is that society surrounds us, and it does it in a coercive way—which we express by saying that society "determines" us.

Nevertheless, this formal structure includes at least three formal features that are necessarily taken to be proper to any kind of society. Accordingly, there is a twofold concept of society in Schutz. At a general level, any experience typified as social is perceived as occurring in the midst of a society (which is only appresented) that works at once as its surrounding and as its determinant. At a specific level, any society is apperceived as having three formal features: it symbolically constructs the natural course of life, it is composed of groups, and it ranks those groups in relation of status and prestige. Let us see this in some detail.

First, society constructs its inner relations in opposition to nature. Interestingly, Schutz describes the apperception of society in parallel with the apperception of nature. His claim is that society symbolically constructs the natural course of life in terms of a life plan. In Schutz's view (1962, p. 330), the order of society "furnishes to everyone the setting of the cycle of his individual life, of birth, aging, death, health and sickness, hopes and fears." Thus, in a given society, individuals will have their life course defined by social typifications that structure their "natural" course of life. Second, society is made of groups. This means that individuals are not directly linked to society but to groups that, in turn, compose society. In other words, the individual's relation to society is mediated by group memberships: "Each of us is a member of the group into which he was born or which he has joined and which continues to exist if some of its members die and others enter into it" (Schutz, 1962, p. 330). Third, groups are related to one another in relations that constitute ranks of status and prestige: "Everywhere there will be systems of kinship, age groups and sex groups, differentiations according to occupations, and an organization of power and command which leads to the categories of social status and prestige" (Schutz, 1962, pp. 330–331).

Consequently, there is a twofold concept of society in Schutz's idea of society as an appresentational apperception. At a general level, any experience typified as social is perceived as occurring in the midst of a society (which is only appresented) that works at once as its surrounding and as its determinant. At a specific level, any society is apperceived as having three formal features: it symbolically constructs the natural course of life, it is composed of groups, and it ranks those groups in relation to status and prestige.

9   CONCLUSIONS

As seen in this chapter, the macro strata of the social world pertain to the most remote and anonymous region of our experience of others. Anonymity refers to the relative scope of the typifying scheme involved in that experience, which is determined by the relative completeness and generality of that segment of the stock of knowledge that guided the selection of the trait to be typified. Generality refers to the kind of previous experiences from which a typifying scheme is derived, whether it is derived from the previous experiences of a particular fellow man or from personal ideal types. Brief, the anonymity of the typifying scheme is in opposition to familiarity, while its generality is in opposition to concreteness. In addition, since each typification involves other typifications, the more substrata of typifying schemes are involved in a given ideal type, the more anonymous it is.

Within these strata, our relationships with others are not experienced in direct perception but indirectly appresented through indications, signs, and symbols. Symbolic appresentation not only gives us the concrete, familiar other but also the abstract, anonymous one who does not belong to the finite province of everyday life but to that of ideal relations. It gives us both intertwined by the pairing of elements pertaining to the lifeworld with elements pertaining to the realm of idealities. In other words, it opens the lifeworld to the transcendence of ideality.

In Western modern societies, the symbolic arrangement of collective experience is strongly structured on three bases that make up the ribbing of their macro strata: institutions, social classes, and the state. These are ways of transcending—and therefore of transforming—concrete, personal experiences into abstract, collective ways of being-together.

Social institutions are reified patterns of social behavior that acquire a certain degree of objectivity whereby they become anonymous and, consequently, no subjective meaning context can be assigned to them. Institutions are the symbolic structuration of human behavior pertaining to the lower range of the macro strata of the social world. They consist of typical patterns of behavior derived, sanctioned, and stocked socially that embody typical social actors, roles, and relationships that any member of an in-group must know and take into account to become a member and have meaningful interactions with other members. In other words, institutions are a basic and a major aspect of the cultural background of groups.

Social classes are typifications imposed by the social conditionedness of relevance systems that are socioculturally codetermined by the structuring of the distribution of knowledge based on political, economic, and other kinds of organizations. Social classes do not address individuals as typical actors or as incumbents of typical social roles. They address typical actors and typified ways of acting as marks and indications of the social groups to which they belong. In other words, marks and indications are not taken from individuals but from group actions, interactions, and relationships. As a typification of group behavior, social classes constitute in-groups whose subjective collective meanings are defined in opposition to objective meanings attributed to an outgroup or outgroups. Its subjective meaning, in turn, is grounded in material conditions that, at the same time, work as their substratum and as an object in dispute. That is why conflict is the most frequent and typical kind of relation among social classes.

The state is a highly anonymous institution of the contemporary world. It is a concrete cultural formation. As a social construct, it is an object of a higher order based on several substrata of typifications of a lower level. It is essentially founded on communities of humans, and it works as an abbreviated designation for a highly complex system of interdependent personal ideal types that the man on the street naively takes for granted. It is a complex structure of typifications and objective matrices of meaning that manifest themselves in the anonymous action patterns of functionaries, which cannot be ascribed to any personal type. It is a kind of typification that cannot be grasped in direct experience. No individual consciousness can be construed for "activities" of the state because it is not a typical "individual" for whom the objective structures would be subjective meaning configurations.

Viewed as a whole, institutions, social classes, and the state are three structuring factors of society resulting from appresentational apperceptions. Society is a representation belonging to the common-sense thinking of everyday life whereby we simply take for granted the existence of an unspecified kind of order. It represents "some kind of order." Still, its essence is unknowable to us. From the individual's perspective, society is experienced in a double sense. On the one hand, he finds himself at any moment of his existence as being "within society." In this way, society is permanently a coconstitutive element of his biographical situation. On the other hand, it constitutes the framework within which alone he has the freedom of his potentialities, which means that it prescribes the scope of all possibilities for defining his situation. In this sense, it is not an element of his situation but a determination of it.

The conclusion follows that phenomenology has contributed to the study of macro phenomena. In accordance, it has not limited itself to the research of microsociological objects. This leads us to oppose the mainstream conception of phenomenology as a microsociological approach focused on face-to-face relationships, everyday life, and subjective processes. In contrast, it is not phenomenology but hegemonic sociology that has missed the importance of macro phenomena.

As seen in the introduction, some contemporary social theorists blamed phenomenologists for being one-sided because of their alleged blindness to the constraining, objective, and macro aspects of social reality. I hope my point has been proven that phenomenology does not neglect the objective macro strata of the social world. In contrast, macro phenomenology has taught that every society has a need for the formalization, generalization, and typification of behavior, and because of that, it includes social institutions and relates individuals within groups. Groups, in turn, are related to each other in rankings of status and prestige. Therefore, every society produces social classes and class relations. All kinds of social behavior are eventually ruled by the state, which is the most general type of social relations after society and works as the subordinating type of all other social types.

There is more to macro phenomenology than what has been said in this chapter. Notwithstanding, the major guidelines for a systematic approach to the higher strata of our indirect experience of others in the social world have been provided. It is the author's best wish that further and more detailed studies will follow. Should that be the case, the history of macro phenomenology would just be beginning.

References

Barber, M. (2017). *Religion and humor as emancipating provinces of meaning*. Springer.

Belvedere, C., & Gros, A. (2019). The phenomenology of social institutions in the Schutzian tradition. *Schutzian Research, 11*, 43–74.

Berger, P., & Pullberg, S. (1965). Reification and the sociological critique of consciousness. *History and Theory, 4*(2), 196–211.

Berger, P. L., & Luckmann, T. (1967). *The social construction of reality. A treatise in the sociology of knowledge*. Anchor.

Bourdieu, P. (1980). *Le sens pratique*. Minuit.

Bourdieu, P. (1989). Social space and symbolic power. *Sociological Theory, 7*(1).

Dreher, J. (2009). Phenomenology of friendship: Construction and constitution of an existential social relationship. *Human Studies, 32*(4), 401–417. https://doi.org/10.1007/s10746-009-9130-4

Embree, L. (2010). From "We" to "I" and back: Still learning from the new school. In *The 41ST annual meeting of the Husserl circle* (pp. 37–46). The New School for Social Research.

Embree, L. (2011). Groups in Schutz: The concrete meaning structure of the sociohistorical world. *PhaenEx, 6*(1), 1–11.

Embree, L. (2015). *The Schutzian theory of the cultural sciences*. Springer.

Giddens, A. (1983). *Profiles and critiques in social theory*. University of California Press.

Giddens, A. (1984). *Central problems in social theory. Action, structure and contradiction in social analysis*. University of California Press.

Schutz, A. (1962). *Collected papers I. The problem of social reality*. Martinus Nijhoff.

Schutz, A. (1967). *The phenomenology of the social world*. Northwestern University Press.

Schutz, A. (1976). *Collected papers II. Studies in social theory.* Martinus Nijhoff.

Schutz, A. (1996). *Collected papers IV.* Kluwer.

Schutz, A. (2013). *Collected papers VI. Literary reality and relationships.* Springer.

Schutz, A., & Luckmann, T. (1989). *The structures of the life-world. Volume II.* Northwestern University Press.

Schutz, A. (2010a). The problem of transcendental intersubjectivity in Husserl. *Schutzian Research, 2,* 9–52.

Schutz, A. (2010b). Problems of a sociology of language (Fall semester, 1958). *Schutzian Research, 2,* 55–107.

Thomason, B. C. (1982). *Making sense of reification. Alfred Schutz and constructionist theory.* Humanities Press.

Macro-social Awareness in Everyday Life: Toward a Phenomenological Theory of Society

Alexis Gros

1   INTRODUCTION

In recent years, a useful conceptual distinction has gained relevance in the field of German-speaking sociology. I am referring to the differentiation between two modes of sociological-theoretical reflection, namely, "social theory" [*Sozialtheorie*] and "theory of society" [*Gesellschaftstheorie*]. As the argument goes, the former deals with the definition of the fundamental features of social reality *as such*, whereas the latter primarily focuses on the analysis of the key structures and processes of *modern* societal formations (see, for instance, Reckwitz, 2016, pp. 8–10; Lindemann, 2009, pp. 19–21).

More precisely, the term "social theory" is nowadays employed to denote what used to be called "general sociological theory" (Popitz, 2011), that is, the "fundamental theory" of sociology concerned with the definition of the discipline's object of research (see Lindemann, 2009, p. 19). Social-theoretical reflection, thus understood, aims at answering the ontological question of what is social reality by elaborating a "basic vocabulary" made up of fundamental sociological concepts, such as "social action," "social structure," "social system," or "social practice" (Reckwitz, 2021, pp. 27, 29). In this sense, it

A. Gros (✉)
Friedrich-Schiller-Universität Jena, Jena, Germany

Universidad de Buenos Aires, Buenos Aires, Argentina

CONICET, Buenos Aires, Argentina

© The Author(s), under exclusive license to Springer Nature Switzerland AG 2023
C. Belvedere, A. Gros (eds.), *The Palgrave Handbook of Macrophenomenology and Social Theory*,
https://doi.org/10.1007/978-3-031-34712-2_3

constitutes a universalistic endeavor focusing on the formal analysis of the *transhistorical invariants* of sociality (Reckwitz, 2016, p. 8).

By contrast, the so-called theory of society mainly deals with the study of the overall organization and processual dynamics of *modern*-type societies. That is, of those capitalistic, rationalized, differentiated, technified, industrialized, secularized, and democratized, large-scale social formations which, with many regional and cultural variations,[1] have become prevalent worldwide since the nineteenth century (Reckwitz, 2021, p. 32; Lindemann, 2009, p. 24). Seen this way, societal-theoretical analysis is not only *historically* situated but also *macro-sociologically* oriented. On the one hand, it seeks to answer the question of what society are we living in *today* by resorting to both empirical research results and historical comparisons (Reckwitz, 2016, p. 8). On the other hand, it adopts a bird's-eye view to provide a *big picture* of the complex macro-processes and structures shaping social life in modernity (Reckwitz & Rosa, 2021, p. 11).

Drawing on this now-popular conceptual distinction, the present chapter intends to take a first, humble step toward the development of a *phenomenological theory of society*—or, more precisely put, a *phenomenologically informed* one. To be sure, I am aware that this idea sounds rather odd to sociological-theoretical ears, and this at least for two reasons. First, phenomenology-based sociology in the Schutzian tradition is rightly regarded as a primarily *social-theoretical* enterprise (see, e.g., Reckwitz & Rosa, 2021, p. 288), given that it seeks to work out the *a priori* features of sociality as a means of providing a "proto-theoretical" foundation for sociology (see Eberle, 2009, p. 493; Luckmann, 1991). And second, it tends to be classified, also with some justification, as a *micro-sociological* approach, as its main focus lies on the infinitesimal analysis of experiences, actions, and interactions as they take place *in vivo* in everyday life (see, e.g., Manzo, 2015, p. 415).

The endeavor of developing a full-blown phenomenological theory of society is far beyond the scope of this chapter. My aim here is to contribute to one of the partial tasks involved in this ambitious project: answering the phenomenological question of *what is it like to experience society in the first-person perspective*. Admittedly, however, I will neither be able to give a complete response to it. For "society," understood as the largest-scale collective entity (Nassehi, 2008, p. 85) or "overall formation of social life" in modernity (Rosa, 2012, p. 273), is experientially encountered in many different ways on the plane of everyday life. In view of this, my analysis will be deliberately restricted to only one of these manifold forms of experience, namely, what I call *macro-social awareness via cognitive mapping*.

The chapter will be divided into three sections. In section "The Project of a Phenomenological Theory of Society", I will sketch the outline of the project

---

[1] In this connection, it is important to acknowledge the existence of "multiple modernities," that is, different versions or modes of manifestation of modernity in divergent geographical and historical contexts (Reckwitz & Rosa, 2021, pp. 263–264).

of a phenomenological theory of society. Section "What Is It Like to Experience Modern Society?" will discuss the general issue of how modern society is experienced in the first-person perspective. Finally, the last and central section of the chapter ("Cognitive Mapping as a Way to Overcome the Transcendence of Society") will offer a preliminary phenomenological analysis of cognitive mapping of society in everyday life.

2   The Project of a Phenomenological Theory of Society

The "Cultural Turn" and Its Radicalization as a Condition of Possibility

To what extent can a supposedly "formalistic-universalistic" and "micro-sociological" approach like life-world phenomenology contribute to a "historically situated" and "macro-sociological" undertaking such as societal-theoretical thought? Are not these two modes of reflection as unmixable as oil and water? Despite this apparent incompatibility, in recent years there has been a growing rapprochement between phenomenology and *Gesellschaftstheorie*. This is evidenced especially, but not only (see Endreß & Lindemann, 2021), in Hartmut Rosa's (2016) current attempt to build a "phenomenological Critical Theory of Society" (Gros, 2019).

Such a development would have been unthinkable without the recent "interpretive" or "cultural turns" in social theory (see Reckwitz, 2002). Since the culturalist and interpretivist "revolutions" starting in the 1970s, the social is generally conceived of as a meaningfully organized reality, that is, as a reality that constitutively depends on cultural-symbolic knowledge operative at the level of everyday life (Reckwitz, 2002, p. 245; Rosa, 2012, p. 104). In the last three decades, this tendency has become more radical. Novel "cultural turns" have emerged, such as the "practice," "affective," "spatial," and "body" turns, which seek to rehabilitate the material, non-intellectual, and pre-linguistic aspects of culture traditionally neglected by social research, including, among other dimensions, corporeality, affectivity, spatiality, and artifactuality (Reckwitz, 2016, pp. 98–99; Bachmann-Medick, 2016).

Classical societal-theoretical thought, tracing back to Marx (see Marx & Engels, 1958, pp. 26–27) and Durkheim (see 1984, p. xxvi), has tended to underestimate pre-scientific knowledge and experience as nothing but an "epistemological obstacle" to "true" scientific knowledge of society (see Celikates, 2009, pp. 27–30).[2] According to this view, which mixes Platonic motifs with others from natural-scientific epistemology, *doxa* systematically "misrecognizes"

---

[2] I am referring here to Marx & Engels' (see 1958, pp. 26–27) conception of "ideology" as "false consciousness" and to Durkheim's (1986, p. 17) account of "pre-notions." Despite the undeniable differences between the Marxian and the Durkheimian theories of society, both conceive of *doxa* as a veil blocking access to true social-scientific knowledge.

(see Bourdieu, 2013, pp. 5–6) the "real" nature of societal structures and processes. Because of its unsystematic and subjectively biased character—so the argument goes—it is incapable of gaining insight into the macro-social as it "objectively" is, even giving a misleading, false, or distorted picture of it (see Hörnqvist, 2022, pp. 6–7). If one follows this account, the social scientist can only provide an accurate theory of society if she eliminates the hindrance of doxic prejudices and moves squarely to the plane of social-scientific *episteme*.

As a result of the "cultural turn" and its current radicalization, this pejorative view of everyday experience and knowledge has declined. More precisely, the idea of society as a purely objective or subject-independent "thing" is now seen as untenable. Today, it is widely assumed, in a very Schutzian vein (Schutz, 1962, p. 53, 1984, p. 298), that lay world- and self-interpretations are a *constitutive* part of societal reality as such—even if they do not exhaust it (Giddens, 1982, pp. 1–18; Habermas, 1981, p. 209; Rosa, 2012, pp. 104–106). From being seen as an "epistemological obstacle" to theory of society, *doxa* has come to be regarded as an essential moment of its subject matter.

In this novel perspective, the genesis, reproduction, and change of societal formations appear as outcomes, either intended or unintended, of everyday socio-cultural practices that are materially embedded and constitutively dependent on embodied meanings (see Reckwitz, 2021, pp. 69–98). Accordingly, it is believed that an adequate theory of society cannot do without a conceptual reconstruction of the participant's cultural perspective, including *all* its crucial aspects: corporeality, affectivity, cognition, materiality, and so on (see, for instance, Rosa, 2016, pp. 83–245). Against this background, it is not difficult to see why phenomenological research is today increasingly being regarded as a relevant resource for societal-theoretical reflection.

Ever since the emergence of the "cultural turn," theorists of society have engaged in a continuing dialogue with different traditions belonging to the so-called interpretive or qualitative paradigm, which, as is well known, focuses on the "meaning-adequate" reconstruction of the emic perspective on the social world (see Eberle & Srubar, 2010, p. 9; Keller, 2012). Among these traditions are pragmatism, symbolic interactionism, hermeneutics, Wittgensteinian philosophy of language, and, of course, phenomenology (see, e.g., Giddens, 1982, pp. 1–18; Habermas, 1981). However, as experts have amply shown (see Belvedere, 2011, pp. 41–62; Srubar, 2007, pp. 68–69), the reading of phenomenology by leading theorists of society of the late twentieth century, like Giddens, Bourdieu, Habermas, or Bauman, has been chronically one-sided and even biased.

It was not until the last few years that societal-theoretical thought has started engaging more seriously with phenomenological reflection proper. On the one hand, this is due to the mentioned materialization of the "cultural turn," which has shifted the focus of social research to the experiential, somatic, and pre-predicative dimensions of the cultural life-world—aspects that always have been at the heart of phenomenology's concerns. On the other, this development owes much to the current "renaissance" of phenomenology in both philosophy and the social sciences driven by different efforts to vindicate this tradition against the unjust prejudices—"solipsism," "idealism," "subjectivism," and so on—of which it has been a victim since its very inception (see Belvedere, 2011; Zahavi, 2018).

A Phenomenologically Informed Theory of Society (Or Why We Need "Perspective Dualism")

A word of caution is needed here. I use the concept of "phenomenological theory of society" only for simplicity reasons. Strictly speaking, the term "*phenomenologically-informed* theory of society" is more accurate for naming the theoretical project I have in mind. For, in my view, it is not possible to develop a full-blown theory of society *solely* by phenomenological means.

More precisely, I consider that in order to develop an adequate *Gesellschaftstheorie* we should adopt what Rosa (2021, p. 171) calls "perspective dualism." That is, an approach that uses two different viewpoints on societal reality *in parallel*, namely, the "emic" or "participant's perspective," typical of phenomenological analysis, and the "etic" or "observer's" one, characteristic of classical macro-sociological accounts like structural-functionalism, systems theory, or historical materialism.

Importantly, this "parallel action," to use a term coined by Luckmann (1979, p. 197) in another context, should not be mistaken for a "conflationist" strategy such as that paradigmatically used by practice theorists like Giddens or Bourdieu (see Archer, 1995, p. 82). What I propose here is *not* to blend or synthetize phenomenology and classical macro-sociological theory into a novel hybrid theoretical outlook. Rather, my argument is that both approaches should be used *simultaneously but separately*, thereby retaining their respective specificities. Only in this way can each of them bring their full potential to societal-theoretical reflection.

As is well known, most classical theories of society tend to depict lay agents as "judgmental dopes" (Garfinkel in Celikates, 2009, p. 19) who are *totally ignorant* of the complex macro-social structures in which their lives are embedded, or even *delusional* about them. This pejorative account of *doxa* is overly exaggerated, as it wrongly underestimates everyday actors' cognitive, interpretive, and reflective skills (see Hörnqvist, 2022). Different sociological theorists have pointed out that lay agents do experience and know modern society's macrostructures in manifold ways. Everyday actors have cognitive "representations" [*Vorstellungen*] (Weber, 1984, p. 31) or "pictures" [*Bilder*] (Popitz et al., 2018) of these structures and also feel pressure from "mute compulsions" [*stumme Zwänge*] emanating from them (see Marx in Marx & Engels, 1962, p. 764; Mau, 2021), like those arising from capitalist competition (see Rosa, 2012, pp. 324–357) or the current hyper-acceleration of social life (see Rosa, 2005).

As life-world phenomenology suggests, these doxic knowledges and experiences may be fragmentary, unclear, flawed, and even partially false (Schutz, 1962, p. 55). However, I have the impression that they can never be *completely delusional*—or at least not on the level of pre-reflective agency.[3] A minimum of *"reality principle"* (see Marcuse, 1955, p. 35), that is, a minimal ability to accurately assess the structure of societal reality and to act upon it accordingly, seems to be necessary for social actors to get by in complex and demanding societies such as capitalist modern ones.

Yet overestimating the scope and accuracy of *doxa* in a demagogic fashion is as dangerous a mistake as its paternalistic underestimation. Bourdieu, Habermas, and others are right when they claim that lay agents do not have a *completely transparent* consciousness of the complex macro-social conditions under which they act. Very often, two central aspects of societal reality, namely, the structural "conditions of possibility" enabling or constraining everyday agency (Bourdieu, 1990, pp. 25–26) and the latter's "unintended consequences" at an aggregate level (Habermas, 1981, p. 384), are neither fully nor thoroughly known by everyday actors (see Reckwitz, 2021, p. 134).

It is in acknowledgment of the possible limits and flaws of the participant's perspective on societal reality that a phenomenologically informed *Gesellschaftstheorie* should adopt "perspective dualism." From what I have said so far, it follows that everyday *doxa* is a constituent moment of that thing called modern society but does not exhaust it. In a sense, macro-social reality *exceeds* common-sense experience, as essential aspects thereof frequently remain only partly know, or even unknown, to lay agents. A theory of society merely restricted to the phenomenological analysis of *doxa* would lose sight of these fundamental dimensions of the societal that remain opaque to everyday experience and knowledge.

In order to gain a comprehensive account of modern society, it is therefore necessary to *complement* phenomenology's "emic" approach with the "etic" approach typical of classical macro-sociological theories. As authors as diverse as Marx, Adorno, Parsons, and Luhmann have shown, by means of conceptual and methodological abstractions it is possible to adopt a bird's-eye perspective on societal reality. This macroscopic view considerably expands upon the narrowness of the participant's perspective, allowing for a *bigger picture* of the totality of society (see Rosa & Oberthür, 2020, pp. 11–12).

It is important to note that recognizing the possible limitations of everyday macro-social awareness does not discredit phenomenology's contributions to societal-theoretical analysis, as especially Bourdieu (see 1989, pp. 14–15) suggests. In a sense, the narrowness of *doxa* constitutes an *essential* aspect of societal reality itself. Modern societies are what and how they are precisely because of this *partial ignorance or not-knowledge* at the common-sense level. Far from romanticizing *doxa*, life-world phenomenology sheds light precisely on these

---

[3] The contemporary influence of conspiracy theories on a large part of the population of Western societies should not be overlooked here (see Butter, 2020). Arguably, however, these theories primarily operate on the level of explicit self- and world-interpretations, not at that of pre-reflective agency. For an analysis of the different levels of self-interpretation and their potential discrepancies, see Rosa (2012, pp. 111–117).

opacities, obscurities, and intransparencies, thereby making significant contributions to an adequate *Gesellschaftstheorie* (see Schutz, 1962, p. 55, 1964, pp. 120–124).

A Working Definition of Phenomenology (and Two Clarifications)

When speaking of a phenomenological theory of society, I use the term "phenomenology" in a broad sense to denote the *sober core* of the "style" of theoretical thought founded by Husserl and further developed by authors such as Heidegger, Merleau-Ponty, or Gurwitsch (see Merleau-Ponty, 1945, p. ii). Specifically, my approach to phenomenological research draws primarily from Schutz's post-metaphysical (Srubar, 2007, p. 178) and social-theoretically oriented (Eberle, 1993, pp. 304–305) "constitutive phenomenology of the natural attitude" (Schutz, 1962, p. 149), which deliberately sets aside the speculative, idealistic, and foundationalist motifs present in Husserl's philosophical project, emphasizing its most concrete contributions to the description of the structures of the life-world (see Schutz, 1984).

Despite their undeniable differences, all phenomenologists share a common focus on the in-depth analysis of "life as we live it" (Van Manen, 2017, p. 39), that is, of pre-theoretical "lived experience" in its full breadth, including essential dimensions such as embodiment, affectivity, reflectivity, ideation, imagination, and cognitive and practical habitualities. Phenomenology is thus concerned not with objects or things in themselves but, rather, with their phenomenality or "mode of givenness" to (inter-)subjectivity (see Henry, 1990, p. 138). Its focus lies not in the objective world in itself—if there is such a thing—but in the "life-world" (Husserl, 1954, pp. 48–54) as it is naively encountered by subjects in the "first-person perspective" (Zahavi, 2007, p. 19).

Importantly, phenomenological analysis does not deal with the study of idiosyncratic or particular events, for example, the headache I had yesterday or the enthusiasm felt in Argentina during the 2022 FIFA World Cup. Rather, it seeks to reconstruct the so-called eidetic invariants, that is, the basal morphological structures of phenomenality in general and of specific types of experiences in particular, such as image-consciousness, collective emotions, or physical pain (see Merleau-Ponty, 1945, p. i; Husserl, 1962, p. 46).

Methodologically, phenomenology operates as a *reflective-descriptive* analysis (see Embree, 2010). On the basis of self-examination, it attempts to provide an adequate structural description of the *what-is-it-likeness* of the experiential life-world. It is crucial to note that phenomenological reflection is strictly methodically controlled, in contrast to everyday reflective practices. It systematically employs various methodological "reductions," especially the "transcendental" and the "eidetic" ones, as a means to lay bare the field of pre-theoretical experience, which tends to remain concealed to both common-sense and scientific thought (see, e.g., Zahavi, 2007, pp. 21–26; Merleau-Ponty, 1945, p. viii).

For the sake of the project of a phenomenological theory of society, two clarifications are in order. The first one (1) refers to the notion of the "first-person perspective," while the second (2) concerns the range of validity of phenomenological analyses.

(1) To start with, phenomenology's focus on the "first-person perspective" should not be mistaken for a solipsistic or subjectivist bias. Far from falling into "robinsonades," phenomenology acknowledges the foundational primacy, either ontological, ontogenetic, or transcendental, of intersubjectivity and sociality over subjectivity (see, e.g., Schutz, 1962, p. 168; Heidegger, 2006, pp. 117–120; Zahavi, 2003, pp. 115–117). For phenomenologists, subjective experience is not only inextricably embedded within complex socio-historical contexts but also mediated and pre-formed by them from the outset (for instance, Schutz, 1964, pp. 229–231; Husserl, 1954, pp. 48–54; Heidegger, 2006, pp. 382–392).

The study of subjective experience constitutes the central interest of most phenomenologists (Zahavi, 2007, pp. 17–21). However, it should be acknowledged that phenomenology not only investigates the "first-person *singular* perspective" but also the "first-person *plural*" one (Zahavi, 2021, p. 2), thus providing a full picture, not a solely egological one, of the participant's viewpoint. This means at least two things. On the one hand, phenomenological reflection is able to analyze the intersubjective constitution via "collective intentionality" of a sense of "we-ness," that is, of the experience of being part of a "we-subject" (see, e.g., Zahavi, 2021; Schutz, 1981, pp. 228–229).

On the other hand, and more importantly for the sake of this chapter, in its "generative" (Steinbock, 2003), "historical-cultural" (Gros, 2023), or strictly "sociological" (Belvedere, 2022) version, phenomenology describes the structure and development of the "objective spirit" of socio-cultural life (see Dilthey, 1981, p. 256) as it is experienced from the "anonymous unified point of view" of large-scale social groups (Schutz, 1962, p. 13; see, e.g., Schutz, 1964, pp. 226–274; Husserl, 1954, pp. 48–54). By this I mean the ensemble of socially established stocks of knowledge, practices, institutions, ideal, and cultural things that constitute the collectively shared "form of life" [*Lebensform*] of a group (Schutz, 1984, p. 360; Jaeggi, 2014). Importantly, all these social constructs possess a layer of anonymous "objective meaning" which, in contrast to "subjective sense," is potentially available as an identical meaning unit to everyone socialized into the group culture (see Bongaerts, 2012, p. 22; Luckmann, 2007, pp. 142–143).

(2) True, classical phenomenological research is mostly generalist in scope, as it seeks to work out the "eidetic" or "*a priori* 'structure[s]'" of universal modes of experience like perception, recollection, empathy, imagination, or action (Husserl, 1962, pp. 17, 43; see Heidegger, 2006, p. 17; Luckmann & Schutz, 2003). However, phenomenologists have also provided, and still offer, what can be called "middle-range" phenomenological analyses.[4] That is, descriptions of the morphology of forms of experience that are not universal but *socio-historically situated*, such as those related to modern technology

---

[4] This concept is loosely inspired by Merton's (1968, pp. 39–40) idea of "middle-range theories."

(Heidegger, 2000) and social classes in capitalism (Merleau-Ponty, 1945, pp. 416–417) or, more recently, to new digital technologies (O'Shiel, 2022) or racism and sexism (Guenther, 2021).

If "generalist" phenomenological analysis is concerned with the description of *a priori* or eidetic structures, "middle-range phenomenology," as I like to call it, deals with the study of "*quasi-a priori*" (Guenther, 2021, pp. 5–23) or quasi-eidetic ones, which are nothing but sedimented outcomes of specific historical processes. It is important to note, however, that middle-range phenomenological analyses are generally founded upon generalist ones, as quasi-eidetic structures of experience might be seen as specific modulations of eidetic ones (see, e.g., O'Shiel, 2022). Yet middle-range analyses can also contribute to revise or correct eidetic reflections, as has been shown especially by Merleau-Ponty (2000, p. 1263).

Toward a Phenomenological Theory of Society

A phenomenological theory of society, as I conceive it, has as its central task offering a "middle-range" description of the specific structural modulations of experience essentially involved in the existence and reproduction of modern societal formations. Importantly, such a theory must operate with a "dialectical" social ontology, acknowledging the reciprocal relation between subjective experience and objective macro-social structures, that is, the fact that the former is a product of the latter, and *vice versa* (Berger & Luckmann, 1966, pp. 208–209). Specifically, a phenomenologically informed *Gesellschaftstheorie* should provide answers to two questions which are two sides of the same coin, namely, (a) *what modes of life-worldly experience are necessary for the subsistence of modern societies?* and (b) *in what ways do societal macro-structures condition, shape, and even constitute everyday actors' experiential life?*

In line with the centrality of subjectivity analysis within the tradition founded by Husserl, a phenomenological *Gesellschaftstheorie*, as I understand it, should place the main focus on the morphological description of our *being-in-modern-society* as it is experienced in the first-person perspective singular. However, as noted earlier, the study of society's "subjective spirit" can never be complete if it does not go hand in hand with a correlative analysis of its "objective spirit." For subjective experience always already moves within a space of objective meaning, being mediated at its core by socio-cultural contents and constantly directed toward them via intentionality.

These rather abstract aims can be operationalized into four more concrete partial tasks. The first one (1) and most basic of them is the one I will attempt to carry out in the present chapter, namely, the analysis of the way in which society *as such* is subjectively experienced in everyday life. As for the second one (2), it consists in describing the manifestations at the level of the life-world of those fundamental macro-processes shaping *all* modern societies, namely, "social differentiation," "rationalization," and "individualization," among others (see Rosa, 2005, p. 89; Gros, 2022). The third task (3), in turn, is related to the sociological diagnosis of the times, focusing on the analysis of the impacts on lived experience of far-reaching developments typical of late modern societies, such as digitalization (see Nassehi, 2019), "singularization" (see Reckwitz, 2017), or hyper-acceleration (see Rosa, 2005).

Finally (4), without denying the all-encompassing nature of those macro-processes, a phenomenological *Gesellschaftstheorie* cannot avoid addressing the experiential effects of societal-structural inequalities, primarily those based on class but also those gender- and race-related. If a theory of society is to be truly phenomenological, that is, adequate to the texture of *actual* lived experience, it cannot overlook that (late) modern social formations, both in the Global North and in the Global South, are far from being monolithic. Each particular society shows a specific "social stratification" primarily based on a hierarchy of economic "social classes," or "strata," with unequal access to relevant social resources like income, education, or prestige (see Geißler, 2014, pp. 1–3). The class position of an individual, along with her race and/or gender, not only pre-defines her life chances but also entails her socialization into particular cultural worldviews and "ways of life" (see Reckwitz, 2019, pp. 63–69; Berger & Luckmann, 1966, p. 151).

3   What Is It Like to Experience Modern Society?

My aim in the next pages is to contribute to the first one of the concrete tasks mentioned above, namely, answering the phenomenological question of *what is it like to experience society as such in the first-person perspective singular*. In doing so, I start from two strong theses. First, I claim that, within the life-world, individual subjects are in fact able to experientially encounter *Gesellschaft*, along with its large-scale structures and processes, in many different ways. And second, that this subjective experience of the macro-social plays a crucial role in the existence, reproduction, and change of modern societal formations.

Two Obstacles to a Phenomenology of the Experience of Society

To date, there has been no systematic response to this concrete question neither inside nor outside the phenomenological tradition, although interesting insights in this regard can be found in the works of phenomenologists like Schutz (for instance, 1962, pp. 354–355) and Luckmann (e.g., 1980, p. 260), and of non-phenomenologists such as Heinrich Popitz et al. (2018, pp. 1–9). The lack of a treatment of this issue in current theory of society is arguably due to at least two epistemological obstacles precluding its discussion.

(1) The first hindrance is a classical misconception still very influential in the social sciences in general and theory of society in particular. I am referring to the assumption that it is not possible to experience society firsthand, for it is imperceptible to our sense organs. As a recent handbook of theory of society puts it: "One cannot without further ado experience [...] 'society': one cannot see, grasp, hear or in any other way 'apprehend' it" (Rosa & Oberthür, 2020, p. 11).

Admittedly, there is a point to this statement. To use Adorno's (2003, p. 65) words, nobody can rightfully say: "*voilà*, there you have society" like one does with concrete material objects. However, this is not the same as affirming that we cannot experience society *at all*. The latter is a misapprehension resting on an unfounded naturalist-empiricist prejudice: "the identification of experience with sensory observation" (Schutz, 1962, p. 54).

As phenomenology's expanded or "radical empiricism" teaches us (Schutz, 1984, p. 260), the realm of life-world experience is not reduced to what sensory perception gives us, namely, real physical things (Husserl, 1950, p. 43). Rather, it includes *everything* that encounter us phenomenally exactly as it is given to us, regardless of its origin, nature, or complexion—ideas, theories, self- and other-experiences, hallucinations, phantasies, cultural objects, social institutions, and so on (pp. 42–49). On this basis, my argument here is that we do experience society within the *Lebenswelt*, but in a different way than we perceive material things like a tree, a book, or a table.

(2) The second obstacle is another prejudice concerning the impossibility of experiencing society within the life-world. At least since Marx (in Marx & Engels, 1962, p. 59), most theories of society, especially the critical ones, assume that the macro-societal structures determining social life in modernity, for example, the capitalist mode of production, essentially operate "behind the backs" of lay actors, thus being inexperienceable or unknowable for them (see, e.g., Gardiner, 2000, p. 7).

For instance, Habermas (1981, pp. 302–303) argues that the macro-economic and political systems typical of modern societies reproduce themselves "silently," completely "bypassing the consciousness of actors." These large-scale systemic mechanisms—so the argument goes—are not part of the life-world of lay agents but actualize themselves in the dark, through the imperceptible concatenation of "unintended" consequences of action (p. 384). From this, it follows that phenomenology has little or nothing to contribute to a theory of modern society. The macro-social as such would be inaccessible to the "participant" or first-person perspective, being only analyzable from an "observer" or third-person one like that used by systems theory (see p. 179).

Another classical phenomenological insight can help us overcome this apparent obstacle. I am referring to the notion of "horizonal awareness" as developed by Husserl, Gurwitsch, and Schutz. Contrary to what Habermas and other theorists of society seem to assume, phenomenology demonstrates that life-world experience is not restricted to what is explicitly and thematically seen or grasped. Every thematic object-experience is always accompanied by a tacit, non-thematic sense of the thing's "context," that is, of the "horizon" within which it is embedded (see Gurwitsch, 2012, p. 501; Schutz, 1984, p. 338; Husserl, 1972, p. 29). Accordingly, it can be argued that lay actors are always somehow aware of what is happening "behind their backs," at least in a rather indeterminate and vague manner. I will discuss the implications of this idea in the third section.

What Is Modern Society?

In current societal-theoretical literature, there seems to be broad agreement, at least in general terms, on the definition of the concept of "society." It is normally used to denote "the largest social unity, which includes all other social unities" (Nassehi, 2008, p. 85) or, put differently, the all-encompassing "total formation" of social life (Rosa, 2012, p. 273). The societal is thus regarded as the macro-social *par excellence*, as opposed to the meso- and the micro-social, that is, institutionalized organizations and interactions, respectively (Weymann, 2020, p. 17).

There is also a consensus that both the concept and the thing "society" [*Gesellschaft*] are of *modern* origin (Rosa & Oberthür, 2020, p. 11). As Adorno (2003, pp. 54–56) classically puts it, "society in the emphatic sense," that is, as a structured totality embracing *all* that is social, does not emerge until capitalist modernity. From the nineteenth century onward, a number of closely linked macro-social processes—such as functional differentiation, rationalization, individualization, and, especially, the establishment of capitalism—start permeating and shaping every aspect of social life—first in the Western world and then globally (see Reckwitz, 2021, p. 32). As a result, the modern stage of "total sociation" [*totale Vergesellschaftung*], in which nothing exists that is not somehow mediated by society, is reached (Adorno, 2003, p. 23).

However, there is no agreement as to the spatial or territorial scope of that thing called society. Here one finds two apparently irreconcilable views. A first position, which in a sense coincides with common-sense thought, speaks of societies *in plural*, equating their respective territorial boundaries with those of particular nation-states (e.g., Giddens, 1995, p. 14; Schimank, 2013, pp. 11–13). A second view, in turn, argues for the existence of *a single* "world society" [*Weltgesellschaft*] (Luhmann in Nassehi, 2008, p. 88), thereby emphasizing the inextricable global interdependence of all socio-cultural phenomena in modern times (see Nassehi, 2008, p. 88; Rosa, 2021, p. 156).

Arguably, far from being mutually exclusive, both outlooks have a moment of truth and should therefore be combined. On the one hand, it is legitimate to speak of concrete national societies as relatively closed and "self-sufficient" social formations with a history and a macro-structure of their own (see Schimank, 2013, p. 11). On the other hand, it is undeniable that, thanks to ever-new advancements in transportation and communication technology, the modern world has become a global societal formation where all fundamental economic, political, and cultural processes are internationally interwoven (Nassehi, 2008, p. 88).

What Is It Like to Experience Society?

Phenomenologically speaking, the realm of human experience includes not only what can be touched, smelled, seen, tasted, or heard but *everything* that appears phenomenally. Modern society, I claim, is one of those non-sensory "things" that encounter us in everyday life. Far from being purely theoretical, this thesis is supported by our concrete life-world experience. As especially reflected in many pre- and extra-scientific discourses, every modern subject is somehow aware that she is a member of a national and/or a global society.

The frequent everyday talk about the inequality, competitiveness, polarization, or mercilessness of contemporary society is not mere "idle talk," to put it in Heideggerian jargon (see Heidegger, 2006, pp. 168–169). On the contrary, it testifies to the lived experience of being part of *large-sized* social formations that surpass by far, both in scope and in number of members, those small- and middle-scale social unities within which we conduct our most daily routines, for example, our family, group of friends, university, or work company.

From this, it follows that the notion of society and the *micro-meso-macro* distinction are not merely social-scientific "constructs of the second degree" in Schutz's terms. Instead, they seem to be firmly rooted in the first-order "common-sense constructs" prevalent in modern everyday life (see Schutz, 1962, p. 59). To be sure, this macro-social awareness is not solely an individual achievement but a form of "socially derived," "approved," and "distributed" knowledge (see Schutz, 2003, pp. 330). The emergence and consolidation of this macro-knowledge are influenced by socio-cultural factors such as socialization processes (see Berger & Luckmann, 1966, pp. 149–166), the impact of the mass media (see Schutz, 1964, pp. 113, 130), and the "double hermeneutic" (see Giddens, 1982, p. 7) between common-sense and social-scientific knowledge.

If one takes modern everyday discourses as a reliable starting point, two fundamental modes of experiencing society within the *Lebenswelt* can be analytically distinguished, namely, one in which it encounters us as an *anonymous collective subjectivity* and another whereby it manifests itself as an *objective context of quasi-spatial nature*. To use two classical concepts from Durkheim and Marx, respectively, in the first case (1) it is given to us as a "collective consciousness" (Durkheim, 1984, p. 39)—*society as subject*—whereas in the second (2) it appears as a set of "societal circumstances"—*society as object* (Marx in Marx & Engels, 1958, p. 5). Given its consistency with the theoretical definition of society offered above, I am mostly interested in the second of these modes of macro-social awareness. However, it is important to note that the two forms of experience are often fused together in common-sense thought, given the latter's unsystematic and fuzzy "style" (see Schutz, 1964, p. 79).

(1) Common everyday statements like "Argentine society is fed up with economic crises," "'society' wants us to be happy all the time," or "German society demands a political change" paradigmatically exemplify the first modality of macro-social awareness. Society is here anthropomorphized as a giant collective consciousness, a sort of *Volksgeist* able to think, feel, and want things just like individual subjects do (see Schutz, 1981, pp. 279–280). More precisely, it appears as a "generalized other" (Mead in Berger & Luckmann, 1966, p. 153), a representation of an anonymous plural subject supposedly embodying the average attitudes of "everyone" within the societal group. This experience of society is well captured by Heidegger's (2006, p. 126) concept of "the They" or "the One" [*das Man*].

(2) My focus here, however, lies on the second experience modality mentioned, which is paradigmatically reflected in quotidian expressions such as "society's economic conditions are changing rapidly" or "Latin American societies are characterized by structural social inequality." I am referring to the experience of society as a set of objectively given "societal circumstances" [*gesellschaftliche Umstände/Verhältnisse*] not freely chosen by the social actors (see Marx in Marx & Engels, 1958, p. 5, 1960, p. 115). In this sense, macrosocial objective circumstances—for example, labor market pressures, bureaucratic constraints, high inflation rates, or structural social inequalities—appear to us as an "imposed" context or situation which sets both limits and possibilities for our everyday agency (see Schutz, 1984, pp. 221, 347).

Not by chance, all the terms used to describe this second mode of encountering society, namely, "circumstances," "context," "situation," and so on, have clear *spatial* connotations. My argument is that in this modality of experience, society manifests itself as an *objective macro-social space*. By this, however, I do not mean the "social space" as conceptualized by Bourdieu (1998, pp. 10–13), who defines it as a sociological model constructed "on paper" to display large-scale social structures that are supposedly invisible to everyday actors. Rather, I am referring to our actual pre-theoretical experience of societal reality as a *lived space* in the phenomenological sense of the term.

Too Much to Handle: The "Exceedance" of the Macro-social Space

In the following pages, I will restrict myself to the analysis of the experience of society as a macro-social space. My argument is that we (late) modern individuals experience the "objective" societal context as an "imposed transcendence" (see Schutz, 1962, p. 330), which, in its mighty immensity, surpasses and overpowers our subjectivities. Drawing on classical and contemporary societal-theoretical reflection, I claim that one can analytically distinguish two—factually closely linked—ways of subjectively encountering society's *exceedance*,[5] namely, an *existential* and a *cognitive* one. Due to space constrictions, I will reserve an examination of the former for future works and dedicate the final section of this chapter to an in-depth analysis of the latter.

What I call the *existential exceedance* of society is particularly analyzed by the "Weberian-Marxist" tradition (see Löwy, 1996; Lukács, 1967). It can be characterized as a chronical *sense of powerlessness* of the individual in the face of the overwhelming "mute compulsions" (Marx in Marx & Engels, 1962, p. 764; Mau, 2021) emanating from modernity's huge capitalist-bureaucratic-technocratic apparatus. Sketching the outlines of a "phenomenology of modernity" (Giddens, 1995, p. 137), Weber (1986, pp. 388–390) has coined the image of the "shell as hard as steel" [*stahlhartes Gehäuse*] to describe this cold

---

[5] Marion (2002) has developed a phenomenological account of "exceedance" or "excess" in connection with his analysis of "saturated phenomena." The idea of conceptualizing the macrosocial as a saturated phenomenon stems from Carlos Belvedere.

and monstrous "machinery" and the feeling of helplessness of those trapped within it.

In turn, the *cognitive* or *experiential transcendence* of macro-social reality, which I will discuss below in detail, consists in the modern subject's inability to obtain a complete knowledge of the social totality in all its vastness and complexity. To put it in Schutz's (1964, p. 120) words, the "outstanding feature of a man's life in the modern world is his conviction that his life-world as a whole is neither fully understood by himself nor fully understandable to any of his fellowmen." This inability, as we will see, is pragmatically palliated in everyday life by means of cognitive mapping (see, e.g., Popitz et al., 2018, pp. 2–8).

4   Cognitive Mapping as a Way to Overcome the Transcendence of Society

As different sociological theorists have suggested (see Popitz et al., 2018, pp. 2–8; Gehlen, 1949, p. 7; Schutz, 1964, p. 120), modern subjects are chronically unable to gain comprehensive knowledge of the society they live in. The societal totality seems to surpass their experiential and cognitive abilities by far, being both imperceptible and unknowable as a whole. This is not only due to the vast immensity of the macro-social space, within which a countless number of relations are interwoven at a transregional and international level, but also because of its great complexity. Modern societies are internally differentiated into specialized social spheres that appear to be indifferent to each other but are in fact deeply interconnected through intricate chains of unintended consequences of action (see Gehlen, 1949, pp. 9, 11, 13). As Arnold Gehlen (1949, p. 11) puts in a still-timely 1949 study, "[I]t may never have been more difficult to acquire a serviceable knowledge of the large-scale circumstances than it is today."

Being unable to act without a sense of the complex societal reality within which they live, everyday actors are forced to overcome the experiential transcendence of modern society life by means of cognitive mapping, that is, by constructing and using cartographical representations of the macro-social space. One of the most detailed theoretical treatments of this process can be found in a classic sociological study by Heinrich Popitz, Hans Paul Bahrdt, and their team, entitled *Das Gesellschaftsbild des Arbeiters* (Popitz et al., 2018). In what follows, I will argue that if combined and supplemented with insights from Schutz's life-world phenomenology, the *Gesellschaftsbilder* theory offers a solid starting point for a phenomenological analysis of cognitive mapping as a way of surpassing the experiential exceedance of society.

Images of Society as Cognitive Maps

According to Popitz et al. (2018, p. 248), modern subjects are unable to experience firsthand, let alone to fully comprehend, the highly complex macroeconomic, political, and social conditions within which their existence is embedded. In modernity, there is an insurmountable gap between the narrowness of an individual's "area of immediate lived experience" (p. 248), that is, that segment of social reality available to her in direct perception and knowledge, and the vast plexus of societal processes having an impact on her daily life. This cognitive discrepancy, as it were, is not only due to the essential spatiotemporal limitedness of the subjective perspective but also due to the specialization process typical of modernity, which binds individuals to partial viewpoints, precluding them from gaining an overall view of social totality (pp. 2–5).

As Popitz et al. argue, every modern individual is well aware of being deeply affected by societal powers and processes that transcend her area of direct experience and knowledge. For instance, she knows that "things" she neither sees nor fully comprehends, like the current "political and economic crisis" in her country, the "global rise of inflation," or the emergence of "a new pandemic," could significantly impact on her daily life. In order to make sense of these transcendences, she has no choice but to go beyond what is directly experienceable, which she does by building a cognitive "representation" [*Vorstellung*] of the macro-social order, namely, an "image of society" [*Gesellschaftsbild*]. Generally speaking, the latter is an "overall picture" of the "totality" of societal conditions utilized by the subject as an "interpretive schema" for making sense of all sorts of social phenomena (pp. 2–8).

An image of society thus understood operates as a "cognitive map" (see Ungar, 2005; Jameson, 1988). It constitutes a cartographic representation of the societal space, including the actor's own "location" or "position" within it, which helps her navigate everyday life (Popitz et al., 2018, pp. 9, 247). More precisely, it should be characterized as a "cognitive-evaluative map" (Rosa, 2012, p. 380), as it is through and through permeated by evaluations: each segment or region of the social world appears as having a higher or lower value for the subject.

Two clarifications are needed here to avoid misunderstandings. First, images of society are not solely an individual achievement but stem mostly from established socio-cultural repertoires: philosophical or sociological knowledge, mass media discourses, artistic works, and so on (see Popitz et al., 2018, p. 5). And, second, even though they are inherently representational in nature, they do not need to be "consulted" thematically every time anew, as it were. Rather, they operate implicitly within pre-reflective experience as a background know-how underlying our ability to find our bearings in the social surroundings (see pp. 8–9).

Interestingly, Popitz et al.'s account stresses that the process of building images of the macro-social always carries a "danger," namely, that of losing touch with reality and falling into the realm of the "imaginary." Since *Gesellschaftsbilder* cannot be controlled, corrected, or corroborated by direct everyday experience, there is always the possibility of fabricating fantasy worlds where mysterious powers, existing in the shadows, govern the fate of society (p. 3). This warning is highly topical in light of the current rise of conspiracy theories worldwide (see Butter, 2020).

What Is It Like to Map Society? Toward a Phenomenology of Cognitive Mapping

The *Gesellschaftsbilder* theory has a phenomenological flair to it. However, it does not offer the conceptual resources necessary for systematically describing the representational-cartographic mode of experiencing society that it calls attention to. I argue that to get those resources, one needs to turn to life-world phenomenology. As I shall show in the following, the Schutzian phenomenological approach provides at least four theoretical contributions relevant in this regard, namely (1) an analysis of the way in which "transcendences" are experienced and dealt with in everyday life, (2) an examination of the structure and workings of "horizonal awareness," (3) a description of the quasi-spatial "structuring of the social world," and (4) some reflections on the cartographic nature of common-sense knowledge and experience.

The Transcendences of the Life-World

The *Gesellschaftsbilder* theory correctly suggests that society transcends our sphere of direct experience and knowledge. As I shall show, this crucial insight might be conceptually refined with the help of life-world phenomenology. Schutz (1984, p. 306) and Luckmann (2002, p. 143) claim that the experience of "transcendences" constitutes a universal feature of human life. Every human being, in all times and places, is well aware of the limited nature of her experiential life. She knows that she is part of a broader world, both natural and social, which harbors much more entities, processes, and events than those she is currently perceiving, either externally or internally. And she also knows that those not-yet-perceived or even unperceivable "things" affect her life in significant ways (see Luckmann, 2002, pp. 140–143; Schutz, 1962, p. 330).

Every day, we encounter different kinds of these "transcendences." We have to turn around to see what is happening behind our back; we never have total access to what another person is thinking or feeling; and we are unable to witness a war taking place in a faraway country, although we might know about it from the news (see Luckmann, 2002, p. 141). As paradoxically as it may sound, our experience of transcendence can be described as *the accessibility of the inaccessible* or, put differently, as the presence of an absence (see Waldenfels, 2007, p. 10).

Now, it is crucial for human beings to gain some knowledge about these *experienced inaccessibilities*, especially of those related to social life, in order to be able to navigate the everyday life-world. Not having some idea of what other persons might think about me, what is happening some blocks from home, or the current state of my country's macroeconomy could be as disadvantageous as dangerous. This is why every socio-cultural group provides its members with a series of cognitive devices to "come to terms" with transcendences of different kinds (Schutz, 1984, p. 338). Among them are sets of socially approved typifications—of things, processes, persons, and situations—and systems of signs, marks, and symbols (see Luckmann, 2002, p. 143; Schutz, 1962, p. 331).

Importantly, our knowledge of the existence and consistency of these transcendences is itself a *constituent part* of our life-world. The latter could not appear as it does, namely, as a structured field made up of entities, persons, events, institutions, and so on, if our experience was confined to the narrow sphere of that which, strictly speaking, is directly perceived. Although we are mostly unaware of it, our common-sense experience involves manifold "contributions" of the mind that enrich the poverty of the immediately given, thereby constituting a meaningful world of objects, subjects, and processes (Schutz, 1962, pp. 3–4).

Even the apparently most "concrete facts" we encounter in the *Lebenswelt*, namely, the material things perceived, "are not as concrete as they seem" (pp. 3–4). The kernel of what is sensory given in strict sense is always less than the mundane thing actually *perceived*. If we would not "complete" what we *actually* see by means of the contributions of the mind mentioned, we would not be able to perceive material objects as such. For instance, I am now certain of *perceiving* my copy of *Das Kapital* on my desk, although what I *actually see* is only one side of it, namely, its cover. This is possible because I tacitly and passively "supplement" my partial perception through "appresentations" anticipating the book's now unseen but potentially seeable parts—its back cover and interior (see p. 295).

In addition to passive "appresentations," our consciousness enriches our life-world experience through various socially pre-formed cognitive operations, including "idealizations" (see p. 4), "categorial intuitions" (see p. 110), and "presentifications" [*Vergegenwärtigungen*] (see pp. 145–146),[6] all of which are grouped by Schutz under Whitehead's concept of "the imagination of hypothetical sense presentations" (p. 3).

Horizonal Awareness and the World as the "All-Encompassing Horizon"

The phenomenological concept of "horizon" in general and that of the "world" as the "all-embracing horizon" in particular (see Husserl, 1954, p. 141; Gurwitsch, 2012, p. 500) allow for an accurate description of how the transcendence of the macro-social space is encountered and navigated in everyday life. If one understands society as synonymous with "social world," that is, as the "all-embracing horizon" or totality of social reality in modernity, then societal cognitive mapping can be reconceptualized as a form of "horizonal consciousness."[7]

One of the main findings of phenomenological research is that objects, whatever their type, never appear as completely self-contained and contextless. Rather, every object is experienced from the outset as inherently exceeding itself in manifold ways, tacitly referring to surrounding phenomena either not currently perceived or not occupying the center of attention (Schutz, 1984,

---

[6] Schutz borrows all these concepts from Husserl.

[7] Gunderson (2021) offers an interesting analysis of the experience of macro-social structures as a form of horizonal or marginal consciousness not far from the one I provide here.

pp. 335–338). As Schutz puts it, the intentional object or noema always carries its "horizons," and our "experience of the transcendence of the experiential content is horizonal intentionality" (p. 338).

The content of lived experience is therefore never an isolated object but one embedded within a complex fabric of phenomenality. Even though we may not realize it, there is always more to phenomenal experience than what our mind concentrates on. Phenomenologists refer to the "totality" of phenomena co-given to me at a certain moment as the "field of consciousness" (see Gurwitsch, 2012, p. 2). If one follows Schutz (2011, p. 94),[8] this field is always and essentially structured into two fundamental domains, namely, the "theme" and the "horizon." As its name implies, the theme is what occupies my explicit center of attention at present, namely, the noema as such (see Gurwitsch, 2012, p. 4). The horizon, in turn, can be described as an implicit co-consciousness of phenomena surrounding the theme, which appear as the "background" over against the latter stands out (p. 4).

Horizonal consciousness is thus a non-thematic "experience of context" that always accompanies our thematic object-experience (p. 5). Phenomenologically, it is possible to differentiate two kinds of horizons, namely, the "inner" and the "outer" one. The former constitutes what might be called the *immanent* context of the object, that is, its now unperceived or unattended sides, which are nonetheless tacitly present as constituent parts thereof—for instance, the now unseen back cover of my copy of *Das Kapital*. As for the outer horizon, the most important for my argumentation, it can be defined as the actually *transcendent* context of the noema including the "co-objects" [*Mitobjekte*] surrounding it, which are not thematized right now but could be at any time (Schutz, 1984, p. 335; Husserl, 1972, p. 28).

Here I come to the core of my argument. According to phenomenologists, the outer horizon of experience includes both the *micro*-context and the *macro*-context of experience. That is, it encompasses not only the object's immediate surroundings but also the larger-scale environment within which the former are necessarily embedded, namely, the "world" (see Gurwitsch, 2012, p. 501). Seeing my copy of *Das Kapital* on my desk, I am not only horizonally aware of the objects immediately surrounding it, such as my lamp, my steaming cup of coffee, and so on, but also of the things "behind my back" in my room, of my whole apartment where I live and work, of the Buenos Aires neighborhood where it is located, of the entire city as such, of Argentina as a country, and so on and so forth up to the *world as a whole* (see Schutz, 1962, p. 108). In this sense, the life-world can be characterized as the "all-encompassing" (Gurwitsch, 2012, p. 500) or "universal horizon" (Husserl, 1954, p. 141) embracing the totality of what is potentially experienceable.

A fundamental insight follows from this: we are *always* somehow aware of the life-world as a whole, whether we notice it or not (see Husserl, 1972,

---

[8] In contrast to Schutz, Gurwitsch (see 2012, p. 4) speaks of three fundamental "domains" of the field of consciousness, namely, the "theme," the "thematic field," and the "margin."

p. 26). The horizonal awareness of the world *qua* totality "pervades all our conscious life," tacitly accompanying *each and every one* of our object-experiences (see Gurwitsch, 2012, p. 504). Importantly, the ubiquity of our world-awareness is not without consequences. It impacts the very mode of givenness of things: every particular object not only appears as belonging to the world but is also marked with a "positional index" denoting its location within it (see Gurwitsch, 2012, p. 503).

To be sure, the life-world as universal horizon is given to us in a rather indeterminate, indistinct, and even vague manner, especially when compared to the direct and/or thematic experience of objects (see Schutz, 1984, p. 335). However, it is essential to note that our horizonal world-awareness is never completely empty. Even without knowing each and every one of its particular regions, entities, and processes firsthand—which is in fact impossible, given the life-world's infinite extension—we always already have some "pre-knowledge" of its general structures and a "familiarity" with it based thereon (Husserl, 1972, pp. 27, 33). To use Schutz's (1962, p. 7) words, the *Lebenswelt* manifests itself from the outset as a "horizon of familiarity and pre-acquaintanceship."

Importantly, this pre-knowledge of the world is essentially of *typical* nature. We know what to typically expect from the life-world in general—it has a "typicality as a totality" (Husserl, 1972, p. 33)—and from its typical "things" in particular, such as "tables," "schools," "institutions," "books," "friendships," or "videogames" (see pp. 33, 35). For instance, even if I have not met my brother's new puppy yet, I have some idea of what it looks like and how it is to interact with it: I know how typical "puppies" typically behave, how they typically play, what they typically like and dislike, and so on. According to Schutz (1962, p. 7, 10), our pre-knowledge of the *Lebenswelt* as lay actors is based on a "stock of knowledge" made up of a system of "typifications," which we acquire and sediment through complex socialization processes and ends up functioning as our "scheme of reference" for defining our situation in the world.

To sum up, our primary mode of encountering and knowing the world as a macro-phenomenon is that of implicit-horizonal consciousness, and not that of thematic "image-like representations" (see Gurwitsch, 2012, p. 496). It is more of a tacit know-how than an explicit know-that. However, and this is crucial, there is always the possibility to "explicate" this rather vague world-awareness via thematic presentifications with a more or less determinate content. I can actively "move along" in my "imagination," as it were, and picture how remote or inaccessible regions of the *Lebenswelt* would look like (p. 498). Arguably, discrepancies and even tensions are likely to occur between our implicit-horizonal and our explicit-representational mode of macro-awareness (see Rosa, 2012, pp. 111–117).

The Social World—Or Society in the First-Person Perspective

The considerations on transcendences and horizonal world-experience introduced above are still too abstract to help us develop a full-blown phenomenological analysis of macro-social awareness via cognitive mapping. I argue that Schutz's application of these general ideas to the more concrete analysis of the "social world" takes us a step further.

Unlike most theories of society, which analyze societal reality from above and in the third-person perspective, life-world phenomenology attempts to describe it exactly as it is experienced from the first-person viewpoint. In this approach, society is conceptualized as *the* "social world," understood as the universal horizon that encompasses the totality of social reality, including not only individual alter egos but also different kinds of supraindividual "socio-facts" (Schutz, 2011, p. 285). Among these are small- and large-scale "social entities" [*soziale Gebilde*], structures, and orders such as families, social classes, states, and markets (see Schutz, 1981, pp. 245–289).

Schutz conceives of the social structuring of the life-world as isomorphic to its spatial stratification (see Schutz, 1984, p. 250). For this reason, it is necessary to say a few words about the latter in order to understand the former. The starting point of any phenomenological analysis of *lived spatiality* is the living body, or *Leib*, which operates as the "center O of my system of coordinates" around which the entire space unfolds and organizes itself (Schutz, 1962, p. 222). The position of my *Leib* is the absolute "Here" in reference to which the elements and segments of my surroundings are spatially grouped. It is only relatively to my body's location at a given moment, and not in an absolute sense, that things and places appear as being far, near, below, above, and so on (pp. 222, 306–307).

To the individual subject, the *Lebenswelt* appears as spatially stratified into two fundamental regions, which differ in their degree of experiential "accessibility," namely, the "world within my actual reach" and the "world within my potential reach" (Schutz, 1962, pp. 134, 224, 307). The former includes all objects, entities, and processes currently within the scope of my sensory perception, some of which I can manipulate directly. As for the latter, it constitutes that sector of the life-world not perceptually accessible right now but potentially perceivable in the near or distant future (pp. 224–226; 307–308). To be sure, the transition between these two regions is fluid, as I can use my own body and other means of transportation to move across the space, transforming my current "There" in a "Here" (see p. 178).

While the "world within my actual reach" is directly and thematically experienced, the "world within my potential reach" constitutes a cognitive transcendence primarily experienced in the mode of horizonal consciousness. I am tacitly aware of the existence of this now invisible spatial sector and know it shows a typically similar structure to that of the "world within actual reach." My specific typifications of it are more or less determinate depending on whether I have been there before or not (see Schutz, 2003, p. 327, 1962, p. 225).

Just as in the case of lived spatiality, the social life-world unfolds around me as a center. My own body's spatial location constitutes the origin of the coordinate system in terms of which social reality is mapped. Metaphorically speaking, however, my social position, for example, my status, role, and class, also plays a key role in this respect. In this sense, terms like "you," "we," or "they," used in everyday life to depict "social distance" and proximity, are not absolute but relative values, obtaining their meaning in reference to my own location in both the physical and social space (see Schutz, 2003, p. 98, 1962, pp. 9, 15).

The social world is also given to me as being structured into two fundamental regions with different experiential accessibility, which correspond to the two zones of lived spatiality mentioned above. I am referring to the "social *Umwelt*," or world of "consociates," and the "social *Mitwelt*," or world of "contemporaries." While the former correlates with the "world within my actual reach," the latter does so with the "world within my potential reach" (Schutz, 1962, p. 134, 2003, p. 329). Again, the transition between these two regions is relatively fluid because of my ability to move across the (social) space (see Schutz, 2003, p. 98). The thesis I want to defend in what follows is that the social *Mitwelt* constitutes the home of our experience of the macro-social in modernity.

My *Umwelt* constitutes the zone of the social world of which I have the most direct and immediate knowledge possible: the *micro-context* in which all my "face-to-face" interactions, ranging from the most superfluous to the most intimate ones, take place. This region is inhabited by my "consociates," a number of alter egos with whom I intercorporeally share a segment of space within reach. As I am able to directly perceive their bodies *qua* psycho-physical units, I vividly experience them "in the flesh" as concrete and individual embodied persons (see Schutz, 1962, pp. 16–17, 1984, pp. 250, 267–268). Importantly, the *Umwelt* also harbors a specific kind of supraindividual formations made up of "consociates," namely, "primary groups." These are small-scale social groups that allow for constant face-to-face contact between their members, such as families, groups of friends, or certain work groups (see Schutz, 1962, p. 354, 1984, p. 365).[9]

The *Mitwelt*, on the other hand, is the sector of the social life-world that lies outside my actual perceptual reach and, arguably, encompasses the entire *macro-context* surrounding the *Umwelt* in modern societies. The lack of spatial-intercorporeal community precludes me from directly experiencing its inhabitants, the "mere contemporaries," as I do with my "consociates." Accordingly, the *Mitwelt* is not perceived "in the flesh" but appears as a cognitive transcendence that we overcome primarily through horizonal consciousness and secondarily by thematic presentifications and categorial intuitions (see Schutz, 1984, pp. 250, 268, 1962, p. 17).

---

[9] Importantly, with the emergence of the cyberspace in the last decades, the *Umwelt* has expanded to include people located in the *Mitwelt* but with whom I can establish *quasi*-face-to-face relationships, either via videotelephony or via chat. These alter egos have been called "consociates contemporaries" (see Zhao, 2004). Along these lines, WhatsApp chat groups could be understood as *quasi*-primary groups.

More precisely, I only have an indirect experience of my "contemporaries" by means of "typifications" or "ideal types," which are mostly socio-culturally originated. I am not able to experience these Others as concrete and unique embodied subjectivities but solely as exemplars of certain "type" of persons, having "typical" motives, attitudes, courses-of-action, and so on (Schutz, 1984, pp. 250, 268, 364, 1981, pp. 256–258). Importantly, the typifying constructs used here show divergent degrees of "fullness and emptiness" or, what is the same thing, of "intimacy and anonymity," which gives the *Mitwelt* a complex, multifaceted character (Schutz, 2003, p. 329).

Consider, for instance, the difference between the typical experience we have of a particular "contemporary" whose personal traits we only know from the media, for example, some prominent politician, and that of the generic bearers of established social functions or roles, such as delivery persons or police officers. In the first case, I resort to a *subjective*, "characterological" typification that shows a certain degree of fullness of content and even of intimacy (see Schutz, 1981, p. 277, 1962, p. 17). By contrast, the typifying constructs operative in the second case are *objective*, "functionary" types, that is, relatively empty and anonymous typifications that do not grasp the Other as a concrete individual but merely as a typical performer of a typical social role or function (Schutz, 1964, p. 45, 1962, p. 17).

However, and this is crucial for my argument, the *Mitwelt* not only harbors typified alter egos but also typified supraindividual sociofacts. I am referring to the anonymous, big-scale groups, institutions, and structures characteristic of modern societies, such as classes, nations, organizations, states, or capitalist markets (see Schutz, 1981, pp. 279–280). In this sense, this region of the social world can be regarded as the home of everyday macro-social awareness, or, put differently, as the very place where complex socio-structural conditions manifest.

Unlike "primary groups," whose workings can be observed *in vivo* within the *Umwelt*, these macro-social entities are perceptually intangible, only being known by their effects. As Schutz (see 1984, p. 364) suggests, they do not appear as material things but, rather, as "ideal objects" apprehended through categorial intuitions, similar to how numbers, social-theoretical notions, or mathematical axioms are experienced (see Schutz, 1962, p. 110). In line with Weber (see 1984, p. 30), life-world phenomenology assumes that, despite escaping sensory observation, our ideal representations concerning the existence, validity, and structure of macro-social entities are a constituent part of social reality (see Schutz, 1962, pp. 354–355). As the "Thomas theorem" has it, if human beings "define situations as real, they are real in their consequences" (p. 348).

More precisely, the organization and functions of these macro-social entities are grasped in everyday life by means of objective-anonymous "ideal-typical conceptual constructs," which are much more abstract and assumption-rich than those used to typify alter egos (see Schutz, 1981, p 251, 279). Modern societies are permeated through and through by "rationalization" processes that involve a growing formalization and anonymization of social organization (see Schutz, 1964, p. 71); however, the typifications of macro-social entities show different degrees of emptiness and anonymity. For instance, the ideal representation of a concrete institution as the German parliament is less empty than those of the global working class, the capitalist system, or the finance markets (see pp. 251, 279).

In the present context, it is not possible to offer a complete account of Schutz's treatment of our experience of large-scale social phenomena in the *Mitwelt*. However, it is worth mentioning three key features of this experience that must be considered. First, in everyday life, we grasp and understand the texture and stratification of complex "institutionalized forms of social organization," for example, the hierarchic structure of a company or a state, through "networks of typifications" (Schutz, 1964, pp. 230, 232). Second, macro-social entities are often anthropomorphized by common-sense thought, being conceived as plural subjects capable to think and act (see Schutz, 1981, p. 279). And finally, symbolic constructions play a critical role in how we make sense of these entities (see Schutz, 1984, p. 364), as is evident in the case of nations, understood as "imagined communities" (Anderson, 1985) condensed into symbols like flags, national anthems, or literary figures (see Dreher & Figueroa-Dreher, 2011).

Rounding Off the Picture: Cartographic Metaphors and the Problem of Relevance

The concepts employed by life-world phenomenology to describe the mode of givenness of the world-phenomenon in general and of the social world in particular are primarily of a spatial nature, including terms like "horizon," "surroundings," "field," "zones," and "regions." This already suggests the usefulness of phenomenological analysis in accurately describing how we mentally map society in everyday life. But Schutz goes even further and uses cartographic metaphors himself to portray the nature and workings of our knowledge of the social world (see, e.g., López, 2021). I would like to conclude this section by saying a few words about this.

In some of his writings, Schutz (1964, p. 99) depicts the socially established stock of knowledge of a group as a "scheme of orientation," that is, as a sort of map used by its members to find their way in the socio-cultural surroundings. Further, he explicitly compares how we navigate the social world on a daily basis with our quasi-cartographic sense of orientation in our hometown, highlighting the differences between this rather unsystematic and intuitive form of cognitive mapping and the scientific maps developed by cartographers (p. 66). Finally, in line with contemporary positions like Rosa's (see 2012, p. 380) account of "cognitive-evaluative maps," Schutz (1964, pp. 124–125) points out that the social life-world is not a homogeneous, value-neutral space but, rather, one stratified into different "zones" with varying degrees of "relevance" according to our specific "interests at hand." In this sense, the world appears to us in a similar way to a "topographic map" in which "peaks and valleys, foothills and slopes, are spread over [...] in infinitely diversified configurations" (p. 124). The relevant "peaks" are those regions we have a deeper and clearer knowledge of, while the opposite seems to be true for the irrelevant "slopes" (see p. 124).

Addressing the issue of "relevance" is crucial for rounding off my attempt of phenomenologically analyzing how we map the macro-social space in everyday life. If one follows Schutz's tenets, the scope and complexion of a social actor's map of society hinges on her specific "system of relevances," which in turn depends to a great extent on her socio-cultural position, for example, her social role, profession, class, and gender (see p. 124). Accordingly, in social formations characterized by constantly growing social differentiation, hyper-specialization, and cultural pluralization like the (late) modern ones the "images of society" tend to multiplicate and diversify.

5 Cognitive Maps in the Post-Truth Era: A Final Reflection

To conclude, I would like to briefly and tentatively reflect on a crucial issue that was only touched upon in passing in the preceding pages but deserves to be the focus of future investigations. I am referring to the problem of the truthfulness or falsehood of everyday cognitive maps of society, or, more precisely, of their adequacy—or lack thereof—to *actual* societal reality. This problem, closely linked to the classical *topos* of ideology as a form of "false consciousness," becomes especially relevant today with the rise of the "post-truth" era (see Zoglauer, 2023). In particular, conspiracy theories can be regarded as delusional macro-social cognitive maps that are not adequate to the factual structures of contemporary societies (see Butter, 2020). "Conspiracy," writes Fredric Jameson (1988, p. 356), "is the poor person's cognitive mapping in the postmodern age."

To be sure, this issue only arises as such if one assumes, as I do in line with authors like Rosa (see 2012, p. 273) and Jameson (see 1988, p. 348), that capitalist modern "societies" do exist as organized social totalities governed by more or less unified logics that can be known through theoretical and empirical social research. Only by accepting the existence of structured macro-social formations of this sort can one classify everyday socio-cognitive maps, or "images of society," as being more or less "accurate." This assumption, however, is systematically denied by different parties both inside and outside social-scientific thought, such as post-structuralists, post-colonialists, methodological individualists, and neoliberals. With different arguments, epistemological, ontological, political, or ethical, they all seem to agree that "there is no such thing as society" (see Rosa, 2012, p. 273).

Today, the possibility of building "inadequate," "inaccurate," or "false" cognitive maps of the macro-social space seems to be especially high. This is not only because of the ever-growing, almost unmanageable complexity of contemporary societies but also because of the proliferation of fake-news, mis-information, and conspiracy theories on social media. As suggested above, however, I have the impression that cognitive maps can never be *completely delusional*, at least not on the level of pre-reflective agency. A minimum of "reality principle" seems to be indispensable for individuals to be able to "successfully" adapt to the inescapable, steel-hard constraints of late modern societal structures. If this is true, then one and the same individual may operate with a conspiracy theory on the explicit level of self-interpretation and be a "capitalist realist," as it were (Fisher, 2009), on that of implicit pre-reflective agency.

As especially Jameson (1988) has shown, building adequate cognitive maps of the "social totality" is crucial for achieving emancipatory political aims, for "the incapacity to map socially is as crippling to political experience as the analogous incapacity to map spatially is for urban experience" (p. 353). Insofar as it contributes to gaining an accurate big picture of societal reality, the project of a phenomenological theory of society should be regarded not only as a social-scientific endeavor but also as a political one.

References

Adorno, T. W. (2003). *Einleitung in die Soziologie.* Suhrkamp.

Anderson, B. (1985). *Imagined communities. Reflections on the origin and spread of nationalism.* Verso.

Archer, M. (1995). *Realist social theory. The morphogenetic approach.* Cambridge University Press.

Bachmann-Medick, D. (2016). *Cultural turns: New orientations in the study of culture.* De Gruyter.

Belvedere, C. (2011). *Problemas de fenomenología social.* Prometeo.

Belvedere, C. (2022). *A treatise in phenomenological sociology: Object, method, findings, and applications.* Lexington Books.

Berger, P., & Luckmann, T. (1966). *The social construction of reality. A treatise in the sociology of knowledge.* Anchor Books.

Bongaerts, G. (2012). *Sinn.* transcript.

Bourdieu, P. (1989). Social space and symbolic power. *Sociological Theory, 7*(1), 14–25.

Bourdieu, P. (1990). *The logic of practice.* Stanford University Press.

Bourdieu, P. (1998). *Practical reason: On the theory of action.* Stanford University Press.

Bourdieu, P. (2013). *Outline of a theory of practice.* Cambridge University Press.

Butter, M. (2020). *"Nichts ist wie es scheint." Über Verschwörungstheorien.* Suhrkamp.

Celikates, R. (2009). *Kritik als soziale Praxis. Gesellschaftliche Selbstverständigung und kritische Theorie.* Campus.

Dilthey, W. (1981). *Der Aufbau der geschichtlichen Welt in den Geisteswissenschaften.* Suhrkamp.

Dreher, J., & Figueroa-Dreher, S. (2011). De Bandido a Héroe: el poder integrador del simbolismo gaucho en la Argentina. In S. Figueroa-Dreher et al. (Eds.), *Construcciones de identidad y simbolismo gaucho en Argentina* (pp. 153–186). Prometeo.

Durkheim, É. (1984). *The division of labour in society.* Macmillan.

Durkheim, É. (1986). *Les règles de la méthode sociologique*. Presses Universitaires de France.

Eberle, T. (1993). Schütz' Lebensweltanalyse: Soziologie oder Protosoziologie? In A. Bäumer & M. Benedikt (Eds.), *Gelehrtenrepublik – Lebenswelt: Edmund Husserl und Alfred Schütz in der Krisis der phänomenologischen Bewegung* (pp. 293–320). Passagen.

Eberle, T. (2009). In search for Aprioris. Schutz's life-world analysis and Mises's praxeology. In H. Nasu et al. (Eds.), *Alfred Schutz and his intellectual partners* (pp. 493–518). UVK.

Eberle, T., & Srubar, I. (2010). Einleitung. In A. Schütz (Ed.), *Zur Methodologie der Sozialwissenschaften. Alfred Schütz Werkausgabe, Bd. 4* (pp. 9–44). UVK.

Embree, L. (2010). Interdisciplinarity within phenomenology. *Indo-Pacific Journal of Phenomenology, 10*(1), 1–7.

Endreß, M., & Lindemann, G. (2021). Phänomenologien und Gesellschaftstheorien, Call for Papers der Interdisziplinären Arbeitskreis Phänomenologie und Soziologie, Sommertagung der DGS-Sektion Soziologische Theorien. https://soziologie.de/fileadmin/sektionen/iaps/6._Tagung_des_IAPS_-_Gesellschaftstheorien__Delmenhorst_2022_.pdf

Fisher, M. (2009). *Capitalist Realism: Is There No Alternative?*. Winchester, UK: Zero Books.

Gardiner, M. (2000). *Critiques of everyday life: An introduction*. Routledge.

Gehlen, A. (1949). *Sozialpsychologische Probleme in der industriellen Gesellschaft*. Mohr (Paul Siebeck).

Geißler, R. (2014). *Die Sozialstruktur Deutschlands*. Springer.

Giddens, A. (1982). *Profiles and critiques in social theory*. Macmillan.

Giddens, A. (1995). *The consequences of modernity*. Polity Press.

Gros, A. (2022). A phenomenology of modernity? Alfred Schutz's contributions to a theory of modern society. In M. Barber (Ed.), *The Anthem companion to Alfred Schutz* (pp. 115–136). Anthem Press.

Gros, A. (2023). ¿Qué es la fenomenología? Una introducción breve y actualizada para sociólogos. *Revista Colombiana de Sociología, 46*(1), 293–324.

Gros, A. (2019). Towards a Phenomenological Critical Theory: Hartmut Rosa's Sociology of the Relationship to the World. *Revista Científica Foz, 2*(1), 8–46.

Guenther, L. (2021). Six senses of critique for critical phenomenology. *Puncta, 4*(2), 5–23.

Gunderson, R. (2021). How do social structures become taken for granted? Social reproduction in calm and crisis. *Human Studies, 44*, 741–762.

Gurwitsch, A. (2012). *The collected works of Aron Gurwitsch (1901–1973): Volume III: The field of consciousness: Theme, thematic field, and margin*. Springer.

Habermas, J. (1981). *Theorie des kommunikativen Handelns, Bd. 2*. Suhrkamp.

Heidegger, M. (2000). Die Frage nach der Technik. In M. Heidegger (Ed.), *Gesamtausgabe, Bd. 7, Vorträge und Aufsätze* (pp. 1–53). Vittorio Klostermann.

Heidegger, M. (2006). *Sein und Zeit*. Max Niemeyer.

Henry, M. (1990). *Phénoménologie matérielle*. Presses Universitaires de France.

Hörnqvist, M. (2022). Critique and cognitive capacities: Towards an action-oriented model. *Philosophy & Social Criticism, 48*(1), 62–85.

Husserl, E. (1950). *Cartesianische Meditationen und Pariser Vorträge. Husserliana I*. Martinus Nijhoff.

Husserl, E. (1954). *Die Krisis der europäischen Wissenschaften und die transzendentale Phänomenologie: eine Einleitung in die phänomenologische Philosophie. Husserliana VI.* Martinus Nijhoff.

Husserl, E. (1962). *Phänomenologische Psychologie: Vorlesungen Sommersemester 1925. Husserliana IX.* Martinus Nijhoff.

Husserl, E. (1972). *Erfahrung und Urteil: Untersuchungen zur Genealogie der Logik.* Felix Meiner.

Jaeggi, R. (2014). *Kritik von Lebensformen.* Suhrkamp.

Jameson, F. (1988). Cognitive mapping. In C. Nelson & L. Grossberg (Eds.), *Marxism and the interpretation of culture* (pp. 347–358). Macmillan Education.

Keller, R. (2012). *Das interpretative Paradigma.* VS Verlag für Sozialwissenschaften.

Lindemann, G. (2009). *Das Soziale von seinen Grenzen her denken.* Velbrück Wissenschaft.

López, D. (2021). Schutzian social cartography. *Sociologia e ricerca sociale, 124*(1), 69–90.

Löwy, M. (1996). Figures of Weberian Marxism. *Theory and Society, 25*(3), 431–446.

Luckmann, T. (1979). Phänomenologie und Soziologie. In W. M. Sprondel & R. Grathoff (Eds.), *Alfred Schütz und die Idee des Alltags in den Sozialwissenschaften* (pp. 196–206). Enke.

Luckmann, T. (1980). *Lebenswelt und Gesellschaft: Grundstrukturen und geschichtliche Wandlungen.* Schöningh.

Luckmann, T. (1991). Protosoziologie als Protopsychologie? In M. Herzog & C. F. Graumann (Eds.), *Sinn und Erfahrung: Phänomenologische Methoden in den Humanwissenschaften* (pp. 155–168). Roland Asanger.

Luckmann, T. (2002). *Wissen und Gesellschaft.* UVK.

Luckmann, T., & Schütz, A. (2003). *Strukturen der Lebenswelt.* UVK.

Luckmann, T. (2007). *Lebenswelt, Identität und Gesellschaft.* UVK.

Lukács, G. (1967). *Geschichte und Klassenbewusstsein: Studien über marxistische Dialektik.* Luchterhand.

Manzo, G. (2015). Macrosociology-microsociology. In J. D. Wright (Ed.), *International Encyclopedia of the social & behavioral sciences, Vol. 14* (pp. 414–421). Elsevier.

Marcuse, H. (1955). *Eros and civilization: An inquiry into Freud.* Beacon Press.

Marion, J. L. (2002). *In excess: Studies of saturated phenomena.* Fordham University Press.

Marx, K., & Engels, F. (1958). *Werke, Bd. 3.* Dietz.

Marx, K., & Engels, F. (1960). *Werke, Bd. 8.* Dietz.

Marx, K., & Engels, F. (1962). *Werke, Bd. 23.* Dietz.

Mau, S. (2021). Stummer Zwang als besondere Form der Macht. Marx' Beitrag zur Theorie der abstrakten und unpersönlichen Herrschaft des Kapitals. *Prokla. Zeitschrift für kritische Sozialwissenschaft, 51*(205), 675–696.

Merleau-Ponty, M. (1945). *Phénoménologie de la perception.* Gallimard.

Merleau-Ponty, M. (2000 [1951–1952]). Les sciences de l'homme et la phénoménologie. In M. Merleau-Ponty, *Œuvres,* C. Lefort (Ed.) (pp. 1203–1267). Gallimard.

Merton, R. K. (1968). *Social theory and social structure.* The Free Press.

Nassehi, A. (2008). Gesellschaft. In S. Farzin & S. Jordan (Eds.), *Lexikon Soziologie und Sozialtheorie* (pp. 85–90). Reclam.

Nassehi, A. (2019). *Muster: Theorie der digitalen Gesellschaft.* C.H. Beck.

O'Shiel, D. (2022). *The phenomenology of virtual technology: Perception and imagination in a digital age.* Bloomsbury.

Popitz, H. (2011). *Allgemeine soziologische Theorie.* UVK.

Popitz, H., et al. (2018). *Das Gesellschaftsbild des Arbeiters. Soziologische Untersuchungen in der Hütterindustrie.* Springer.

Reckwitz, A. (2002). Toward a theory of social practices: A development in culturalist theorizing. *European Journal of Social Theory, 5*(2), 243–263.

Reckwitz, A. (2016). *Kreativität und soziale Praxis: Studien zur Sozial- und Gesellschaftstheorie.* transcript.

Reckwitz, A. (2017). *Die Gesellschaft der Singularitäten. Zum Strukturwandel der Moderne.* Suhrkamp.

Reckwitz, A. (2019). *Das Ende der Illusionen: Politik, Ökonomie und Kultur in der Spätmoderne.* Suhrkamp.

Reckwitz, A. (2021). Gesellschaftstheorie als Werkzeug. In A. Reckwitz & H. Rosa (Eds.), *Spätmoderne in der Krise. Was leistet die Gesellschaftstheorie?* (pp. 23–151). Suhrkamp.

Reckwitz, A., & Rosa, H. (2021). *Spätmoderne in der Krise: Was leistet die Gesellschaftstheorie?* Berlin: Suhrkamp.

Rosa, H. (2005). *Beschleunigung. Die Veränderung der Zeitstrukturen in der Moderne.* Suhrkamp.

Rosa, H. (2012). *Weltbeziehungen im Zeitalter der Beschleunigung. Umrisse einer neuen Gesellschaftskritik.* Suhrkamp.

Rosa, H. (2016). *Resonanz: Eine Soziologie der Weltbeziehung.* Suhrkamp.

Rosa, H. (2021). Best account. Skizze einer systematischen Theorie der modernen Gesellschaft. In A. Reckwitz & H. Rosa (Eds.), *Spätmoderne in der Krise. Was leistet die Gesellschaftstheorie?* (pp. 151–253). Suhrkamp.

Rosa, H., & Oberthür, J. (2020). Einleitung. In H. Rosa et al. (Eds.), *Gesellschaftstheorie* (pp. 11–35). UVK.

Schimank, U. (2013). *Gesellschaft.* transcript.

Schutz, A. (1962). *Collected papers I: The problem of social reality.* Martinus Nijhoff.

Schutz, A. (1964). *Collected papers II: Studies in social theory.* Martinus Nijhoff.

Schutz, A. (1981). *Der sinnhafte Aufbau der sozialen Welt.* Suhrkamp.

Schutz, A. (1984). Die Notizbücher. In T. Luckmann & A. Schutz (Eds.), *Strukturen der Lebenswelt, Band 2* (pp. 215–405). Suhrkamp.

Schutz, A. (2003). *Theorie der Lebenswelt 1: Die pragmatische Schichtung der Lebenswelt. ASW, Bd. V.1.* UVK.

Schutz, A. (2011). *Collected Papers V. Phenomenology and the Social Sciences.* Dordrecht: Springer.

Srubar, I. (2007). *Phänomenologie und soziologische Theorie.* UVK.

Steinbock, A. (2003). Generativity and the scope of generative phenomenology. In D. Welton (Ed.), *The New Husserl. A critical reader* (pp. 289–327). Indiana University Press.

Ungar, S. (2005). Cognitive maps. In R. Caves (Ed.), *Encyclopedia of the City.* (pp. 79–80). London: Routledge.

Van Manen, M. (2017). Phenomenology in its original sense. *Qualitative Health Research, 27*(6), 810–825.

Waldenfels, B. (2007). *The question of the other.* The Chinese University Press.

Weber, M. (1984). *Soziologische Grundbegriffe.* Mohr Siebeck.

Weber, M. (1986). *Gesammelte Aufsätze zur Religionssoziologie, Bd. 1.* Mohr Siebeck.

Weymann, A. (2020). Interaktion, Institution und Gesellschaft. In H. Joas & S. Mau (Eds.), *Lehrbuch der Soziologie* (pp. 107–135). Campus.

Zahavi, D. (2003). *Husserl's phenomenology.* Stanford University Press.

Zahavi, D. (2007). *Phänomenologie für Einsteiger*. UTB.

Zahavi, D. (2018). *Phenomenology: The basics*. Routledge.

Zahavi, D. (2021). We in me or me in we? Collective intentionality and selfhood. *Journal of Social Ontology, 7*(1), 1–20.

Zhao, S. (2004). Consociated contemporaries as an emergent realm of the lifeworld: Extending Schutz's phenomenological analysis to cyberspace. *Human Studies, 27*, 91–105.

Zoglauer, T. (2023). *Constructed truths*. Springer.

PART II

Phenomenology and Politics

Democracy as a Way of Being in the World: Responsivity as the Essence of the Common Good

Hartmut Rosa

1   The Common Good as a Way of Relating to the World

In my view, the reason why the democratic ideal has been able to develop such mass, almost universal, power is that democracy delivers a promise of a very specific way of *being in the world*. This promise is based on the concept that everyone should be given a voice that enables them to be heard and to contribute. Yet it is not enough for this voice just to be heard; democracy only becomes attractive when people believe their voices can actually be *effective*. This attractiveness is based on the premise that it will and in fact should be possible for us to *collectively* shape the world in which we live such that we can see ourselves reflected in that world and that it both responds to us and can give expression to our voices. Thus, even in a secular or post-secular age, which no longer rests on the assumption that the institutions of public life are *God given* or that there is a higher natural order creating and preserving them, the structures within which we act can be experienced as responsive or accommodating if and for the very reason that people have a sense of collective self-efficacy, of taking part in *cooperative action*.

H. Rosa (✉)
Institut für Soziologie, Friedrich-Schiller-Universität, Jena, Germany
e-mail: hartmut.rosa@uni-jena.de

C. Belvedere, A. Gros (eds.), *The Palgrave Handbook of Macrophenomenology and Social Theory*,
https://doi.org/10.1007/978-3-031-34712-2_4

This republican idea of democracy is quite different to the liberal, individualistic form, where politics is about articulating and pushing through interests, demanding rights, and creating and resolving conflict. The difference between these two notions of democracy is the relationship people have, first, with one another and, second, with the community that political action brings about and shapes. With respect to the first of these relationships, the republican concept of democracy rests on the belief that democracy goes way beyond members of a community sharing certain values and resolving conflict by means of compromise. In fact, it is also about members of a community being able to *reach out* to one another, using arguments and their voices. It is about joint political action transforming the positions, voices and even identities of those individuals such that it becomes possible to create a shared community that goes beyond compromises or the will of the majority.

Here, self-efficacy does not mean asserting one's interests but rather *reaching out to one another*. A prerequisite for this, however, with respect to the latter relationship between members of the community, is that the notion of a common good has an effective regulatory impact on political action. This chapter aims to show that, in the absence of this notion, a democratic culture or the creation of a shared world by democratic means is not entirely conceivable, nor would it be permanently achievable. This still applies irrespective of three imponderables regarding the common good: *what* and *whose* "good" this might be, and how the *common* that is a constituent part of this concept might be defined. In fact, it seems that the common good can (and indeed must) serve to regulate political action precisely *because* it remains a notoriously vague, even "essentially contested" concept (see Gallie, 1956). It is thus this struggle for the common good that can be found at the very heart of political culture. It is central even in situations where other political concepts such as interests, power or competition claim to be able to effectively guarantee the proper functioning of the (democratic) political system. This realization is one of Peter Graf Kielmansegg's (1977, 2013, 2016; see Zittel & Kaiser, 2004) key insights. In his writing, Kielmansegg emphasizes at almost every opportunity that it is impossible to sustain the distinction between the concepts of politics and the pursuit of interests without the regulatory effect of the common good. This creates an inextricable link between politics *per se* and the concept of the common good. Those involved in politics must at least implicitly maintain that their actions are linked to the common good, while those (exclusively) pursuing their own interests do not have to make such a claim. According to Kielmansegg, there is thus a necessary and constitutive link between legitimacy and the common good: a form of government can only claim to be legitimate if it can present sound and convincing arguments that it serves the common good—even if the definition of a *sound argument* may change over time.

For modern societies, the principle of democracy is now virtually uncircumventable: without democratic legitimacy, the claim to be serving the common good seems hollow. And this, in turn, means that the common good can only ever be achieved through ongoing processes, that is, *politically*.

Having said that, if we define democracy as a means of identifying the political will of the majority, the democratic principle alone is *not enough* to protect or achieve the common good. Accordingly, Kielmansegg suggests that the principles of constitution and good governance must form constituent parts of the concept of democracy (Kielmansegg, 1985). His reasoning was that the common good also implies, and indeed must imply, the good of minorities and of the underdogs in democratic competition. Although sectional interests play a crucial role in democratic debate, the common good must never be defined exclusively by sectional groups. Serving to protect the common good from overt and unrestricted access by majorities, legal and constitutional safeguards and restrictions on this access are thus in place. The idea of the common good, however, also always includes a historical aspect which goes beyond the isolated point in time when a political decision is made "in the fray." This historical dimension implies taking not only the interests of future generations into account but also the obligations and, moreover, the *experiences* emanating from a community's history or past (see, e.g., Buchstein, 2018).

Beyond this temporal dimension, another intrinsic part of the concept of the common good is the *spatial* dimension. From the Ancient Greek *polis* to the modern state, the common good is not just the good of an abstract political community but also entails the creation of a common territory, a "transformative appropriation" of a world that is shared both institutionally and materially. The common good also always implies a specific, successful relationship with a space that is shaped by politics and has developed over time. This does not preclude the possibility of the shared world that is to be shaped expanding to global dimensions, however. This is something which is encountered, for instance, where the protection of the polar bear or conservation of deep sea flora and fauna is perceived as a task that serves the common good.

Defining the elusive common good conceptually would be rather like trying to catch the proverbial eel. If, however, despite the difficulties outlined above, we would still like to attempt to pin the concept down, I believe that, in light of the aforementioned considerations, it would make sense to view the common good as a specific *type of relationship*. My thesis is that the idea of the common good is at its most tangible and has most substance if we try to understand it in the context of a specific way of relating to the *past and future* of a political community, to a lifeworld that is shared both materially and institutionally (and is thus always spatially constituted), as well as to other *members* of this community. A more detailed definition of this relationship is provided below. This is based on and draws upon another theory of mine, the concept of resonance (Rosa, 2016d). Using this concept I will demonstrate the *normative* character of this regulatory idea: *the common good can only be pursued and achieved where a body politic succeeds in establishing relationships of resonance, or, more precisely: axes of resonance, first, between the members of the community, second, with the shared institutions and practices of the collective lifeworld, and, third, with the past and the future.* Then (and only then) can democracy's promise—in practice, as an ongoing process—be delivered. In the second part of this chapter, I will turn to the question of why this promise is, in fact, not being fulfilled under today's conditions of late modernity and, finally, I will conclude by asking what might be done about this. Thus, my proposition is that *the common good*, understood as a successful democratic process, should be *seen as a relationship of resonance*. But what could this mean?

In the history of political thought, from times immemorial to very recently, scholars have repeatedly questioned what the "social bond" between members of a community constitutes exactly or what such a bond is capable of bringing about. Recently, this question has been posed not only by communitarian, republican or Neo-Durkheimian minded thinkers (e.g., Adloff & Leggewie, 2014) but also, and in fact in particular, by post-structuralist authors (see, for instance, Bedorf & Herrmann, 2016). My theory of resonance would provide us with the following response: this bond does not evolve from a predetermined foundation—shared values, customs, traditions or stories, for instance—but rather is formed by a specific type of relationship between individuals, one that can be described as being based on *listening* and *responding*. Listening and responding are the two poles that constitute a resonant relationship. This relationship is characterized by four key qualities: first, the willingness and ability to allow ourselves to be affected and *moved* by the voices of others (or other voices). This implies that one of the first preconditions for the common good is the basic assumption and acknowledgment among citizens that when they encounter one another they will *have something to say*. This prerequisite is undermined, for instance, when political actors perceive one another as racists and fascists or traitors and are not interested in *hearing anything the others have to tell them*, instead attempting to shout them down or silence them. Second, according to this understanding, the social bond is not confined to pure receptiveness but essentially also evolves as part and as a result of the experience that everyone is able to make their voices heard and to contribute. This is the fundamental promise of democracy: everyone receives a voice, a vote, which they do not simply *hand over* but use to *contribute* in a responsive, proactive and reactive manner. To my mind, it is utter nonsense to see the casting of this vote as a *cost* incurred by each individual in their endeavor to pursue personal interests, as described by rational (or public) choice theorists, who then go on to wonder why people bother participating in elections at all (see, e.g., Caplan, 2008; Wittman, 1997). Having a voice by casting a vote provides citizens with an inimitable experience of political *self-efficacy*: their voice and vote connects them with others and with the community and enables them to participate in the collective shaping of the world. It is not simply a (very limited) tool that enables us to *achieve something* in the sense of asserting our own interests but is an instrument—by all means of the musical kind (see Love, 2006)—which we use to reach out to *others* with whom we then enter into a relationship. The second condition of the common good is thus that the political process is organized so as to permit and facilitate this experience of *self-efficacy*.

Third, and I believe this to be paramount, one consequence of *entering into a resonant relationship* is the inevitable *transformation* of the participating voices. Resonance means allowing ourselves to be "called" or moved by one or several other individuals in such a way that when we respond and react to those individuals, we are personally transformed (see Rosa, 2016b, 2016d; Latour, 2014, pp. 614–616). Resonance is a dialogical process of reciprocal "transformative appropriation," where participants do not remain the same people they were before. This has always been at the core of republican thinking (see Buchstein, 2018): the common good is not conditional on citizens having shared specific values or goals all along, but rather is based on them being accessible and open to one another, on them being able to transform themselves for the purpose of (achieving) something shared (or a joint project). The fact that this shared world also includes conflict and dispute and is even based on and results from such conflict, is irrefutable and unavoidable. It is thus entirely wrong to define the concept of resonance simply as *consonance* or *harmony*: in fact, conceptually, resonance always requires difference and thus also dissonance, because only then is an encounter with a genuine "other" and the associated self-transformation possible.

Thus, fundamentally, resonance lies *between* identity and difference, between consonance and dissonance; it bridges the gap between these concepts via the principle of transformation (see Rosa, 2017). Accordingly, the third condition of the common good is the ability and willingness of the community and its members to substantively transform. This ability is undermined when a priori stipulations outside the political process or socially constructed, naturalized practical constraints cause the structures of that community to reify or fossilize (see Rosa & Sörensen, 2014; Sörensen, 2016).

The fourth crucial quality of a resonant relationship is, however, its fundamental elusiveness. This means that a relationship of resonance cannot be forced or guaranteed, neither institutionally nor instrumentally. What is more, the result of an experience of resonance is impossible to predict, anticipate or control. In the context of this chapter, this means that there is no possible way of guaranteeing democratic resonance institutionally. Thus, it is impossible to create constitutional, procedural or other guarantees that the political process will be implemented in a mode of resonance. Torpor, alienation, instrumentalization and reification as alternative modes of political relations are always a possibility and a risk. Having said that, much to the chagrin of authoritarian and totalitarian rulers, this elusiveness does also mean, however, that there is no way to suppress or prevent the emergence of political relations of resonance in the democratic and transformative sense outlined here.

Yet, elusiveness does not mean that it would be impossible to use social, legal and organizational means to create the dispositional and institutional *conditions* for resonant relations. Thus, the role of the institutions embodying constitutional law and policy and the principles of democratic participation and representation is to establish and protect the lines of connection, as it were, or the *axes of resonance* along which vibrant relations of resonance can develop. Given the elusive nature of resonance, the quality of democracy and equally of the common good can never be determined or measured using predefined *output* criteria. The fundamental outcome of processes of resonance is, by necessity, undetermined.

If we assume that it is plausible to use the notion of resonance to understand the concept of the common good as a *specific type of relationship between citizens*, this then makes the present attempt to reframe the common good all the more attractive since this four-sided type of relationship can also be applied to how people relate to the past and the future of a community.

From a temporal perspective, the common good is thus achieved when a *resonant relationship* to both the past and the future materializes. With regard to the past, this means: the common good implies that, as citizens, the history of the community "concerns us" and has "something to tell us," that we are in a *responsive relationship* with that community and, in fact, the success of the democratic process where this common good is attained is conditional on this. This involves all four principles of a relationship of resonance: the past event affects or moves us. By no means do we have to be moved in a positive or pleasant way, however. For instance, someone visiting a concentration camp museum or holocaust memorial may experience an existential obligation arising from a memory of the past brought to life by the location. The individual may react with a response that is transformative, one which affects who they are at present and how they will act in the future, despite the fact that they would not be able to specify exactly *what* the obligation is that arises from this situation (elusiveness). Such resonance creates a link, however, or an *axis of resonance* between the past and the future.

When someone feels a vibrant and responsive connection not only with past but also with future generations, he or she has a direct sense, as it were, both emotional and physical, of the relevance of his or her actions for those who come after them. Once again, the consideration of future needs and interests then stops being an irksome obligation or a cost that outweighs the benefits and, instead, creates an experience of *accessible* and transformative *self-efficacy*. I am therefore of the opinion that the quality of a democratic system can most certainly be "measured" by the quality of the trans-historical connection: the common good tends to be achieved where there is a vibrant axis of resonance spanning the past and the future. This axis of resonance does not determine each action in the present but rather inspires and motivates those actions.

However, what emerges (in the mode of transformation and elusiveness) is a shared world arising from joint political action, in line with Hannah Arendt's (1958b, 1994; see Sörensen, 2016) concept. People living in the modern world heavily influenced by the West generally no longer see themselves as being part of a cosmic system inhabited by spirits or decreed by God—"the great chain of being" (see Taylor, 1995, p. 11)—but rather as placed in a world that has become more or less arbitrary and shaped by historical coincidences, a world which strikes them as a contingent result of countless historical conflicts (of interest). As a result, the rules and institutions of the lifeworld and hence also the socio-territorial space are initially perceived as something external, something determined by others, something which limits them and subjects them to all manner of restrictions. And yet, this modern world, with its strategy of democratic representation and participation, provides people with a powerful instrument enabling them to *appropriate* this lifeworld in a way that is transformative. This encapsulates the fundamental idea of modern political republicanism and the key promise of democracy (see Buchstein, 2018): the joint shaping of the world is the instrument by means of which society and public space can become a "sphere of resonance" for the citizens, a world which "responds" to their desires, values and needs, and in which they recognize themselves. The socio-political system thus becomes a structure that *is their own*. Again, when I say a structure that *is their own*, this does not mean that that system is fully consistent or in total harmony with all their desires, needs and interests, but rather that there is a constitutive *responsive* relationship between the citizens and all the institutions and practices, spaces and buildings, rules and traditions. Here, opposition or conflict is an important and inevitable form of this response—without contradiction, and this applies to our context too, there can be no transformation or encounter, and without the opposition of an *other*, there can be no *experience of resonance*.

If we redefine the conceptual pairing of the common good and democracy as a multidimensional relationship of resonance, the fundamental problem of the notion of the common good initially remains unchanged: where are *the boundaries* of the community whose good we are referring to, how does this community relate to the social or material outside world? My thesis (and my hope) here is that a society cannot be unjust, violent, repressive or destructive to the *outside world* if it wishes to maintain the capacity to be resonant *within*. If we define the common good using the concept of resonance, resonance describes a way of relating to the world as a whole, a way of *being in the world*. Repression, violence and suppression, however, force not only the victims but also and particularly the perpetrators into an objectifying, repulsive mode of relating to the world. This relationship is characterized by the dispositional suppression of resonant relations in oneself and in others and the ruthless obliteration of the corresponding impulses. This repression and violence impose a relationship with the world in which the transformative listening to the voice of the (genuine) other is systematically impeded or rendered impossible, while the echo-like amplification of our own unvarying voice is systematically promoted or enforced (see Rosa, 2016c, pp. 97–108).

Interestingly, the exact same also applies to our relationship with the natural world: those who treat the material (and especially the living) environment simply as a resource to be exploited and processed, to be used instrumentally and to be shaped, cannot experience that environment as a sphere of resonance or a vibrant *other* that is in a lasting and responsive reciprocal relationship with us as human beings. The reverse also holds true: those with a stable resonant relationship with the natural world (whatever your definition of that might be) need not *force* themselves to protect or sustainably manage the environment. This is something they will do automatically to avoid rendering the voice of that "other" inaudible, losing their own voice in the process (see Rosa, 2014, pp. 123–141).

I am thus proposing that we try to grasp the democratic common good as the creation of axes of resonance: a social axis (the type of relationship people have with one another), a material axis (the type of relationship people have with the shared lifeworld) and a vertical axis (the type of relationship people have with the world, history, nature or life as an all-encompassing whole). If we take this approach, then the common good and community spirit do indeed prove to be complementary reciprocal conditions and the key components of a successful democracy (see Münkler et al., 2002). *Community spirit* then describes people's capacity for and openness toward resonance. *The common good*, however, is achieved where the social and material, temporal and spatial conditions allow the social, material and vertical axes of resonance to be established and maintained.

2   THE CRISIS OF DEMOCRACY AS A CRISIS OF RESONANCE

Nowadays, the notion of a common good as a point of reference for the democratic political process seems to have become a defunct relic of the past and, moreover, it arouses suspicions of hegemonic, paternalistic structural and cultural conservatism. In light of the observations made here, this could perhaps be interpreted as an unequivocal sign of a serious *crisis of democracy*. The essence of this crisis is that all three dimensions of the axes of resonance—social (between citizens), material (with the material lifeworld) and vertical (with the past)—are at risk of being silenced or have already fallen silent. Consequently, a democracy whose default mode is *listening and responding*, whether in terms of our relationship with our fellow citizens, our perception of the past and the future or our institutional and material environment might seem unattainable and unrealistic. But is there any evidence to support such an assumption?

First, I believe it is important to emphasize that empirical evidence of this crisis of alienation most certainly exists. The decline of established political parties and the loss of the legitimacy of the political establishment observed throughout western democracies and, to some extent, also in the newly democratized states are accompanied by the vociferously expressed allegation that politics and politicians have become "unresponsive." Many have the impression that politics no longer has an impact (believing that in fact it is businesses, Wall Street, the media or the bureaucrats in Brussels, Washington and elsewhere that call the shots) and/or politicians no longer listen to them, see them, acknowledge them and, in fact, are no longer accessible to them. This perception reflects a profound lack of expectation or experience of self-efficacy and is based on the conviction that the shared world, the structures of the community can no longer be *accessed* by democratic means. All manner of rightwing populists have responded to this, from Trump in the US to Germany's Alternative for Germany (AfD) party and Austria's Freedom Party (FPÖ). These political movements are all sustained by the protest against such a feeling of alienation and feed on people's longing for resonance in the sense of their need *to be heard*. It is no coincidence that Trump's electoral campaign speeches culminated in the promise: "I am your voice!" (Trump, 2016), and that the Brexit campaign was built on the pledge to the British people that they would be able to "take back control" from the abstract, distant Brussels bureaucracy and once again become subjects of political action. *We are listening to you, we can see you, we are giving you back your voice and with it your self-efficacy.* This is thus the essence of the rightwing populist message which without a doubt alludes to the key promise of democracy.

Yet, as I have attempted to demonstrate elsewhere (Rosa, 2016a), the rightwing populist strategy for responding to this situation single-handedly undermines this promise of resonance in three different ways. First, the primary aim of political parties and movements driven by identitarianism and nationalism is to silence all other voices: anyone who doesn't fit the image conjured up by the imagined public sentiment does not belong and should either be silent or simply disappear. This includes *Jews, blacks, Muslims, transsexuals, migrants, leftwing activists*, none of whom belong "here" or are "one of us," meaning they most definitely should *not be heard*.

The fundamental belief, often felt more than articulated, which makes people gravitate toward Patriotic Europeans Against the Islamisation of the West (PEGIDA), AfD, etc., can be roughly described as follows: "We want to be and remain exactly as we are; we perceive the 'homeland' as the embodiment of the notion that nothing must be allowed to change. We do not welcome outsiders, ideas that are not our own, customs that are not familiar to us, people who look different or live differently. We reject everything that is different—religious belief, sexual orientation, political persuasion, forms of worship, ways of speaking and celebrating. In a nutshell, the desire to banish all that is different."

This attitude expresses a sclerotic relationship with the world. When people perceive the world around them and the world they encounter as a battle zone, a world that is at best indifferent, at worst hostile, toward them, a world in which the position they occupy is all but precarious, anything vibrant, foreign or unknown will seem potentially dangerous and threatening. Admittedly, their actual experience of change has, more often than not, been associated with demise and decline (see Nachtwey, 2016). Such a relationship with the world can be described, in a nutshell, as *alienation*: alienated people shun encounters with outsiders because they only associate them with the risk of being hurt. They have limited experience of the self-efficacy that would allow them to engage in an open and active debate with the unfamiliar (whether this be a person, an idea, a practice or a piece of architecture in the form of a minaret) or even enable them to appropriate these experiences in a (self-)transformative way.[1] Their relationship with the world is precarious and repellent. They feel unheard, unseen, isolated and voiceless in an indifferent or even threatening

---

[1] For an explanation of the difference between *instrumental appropriation* in the sense of taking control or possession of something and transformative *appropriation* meaning to *engage with something*, where the encounter (with an individual, but also, for example, with a book, a piece of music, scenery or a life form) results in a transformation, see Rosa (2016d).

environment, where it is essential to literally keep this very world *at arm's length* (see Von Thadden, 2018), as far away as is humanly possible. They believe that the other, the vibrant, the young, the elusive should not be allowed to touch them, either physically or spiritually, let alone transform them. The more disenchanted and despondent and the more alienated people are the more extreme their need for a strategy of immurement. The world that appears threatening must be kept at a distance and the ties with that world severed.

Today's refugee crisis is a clear reflection of this way of relating to the world: the figure of the refugee appears to be the reason for one's own world alienation. Consequently, the recent success of rightwing populist and far-right extremist parties and movements across the continent and, indeed, across virtually the entire world is hardly surprising. What all these parties—the AfD in Germany, the Law and Justice Party (PiS) in Poland, the Party of Civic Rights (SPO) in the Czech Republic, the Front National in France, the Partij voor de Vrijheid in the Netherlands and the FPÖ in Austria—have in common is undoubtedly their repressive, at times racist, refugee policies, which are geared toward the radical exclusion of foreigners. This is, if you like, their brand essence, and it is no coincidence that it has also turned out to be Donald Trump's recipe for success. Foreigners and their peculiarities are to be kept out with walls and fences and, if necessary, even mines and guns. Rightwing populists in almost every country seem to have exactly the right strategy to profit from this rampant sense of alienation. Even in countries where rightwing populists are not (yet) in power, government policies have eagerly picked up on this supposed panacea. Consequently, today's political coverage is inundated with images of border walls and fences reinforced with barbed wire or of the threat of war.[2] These images express the urge to stop the world from bearing down on us, to shut out the vibrant, intangible other, to keep it at arm's length—if necessary, by force.

But in silencing everything and everyone that is not identical to you, you will also not hear any other voices to which you could respond and by which you could be affected. You become incapable of experiencing relationships of resonance. However, the logical consequence of this is that, paradoxically, your *own voice* can then no longer be discerned or articulated either. We can only hear, develop and unfold our own voice if and when it is in dialog with others. Yet rightwing populism promises (or aspires to) the convergence of the individual into a homogenous "national whole," where the voice of the people is undifferentiated and identical, articulated through the *single* voice of the movement (see Müller, 2016). Trump himself claims that his voice is "ours." Instead of resonance between two or many individual voices, each with their own timbre, a hollow echo emerges: the same sound is to be heard everywhere, and that same voice must echo back, greatly amplified. It is telling that Trump does not say: *I will make your voices heard*, but rather *I am your voice*—in the singular. The Trumps, Höckes, Haiders, Wilders and others like them thrive on this

---

[2] For an account that draws on contemporary political theories, see Wendy Brown (2014).

vision of a noisy fusion into collective harmony, which is to replace silent fos-silization. Yet there is a high price to pay for this. Not only must everything that is different or deviant be excluded, silenced or even destroyed (first attack on resonance), the direct consequence being that individuals are denied an experience of their own self-efficacy (second attack on resonance), but also—and this is the third attack on resonance—the ultimate price is that we have to shut ourselves off from any and all change, development, progress and, in the end, vibrant encounter—and thus life itself. The rightwing populist response to the problem of alienation in late modern capitalist societies is thus not an expression of a resonant but rather deeply repellent relationship with the world that is in no way suited to fostering the democratic common good in any shape or form.

What I have attempted to illustrate so far is that, first, the political sphere in late modern societies is characterized by a massive lack of resonance and that, second, the rightwing populist strategy for plugging this gap is completely ineffectual. But what form would a better solution take? To respond to this, we first need to take a closer look at the *cause* of the crisis of resonance. What is the root of the increasing feelings of hopelessness among today's citizens that they are unable to shape their world by political means, the sense that they have no effective voice, that the future remains closed to them and that the structures of the lifeworld are all but hostile toward them? For reasons of space and because I have already developed this argument in detail elsewhere, I will keep my response to this question brief. This impression exists because *it is correct*: under the prevailing conditions, the world and the future *are* virtually impos-sible to shape using political means; they are sclerotic and unresponsive because, on the macro (or institutional) as well as the micro (or individual) levels, the forces that do change the lifeworld are structural and systemic. *Modern society is characterized by the fact that it is only capable of stabilizing dynamically; in other words, that it systematically depends on (economic) growth, (cultural) inno-vation and (technical) acceleration to maintain and reproduce its structure.* This is the guiding principle of my two books *Acceleration (Beschleunigung)* and *Resonance (Resonanz)*, and, although, on many levels, my fellow researchers in the Research Group on Post-Growth Societies in Jena have interpreted the principle of dynamic stabilization differently, this principle still essentially underpins our common research work (Rosa et al., 2017). It is the need for constant growth, optimization and rationalization in the means-end chains that is reflected in equal measure in the economic *appropriation* of raw materi-als and physical functions, of population groups and spheres of life, as well as in the political activation of pensioners, children, the unemployed and civic activ-ists and in the relentless acceleration of technology, social change and the pace of life. According to my thesis, the defining features of the political and cultural reality of late modernity are the escalatory forces of growth, on the one hand, and institutional and structural standstill, on the other. This is because, rather than being geared toward change, all efforts are focused solely on preserving the institutional *status quo* (jobs, the social system, pension levels, healthcare, science, education, the state budget, and thus, ultimately, the political system and its legitimacy). I have described this situation as a "frenetic standstill," reflected in the everyday reality that people *are forced to run faster and faster each year, not to get anywhere, but just to keep pace and stay in the same place in their society and thus their world* (Rosa, 2005). Since this logic of growth ultimately dominates all areas of society and all population groups (albeit in different ways: cultural and economic elites generally *internalize* and *habitualize* this logic, whereas it often impacts workers and those in precarious life situations in the form of an *external, institutional compulsion to optimize*), and since neither the left-leaning democratic nor rightwing populist or even the green political parties and agendas have come up with a plausible proposal as to how to quash this need for growth, the body politic's shared lifeworld does in fact prove to be unresponsive, and political action fails to give people a sense of self-efficacy. Acts of apparent self-empowerment, reflected in belligerent actions, headscarf bans, tax hikes or punitive tariffs, for instance, only have a peripheral impact on the aforementioned escalatory logic of growth, despite the fact that they can be a matter of life or death for those affected.

With the relationship of resonance between people and the community thus fundamentally compromised and the structural logic of that community "deafened" to all political callings, the axis of resonance with the past and the future also proves to be rigid: the future appears to be a hopeless recurrence of the "same old" but under increasingly bleak conditions. And so it continues, although more and more material, cultural, political and emotional energy have to be invested just to keep up this game of growth or stay in the competition. As a result, the scope that people have to shape their lives on all these levels withers away more and more.

This reduced scope ultimately also determines the dominant relationship with the natural environment: nature is seen as a resource to be exploited and appropriated (including for emotional and physical recreation and cultural production), an object to be shaped, but not as an autonomous sphere of resonance.

One aspect that I believe to be crucial when trying to understand *what is "wrong"* in the narrow sense of the word *with the democratic process* in modern societies is the fact that this experience of a fundamental loss of resonance or profound alienation from the "world" or the community as a whole, that is, in the aforementioned vertical axis of resonance, also applies to the dispositional attitudes along the horizontal axis. In each case, the *other voices* in society— irrespective of whether we are talking about the class enemy, religious groups, political parties or ethnic differences—are perceived as adversaries, against whom we must assert ourselves, defend our interests, rights and normative demands. The democratic process is understood as agonistic, but not in the sense of wanting to *reach others*, to achieve something shared and obtain the common good through a process of reciprocal transformation. But rather agonistic in the sense of drawing a distinction between friends and enemies and consequently not being remotely interested in what the *enemies of the people* and *traitors to their country* or *the fascists* and *racists* have to tell us, and in the sense that everything is about *winning through* and gaining hegemony. Political struggle thus involves the respective sides trying to make their voices heard as loudly as possible, trying to make themselves as accessible as possible by delegitimizing the others so their voices become inaudible. Here, participants strive for self-efficacy in the mode of (maximum) availability and not in the mode of (reciprocal) accessibility, however, and politics is not perceived as a process of resonance but rather as an antagonistic conflict of interests and a struggle for power. Theories of democracy which recognize this antagonism as the very nature of politics in the first place take this idea one step further by identifying the essence of political culture not as *listening and responding* but rather as *battling and pushing through*, establishing this (repellent) mode of political debate as the default (see Bedorf & Röttgers, 2010; Marchart, 2010; Mouffe, 2007; Rancière, 2002; Reitz, 2016). This *modus operandi* is rehearsed and demonstrated in talk shows and, regrettably, also in parliamentary debates, where the objective of the politicians is precisely *not* to allow themselves to be reached or affected by the arguments, concerns and beliefs of the others and *by no means* (or at least certainly not *strategically*) to allow themselves to be "moved," but rather ideally to expose and delegitimize the opposition. This logic of debate spills over onto the streets when angry people come to blows with anti-fascists.

From this perspective, it is then rather irksome that social sciences experts in the liberal West would appear to be in agreement—and this is something that is expressed in publications and at conferences—that the arguments put forward by the likes of Trump or Putin, the opinions of leaders such as Xi Jinping or Modi, as well as the positions of Erdogan, the Iranian government or Duterte are not to be taken seriously. Indeed, we should not even listen to these people in the first place: first, because we already know *a priori* that these are authoritarian, dictatorial, totalitarian or criminal voices and, second, because, by extension, these others, with their categorical opposition to behavior that is geared toward common understanding, cannot be reached. This assumption prevails despite the fact that these political actors have evidently found both a voice and support among what is increasingly becoming a majority of the population in their respective countries (and thus in the world population). I therefore cannot be sure to what extent the academic discourse in the liberal-democratic West can be described as being in a relationship of resonance with its own "others," even in countries where the debate takes post-colonial arguments seriously. Perhaps it is no coincidence that even the relationship between the academic elites and the majority of the population can be described as alienated or non-resonant; at the very least, the resonance fibers are rather strained: the voices of these elites are not really heard by broad swathes of the population, just as the views of the latter do not resonate with the former. This gives populist leaders a dangerous opportunity to silence social science and social philosophical discourse.

3   THE ESTABLISHMENT OF DEMOCRACY AS A SPHERE
OF RESONANCE

If we are trying to work out how to achieve a (re)democratization of society in the form of a robust process of resonance oriented toward the common good along the three axes outlined, it would certainly seem logical to start with our own social science theory and practice. In practice, resonance means not always claiming to know better than the "deluded masses," the corrupt economic elites or the power-crazed politicians. Having said that, it is not enough to simply record and categorize the voices and positions of those "others." Instead, we have to *listen* and *respond with our own voice* in a process that is dialogical on multiple levels, in doing so always remaining open and willing to self-transform. As to the theory, in my view, we urgently need to overhaul the hegemonic understanding of democracy and rejuvenate the concept of the common good. Provided it is possible and desirable to have a field of resonance within the social sciences, this field certainly gives us the chance to, indeed the responsibility of, responding to the preponderance of political alienation that has been diagnosed and to make a productive contribution to the shaping of the community by introducing coherent theoretical, empirically sound and normatively substantive insights. The re-conceptualization of democracy as a sphere of resonance would take us one giant step closer to (re)gaining the ability to shape using political means. The reason being that social science concepts have always implicitly "responded to" the perceived political reality and are in a double-sided relationship of interdependence with that reality. In this vein, as early as 1982, William Bluhm (1982, pp. 3–4) writes: "Every descriptive framework arises from a total, normladen view of the world. Each framework is rich with implications for understanding the way the world is as a moral order. The way the world is includes, of course, the way the human person is, as a moral animal. And this conception obviously includes a view of the way a human being reasons morally. Thus, if the political world consists of overlapping interest groups ... then the rules of moral reasoning of its members will enjoin calculations of group interest ... If the world consists of fundamentally antagonistic classes, men will develop class identities as an aspect of their moral reasoning and will support the class struggle ... If the world consists fundamentally of autonomous, rational (logical) and self-interested individuals who also have an ethical sense, notions such as 'universalizability' will be prominent components of the structure of moral reasoning." What is missing from this list of options, however, is a conceptual framework that would enable us to understand democracy as a process of resonance.

A simple reevaluation of concepts and social theory, however, would quite clearly not suffice; such an approach would not be able to make political opinion-forming and decision-making processes themselves resonant; at best, it would be no more than a building block for creating such resonance. The broader question that now arises is how the institutional practices of political action can be organized such that people are able to experience a form of self-efficacy that is receptive to resonance even under conditions of global integration. I have neither the space here nor the conceptual means, or even sufficient imagination to propose a coherent democratic institutional structure based on resonance. What I can do, however, is briefly outline—under the headings of participation, representation and synchronization—the main considerations in the development of such a structure.

(A) *Participation*: In a recent paper, referring to the works of James Fishkin and his team (see 1991, 1995; Fishkin & Farrar, 2005; Fishkin & Luskin, 2005), Hubertus Buchstein (2018, pp. 24–25) puts forward some highly inspirational thoughts on how the institutions of an aleatory democracy and even of aleatory parliamentarianism, that is, advisory and possibly even decision-making bodies whose representatives are selected randomly from among the citizens, can encourage resonant democratic action and experiences. He cites empirical evidence for the notion that such bodies make a wider range of voices heard than conventional representative organs, generate significant experiences of self-efficacy among participants and also give them a deeper understanding of *other* positions—the consequence being they *listen and respond*.[3] As the theory of resonance leads us to expect, this results in a dramatic transformation in the participants' opinions and positions: "Accompanying empirical research produced solid evidence substantiating the fact that, in the course of discussions the participants' opinions were found to change drastically at the aggregate data level" (p. 25). Further, and this insight is particularly interesting in terms of the capacity for resonant transformative appropriation of the future, it has been shown that aleatory institutions develop a substantially longer temporal horizon and a stronger connection with the future that goes beyond the mere fixing of election dates and legislative periods.

(B) *Representation*: However interesting these ideas might be, they should not and indeed cannot replace or supersede the institutions of conventional political representation. That said, the concept of resonant democracy centered on the regulatory idea of the common good does imply a substantial change in the practical mode of relations of representation. In the vast majority of established democracies, over the course of the twenty-first century, polls have become almost paramount when drawing up political parties' and candidates' agendas and policy proposals (see, e.g., Genovese & Streb, 2004; Hennis, 1999). As a result, the relationship between politicians and the population involves parties and politicians asking, sensing and exploring "what the people want," and then attempting to deliver this. The political representatives thus become "delegates," as it were, although they do still try to use spin doctors to influence public opinion in their favor. In some ways, at first glance we could be led to believe that this is a very clear case of "listening and responding." However, if we look more closely, it becomes obvious that the relationship between the electorate and the representatives is most definitely not a resonant

---

[3] "Participants develop a significantly and measurably better understanding of the positions of others and are more inclined to compromise their own convictions" (Buchstein, 2018, p. 24).

one. This relationship does not consist of listening and responding with both sides reaching out to one another, because the representatives' "own voices" are not articulated or heard. Instead, the political agendas that are developed on this basis form a sort of echo of the aggregate of a large number of individuals' opinions. They are not the result of a process of political resonance but in fact precede political debate. Voters and politicians do not "reach out" to one another in a reciprocally transformative process. Instead, they are in a relationship which is based partly on delegation and partly on manipulation. The voice that is articulated in this process is ultimately *no one's voice*, and it has no power to generate the different relationships of resonance among citizens, with the community or with the future.

For this reason, beginning with Max Weber and perhaps even Edmund Burke, critics of this type of "representation" have repeatedly called for political "leadership": politicians should *shape* public opinion and not allow themselves to be driven by it (see, e.g., Hennis, 1999). This belief is based on the idea that the people will follow the voice of a political "leader" if that voice is sufficiently charismatic and authentic. The relationship between the voters and the politicians is thus a (one-sided) relationship of trust. Its fundamental structure resembles what I have referred to above as the rightwing populist notion of fusion into a single voice—"I am your voice!"—which leads to a structural immobilization of the process of resonance on both sides.

On the other hand, in a resonant democracy, the concept of representation is based on the idea that the relationship itself (between the voters and the politicians) follows the model of voices reaching out to one another. Politicians and political parties make themselves "audible" by articulating and advocating their *own specific and substantive* idea of the common good or policy that serves the common good. At the same time, however, they are receptive to the arguments, objections and counterproposals of the people or of "public opinion," though not by simply adapting their positions to the latter but rather by attempting to reach the people with their agendas and facilitate a process of co-transformation (Pitkin, 1972).[4] A relationship of this type, however, is only possible in an *accommodating sphere of resonance* (see Rosa, 2017), which, taking temporal conditions into account, also facilitates political decision-making and action in a mode of resonance.

(C) *Synchronization*: Democratic resonance and the community's transformative appropriation brought about by this resonance are time-consuming and also very *slow* processes. They are not based on aggregated opinions or interests but rather on dynamic and deliberative reciprocal relationships of listening and responding, which transform positions (and individuals) and, moreover, are always (by definition) shaped by instances of *elusiveness*: it is impossible to predict when these processes of resonance will occur (and when not), how long they last and what they will result in. Yet the logic of growth and acceleration

---

[4] Hanna F. Pitkin's (1972) influential conceptualization of representation and particularly her term "responsiveness" (between politicians and voters) closely resembles this notion of resonant.

that dominates modern societies calls for speed, predictability and availability—including and especially in political decision-making. Markets and the media, in particular, require quick decisions and for positions on current events to be taken immediately. This bears the risk of increasing "desynchronization" at the interfaces between politics and the economy, the sciences, media, the environment, etc. An empirical study conducted by the University of Jena in collaboration with the University of Bremen showed that although hybrid organizations made up of experts such as the German Ethics Council (*Deutsche Ethikrat*) (at the interface between politics and science) or the Federal Financial Supervisory Authority (*Bundesanstalt für Finanzdienstleistungsaufsicht, BaFin*) (at the interface between politics and the financial markets) are able to achieve a resynchronization between political decision-making processes and the sectors of society regulated or shaped by these processes, this is at the cost of increasing desynchronization between political decision-making and democratic will-formation and thus also at the cost of political alienation (see Bohmann et al., 2018).

And so we arrive at the fundamental problem faced by any attempt to honor the basic promise of democracy under the conditions that prevail in globalized modern societies. Democracy can only be established as a sphere of resonance (as outlined at the start of this contribution) when and if it manages to immobilize the forces of growth and acceleration that are linked to the mode of dynamic stabilization, thus making it possible to shape and "transformatively appropriate" the fundamental structures of the community, the future and the material and institutional environment, and, in turn, to activate the axes of resonance. As long as these forces of growth and acceleration are at play, it will remain impossible to shape the world, and democratic politics will not allow individuals to experience self-efficacy. At least this is what I have attempted to show here. The powers and forces that determine the underlying trends of our lives are beyond our sphere of influence; they prove elusive and naturalized. However, if dynamic stabilization is a core feature of modernity, this means that it is only possible to substantively establish a durable and genuinely democratic sphere of resonance (as described at the beginning of this chapter) *beyond modernity, in another society*. And now we need to square the circle: working out what form this "other society" might take is not something we can do using the tools at our disposal in the social sciences. As I have attempted to demonstrate with my reference to Graf Kielmansegg, legitimacy for a concept of the common good can only be achieved via democratic means, through resonant joint action. The logical consequence of this is that democratic resonance *is* the alternative to the dominant mode of dynamic stabilization. It should not be the blind, mute growth imperatives of this latter mode that determine the community's form, structure and direction but rather the formative capacity of democratic resonance, with its open-ended outcome and its power to generate a sense of self-efficacy that fulfils this function. What this implies, however, is that the prerequisite for overcoming the forces of growth and reclaiming the ability to shape the future is an intact sphere of democratic resonance. At the same time, this is *structurally impossible*, given the conditions created by dynamic stabilization.

Yet is this really the case? *Under today's prevailing conditions, the world and the future are virtually impossible to shape using politics; they are sclerotic and unresponsive because, on the macro (or institutional) as well as the micro (or individual) levels, the forces that do change the lifeworld are of a structural and systemic nature.* This is the hypothesis I put forward above. What this means, however, is that the vertical and material axes of resonance are obstructed. *The structures of the community, nature as the world around us, the future*: none of them prove to be resonant under the influence of the forces of dynamic stabilization. But this does *not* mean that the horizontal axes of resonance between people are, by extension, also irrevocably devoid of resonance. In fact, the main insight delivered by this contribution is that democratic relations only function effectively as horizontal relationships of resonance. Resonance between individuals, however, can never be completely immobilized. Elusiveness not only means that resonance cannot be forced but also that it can never be permanently institutionally immobilized either. The transfer of the dispositional alienation from the vertical and material structure of the lifeworld to the horizontal dimension, as observed here, *is not mandatory*. Even when people are slaving away under the yoke and the wheels of the forces of growth, they can still engage with one another in an exchange over what form the structure of their community and the shared lifeworld *might* take and how they *should* pursue the common good. Hence, a democratic sphere of resonance can be recreated and, at the same time, *recreate the world* from within itself, as it were. Perhaps the most powerful expression of this idea can be found in Hannah Arendt's (1958a, p. 300) essay "Kultur und Politik" (Culture and Politics), where she says that political action is a question of "what the world *qua* world [...] is supposed to look and sound like, how it is supposed to be looked at and listened to." Through the process of reaching a common understanding on this, resonant political action emerges, providing people with a sense of self-efficacy. According to Arendt, this type of collective production of political resonance has the capacity not only to *transform* the world but also to *create* the world. This alone gives us hope "that we, who are not of the desert though we live in it, are able to transform it into a human world" (Arendt, 2003, p. 181).

Such a transformation of the political desert into a democratic sphere of resonance presupposes one condition in particular (or perhaps just one *per se*): the existence of an intact public space as a meeting place and thus as a sphere of resonance where different voices can be articulated and those voices can hear and respond to one another, making them capable of self-transformation. The element of socio-structural development in today's late modern societies that is, from a sociological, social theory and political perspectives, the most striking and at the same time the most unsettling is thus possibly the emerging dramatic *structural transformation of the public sphere*. This entails an increasingly strict separation of the lifeworlds of different population groups or social strata and the progressive drifting apart of their cultural practices, opinions and knowledge.[5] This drift is not necessarily, or at least not primarily, characterized by the fundamental *incompatibility* of practices and knowledge or opinions. Rather, it has much more to do with the fact that the spheres where people move, practice and share information barely come into contact let alone interact with one another. This goes far beyond the growing residential segregation—people with different social backgrounds inhabiting different neighborhoods. The problem is in fact compounded when and where members of different social, cultural or ethnic groups live in close proximity to one another. But, due to increasing geographic mobility trends and the relaxation of neighborhood socio-spatial anchoring, these groups then attend different pre-school establishments and schools and work in heterogeneous contexts, etc. (see Maaz et al., 2014). However, beyond the sphere of work, education and housing, this differentiation also becomes radicalized with regard to other lifestyle indicators: people from different social backgrounds shop in different clothes and grocery stores (from exclusive designers to textile discounters), eat in different restaurants (from McDonalds and kebab shops to five-star establishments), attend different cultural activities, have different leisure pursuits, watch different films, listen to different radio stations, watch different television channels and formats, read different print media, surf on very different websites, etc. The result of this fragmentation is that there is virtually no overlap between their lifeworlds; people with different social (and ethnic) milieus reside in very different knowledge, practice and discourse universes, with some of the same segregation effects also being applicable to different age groups. Indeed, strong differences can be seen between the lifeworlds of the young and the old. Of course, it can be said (with reference to Pierre Bourdieu's studies and those rooted in his line of tradition) that such differences in lifestyle are nothing new; quite the contrary, in fact, social groups have always strived to distinguish themselves from one another. But such distinctions played and continue to play an important role in *shared* lifeworlds where the members of different groups encounter and interact with one another. The visible erosion of these spaces—including and in fact especially media spaces—presents a major challenge, perhaps even one of the biggest challenges of the present day. The populist shocks of recent years and debate over postdemocratic conditions are not the first to highlight this (see Crouch, 2008; Müller, 2016). Without these spaces, a democratic sphere of resonance as a meeting place is quite simply inconceivable.

Interestingly, it is in the very erosion of these spaces that we find the structural cause of the current political debates on "fake news," "the lying press" or the "post-factual age"—and the associated social problems: if discourse universes, spheres of practice and lifeworlds barely come into contact any more, if the public sphere is fragmented and there is no longer a single public, it is

---

[5] The available empirical data for this finding is still unsatisfactory; research on the drifting apart of lifeworlds has been conducted in the field of urban sociology, in particular. See, for example, Kronauer and Siebel (2013). Another interesting study here is by Beck and Perry (2008).

hardly surprising when each world starts to produce its own realities and knowledge. There can be no doubt that this separation into parallel worlds has a central *media world* aspect. The media construct of a shared, common world comprised facts, interpretations, stories and people conveyed via the main news programs on the radio, television and in the leading print media is a thing of the past. It has given way to a confusing multiplicity of partial media universes that are not always in competition with one another but often simply closed to one other, although they do produce referential connections between print, broadcast and internet media, each creating their own worlds from facts, interpretations, stories and faces. This reinforces the creation of "echo chambers" observed on every level: in the (digital, but, to some extent, also still analog) media world, people seek out forums where they expect to find and in fact do encounter like-minded individuals. Their own voices are then greatly amplified, overtones disappear or are silenced, and the "others" in other chambers are seen as irrelevant or even as enemies with whom only indifferent or repellent relationships are possible. The emergence of such political echo chambers and milieus that are segregated from one another is also mutually reinforcing—and they undermine the possibility of a democracy based on resonance (and thus of democracy *per se*).

In this context, the main challenge in establishing a democratic sphere of resonance is obvious—this sphere of resonance is simply impossible to achieve without strong, politically institutionalized and guaranteed, public service broadcasters and also without the guarantee of physical civic meeting places. The role of this democratic sphere of resonance is to connect and bind together the social multiverse, first by creating and safeguarding a shared knowledge space and, second, by establishing a forum for democratic participation and exchange which can serve as a meeting place for *any and all* groups, milieus and strata.

If we see democratic politics as a vital sphere of resonance in the modern era, it must not look to subsume its own diversity in identitary harmony. As I have already demonstrated, resonance certainly does not mean (also etymologically) harmony, accord or consonance, but rather, it is a process of responding, moving and being moved, and affecting and being affected. Particularly in politics, this also includes resounding contradiction. The theory of resonance in fact depends on the difference between this form of contradiction and the silent resistance presented by sclerotic relations that appears to have become prevalent in late modernity. A theory of resonant democracy thus oscillates between the different associative and dissociative understandings of politics developed, for example, by Oliver Marchart drawing on Arendt, on the one hand, and Carl Schmitt, on the other. By centering on the contradictory nature, the viscerality and diversity of people's voices, the theory of resonance tends toward the dissociative view. In its notion of harmony and affective, responsive relationships, however, it also includes the associative republican vision of joint action and the productive, transformative appropriation of public spheres and institutions. If we thus succeed in establishing a horizontal political sphere of resonance, this will enable us to find the ways and means of creating new institutions to replace the incessant need for growth that is inherent in dynamic stabilization and relentless accumulation. Such a sphere of resonance would, in turn, facilitate the transformative appropriation of every dimension of the world and the future.

References

Adloff, F., & Leggewie, C. (Eds.). (2014). *Das konvivialistische Manifest. Für eine neue Kunst des Zusammenlebens.* transcript.

Arendt, H. (1958a). Kultur und Politik. In I. H. Arendt (Ed.), *Zwischen Vergangenheit und Zukunft. Übungen im politischen Denken* (pp. 277–302).

Arendt, H. (1958b). *Zwischen Vergangenheit und Zukunft: Übungen im politischen Denken.* Piper.

Arendt, H. (1994). *Vita activa oder Vom tätigen Leben.* Piper.

Arendt, H. (2003). *Was ist Politik? Fragmente aus dem Nachlass.* .

Beck, S., & Perry, T. (2008). Studie Soziale Integration. Nebeneinander und Miteinander in der Stadtgesellschaft. *VHW FW, 3,* 115–122.

Bedorf, T., & Herrmann, S. (Eds.). (2016). *Das soziale Band: Geschichte und Gegenwart eines sozialetheoretischen Grundbegriffs.* Campus.

Bedorf, T., & Röttgers, K. (Eds.). (2010). *Das Politische und die Politik.* Suhrkamp.

Bluhm, W. (1982). Introduction. In W. Bluhm (Ed.), *The paradigm problem in political science. Perspectives from philosophy and from practice* (pp. 1–12). Carolina Academic Press.

Bohmann, U., et al. (2018). Desynchronisation und Populismus. Ein zeitsoziologischer Versuch über die Demokratiekrise am Beispiel der Finanzmarktregulierung. In J. Beyer & C. Trampusch (Eds.), *Finanzmarkt, Demokratie und Gesellschaft, KZfSS, Special Edition.*

Brown, W. (2014). *Walled states, waning sovereignty.* Zone Books.

Buchstein, H. (2018). Der Kernbestand der Demokratie – Resonanztheorie der Demokratie und Aleatorische Demokratietheorie. In K. Becker & K. Dörre (Eds.), *Berliner Journal für Soziologie, Special Volume: Wachstum und Demokratie.*

Caplan, B. (2008). *The myth of the rational voter: Why democracies choose bad policies.* Princeton University Press.

Crouch, C. (2008). *Postdemokratie.* Suhrkamp.

Fishkin, J. (1991). *Democracy and deliberation. New directions for democratic reform.* Yale University Press.

Fishkin, J. (1995). *The voice of the people. Public opinion and democracy.* Yale University Press.

Fishkin, J., & Farrar, C. (2005). Deliberative polling. From experience to community Resource. In J. Gastil & P. Levine (Eds.), *The deliberative democracy handbook* (pp. 686–697). Jossey-Bass.

Fishkin, J., & Luskin, R. C. (2005). Experimenting with a democratic ideal: Deliberative polling and public opinion. *Acta Politica, 40,* 284–298.

Gallie, W. B. (1956). Essentially contested concepts. *Proceedings of the Aristotelian Society, 56,* 167–198.

Genovese, M. A., & Streb, M. J. (Eds.). (2004). *Polls and politics. The dilemmas of democracy.* State University of New York Press.

Hennis, W. (1999). Meinungsforschung und repräsentative Demokratie. In W. Hennis (Ed.), *Regieren im modernen Staat* (pp. 37–88). Mohr Siebeck.

Kielmansegg, P. G. (1977). *Volkssouveränität. Eine Untersuchung der Bedingungen demokratischer Legitimität.* Klett.

Kielmansegg, P. G. (1985). Die "Quadratur des Zirkels". Überlegungen zum Charakter der repräsentativen Demokratie. In U. Matz (Ed.), *Aktuelle Herausforderungen der repräsentativen Demokratie* (pp. 9–41). Heymann.

Kielmansegg, P. G. (2013). *Die Grammatik der Freiheit. Acht Versuche über den demokratischen Verfassungsstaat.* Nomos.

Kielmansegg, P. G. (2016). Repräsentation und Partizipation. Überlegungen zur Zukunft der repräsentativen Demokratie. *Goethe University Frankfurt, Scientific Society, Meeting Minutes, 53*(3). Stuttgart: Franz Steiner Verlag.

Kronauer, M., & Siebel, W. (Eds.). (2013). *Polarisierte Städte. Soziale Ungleichheit als Herausforderung für die Stadtpolitik.* Campus.

Latour, B. (2014). *Existenzweisen. Eine Anthropologie der Modernen.* Suhrkamp.

Love, N. S. (2006). *Musical democracy.* State University of New York Press.

Maaz, K. et al. (Eds.). (2014). Herkunft und Bildungserfolg von der frühen Kindheit bis ins Erwachsenenalter. *Zeitschrift für Erziehungswissenschaft, 24* (Special Edition).

Marchart, O. (2010). *Die politische Differenz.* Suhrkamp.

Mouffe, C. (2007). *Über das Politische.* Suhrkamp.

Müller, J. W. (2016). *Was ist Populismus? Ein Essay.* Suhrkamp.

Münkler, H., et al. (2002). *Gemeinwohl und Gemeinsinn.* Akademie Verlag.

Nachtwey, O. (2016). *Die Abstiegsgesellschaft.* Suhrkamp.

Pitkin, H. F. (1972). *The concept of representation.* University of California Press.

Rancière, J. (2002). *Das Unvernehmen. Politik und Philosophie.* Suhrkamp.

Reitz, T. (2016). *Das zerstreute Gemeinwesen. Politische Semantik im Zeitalter der Gesellschaft.* Springer VS.

Rosa, H. (2005). *Beschleunigung. Die Veränderung der Zeitstrukturen in der Moderne.* Suhrkamp.

Rosa, H. (2014). Die Natur als Resonanzraum und als Quelle starker Wertungen. In G. Hartung & T. Kirchhoff (Eds.), *Welche Natur brauchen wir? Analyse einer anthropologischen Grundproblematik des 21. Jahrhunderts* (pp. 123–141). Karl Alber Verlag.

Rosa, H. (2016a). Der Versuch einer sklerotischen Gesellschaft, sich die Welt vom Leibe zu halten – und ein Vorschlag zum Neuanfang. In K. Rehberg & F. Kunz (Eds.), *Pegida: Rechtspopulismus zwischen Fremdenangst und "Wende"-Enttäuschung? Analysen im Überblick* (pp. 289–296). transcript.

Rosa, H. (2016b). Einem Ruf antworten. Bruno Latours andere Soziologie der Weltbeziehung. *Soziologische Revue, 39,* 552–560.

Rosa, H. (2016c). Politik ohne Resonanz: Wie wir die Demokratie wieder zum Klingen bringen. *Blätter für deutsche und internationale Politik, 61*(6), 97–108.

Rosa, H. (2016d). *Resonanz. Eine Soziologie der Weltbeziehung.* Suhrkamp.

Rosa, H. (2017). Für eine affirmative Revolution. Eine Antwort auf meine Kritiker_innen. In C. H. Peters & P. Schulz (Eds.), *Resonanzen und Dissonanzen. Hartmut Rosas kritische Theorie in der Diskussion* (pp. 311–330). transcript.

Rosa, H., & Sörensen, P. (2014). Wenn die Kommandobrücken verstummen: Politiktheoretische und sozialphilosophische Perspektiven auf Entfremdung im Werk Charles Taylors. In U. Bohmann (Ed.), *Wie wollen wir leben? Das politische Denken und Staatsverständnis Charles Taylor* (pp. 117–139). Nomos.

Rosa, H., et al. (2017). Appropriation, Activation and Acceleration: The Escalatory Logics of Capitalist Modernity and the Crises of Dynamic Stabilization. *Theory, Culture & Society, 34*(1), 53–73.

Sörensen, P. (2016). *Entfremdung als Schlüsselbegriff einer kritischen Theorie der Politik: Eine Systematisierung im Ausgang von Karl Marx, Hannah Arendt und Cornelius Castoriadis.* Nomos.

Taylor, C. (1995). *Das Unbehagen an der Moderne.* Suhrkamp.

Trump, D. J. (2016, July 21). Acceptance speech at the 2016 republican national convention [Video]. YouTube. https://www.youtube.com/watch?v=pWcez2OwT9s

Von Thadden, E. (2018). *Die berührungslose Gesellschaft.* Beck.

Wittman, D. A. (1997). *The myth of democratic failure: Why political institutions are efficient.* Chicago University Press.

Zittel, T., & Kaiser, A. (2004). Demokratietheorie und Demokratieentwicklung: Fragestellungen im Werk von Peter Graf Kielmansegg. In A. Kaiser & T. Zittel (Eds.), *Demokratietheorie und Demokratieentwicklung, Festschrift für Peter Graf Kielmansegg.* VS Verlag.

Phenomenology of Power: Reflections on Social Construction and Subjective Constitution

Jochen Dreher

1   INTRODUCTION

Power in a wide range of socio-scientific research is mainly considered a macro-sociological phenomenon with respect to the objectivity of structural preconditions in societies that are relevant to establish structures or hierarchies of power. On the one hand, power in a collectivity is a means of effectively mobilizing obligations in the interest of collective goals, as Talcott Parsons argues (Parsons, 1963). His structural functionalism claims that within the societal system, power on the one hand is exchanged for other generalized media, specifically money and influence, and on the other hand for significant rewards, for example, services and support, and factors of effectiveness. From a different perspective that we prefer, on the other hand, power according to Max Weber's argumentation is "the probability that one actor within a social relationship will be in a position to carry out his own will despite resistance, regardless of the basis on which this probability rests" (Weber, 1978 [1920/1921], p. 53). From Weber's viewpoint of methodological individualism, it is possible to examine power as a mechanism which serves as an asymmetrisation of social situations, in which an enforcement of one's own will opposing a foreign one becomes possible. It is decisive for Weber's model that power has to be

J. Dreher (✉)
Social Science Archive Konstanz, Department of History and Sociology, University of Konstanz, Constance, Germany
e-mail: jochen.dreher@uni-konstanz.de

considered as individual and collective power, which decides upon situations by means of asymmetric design of interactions in favor of one party.

From the perspective of a *phenomenology of power*—the focus of this outline—it is insufficient to conceptualize power exclusively as a macro-sociological phenomenon since power is established on the interface of collectivity and individuality as well as of objectivity and subjectivity. Power is not only implemented in structural preconditions of societies; it is also implemented in the structures of the life-world of the individual actor. To understand power, it is necessary to analyze the *social construction* and the *subjective constitution* of power, combining a social science with a phenomenological perspective. Society is perceived as objective as well as subjective reality (Berger & Luckmann, 1989 [1966]), which is why power has to be analyzed with respect to its objective construction as well as to its subjective constitution. From this perspective, the micro/macro distinction becomes obsolete and results to be not suitable for the considerations of a phenomenology of power.

The following reflections on a phenomenology of power specifically part from Alfred Schutz's theory of the life-world and in particular from his concept of "relevance," which establishes the bridge between objectivity and subjectivity. The concepts of life-world and relevance serve to reconstruct the complexity and dynamics of power constitution on the interface of objective and subjective reality. As individuals, we are subjected to *imposed structures of relevance* including power hierarchies that are part of our subjective motivation. But based on intrinsic structures of relevance, we confront the objectively given by spontaneous volitional decisions and we can act against pre-given power hierarchies.

Starting from Schutz's concept of the life-world and his reflections on the problem of relevance, the present analysis at the interface of phenomenology and the social sciences reconstructs typification procedures and systems of relevance that are effective within the constitution of power within specific social groups and collectivities. According to Schutz, the subjectively centered life-world not only includes stratification related to time, space, the social world, or multiple reality spheres; the life-world is also characterized by specific structures of relevance. To be able to explain power differences or power relations from a phenomenological perspective, the Schutzian differentiation between *intrinsic relevances* and *imposed relevances* turns out to be of major importance. The knowledge of our life-world as it is subjectively experienced is stratified on the one hand by *systems of imposed relevances* depending on the pre-given world. On the other hand, *systems of intrinsic relevances* are the product of our chosen interests and of spontaneous decision-making and problem-solving.

A theoretical focus will be presented which serves to reconstruct typification procedures and systems of relevance that are effective within the construction and constitution of power differences. Following and going beyond the theoretical conceptions of Alfred Schutz, Peter L. Berger/Thomas Luckmann, Maurice Merleau-Ponty, Pierre Bourdieu, and others, I argue that the constitution of power has to be analyzed with reference to the subjective perspective of the individual actor within relationships of interaction in a specific social world. If we concentrate on the dialectical relationship between individual and society, it is possible on the one hand to analyze the subjective constitution of power based on incorporated knowledge typifications. On the other hand, power hierarchies are constructed through collectively shared knowledge structures that are established in processes of symbolization.

2   Parallel Action of Sociology and Phenomenology: "Construction" Versus "Constitution"

The analysis of power with roots in Weberian sociology requires considering the individual actor who is exposed to specific power structures, at the same time possessing the probability to act against imposed objective power structures. This brings us to the point that the question of power has two sides that have to be considered. Power on the one hand is imprinted in *objective structures* such as social inequalities, chances for access to education, and so on. On the other hand, power is *subjectively perceived and experienced* by the individual actor who is not completely subjected to imposed power structures, but does have the potential to act against and break out of these structural preconditions. Therefore, the analysis of power has to negotiate between the two poles of "objectivism" and "subjectivism."

For the argumentation with respect to a phenomenology of power, we open up the distinction between subjective constitution and social construction which results to be highly relevant for the analysis of power. This differentiation of viewpoints is connected to the diverging epistemological perspectives of phenomenology and the social sciences. According to Thomas Luckmann, both perspectives have to be kept apart as far as their methodical approach is concerned. Phenomenology concentrates on the analysis of the subjective *constitution* of the phenomenon of power, to be precise, on constitutive processes of the subjective consciousness that are the basis to build up the individual's world structured by power hierarchies. Social sciences focus on historical and social realities, analyzing the *construction* of the socio-historical expression of a concrete phenomenon (Luckmann, 2007 [1999], p. 131; Dreher, 2009, p. 405 f.), in this case the phenomenon of power. The division of phenomenology and social sciences also has a reference to the introduced distinction between subjectivism and objectivism, decisive for the analysis of power. The differentiation between the phenomenological and the social science perspective specifically allows reflecting on the challenges which result from subjectivism. On the one hand, the phenomenological viewpoint describes general principles of power *constitution* related to the subjective consciousness. On the other hand, the social science perspective reconstructs concrete social circumstances of power *construction*, in the first instance taking the standpoint of methodological individualism.

To combine the two perspectives with each other, Luckmann introduces the program of a "parallel action" of sociology and phenomenology (Luckmann, 1983 [1970]) which serves to relate the empirical focus on the social construction of the phenomenon—in our case power—to the phenomenological focus on the subjective constitution of it. The sociological and the phenomenological perspective in a "parallel action" serve as a corrective for each other and mutually enrich their findings. We will not realize a "parallel action" with respect to concrete historical, empirical power constellations and the constitutive processes of power in human subjectivity. But we will use the distinction between "construction" from a sociological and "constitution" from a phenomenological perspective for our reflections on power between subjectivism and objectivism.

3   POWER BETWEEN SUBJECTIVISM AND OBJECTIVISM

If we follow Maurice Merleau-Ponty, the problem of power constitution is bound to the discrepancy between two apparently incompatible points of view: objectivism and subjectivism. For this author philosophizing concentrates on a continuous negotiation between objectivism or realism and subjectivism or idealism/intellectualism. From this phenomenological perspective, human existence can be considered neither as pure thing nor as pure consciousness. If we follow Merleau-Ponty, the most important achievement of phenomenology is exactly to have united extreme objectivism and extreme subjectivism. The problem of "rationality" in this context demonstrates the relevance of the two different epistemological positions. Rationality is established on the intersection of diverse subjective perspectives; it is the product of perceptions confirming each other and of sense giving within interactional processes.

But rationality cannot be posited apart or transformed into absolute Spirit, or into a world in the realist sense. The world and the idea of rationality according to Merleau-Ponty are inseparable from subjectivity and intersubjectivity, which are based on past and present experiences of the individual and respective others (Merleau-Ponty, 2007, p. 67). "If reflection consists in seeking the first-hand, or that by which the rest can exist and be thought about, it cannot confine itself within objective thought, but must think about those thematizing acts which posit objective thought, and must restore their context" (Merleau-Ponty, 1966, p. 289). Bourdieu, who borrows the idea of a philosophy between objectivism and subjectivism from Merleau-Ponty, argues that social science oscillates between the two poles, the main task of which is to overcome this conflict. Specifically, the discussion of the phenomenon of power requires reflections oscillating between objectivity and subjectivity since on the one hand objectified power structures of a society or a social group, for example, social inequalities, are the product of social interaction processes in which individual actors are involved. On the other hand, the subjectivity of the individuals is determined by these power structures which frame their perception and experience, but at the same time individual actors not only reproduce power differences, but are able to produce change against imposed objective structures through their action.

Max Weber, one of the most important theorists of power within the German-speaking context of the social sciences, dealt with the concept of power in a distanced and careful manner and describes "power" as "sociologically amorphous." Weber refused to consider the concept of "power" in its diffuse and unstructured form. Instead of focusing on "power," Weber prefers to concentrate on "authority" as a specific form of political power that is anchored in firmly established hierarchies and institutions. In his well-known definition, "power" is already present as "probability that one actor" can carry out his or her own will despite resistance, independent of the social constellations or resources on which power is based.

Considering the diverging theory of power by Michel Foucault, power is described as diffused in social space and only appears in transient figurations of discourse structures (Foucault, 1981). If from such a position we consider political power in the sense of authority that is grounded in a stable hierarchy of institutions, the Weberian viewpoint would become obsolete. From a Foucaultian perspective, it results to be difficult to analyze power as a mechanism which serves as an asymmetricisation of social situations, in which an enforcement of one's own will opposing a foreign one is the case. If we start, like Weber, from the assumption of a model of power as an individual and collective power to act, in which the focus is on asymmetric situations of interaction in favor of one party, then other models with a focus on communication or symbolic representation appear as mechanisms of power (Srubar, 2009, p. 201). The argumentation of a phenomenology of power takes exactly this path, considering the acting individual entangled in symbolic knowledge structures of power that form part of the objective world.

If we follow Weber, power in the form of political authority can access its subjects in two different modes. Power over the state's monopoly on violence first of all appears as an external force on the body and its corporeality. Second, we need to focus on the symbolic meaning dimension of action which is provided through the legitimacy of authority. From this viewpoint, legitimisation is based on symbolisations that do not only have an effect on the asymmetricisation of interactions. Legitimisation is based on the inclusion/exclusion of possibilities to act by means of meaningful interpretation of reality. Furthermore, it has a selective effect on what qualifies as normative and accepted, why it is possible to encounter a selection of acting possibilities. Following this argumentation, Ilja Srubar explains power as *meaning selection* based on processes of the meaningful structuring of the social world. This meaning selection functions through practices, mechanisms, and acts which establish a "Kosmion" as a symbolic meaning world that is relevant to individual actors (Srubar 1988, 2009, p. 202). Individuals generate the "pragmatic motive" as something meaningful and symbolically "modified" in the process of acting itself, which is based on their life-world.

To further elaborate the standpoint of an analysis of power between objectivism and subjectivism, we first turn to the perspective on the *social construction of power*. In a second step, the *subjective constitution of power* is theoretically investigated taking over a decidedly phenomenological point of view.

4   THE SOCIAL CONSTRUCTION OF POWER

If we consider the phenomenon of power from the perspective of the social sciences, we find a variety of diverse conceptions that (sometimes strongly) differ from each other because they originate from divergent epistemological perspectives. This outline serves to frame the reflections on a phenomenology of power, at the same time highlighting the specific potential of this theoretical perspective. The conceptions of power can briefly be described following three lines: the first one distinguishes between "universality" and "particularity" considering fundamental anthropological forms of power on the one hand (Friedrich Nietzsche, Heinrich Popitz) and historical ideal types on the other (Max Weber, Norbert Elias). The second one differentiates between "intentionality" (Heinrich Popitz, Max Weber) and "structure" (Michel Foucault), coming on the one hand from the conviction, that power is exerted on others based on intended action and on the other hand, that it is an effect of structurally established discourses. The third line of argumentation distinguishes between "objectivity" (Karl Marx, Emile Durkheim) and "subjectivity" (Peter L. Berger/Thomas Luckmann, Pierre Bourdieu), reflecting the possibility of contradicting definitions of the situation between power holders and those exposed to it (and thus the possibility of latent power). This third distinction between "objectivity" and "subjectivity" results to be specifically decisive for the perspective of a phenomenology of power since it highlights the relevance of life-worldly power structures involved in subjective experience and action. The reflections on a phenomenology of power basically follow Merleau-Ponty's standpoint of bridging the gap between objectivity and subjectivity, taking into consideration the specific dynamics of the subjective constitution of power.

The forms in which power is exerted on human beings differ strongly. The German sociologist Heinrich Popitz from an anthropological perspective describes four different forms of power: (1) bodily superiority or violence can be used to exercise "power of action," which is based on the potential vulnerability of human beings; (2) "Instrumental power" results from the ability to give and take (resources, affection, knowledge, etc.) and the possibility to give gratification or punishment; (3) and there is also "authoritative power," functioning through the voluntary, consenting agreement of those human beings who are in an inferior situation, who are subordinates; and (4) the fourth type of "power of data constitution" is based on technological progress leading to an increase of power of human beings over others. The power to constitute and control data can lead to a tremendous amount of power over a tremendous amount of human beings (Popitz, 2017, pp. 9–22). "Power" from the perspective of game theory can be considered as the "relative playing ability" as formulated by Norbert Elias as part of his relational concept of power (Elias, 2006 [1970], p. 77). Or power functions through knowledge discourses that are charged with a certain degree of truth following Michel Foucault. According to him, "[T]here is no power relation without the correlative constitution of a field of knowledge, nor any knowledge that does not presuppose and constitute at the same time power relations" (Foucault, 1991 [1975], p. 27).

We discover a great variety of sociological, anthropological, discourse analytical, game theoretical, and so on positions on power; they all dispose of a distinct focus on the social "construction" of power related to language, knowledge, physical superiority, natural resources, and so on. After this sketch of different theoretical orientations rather related to the social construction of power in concrete socio-historical circumstances, I will now move to the phenomenological perspective on the subjective constitution of power.

5   THE SUBJECTIVE CONSTITUTION OF POWER

It is specifically the concept of the life-world that serves for an analysis of power constitution with respect to the subjectivity of the individual actor. Of course, "life-world" has different connotations; for Husserl it is the place of world acceptance, which lies in activities and the productivity of our consciousness. If we follow Alfred Schutz, the life-world is considered a social world as a constituted and interpreted world shared with other human beings. It is a socially solidified reality with a relevance and typicality structure that is produced by individual actors. The subjective experience of the individuals is formed by this reality; social identities are generated and patterns of action are habitualized. But the process of socialization is not passively experienced by the subjects; they are able to modify, acquire, and process social reality. Therefore, the life-world receives a specific dynamic; it is on the one hand experienced as social reality and on the other hand can be acquired and modified. This form of pragmatic constitution of the life-world as social world develops in the field of tension between an intersubjective/social and a subjective pole (Srubar, 2007, p. 23). With Schutz, we conceptualize the life-world as social world with the pragmatic world of everyday life; our world of working as core reality, but life-world also includes everyday transcending realities such as religious experiences, political thought, dream worlds, digital worlds, scientific realities, and so on.

To deal with the concept of power parting from the life-world concept, it is specifically important to consider Pierre Bourdieu's criticism of the phenomenological conception with respect to an alleged oblivion of power of phenomenologically oriented sociology, specifically of Alfred Schutz and Peter L. Berger/Thomas Luckmann. What is highlighted by Bourdieu in his criticism actually demonstrates the strength of the phenomenologically founded outline on power. Bourdieu sees a supposed epistemological problem of phenomenology; he asks the question of whether the contours of the life-world in the "natural attitude" which are "taken-for-granted" in everyday life are by themselves universal boundaries of the social world? Or do they have a history of their own which therefore sociology has to take into account? According to Bourdieu, this history of the life-world, the historically grown preconditions of the life-world have to be taken into consideration to understand the "forgotten fields of power" involved in the constitution of the life-world. The aim is to discover the un-thought categories of thought limiting the thinking and predetermining of what is actually thought. Bourdieu criticizes phenomenologically oriented sociology for its—supposed—lack of any analysis of knowledgegenerating processes as always structured by power. Phenomenologists accordingly would obliterate the presuppositions of their thought, the social conditions of possibility of the scholastic point of view, and the unconscious dispositions that are productive of unconscious theses (Endress, 2005, pp. 58, 60). Apparently forgotten are the subjectified "dispositions" that include categories and hierarchies of power since they were constituted dependent on objectively established concrete expressions of power.

To confront Bourdieu's criticism, I will demonstrate that these argumentations are not justified, because Schutz's theory of the life-world and of relevance specifically serves to analyze the subjective constitution of power. The "unknown" field of knowledge active in everyone's consciousness, identified by Bourdieu, can be reconstructed with Schutz's phenomenological conception. The life-world cannot be considered "a harmless place" (Srubar, 2005, p. 243), as Jürgen Habermas argues (Habermas, 1987). As the subjective world of our experience it includes all the dynamics related to power structures and knowledge structured by power hierarchies. The life-world is constituted in processes of action and interaction, in which the we-world is created in communicative processes. In our natural attitude we experience structures of relevance and typification (Srubar, 2007, p. 27) that involve structures of power.

6   RELEVANCE AND POWER

In taking over a life-world perspective, Alfred Schutz's and also Thomas Luckmann's reflections on the problem of relevance are very suitable to explain the subjective constitution of power. The notion of "relevance" specifically serves to explicate power at the interface of objective and subjective reality, since it functions as a regulative principle of reality construction. It coordinates the knowing and experiencing of objects and it serves the individual actor for the definition of the situation (Nasu, 2003, p. 91). The social world possesses a structure of meaning and relevance for all those who live, think, and act in it (Schutz 1962b [1953], p. 5 f.). The social world with its power structures is already pre-interpreted and contains a stratification based on typifications and symbolizations that are unquestionably given to the members of the social group. The knowledge of the everyday life-world of the individual is structured in relation to degrees of familiarity and acquaintance and it is relative to his or her biographical situation; the knowledge of the social group is relative to its respective historical situation. The relevance concept enables us to investigate the subjective motivation of the individual entering into processes of action. Therefore, the theory of relevance is based on the assumption that the individual actor living in the world experiences him- or herself in a certain situation which—following the Thomas theorem (Thomas & Thomas, 1928, p. 572)— has to be defined by him- or herself.

The definition of the situation includes two decisive components: the first one is the result of the ontological structure of the pre-given world and the other one is defined by the actual biographical state of the individual. The first component cannot be changed by the individual and determines the *imposed systems of relevance* that are not connected with his or her chosen interests; there is no possibility to change them. The second component determines our *intrinsic systems of relevance* that are related to our chosen interests, established by our spontaneous decision to solve a problem by our thinking, to attain a goal by our action, and so on (Schutz, 1964 [1946], p. 126 f., 1970a, p. 26ff.). The theory of relevance allows us to establish a bridge between subjective motivation and objective knowledge structures imposed on the individual (Dreher & López, 2014, p. 18 f.). Power structures as part of the objective reality of society are implemented in the stock of knowledge of the individual specifically in the form of imposed systems of relevance. The subjective motivations of the individual actor depend on imposed and intrinsic relevances; they are simultaneously the starting point for challenging the objectively given determinations of imposed power structures.

The theory of relevance is designed on the interface of objectivity and subjectivity and not only establishes a theoretical bridge between the two perspectives; it also negotiates with respect to the micro-macro distinction of the social sciences. Relevance systems cannot be ascribed to individual actors only; they are socially derived and approved and therefore reach beyond the egological sphere. With the concept of relevance, biographical and social circumstances are brought together, which is why "relevance" functions as a hinge between micro- and macro-analysis (Göttlich, 2022, p. 23). From the perspective of methodological individualism, the reflection is decisive that a collectivity of individual actors based on their structures of relevance is immersed in structures of power. The individual members of a collectivity share imposed relevances and also in part may share their intrinsic relevances and motivations. With respect to the problem of power, specifically based on intrinsic relevance, the possibility to act against imposed power structures evolves.

A further aspect of the theory of relevance that is important with respect to the notion of power is the fact that the relevance concept is also connected to a conception of social action. In Schutz's paper "Choosing Among Projects of Action," he applies the relevance concept for the analysis of the process by which an actor in everyday life determines his or her future conduct "after having considered several possible ways of action" (Schutz, 1962a [1951], p. 67). Our biographical situation determines what is relevant for the actual purpose at hand and this purpose, in turn, is responsible for our choice of action. In this sense relevance also establishes a connection to social action, since it explains how the "definition of the situation" is involved in the decision of action (Göttlich, 2022, p. 14). So the explication of a social situation—following Weber's concept of power—in which one actor can impose his or her own will despite resistance needs to be analyzed with respect to imposed and intrinsic relevances that are the basis and the motivation for the exertion of power as well as the intrinsically motivated exertion of counter-power.

If we sociologically extend the theory of relevance, then specifically "imposed relevances" are related to social interactions that involve the exertion of power. This is the case when starting from a wide power conception in Weber's tradition based only on the probability that one actor can carry out his or her own will despite resistance. This concept of power also includes cases in which no opposed will goes against the striving for power. Following a theory of relevance, power cannot only be articulated in a form that one actor imposes the own relevances against the will of the other. The other possibility would be to define and declare the own relevances of one actor as shared relevances and ensure them (Göttlich, 2012, p. 163).

In a discourse analysis related to the Third Gulf War based on the Schutzian theory of relevance, Andreas Göttlich distinguishes the moral orientations and interpretive schemes of four different actors that deal with this conflict: the US American government, the British government, the Catholic Church, and the Protestant Church in Germany. The empirical analysis parts from the reflection that the controversial judgments of the Gulf War are based on differing interpretive schemes of the four parties. Their respective action and argumentation related to the conflict is based on certain relevance decisions, namely the aspects of the topics that are focused and considered as important, which facts are presupposed, which stock of knowledge is used for the argumentation, and which motivations underlie their interpretations (Göttlich, 2012, p. 74). This case demonstrates that the two churches part from a wider scope of options with respect to possibilities of action compared to George W. Bush and Tony Blair as the representatives of the US American government and the British government, who describe certain necessities of action. While the US president designates the military invention as "pre-emptive strike" with the intention of an attack of the opponent Iraq, the representatives of the two churches decidedly speak of a "preventive war" and therefore do not assume the existence of such an intention (ibid. 145). The divergent relevances of the actors are connected to certain power interests that can be reconstructed through the relevance analysis.

The theory of relevance has the potential to illuminate determination and freedom of action and, in this sense, subjection to power structures as well as resistance to them. Schutz establishes three ideal types of relevance, which, as we argue, serve to explicate the subjective dimension of power constitution: he introduces "motivational," "thematic," and "interpretational relevances." They are ideal typical constructions in the sense of Max Weber and not real types, that is, they are created for theory formation, not with the intention of representing reality.

(1) As far as *motivational relevances* are concerned, they explain the subjectively experienced motives in order to define the situation and characterize the interests that are pre-given and pre-structured by the objective world. Imposed categories of power enter into the subjective stock of knowledge and are expressed by motivational relevances. Based on these relevances, the individual defines the situation thinkingly, actingly, and emotionally to be able to come to terms with the world. Motivational relevances result from our taken-for-granted knowledge. They are determined by a pre-given world of meaning and the symbolic universes as part of the objective reality of the social world (Schutz, 1970b [1957], pp. 123–124). They are based on routinized action and they are not questioned by the individual. Following Schutz, motivational relevances can be expressed as *in-order-to motives* and *because motives*; if our motivation is related to some future action, then we can speak of in-order-to motives. If the action has not been performed yet, then in-order-to motives refer to volitional, future-oriented projects; but if actions based on in-order-to motives already have been performed, then past in-order-to motives cannot be changed voluntarily any more. Because motives are the complement to in-order-to motives and they aim at subjective motivations deriving from dispositions that are biographically determined, which means that they are rooted in the past. Our action is performed in a certain manner, because we are disposed in a certain way (Göttlich, 2022, p. 16); because motives are generally imposed.

Concerning the example of the Third Gulf War, the actors involved—the US government, British government, Catholic Church, and Protestant Church—describe their in-order-to motives as safety and hazard defense, self-defense, and the overcoming of Islamic terrorism to "reach a better world" or a "positive future." Bush and Blair formulate that they intend to help the Iraqi people, while the Catholic Church generally wants to prevent the Iraqis from suffering, and this also means from suffering caused by a military operation intended for help. Both Christian churches principally name strong pacifistic elements which define de-escalation and the avoidance of war as their major aims. The churches as opposed to the British and US governments do not describe the termination of the Saddam Hussein dictatorship as their in-order-to motive, since this is on short notice only realizable with violence. As far as the because motives of the four actors are concerned, they differentiate specifically with respect to the profane self-interest of the two nations, namely self-defense, which is not decisive for the churches. Concerns, sorrows, and fears are mentioned by all the actors as emotional states and because motives; these may result from Islamist terrorism, but also as an answer to Western politics on the War, which according to the churches increases the problem instead of solving it (Göttlich, 2012, pp. 156–157).

(2) The second ideal type of *thematic relevances* differs from the first one, because specifically what is taken-for-granted is *not* recognized as relevant. The unknown and the unfamiliar become relevant, because the taken-for-granted proves to be questionable and uncertain. The actual stock of knowledge does not provide the necessary options for problem-solving within the course of

action, which is why our knowing consciousness needs to focus on a new thematically relevant topic. The creative acquisition of additional knowledge becomes important because the current explanations and existing worldviews do not offer a consistent possibility to solve a situation of action. Thematic and motivational relevances can be either imposed or intrinsic, but intrinsically motivated thematic relevances contain the subjective potential to confront or challenge pre-given structural conditions, for example, situations experienced as unequal. In this way, objectively imposed power structures can be contested on the basis of thematic relevances, which reject taken-for-granted imposed knowledge and initiate action against it. A standpoint for a critique of social reality based on the subjectivity of the individual actor becomes obvious (Dreher & López, 2014, p. 20). This confrontation with and resistance against established power structures is based on thematic relevances that achieve a differentiation from the status quo.

The investigation of the Third Gulf War shows that the four actors thematically focus on consistent topics; they concentrate on the government and people of Iraq, the region, and also Islamist terrorism, topics present in all of their discourses. But an asymmetry can be encountered in that the churches take over the perspective of the observer and it becomes clear that they are unable to influence the war conflict in an institutionalized form. This means that the discourse of the churches comes chronologically after the discourse of politics; it is thematically focused on the military intervention of the US government (Göttlich, 2012, p. 146). Since the churches have the role of the observer without the power to decision-making and without the possibility to directly interfere in the political process. The consequences of the actions of the churches are first and foremost the establishing of a commitment of their members; in their role as an observer they possess the possibility of delegitimizing politics. Based on their thematic relevances, they are able to contest unjust power relations and focus on them within the discourses.

(3) *Interpretational relevances* are the outcome of former thematic relevances. When a specific solution is found for an occurring problem within the course of action, it can be established as a typical solution for frequently occurring problems of a similar expression. They are biographically and ontologically determined and have their origins in motivational relevances (Schutz, 1970b [1957], p. 127). Different interpretations of social reality, for example, religious interpretations, magical understandings, or natural scientific explanations, and so on, may be used to propagate new perspectives and solutions to problems (Dreher, 2011, p. 499). Legitimations of power, if thematically relevant, can therefore be diversified and the individual actor has the freedom to accept or confront biographically, culturally, or socially determined interpretational relevances that are "imprinted" by power structures.

In the case of the four different actors involved in the controversy on the Third Gulf War, diverging interpretational relevances become obvious. While the US and the British governments part from the conviction and underline the presumed fact of the possession of weapons of mass destruction of the Iraqi government, the assessment of the churches in this relation is rather reserved. Also, the allegation of a supposed connection between the Iraqi government and Islamist terror groups is strongly mentioned by Bush and Blair, but rather of less significance for the two churches. A major difference with respect to interpretational relevances becomes apparent between the two political actors and the two churches especially when they focus on Saddam Hussein. The US and the British governments consider him as fundamentally evil and without a sound human understanding, which is why international political pressure cannot stop Hussein from acting. But for the churches, the Iraqi regime is not considered principally uninfluenceable through political pressure. Here a differing reciprocity assumption with relation to Hussein becomes obvious. While Bush and Blair deny Hussein reason, they part from an incongruence of systems of relevance. They deactivate the general thesis of reciprocity in the Schutzian sense. A communication based on understanding for them seems to be only possible to a limited extent. Hussein therefore is discarded as a political dialogue partner, which is why based on the refusal of discourse the military option comes into the foreground. This is different with the churches, specifically the Protestant Church, which does not fundamentally give up the reciprocity assumption. Hussein therefore remains within the circle of potential partners for a dialogue (Göttlich, 2012, p. 148). Each of the actors following interpretational relevances achieves a specific legitimation of its own power position with diverse possibilities to symbolically interpret the war conflict.

7   Synthesis

In between the perspectives of sociology and phenomenology, inspired by the idea of "parallel action," an analysis was presented to on the one hand demonstrate the social construction of power in situations of interaction and on the other hand the constitution of power with respect to the subjectivity of the individual actor. From the sociological perspective, we can investigate objectively given power structures, as expressed in social structure, in social interaction, and so on. Power is considered as *universal* and *particular* phenomenon; power is exerted on others through intended action or can be an effect of structurally established discourses. But furthermore, it is not only an effect of *objective* structural preconditions, but also based on *subjectivity* as structured by power.

Phenomenological analysis can explain the subjective constitution of power or counter-power. We argue against Bourdieu that the "forgotten fields of power" of our everyday life-world are not forgotten at all, since the theory of relevance specifically allows us to reconstruct the complexity of subjective power constitution. The life-world of the individual is not a "harmless place," as Habermas argues. It is influenced by the dynamics of power hierarchies and as a theoretical concept; life-world serves to understand the complexity of the effects of power related to the subjectivity of the individual.

As individuals, we are subjected to *imposed structures of relevance* including power hierarchies that are part of our subjective motivation. But based on intrinsic structures of relevance, we confront the objectively given by spontaneous volitional decisions and we can act against the pre-given power hierarchy. Even though *motivational relevances* impose on us what we have to think, feel, and take for granted, we can deviate from them based on *thematic relevances*. We experience power hierarchies as unjust. Military conflicts as in the example of the Third Gulf War can be considered as unjust, not legitimate, based on false assumptions such as the existence of weapons of mass destruction in Iraq, and so on, always dependent on the respective motivation and interest of the respective actors. And furthermore, based on *interpretational relevances*, possible solutions parting from new interpretations may be established against the existing symbolic universes. It is phenomenology and specifically the theory of the life-world that serve for an analysis of power, since it captures the dynamic processes of power constitution on the interface of objectivity and subjectivity. It is the life-world with its structures of relevance, in which the unforgotten fields of power can be reconstructed in all their complexity.

For a phenomenology of power, based on the theoretical distinction between social construction and subjective constitution of power, furthermore based on methodological individualism, the micro/macro distinction of the social sciences becomes obsolete. We argue that the exertion of power needs to be investigated on the interface of objectivity and subjectivity, based on the idea that power structures are established as objective as well as subjective reality. The analysis of power following Max Weber requires to reconstruct the relevances or motives of individual and collective actors involved in power processes. The dynamics of the construction and constitution of power can be analyzed in all their complexity based on a theory of relevance that bridges the gap between micro- and macro-sociological reflections and therefore makes the micro/macro distinction with respect to its theoretical potential obsolete.

REFERENCES

Berger, P. L., & Luckmann, T. (1989 [1966]). *The Social Construction of Reality. A Treatise in the Sociology of Knowledge*. Anchor Books.

Dreher, J., & López, D. (2014). Subjectivity and Power. In *Human Studies*, published online, pp. 1–26.

Dreher, J. (2009). Phenomenology of Friendship: Construction and Constitution of an Existential Social Relationship. *Human Studies, 32*(4), 401–417.

Dreher, J. (2011). Alfred Schutz in Major Social Theorists. Volume I Classical Social Theorists, edited by George Ritzer/Jeffrey Stepnisky: Wiley-Blackwell, pp. 489-510.

Elias, N. (2006 [1970]). *Was ist Soziologie?* Suhrkamp.

Endress, M. (2005). Reflexivity, Reality, and Relationality. The Inadequacy of Bourdieu's Critique of the Phenomenological Tradition in Sociology. Explorations of the Life-World: Continuing Dialogues with Alfred Schutz, edited by Martin Endress/George Psathas/Hisashi Nasu: Springer, pp. 51–74.

Foucault, M. (1991 [1975]). *Discipline and Punish. The Birth of the Prison*. Penguin Books.

Foucault, M. (1981). The Order of Discourse. Inaugural Lecture at the Collège de France, given 2 December 1970. In P. Young (Ed.), *Untying the Text: A Post-Structuralist Reader* (pp. 48–78). Routledge.

Göttlich, A. (2012). *Geteilte Moral. Die westliche Wertgemeinschaft und der Streit um den Dritten Golfkrieg.* Campus.

Göttlich, A. (2022). Alfred Schutz's Theory of Relevance. In M. D. Barber (Ed.), *The Anthem Companion to Alfred Schutz* (pp. 9–27). Anthem.

Habermas, J. (1987). *The Theory of Communicative Action, Vol. 2: Lifeworld and System: A Critique of Functionalist Reason.* Beacon Press.

Luckmann, T. (1983 [1970]). On the Boundaries of the Social World, in *Life-World and Social Realities* (pp. 40–67). Heinemann.

Luckmann, T. (2007 [1999]). Wirklichkeiten: individuelle Konstitution und gesell-schaftliche Konstruktion. In J. Dreher (Ed.), *Lebenswelt, Identität und Gesellschaft. Schriften zur Wissens- und Protosoziologie* (pp. 127–137). UVK.

Merleau-Ponty, M. (1966). *Phenomenology of Perception.* Routledge & Kegan Paul.

Merleau-Ponty, M. (2007). What is Phenomenology? In T. Toadvine & L. Lawlor (Eds.), *The Merleau-Ponty Reader* (pp. 55–68). Northwestern University Press.

Nasu, H. (2003). A Schutzian Approach to the Problem of Equality-Inequality. In C.-F.Cheung, I. Chvatik, & I. Copoeru, et al. (Eds.), *Essays in Celebration of the Founding of the Organization of Phenomenological Organizations.* Published at www.o-p-o.net

Parsons, T. (1963). On the Concept of Political Power. *Proceedings of the American Philosophical Society, 107,* 232–262.

Popitz, H. (2017). *Phenomena of Power. Authority, Domination and Violence* (G. Poggi, Trans., A. Göttlich, & J. Dreher. Columbia University Press.

Schutz, A. (1962a). Choosing Among Projects of Action. In M. Natanson (Ed.), *Collected Papers, Vol. I: The Problem of Social Reality* (S. 67–96). Nijhoff.

Schutz, A. (1962b [1953]). Common-Sense and Scientific Interpretation of the Social World. In M. Natanson (Ed.), *Collected Papers, Vol. I: The Problem of Social Reality* (pp. 3–47). Nijhoff.

Schutz, A. (1964 [1946]). The Well-Informed Citizen: An Essay on the Social Distribution of Knowledge. In A. Brodersen (Ed.), *Collected Papers, Vol. II. Studies in Social Theory* (pp. 120–134). Nijhoff.

Schutz, A. (1970a). *Reflections on the Problem of Relevance.* Yale University Press.

Schutz, A. (1970b [1957]). Some Structures of the Life-World. In I. Schutz (Ed.), *Collected Papers, Vol. III. Studies in Phenomenological Philosophy* (pp. 116–132). Nijhoff.

Srubar, I. (1988). *Kosmion. Die Genese der pragmatischen Lebenswelttheorie von Alfred Schütz und ihr anthropologischer Hintergrund.* Suhrkamp.

Srubar, I. (2005). The Pragmatic Theory of the Life-World as a Basis for Intercultural Comparisons. Explorations of the Life-World. Continuing Dialogues with Alfred Schutz, edited by Martin Endress/George Psathas/Hisashi Nasu: Springer, pp. 235–266.

Srubar, I. (2007). Ist die Lebenswelt ein harmloser Ort? Zur Genese und Bedeutung des Lebensweltbegriffs. In I. Srubar (Ed.), *Phänomenologie und soziologische Theorie. Aufsätze zur pragmatischen Lebenswelttheorie* (pp. 13–33). VS-Verlag.

Srubar, I. (2009). Wo liegt Macht? Zur Semantik- und Sinnbildung in der Politik. In *Kultur und Semantik* (pp. 201–220). VS.

Thomas, W. I., & Thomas, D. S. (1928). *The Methodology of Behavior Study, in The Child in America: Behavior Problems and Programs* (pp. 553–576). Alfred A. Knopf.

Weber, M. (1978 [1920/1921]). *Economy and Society. An Outline of Interpretive Sociology.* University of California Press.

Understanding Opinions:
A Phenomenological Analysis

Jerry Williams

1   INTRODUCTION

In the United States, public opinion about global climate change is deeply divided. While most Americans believe that change is happening, less than half think it is human-caused (Yale, 2020). Of course, this directly contradicts the scientific evidence that leaves no room for doubt (Shwom et al., 2015). What explains the disjunction between public opinion and scientific evidence? Some have argued it results from a lack of information or education on the part of the public (Marquart-Pyatt, 2012). Others have concluded powerful interests with connections to fossil fuels have shaped public opinion (Jenkins, 2011). Yet others suggest it is a matter of religion or politics (Arbuckle & Konisky, 2015).

Concerning this very large-scale problem, this disjunction is undoubtedly curious. For that reason, I have devoted a substantial amount of effort over the last twenty years considering the related epistemological and empirical issues (Williams, 1998, 2000, 2007). This chapter extends that work by examining the constitution of public opinion in everyday experience. Environmental sociologists in the United States often do not consider this type of question because of their empirical orientation and consequent aversion to philosophical introspection. However, precisely these types of foundational questions informed Alfred Schutz's methodological writings (Schutz, 1962a, 1996). Consistent

J. Williams (✉)
Department of Anthropology, Geography, and Sociology, Stephen F. Austin State University, Nacogdoches, TX, USA
e-mail: jwilliams@sfasu.edu

C. Belvedere, A. Gros (eds.), *The Palgrave Handbook of Macrophenomenology and Social Theory*,
https://doi.org/10.1007/978-3-031-34712-2_6

with the Schutzian impulse, two related questions about opinion must be pursued. First, what is your opinion on the individual level of experience? For example, to say, "I have an opinion," or "I hold an opinion" infers that I have a static bit of "knowledge" tucked away in my "stock of knowledge" (a repository of such knowledge bits). What exactly can this mean?

The second question requiring clarification relates to the nature of public opinion? Is public opinion simply the empirical aggregation of individual opinions as commonly held in the sociological literature?[1] If we consider public opinion as credibly different from an aggregate of personal opinions, how does public attention stand in relation to individual opinion? Answers to these questions are not to be found in the quite substantial sociological literature concerning opinion, which treats public opinion in a reified and taken-for-granted manner as something to be enumerated. Instead, we must analyze how opinion and public opinion are experienced on the conscious level of the social actor engaged in life-worldly activities. We must consider a phenomenological understanding of opinion.

Here Schutzian analysis is utilized to understand public opinion about issues like global climate change. The central point is that public opinion is not simply an aggregation of individual opinions. Instead, public opinion represents what Berger and Luckmann (1966, p. 67) call the intersubjective sedimentation of collective experience. Public opinion is an element of subjective experience derived not from our originary experiences but from our interactions in a shared social and cultural matrix in which sedimented social meanings are disseminated using a sign system (language). To successfully make this point will require an inquiry into the nature of opinion in individual experience, an issue about which Schutz had little to say. It will be necessary to investigate Schutz's phenomenological conceptions of experience, leaning heavily on his discussions of sedimentation and typification, an understanding of which will allow us to see public opinion as resulting from intersubjective sedimentation on the group level. The results of this analysis will be a bridge of sorts between individual subjectivity and the intersubjectivity of the group.

Three points are elaborated here. First, on the level of individual experience, an opinion does not exist as a preconceived facticity—"I hold an opinion." Instead, opinions are sedimentations or amalgamations of prior experiences that are part of a socially derived stock of knowledge framed by social, political, and historical circumstances. For this reason, opinions are not static "bits" of knowledge. Opinions arise in specific social and rhetorical circumstances that carry with them horizons of relevance that trace out those aspects of reality appropriate for the holder's particular purpose.

The second point considered here is that public opinion is a social fact in a sense articulated by Durkheim. It is produced by the subjective processes of individuals yet exists as an exteriority that transcends them. I maintain that public opinion is an intersubjective sedimentation of ideas, a group-level

[1] For example, in regard to global warming see Shwom et al. (2015).

phenomenon that in its expression as social fact, thus, relates in a dialectical fashion with individual opinion (Berger & Luckmann, 1966). That is, as Igo (2007) argues, humans have an insatiable desire to know how their individual opinions stand in relation to the larger group of which they are part. Collections of individuals form public opinion, but their opinions are also shaped by public opinion.

This essay's third and final point is that a dialectical understanding of public opinion and individual opinion provides an opportunity to consider a nagging problem. How can public opinion be changed? If public opinion is simply an aggregation of individual opinions, social change must come one person at a time, perhaps as the result of education. This seems a naïve proposition. More realistically, considering opinion and public opinion as dialectically related suggests that public opinion is much harder to change than we would like to believe.

2   OPINION

The nature of opinion is one of the most commonsense and taken-for-granted ideas in modern societies. To have an opinion is to possess a belief or judgment about something; for example, "I believe that climate change is a threat to human societies." Considered in this way opinion seems to be thing-like and individualistic, much like the possession of material things. However, this way of thinking brackets or sets aside what opinion is. Of course, this unthinking approach is a diagnostic feature of the life-world, our everyday reality. Schutz referred to this feature of our daily life as the "epoche of the natural attitude," a postulate that the world is what it appears to be. He states:

> The suggestion may be ventured that man within the natural attitude also uses a specific epoché, of course quite another one than the phenomenologist. He does not suspend belief in the outer world and its objects, but on the contrary, he suspends doubt in its existence. What he puts in brackets is the doubt that the world and its objects might be otherwise than it appears to him. We propose to call this epoché the epoché of the natural attitude. (Schutz, 1962b, p. 224)

It is not surprising, then, that the nature of opinion is taken for granted, so too is reality in a general sense. While this may be a satisfactory approach in everyday life, scientific thinking about opinion should take place in a finite province of meaning articulated on a level different than the commonsense conceptions of everyday life (Schutz, 1962c, p. 346). A close look at the scientific literature concerning opinion, however, tells a different story. Everyday thinking about the nature of opinion is often coextensive with its scientific use. This requires clarification.

As a matter of scientific interest, opinion first became a sociological concern in the early twentieth century as researchers sought to describe how people in the United States thought and behaved. One of these efforts was the

Middletown project, an attempted anthropological description of an average American town (Igo, 2007, pp. 37–38). In this way, describing public opinion resembled the ethnographic description of the lifeways of indigenous people.

Following Middletown, scientific surveying became widely used. Describing the ascendancy of surveying in the United States, Igo (2007, p. 13) states:

> At the turn of the century, surveys were the province of statisticians, social reformers, the federal Census Bureau, and scattered businessmen and entrepreneurs. By the century's end, social scientific methods, findings, and vocabularies were omnipresent.

As surveying grew, American capitalism saw an opportunity. To know what Americans think and how they behave might well provide insight into their consumptive behavior, and thus, surveys could provide an essential tool for marketing. Of course, none of this required insight into what constitutes an opinion, and therefore opinion was treated in a rather unsystematic fashion. Opinion was treated as a social artifact to be measured and perhaps exploited. From the early twentieth century onward, opinion came to be thought of in a very reified and fact-like manner. Theorizing about public opinion was modest at best. To this end, Clark (1933, p. 311) observes:

> In spite of their growing importance in affairs, the public and public opinion as concepts for group analysis remain wrapped in a haze of confusion and doubt. Their definitions and interpretations seem likely to rival in variety the views of political theorists as to the nature of the state. This situation became acutely apparent In 1924 when a Round Table on Political Statistics of the National Conference on the Science of Politics found it impossible to agree on a standardized meaning, and concluded it best "to avoid use of the term public opinion, if possible."

Ironically, Hyman (1957, p. 54) suggests that theorizing about public opinion could be aided "if greater emphasis was placed on certain aspects of empirical research: for instance, on establishing better series of data, and on probing the social substratum of public opinion." He goes on to argue for greater sophistication in index and scale construction to measure public opinion, not for a foundational understanding of what public opinion is.

Perhaps the most important theoretical discussion of public opinion was articulated by Ferdinand Tonnies (Palmer, 1938). Tonnies suggests that the common usage of public opinion can refer either to publicly expressed opinions or to a "unified social will." According to Tonnies, the latter is what is truly meant by public opinion (Arnold, 2007; Palmer, 1938, p. 586). That is, public opinion represents a feature of the collective distinct from the public expression of opinion by individuals. Palmer (1936, p. 586), however, also points out that Tonnies's work on public opinion has had little impact in the United States, where theorizing about public opinion has been uncommon.

Absent adequate theoretical specification of public opinion, sociologists in the United States were left in a peculiar position. To be a scientist of public opinion was to use scientific techniques (surveys, indexes, scales, etc.) to measure a commonsense and unexamined concept. The reasons for this lack of scientific and theoretical rigor are not complicated. Marketing surveys and political polling offered funding for sociological programs engaged in opinion research. Opinion research also offered something else. It showed sociology the potential to be seen by the public as legitimate science in much the same way that psychology had earlier been legitimated by way of its use of the experimental method (Berger, 1963, p. 10). In this context, the enumerators of public opinion had little use for theorizing. As a result, it was treated in a commonsense fashion as simply an aggregate of individual opinion. To see why this is problematic it is important to consider more carefully what opinion actually is on an experiential level.

As a starting point, let us imagine a particular moment in which a survey respondent is asked to answer a telephone survey item as part of a project to measure public opinion about global warming. Using a Likert response format, the item might look like this.

> I believe that global warming is caused by human activities.
> Strongly Agree – Agree – Disagree – Strongly Disagree

Operationalized in this way opinion is treated as "thing-like," as a cognitive construct that exists much like a computer stores data. Surveys, then, are seen as means to collect these "things." This understanding, however, requires clarification. How do opinions arise? What does it mean to hold an opinion? What function, if any, do opinions have for those who hold them, and to what extent are these opinions connected to the intersubjective opinions of others?

Phenomenologically speaking, opinions are at their base typifications. That is, they are "types" formed in the same way as other experiences in everyday life. Typifications are preconceived mental constructs derived from a shared, social stock of knowledge. Schutz (1962d, pp. 7–8) states, "the outer world is not experienced as an arrangement of unique individual objects, dispersed in space and time, but as "mountain," "trees," "animals," "fellow-men." On a cognitive level, typification, the social process of turning the world into types, is a necessary human activity. Reality is a cacophony of possible experiences—a bewildering array of sights, sounds, and other sensory experiences. Even in a quite restricted environment such as my office, the multitude of possible sensory inputs is overwhelming. I make sense of this chaos in two ways. First, through the process of intentionality, I only become aware of those things toward which I turn my attention. For example, at this moment, even though there are countless possibilities, I intentionally retain in my consciousness only those phenomena that are relevant for my purposes—typing on my computer and other things. At the same time, until just now, I am unaware of the sound of my clock ticking in the background. To put this differently, my duration contains those elements retained by my intentional activities (Schutz, 1962e).

I filter out extraneous sensory input in favor of those phenomena that meet my purposes and system of relevance.

Typifications also help us make sense of the world in yet another way. They provide explanatory templates. As an example, imagine your first experience with a tree. There retained in our consciousness is the sight of a tree with specific characteristics—tall, green, and so on. Of course, making sense of this experience will require help from those around us. "What is this thing?" "It is a tree." Based on this experience and assistance from others, I then polythetically (step-by-step) construct a type "tree" by assigning certain typical features that correspond to an intersubjectively shared preexisting type; it has bark, leaves, and so on. As I grow older, I experience many other trees. Some have leaves, others have needles, some are large, and others are small. Each of these new experiences does not replace the original type; instead, they modify it in ways that correspond to the new experiences. That is, typifications are synthetic in nature. Over time this synthetic type becomes sedimented in my consciousness as an explanatory template for all future experiences of trees. This is important. Our future experiences of trees, then, are not generally of particular trees experienced polythetically (step-by-step in their uniqueness) but instead of an earlier constructed typification that we experience monothetically, as a preconceived and anonymous type (Schutz, 1962f, p. 143). The efficiency of this process is worth noting. In terms of cognitive effort, we experience particular trees as typical and anonymous trees, thus saving the effort it might take to experience the specific features of the tree in front of us. Of course, if required by our purpose at hand, we could make an effort to know this specific tree in its particularity, but for most of our purposes that is unnecessary.

To understand opinion about global warming as a typification, we must explore some additional features of typifications. To continue our example, our daily experiences of trees, as we have said, are not generally of a particular tree but instead of typified trees. In consciousness, typifications exist not as discrete objects to be recalled but rather as halos or fringes—a complex of sedimented characteristics derived from previous experiences (Schutz, 1962e, p. 108). Because these experiences stem from specific purposes, our typification contains elements relevant to only those purposes from which they are derived and therefore not relevant to others. For example, having once used a chainsaw to cut down a tree, my typification of "tree" contains sights, smells, and other sensations that go unnoticed when I merely experience a tree in the distance and admire its beauty. In addition to a tree's observable features, I might also include an action orientation in my typification. That is, under the right circumstances, I could do something with the tree—climb it, chop it down, or just touch it. Also possibly included in the typification is a value assessment—it is a good thing, a bad thing, or neither. Further, under the right circumstances, this typification can also be connected to other preexisting typifications. For example, depending upon my purpose, I might connect "tree" to the typification "plant" or an aesthetic typification of "beauty," and so on. Still, I might connect preexisting typifications about the tree's origin, purpose, and existential meaning. In total, typifications are usually a complex of descriptive, explanatory, or evaluative features.

Typifications, including opinions about global warming, then, are best thought of as halos or orientations, not discrete objects in consciousness. At any one moment, my utilization of a typification only includes those elements of the typification relevant to my purposes at hand. With respect to global warming, my answer to the Likert item "I believe that global warming is caused by human activities" demands of me the recollection of the type "global warming." That is, my response happens in a particular rhetorical situation. My answer draws upon my typification of "global warming" not in the totality of its halo of meaning but rather only upon those aspects relevant to the particular rhetorical situation—audience, occasion, purpose, and so on. For example, a different rhetorical situation, perhaps explaining global warming to my young daughter, would require a different intentional selection from my type's halo or fringes. Typifications, then, are not discrete kernels in my consciousness but rather are halos of possibilities that are never experienced at any one time in their entirety. Which aspects of this halo I experience depends entirely upon my particular purposes and relevance at any given time.

While convenient, the tree example used to illustrate the process and use of typifications requires further elaboration if it is to help us understand opinions about global warming. While the typification "tree" corresponds to a tangible phenomenon ubiquitously present in our daily experience, global warming, on the other hand, is much less tangible. Our everyday understanding of global warming is primarily an idea about the physical world drawn from scientific and authoritative sources. To date, climate changes have been too subtle and distant for most people to directly associate them with global warming.[2] Global warming is a mental construct or typification nearly absent immediately apparent corresponding features in everyday life. At best, we can point to knowledge of record heat, melting glaciers, and massive storms as evidence, but these often lack the immediacy that objects like a tree have in our experience. Our knowledge of global warming is almost exclusively passed down or obtained through education and information from authoritative sources.

An important consequence of the intangibility of "global warming" is that its specification in our stock of knowledge requires legitimation and explanation in a way that more tangible typifications do not. Our originary experience of a tree only requires that it be named and described—"it is a tree with rough 'bark' and 'leaves.'" In its "treeness," it speaks for itself. If I have doubts about its realness at some point, I must only touch it, and if I have further doubts, I might ask for another opinion. My interpretive efforts are, in sum, very meager. To locate the tree in my stock of knowledge, I may understand it as a

---

[2] For a discussion of perceptions of local weather and their connection to global climate see Szafran, Williams and Roth Robert Szafran, Jerry Williams, and Jeffery Roth. 2013. "If Local Weather Was Our Only Indicator: Modeling Length of Time to Majority Belief in Climate Change." *Simulation and Gaming* 44(2–3): 409–426.

"plant" or a "living thing," but in the end, these are insignificant details when compared to our experience of "global warming." Without direct correspondence in the field of immediate physical things, I rely heavily upon knowledge passed down to me by people I trust. Further, my understanding of it will rely upon how I connect it to other preexisting typifications—it is an "environmental problem," it is another example of "living beyond our limits," or it is an example of a "liberal conspiracy." We might also connect it to more metaphysical typifications—"God is in control," "Gaia will prevail," and so on. While the process of fitting global warming into our social stock of knowledge is like our experience of the tree, the cognitive connections to preexisting typifications are substantially more important. So too are the authoritative sources we rely upon to make sense of things. The day-to-day signs of global warming are subtle and often do not provide an adequate corrective to the typifications we hold about it (Williams, 1998).

So far, opinion has been described on the level of an individual who builds and maintains her opinions. The question of legitimation, however, brings into view the obvious fact that opinions are never solitary and individualistic. They are, instead, social and intersubjective. For example, my opinion about global warming stands in a dialectical relationship with my society's opinion about global warming. Public opinion is the framer and source of my opinions but also the way in which those opinions are maintained over time. Public opinion is not just a collection of individual opinions. It is an exteriority that appears to us in everyday life as, using Durkheim's term, a "social fact" (Durkheim, 1984, p. 326). The key to understanding this aspect of public opinion is the process of intersubjective sedimentation.

3   Intersubjective Sedimentation

Earlier it was noted that as part of the experiential process, individuals synthetically typify experiences as types transforming polysynthetic experiences into monothetic types. However, typifications, including opinions, are never uniquely "mine." They are rather collective products of the group with whom I share an affinity. They are intersubjective. Paradoxically the intersubjective foundation of my typifications and opinions is often not apparent to me. That is, I believe my opinion to be "my opinion," not a product of my social group. This social amnesia is a product of what Berger and Luckman have called the paradox of social existence (Berger, 1963, p. 129). Individuals actively engage with others in a social world-building process while, at the same time, the social world makes and shapes the very individuals involved in social world-building. Only rarely and only upon reflection do participants become aware of the inner workings of this dialectic and perhaps see the social roots of their subjectivity. In fact, a perceived sense of social order is probably only possible so long as the social dialectic is obscured from everyday experience. As we go about our daily lives, we apprehend ourselves and the social world as accomplished facts— "that's just the way it is." In doing so, we give the socially constructed world a nomothetic quality that blinds us to the often arbitrary and capricious nature of the social world-building process while at the same time providing a sense of order.

Society and its institutions are, then, experienced by us as a duality. On the one hand, we experience them as anonymous exteriorities independent of our subjectivity—"they are out there." On the other hand, I individualize or appropriate their associated roles, recipes, and ideas as my own. At precisely the same time, as society appears to me to be external and objective, aided with social amnesia, I experience myself and my ideas as "mine," as products of my subjectivity. For example, I think of my role as a parent as an aspect of my biography, not generally as a product of my social and cultural circumstances. While it is often not apparent to me, my role as a parent was my subjective response to the social expectations of my society, a dialectic. Nevertheless, my roles, identity, and ideas result from a working back-and-forth between what is experienced by me as an anonymous and objective externality and the persistent and subjective sense that I am an individual independent of that externality.

The social dialectic illustrates why the common conception of public opinion as an aggregate of individual opinion is inadequate. Such conceptions implicitly see only one side of the social dialectic—the constitution of social reality by individuals. They ignore the obvious fact that individuals experience public opinion as an anonymous and objective reality independent of their subjectivity, a reality that exists in our experience as a dialectic with what we think are "our individual opinions." Opinion, then, is an ongoing conversation with society, not simply static elements of knowledge held in our subjective repositories. Intersubjective sedimentation is the key to understanding how this conversation works.

Intersubjective sedimentation is the process by which individual consciousness, by way of participation in a social group, is externalized and thus becomes an anonymous exteriority transcending individual subjectivity. It is also, however, the way in which these authorless (anonymous) exteriorities are later individualized (internalized) by individuals.[3] Berger and Luckmann (1966, p. 67) state:

> Intersubjective sedimentation also takes place when several individuals share a common biography, experiences of which become incorporated in a common stock of knowledge. Intersubjective sedimentation can be called truly social only when it has been objectivated in a sign system of one kind or another, that is, when the possibility of reiterated objectification of the shared experiences arises.

---

[3] Intersubjective sedimentation is closely related to Durkheim's (1984, p. 117) collective consciousness. Durkheim defines collective consciousness as: "the totality of beliefs and sentiments common to the average members of a society forms a determinate system with a life of its own. It can be termed the collective or common consciousness. Undoubtedly the substratum of this consciousness does not consist of a single organ. By definition it is diffused over society as a whole, but nonetheless possesses specific characteristics that make it a distinctive reality."

Only then is it likely that these experiences will be transmitted from one generation to the next and from one collectivity to another.

Language allows for intersubjective sedimentations to be individualized and appropriated by individuals who share that language as the building blocks of their individual sedimentations. Confronted with a novel experience, they rely on these sedimentations monothetically without recourse to their original constitution. Berger and Luckmann (1966, p. 68) argue:

> Language becomes the depository of a large aggregate of collective sedimentations, which can be acquired monothetically, that is, as cohesive wholes and without reconstructing their original process of formation.

Importantly for understanding public opinion, language not only serves as a "depository" for collective sedimentations but also provides these sedimentations with a degree of anonymity, as not connected to "concrete individual biographies."

> An objectively available sign system bestows a status of incipient anonymity on the sedimented experiences by detaching them from their original context of concrete individual biographies and making them generally available to all who share, or may share in the future, in the sign system in question. (Berger & Luckmann, 1966, p. 68)

The anonymity of intersubjective sedimentations provides insight into the dialectic involved in opinion formation. Individual opinions are formed in a dialectical fashion with the disconnected and abstract intersubjectivity of others (public opinion). Take as an example my hypothetical experience of global warming.

Recently, perhaps, I have heard much about global warming from friends, the news, and other sources. I also know that others have formed opinions about it. In creating and maintaining my opinion about global warming, I rely upon my subjective experiences of climate and my understanding of news reports and climate science. Importantly, however, I do not need to polythetically (step-by-step) form my own opinions. Instead, I avail myself of typifications intersubjectively sedimented in public opinion and thus adopt their monothetic explanations as my own. In dialectic relation with my subjective experiences, I individualize and tailor these intersubjective sedimentations. Public opinion about global warming, then, is not just an aggregation of individual, subjective opinions; it is experienced by me as an external facticity—as real.

4   CHANGING PUBLIC OPINION

Understanding public opinion as the product of intersubjective sedimentation provides insight into a nagging question—how does public opinion change? Regarding global climate change, this is a crucial question. The projected consequences of inaction on climate change paint a dark picture for the future of the planet: decreased sea ice, ocean level rise, disruption of climate patterns, and the prospect of climate refugees (Méndez, 2020; Noussia, 2020). If we are to reduce or eliminate fossil fuel use to avoid the worst of these consequences, it will require some level of consensus. At least in the United States, this seems a distant hope. We are far from consensus. How might this change? The answer to this question is perhaps related to how we think of public opinion—as an aggregation of individual opinion or, as argued here, the result of a dialectical relationship between individual and public opinion.

To see public opinion as an aggregation of individual opinion commits us to see change as occurring one person at a time. Consequently, we envision individuals as divorced from the social dialectic that gives rise not only to their opinions but also to their identities, social roles, and institutional arrangements. Disconnected from the social matrix, we attribute to social actors a greater capacity for agency and theoretical thinking than they routinely exercise. Along those lines, Schutz (1962b, p. 208) contends the world of everyday life is primarily pretheortical, pragmatically motivated, and not often concerned with ideas. Berger and Luckmann (1966, p. 15) sum it up this way:

> Theoretical thoughts, "ideas," Weltanschauungen are not that important in society. Although every society contains these phenomena, they are only part of the sum of what passes for "knowledge." Only a very limited group of people in any society engages in theorizing, in the business of "ideas"… To exaggerate the importance of theoretical thought in society and history is the natural failing of theorizers.

This prevailing tendency to attribute too much importance to human agency and rationality has been called naïve rational humanism (Williams, 2003). Naïve rational humanism assumes that once an environmental problem is identified by elites or other theorizers, the next step in changing public opinion is to educate the public about the problem and its threats. This amounts to the differential knowledge thesis (Dietz et al., 1989, p. 53). That is, public opinion is thought to change once information about the problem has been disseminated by elites and the public is educated about it. Again, change is sought on an individual level. When enough individuals change their opinions, we can then say public opinion has changed.

To examine this formulation, consider how individual opinions are thought to change. William James (1907, p. 57) describes the process consistent with the differential knowledge thesis. He states:

The individual has a stock of old opinions already, but he meets a new experience that puts them to a strain. Somebody contradicts them; or in a reflective moment he discovers that they contradict each other; or he hears of facts with which they are incompatible; or desires arise in him which they cease to satisfy. The result is an inward trouble to which his mind till then had been a stranger, and from which he seeks to escape by modifying his previous mass of opinions. He saves as much of it as he can, for in this matter of belief we are all extreme conservatives. So he tries to change first this opinion, and then that (for they resist change very variously), until at last some new idea comes up which he can graft upon the ancient stock with a minimum of disturbance of the latter, some idea that mediates between the stock and the new experience and runs them into one another most felicitously and expediently.

Scientists and others wishing to change individual opinions then educate the public and put an individual's "stock of old opinions to a strain." As a result, they try to fit the new information with their existing stock of knowledge with a "minimum of disturbance," all the while preserving as much of their old "mass of opinions" as possible.

While James provides an important account of how opinions change on an individual level, it is apparent that it also fails to consider the part public opinion as an exteriority, a social fact, might also play in this process. In James's formulation, the individual wrestles with new and contradictory information alone. However, such information is never weighed in solipsistic darkness. Instead, contradictory information is balanced against intersubjective sedimentations from the social group of which individuals are part. That is, they experience these opinions monothetically and as having substantial anonymity. Put differently, they weigh contradictory information in a dialectic conversation between their individual opinions and that of the group. This realization fixes the importance of seeing public opinion as more than an aggregation of individual opinion. The problem of the perceived legitimacy of the claims maker will help clarify why this understanding is critical.

As mentioned earlier, much of our existing stock of knowledge is passed down to us from the society in which we live. As part of this process, we come quite naturally to "trust" some sources and to "distrust" others. While it is impossible to draw out this problem here fully, it is important to point out that legitimacy and authority are closely related. Much of the day-to-day knowledge in my social stock of knowledge, either directly or indirectly, results from authoritative sources—parents, teachers, and so on. As a young child, my initial trust in these authorities derives first from my familial connections and second from the trust I place in my parents' judgments about such matters. In other words, I vest authoritative sources I trust with a determination of legitimacy. This is also true in adulthood. When judging which claims about reality are true and which are not, I consider the legitimacy of their source.

To determine their legitimacy, I might, in a pretty rational way, assess the claim using whatever scientific knowledge I have about the matter combined with additional research. I might also investigate the source itself—asking how it is funded and to what other groups it is related. These efforts, while possible, are not likely. Elements in my stock of knowledge are passed down to me monothetically as typifications derived from others, thus providing explanatory templates for my experiences. Deconstructing them in the face of contradictory information risks stripping them of their anonymity and order-making function.

A much more likely approach when assessing the legitimacy of contradictory sources is to compare them to what I already know, as James suggests, and in relation to what I perceive to be the mean attitude of my social group. If the new information contradicts what I already know or what I see to be the opinion of my social group, I will likely dismiss these claims as not legitimate and therefore alleviate any need on my part to reconcile the contradictory information. This is true even if the conflicting information comes from scientific sources. In everyday life, because most people are not climatologists or scientists, scientific claims about global warming are mostly understood in nonscientific terms (Williams, 2003). Their truth or falsity is assessed with respect to how well they correspond to what is already known and accepted by both my social group and me, therefore, allowing me to judge the perceived legitimacy of their source.

The perceived legitimacy of claims makers illustrates the importance of a dialectical understanding of public opinion and points to the difficulty of changing public opinion. Rather than changing the individual minds of fully aware rational social agents, claims makers are faced with changing the intersubjectively sedimented monothetic explanations of the social group against which individuals form and maintain their individual opinions. This is quite a daunting task. Nevertheless, those interested in changing public opinion must understand that change is necessarily slow, and if a change is possible through the intentional efforts of claims makers (a fact that is far from certain), that change must be accomplished by a slow and incremental reshaping of the shared social stock of knowledge.

5   CONCLUSION

The foregoing has considered the nature of opinion and public opinion on the level of experience. It was argued that individual opinion exists in a dialectic with public opinion. Individual opinions are never truly individual phenomena. Rather, they are formed when individuals make sense of their subjective experiences by reappropriating and individualizing the intersubjective sedimentations of the group with which they share an affinity. That is to say, public opinion is more than simply an aggregate of individual opinions. It is experienced by individuals as a social fact.

Understanding public opinion as a social fact runs counter to the prevailing conception of public opinion as an aggregation of individual opinions. Not a vigorously considered stance, the conception of public opinion as an aggregate of individual opinions is rather a taken-for-granted and unexamined presupposition. It is precisely these types of unexamined concepts that Alfred Schutz argued must be examined if they are to be scientifically explained. About this Schutz and Luckmann argue, "the sciences that would interpret and explain human action must begin with a description of the foundational structure of what is prescientific" (Schutz & Luckmann, 1973, p. 3). Schutz's admonition to examine the pre-theoretical world of everyday life is often taken as a direction to explore the subjectivity of individual social actors. Certainly, this approach has yielded important results. This analysis, however, suggests that even large-scale phenomena like public opinion about global warming can also benefit from an examination of the subjective constitution of social phenomena.

REFERENCES

Arbuckle, M. B., & Konisky, D. M. (2015). The role of religion in environmental attitudes. *Social Science Quarterly (Wiley-Blackwell), 96*(5), 1244–1263. https://doi.org/10.1111/ssqu.12213

Arnold, A.-K. (2007). Tonnies' concept of public opinion and its utility for the academic field. *Javnost—The Public, 14*(2), 7–30.

Berger, P. L. (1963). *Invitation to sociology: A humanistic perspective*. Doubleday.

Berger, P. L., & Luckmann, T. (1966). *The social construction of reality: A treatise in the sociology of knowledge*. Doubleday.

Clark, C. D. (1933). The concept of the public. *The Southwestern Social Science Quarterly, 13*(4), 311–320.

Dietz, T., Stern, P. C., & Rycroft, R. W. (1989). Definitions of conflict and the legitimation of resources: The case of environmental risk. *Sociological Forum, 4*, 47–70.

Durkheim, E. (1984). *The division of labor in society* (S. Lukes, Ed., W. D. Halls, Trans.). Free Press.

Hyman, H. (1957). Toward a theory of public opinion. *Public Opinion Quarterly, 21*(1), 54–60.

Igo, S. E. (2007). *The averaged American*. Harvard University Press.

James, W., & Herman Finkelstein Collection (Library of Congress). (1907). *Pragmatism: A new name for some old ways of thinking: Popular lectures on philosophy*. Longmans, Green.

Jenkins, J. C. (2011). Democratic politics and the Long March on global warming: Comments on McCright and Dunlap. *Sociological Quarterly, 52*(2), 211–219. https://doi.org/10.1111/j.1533-8525.2011.01201.x

Marquart-Pyatt, S. T. (2012). Contextual influences on environmental concerns cross-nationally: A multilevel investigation. *Social Science Research, 41*(5), 1085–1099. https://doi.org/10.1016/j.ssresearch.2012.04.003

Méndez, M. J. (2020). The silent violence of climate change in Honduras: In one of the most environmentally vulnerable regions in the world, indigenous and rural communities are fighting to stay in the face of climate-driven displacement. Still, the immediate exodus demands new international forms of protection for climate refugees. Vol. 52. 10714839. Taylor & Francis Ltd.

Noussia, K. (2020). On modern threats to environmental sustainability in the Arctic: The climate change factor. *European Energy & Environmental Law Review*, *29*(3), 98–109.

Palmer, P. A. (1938). Ferdinand Tönnies's theory of public opinion. *Public Opinion Quarterly*, *2*(4), 584–595. https://doi.org/10.1086/265233

Schutz, A. (1962a). Common-sense and scientific interpretation of human action. In M. Natanson (Ed.), *Collected papers I: The problem of social reality* (pp. 3–47). Martinus Nijhoff.

Schutz, A. (1962b). On multiple realities. In M. Natanson (Ed.), *Collected papers I: The problem of social reality* (pp. 207–259). Martinus Nijhoff.

Schutz, A. (1962c). Symbol, reality, and society. In M. Natanson (Ed.), *Collected papers I: The problem of social reality* (pp. 287–356). Martinus Nijhoff.

Schutz, A. (1962d). *Common-sense and scientific interpretation of human action* (M. Natanson, Ed.). Martinus Nijhoff.

Schutz, A. (Ed.). (1962e). *Some leading concepts of phenomenology* (M. Natanson, Ed.). Martinus Nijhoff.

Schutz, A. (Ed.). (1962f). *Husserl's importance for the social sciences* (M. Natanson, Ed.). Martinus Nijhoff.

Schutz, A. (1996). Basic concepts and methods of the social sciences. In H. Wagner, G. Psathas, & F. Kersten (Eds.), *Collected paper IV*. Springer.

Schutz, A., & Luckmann, T. (1973). *The structures of the life-world*. Northwestern University Press.

Shwom, R. L., McCright, A. M., Brechin, S. R., with Dunlap, R. E., Marquart-Pyatt, S. T. (2015). Public opinion about climate change. In R. E. Dunlap & R. J. Brulle (Eds.), *Climate change and society* (pp. 300–332). Oxford University Press.

Szafran, R., Williams, J., & Roth, J. (2013). If local weather was our only indicator: Modeling length of time to majority belief in climate change. *Simulation and Gaming*, *44*(2–3), 409–426.

Williams, J. (1998). Knowledge, consequences, and experience: The social construction of environmental problems. *Sociological Inquiry*, *68*(4), 476–497.

Williams, J. (2000). The phenomenology of global warming: The role of proposed solutions as competitive factors in the public arenas of discourse. *Human Ecology Review*, *7*(2), 63–72.

Williams, J. (2003). Natural and epistemological pragmatism: The role of democracy in confronting environmental problems. *Sociological Inquiry*, *73*(4), 529–544.

Williams, J. (2007). Thinking as natural: Another look at human exemptionalism. *Human Ecology Review*, *14*(2), 130–139.

Yale. (2020). Yale Project on Climate Change. Retrieved 1/2, 2020 from https://climatecommunication.yale.edu/visualizations-data/ycom-us/

PART III

Phenomenology of Organizations and Institutions

Some Reflections on a Phenomenology of Organizations

Thomas S. Eberle

The late Husserl (1936/1970) argued that the crisis of modern sciences was caused by the fact that they had taken their idealizations and abstractions, their mathematical and geometrical formulae, for bare truth, and had forgotten that they originated in the lifeworld. Husserl meant, as always, the natural sciences, but it also applies to the social sciences, which sometimes only see numbers, graphs and statistical distributions but not the society as it is *experienced* by its members. The same applies to the positivist versions of organizational theory which attempt to grasp organizations by constructing mathematical indices of all sorts and modeling hypothetical causal relationships. All these constructions rest upon the unquestioned fundament of the lifeworld, the world as we subjectively experience it. The goal of phenomenological lifeworld analysis is to describe how the lifeworld is experienced and elucidate how scientific methods work—in order to solve the "crisis of modern sciences."

Modern society is rife with organizations; hence, each of its members encounters a multitude of organizations in his or her everyday life. However, how is an organization experienced? Can an 'organization' be experienced at all? Or is it only some aspects and fragments that can be perceived? And if so, in which way are other realms of an organization given to our experience? Nobody would object that social phenomenology and phenomenological sociology have contributed much on the micro level. The basic question of this

T. S. Eberle (✉)
Research Institute of Sociology, University of St. Gallen, St. Gallen, Switzerland
e-mail: thomas.eberle@unisg.ch

C. Belvedere, A. Gros (eds.), *The Palgrave Handbook of Macrophenomenology and Social Theory*,
https://doi.org/10.1007/978-3-031-34712-2_7

book is if they also can explore the macro level? In this essay I try to approach this question on the so-called meso level, the level of organizations. I begin with Husserl's concept of 'personalities of a higher order' and track how eidetic analyses of collectives are conducted. Then I have a look at Schutz's alternative approach which complemented the egological perspective by a pragmatic, intersubjective perspective. On this basis, I then make some reflections on a phenomenology of organizations. I conclude with the suggestion to relate micro, meso and macro level; these levels can only be analytically distinguished, in social reality they are closely intertwined.

1   Eidetic Analyses of 'Personalities of a Higher Order'

Husserl (1928/2012) showed convincingly that conventional dualisms such as rationalism vs. empiricism, subjectivism vs. objectivism, or idealism vs. realism are non-sense as both are mutually dependent. All we can cognize are phenomena, and phenomena are objects as perceived by subjective consciousness. Hence, consciousness and world, subject and object cannot be separated, they are intertwined. This is sometimes called "correlationalism" (cf. Zahavi, 2016, pp. 4–9). There is no objective thing in itself, and there is no consciousness in itself. Consciousness is always 'consciousness of *something*.' The 'intentionality' of consciousness is a central phenomenological concept, and these intentionalities are in a continuous flow, Husserl speaks of the 'stream of consciousness.' This temporal dimension of perceived phenomena is fundamental to phenomenology as is the spatial dimension for objects of the outer world. In addition, every subjective consciousness is bound to a lived body whose different senses provide a variety of sensuous data. A crucial insight of phenomenology is that phenomena do not just consist in sensuous data, they are at the same time *meaningfully constituted*.

Husserl developed several methods to pursue a phenomenological analysis. All of them are descriptive and mainly egological, that is, a phenomenologist investigates the phenomena in his or her own subjective consciousness. One of these methods is the *epoché* or *phenomenological reduction*, the 'bracketing' of the assumptions of the natural attitude that we regularly rely upon in everyday life. It reduces iteratively the beliefs, the theoretical and pre-theoretical presuppositions, hypotheses and elements of knowledge that are usually involved in the constitution of a phenomenon. Elucidating all these presuppositions helps to clear the way from the particulars to the universal *eidos (essence)* of a phenomenon. Another method is the *constitutive analysis* which starts at the other end and asks *how we constitute the sense of phenomena*. The core is *apperception*: what is actually perceived? Phenomena are constituted with an outer horizon—against a 'background,' within a 'context'—but they have also an inner horizon which is constituted by *appresentation*: We not only perceive what is perceivable, but 'appresent' also aspects that are not perceivable (e.g., we see a 'house' although we just perceive its front side). Phenomena are constituted in passive syntheses and include sensuous apperception as well as meaning. A crucial difference to many other, especially linguistic, approaches is that phenomenology analyzes meaning constitution on a *pre-predicative level*. Subjective experience is always more and different from what is formulated in language. It is therefore crucial to pursue an analysis at the pre-predicative level of subjective experience and not only at its representations on the *predicative level of language*.

Husserl introduces the analytic distinction between noesis and noema. Noetic aspects concern the processes of consciousness; noematic aspects originate in the perceived thing. I can, for instance, vary my mode of attention and perceive a thing as clear-cut or as blurry. But there are also properties of the noema: I cannot see an elephant if there is only a mouse. In a concrete act of perception, noesis and noema are always intertwined. But on the basis of this analytical distinction, a phenomenological analysis can go different ways: It can focus exclusively on the noetic aspects which are constitutive of whatever the concrete correlate of experience may be. Or it can describe the 'material essence' of a concrete phenomenon. Husserl proposed to go both ways: First, formal ontology "deals with 'anything in general' and studies the forms of any possible entity meant in the most extended logical sense." Second, regional ontologies or material ontologies are "grounded in the 'material essence' that defines a certain type of entity" (De Vecchi, 2016, p. 309).

The late Husserl (1936/1970) argues that the lifeworld is experienced as a universe of things, which are given in a concrete typology and are represented by the substantives of the language concerned. These are relevant for practice, but only the phenomenological reduction can reveal regional eidetics or regional ontologies. Husserl identifies basic eidetic distinctions such as those between living and inanimate things, between animals and plants or between animals and humans. And he claims that such distinctions are fundamental for the distinction of different scientific realms. A particularly important distinction is the one between nature and mind or culture (*Geist*): The methods of natural sciences cannot be adequately employed for matters of the cultural, moral and social sciences (*Geisteswissenschaften*). He agrees in this respect with Dilthey (1927/2002) and trusts in phenomenology to clarify the invariant eidetic necessities.

Husserl (1973) recognizes early on the necessity of an intersubjective extension of egological phenomenology. In his material analyses, social acts build 'personalities of a higher order,' intersubjective communities such as marriages, families, associations, the State or religious communities. They are characterized by sympathy as well as volition and the unity of a goal; they have a common environment and produce community achievements that refer to common tradition and culture. Like any monad, a social community has a specific genesis, too, namely the history of the we-community. Analogously, there is not only the intentionality of the subjective consciousness of the individual monad, but also the we-intentionality of a community (Schmid, 2005). Husserl and his students invest considerable efforts to explore such collectives.

Gerda Walther (1923) writes a thorough phenomenological analysis of the ontology of social communities, with an appendix on the phenomenology of social communities. Taking up the distinction between society (*Gesellschaft*) and community (*Gemeinschaft*), which was current at the time (cf. Tönnies, 1887/2002), she argues that shared knowledge or shared experiences are constitutive, but not sufficient to speak of a community. Actors working together, for instance, interact with each other and orient to the same environment, but if they lack an inner bond or a feeling of togetherness, they are not yet a community. A community presupposes a unification. An inner bond between individuals can exist because they share a relation to specific objects or because they directly bond to each other. Walther therefore distinguishes different types of communities (cf. Léon & Zahavi, 2016 for a careful account) and stages of development. In the course of time, communities produce a community law, ethical and legal norms that regulate the behavior of its members in regard to each other as well as to the community. Communities are called and enabled to higher things than single individuals; they are more than the sum of individual members or the relations between them. Hence they require a special intentionality, a particular cognitive focus (*Erkenntniseinstellung*) on the supraindividual social. Social communities are relatively autonomous, real, psychic-mental (*seelisch-geistig*) units of a higher order. They have no bodies but rest on the bodies of their individual members and their lives and are intertwined with them, but they lead a psychic-mental life of their own (Walther, 1923, p. 143–148). Communities, in other words, cannot be reduced to the actions and interactions of their members; they are more than that, and they have their own history, tradition and community norms.

In the same way, Husserl (1973) and particularly Edith Stein (1925) develop an eidetic analysis of the State which is also considered a personality of a higher order by means of law and power. The State imposes norms on its citizens, assigns them functions, prohibits certain behaviors and regulates their degree of freedom (see Walton, in this volume). And it has its own history, as do communities.

These material analyses can be considered as contributions to a *social ontology*. As Salice and Schmid (2016b) state, they center essentially around three general concepts: social and institutional facts, collective intentionality, and values. Humans are born into a community and are socialized in it; they learn to participate in a we-intentionality. Interestingly, these contributions are hardly discussed in phenomenological sociology, although they deal with its very subject matter. In philosophical phenomenology, however, they are, also enriched by Heidegger's thinking about the fundamentals of human sociality, still vividly debated, as is illustrated by the recent book of Salice and Schmid (2016a). The search for aprioris persists.

2   ALFRED SCHUTZ'S ALTERNATIVE APPROACH TO SOCIAL PHENOMENA

Methodological Individualism and Egological Analysis

It is due to Alfred Schutz's eminent influence on phenomenological sociology that these paths to a social ontology were disregarded. In his essay on *Husserl's Importance for the Social Sciences*, Schutz (1962, pp. 140–141) accuses Gerda Walther (1923) and Edith Stein (1925) of their "naive use of the eidetic method in analyzing the problems of the social relations, of community, and of the state" and contends that their "formulation of certain apodictic and purportedly aprioristic statements ... have contributed toward discrediting phenomenology among social scientists." Interestingly, he attributes this failure to "the first group of Husserl's close personal students" and not to Husserl himself, although Husserl had guided their work and made own contributions in this respect. Schutz also criticizes Max Scheler for using "the same unfortunate approach" (p. 141) in his early work, but he relies heavily on his later work. There Scheler declared that "our grounds for assuming the reality of other selves and the possibility and limits of our understanding them ... is virtually *the* problem for any theory of knowledge in the social sciences" (p. 141). And he proposes that "general theses of reality in the natural attitude and its anthropomorphic character" as well as the *structure* of the given and unquestioned lifeworld can be analyzed by phenomenological methods (p. 142). The *content* of the relative natural attitude differs from group to group, culturally as well as historically. "To describe its features is the task of the empirical social sciences" (p. 142). Hence, sociology must be founded upon a philosophical anthropology.

This became exactly Schutz's program: a constitutive phenomenology of the natural attitude, a formal analysis of the structures of the lifeworld. From the outset, he ties his investigations to Max Weber's definition of sociology as an interpretive theory of action. Understanding the subjective sense that the actor bestows upon his or her action and thereby explaining social action requires, in Schutz's view, a phenomenological clarification of the basic concepts. This sets the path and the way in which Schutz (1962, pp. 145–149) makes fruitful use of Husserl's insights:

1. As *meaningful action* is conduct motivated by a preconceived project, Husserl's analysis of the consciousness of inner time and of phantasy (projecting) are important.
2. As any projected action refers to the sedimentation of previous experiences and their generalizations, formalizations and anticipations, the *subjective stock of knowledge at hand* is the ground of all protentions and anticipations as well as of idealizations such as 'and so forth and so on' and 'I can do it again.' It contains manifold degrees of clarity and distinctness, infinite open horizons and relevance structures of different types. Retrospectively, polythetically constituted acts are grasped mono-

thetically by way of synthetic operations of our consciousness. Husserl had provided all these ideas in his "Ideas" (1928/2012), and Schutz considers them as crucial for the concrete problems of the social sciences.

3. All acting involves *choosing*, choosing among different actions but also choosing if a projected action shall be carried out or dropped. For this, Schutz refers above all to Husserl's analysis of open and problematic possibilities and of the various meanings of "I can."

4. To analyze a *face-to-face relationship*, Husserl's distinction between the 'here' and 'there' are important. Each 'here' of an individual is the zero point or the center around which zones within actual or potential reach are perceived. I and the Other have different perspectives on the environment, not only spatially but also socio-culturally and historically. A crucial problem is therefore how an interchange of these different standpoints and how a reciprocity of perspectives can be achieved (see pt. 6).

5. Husserl's analyses of the consciousness of *inner time* also reveal why I can partake in the Other's stream of consciousness in his or her vivid present, whereas I can grasp mine only retrospectively with a reflective attitude.

6. Husserl has clearly seen that the Other's stream of consciousness is not directly accessible, only by means of *appresentation*. His earlier analyses on signs and symbols as well as his later theory of appresentation prove very helpful to clarify the process of understanding the Other, but also to analyze the constitution of symbolic systems such as language, myth, religion, art and so on. Schutz's analysis of multiple realities is closely linked to this.

7. The different dimensions of the social world such as proximity vs. distance in space and time or of intimacy vs. anonymity have a specific *experiential style*. Schutz refers to Husserl's analyses of prepredicative experiences and types. *All experiences are prepredicative* and their style is different when relating to contemporaries, predecessors or successors. Actions of our fellow-men are constructed in terms of course-of-action types and of personal types, or as social roles. All *typifications* are integral elements of the concrete historical and socio-cultural lifeworld, taken for granted and socially approved, and their structure point to the distribution of knowledge and its relevance to a concrete social situation.

In this summary and in detail in his book (Schutz, 1932/1967), it becomes clear how Schutz was guided by basic problems of *sociology* which he tried to solve by phenomenological analysis. And the chosen sociological approach of Max Weber was intimately tied to methodological individualism. This has primarily biographical reasons: Max Weber had left a lasting impression in Vienna after he had spent one semester there as a university professor in 1918. Moreover, Austrian Economics, which was the second strong influence on Schutz, also advocated a methodological individualism, in contrast to Weber not only by methodological but also by ideological reasons. Free individuals, free actions, free choice were the core of liberalism, which believes in a free market economy as sole steering mechanism and strongly opposes all forms of collectivism (like socialism) and state interventions (Mises, 1949/1998; see also Hayek, 1944). Beyond biographical reasons there was also a certain elective affinity between Weber's subjective sense of action and Husserl's analysis of egological experiences in subjective consciousness.

It was this background which made Schutz oppose to Husserl's intersubjective expansion of the egological analysis and his concept of 'personalities of a higher order' such as communities (Walther, 1923) and the State (Stein, 1925) (Schutz, 1962, p. 149). Instead, "all phenomena of the socio-cultural world originate in social interaction and can be referred to it" (p. 145). This implies two things: First, Schutz considers eidetic analyses of social entities such as communities or the State as an aberration in phenomenology; and second, as he formulates in his postulate of subjective interpretation (p. 43), Schutz contends that sociological analyses of such entities must always be analyzed on the level of actors and their (social) actions. It is noteworthy here that this is not the only way to go. As Niklas Luhmann (2013) skillfully demonstrates, phenomenology can also be fruitfully integrated with systems theory which deals with operative processes of systems, not with the action of actors. Due to a process of increasing social differentiation, modern society consists of ever more functional communication systems such as the economy, law, science, education, mass media, art, religion and so on—which is obviously quite a different approach to conceive of social phenomena.

The Intersubjective Pole of the Lifeworld

In his egological analyses, Schutz (1932/1967) radicalizes Weber's subjective sense of action and discerns three different meanings: S1, the sense in self-explication by the actor himself or herself (subjective meaning); S2, the sense attributed by another actor (objective meaning); and S3, the sense attributed by a scientific observer. He infers that Ego's understanding of the Other's action is only possible by means of indications and signs and is at best an approximation because they have different perspectives on an action and because their subjective stocks of knowledge differ. Mutual understanding and reciprocity of perspectives, hence, is always based on two idealizations, the interchangeability of standpoints and the congruence of relevances. How can two or more persons ever arrive at a 'we'? Schutz carefully analyzes the 'we-relationship' in a face-to-face situation and the constitution of a 'unity' of two persons by direct perception of each other and attention to each other, a co-existence of streams of consciousness and an interlocking of experiences on a pre-reflective level. Léon and Zahavi (2016) criticize this analysis as insufficient as it would also apply to a relationship where people argue with each other and even insult each other, which hardly constitutes a 'we-experience' or a sense of unity. Hence, they turn to Walther's (1923) analysis of we-experiences in communities.

Methodological individualism as well as egological analysis are confronted with the same problem: how are shared experiences, how are we-experiences, how are we-intentionalities possible? Schutz recognizes that he must also go beyond the egological analysis and adds a sociological perspective. In his *Personality manuscript* (Schutz, 1936/2013), he makes a pragmatic turn which complements the subjective pole of the lifeworld with a pragmatic, intersubjective pole (Srubar, 1988). The sense of actions is constituted not only in subjective consciousness but also in social interaction and communication. And above all, each individual is born and gradually socialized into a pre-existing society and culture with its extensive social stock of knowledge and its wealth of typifications and relevance systems. Sociality founds subjectivity: the individual, subjective stock of knowledge is socially derived. Schutz considers common-sense knowledge of everyday life as socialized in three respects: First, structurally socialized, since it is based on the idealization of the reciprocity of perspectives, which means that I would experience a situation in substantially the same way as the Other does if we changed places. Second, genetically socialized, as the greater part of our knowledge is socially derived in socially approved terms. Third, socialized in the sense of social distribution of knowledge, "each individual knowing merely a sector of the world and common knowledge of the same sector varying individually as to its degree of distinctness, clarity, acquaintanceship, or mere belief" (Schutz, 1962, p. 61).

That members of a society get socialized, that they constitute society by their actions and interactions, and that the society's knowledge is socially distributed are clearly sociological propositions. This is why Schutz's lifeworld analysis is often called a social phenomenology or a phenomenological sociology. The adoption of a sociological perspective enables Schutz to formulate the conditions under which a successful mutual understanding of interactants is likely: the more two or more persons' individual stocks of knowledge coincide in their typifications and relevance systems, and the more similar their experiences were in the past and are in the present, the easier it will be for them to understand each other.

Schutz's analysis of the natural attitude of everyday life is consistently formal; the structures of the lifeworld (Schutz & Luckmann, 1973/1989) are independent of concrete contents. In this respect, he stays in line with Scheler's proposition to devise a philosophical anthropology on which the social sciences are based, while the concrete socio-cultural and historical contents are investigated by the empirical sciences. Most of Schutz's results are very plausible and seem to work whatever the concrete correlates of experience may be—for instance, that every society or tribe has a social stock of knowledge structured by typifications and relevance systems; that knowledge is socially distributed; that newly born members are socialized into this society and culture; that each individual acquires a subjective stock of knowledge at hand that is socially derived but also a biographically determined and therefore in certain aspects specific; that subjective experiences are pre-predicative; that perception is combined with appresentations; that we use idealizations to bridge transcendencies, and so on. Are these formal structures also universal and invariant? This is difficult to assess as phenomenological analyses are inevitably bound to a concrete language which may be difficult to translate into another one. If we consider the enormous difficulties to translate German phenomenological texts into English, how much more difficult it must be to translate them into Japanese, Chinese or Hindi?

Besides his formal analyses, Schutz (1964) also conducts some material ones such as "The Stranger," "The Homecomer," "The Well-informed Citizen" or his reflection on equality and responsibility. In the first three essays, he sticks to his postulate of subjective interpretation and builds a personal type with an individual mind who makes certain experiences. Already in the "Stranger," he introduces the sociological concepts 'in-group' and 'out-group,' concepts which designate *collectives*. He hesitates at first as this concept itself depends on the question how the social categories of strangeness and familiarity are constituted. But then he decides: "As a convenient starting-point we shall investigate how the *cultural pattern of group life* presents itself to the common sense of a man who lives his everyday life within the group among his fellow-men" (Schutz, 1964, p. 92, my emphasis). The difference to established sociological studies is that Schutz does not consider a cultural pattern of group life from the objective perspective of a scientific observer, but rather asks how it is subjectively experienced by an individual actor (cf. Eberle, 2021). And he talks of 'groups,' not of abstract collectivities such as 'society' or 'culture.' Immigrants are always interacting with concrete individuals of a concrete group. Schutz keeps operating with this concept of in- and out-group.

3   Toward a Phenomenology of Organizations

The term 'organization' has different meanings in everyday life. On the one hand, it can designate the activities and practices of organizing, for example, organizing a birthday party or a festival. It then encompasses all the planning and preparatory activities in advance as well as the coordinated course of the event when it happens. We then speak of a 'well organized' or 'poorly organized' event. After the cleanup, the organization ends. Such an organization can be managed by one person or a group of persons. On the other hand, the term 'organization' can designate an institution that endures. Classically, an organization resides in a (number of) buildings and is a legal personality, that means, it has legal rights and obligations as an institution. In face of the ever-increasing variety of empirical forms of organization, it is difficult to define definite features, but maybe we can agree on the following typical properties: First, every organization distinguishes between members and non-members, between insiders and outsiders (which reminds us of the in-group/out-group distinction and the subjective vs. objective perspective). Second, every organization has a division of labor in which each member performs a specific function. This implies that every organization has a certain distribution of knowledge. And usually there is also some kind of hierarchy between different functions and positions to exercise control. Third, every organization consists of coordinated work activities. These often involve some kind of cooperation and the use of machines such as computers, tools or robots. All of these constitutive features are also perceived by members in work life and are part of common-sense knowledge.

In the following, I will use the term 'organization' in this latter meaning, organization as an institution. It can be considered in two perspectives, in a static and a dynamic one. In a static perspective, we construct a picture at a certain moment in time and see how the organization is structured, for instance, different workplaces in spatial arrangements or characteristic properties. In a dynamic perspective, we look at the processes that are going on in that organization, and this is the very essence of an organization: all the enacted and coordinated work activities and interactions, including the organizational work. Based on the two poles of Schutz's lifeworld analysis, let us first consider an organization from the subjective view of a person's experience and then, second, from an intersubjective, interactional view.

The Subjective Experience of Organizations

Modern society is a society of organizations and institutions—"none of them of my own making" (Schutz, 1962, p. 145). In the natural attitude, they are part of the pre-given social world and taken unquestionably for granted. How is a concrete organization experienced by a subjective actor? An organization can be experienced from the inside or from the outside. An outsider's knowledge of an organization depends on his or her interest, on his or her relevance system. Many customers are only interested in the product, but not in the way it was produced. The features and quality of the product is all that matters. If they have direct contact with an organization, they may perceive the Other just in a specific social role. As Schutz (1962, pp. 25–26) describes: I bring a letter to the post office and expect that the person at the counter behaves as a typical post office employee while I behave as a typical customer. And I expect that post office employees will perform typical actions and finally deliver my letter to the addressee within a reasonable amount of time.

In everyday life this depends, according to Schutz, on the actor's pragmatic interests at hand. However, some people may also develop an interest in an organization for educational purposes as Schutz's ideal type of the 'well-informed citizen.' They read newspaper and journal reports about an organization or watch documentary films and videos on TV or on the Internet. Or they participate, in order to acquire first-hand knowledge, in an official tour of the company when it opens up to the public. Schutz's analysis of typifications and relevance systems proves very helpful here—the less someone is interested in a concrete organization, the more abstract, anonymous and diffuse the knowledge of it remains, and the greater the interest, the more concrete, intimate and specific it becomes. However, the latter is relative as an outsider normally does not have personal access to the organization.

For insiders this is different. Members of the organization do have direct access, at least to their workplace. And members participate in routine activities at the workplace and usually display the required skills to perform the work tasks. Members' lived experience consists in the polythetic acts of subjective consciousness in which they perceive and make sense of the immediate environment of the workplace, of the room, the equipment, the tools, of other persons in the room and the interactions with them. All the members have been socialized into their specific work, have been instructed of the tasks to do and how to perform them. The lived work experiences have sedimented and were interpreted with certain typifications and frames in a reflective attitude. The more the work became routine, the more segments turned into an unquestioned matter of everyday life, and special attention is given above all to those matters that become problematic. In other words, members experience their organization from the perspective of their specific position in it. They gather concrete, intimate and specific knowledge of their own workplace and embody their own work routines. All other areas of organization that members do not have personal experiences with, remain transcendent and must be appresented somehow.

At their workplace, members experience 'the organization' by all the relevances that are imposed on them. These are communicated by, among others, job descriptions and compliance rules, by work flow diagrams and organizational charts which point out their position within the hierarchy, the chain of command and the chain of reporting in the organization as a whole. They have to fulfill the prescribed tasks and must cooperate with others. And they are expected to perform well. Members' work and performances are supervised by a direct superior who represents 'the organization.' How much a member has personal experiences of other areas of the organization depends on its size and on the kind of work. Workers at the conveyor belt may be only interested in the area of their own responsibility and just do their job, while personnel managers have contact to all the areas of the organization. Beyond the requirements of their job, the extent and kind of knowledge also depends on the individual relevance systems—are they intrinsically interested in learning more about other areas? In any case, it is much easier to have a comparatively good grasp of what is going on in a small company with only a few members than in a large corporation such as a car or pharma industry. In large organizations, most areas remain abstract, anonymous and diffuse for most of their members. They are insiders to their own concrete work environment, but outsiders to other areas of the organization.

How are other areas appresented if not directly experienced? By means of communication, above all of narrations (cf. Czarniawska, 1998). On the one hand, members receive regular messages from the top, by the CEO or their department manager as well as from the public relations department. Large organizations spend much energy and money to keep their members informed about the 'big picture' and to transmit a favorable image to the public. They produce glossy brochures and attractive websites, press releases, videos and films, ads in journals and newspapers as well as on TV and on the Internet, in which they present not only the quality of their products and services but also the organization's history, its achievements and successes, present and upcoming challenges and future goals. They communicate an official version of their 'common' vision, their mission statement and their values. And they provide training for their members with the intention that these recognize the implications of the official policy, identify with them and learn to adjust their behavior at their workplace accordingly.

On the other hand, there is a lot of informal communication going on in any organization, interpersonal as well as by social media, narrations of all kinds, comparatively truthful descriptions of happenings, but also rumors, gossip and so on. To capture all these multiple referrals, Schutz (1962, p. 299) extended Husserl's theory of appresentation. Apperceptions are not only complemented by appresentations that make them meaningful; there are also references to other realities that are appresented by symbols such as, for instance, the company's logo and brand, its visions, mission statements and 'big' values. Much of what is known about the 'whole' organization is conveyed by symbolic communication. Besides the apperception, appresentation and reference schemes, there is also a contextual or interpretational scheme that also addresses the personal relationship of a user to the appresented. For example, do the communicated goals and values make a member proud of his or her organization or does s/he distrust the management and rather see it as a hypocritical, capitalist agent who primarily maximizes the profit?

It is crucial to see all these kinds of appresentations in a time perspective. The appresentations of other areas or of the 'whole' of the organization are not permanently enacted, but only occasionally and situationally. They are initiated either by imposed relevances, for instance, when stories are heard, seen or read, official or private ones, or by intrinsic motivation, for example, when a narration comes to a member's mind and/or when s/he retells a story to others. Most of the time in everyday work life, other areas of the organization or the organization as a whole only become relevant when related to a member's own situated work.

It is important to add that the examples in my reflections here relate mainly to a large industrial corporation. In modern society, however, there is a great variety of different types of organizations which must be discerned. With recent communication technology, new types of labor and cooperation in virtual networks have emerged, which in some aspects may be quite different from industrial companies. How members experience their organization must therefore be investigated empirically. A number of phenomenology-based ethnographical approaches have developed, which I will discuss later on.

Intersubjective Constitution of Organizations

After the reflections on the subjective pole, let us turn now to the pragmatic, intersubjective pole of the lifeworld. An organization is not only experienced subjectively by individual actors; it is at the same time enacted by concerted actions and interactions of its members. How this is done is meanwhile well researched empirically by ethnomethodological studies.

Harold Garfinkel (1967) embarks on the intersubjective pole of Schutz's phenomenological lifeworld analysis and turned it into a radically new, sociological program. He adopts Parsons's quest for solving the problem of social order, but attempted to find new ways of explaining it. Inspired by Husserl, Gurwitch and above all Schutz, he gradually develops what he later called 'ethnomethodology.' In his first text from 1948, which was published posthumously, Garfinkel (2006, pp. 109ff.) refers to Schutz's (1962, pp. 207–259) text on manifold realities and the six features of a 'cognitive style,' and he tries to find the empirical specifications of each feature and eventually to reveal even more such features. He illustrates this with the example of a library guard at the university. He defines a 'library' as a "system of coordinated actions" and a 'library guard' a class of social persons who are responsible for preventing theft (Garfinkel, 2006, p. 110) and then asks which cognitive attitude is characteristic of them. In his dissertation, Garfinkel (1952, pp. 90–150) compares the constitutive premises of Parsons's approach with those of Schutz's lifeworld analysis and treats them as two alternative paradigms for explaining social order: the "correspondence theory" and the "congruence theory," both of which he characterizes and compares along six criteria. Although a doctoral student of Parsons, Garfinkel favored the congruence theory of Schutz to explain social order and attempted to demonstrate empirical evidence of that by his first incongruity experiment. In the following years, he experimented with many different subjects and various empirical methods in order to work out the ethnomethodological program (cf. Eberle, 2012).

Garfinkel (1967) shared Schutz's skepticism toward abstract, general concepts in sociology and pejoratively referred to conventional sociology as a 'folk science.' The established concepts of social science make actors 'judgmental dopes.' Instead, ethnomethodology makes actors' common-sense reasoning the very subject of its research. How do actors make sense? How do actors make their actions observable, tellable, reportable, accountable? It is obviously by their 'communicative efforts' that actors make actions recognizable, interpretable and intelligible. And the task of ethnomethodology is to analyze the methods, or the practices, with which such a concerted sense-making in its temporal sequence is achieved. The epistemological status of such ethnomethods—later Garfinkel prefers the notion 'members' methods'—have never been clarified. Garfinkel seems to strive for some kind of formal methods that are similar to Husserl's or Schutz's formal properties or formal structures. He sticks to the phenomenological question of How (instead of What and Why), analyzes concrete phenomena and asks how they are constituted. This way he fulfills the original dictum of phenomenology, "to the things themselves." At the same time, however, he disposes of the subjective consciousness and the egological perspective and replaces them by empirical observation. He also eliminates all the anthropological premises in Schutz's work: Actors in the ethnomethodological perspective are no concrete individuals with flesh and blood, who act on the basis of their intentions, who play different roles in different settings and who have a self or a personal identity, a biography or plans for their future. Actors are rather meaningful constructions that are produced in a given sequence of interaction. It is actions that produce actors, not the other way round. In an ethnomethodological perspective, social settings are, thence, 'self-organizing.' Despite these significant differences, ethnomethodology can still be categorized, for good reasons, as a phenomenological sociology (Psathas, 1989; Belvedere, 2020, 2022).

An organization, such as a university library, defined as a "system of coordinated actions" is not empirically observable as a whole. In ethnomethodological research, an organization is therefore reduced to a concrete, self-organizing social setting where the details of interactions can be carefully investigated. Bittner (1965) argues, for example, that organizational theories such as Weber's ideal type of bureaucracy are inadequate descriptions of organizational reality as they operate with much common-sense reasoning that remains unexplicated. Instead, one should examine the methodological use of concepts of organization by competent users in everyday life. Striking in the same notch, Silverman and Jones (1976) propose not to study 'organizations,' but rather how 'organizational work' is carried out in organizations. Many such studies of organizational settings have been conducted, a number of rich ethnographies with quite illuminating methodical and theoretical reflections; however, the identification of 'ethnomethods' remained rather poor. Many ethnomethodologists, hence, turned to conversation analysis, which was much more successful in describing concrete conversational practices. How did conversation analysis deal with organization or, in its own terminology, with institutional settings?

Conversation analysis was founded by Harvey Sacks (1963, 1992) in close cooperation with Garfinkel. It studies the sequential organization of ordinary conversation. As in ethnomethodology, only 'naturally occurring situations' are analyzed, and each analysis must be data-guided, not theory-guided. The use of audio-visual recordings enables the researchers to watch a sequence again and again in order to attend to every detail. An interaction is always context-dependent but also context-renewing, as each statement depends on what has been said before and forms the context for what follows. Hence, the formal principles that conversation analysis strives for must have the double feature of context-dependency as well as context-sensitivity. On the one hand, they must be valid for many situations; on the other hand, they must be applicable to the specific context of a concrete situation. What counts as context is handled restrictively, it consists only in what was said before and in what was made accountable in that conversation (Schegloff 1991, 1992, 1997). This means, for instance, that a researcher may not designate a conversation as a 'doctor-patient-interaction'; instead, it must be observable from within the interaction that one person is a doctor and the other a patient.

This methodological rigorism was abandoned by many who studied 'institutional interactions.' This term refers to interactions that are work- or task-related and in which at least one participant represents a formal organization (such as a doctor in a hospital). Drew and Heritage propose a cumulative research program that first performs the normal conversation analytic tasks. Then, second, it moves on to study how actors' behaviors and their social organization manifest orientations that are specifically institutional or react to institutional constraints. To detect them they suggest conducting a comparative analysis between institutional and ordinary conversations. Heritage (2005) finds differences in the turn design, certain asymmetries, and also typical phases and patterns of interaction in special contexts such as medicine, education, the law and mass media.

Another type of research are the workplace studies (Knoblauch et al., 2000), which explore work processes in complex technical environments, for example, the activities of air traffic controllers in a control tower, of supervisors in the control room of a subway line, of officials in an emergency call center, of architects at the computer, of traders on the stock exchange (Heath & Luff, 2000), or of the dynamics of auction (Heath, 2013). All of these authors were ethnomethodologists or/and conversation analysists by training, but many of them added complemented the audio-visually recorded data by ethnographic data of the specific context. As the relationship between ethnomethodology and conversation analysis on the one hand and ethnography on the other has always been characterized by tensions, this evoked some noteworthy methodological discussions (e.g., Duranti & Goodwin, 1992; Maynard, 2006; Button et al., 2015; Meyer & Meier zu Verl, 2022).

In sum, ethnomethodology and conversation analysis have greatly enriched qualitative methods and qualitative research, especially with its research attitude that no proposition is accepted if it cannot be substantiated in the data at hand. And the rigorous stance that all relevant context is to be produced within the setting prohibited an observer or analyst to introduce contextual knowledge from the outside—either it is observably made relevant within the setting or it is of no importance for the analysis either. This methodical principle helped, as in hermeneutics, to discern very carefully which knowledge was in use in the observed setting and what could not be seen properly in the data. However, this also implied that all studies remained micro- or even nano-sociological. Therefore, institutional researchers began to compare different settings, and workplace researchers added ethnographic data regarding the organizational context.

4   Conclusion

Husserl provided a wealth of phenomenological insights from an egological perspective in the transcendental sphere. In his material analyses, he also went beyond and explored 'personalities of a higher order.' His students Walther and Stein followed this track and produced fine analyses, eidetic descriptions, of communities and the State. As humans are born into a community and are socialized in it, they learn to participate in a we-intentionality. Salice and

Schmid (2016a) demonstrate that such phenomenological reflections on a social ontology are persisting and center around the key concepts of social and institutional facts, of collective intentionality, and values. It is puzzling that these studies are hardly taken note of in phenomenological sociology, and I do not agree with Schutz to resolutely thrust them aside. We have the same problem here as in sociology between individualist and collectivist approaches, two perspectives that complement each other. Especially in regard to organizations, Walther's point is worth considering that they are more than the sum of individual members and the relations between them—a view that is very common among organizational theorists. Walther also emphasizes the importance of emotions such as the feeling of togetherness. Emotions play a vital role in organizations (cf. Fineman, 2000), for instance, in relationships (including conflicts), for motivation, for members' identification with their organization, and so on. As Schutz considers emotions as "ineffable" (1964, p. 100), he disregards them in his social phenomenology, which is, in my view, a serious problem (Eberle, 2021). However, there are also two caveats regarding Walther's and Stein's approach. First, if it is phenomenology's goal to strive for universal and invariant aprioris, it will prove difficult to deal with phenomena such as a community or a State—both are historically and culturally variable. Second, as modern society has been increasingly characterized by individualization and pluralism, the degree of common values and of a collective we-intentionality is probably in decline—regardless of the symbolic declarations. For these reasons, I left this track and went on with Schutz's lifeworld analysis.

My reflections on how an organization is subjectively experienced distinguished between the perspectives of outsiders and insiders. Insiders experience 'the organization' by all the relevances that are imposed on them, the social role to be performed, the tasks as defined in the job description and the instructions given by the superior (who locally represents 'the organization'). Other organizational areas or the 'organization as a whole' are symbolically appresented in many forms and by means of diverse media. There is official information from the top or the public relations department, and there is informal communication such as rumors and gossip. Much of it is imposed at a given moment, some of it is intrinsic (stories that an actor retells). Such appresentations are not permanently enacted, but only occasionally and situationally. I made some basic reflections and operated with illustrative examples, but of course, empirical studies will bring more tangible results.

At the pragmatic, intersubjective pole of his lifeworld analysis, Schutz also exceeds the mundane egological perspective. He argues that humans are born into a pre-existing society and socialized in it, and that their subjective stock of knowledge is, thence, socially derived. Sociality founds subjectivity. In addition, knowledge is socially distributed in society, each individual is socialized into a specific socio-cultural milieu. These are explicitly sociological propositions. Srubar (1988, 2005) demonstrates that Schutz also delivered a comprehensive pragmatic lifeworld theory that can be considered as a social anthropology. This, however, does not contribute much to the question of how an organization is intersubjectively constituted. Hence, I turned to ethno-methodology and conversation analysis which embarked on the pragmatic, intersubjective pole of Schutz's lifeworld. They produced many empirical studies of organizational, or institutional, settings. Their history of the last three decades shows that they remain not only a micro- but a nano-sociology if they do not extend their analyses to data of a wider context, too.

In fact, it was Schutz who placed this emphasis on the micro level. In the common-sense attitude, members take the existence of organizations and institutions as natural facts of everyday life. How they typify them depends on their accumulated (intimate or superficial) knowledge about them and upon their subjective relevance system at hand. But treating them as entities, rather than social constructions, means reifying them. "Social collectivities and institution-alized relations" can be apprehended "only symbolically"; "they are constructs of common-sense thinking which have their reality in another subuniverse" such as "the subuniverse of ideal relations" (Schutz, 1962, p. 353). They must be analyzed as constituted by individual actors' actions in their concrete life-world. In this perspective, 'organizations' and 'institutions' are interpretive schemes or, in Goffman's terminology, 'frames' that members use to situate their work in a wider context. Does this necessarily imply a micro-sociological perspective?

In my view, there are two basic ways to explore the meso level of organiza-tions or even societal macro-phenomena from a phenomenological perspec-tive. The first one is to conduct phenomenological ethnographies, or in vom Lehn and Hitzler's (2015) term, 'phenomenology-based' ethnographies, which thoroughly investigate members' experiences. A number of such approaches has emerged, such as lifeworld analytic ethnography, phenomeno-logical hermeneutics and ethnophenomenology (cf. Eberle, 2014), plus go-along ethnography and focused ethnography (cf. vom Lehn, 2019). As all of them share their common origin in Schutz's social phenomenology, they com-plement each other perfectly. And they clearly differ from other ethnographic methods. By "revealing participants' subjective experiences, their aim is to arrive at an understanding of the social structure of knowledge underlying those subjective experiences" (vom Lehn, 2019, p. 198). In organizational set-tings, it is not only the collaborative work that is of interest, but also how members relate to their organization, what images they have of it, how they identify with it, if they are proud or disappointed of it, and so on. And as mem-bers are not only seen in their local interactional role, but as human beings who also have a life beyond their work and outside their organization, we may also detect a number of references to the outside world that are relevant to them. When a trade union calls for a workers' strike and common protest, for instance, a mother or father of a family may be afraid to lose the job and resist to join. Phenomenology-based ethnographies, hence, can reveal how members person-ally relate to phenomena on the meso and macro level, although their work activities are situated in a local interactional context. In an organizational context, several members in similar positions and several in other positions can be compared and commonalities and differences among them identified.

Another road to go is to elaborate the theoretical approach and to introduce sociological concepts on the meso- and macro level. Berger and Luckmann (1966) go this way. They show how it is possible to talk about institutions without reifying them. Rather, they view them as social processes, as 'institutionalization' (and legitimation and socialization). This process proceeds from habitualization, typification, objectivation to sedimentation and culminates in social roles as reciprocal typification "in the context of an objectified stock of knowledge common to a collectivity of actors" (pp. 73–74). Institutionalization ensures a certain degree of intersubjectivity. It is noteworthy here that institutions—and analogously: organizations—are considered as social constructions, but they are not fictions, they are real for the actors involved. Organizations do exist; industrial corporations produce tangible products after all, such as cars, computers or pharmaceutical drugs. However, due to the social distribution of knowledge in an organization, actors' perspectives differ. It is difficult even for top managers who try to control all the company processes, to see the whole of their complex organization and keep track of it all—each has a specific perspective. And the same applies to organizational theories, too, even when attempting to view an organization as a whole. Morgan (1997) therefore suggests treating organizational theories as images and metaphors: Each sheds light on some aspects of an organization, but each has also its blind spots.

In their comprehensive and detailed overview on "phenomenology and organization theory," Holt and Sandberg (2011) argue that Berger and Luckmann's "social constructionist interpretive perspective" has affected organization theory and organizational studies in many ways: First, investigating people's lived experience; second, the study of social action within collectives (teams, departments, the whole organization); third, to study how human reality is constructed through interaction, on the micro level (ethnomethodology) or at the macro level (institutional theory) (pp. 229–230). "In contrast to Garfinkel's microfocus, the institutionalist approaches focus on how the macrocontext in the sense of specific socially constructed institutions, such as 'gender', 'leadership', 'professions', 'marriage', and 'money', shapes the social interaction at the microlevel" (p. 228). Institutional theory developed based on Berger and Luckmann (1966) (Meyer & Rowan, 1977; Zucker, 1977) and became very influential in organizational theory. Holt and Sandberg also integrate "the second road to phenomenology" (Aspers, 2010), namely Heidegger (1927/1962, 1949) who is referenced in the recent practice-based studies within strategy and knowledge in organizations. In regard to phenomenology's potential, the two authors suggest "reorienting research in organization studies away from an entitative epistemology in which things are seen in increasingly causally linked, detailed isolation, and toward a relational epistemology in which what exists is understood in terms of its being experienced within everyday lives" (Holt & Sandberg, 2011: 215–216).

What is experienced as imposed relevances at the workplace comes to a great deal from higher up in the hierarchy. The top management determines certain strategies and policies which are communicated down in form of rules and instructions to lower levels of the hierarchy. Such imposed relevances invite to empirically analyze the power structure of organizations (cf. Dreher & López, 2015). And it is certainly eye opening to reflect as well how much the local, situated interactions and collaborations are shaped by institutions from the macro level, as mentioned above. Furthermore, the imposed relevances also mirror constraints that result from the social and economic state of a society and factors such as culture, demographics, climate, and so on. The working conditions in many African and Asian countries are often very different from those in Europe or the U.S. In other words, subjective experiences of local working situations are also shaped by events and constraints on the meso and macro level.

Micro, meso and macro level is an analytic distinction that is perpetuated by established sociological approaches and corresponding research questions. In social reality, these levels are inseparably intertwined. It is therefore wise to search for ways to better link what was analytically separated (Gros, 2022). Inspired by the social constructionism of Berger and Luckmann, Knoblauch (1995) proposes to view the contexts of direct, immediate communication, the contexts of indirect, mediate communication and societal contexts in their interconnection. In his recent "Communicative construction of reality" (Knoblauch, 2020), he develops, based on his vast experience in empirical, qualitative-interpretative research, an updated interpretation of Berger and Luckmann's approach that takes into account some crucial developments of social theory during the recent decades as well as the on-going fundamental transformation of society by processes of digitization and mediatization. It is worth examining this approach to see what it contributes to resolving the issues raised here. Promising is also Gros's (2020) project to link phenomenology with critical theory: when people suffer, how is this linked to social processes and constraints of the larger societal context? On the level of organizations, a similar link can be attempted, for example, between phenomenology and critical management studies: how is the suffering from certain work conditions linked to specific management practices? In any case, the analysis of subjective experiences and social interaction in everyday life situations form the core of a phenomenological approach, but to interpret them in a wider context, too, can be illuminating.

References

Aspers, P. (2010). The second road to phenomenological sociology. *Sociology*, *47*, 214–219.

Belvedere, C. (2020). Ethnomethodology as an experimentation with the natural attitude. George Psathas on phenomenological sociology. *Human Studies*, *43*(3), 327–342.

Belvedere, C. (2022). *A treatise in phenomenological sociology.* Lexington.

Berger, P., & Luckmann, T. (1966). *The social construction of reality: A treatise in the sociology of knowledge.* Anchor, Doubleday.

Bittner, E. (1965). The concept of organization. *Social Research, 32*(3), 239–255.

Button, G., Crabtree, A., Rouncefield, M., & Tolmie, P. (2015). *Deconstructing ethnography.* Springer.

Czarniawska, B. (1998). *A narrative approach to organization studies.* Sage.

De Vecchi, F. (2016). A priori of the law and values in the social ontology of Wilhelm Schapp and Adolf Reinach. In A. Salice & H. B. Schmid (Eds.), *The phenomenological approach to social reality* (pp. 279–316). Springer.

Dilthey, W. (1927/2002). *The formation of the historical world in the human sciences* (R. Makkreel & F. Rodi, Eds.). Princeton University Press.

Dreher, J., & López, D. G. (2015). Subjectivity and power. *Human Studies, 38,* 197–222.

Duranti, A., & Goodwin, C. (Eds.). (1992). *Rethinking context: Language as an interactive phenomenon.* Cambridge University Press.

Eberle, T. S. (2012). Phenomenological life-world analysis and ethnomethodology's program. *Human Studies: Special Issue in Memory of Harold Garfinkel, 35*(2), 279–304.

Eberle, T. S. (2014). Phenomenology as a research method. In U. Flick (Ed.), *The Sage handbook of qualitative data analysis* (pp. 184–202). Sage.

Eberle, T. S. (2021). A study in xenological phenomenology: Alfred Schutz's Stranger Revisited. *Schutzian Research, 13,* 27–50.

Fineman, S. (2000). Emotion in Organizations. London: Sage.

Garfinkel, H. (2006). *Seeing sociologically. The routine grounds of social action.* Rowman & Littlefield.

Garfinkel, H. (1952). *The perception of the other. A study in social order.* Unpublished dissertation, Harvard University.

Garfinkel, H. (1967). *Studies in ethnomethodology.* Prentice-Hall.

Gros, A. (2020). The reification of the other as a social pathology: Traces of a phenomenoloogical critical theory in Alfred Schutz. *Schutzian Research, 12,* 13–44.

Gros, A. (2022). A phenomenology of modernity? Alfred Schutz's contributions to a theory of modern society. In M. Barber (Ed.), *The anthem companion to Alfred Schutz* (pp. 115–136). Anthem Press.

Hayek, F. A. (1944). *Roads to serfdom.* Routledge.

Heath, C. (2013). *The dynamics of auction.* Cambridge University Press.

Heath, C., & Luff, P. (2000). *Technology in action.* Cambridge University Press.

Heidegger, M. (1927/1962). *Being and time* (J. Macquarrie & E. Robinson, Trans.). SCM Press.

Heidegger, M. (1949). *Existence and being.* Regnery Co.

Heritage, J. (2005). Conversation analysis and institutional talk. In K. L. Fitch & R. E. Sanders (Eds.), *Handbook of language and social interaction* (pp. 103–147). Routledge.

Holt, R., & Sandberg, J. (2011). Phenomenology and organization theory. In H. Tsoukas & R. Chia (Eds.), *Philosophy and organization theory* (Research in the sociology of organizations 32) (pp. 215–249). Emerald.

Husserl, E. (1928/2012). *Ideas: General introduction to pure phenomenology.* Routledge.

Husserl, E. (1936/1970). *The crisis of European sciences and transcendental phenomenology: An introduction to phenomenological philosophy* (D. Carr, Trans.). Northwestern.

Husserl, E. (1973). *Zur Phänomenologie der Intersubjektivität. Texte aus dem Nachlass. Zweiter Teil: 1921–1929* (I. Kern, Ed.). *Husserliana 14.* Martinus Nijhoff.

Knoblauch, H. (1995). *Kommunikationskultur. Die kommunikative Konstruktion kultureller Kontexte.* de Gruyter.

Knoblauch, H., Heath, C., & Luff, P. (2000). Technology and social interaction: The emergence of 'workplace studies'. *British Journal of Sociology, 51*(2), 299–320.

Knoblauch, H. (2020). *The communicative construction of reality.* Routledge.

Léon, F., & Zahavi, D. (2016). Phenomenology of experiential sharing: The contribution of Schutz and Walther. In A. Salice & H. B. Schmid (Eds.), *The phenomenological approach to social reality* (pp. 219–234). Springer.

Luhmann, N. (2013). *Introduction to systems theory.* Polity.

Maynard, D. W. (2006). Ethnography and conversation analysis. In S. N. Hesse-Biber & P. Leavy (Eds.), *Emergent methods in social research* (pp. 55–94). Sage.

Meyer, C., & Meier zu Verl, C. (2022). Ethnomethodologische Fundierungen. In A. Poferl & N. Schröer (Eds.), *Handbuch Soziologische Ethnographie* (pp. 85–99). Springer VS.

Meyer, J. W., & Rowan, B. R. (1977). Institutionalized organizations. Formal structure as myths and ceremony. *American Journal of Sociology, 83*(2), 340–363.

Mises, L. (1949/1998). *Human action. The Scholarly Edition.* Ludwig von Mises Institute.

Morgan, G. (1997). *Images of organization* (2nd ed.). Sage.

Psathas, G. (1989). *Phenomenology and sociology. Theory and research.* The Center for Advanced Research in Phenomenology, University Press of America.

Sacks, H. (1963). Sociological description. *Berkeley Journal of Sociology, 8*, 1–17.

Sacks, H. (1992). *Lectures on conversations* (Vol. 1 & 2). Blackwell.

Salice, A., & Schmid, H. B. (Eds.). (2016a). *The phenomenological approach to social reality.* Springer.

Salice, A., & Schmid, H. B. (2016b). Social reality—The phenomenological approach. In A. Salice & B. Schmid (Eds.), *The phenomenological approach to social reality* (pp. 1–14). Springer.

Schegloff, E. A. (1991). Reflections on talk and social structure. In D. Boden & D. H. Zimmermann (Eds.), *Talk and social structure* (pp. 44–70). Polity.

Schegloff, E. A. (1992). On talk and its institutional occasions. In P. Drew & J. Heritage (Eds.), *Talk at work. Interaction in institutional settings* (pp. 101–134). Cambridge University Press.

Schegloff, E. A. (1997). Whose text? Whose context? *Discourse & Society, 8*, 165–187.

Schmid, H. B. (2005). *Wir-Intentionalität.* Freiburg/München.

Schutz, A. (1932/1967). *The phenomenology of the social world* (G. Walsh & F. Lehnert, Trans.). Northwestern.

Schutz, A. (1936/2013). The problem of personality in the social world. In M. Barber (Ed.), *Collected papers VI. Literary reality and relationships* (pp. 199–308). Springer Science+Business.

Schutz, A. (1962). *Collected papers 1: The problem of social reality* (M. Natanson, Ed.). Nijhoff.

Schutz, A. (1964). *Collected papers 2: Studies in social theories* (A. Brodersen, Ed.). Nijhoff.

Schutz, A., & Luckmann, T. (1973/1989). *The structures of the* Life-World. Vol. I (1973). Trans. R. Zaner & T. Engelhardt. Vol. II (1989). Trans. R. Zaner & D. J. Parent. Northwestern University Press.

Silverman, D., & Jones, J. (1976). *Organizational work. The language of grading / the grading of language*. Collier-Macmillan.

Srubar, I. (1988). *Kosmion. Die Genese der pragmatischen Lebenswelttheorie von Alfred Schütz und ihr anthropologischer Hintergrund.* .

Srubar, I. (2005). The pragmatic theory of the lifeworld as a basis for intercultural comparison. In M. Endress et al. (Eds.), *Explorations of the lifeworld* (pp. 235–266). Springer.

Stein, E. (1925). Untersuchung über den Staat. *Jahrbuch für Philosophie und phänomenologische Forschung, 7*, 1–125.

Tönnies, F. (1887/2002). *Community and society* (C. P. Loomis, Trans. and Ed.). Dover.

vom Lehn, D. (2019). Phenomenology-based ethnography for management studies and organizational analysis. *British Journal of Management, 30*, 188–202.

vom Lehn, D., & Hitzler, R. (Eds.). (2015). Phenomenology-based ethnography. *Journal of Contemporary Ethnography, 44*, 5.

Walther, G. (1923). Zur Ontologie der sozialen Gemeinschaften. *Jahrbuch für Philosophie und phänomenologische Forschung, 6*, 1–159.

Zahavi, D. (2016). The end of what? Phenomenology vs. speculative realism. *International Journal of Philosophical Studies, 24*(3), 289–309.

Zucker, L. G. (1977). The role of institutionalization in cultural persistence. *American Sociological Review, 42*, 726–743.

Institutions, Imposed Relevances, and Creativity

Michael D. Barber

1   INTRODUCTION: THE PROBLEM AND THE GENETIC CONSTITUTION OF INSTITUTIONS

In the invitation to contribute to this book, the editors posed the penetrating question about whether phenomenology, usually concentrating on micro-social phenomena, has anything to say about macro-social phenomena. Belvedere and Gros (2021) pose the objection:

> Phenomenological analysis, it is said, can help us understand everyday experiences, actions, and interactions, but when it comes to dealing with the workings of wide-reaching social processes, structures, and institutions, we would be better off resorting to approaches such as Marxism, systems theory, (post-) structuralism or Critical Theory.

These editors, though, were convinced that phenomenology can make original contributions to the analysis of macro-social phenomena (e.g., the state, history, class relations, religions, social movements and protests, democracy) and that it can account for the "inextricable link between these large-scale phenomena and (inter-)subjective experience, that is to say, of the manners in which they are lived, constituted, suffered, and changed in the lifeworld" (Belvedere & Gros, 2021).

This chapter will show the linkage between micro-phenomenology and macro-social phenomena through the general idea that Edmund Husserl and

M. D. Barber (✉)
Department of Philosophy, Saint Louis University, St. Louis, MO, USA
e-mail: michael.barber@slu.edu

Alfred Schutz both make use of, namely that one can start with higher-level meanings that appear as established and complete and think back to the lower-level meanings and experiences through which those higher-level meanings were built up or "founded." Husserl, for instance, demonstrates that even the researchers of nature presuppose as a fundament for their (subjective) work of thought the surrounding life world with its conscious activity (Husserl, 1970a; Husserl, 1970b); that the idealizations of geometrical science depend on pre-scientifically intuited nature, apparent in everyday induction (Husserl, 1970a); that one can trace genetically "*predicative evidences back to the non-predicative evidence* called *experience*" (Husserl, 1969, p. 209, the italics are Husserl's). Likewise, Schutz, too, works back from social-scientifically constructed ideal types to underlying processes of everyday-life understanding and claims that in thinking in everyday life about another I am already taking up toward this other the attitude of a social scientist (Schutz, 1967).

Robert Sokolowski (1970, p. 208) comments on how the concept of philosophical genetic constitution can be extended to diverse areas (such as sociology):

> Each type of experience and encounter has its own way of developing, and goes through stages of evolution proper to itself. Genetic constitution will allow such individual differences to come to the fore. Most important, it will allow us to see how each region of being becomes conceptualized on the basis of pre-predicative encounter. It gives us a framework in which we can show, for example, how ethical concepts become fixed in judgments, and what pre-predicative consciousness has preceded them; then we would be able to contrast this form of conceptualization with the fixation of concepts proper to science or esthetics, for example. Thus the sources from which these regions of reality and encounter arise can be studied, and the great complexity and richness that lies in the "lived encounter" at the base of our concepts can be revealed.

It should be possible, then, to begin with institutional structures and their evolution and inquire about the genesis of such structures by a consideration of how lower-level experience-contexts generate new syntheses that build up to such institutional structures and development on a higher level (Husserl, 1973). "Founding" in the institutional sense would be used analogously insofar as it is not a matter of showing how higher-level cognitive processes depend upon lower ones and grow out of them, but rather in presenting how institutional patterns of action mirror more basic behavioral patterns, including the physical movements of infants, to which their origins can be traced. In fact, seeing institutions as "founded" in everyday life action patterns may be more appropriate insofar as such institutions and actions are much more than a matter of mere cognitive processes or ideal "meanings" freely floating above actional/institutional engagements with others.

To exemplify such a genetic account with reference to institutions, I will explain how African-Americans, seeking to share and create humor under the crushing weight of slavery in the United States, evaded the obstacles, that is, imposed relevances, they encountered by creatively giving birth to a separate institution, oral folklore. This entire process of institutional creation on the macro-sociological plane is linked to and grows out of the social-pragmatic process of coming to terms with imposed relevances in everyday life at the micro-sociology/micro-phenomenological level.

2   The Suppression and Resurgence of African-American Humor

In the history of African-American humor in the United States, one can observe the very coming to birth of the institution of folkloric humor, however amorphous and undefined its boundaries may have been. Mel Watkins's *On the Real Side* surveys what he calls the history of "The Underground Tradition of African-American Humor," which needs to be understood against the background of repressive slavery that "was, ironically, the primary factor molding the style and content of both private and public black humor" (Watkins, 1994, p. 48). It was to humor, which can be deployed as a strategy of resistance that can at once express and disguise one's true feelings, that African-Americans resorted when subjected to the brutality and violence of the institution of slavery from its inception in the 1600s until the Civil War and to the ruthless suppression of the Jim Crow era that followed on the Reconstruction up until the civil rights movement in the mid-twentieth century. Watkins sums up why African-Americans embraced such a strategy of venting their outrage at slavery through the masked mechanism of humor by observing that "calculated cunning and deceit" (Watkins, 2002, p. 1) were "the first line defense for any vanquished people" (Watkins, 2002, p. 1).

Slaves, for instance, utilized a kind of subdued humor as a protective device insofar as "No master could be thoroughly comfortable around a sullen slave; and, conversely, a master, unless he was utterly humorless, could not overwork or brutally treat a jolly fellow, who could make him laugh" (Weatherford & Johnson, 1934, p. 284; Watkins, 1994, p. 46). As a result, slaves could manifest superficial happy-go-lucky, mirthful, joke-cracking behavior as part of strategy to placate the master's suspicion that they harbored resentments about being enslaved or to dissipate the slave-owner's proclivity to wring from them back-breaking labor. Through such humor, slaves sought to give vent to while also veiling inner sentiments of anger, just as their laxity regarding disciplined work or carelessness with equipment might have both expressed and hidden their protest against exploitation, although the masters might have interpreted such behavior as laziness or ignorance (Watkins, 1994). In fact, slave-owners would take advantage of slave's simple, congenial humor and their tactics to resist cruel labor as evidence to prove that slaves were by nature childlike and dependent and that the institution of slavery should be maintained because slaves found joyful fulfillment within it (Watkins, 1994).

Slaves circumscribed their humor around slave-owners because they knew that any hint even in humor that they were not completely content with their lot or protested it could have brought down slave-owner's ire upon them in the form of lashings or even lynchings. Black comedian Richard Pryor, much later in the 1960s, commented on how whites were continually wary of Black humor, often interpreting it as "inappropriate or aggressive" (Watkins, 1994, p. 17), and he added, "White folks get upset when they see us laughing ... Are they laughing at us?" (Watkins, 1994, pp. 17–18).

Walking the tightrope between the extremes of producing insipid humor or risking humor that might be taken to object to the brutal institution of slavery, some Blacks resorted to forms of comic, narrative folklore such as the Uncle Remus tales that portrayed Brer Rabbit (representing slaves) outwitting and escaping Brer Fox (slave-owners). However, the critical sharpness of the humor in these tales was so blunted that Joel Chandler Harris, the white collector of these tales, denied that they had any edge on them and considered the narrator, Uncle Remus, who conveyed the stories to a young white child, to be a "faithful darky" (Watkins, 1994, p. 71), a happy slave, who was living proof of the beneficence of institutional slavery. Only later in the nineteenth century, it was publicly revealed that another group of comic, folkloric tales, the John/Ole Massa stories, had been developed and circulated among Blacks only, since their portrayal of a slave repeatedly outwitting and embarrassing his white master might have provoked white retaliation. This revelation indicates how a parallel, subterranean institution of African-American folklore existed in tandem with the institution of slavery (Watkins, 1994; Watkins, 2002).

From the 1820s onward into the twentieth century, white minstrelsy groups, wearing black-face and attaining "an unprecedented level of national popularity" (Watkins, 1994, pp. 71–72), expanded earlier portrayals of Blacks as childlike simpletons, and they belittled Black modes of speaking, acting, singing, and dancing—essentially Blacks as fools before white audiences (Watkins, 1994). Indeed, the spasmodic movements that a disabled black stable groom exhibited in a dance were mocked by minstrels and became the origin of the figure of "Jim Crow," in whose name the cruel laws isolating blacks from whites after Reconstruction were designated. These white constructions in effect promulgated a deeply sedimented stereotype about who Blacks were and with which Blacks, even in their own humor, had to conform if they wished to avoid appearing "uppity" (Watkins, 1994, p. 89). Such compliance with stereotypes, consequently, governed even Black minstrelsy groups, which, beginning around 1855, imitated white groups by darkening their faces with burnt cork and, tragically, repeating "demeaning images of blacks" (Watkins, 1994, p. 100) that were "no different in most respects from those projected by white minstrels" (Watkins, 1994, p. 112). Nevertheless, it would have been almost impossible for Black groups to present any biting humor that might criticize whites or white stereotypes of Blacks, given the omnipresence of the Ku Klux Klan, vigilante groups, lynching, and Jim Crow practices that compelled Black minstrel groups and other performing companies, particularly in tours of the

South, to submit to white norms of humor (Watkins, 1994). Given such abasement of Black people in shows popular even among Black audiences, critics like W.E.B. DuBois protested and upheld counter-images of Blacks through encouraging the African-American Talented Tenth. Even much later, the 1950s television series *Amos n' Andy* continued this tradition by having Black actors present corrupt characters, until the The National Association for the Advancement of Colored People (NAACP) objected so strongly that the show was removed. Only when Black comic performers appeared like Moms Mabley, Hattie McDonald, Redd Fox, Dick Gregory, and Richard Pryor, did it become possible for Black comic artists to engage in a humor that was critical of norms governing racial relationships, even to the point of impugning white supremacist suppositions themselves (Watkins, 1994). This history justifies Mel Watkins's sobering summary of the suppression of Black humor (1994, p. 381):

> In an era when anti-Negro sentiment and lynching were at their peak, publicly discarding the mask of naïveté, revealing the aggressive aspects of their humor, and openly challenging tacit assumptions about the nature of black comedy (indeed about black *nature*) on a circuit that not only regularly toured the deep South but also played theaters owned by outspoken racists would have been suicidal.

What is extraordinary is that around the time when all these constraints were in place circumscribing African-American humor (e.g., from the nineteenth century to as late as the 1960s), the institution of African-American folkloric humor developed more sharply the critical dimensions implicit in the Uncle Remus tales. The comic stories and jokes making up this more critical stream in Black folklore were originally communicated orally (since Blacks were often denied access to literary or writing facility) among Blacks themselves and concealed from whites, although they were finally collected and recorded eventually by prominent anthropologists and authors, such as Zora Neale Hurston. Many of the materials in this folkloric current narrated encounters between John (a Black slave) and his white slave-owner, Ole Massa, in which John frequently outwits the Massa and makes a fool of him. One anthropologist, Harry Oster, contends that these narratives are among the least discussed but more significant areas in African-American folklore (Oster, 1968; Watkins, 2002). For Hurston (1995a, p. 836), these comic folkloric tales were bold and lacking in reverence, whether for God or the devil or for Rockefeller or Ford (whose names are repeatedly found in the materials), but she believed that there are "no bitter tragic tales at all" (Hurston, 1995b, p. 927). For Bruce Dickson (1974), the stories served as symbolic denials of white Southerners' belief that they were superior to Black slaves.

Despite Hurston's final comment, an undercurrent of antagonism can be found in these tales in which slaves equate the master with a jackass, poison with joy a Black woman who informed the master of some slaves' misbehavior that eventually cost them their lives, look at Ole Missus's drawers (but on the clothes line) or even slap her in the face, highlight in a party-toast how slave-owners unfairly profit from slaves' uncompensated labor, or even rejoice in a funereal song over a cruel master's demise. In addition, though, slaves some-times in the folklore cooperate with white owners, agreeing that the white post-death paradise is more luxurious than the Black abode after death (though the former is empty), showing how food stolen from the master enables the slave actually to offer the master better service, pleasing the master so much with jokes about food stolen from the master that the master decides to pro-vide food freely to slaves, and presenting slaves as conniving with masters to win bets against other slave-owners. Slave masters are presented at times as genuinely caring about the protection and well-being of slaves (e.g., when one owner bakes $1000 in a cake given to the slave), and there are even cases where a slave's humor runs circles around a master but in such a way as to establish a kind of bond between both that results finally in the master emancipating the slave (Hurston, 1995b; Hurston, 2001; Watkins, 1994; Watkins, 2002).

Part of the danger inherent in humor is that it is what Alfred Schutz called a finite province of meaning, which is characterized by a relaxed tension of consciousness, of which dreaming or phantasy are other variants. In such prov-inces, the controlling ego withdraws to a degree and so unconscious, passive syntheses are effected and surge into consciousness or burst into public expres-sion. Further, one theoretic understanding of humor—the one probably enacted regularly among oppressed peoples—is the superiority theory, accord-ing to which the humorist conveys the humor involved when a misfortune befalls those who are powerful and mighty. For example, a community of poor people might circulate a story, particularly comical for them, of how the wealthy white person charging them high rents slips and falls into a swimming pool and ruins his high-priced suit. If one is engaging in humor that one's consciousness never completely monitors and if one develops the kind of humor the superior-ity theory explains, then humor wielded by African-American slaves against white slave-owners would have been quite precarious insofar as those slave-owners were usually inclined to punish severely any expression of discontent by slaves against their lot. But, in folkloric tales, one could relax one's conscious-ness, express what came to mind, and even humiliate those in power—as long as these processes were carried on orally within the institution of folklore shared only among Blacks and concealed from whites. Folklore, then, as an institu-tion, provided a safe space for the production of authentic, honest Black humor.

3   SCHUTZIAN ELEMENTS IN THE BIRTH OF AN INSTITUTION (FOLKLORE)

This brief tour through the history of African-American humor reveals how and why an institution such as oral folklore develops and what its constitutive features are—all this as prelude to discussing how institutions can be "founded" in the features of Schutz's phenomenology of the natural attitude. Such folklore is a loosely structured institution and its rules much less rigid and well-defined than a government's social welfare office might be, with well-defined procedures and a battery of appropriate forms clients need to fill out, for example. In fact, folklore might appear to be more of a practice than an institution, though the boundaries between the two structures may not be that clearly delineated. Both practices and institutions (and African-American folklore, for that matter) would fall under the definition of an institution given by Peter Berger and Thomas Luckmann (1966, p. 54):

> Institutionalization occurs whenever there is reciprocal typification of habitualized actions by types of actors. Put differently, any such typification is an institution. What must be stressed is the reciprocity of institutional typifications and the typicality of not only the actions but also the actors in institutions.

There is no space here to argue that the history of the development of the institution of African-American folkloric humor as a kind of bypass in response to the coercion brought to bear against slaves can be generalized to the development of other institutions, but it seems quite possible to imagine how a variety of institutions could follow an evolutionary trajectory similar to that of this specific institution.

Three features appear prominent in the development of the institution of African-American folkloric humor: the experience of imposed relevances; a protective system of typifications developed in response, as Berger and Luckmann (1966) explained; and distinctively arranged social relationships—all of which are intertwined with each other. As regards imposed relevances, one can imagine that peoples in Africa prior to the onset of the Middle Passage no doubt would have valued an ability to determine their own lives, to escape brutally imposed labor, and to engage in humor with their comrades—all these would have constituted their system of intrinsic relevances (and probably those of most human beings in general). As a consequence, being captured, forced to undergo the debasing middle passage to a new continent and culture, and finding their lives there totally subjected to an authoritarian, state-approved structure of governance by slaveholders—all would have been experienced by them as a system of imposed relevances, if ever there were such a thing as imposed relevances. Common experience would suggest that one way of coming to terms which such imposed relevances, of accommodating them within one's intrinsic relevances, might have been to seek a least some small relief for at least a small period of time from the cruel and excessively burdensome pressures of everyday life by leaping with others into the finite province of meaning of humor. In that province's relaxed tension of consciousness, slaves might have experienced something like what Bergson (1920, p. 132) described as occurring during dreaming in which one's tension of consciousness abates to a degree and in which one can discover "a distraught self, a self which has let itself go." Encountering the imposed relevance of the system of slavery no doubt heightened the desire to take refuge in the finite province of humor, but it also circumscribed the shape of humor that slaves might engage in. Slaves learned that any critical humor could bring down up on them fierce punishments, and so they at first prudently embraced the form of simplistic happy-go-lucky humor, so as to avoid the appearance of being sullen or to soften any tendencies of a master to exact from them excessive labor.

But such humor would have submerged most of the aggressiveness and justifiable indignation that slaves might have naturally felt and that they might have vented albeit disguisedly in humor, as the superiority theory of humor explains. Slaves, however, did manage to work around slavery's imposed relevances and act in accord with what their intrinsic relevances might have called for, timidly though at first, through the folkloric humor represented by the mollifying Uncle Remus tales. These tales, despite their anticipating the assertive John/Ole Massa narratives, consisted in contents shared with whites and therefore muted any aggressive tendencies to such a degree that whites, such as Harris, considered these stories to be free of any bitterness. Black humor was further circumscribed insofar as Black minstrelsy could only cope with the massive demeaning stereotypes of Blacks propagated by white minstrelsy and enforced by lynching and lashings, by repeating them even up until the mid-twentieth century, despite protests by W.E.B. DuBois and the NAACP.

It is quite remarkable that in the face of all these imposed relevances pervasively manufactured for centuries by white supremacist patterns of action, African-Americans were nevertheless able to develop creatively a critical, defiant humor of their own in versions of their own oral folklore. Of course, the only way for them to engage in such humor safely was for them to develop such folklore as a separate, insulated institution dependent on typifications, such as the typical concealment of such humor from whites. In consequence, one could say that faced with the imposed brutality of slavery, slaves, adapting their intrinsic relevances, creatively resorted to the finite province of humor, at first modified and muzzled, until they were able to devise an outlet for kind of honest, transgressive humor found in the folkloric John/Ole Massa stories. The only way to venture such a type of humor, though, was to surround it with a protective institutional infrastructure, that typically included some participants and excluded others, that typically allowed expressions typically forbidden elsewhere. Hence, the creative response in the face of imposed relevance of slavery involved not only resorting to humor and modifying humor to make it safe, but also to underpin that humor with the institution of oral folklore through a system of typifications, enhancing the humorists' freedom as never before.

It is also interesting that in addition to these methods for coming to terms comically with the imposed relevances that slavery and racism had put in place, Blacks, even within the well-protected humor of folklore, thematize regularly and comically the struggle with imposed relevances. The John/Ole Massa stories are all about the slave John being faced with insuperable obstacles and yet devising ingenious ways of eluding traps, out-strategizing and humiliating the master, or even winning his freedom from the entire institution of slavery. At the same time, although one might anticipate that the freedom possible within the institution of folklore might unleash all the pent-up hostility that African-Americans legitimately would have felt against white slave-owners and the white supremacist practices of Jim Crow regulations, it is striking that in the John/Ole Massa stories there are whites displayed who cooperate with Black slaves. Whites, on occasion in that folklore display moments of genuine care or, even in the most hardened of cases of cruel slave-owners, emancipate the slaves who brought them to laughter. It is as almost as though whites themselves in those narratives constitute an imposed relevance that African-American folklore narrators felt compelled to take into account, as though whites were not to be run roughshod over, as though they exceeded the stereotypes often depicting them as cruel—in brief, having the kind of moral dignity that whites repeatedly denied to African-Americans.

The establishment of the institution of folklore in which slaves experienced themselves as able to indulge in honest, relatively unconstrained humor regarding themselves and white masters all depended on the use of the kinds of typifications that Berger and Luckmann mention and that are constitutive of the social relationships that characterized the institution of African-American folklore. For instance, insofar as slaves would typically share John/Ole Massa tales only with other slaves and not with slave-owners, they thereby determined themselves as an in-group whose membership they from their viewpoint, that is, subjectively, determined and assigned slave-owners to the out-group. It must be admitted, though, that slaves developed their own identity as an in-group because slave-owners had already assigned them from a viewpoint outside themselves, that is, objectively, to out-group status, thereby imposing a relevance on them to which they responded by forming their own in-group. By specifying the boundaries of the in-group, slaves determined those with whom one might reciprocally and habitually speak and in whom one could confide, typically communicating stories with each other about outsmarted white masters, with no expectation that any offense would be taken. It is as though the typical regulations governing separate group memberships provide a typical, taken for granted, "safe space" (another typification). Within that space, slaves were able to engage in rich processes at an ever-ascending level of humor-making, much as the taken for granted but prescriptive rules of language make possible the higher-level creative activities of writing poetry or novels, as Robert Brandom (1979, p. 192) has observed. Given that African-American oral folklore depended on this structure of social relationships in which an in-group and an out-group stood poised over against each other, both groups were prone to engage in "looking glass" interactions with each other, with each group typifying how the other group was typifying them, as Richard Pryor suggested, when he observed that white people interpret Blacks as secretly laughing at them when Black people laugh in the presence of whites. Pryor's interpretation of whites itself involves a Black interpretation, or typifying, of how whites typify Blacks within the looking glass. The tales themselves follow typified patterns that structure the social relationships appearing in the narratives: with slaves typically free to vent aggressive feelings toward white masters, but also with slave-owners typically portrayed as at times entering into cooperative arrange-ments with slaves that typically benefit both owners and slaves and with slaves being able to deploy humor to depose masters from their sense of superiority over slaves to the point that they even consent to emancipating slaves.

The picture that emerges is that the institution of folklore was built in the face of ruthlessly imposed relevances, but those relevances did not deterministi-cally, in a causal way, suppress the humor of African-Americans, who instead of capitulating to severe domination, explored often tentatively and timorously a variety of responses in line with their intrinsic system of relevances, namely to deal with the misery of slavery through humor. Finally, the John/Ole Massa narratives proved themselves most suitable for allowing an honest, authentic, critical, assertive, self-determined locus for addressing slavery through humor, including even presenting whites on occasion in a favorable light. However, these narratives could only have survived because the community constructed as an infrastructure for them, namely an institution, that is, an intricate net-work of "reciprocal typification of habitualized actions by types of actors." The institution of folklore consisted of typifications of persons, of group member-ship, of regulations, of self-typifications, and typifications of other groups, and even typifications of others' typifications of oneself.

It must be noted that it becomes clear in this dialectic between in-group and out-group that the establishment of institutions is not simply a matter of micro-sociological interaction between two persons in a dyad. Ways of controlling and subordinating slaves, Jim Crow restrictions, African-American engagement in humor and giving birth to an institution like folklore with its various ver-sions of narratives—all depend on myriads of individuals acting in typified man-ners, learning from and imitating, more or less, others—with the result that institutions emerge and are maintained. It is impossible to identify single indi-viduals who produce by themselves such results. Rather, the legion of anony-mous individual actors whose incremental interventions contributed to the rise of such institutions within which in-groups and out-groups function makes it possible to see institutions as products of social groups rather than actions taken by individuals in relationship to each other, however important such actions may have been in the gradual construction and maintenance of such institutions. As Burke Thomason comments, when one states that "*collectivities* construct social reality" (1982, p. 141), one means that social realities like institutions are "being built-up over time out of the actual patterned doings of human beings." At the same time, it is no wonder that such institutions are experienced as an objective reality over against individuals, as Berger and Luckmann (1966, p. 60) observe, insofar as individuals always find themselves already within such institutions whose norms they internalize and experience as shaping who they are. Berger and Luckmann (1966, p. 61, italics theirs) pithily conclude their account of this circular process: "*Society is a human product. Society is an objective reality. Man is a social product.*"

4   The Genetic Constitution of Institutions (e.g.,
African-American Folkloric Humor)
in the Natural Attitude

Husserl and Schutz found the complex, higher-level cognitive processes taking place in logic and the natural and social sciences as paralleling, reflecting, and growing out of analogous cognitive processes taking place on a lower, pre-predicative, intuitive, or everyday-life plane. So one can inquire whether the patterns of activity at play in the development and maintenance of institutions that we have identified, namely imposed relevances and the generation of novel typified responses, both taking place within the context of a variety of social relationships, might also be operative in the fundamental, pre-predicative, intersubjective, and pre-institutional practices of everyday life. Such practices are isolatable, even though intersubjective interchanges in everyday life are to some degree already affected and influenced by the institutions one finds in the everyday life world.

Indeed, this general pattern at work in the already discussed establishment of the institution of African-American folklore is pervasive and fundamental in everyday life, in the domain of micro-sociology or micro-phenomenology. For instance, this pattern appears in the very structure that makes interpersonal relationships possible: the reciprocity of perspectives. Schutz (1962a) acknowledges that we know and take for granted that the same object means different things to different people insofar as we occupy different spatial positions with different aspects of the objects being accessible to us (and certain objects accessible to us are out of reach for the other). In addition, objects have different meanings insofar as our biographically determined situations, and our adopted purposes, with differing configurations of (intrinsic) relevances that accompany them, differentiate the meanings we give to such objects from those that others give. These differences in bodily location and biography that inflect the meanings we give constitute imposed relevances that make it inescapable that the objects we as individuals confront will have different meanings. But then Schutz argues that we engage in the idealizations of the interchangeability of standpoints, by which I assume that if moved to your location I would see things as you do and of the congruency of the systems of relevance by which we each assume that our differences in relevances are irrelevant for a common purpose we have at hand. As a result of these idealizations, we are therefore able to share objects as common for all practical purposes, and we take the knowledge of objects we attain as knowledge available for everyone. The fundamentally shared knowledge of a common world, which is the basis of all kinds of higher-level commonalities, rests on an encounter with an imposed relevance that actors repeatedly overcome through idealizations, typically deployed suppositions that I would see what you see (and vice versa) if I were in your place. Through these typically deployed idealizations, the world I mean is the same as yours, at least for certain pragmatic purposes and certainly for the sake of social relationships that could not exist without this idealization of the reciprocity of perspectives. The very pattern occurring at the higher level of institutional establishment—imposed relevances with the implementation of typifications in an interpersonal setting—is at play in the simplest meeting between two persons in everyday life.

Many other instances of this pattern can be found in everyday life. For example, according to Schutz, while I am unavoidably situated in my body, the 0-point of my system of coordinates, various worlds of reach spread out from my body. While our being so situated because of our body is experienced as an imposed relevance, yet through locomotion we inevitably bring within reach what is distant. Furthermore, this manner of overcoming what is imposed upon us generates a deeper sense of "I can do it again," through which we typify ourselves as able repeatedly to overcome whatever situational limits will be imposed upon us in the future, including accessing through type-constructions temporally and spatially distant others (such as Predecessors and Contemporaries) and their experiences (Schutz, 1962b) or moving beyond the present to retrieve the past through memory or anticipate the future in imagination. Similarly, Schutz and Luckmann comment on how cumbersome it would be if we had to resort constantly to pre-symbolic objectivations of something like a river and its crossing point. If this were the case, anytime an interlocutor inquired about where the river or its crossing point was, we would have to accompany them, perhaps over a long distance, to be able to bring them face to face with the river and to point out (literally digitally) the site where it might be forded. Faced with such an imposed relevance, we fortunately have developed the "'idealizing' and 'anonymizing' interpretive matrices of sign systems" (Schutz & Luckmann, 1974, p. 281). Confronted with the imposed relevance of having to travel all the way to the river to provide an interlocutor with information, we have built up the system of typifications and typified ways of acting that constitute language, itself a basic institution—and so we can linguistically explain from the hotel how to get to the river and where to cross. Indeed, significative devices on every level, that is, marks and indications and especially signs and symbols, represent typified and typifying devices by which we more or less come to terms with relevances imposed upon us (e.g., our lack of originary access to other's consciousness in the case of signs). Although Schutz (1962b) tends to avoid genetic accounts of patterns of action insofar as he limits himself to painting a picture of the grown-up adult, one could imagine the infant finding an imposed relevance in the distance between her and her parents across the floor and commencing the typified behavior of crawling to her parents whom she wishes to join, establishing a reliable, repeatable behavior—thereby coming to terms with an imposed relevance in such a way as to satisfy the needs originating in her intrinsic relevances—though none of this would be deliberate or consciously planned by her.

5   CONCLUSION

Many of the points made in this chapter coincide with the interesting discussions in the recently published *Fenomenología de Poder* edited by Jochen Dreher and Daniela Griselda López that criticizes the view that Schutz is basically a subjectivist who has little to say about the objective order (Lopéz, 2014). I would concur with Jochen Dreher who opposes Pierre Bordieu by suggesting that his notion of "habitus" should be replaced by the idea of typifications, which in the Schutzian phenomenological paradigm, retain a space for the free functioning of human consciousness, keep us from being the prisoners of a habitus, and permit us to oppose structures of power (Dreher, 2014a, 2014b). Likewise, Carlos Belvedere (2014) locates objective power in the bodily interaction between individuals, who have acquired through corporeity the sense of "I can" and mutually impose relevances on each other. Finally, Daniela Griselda López; (2014) criticizes earlier subjectivistic readings of Schutz and offsets such interpretations by locating the objectivistic dimension of Schutz's thought in economic interaction and the production and reproduction of linguistic communication in everyday life. Converging with López, Dreher, and Belvedere, I have used the example of how African-Americans responded to the imposed relevances of the institutions of slavery and Jim Crow, objectivistic impositions at the maximum, and yet through creative, free, "subjective" (i.e., from their group's perspective) exploration ventured to create diverse forays into how to execute authentic forms of humor until arriving at the systematic network of typifications that constitute the practice of folkloric humor, particularly the John/Ole Massa tales. My approach, based on a concrete example of the development of an institution, preserves through different, but related means the interaction between subjectivistic and objectivistic dimensions that one might find in a Schutzian account of institutions whose fundaments can be found in the most basic interactions of everyday life. In addition, my account would converge with Thomason's criticism of "reification" as a "cognitive process whereby various aspect of experience come to acquire a king of inappropriate ontological fixedness" (Thomason, 1982, p. 88). Typifications can be hardened and appear as imposed relevances, but the account of the genesis of the institution of folkloric shows the freedom and creativity of a group in the face of the rigidity of typifications imposed by slavery and Jim Crow and that group's ability to develop new institutional arrangements, which function in turn as imposed typifications (e.g., protecting African-Americans by excluding slavemasters). However, even then the somewhat benign treatment of whites in the John/Ole Massa tales suggests the possibility of a different network of typified roles and expectations in which possibly even whites might be included.

Finally, one might object the most institutions function by the regular application of typified rules, and that my genetic account of how an institution can spring into being in the face of (severely) imposed relevances really ignores the regular ongoing functioning of institutions whose typifications remain fairly immutable, constant, and smoothly applied. As a result, one might say that my genetic account tends to overlook the reification of typifications that takes place in *normal* institutional functioning as opposed to the *revolutionary* institutional building exemplified in an out-of-the-ordinary institution like African-American folklore—to paraphrase and apply a distinction drawn by Thomas Kuhn in *The Structure of Scientific Revolutions.*

However, my reversion to everyday life suggests that even more basic than the imposed relevance/typification/social pattern that I have articulated is the way that typifications themselves operate. A typification integrated within a system of typifications that has proved itself "successful" (which depends on a group being satisfied with such a system) carries with it a kind of value in itself, it becomes a part of the intrinsic relevances of those who wish to keep that system of typifications unchanged. Nevertheless, such a system of typifications must be regularly applied, and frequently the one applying such typifications runs up against an imposed relevance, a situation not clearly covered by these typifications and at times resistant to them. As a result, when those operating with a favored system of typifications refrain from revising their typifications when faced with imposed relevances, *that very refusal to respond to those imposed relevances is itself a response to such relevances.* Thus, when the white power structure was confronted by the imposed relevance of African-Americans seeking to express themselves and exercise their freedom, it chose to double-down on the typifications already in place, that is, the brutally enforced typical norms of slavery and Jim Crow. One might say that this response to this imposed relevance by reifying typifications and seeking to suppress by force this imposed relevance never definitively or effectively removed it; instead, it persisted underground. One might say that very attempt to suppress imposed relevances, the very reification of typifications of intrinsic relevance to the group in power, is inevitably part of social relationships insofar as they consist in a continual struggle between in-groups and out-groups within an institutional framework. Consequently, the pattern of imposed relevances evoking typified responses in a social setting is not only something that takes place in the creative genesis of new institutions; the pattern is at play in even the most rigidly reified institutions as they seek to preserve their ongoing self-maintenance. But, as history shows, the reified, typified norms of slavery and Jim Crow in the end proved themselves to be a mistaken, immoral, and ultimately ineffective way of coming to terms with the imposed relevances of African-Americans clamoring for their freedom.

References

Belvedere, C. (2014). En primera persona: Reflexiones fenomenólogicas sobre el poder. In J. Dreher & D. Lopez (Eds.), *Fenomenología de poder* (pp. 37–63). Universidad Santo Tomás.

Belvedere, C., & Gros, A. (2021). Invitation to contribute to *macrophenomenology: The entanglement between experience and large-scale social phenomena.*

Berger, P., & Luckmann, T. (1966). *The social construction of reality: A treatise in the sociology of knowledge*. Anchor, Doubleday.

Bergson, H. (1920). *Mind-energy: Lectures and essays* (H. W. Carr, Trans.). Henry Holt and Company.

Brandom, R. (1979). Freedom and constraint by norms. *American Philosophical Quarterly, 16*, 187–196.

Dickson, B. (1974). The "John and Old Master" stories and the world of slavery: A study in folktales and history. *Phylon, 35*(4), 418–429.

Dreher, J. (2014a). *Fenomenología de poder*. In J. Dreher & D. Lopez (Eds.), *Fenomenología de poder* (pp. 65–86). Universidad Santo Tomás.

Dreher, J. (2014b). Mundo de vida, constitucion de desigualdades sociales y jerarquías de poder simbólicas. In J. Dreher & D. Lopez (Eds.), *Fenomenología de poder* (pp. 111–127). Universidad Santo Tomás.

Hurston, Z. N. (1995a). Characteristics of Negro expression. In *Selected articles*, published in *Folkore, memoirs, and other writings* (pp. 830–846). The Library of America.

Hurston, Z. N. (1995b). High John de Conquer. In *Selected articles*, published in *Folkore, memoirs, and other writings* (pp. 922–931). The Library of America.

Hurston, Z. N. (2001). *Every tongue got to confess: Negro folk-tales from the gulf states* (C. Kaplan, Ed.). Harper Collins.

Husserl, E. (1969). *Formal and transcendental logic* (D. Cairns, Trans.). Nijhoff.

Husserl, E. (1970a). *The crisis of European sciences and transcendental phenomenology: An introduction to phenomenological philosophy* (D. Carr, Trans.). Northwestern.

Husserl, E. (1970b). The Vienna lecture. In *The crisis of European sciences and transcendental phenomenology: An introduction to phenomenological philosophy* (D. Carr, Trans.) (pp. 269–299). Northwestern.

Husserl, E. (1973). *Zur Phänomenologie der Intersubjektivität: Texte aus dem Nachlass, Dritter Teil. 1921–28. Husserliana* 14 (I. Kern, Ed.). Nijhoff.

Lopéz, D. G. (2014). El "Schutz objectivista": Aportes de la reflexiones schutzianas al problema del orden social. In J. Dreher & D. Lopez (Eds.), *Fenomenología de poder* (pp. 21–35). Universidad Santo Tomás.

Oster, H. (1968). Negro Humor: John and old master. *Journal of the Folklore Institute, 5*(1), 42–57.

Schutz, A. (1962a). Common-sense and scientific interpretation of human action. In M. Natanson (Ed.), *Collected papers 1: The problem of social reality* (pp. 3–47). Nijhoff.

Schutz, A. (1962b). On multiple realities. In M. Natanson (Ed.), *Collected papers 1: The problem of social reality* (pp. 207–259). Nijhoff.

Schutz, A. (1967). *The phenomenology of the social world* (G. Walsh & F. Lehnert, Trans.). Northwestern.

Schutz, A., & Luckmann, T. (1974). *Structures of the life world* (Vol. 1). Heinemann.

Sokolowski, R. (1970). *The formation of Husserl's concept of constitution*. Nijhoff.

Thomason, B. (1982). *Making sense of reification*. Macmillan.

Watkins, M. (1994). *On the real side: Laughing, lying, and signifying—The underground tradition of African-American humor that transformed American culture, from slavery to Richard Pryor*. Simon & Schuster.

Watkins, M. (Ed.). (2002). *African-American humor: The best black comedy from slavery to today*. Lawrence Hall Books.

Weatherford, W. D., & Johnson, C. S. (1934). *Race relations: Adjustment of whites and Negroes in the United States*. D. C. Heath.

The Durable Dimensions of Social Institutions: A Generative Phenomenological Approach

Daniela López

1   Introduction. Following the Footsteps of a Generative Phenomenology

How may one approach the study of institutions from a phenomenological perspective? In a group of texts from the end of the 1990s, Anthony Steinbock reflected upon the phenomenological method and emphasized the fact that "[*w*]hich 'matters,' which '*Sachen*' can be given to the phenomenologist depends in part upon how the phenomenologist approaches them. The way of approach we call a 'method'" (Steinbock, 1998, p. 127). From this viewpoint, investigating certain topics involves deploying appropriate tools according to the topic in question. Edmund Husserl developed different devices to account for different aspects of phenomenality. In short, Husserl drew a distinction between two approaches: the static approach and the genetic approach. Static phenomenology entails both an ontological enterprise and a constitutive analysis (Steinbock, 2003, p. 290). As an ontological enterprise, it aims at analyzing the *structures* of stable intentional objects. It seeks to describe the structures and essences within the natural attitude. As a constitutive analysis, it inquires into the way something is given, that is, a constitutive inquiry "into how something takes on sense, carried out in the transcendental attitude" (Steinbock, 1995, p. 79). However, within static analysis, there is no place for the question of temporal development. To fill this gap, genetic phenomenology aims at

D. López (✉)
CONICET/Instituto de Investigaciones Gino Germani, Universidad de Buenos Aires, Buenos Aires, Argentina

© The Author(s), under exclusive license to Springer Nature Switzerland AG 2023
C. Belvedere, A. Gros (eds.), *The Palgrave Handbook of Macrophenomenology and Social Theory*,
https://doi.org/10.1007/978-3-031-34712-2_9

studying the temporal becoming of sense. Genetic phenomenology is concerned with the origins of egological constitution, self-temporalization, and individual facticity. Proceeding from the static to the genetic method means, briefly, moving from a study of "something at rest" to a study of "something in motion" (Steinbock, 1998, p. 129).

In recent years, reference has been extended to a generative dimension, which aims at accounting for geohistorical, cultural, and intersubjective phenomena. Steinbock introduced a third dimension of experience peculiar to phenomenology, generative phenomenology (Steinbock, 1995). Although Husserl did not explicitly formulate the dimension of phenomenology as generative, Steinbock elaborated it on the basis of a wide range of Husserlian texts that mention "generative problems" and describe phenomena as "generative":

> In distinction to genetic analysis, which is restricted to the becoming of individual subjectivity, a synchronic field of contemporary individuals, and intersubjectivity founded in an egology, generative phenomenology treats phenomena that are geo-historical, cultural, intersubjective, and normative. For Husserl, *generativity suggests both the process of becoming, hence the process of generation, and a process that occurs over the generations as socio-geohistorical movement.* (Steinbock, 2003, p. 292. Emphasis added)

According to Steinbock, generativity becomes Husserl's new "Absolute" and in this sense, ultimately, the matter of generative phenomenology. With this attention given to the historical-cultural and the intersubjective in the foreground, the reference to consciousness is markedly blurred (Inverso, 2018, p. 470). Within genetic phenomenology, the sphere of intersubjectivity does not go beyond the limits of a transcendental sociology oriented to the synchronic field of contemporaries. The generative approach, on the other hand, transcends that limit and is concerned with issues in which historicity is brought to the fore. Attention is drawn, then, to the life-world and its "texture of rites, traditions, language, and intergenerational, cultural, and multicultural relationships that take place in the dialogue between the homeworld and the alienworld" (Inverso, 2018, p. 471). Husserl's work allows unveiling a generative formulation of intersubjectivity articulated as the structure of homeworld/alienworld [*Heimwelt/Fremdwelt*]. This structure is a new point of departure for a philosophy of the social world that is most concretely a generative phenomenology (Steinbock, 1995, p. 220).

Additionally, genetic phenomenology has its "limits" concerning the constitution of the "I-Other relation" of intersubjectivity (Steinbock, 2003, p. 292). The "co-constitutional" and "non-foundational" relation of homeworld/alienworld stands in stark contrast to the foundational relation of I and Other. One of the key differences in these two diverse formulations of intersubjectivity is the difference between the emphasis on the "world," in the first instance, and on "consciousness" *qua* egological subjectivity, in the other (Steinbock, 1995,

p. 17. Emphasis in original). A non-foundational phenomenology of the social world means that we are dealing with a phenomenology that describes and participates in geologically and historically developing structures of existence and coexistence, as well as their respective modes of constitution, without reducing those modes of constitution or structures to consciousness or to an egological subjectivity as foundational account does. The problem of the world[1] in phenomenology is, according to Steinbock, the basis for this new departure for intersubjectivity.

Shortly, the various methods and matters of phenomenology are characterized by Steinbock as follows:

(1) Generative phenomenology whose matter is generativity is the most concrete dimension of phenomenology; it concerns intersubjective, historical movement. (2) Genetic phenomenology treats generativity shorn of its historical/generational dimension. The movement between levels here would be from generational temporalization or historicity to individual, self-temporalization or facticity. (3) Finally, generativity can be addressed statically through yet another level of abstraction, shorn of all temporal becoming. This would be a static analysis that treats generativity in terms of structure, or again, the structure of generativity. (Steinbock, 2003, pp. 314–315)

The possibility of movement between methods and matters is analyzed by highlighting aspects of progression and regression as directional features that connect the different approaches. The idea is that directionality can be reversed or act locally on two or more dimensions. This complementarity thus shapes the methodological framework.

The Husserlian zigzag figure serves as an illustration (Steinbock, 1995; San Martín, 1990). In the general spectrum, the phenomenological analysis allows one to go from the life-world to the appearance of things in consciousness in both directions, appealing to progressive or regressive procedures that lead us to the idea of a methodology based on what Husserl calls "zigzag" (Inverso, 2018, p. 479). In the general methodological framework, the zigzag enables various layers of examination, a back-and-forth movement that research can undertake within its orbit or go through it by connecting several layers in such a way that the analysis of each one complements and illuminates the others. The fact that some methods are better adapted to certain topics underlines an important aspect of the methodological universe of phenomenology, which is not limited to a single device but, on the contrary, is open to variation by conceiving that "the methodological motivation is oriented by the phenomena" (Inverso, 2018, p. 481).

The complementarity of the approaches that make up a methodological framework makes it possible to understand the phenomenological affiliation of different phenomenological strands as part of a common framework (Inverso,

---

[1] See Steinbock (1995, pp. 78–80) for an analysis of the motives for Husserl's undertaking of the regressive procedure and how it oriented phenomenology on the natural world of life.

2018). Husserl never considered phenomenology to be an undertaking accomplished by a single thinker. As he himself cautioned again and again, phenomenology is a communal enterprise that is learned not merely by studying it but by actively taking it up. For Husserl, "phenomenology as a scientific enterprise consisted in an ongoing historical project in which one participated" (Steinbock, 1995, p. 258). In this sense, phenomenology is not only contained in the works of Husserl but is constantly increased and revitalized by the continuous exploration of new structures of meaning (Inverso, 2018).

From the understanding of the Schutzian phenomenological project as part of the phenomenological communal enterprise that we propose in this chapter, generative problems emerge from the point of view of his philosophical anthropology in different parts of his work, unsystematically but with an enormous heuristic potential. In his account of the life-world, the historical-cultural and the intersubjective are brought to the foreground. The world is for Schutz a "texture of meaning," a world of physical and cultural objects, such as symbols, language systems, works of art, social institutions, traditions, and legal and economic systems, which originate in and have been instituted by human actions and are embodied in the intersubjective encounter between social groups. Thus, in the terms proposed by Steinbock, Schutz developed a generative formulation of intersubjectivity that is articulated as the structure in-group (home-group)/out-group.[2] Following in the footsteps of a generative phenomenology, we will assert that the generative framework is best suited to approach the matter of social institutions. We claim that Schutzian generative formulation of intersubjectivity allows the unraveling of the different layers of phenomenality that the specialized discussion considers to be macro-social.

2   Alfred Schutz and the Generative Formulation of Intersubjectivity

As mentioned, generative phenomenology begins with the problem of the world rather than consciousness. Taking the lived-experience of the subject as an integral component of the world, Husserl coins the neologism "world of life" or "life-world" [*Lebenswelt*] (Steinbock, 1995, p. 87). The notion of life-world gradually evolved as the central theme of Husserlian writings during the 1920s and especially in the 1930s until its definitive elaboration in *The Crisis of the European Sciences* (1970 [1936]). According to Husserl, the life-world "is the spatiotemporal world of things as we experience them in our pre- and extra-scientific life and as we know them to be experienceable beyond what is [*actually*] experienced. We have a world-horizon as a horizon of possible thing-experience" (Husserl, 1970 [1936], p. 138). By "things," he meant "stones, animals, plants" and also "human beings and human products" (Ibid.). Among the objects of the life-world, "we also find human beings, with all their human

---

[2] Schutz deployed the concepts of homegroup, home group, and home-group interchangeably. For the sake of consistency, hereafter we will refer to this concept as home-group.

action and concern, works and suffering, living in common in the world-horizon in their particular social interrelations and knowing themselves to be such" (Husserl, 1970 [1936], p. 146). Life-world is understood, in the terms used by Steinbock, as a territory and is designated in two modalities as "world-horizon" and "earth-ground" (Steinbock, 1995, p. 97).

Schutz's generative formulation of intersubjectivity can be recovered from several of his manuscripts. In "The problem of transcendental intersubjectivity in Husserl" (Schutz, 1966a), a text written in 1957, he approached the concept of the life-world and explicitly disregarded the matter of consciousness. He concluded that Husserl's attempt to account for the constitution of transcendental intersubjectivity "in terms of operations of the consciousness of the transcendental ego has not succeeded." He also asserted that intersubjectivity "is not a problem of constitution which can be solved within the transcendental sphere, but is rather a datum [*Gegebenheit*] of the life-world." Accordingly, intersubjectivity "is the fundamental ontological category of human existence in the world and, hence of all philosophical anthropology." In this sense, "intersubjectivity and the we-relationship will be the foundation for all other categories of human existence" (Schutz, 1966a, p. 82).

Therefore, there is in Schutz's perspective an identification of the life-world with the social world, that is, intersubjectivity is conceived as a fundamental ontological category of human existence in the world. For him, intersubjectivity is a mundane problem. Aron Gurwitsch argued that this is one of Schutz's most original contributions, namely the contention that "the social character belongs to the life-world essentially and intrinsically." Such a world is a social and intersubjective world from the outset (Gurwitsch, 1966: XXIII). Our everyday world is, from the start, an intersubjective world of culture. It is a world of culture because the life-world is a universe of significations to us, that is, "a framework of meaning [*Sinnzusammenhang*] which we have to interpret, and of interrelations of meaning which we institute only through our action in this life-world." It is a world of culture also because we are always conscious of its historicity, which we encounter in tradition and habituality and which is capable of being examined because the "already-given" refers back to one's own activity or to the activity of Others, of which it is the sediment (Schutz, 1962d, p. 133). Thus, Schutz's ontology of the social world "can be summed up by what Husserl calls the 'general thesis of the natural standpoint' " (Kim, 2005, p. 207). In other words, within the natural attitude of everyday life, the existence of other human beings is taken for granted. Schutz conceived the intersubjective social world as unquestionably given in the natural attitude, and he took as his point of departure "the existence of the social world as it is always accepted in the attitude of the natural standpoint" (Ibid.). As human beings living in a situation within the world, we take for granted that fellow human beings exist; that we act upon each other; that communication by symbols and signs is possible; that social groups and institutions, legal and economic systems, and the like are integral elements of our life-world; and that this life-world has its own history and its special relationship to time and space

(Schutz, 1962e, p. 116). This conception of the life-world concerns intersubjectivity and historical movement.

The notion of "situation" played a key role in this generative formulation of intersubjectivity. Inspired by Maurice Merleau-Ponty, Schutz stated that human beings should be understood in "situation within the world": "[*w*]e are in the world, mingled with it, compromised with it" (Merleau-Ponty, 1964 [1945], p. 147). Our subjectivity is, according to this view, inseparable from the world. In his *Collected Papers I* (Schutz, 1962a), following Merleau-Ponty, Schutz argued that human beings find themselves at any moment of their daily life "in a biographically determined situation," that is, in a physical and sociocultural environment as defined by them, within which they have their position, not merely in terms of "physical space and outer time" or of their status and role within the social system, but also in terms of their "moral and ideological position" (Schutz, 1962b, 1962c). We are within a world in a physical geohistorical situation, but we also find ourselves within a social structure, and we occupy a moral and ideological position. Therefore, time, space, and sociality are three formal dimensions of the structure of the life-world.

Schutzian phenomenological sociology of social groups is another important aspect of his generative conception of intersubjectivity. The private situation of the individuals as defined by them is always a situation "within the group, his private interests are interests with reference to those of the group" (Schutz, 1964a, p. 238). This means that whether by way of particularization or antagonism, the individual's private problems are necessarily in a context with the group's problems. It is the socially approved knowledge that helps the members of the group to define their situation in the reality of everyday life in a typical way. In the words of Schutz, only a very small part of our knowledge of the world originates within our personal experience. The greater part is socially derived, handed down to us by friends, parents, teachers, and teachers of my teachers. We are taught how to define the environment, that is, the typical features of the relative natural aspect of the world prevailing in the in-group as the unquestioned. This includes ways of life, methods of coming to terms with the environment, and efficient recipes for the use of typical means for bringing about typical ends in typical situations.

Thus, the world, the physical as well as the sociocultural one, is experienced from the outset in terms of types; the objects of the world, including the cultural ones, are typified and so are subjects or groups. Typicality emerges in the projects of groups and in the way in which they typically carry out these projects in relation to others in their common world. The typifying medium *par excellence* for the transmission of the "socially derived knowledge" is the "vocabulary and the syntax of everyday language" (Schutz, 1962b, pp. 13–14. Emphasis in original). The stock of knowledge includes the socially approved system of typifications, relevances, and appresentational references, which stabilize a common, familiar world for the members of a group. All the elements of the stock of knowledge "if believed to be true, are real components of the 'definition of the situation' by the members of the group" (Schutz, 1962f,

p. 348). The socially approved system of typifications and relevances forms part of the relative natural conception of the social world that not only provides a group and its individuals with the means to define their situation within the social cosmos but also becomes an integral element of the situation itself.

The "principal ambivalence of the meaning of all social phenomena" is many times ignored by Schutz's critics. This ambivalence refers to the fact that meaning differs depending on whether it is interpreted by members of the group under scrutiny (in-group) in terms of its own system of typifications and relevances or by the members of other groups (out-groups) in terms of theirs (Schutz, 1964a, p. 227). This distinction coincides with that made by William Graham Sumner between the in-group or We-group and the out-group or Others-group (Schutz, 1964a, p. 244). A special case of that "principal ambivalence of meaning" refers to the definition of the situation within the social cosmos by the actor or the group within it, and the situation as defined by the outsiders.

The "family resemblance" between the in-group/out-group division and the one proposed by Husserlian generative phenomenology between home-world and alienworld is quite apparent. Bernhard Waldenfels confirms this correspondence by mentioning that the difference, which stems from Husserl, "corresponds to the well-known difference between in-group and out-group" (Waldenfels, 1997, p. 72). As a consequence, consistent with Husserlian distinction, Schutz delineated the in-group (We-group) and out-group (Others-group) divisions from the understanding of those groups as intersubjective worlds. In his article "The Homecomer" (1964b), Schutz connected the membership in the in-group with the idea of home. The home is the starting point as well as the terminus. It is the null point of the system of coordinates that we ascribe to the world in order to find our bearings in it (Schutz, 1964b, p. 107). "To feel at home," said Schutz, is an expression of the highest degree of familiarity and intimacy. This intimacy is independent of the face-to-face relation (Schutz, 1964b, p. 110); rather it merely designates the degree of reliable knowledge we have of another person or of a social relationship, a group, a cultural pattern, or a thing (Schutz, 1964b, p. 113). Life at home refers to the "life within primary groups," which means that it follows an organized pattern of routine. At any given moment of its history, any home-group is characterized by a "cultural pattern of group life." The cultural pattern designates "all the peculiar valuations, institutions, and systems of orientation and guidance (such as the folkways, mores, laws, habits, customs, etiquette, fashions)" (Schutz, 1964c, p. 92). It constitutes a "frame of reference" in terms of which not only the sociocultural, but also the physical world has to be interpreted, a frame of reference that is used for solving most of the practical problems at hand. This cultural pattern of the group's life, which stands in "correlation" with the stock of knowledge, is also mentioned by Schutz as the "the ways of life of the in-group," the "thinking as usual," and the "relatively natural conception of the world" (Schutz, 1964c, p. 95). It is also called "a normal way of life" (Schutz, 1964c, p. 104). This familiar, common way of life stabilizes the institutionalization and organization of collective, group activities, and in this sense, it is taken for granted but also linked to the dynamic of the social structure that exists at any historical moment. Thus, the in-group relative natural conception of the social world can be defined as an intersubjectively typically familiar way of life in which we feel "at home" and which is also endowed with a durable dimension. In the vocabulary of a generative phenomenology, the intersubjective worlds of the in-group and of the out-group are "normatively significant, geo-historical life-worlds" or "normal environing-worlds" (Steinbock, 2003, p. 296).

Even though Schutz did not use the term "normality," he referred to the durable and stable dimensions of the processes of institutionalization of meaning by highlighting the typicality and familiarity of the features of the relative natural aspect of the world prevailing in the in-group as the unquestioned, but always questionable, sum total of things taken for granted until further notice. The relative natural conception of the world shared by a group allows the stabilization of a typical environing-world. In Schutz's work, this stability is understood in terms of familiarity. In his generative formulation of intersubjectivity, a gradation of familiarity and strangeness is what characterizes the in-group and out-group relationship, or said otherwise, this structure has its correlation in the relationship between in-group and out-group. The structure of familiarity and strangeness characterizes the horizons that extend out from each group's situation within the world. The temporally, spatially, and socially arranged horizons of every actual experience or situation, in general, extend in the direction of decreasing familiarity, determinateness, and credibility (Schutz & Luckmann, 1974, p. 167). We might say that the life-world is, from the very beginning, divided into homeworld and alienworld and, at the same time, that "ownness and alienness are present with equal originality" (Waldenfels, 2001, p. 119). Then, the life-world is understood generatively as our homeworld, our familiar world, and as non-familiar and inaccessible as alienworld.

These worlds are stable for social groups; the stability of a typical environing-world is institutionalized in the group life. The next section deals with this matter and emphasizes that social types confer stability to the intersubjective worlds so that they are institutionalized as "normal," "familiar" worlds. However, typicality, familiarity, and stability do not always mean reification, as Zygmunt Bauman would claim: "Schutzian analysis convincingly demonstrates that reification, and hypothetical types replacing the intimate, I-Thou experience of others, are built into the very fabric of the member's existence. They can perhaps be re-negotiated and re-made, but in one form or another they are there to stay forever" (Bauman, 1976, p. 57). Rather, the Schutzian notion of typicality is generative, and this dynamism is linked to the fact that a future dimension is implicit in typical experience.

It is for this reason that we can assert that beyond stability, the intersubjective worlds are characterized by their plasticity and elasticity. As a typical environment for a certain group, each intersubjective world is "constantly" there throughout various divergences and discordances. It is important to mention this trait because the phenomenological notion of the life-world, within social theory's narrative, is usually reduced to the cultural world of ideas, a world that lacks any structural dimension, which is also understood as the quintessential microsocial sphere of everyday interactions. The trivial world of common sense is the traditional world of culture that appears deprived of aspects connected to conflict and power relations (Habermas, 1990, p. 213). The life-world is then relegated to the realm of cultural reproduction and of consensus, a homogeneous world that is devoid of "macro" dimensions usually connected to conflict and social change. In contrast, the membership of social groups and the dynamic relations between one's own group and others' group constitute central elements in Schutz's conception of mundane intersubjectivity. The author analyzed the ways in which groups define their situation in the world as opposed to other groups. He studied how each group approaches and distances itself in different ways from other social groups and the dynamics of inclusion and exclusion that shape social ordering processes. Thus, we would like to emphasize the idea that the same mechanisms that constitute those intersubjective worlds and give them stability and identity also affect the differences between them.

3   THE STABILITY OF A TYPICAL ENVIRONING-WORLD

In line with Husserl, Schutz argued that within our physical and sociocultural environment, "[n]o object is perceived as an insulated object; it is from the outset perceived as 'an object within its horizon,' a horizon of typical familiarity and preacquaintanceship" (Schutz, 1962c, p. 279). Following the vocabulary of a generative phenomenology, the familiarity we perceive in the objects of the world is an expression of the typical that, in turn, is an expression of the optimal in its genetically dense concordance (Steinbock, 1995, p. 163). This definition encompasses four notions that are worth analyzing in detail since they allow visualizing the durable dimensions of the relative natural conception of the world shared by a group and the stability of a typical environing-world. According to the generative method, this stability is connected with the matter of normality and abnormality, which are meant to be constitutive features of the problem of homeworld and alienworld. Following Steinbock, the home-world is a "normal environing-world in the sense of being optimal as typically familiar."

Husserl distinguished four notions of normality: concordance and discordance, optimality and non-optimality, typicality and a-typicality, and familiarity and unfamiliarity (Steinbock, 2003, p. 310). The discussion on the "normal and abnormal significant worlds" is the point of departure for an analysis of normality and abnormality. Husserl did not understand these terms in a medicinal or psychological sense but rather as "modalities of sense constitution" (Steinbock, 1995, p. 179). Nor is the phenomenology of normality and abnormality[3] concerned with the assumption of normality to be the derivative or averageness and abnormality to be a matter of deviance, unnaturalness, or artificiality. Normality and abnormality are not psychological, therapeutic, or medical notions, but constitutive ones since they concern the very becoming of sense: "This sense is constitutionally normal (or abnormal) depending upon whether it is concordant, optimal, typical, or familiar in relation to other acts (past or present), to a task, to an event, or within the context of an individual's environing-world or community" (Steinbock, 2003, p. 293). On the other hand, when modes of comportment veer from what is concordant, optimal, or typically familiar, they can be called "abnormal" with respect to the constitution of sense (Steinbock, 2003, p. 294).

Concordance is tied to the very constitution of sense. It refers to the concordant process of sense endowment. When revising the concept of concordance, Steinbock broaches certain prejudices that conceive norms are static and imposed from outside. Emile Durkheim is an example of this view. He defines normal as the "average" or that which is most generally distributed. Whatever falls outside these parameters is "morbid" or "pathological." This also enables him to define a norm as what can be observed in the greatest number of cases. However, "beginning with the phenomenon of concordance, one is obligated to take normality as something that is instituted through its development over time" (Steinbock, 1995, p. 136). Institutionalization of meaning is at the core of the constitution of a normal-environing-world. Thus, normality is "the way in which sense unities fit or pass together in the concordant formation and confirmation of sense" (Steinbock, 1995, p. 130). Experience progresses concordantly, and a sense of "normal," familiar phenomena is instituted through its development over time. This does not mean that the phenomena would be less coercive or that they will not exert an influence on people's actions; on the contrary, it implies that at the base of even the most crystallized institutions there are processes of sense constitution in which differences interact in the formation of identical sense, namely, concordantly or discordantly.

Normality and abnormality are pairs also understood in terms of optimality and non-optimality. They depend upon whether or not they are optimal for experience (Steinbock, 1995, p. 138). If the lived-body is intermeshed in a network of phenomena, as Husserl pointed out, then there will be a perspective or a situation that will be *preferred* as *better* or *best* for experiencing. By optimal, it is meant that normal experiences are "richer," differentiated. To say that we "prefer" such a situation means that "normally" we tend toward the "maximum of richness" or "maximum of focus" in which the object is both sharp and differentiated. The normal as optimal is what enriches experiences (Steinbock, 1995, p. 139). Steinbock reviewed Husserl's contribution to the theory of "relief" or prominence and his contention that what comes into relief

---

[3] Steinbock argued that "among Husserl's persistent albeit scattered occupation with the problems of normality and abnormality, one can articulate a cogent theory of these notions" (Steinbock, 1995, p. 126).

is always charged with significance, effective in the sense of exerting an "affective force" (Steinbock, 1995, p. 153). The concepts of affective relief or affective perspective suggest that if something is prominent in our field of comportment, it is prominent because it "says" something to us in a way that *"makes a difference"*; it exerts an affective efficacy on us in a specific context and does not achieve prominence in an indiscriminate manner. This means, further, that "a relief or perspective is *better* or more *favorable* than others and that an affective relief can be optimal and function as a norm for normal life" (Steinbock, 1995, p. 156. Emphasis in original). If we connect these ideas with concordant comportment, concordance is the capacity to take up the optimal and to repeat it in an internally coherent manner. With its repetition over time, "the normal acquires a genetic density" (Steinbock, 1995, p. 158). As a corollary, when normality acquires a "genetic density" it structures a normatively significant environing-world (Steinbock, 1995). In concordant comportment, there is a process of selection and exclusion of the optima, and through this process, a "genetic density" of the optimal is established. In the same process, the typical is established.

According to Steinbock, if not directly from Husserl, then at least through the works of Schutz, "it is well-known that type, the typical, and typicality are notions consistently associated with the normal and the optimal" (Steinbock, 1995, p. 159). The typical is defined as the optimal in its genetic density or development over time. Then the optimal becomes a type when it is repeated concordantly and integrated into the rapport of lived-experiences with the environing-world. Thus, the typical is the optimal in its genetic density or, put another way, "the typical is the concordant repetition of the optimal" (Ibid.). As a consequence, the concordant iteration of the optimal is constitutive of typicality. Or, in other words, typicality is the concordant repetition or iteration of that which is charged with significance, that is, the optimal.

It should be mentioned that the typical is not a mere repetition of that which is charged with significance. The typical is generative because a future dimension is also implied in typical experience. In this regard, typification and typical experience can be seen as guiding experience, sketching a style of a "normal, familiar world" or typical environing-world. Schutz elaborated a dynamic point of view on the formation of typicality (Schutz, 1966b, 1966c) through Husserl's phenomenology of association and connected the formation of typicality to experiences that become sedimented and are "called forth," "awakened" from their latency in the past to bond as the same type in the present (Schutz, 1966c, p. 96).

According to Steinbock, it is not possible to find in Schutz's reflection any explicit connection of typicality with the optimal. Only implicitly did Schutz refer to the relation of the typical to the optimal. It is through a quotation that Schutz alluded to the Husserlian idea of optimality and linked it to the idea of interest. If certain characteristics are "paired" with others as typically similar, it is because "Our interest is thereby not indifferently parceled out to all the characteristics that become prominent; rather our gaze is directed towards especially impressive properties, through which the object of precisely this type or this individual object distinguished itself from other objects of an equal or similar type" (Quoted in Steinbock, 1995, p. 162). Typicality is not analyzed through the notion of optimality but through Schutz's central category, the notion of relevance:

> What Husserl has not explained […] is that this typification takes places according to particular structures of relevancy […] Which typical structure I choose depends upon the thematic relevancy which this object has for me. (Schutz, 1966b, p. 125)

Our "interest at hand" is what determines our system of relevances. This interest is only an element within a hierarchical system, or even a plurality of systems, of interests which in everyday life can be named "plans" (plans for work and thought, for the hour and for our life, and so forth). Schutz also developed a theory of relief,[4] but in contrast with Husserl, this theory does not refer to optimality but to relevance. The system of relevances is not to be conceived as homogeneous. It has its profile. Some of the relevances stand out over the others. It is a system of isohypses more comparable to the reproduction of a mountain chain in relief than on the usual map (Schutz, 1970, p. 34). These are our coordinates, our grid references for mapping the terrain, our life-world. What comes into relief is always charged with significance. Firstly, which typical structure I choose depends upon the *thematic relevance* this object has for me. Secondly, the phenomenon now perceived as thematically relevant is given to us for interpretation. Therefore, the system of *interpretative relevances* depends upon the system of topical relevances, since there is no interpretational relevance as such, but only referring it to a given topic. We must interpret it, that is, subsume it as to its typicality under various typical prior experiences constituting our actual stock of knowledge at hand. Finally, *motivational relevances* point to the importance attributed to the interpretative decision for the planning of future conduct. It is possible to understand this relevance as "causal relevance" in terms of "in-order-to and because-motives." The "in-order-to motive" makes reference to the future tense and involves ends to be achieved or goals sought from the point of view of the actors. For its part, the "because motive" alludes to their past experiences, which have determined their actions, that is, the actors' background, environment, or psychic disposition. Thus, prominence is given for Schutz by our present interests and systems of relevances. According to the type in question, certain aspects, features, and characteristics of the object acquire emphasis and prominence, while others may pass almost unnoticed. Some features of the object are selected, and others are excluded. "My present interests and the system of relevances corresponding to them determine which form of typification will prevail at a given moment, every shift in my interest being accompanied by, and entailing, a change in typification" (Gurwitsch, 1966: XV). In concordant comportment, there is a

---

[4] For a more detailed presentation of the Schutzian theory of relief see López (2021).

process of selection and exclusion of the relevant, and through its development over time, a genetic density of the relevances is established and, as a consequence, typicality is instituted. The genetic density of relevance in the formation of the type is a vantage point from which familiarity and stability of the intersubjective worlds can come into being. It is this perspective from which the "familiar" context for lived-experience of different intersubjective worlds or collectivities can be addressed, from the understanding of them as stable and typical environing-worlds.

The typical is, in the Schutzian view, the origin of the familiar: "typicality is the origin of the preacquaintedness and the familiarity of the objectivities within the world" (Schutz, 1966c). The temporal genesis of relevance that yields the typical produces enduring typical institutions. The typical is expressed again and again in a concordant, constant manner so that the type becomes valid over time. Steinbock mentions that typical can also be referred to as "practical constants," which implies conceiving them as typical constants whose iteration over time institutes orders and, at the same time, expresses the enduring efficacy of a type. "The type acquires the idealization of the 'again and again' so that 'typicality' the normal 'I can' becomes a typical 'I can ... again and again' " (Steinbock, 1995, p. 160). To say that the typical has the trait of being valid over time does not mean that its ideality is eternal and atemporal. It is its "inveteracy" and "persistently possible relevance" for future action that makes it seem natural in the sense of eternal. However, the typical is generative: it does not correspond to fixed and immutable values but "achieves a flexible stability" (Steinbock, 1995, p. 163); it stabilizes a typical environing-world but is also founded in intersubjective processes of sense constitution in which differences interact.

Therefore, the in-group relative natural conception of the social world, that is, the intersubjectively typically familiar territory in which their members feel "at home" is endowed with stable, durable dimensions. The very idea of familiarity is based on the notion of typicality, which in the Schutzian view involves the institution of sense of the typical group's environing-world through its development over time, that is, genetic or temporal density, and through the concordant repetition or iteration of the group's system of relevances. The typical has enduring effectiveness, and it is constantly there available for action or groups, thus allowing the institution of social orders. Relevance, concordance, typicality, and familiarity are modalities of sense constitutions that make it possible to achieve the stability of a typical environing-world. A typical environment for a certain action or group is "constantly" there as "the milieu we especially count on, the 'familiar' or as that to which one is accustomed" (Steinbock, 1995, p. 163). This typical environment is constantly there also throughout various divergences and discordances. Thus, the stability of a typical environing-world does not necessarily mean reification. It can be true that certain social institutions can be reified in their historical development and that the reference to the generating activities, to the instituting processes "behind" institutions, may be lost. Schutz was aware of this process of anonymity (Schutz,

1964d). But no matter how reified social relationships and institutions become, such reification "only defines a historical process" (López Sáenz, 1996, p. 210) in which the intersubjective fabric "behind" and the generative constitution of institutions are overlooked. In the following section, we will analyze the specific traits of an economic institution, commodity, as an example of the process of reification.

4   On Social Institutions

The stability of a typical environing-world is accompanied by the stability of social action. Socially approved behavior patterns for coming to terms with typical problems are frequently institutionalized and, therefore, ordered in a particular configuration of domains of relevances, which in turn has its origin in the relative natural world view of a group, in their habits, customs, moral, and so forth. The more institutionalized or standardized such a behavior pattern is, the more typified it is in a socially approved way by laws, rules, regulations, customs, habits, and so on, and the greater is the chance that my own self-typifying behavior will bring about the state of affairs aimed at (Schutz, 1962b, p. 26).

As mentioned in the previous section, this world of cultural objects and social institutions can best be understood as realms of intersubjectivity: they "point back by their very origin and meaning to the activities of human subjects" (Schutz, 1962b, p. 10). The whole world of cultural objects includes everything from artifacts to institutions and conventional ways of doing things. These contain within themselves implicit references to my contemporaries (Schutz, 1967 [1932], p. 182). They originate in and have been instituted by human actions, our own and our fellow human beings, contemporaries, and predecessors. Rephrasing this idea in the words of William Hamrick, an institution should be understood as that which is created out of the events of an experience which can endow it with durable dimensions, by relation to which a whole series of other experiences will have meaning, will form a thinkable continuation or a history—or again, the events which depose in me a meaning, not as a relic and residue, but as an appeal to a continuation, the demand of a future (Hamrick, 1987, p. 43). In this sense, generativity goes beyond inter-subjectivity in the sense of co-presence. Generativity of the homeworld runs through the normal human community of the generations, which allows thinking not only of their origin in contemporaries and predecessors, but of its orientation toward our successors to which we orient our actions.

This demand of a future or, in other terms, the generativity that exceeds the intersubjectivity understood as co-presence is inherent to the processes of institutionalization and refers to the "recurrent character of social relationships." This recurrent character is a feature of "life at home" or, in other words, of "life within primary groups." Primary groups imply the recurrent character of certain social relationships (Schutz, 1964b, p. 112). More precisely, the so-called 'primary groups' are institutionalized situations which make it possible to re-establish the interrupted we-relation and to continue where it was broken off last time. There is, of course, no certainty, but just a mere chance, that such a re-establishment and continuation will succeed [...] the existence of such a chance is taken for granted by all its members. (Schutz, 1964b, p. 111)

Thus, the appeal to continuation, the mere chance of the re-establishment of the interrupted typified social relationship, is a generative trait of social institutions. Typicality of action is generative because a future dimension is inherent to this typical intersubjective experience. The members of the group have in common with others a section of space and time and surrounding objects as possible ends and means; they also have interests based upon an underlying more or less homogeneous system of relevances. Each of them has the chance to re-establish the we-relation, if interrupted, and to continue it as if no intermittence had occurred. Each member expects a continuation in the future of the typicality of objects and actions and the concordant repetition or iteration of the group's system of relevances. A continuation of the member's activities in the routine work of everyday life is expected and so is the reactivation of their "recurrent relations with men and things" (Schutz, 1964b, p. 116). Thus, the stability of the way of life at home, the typical environing-world, and the stability of social action could be reactivated in our recurrent relations with persons, groups, and things. This stability of institutions makes them acquire a high degree of anonymity and could give rise to processes of reification, in which they may appear as perennial. Our consciousness of the historicity that we encounter in tradition and habituality is then blurred, and it is no longer possible to refer back institutions to one's own activity or to the activity of Others.

Social institutions can adopt an anonymous character; they are "objective configurations of meaning which have been instituted in the world of my contemporaries and which live a kind of anonymous life of their own, such as the interstate commerce clause and the rules of French grammar" (Schutz, 1967 [1932], p. 181). The fact that social institutions acquire a kind of anonymous life is clear in the case of economic institutions. Schutz conceived every institutionalization as departing from the institution of meaning, both as an instituting and as an instituted process. This, together with a reference to the generating activities, is what has been lost in our institutions and what has led to the disaffection of the citizens toward them. Schutz was aware of the development of this type of anonymity, together with the restriction of our autonomy to decide our own relevances (Schutz, 1964d). However, he was convinced that it was essential to get to know and distinguish them from the relevances imposed by other groups (López Sáenz, 2018, p. 140).

The type of anonymity of institutions defined as reification should be understood as the tendency to "forget" the reference to the generating activities, in other words, to the instituting processes "behind" institutions. Therefore, institutions are divested of social relationships, which sometimes are "forgotten" when certain social and historical forces come into play. The estrangement between citizens and institutions is a trait of modern life, according to Schutz. The tendency manifests in varying degrees and in different areas of the workplace and in everyday life. Wade Bell asserted that reification "is primarily connected to capitalism's ability to 'obscure' the lived experience" (Bell, 2014). In this process, our way of viewing the other is fundamentally transformed, as human beings are reduced to the objective, calculable properties of things. As a consequence, we begin to see the natural world as a mere object for exploitation and social relations become more thing-like. From this viewpoint, reification is "a form of forgetting precipitating from our participation in the capitalist system" (Bell, 2014, p. 15). The commodity institution is an emergent of this process. We can see examples of this phenomenon in everyday life. Children, women, and men in developing countries are forced to work under exploitative conditions in sweatshops to produce cheap commodities for Western consumers. The citizens do not usually take into account the fact that the production process of goods pollutes and exploits children and women, hurts animals, or consumes too much energy. Thus, commodities appear to us stripped of social relationships. The others behind the things that circulate in the market space stay in the shadows. Intersubjective relationships are reduced to a calculable property of those things.

Commodity designates a way of being of a thing, precisely determined by the fact money is the necessary condition to obtain it. The mode of being of commodity is directly linked to the human experience of space (González, 2009, p. 294). The thing that appears to me as commodity is exposed there. The ex-position points out the specific character of commodity's spatiality (González, 2009, p. 292). The spatial dimension of commodities shows that they are also things in circulation, that is, they are things exchanged between different types of economic actors. Thus, not only spatiality but also intersubjectivity constitutes its characteristic feature. Commodity involves an exchange between at least two persons. It is, at the same time, a crystallized human work. We could go even further and say that commodity expresses the appropriation of the surplus value of one social group with respect to another. This necessary reference of commodity to others configures the analysis of commodity as an institution, in other words, as an "institutional social object" (González, 2009, p. 296). Social actors, be they buying or selling, are constantly immersed in the universe of commodities. The order of commodities emerges in a process through which each thing is assigned a price in monetary terms every time it changes hands (Boltanski & Esquerre, 2020, p. 1). These products are just reduced to faceless number-identifications with price-tags attached to them. In short, "the capitalist system and its commodity relations have the tendency to transform human beings and social relations into things" (Bell, 2014, p. 2).[5]

---

[5] It is important to mention that we are referring here to the "standard form" of commodity, and we intentionally set aside the diversification of the cosmos of commodities linked to the new economic arrangements upon which capitalist accumulation relies. The diversification of the cosmos of commodities was studied by Luc Boltanski and Arnaud Esquerre (Boltanski & Esquerre, 2020) and depends, from their viewpoint, on the modalities according to which value is assigned to them. They identified three forms of value, which correspond, respectively, to three different types of capitalist economy and different types of commodities: industrial economies utilize the "standard form," financial economies the "asset form," and enrichment economies the "collection form." Though relevant, this reflection is beyond the scope of our work.

5   THE EXPERIENCE OF INCONGRUENCE BETWEEN SOCIAL GROUPS

Thus, the social relationship between groups should be brought to the foreground in order to avoid the understanding of institutions as eternal and atemporal. From the point of view of generative phenomenology, institutions should be reconducted to the relationships between social groups. These relationships are diverse and can range from consensus to conflict and social change. On the one hand, Schutz mentioned that congruency, iterability, and familiarity of the cultural pattern are expected between the members of the home-group. Familiarity is a characteristic of the stock of knowledge inherent to a group. According to Schutz, the "chances of success of human interaction" are linked to the "establishment of a congruency between the typified scheme used by the actor as a scheme of orientation and by his fellow men as a scheme of interpretation" (Schutz, 1964a, p. 238). Those chances increase if the scheme of typification is standardized and the system of pertinent relevances is institutionalized. The various means of "social control (mores, morals, laws, rules, rituals) serve this purpose." Congruency of cultural patterns and their interpretive schemes, which include structures of relevance and typicality, can be expected among members of in-groups. Schutz delved into the experience of familiarity and reciprocal strangeness between groups and analyzed the experiences of congruency and incongruence of the stock of knowledge and its correlative cultural pattern. Cultural reproduction and consensus are possible experiences between groups in the intersubjective coordination of their actions. Notwithstanding, intersubjective relationships between groups can be conflictive and can also lead to the promotion of social change.

As mentioned, Schutz's generative formulation of intersubjectivity suggests that what characterizes the in-group and out-group relationships is a gradation of familiarity and strangeness. Said differently, this structure has its correlation in the relationship between in-group and out-group. The position of each social group in the social structure is accompanied by a definition of its situation within the social territory, and the discrepancy between definitions is at the origin of the differences between groups and of the experience of strangeness between them. The "ways of life of the group" establish the standard in terms of which the in-group "defines its situation." This discrepancy is developed by Schutz when analyzing the experience of being a "Stranger" (Schutz, 1964c). When we mentioned that the cultural pattern of the in-group and its corresponding stock of knowledge function as a scheme of orientation in the social territory, we meant that the stock of knowledge acts as a map that helps the members of the group to locate themselves in the social life-world. The stranger "starts to interpret his new social environment" in terms of the "thinking as usual," that is, within the scheme of reference brought from his or her home-group. However, the stranger lacks any status as a member of the social group he or she is about to join and is therefore unable to obtain a starting point to orientate within it: "He finds himself a border case *outside the territory* covered by the scheme of orientation current within the group" (Schutz, 1964c, p. 99. Emphasis added). The strangers meet obstacles in their attempts to interpret the approached group and face "incongruence" and "distortion" of their stock of knowledge at hand and the corresponding contour line of their own group relevance system.

This incongruence is generative; strangeness and misunderstanding emerge in social interaction between groups. According to the Schutzian perspective, the definition of the situation is in no sense a-problematic, as it is derived from principal ambivalence of the meaning of all social phenomena, because when defining their situation in the world, the actors draw the limits of group differences. This definition draws boundaries and delimits the social distance between the in-group and the out-group. According to Schutz, one's own group considers itself the center of everything and all others are scaled, rated, and valuated in reference to it (Schutz, 1964a, p. 244). As mentioned, the home-group, one's own group is the null point of our system of coordinates within the world, and all others are classified with reference to it. The members of an out-group do not consider the ways of life of the in-group as self-evident truths. Each group thinks that its own "folkways" are the only right ones, and if it observes that other groups have other folkways, valuation processes take place within intersubjective relationships. The alienworld of the others could appear colored by the prejudices of the home-group. Moreover, the valuation of other groups is accompanied by logics of justification. Every society considers itself a *cosmion,* a little cosmos, which is illuminated from within by symbols. The symbols and "central myth" governing the ideas of a concrete group and of the rationalization and institutionalization of such a myth constitute the keys to the justification of the different practices of valuation between groups. Schutz even links this justification to the notion of "dominating ideology" (Schutz, 1964a, p. 245). This refers to what Schutz mentioned as an "ideological and moral situation." This source of incongruence in social relationships between groups could also explain the experience of discrimination.

The "folkways" and relevances of others may also be imposed upon us in the social world. The system of "imposed relevances" and typifications of others may seem strange and opaque to us. In the words of Schutz, the interpretation of the group by the outsider will never fully coincide with the self-interpretation of the in-group. Put another way, the relevances imposed by the outsider will not match the intrinsic relevances of the in-group. For this reason, the system of relevances leading to such typification is taken for granted by the outsider but is not necessarily accepted by the individuals who may not be prepared to perform the corresponding self-typification. The subsequent discrepancy may remain harmless "so long as the individuals thus typified are not subject to the outsider's control." The problem arises if the outsider, the out-group, has the power to impose its system of relevances upon the individuals typified by them, and "especially to enforce its institutionalization, then this fact will create various repercussions on the situation of the individuals typified against their will" (Schutz, 1964a, p. 255). There are many ways in which the interpretation by the out-group of the natural aspect of the world prevailing in the in-group changes the latter. There are also many possible responses of the group typified against its will. The reflection of these generative notions opens the path to empirical research (Schutz, 1964a, p. 248) around the institutionalization of excluding and discriminatory typologies, as well as the study of the actions carried out by certain social groups to reverse or contest these processes.

From this framework, there is an undeniable connection between the generative formulation of intersubjectivity and the problems that social theory considers macro-dimensions of the social world, such as power, conflict, and social change. Social theory's narrative develops as follows: sociologies that take and build upon the categories of common-sense knowledge, situation, and social interactions are often regarded as micro-social analysis. On the other hand, phenomena such as social structure, order, power, and conflict are considered to be relevant to macro-social analysis (Coulon, 1995, p. 31). As we suggested, although his analysis was based on categories such as common-sense knowledge, situation, and social interactions, usually characterized as micro-social, Schutz's generative formulation of intersubjectivity makes it possible to reveal macro layers of social phenomena.

6   GENERATIVE PHENOMENOLOGY AND THE MICRO-MACRO DEBATE

Ilja Srubar made explicit the discussion of Schutz's work in terms of what academic debate defines as the micro-macro divide.[6] His most relevant contribution is his recovery of Schutz's generative formulation of intersubjectivity to explain issues related to the micro or macro layers of phenomenality. Srubar made the life-worldly in-group and out-group structure visible in a way that accentuates that both micro- and macro-dimensions are profoundly intertwined:

> First of all, we would have to expose the dynamics, and consequently, the historicity of the structure of the lifeworld and, secondly, we must show that the matrix of the lifeworld structure cannot only be used microsociologically, but also macrosociologically, that is, also on the level of social change. (Srubar, 1998, p. 122)

Srubar emphasized "the dynamic and elastic character of the structure of the life-world from which its historicity emerges" (Srubar, 1998, p. 123) and stated that behind the intersubjectivity of the meaning structures of the life-world there exist constitutional mechanisms that transform its dynamics and plasticity; in other words, they transform the life-world's implicit historicity into history. The dynamic character of the structure of the life-world is anchored in the

---

[6] Alain Coulon asserted that "the micro-macro relationship is artificial; it is not found in the data but is the work of the sociologist" (1995, p. 44). Schutz would agree with that statement. He mentioned that the social divisions that the sociologists approach with terms such as "social classes," "system," "role," "status," and "role expectation" are "experienced by the individual actor on the social scene in entirely different terms" (Schutz, 1964a, p. 232).

need to approach the otherness of the world, on the one hand and, on the other, to transfer strangeness into familiarity (Srubar, 1998, p. 124). Therefore, in line with the generative approach, the dynamic character of the structures of the life-world alludes to the structure of familiarity and strangeness, which corresponds within the social field to the in-group/out-group division. The social dimension of the life-world "is organized on the familiarity axis, or as Schutz put it, on the intimacy and anonymity scale" (Srubar, 1998, p. 127). The Schutzian stock of knowledge, which is available at a certain moment of time for the individual or for the group, has several gradations and degrees of familiarity. The content of what is known, familiar, believed, and unknown is therefore relative: for the individual relative to his biographical situation, for the group to its historical situation (Schutz, 1966c, p. 121).

A significant universal characteristic of intersubjective worlds or life-forms—in the terms used by Srubar—and their reciprocal relationship is that "the same mechanisms that constitute life-forms (identity) also affect their differences" (Srubar, 2005, p. 237). Thus, "the lifeworld has not in any way manifested itself as a homogenous cultural world [...] but as a formal structure that is differentiated by its constitutive mechanisms and that generates heterogeneity and contradiction" (Srubar, 2005, p. 247). The structures of the life-world can be used as a "formal" descriptive language, and yet these structures can be generated from mechanisms that have to be understood as constitutive mechanisms of social reality, therefore "quasi representing the 'autopoiesis' of the life-world" (Srubar, 2005). As far as the stable characteristics of social groups and their identity are concerned, the familiar, common way of life of social groups stabilizes the institutionalization and organization of collective, group activities, and in this sense, it is taken for granted. Srubar defined this process as objectivization. The generative features common to every life-form stabilize the common environment and human acts by their objectification or institutionalization. On the other hand, the differences between life-forms result from the generative mechanisms themselves or, said differently, from divergent types of experience, action, and interaction belonging to each intersubjective world. Objectification can be identified then as the common mechanism that not only stabilizes but at the same time differentiates life-forms.

Time, space, and sociality are the formal dimensions of the universal matrix of the life-world and constitute three moments of a subject's activity that "make up the plasticity, dynamics, and historicity of the life-world." Likewise, these dimensions are traversed by the structure of familiarity and strangeness. The three dimensions do not simply appear as structures of knowledge of the subject's field of action. As mentioned, they acquire stability and are "objectivized" as "institutionalized forms of the intersubjective coordination of actions." Srubar mentioned that such objectivization can be semantic (e.g., linguistic) as well as materialistic. "The market, bureaucracy, factories, and schools are materialized coordinations of the temporal, spatial and social dimensions of a collective field of action" (Srubar, 1998, p. 125). Accordingly, a phenomenological analysis of society "can be conducted as a study of the emergence and change of this kind of objectivized time, space, and social structures, as well as, of their influence and reproduction in the framework of everyday living." Consequently, this kind of analysis is no longer limited to the microanalytic area of everyday interaction but also finds access to the macroanalytic level of society and its change (Ibid.).

The temporal coordination resulting from the division of labor requires specific stabilizing forms that occur in different types of institutionalizations and organization of collective activities beginning, for instance, with ritualized hunting, planting, or harvesting procedures and extending to computerized stock exchange dealings. The temporal structure of interaction and its semantics are, in this way, closely interwoven with social structure and groupings (Srubar, 1998, p. 126). Like the time dimension, the space dimension of the life-world is a structure of the human field of action and represents a structure of meaning; in other words, it is an interpretation of the environment carried by action's pragmatic relevances and types and also by the borders and zones that guide actions. The spatial dimension is connected with spatial semantics, which changes the environment into a linguistically and symbolically structured meaningful space of action. This structure of the area of action and its semantics "follows the differentiation of familiar/unfamiliar" (Srubar, 1998, p. 126), not only as regards the pragmatic access to the objects of the world (the zones of the world are organized into actual, potential, and within reach) but also with reference to other subjects or groups we encounter in the social field of action. "The border of validity of such spatial semantics also defines the borders of the collective area of action, outside of which lies an unfamiliar or foreign realm where only limited meaningful action is possible for group members" (Srubar, 1998, p. 127). Differentiation, hierarchization, and segregation between social groups also occur in this dimension. The organization of social groups and their social networks and the "organization of social distance between groups and individuals" (Srubar, 1998, p. 133) are concomitant processes. Schutz expressed this fact as follows:

> the whole system thus extended over all the different strata of the social world shows altogether all the shades originating in the perspectives of sociality such as intimacy and anonymity, strangeness and familiarity, social proximity and social distance, etc., which govern my relations with consociates, contemporaries, predecessors, and successor. (Schutz, 1962f, pp. 225–226)

Thus, Srubar dealt with a "matrix" of the structure of the life-world. This matrix can be outlined as the temporal, spatial, and social dimensions of the structure of the life-world and is generated from the intersubjectivity of the human approach to the world. Srubar argued that, contrary to Thomas Luckmann's concept, "our matrix here is not static but rather the constituting mechanisms are seen as the—at least potential—generators of the dynamics, historicity, and differentiation of the life-world" (Srubar, 2005, p. 50). In this way, Srubar revealed the structures of generativity employed by Schutz, not only in static terms, shorn of temporal becoming, but also from a generative viewpoint, as the intersubjective and historical becoming of the framework homeworld/alienworld.

7   Final Comments

In this chapter, we asserted that the generative framework is the most convenient method to approach the matter of social institutions in order to address the micro and macro layers of phenomenality. The analysis of institutions we presented here made it possible to identify two phenomenological approaches in the work of Schutz. One of them concerns the static method focused on describing the structures within the natural attitude, the structures of generativity. The other one is the generative approach, which accounts for geohistorical, cultural, and intersubjective phenomena in terms of homeworld/alienworld, that is, in terms of the axis of familiarity/unfamiliarity which characterizes the relationships between groups. Srubar mentioned both methods when he clarified that the universal "matrix" of the life-world is not static but generative, engendering the dynamism, historicity, and differentiation of the life-world. Srubar made explicit the differences between his approach and that of Luckmann. On the one hand, the ontological life-world analysis aims to describe "the universal and invariant structures of the life-world," and on the other, the purpose of the empirical social sciences is "to research the historical and cultural variety of concrete situations" (Eberle, 2012, p. 282). Luckmann departed from this distinction. He stated that "it hardly needs to be pointed out that any concrete experience may be either 'reduced' to its invariant formal properties or analyzed as a complex socio-cultural phenomenon" (Luckmann, 1983a [1970], p. 42). The concept of "constitution," pertaining to the phenomenological viewpoint, refers to the constitutive processes of the subjective consciousness, the universal structures of subjective orientation. In contrast, the term "construction" is used from a sociological perspective because it refers to the socio-historical expression of a specific phenomenon. Both terms refer to different approaches, which can be held in relation to a specific phenomenon: the phenomenological viewpoint and the sociological perspective. These different approaches—the phenomenological analysis of constitution and the reconstruction of historical human constructions of reality—"can complement each other" (Luckmann, 2007, p. 131). However, both disciplines "have to be decidedly kept apart," and as regards their relationship, the term "parallel action" should be reserved to show the interplay between phenomenological and social science research (Dreher, 2009, p. 405). Concerning the constitutive processes of subjective consciousness and the universal structures of subjective orientation, the method used in approaching this elementary question is that of phenomenological proto-sociology (Luckmann, 1983b [1973], p. 69). The project of a proto-sociology is understood as the "phenomenology of the life-world" insofar as it is able to create a link between the universal structures of subjective orientation, the basic forms of intersubjective action, and the objective properties of historical and social realities (Dreher, 2009).

We would like to offer here an alternative interpretation of the idea of parallelism between the phenomenological methods. We contend that the zigzag analogy is best suited to address the analysis of the phenomenological methods employed by Schutz. As Srubar clearly showed, there is a movement between levels, from static (the so-called matrix, the structures shorn of temporal becoming) to generative methods (the generative matter principle of generative phenomenology, the intersubjective and historical becoming of the framework, homeworld, and alienworld). The possibility of movement between levels would explain why, for instance, in his early work, with the aim to ground Max Weber's interpretive sociology from the point of view of a constitutive analysis of meaning, Schutz opted for a genetic analysis. In fact, he addressed the foundations of a theory of intersubjective understanding by referring to the "Thou consciousness," moving from the consciousness of the solitary Ego to the Thou stream of consciousness (Schutz, 1967 [1932], p. 98). Michael Theunissen also took account of these leaps or movements between levels of analysis when he mentioned that in the transition to the social world, Schutz "leaps out of the transcendental into the natural attitude," which "only means that he situates his social ontology at a level on which the transcendental constitution of the Other is already presupposed" (Theunissen, 1986, p. 345). This chapter does not attempt to be conclusive on this issue. In fact, its central objective is not to analyze the complete work of Schutz or the different phenomenological methods used to approach different matters. However, having touched the limits of this problem, we can glimpse, in Schutz's approach, a zigzag strategy more akin to Husserl's than to the strict differentiation between levels proposed by Luckmann.

References

Bauman, Z. (1976). *Towards a Critical Sociology. An Essay on Commonsense and Emancipation*. Routledge & Kegan Paul.

Bell, W. (2014). A Phenomenological take on the Problem of Reification. *Moderna språk, 2*, 1–16.

Boltanski, L., & Esquerre, A. (2020). *Enrichment. A Critique of Commodities*. Polity Press.

Coulon, A. (1995). *Etnometodología y Educación*. Paidós.

Dreher, J. (2009). Phenomenology of Friendship: Construction and Constitution of an Existential Social Relationship. *Human Studies, 32*(4), 401–417. https://doi.org/10.1007/s10746-009-9130-4

Eberle, T. (2012). Phenomenological Life-World Analysis and Ethnomethodology's Program. *Human Studies, 35*, 279–304. https://doi.org/10.1007/s10746-012-9219-z

González, J. (2009). Materiales para una investigación fenomenológica sobre el dinero. *ARBOR. Ciencia, Pensamiento y Cultura, CLXXXV*(736), 289–302.

Gurwitsch, A. (1966). Introduction. In I. Schutz (Ed.), *Collected Papers III. Studies in Phenomenological Philosophy* (pp. XI–XXXI). Martinus Nijhoff.

Habermas, J. (1990). *Teoría de la acción comunicativa II. Crítica de la razón funcionalista*. Taurus.

Hamrick, W. (1987). *An existencial phenomenology of law: Maurice Merleau-Ponty*. Springer.

Husserl, E. (1970 [1936]). *The Crisis of the European Sciences and Transcendental Phenomenology*. Northwestern University Press.

Inverso, H. (2018). Fenomenología de lo inaparente: la inapariencia como cuarto estrato de análisis fenomenológico. *Revista de Filosofía Aurora, 30*, 466–485.

Kim, H. (2005). In Search of a Political Sphere in Alfred Schutz. In M. Endress, G. Psathas, & H. Nasu (Eds.), *Explorations of the Life-World* (pp. 203–234). Springer.

López, D. G. (2021). Schutzian Social Cartography. *SOCIOLOGIA E RICERCA SOCIALE, 124*, 69–90.

López Sáenz, M. C. (1996). La fenomenologia existencial de M. Merleau-Ponty y la sociologia. *Papers. Revista de Sociología, 50*, 209–231.

López Sáenz, M. C. (2018). A. Schütz (1899–1959). Fundamentación fenomenológica delasociologíacomprensivaysociofenomenologíadelMundodelavida.InJ.E.González (Ed.), *Fenomenología y hermenéutica en la sociología contemporánea* (pp. 103–144). Universidad Nacional de Colombia.

Luckmann, T. (1983a [1970]). On the Boundaries of the Social World. In T. Luckmann (Ed.), *Life-World and Social Realities* (pp. 40–67). Heinemann.

Luckmann, T. (1983b [1973]). Elements of a Social Theory of Communication. In T. Luckmann (Ed.), *Life-World and Social Realities* (pp. 69–91). Heinemann.

Luckmann, T. (2007). Kapitel II: Sinnrekonstruktion in den Sozialwissenschaften. In J. Dreher (Ed.), *Lebenswelt, Identität und Gesellschaft*. UVK Verlagsgesellschaft mbH.

Merleau-Ponty, M. (1964 [1945]). The War has Taken Place. In *Sense and Non-Sense* (pp. 139–152). Northwestern University Press.

San Martín, J. (1990). El zigzag Husserliano. *Investigaciones Fenomenológicas, 4*, 2–7.

Schutz, A. (1962a). *Collected Papers I. The Problem of Social Reality*. Martinus Nijhoff.

Schutz, A. (1962b). Common-sense and Scientific Interpretation of Human Action. In M. Natanson (Ed.), *Collected Papers I. The Problem of Social Reality* (pp. 3–47). Martinus Nijhoff.

Schutz, A. (1962c). Language, Language Disturbances, and the Texture of Consciousness. In M. Natanson (Ed.), *Collected Papers I. The Problem of Social Reality* (pp. 260–286). Martinus Nijhoff.

Schutz, A. (1962d). Phenomenology and the Social Sciences. In M. Natanson (Ed.), *Collected Papers I. The Problem of Social Reality* (pp. 118–139). Martinus Nijhoff.

Schutz, A. (1962e). Some Leading Concepts of Phenomenology. In M. Natanson (Ed.), *Collected Papers I. The Problem of Social Reality* (pp. 99–117). Martinus Nijhoff.

Schutz, A. (1962f). Symbol, Reality, and Society. In M. Natanson (Ed.), *Collected Papers I. The Problem of Social Reality* (pp. 287–356). Martinus Nijhoff.

Schutz, A. (1964a). Equality and the Meaning Structure of the Social World. In A. Brodersen (Ed.), *Collected Papers II. Studies in Social Theory* (pp. 226–269). Martinus Nijhoff.

Schutz, A. (1964b). The Homecomer. In A. Brodersen (Ed.), *Collected Papers II. Studies in Social Theory* (pp. 106–119). Martinus Nijhoff.

Schutz, A. (1964c). The Stranger. An Essay in Social Psychology. In A. Brodersen (Ed.), *Collected Papers II. Studies in Social Theory* (pp. 91–105). Martinus Nijhoff.

Schutz, A. (1964d). The well-informed Citizen: an essay on the social distribution of knowledge. In A. Brodersen (Ed.), *Collected Papers II. Studies in Social Theory* (pp. 120–134). Martinus Nijhoff.

Schutz, A. (1966a). The Problem of Transcendental Intersubjectivity in Husserl. In I. Schutz (Ed.), *Collected Papers III. Studies in Phenomenological Philosophy* (pp. 51–91). Martinus Nijhoff.

Schutz, A. (1966b). Some Structures of the Life-World. In I. Schutz (Ed.), *Collected Papers III. Studies in Phenomenological Philosophy* (pp. 116–132). Martinus Nijhoff.

Schutz, A. (1966c). Type and Eidos in Husserl's Late Philosophy. In I. Schutz (Ed.), *Collected Papers III. Studies in Phenomenological Philosophy* (pp. 92–115). Martinus Nijhoff.

Schutz, A. (1967 [1932]). *The Phenomenology of the Social World.* Northwestern University Press.

Schutz, A. (1970). *Reflections on the Problem of Relevance.* Yale University Press.

Schutz, A., & Luckmann, T. (1974). *The Structures of the Life-World.* Heinemann Educational Books.

Srubar, I. (1998). Phenomenological Analysis and its Contemporary Significance. *Human Studies, 21,* 121–139.

Srubar, I. (2005). The Pragmatic Theory of the Life-World as a Basis for Intercultural Comparison. In M. Endress, G. Psathas, & H. Nasu (Eds.), *Explorations of the Life-World* (pp. 235–266). Springer.

Steinbock, A. J. (1995). *Home and Beyond. Generative Phenomenology After Husserl.* Northwestern University Press.

Steinbock, A. J. (1998). Husserl's Static and Genetic Phenomenology: Translator's Introduction to Two Essays. *Continental Philosophy Review, 31,* 127–134.

Steinbock, A. J. (2003). Generativity and the Scope of Generative Phenomenology. In D. Welton (Ed.), *The New Husserl: A Critical Reader.* Indiana University Press.

Theunissen, M. (1986). *The Other: Studies in the Social Ontology of Husserl, Heidegger, Sartre and Buber.* MIT Press.

Waldenfels, B. (1997). Phänomenologie des Eigenen und des Fremden. In H. Münkler (Ed.), *Furcht und Faszination. Facetten der Fremdheit* (pp. 63–86). Akademie Verlag.

Waldenfels, B. (2001). Mundo familiar y mundo extraño. Problemas de la intersubjetividad y de la interculturalidad a partir de Edmund Husserl. *IDEAS Y VALORES, 116,* 119–131.

PART IV

Phenomenology of Culture

Cultural Integration: A Macrophenomenological Analysis

Evandro Camara

1   INTRODUCTION

The integration of cultural systems within pluralist societies is a theme to which scholarly and popular attention, mostly negative, has been increasingly devoted in recent decades. This is a topic closely associated with the society's political life, insofar as it relates to the dynamics of power in the interaction between dominant and subordinate social (ethnic-racial, in the present context) groups.

The main focus of this chapter is on society-wide cultural integration as a crucial aspect of social inclusion and equality in intergroup relations. The alternative condition, cultural separatism, maintains race-based social inequality and the permanent confinement of minority racial groups to the space of *otherness* in the social system. The study takes its theoretical bearings from the work of Alfred Schutz—his phenomenological social psychology—to show how aspects of intersubjective life can be fruitfully used in the investigation of the larger processes in society.

Throughout the period known as the Age of Discovery, the cultural ways of colonized populations of non-European extraction, which came eventually to be seen as products of their racial status, were construed as the mark of their innate inferiority, in relation to the superior nature of European cultural life. This perception of the permanent *otherness* of colonized groups, and the latter's phenotypical distinctions and variations *vis-à-vis* the European physical

E. Camara (✉)
Emporia State University, Emporia, KS, USA
e-mail: ecamara@emporia.edu

archetype, strongly legitimized and maintained their subordination under European colonial rule. This led eventually, by the late 1700s and through the 1800s, to the emergence of a full-blown repertoire of degrading references and attributions imposed on the colonized groups, such as *the inferior societies* (Lévy-Bruhl, 1910), *primitive behavior* (Thomas, 1937), the *dark races of men* (Knox, 1850), and *savage and civilized societies* (Sumner, 1906/1960). This was fully articulated in the discourse of late 1800s' scientific racism.

Race endures as a structural element of great import in modern ethnically pluralist societies organized on the basis of racial bipolarity, such as U.S. society, as evidenced in the latter's persisting racial tensions, divisions, hierarchies, and antagonisms, and more basically still, in the structuring and normative functions of race in the society as a whole. The primary substantive interest here is on intergroup life in U.S. society, and the relations between the dominant Anglo-American part of the population (which, together with the other *white ethnics*, make up the designated white group) and the African-American part of the population.[1]

In multiethnic/multiracial societies of the modern era marked by established cultural separatism between the majority and minority racial segments of the population, this is typically associated with the crystallization of the *otherness* of the minority group(s), hence, with their permanent cultural marginalization. On the other hand, in polyethnic societies where tendencies of cultural integration or unification have prevailed, the general emphasis is on the inclusion of racial minorities and all other groups into the mainstream of national life.

Cultural integration is the model of interethnic life whereby heterogeneous cultural traditions coexist with and complement one another, in a dynamic interrelation and *rapprochement*. The model of integration considered here conforms to Bastide's concept of the *principe de coupure* (1971). The fact that in the syncretic situation the diverse cultural streams do not merge perfectly into a new cultural product, and that the syncretic process itself is hierarchized (inasmuch as it occurs within the context of asymmetrical political relations between the groups involved), does not prevent their interpenetration, as de Queiroz (1979: 152) points out. This model of assimilation has been associated with some major civilizations throughout history, such as the Roman Empire, or the Arab civilization in the Iberian Peninsula, *inter alia*.

Foremost among the cultural resources merging to form the national culture are aspects of consciousness, the group's world of intersubjectivity. From the nonmaterial standpoint, the society's culture may be considered as a complex of typified knowledge, assumptions, linguistic practices, ways of thinking, and so on. Moreover, a case is made here for cultural integration as a necessary component of the full-scale social inclusion of minority segments. In phenomenological terms, this refers to their integration into the dominant meaning-system of the society-at-large.

---

[1] The white and nonwhite designations are used here *under erasure* (Derrida) to denote their relative (i.e., culturally specific) nature.

Schutz puts forward an essentially cultural model of the world of everyday life, as based on his idea that this world is "from the outset an intersubjective world of culture" (cited in Ferguson, 2006: 93). Human group life is oriented by the unquestioned perceptions of reality by society's members. In fact, understanding collective life and how it works from this angle—that is, in terms of the subjective meaning-context of the group—is, for Schutz, no less than "one of the most important tasks of sociology" (1997: 200). The potential of factors of subjectivity for bringing into view the political (power) dimension of cultural institutions is suggested in the assertion that these institutions "are not only places where norms are enforced, but also places where powerful ideas of what is normal and natural are shaped" (Guest, 2017: 50).

The present analysis centers on the question of meaning and such key Schutzian concepts as typifications, stock-of-knowledge-at-hand, structures of relevance, direct and indirect relationships, the They-orientation, anonymity, and the world of contemporaries, toward further clarification of intergroup relations, specifically in the area of race. It aims to bring into sharper focus the connections between phenomenological description and the dynamics of power inequality between dominant and subordinate racial groups. In this way, the potential of phenomenology for macrosociological study shall be high-lighted, in the sense of addressing the larger structural patterns and processes of the social system and, in the particular case here, the political relations between dominant and minority racial groups.

2   The Emergence of Identity Politics

Recent decades have witnessed the growing spread and influence of the idea that cultural integration exerts a negative impact on minority populations in that it suppresses the cultural manifestations of said populations. The rise of this viewpoint has been related to the concomitant rise of the multiculturalist and postmodernist movements of the 1990s, and their corollary politics of difference, or identity politics. The latter continues to be very influential in modern polyethnic societies of the Western industrialized world, in particular the U.S. It advocates the preservation of the cultural separateness of minority ethnic-racial communities that have historically been kept, formally as well as informally, from fully blending into the society's cultural mainstream. The postmodern reaction to cultural integration, therefore, has been the formal and informal enforcement of identity politics as a mechanism that is claimed to enhance the socio-political representation of minority groups while protecting their cultural distinctiveness.

In racially binary societies the status of minority persons is established on the basis of the white/nonwhite dualism. This model of racial classification is deeply rooted in U.S. history but has also gained increasing ground in other industrialized multiethnic societies in recent decades. Racially binary social organization essentializes racial status as such, making it a fixed, quasi-metaphysical condition: race as an ontological state (see, e.g., Camara, 2003,

2021). Consequently, the cultural ways of the groups codified as white and nonwhite, respectively, are also considered to be intrinsic to them.

The pursuit of the politics of identity fosters the cultural division of the society *ad infinitum*. While this orientation is ostensibly intended to protect the cultural make-up of minority populations, its latent function is in fact to maintain the racialization of these populations (i.e., their nonwhite designation) and, consequently, in the manner of classic racism, the construction of their cultural life as the fixed, essential product of their racial background. This, in turn, causes these groups to be characterized as *innately* different in relation to the dominant cultural standard. The end result is the hardening of race-based political stratification. Addressing this issue in reference to the assimilation of incoming groups in the U.S., Franklin (1997: 18) had this to say: "The ethnic grouping that was a way-station, a temporary resting place for Europeans as they became American, proved to be a terminal point for blacks who found it virtually impossible to become Americans in any real sense."

Modern-day industrialized, ethnically and racially diverse societies in which intergroup life is regulated on the basis of racially dichotomous classification promote, in most cases, the *structural* inclusion of minority racial groups while preserving their subcultural difference. In contradistinction, assimilationist multiethnic systems where race is defined and essentially handled in terms of multiple-category racial classification typically favor the absorption of *all* social segments at all levels—structural, cultural, biological, and psychological. This means that these segments are absorbed into the national identity, and the latter normally overrides all other subsidiary social identities and statuses.[2] The outstanding part of this assimilative process is cultural assimilation, which has as its corollary psychological assimilation. The structural and biological aspects of assimilation do not typically advance at the same pace and in the same degree as the cultural and psychological ones.

Being assimilated culturally enables incoming groups and their descendants to maintain a connection with their particular ancestral background, without this constituting a condition of *preserved otherness*. Such would be the case, in the context of U.S. society, of the *white ethnics* (e.g., German-Americans, Irish-Americans, Polish-Americans, and Swedish-Americans). Their full assimilation affords them the ability to function as ideal-typical units of the society, a condition of anonymity or interchangeability in relation to every other fully assimilated formative group of the society, notwithstanding their continuing attachment to their ancestral ethnic background. This is exemplified by such festivities as Oktoberfest and St. Patrick's Day Parade, which, if anything, enhance or add a distinctive flavor to the membership of these individuals in national life.

---

[2] Regarding minority-group cultural assimilation, the prevalence of assimilationist tendencies may be detected in Gates's late 1990s' account of young black culture in London, which he characterizes simply as being part of British "youth culture." This is the culture of the *wiggers* (i.e., "white wannabes") of British culture (1997: 198).

The foregoing should have indicated that the enforcement of structural (i.e., political, economic) assimilation by itself leaves much to be desired when this comes together with cultural separatism, because the latter, particularly when enforced formally over time, tends to hinder the former. For instance, the destruction of the Jim Crow system in U.S. society has been followed precisely by this model of progressive structural absorption of the minority (racial) communities, but in tandem with the white/nonwhite cultural separatism of the Jim Crow era (*sans* the legally upheld physical segregation and oppression of that era).[3] The fact that in recent decades there has been a sacralization of the *modus vivendi* of minority populations on the part of the wider society does not remove the stigma of *difference*, as in perpetual otherness, for the minority groups, nor their disadvantaged political standing. At the level of subjectivity, they remain perpetual strangers in the society-at-large at the level of meaning.[4]

3   THE PROBLEM OF MEANING

This chapter enlarges upon an earlier effort to characterize meaning as a major shaping force of intergroup relations and, more specifically, of race-based relations of power inequality.[5] The cultural life of individuals is their existential grounding and mode of expression. It is through culture that we *are*, in the sense of *being-in-the-world*. Additionally, life in society determines *how* and *what* we are and in this way bears directly on the question of identity. This issue becomes particularly relevant when it is associated with nondominant groups that have been relegated to subcultural spaces in the wider society.

The prevalence of meaning in the lifeworld is reflected in the daily reliance of social actors on *typifications*, the group's habitual or typified cultural objects and practices, behavioral and linguistic patterns, and interpretations, which in turn make up the group's *stock-of-knowledge-at-hand*. The latter refers to the commonly shared complex of knowledge and understandings used by social actors as their basis of orientation in the social world. These two concepts stand foursquare in the center of Schutz's theoretical system. Understanding how social actors construct reality, and structure their life together on the basis of intersubjectively shared typifications, must be treated as the paramount concern of those who seek to understand society.

---

[3] In contradistinction to the U.S. situation. Gates's investigations appear to indicate that being black (i.e., Jamaican, in his analysis) and fully British was a phenomenon that seemed to have reached full fruition by the late 1990s. The situation presented counters the widely upheld premise in racially bipolar models of social organization, of the static nature of cultural divisions and black/white cultural separatism.

[4] See the Schutzian treatment of subjective and objective meanings and its political implications (e.g., 1997: 33–38). Groups that will simply not consider any "truth" that does not conform to their interests not only express the fundamental tenet of prejudiced thinking but also demonstrate the operation of power, thus making meaning a key aspect of intergroup political relations.

[5] On the operation of meaning in intergroup power relations, see, for example, Lengermann & Niebrugge, 1995; Camara, 2014.

The importance of meaning as a fundamental regulatory mechanism of human relations may be further explored in reference to the notions of *causal-adequacy* and *meaning-adequacy*. A given course of conduct by individuals will be correctly apprehended when its constituent parts—the overt behavior and the motives behind such behavior—express a "typical complex of meaning," that is, when they are consistent with and reflect what is collectively perceived as "habitual modes of thought and feeling" (Schutz, 1997: 230). The causal-adequacy of such a course of conduct is the probability that, based on experience, it is likely to repeat itself,[6] in accordance with the ideal-typical construct. This general rule, of course, will not obtain, if the course of action does not meet the criteria for adequacy *at the level of meaning*. The calculations (of statistical probability) involved in causal-adequacy must, therefore, in all cases, be subordinate to the requirements pertaining to meaning-adequacy. As Schutz remarks, "all causal adequacy which pertains to human action is based on principles of meaning-adequacy of some kind or another.... [thus being]......*only a special case* of meaning-adequacy" (emphasis mine) (1997: 233–234).

The motivational basis of the behavior of others can only be apprehended (in sufficient measure) in *direct*, face-to-face relationships (i.e., *the We-relation*). In the larger context of daily life, however, people interpret, and relate to, the behavior of others *indirectly*, that is, through *observational understanding*. This type of understanding of the behavior of our contemporaries in the world of everyday life is gained by reference to objective meaning, which, in Schutz's words, is "already constituted and established [in the wider community], abstracted from every subjective flow of experience ...[and]... grasped as an objectification endowed with 'universal meaning' " (1997: 135). Phrased differently, the Other's behavior is interpreted "in a predicative fashion" (Schutz, 1997: 194), that is, in terms of the behavior's externality—the physical body functioning *qua field of expression* (Schutz, 1997: 23) as it manifests itself in the social world. The conduct of the Other, in this sense, is assessed in terms of whether or not it conforms to typical modes of thought and behavior, or ideal types, as already indicated. The *motivational understanding* of the behavior of the other people, on the other hand, entails the apprehension or grasp of the *subjective* meaning of their conduct—of what they have in mind.

The considerations bring to the fore the pivotal role of meaning in social interaction. Intergroup cultural separatism represents the fragmentation of the sociocultural environment—the world of meaning—in which social groups live (Landgrebe, 1940: 46). Therefore, it seems incontrovertible that this condition creates serious problems of mutual communication and understanding in the relations between members of the groups designated as white and non-white. It is true, of course, that despite the impact of established race-based cultural separatism, the coexistence of dominant and nondominant groups within the same sociocultural system, together with their experience of socialization into the core aspects of the national culture, makes it possible for

---

[6]What Schutz called "the coherence of experience" (1997: 232).

everyone, including members of subcultures, to experience others in general "in their typicality" (Schutz, 1970b: 13), at least at the basic level. This process involves the ability to construct ideal-typical patterns of motives, attitudes, goals, and so on, of people as such, toward mutual understanding of the conduct of others. (This process of putting oneself in someone else's shoes parallels the Meadian formulation of *taking the role of a generalized other.*) Still, this process of mutual interpretation will remain beset by difficulties, which are manifested as tensions and antipathies that flare up from time to time. This becomes a more pressing matter for the wider society whenever more forceful and violent public confrontations occur.

4   The Typification of the World

Social life in every society rests on the operation of a vast complex of shared, culturally prescribed, constantly evolving, recipes for collective behavior and understanding, which society's members internalize, take for granted, and follow daily to orient themselves in the lifeworld. Schutz categorizes these as *typifications.* Typifications integrate the social world, and have in fact been called the very blood of daily life (Natanson, 1973: 16), and "the underlying order that sustains our world" (Weigert, 1983: 28–29).They are, essentially, what culture is about.

Social and cultural practices that become established as part of the complex of social typifications are widely objectivated in language. The relationship between language and typification is "an important factor in the formation of customary thought and conduct." Not all of society's typifications are objectified in language, but Schutz and Luckmann still maintain that "[b]y far the largest province of lifeworld typifications is linguistically objectivated" (1973: 234–235, vol. I).

The typifications of a social system are internalized at such a deep level as to acquire an ontological character. That is, members of the society come to equate their very existence with the typified cultural ways they have grown up with. Thus, in the natural attitude, not only do we take for granted the manifold of concrete elements associated with their life in the social world, but also, the naturalness of these elements constitutes the foundation of our social existence. Gurwitsch (1962: 56) addresses thusly this attitude of unquestioning acceptance of the world around us: "Growing into our world and into our society, we have acquired a certain language that embodies the interpretations and typifications ... that prevail in our society and come to be accepted by us as patterns to be followed unquestioningly."

Social interaction is incredibly complex and nuanced. At both the individual and collective levels of human relations, the sharing of the society's majority system of meanings and symbols—which is associated with cultural integration is essential. When this criterion is not operative, the likelihood of intergroup communicative conflict and chaos, and its attendant ramifications, is greatly increased. In this respect, Schutz (1957/1964: 237) asserts, in reference to the

level of mutual understanding required for establishing direct social relationships, that the parties involved must "apply the system of typifications to which
[they] belong," which immediately suggests the difficulties that may arise in
the interaction between ruling and minority groups when their respective
stocks-of-knowledge differ in content—that is, they contain different sets of
typifications. A pertinent example concerning this issue is that of intrasocietal
variations in speech, when the latter are a product of intrasocietal cultural separatism, and manifested as subcultural speech forms.[7] This example not only
brings into focus the importance of linguistic typifications as such, but also,
because these minority speech forms are normally codified as a distinct manifestation of minority-group otherness and inferiority, ties in with the dynamics
of power and power inequality in intergroup life. In this regard, Schutz and
Luckmann maintain that "by far the largest province of lifeworld typifications
is linguistically objectivated" (1973: 234, vol. I), suggesting the macrolevel
significance of this aspect of social life.

Society is a dynamic entity, constantly evolving, which means that social
conditions are always in a provisional state. At any point in the society's evolutionary development, the dominance of majority over minority segments is
clearly shown in the power of the former group to establish the primacy of its
relevance structures (Schutz, 1970a)—sets of interests—over those of the latter.
The concept of relevance runs like a *leitmotif* in Schutz's discussion of social
relations. He distinguishes between three, closely interrelated, classificatory
categories: motivational, thematic, and interpretational. Without dwelling at
length on any of these categories, it may be briefly indicated that they are all
representations of group interest, which then potentially discloses the group's
motivational structure. They comprise, specifically, what group members consider to be relevant in assessing their objective situation—their *definition of the
situation* (Thomas & Thomas, 1928)—and the determination of appropriate
interpretational rules and typifying schemes prior to embarking on specific
courses of action. Taken together, these aspects of relevance have enormous
importance in providing a blueprint and motivational impetus for social action
and are, in this regard, as Dreher reminds us (2011: 499), "a most significant
regulative principle of reality construction."

These relevances are hierarchically organized in the society, being therefore
connected with the dynamics of social power. The ability of ruling groups to
determine what is to become typical or "normal" in the social world comes
down to the process of making their relevance structures (more concretely
understood as their practical interests) prevail over those of less powerful, nondominant groups. As an aspect of the community's stock-of-knowledge,
schemes of relevances do not operate in abstraction from the political life of the

---

[7] In the 1990s the emergence of what came to be known as *ebonics*, a dialectal variation of
S.E. (Standard English), received a great deal of attention and formal support under the auspices
of the politics of identity. This would be interpreted here as minority-group *otherness* manifested
linguistically and supported formally (also see, e.g., Harris, 1997).

society, insofar as dominant-group relevances have primacy over those of everyone else.

Regarding the question of race, this means that the majority racial part of the population has the power to impose its relevance structures and typification systems over those of racial minorities—and ultimately over the entire society. This translates, *latu sensu*, into the ability to determine the nature of social arrangements and practices—and naturally, the patterns of white-nonwhite relations—according to their interests. The conditions of daily life, normally taken for granted by everyone as they engage in the *natural attitude*, stand for the greater power of society's hegemonic groups—those codified as racially white, in this discussion—to build society according to their interests. A useful illustration of the suppressive effect of dominant-group power over minority-group typifications (cultural expressions) may be taken from the historical situation of colonialism: this was the systematic suppression of aboriginal dance forms in Tahiti, Hawaii, and so on, by Protestant missionaries in the early 1800s.

5   ANONYMITY AND SOCIAL INCLUSION

Representation and identity per se are not indicative of social advantage. In fact, from the standpoint of a Schutzian social psychology, the notion of anonymity will be examined as a significant indicator of social inclusion. It confers upon the individual the possibility of being recognized in her/his general relations with others in the *mitwelt* (i.e., the world of contemporaries) in terms of "typical characteristics" (Schutz, 1997: 194), not of what is *atypical*, that is, of the dominant-group constructions of minority subjectivity, which are geared to the designation of otherness. In this connection, fully acculturated persons acquire a quality of generalizability and universality in the social world.

Ordinary (i.e., culturally integrated) individuals normally go about their daily round of activities—the performance of their social functions—in the manner of every other person who performs the same functions. For example, meeting with a group of friends in a public place for conversation and entertainment. Like most other such instances of social action, this situation is carried out fundamentally in the same basic fashion, across the society, but it may deviate, in varying degrees, from the predominant society-wide pattern when the people involved are members of outside groups (i.e., tourists), first-generation immigrants, or subcultures.

Two main versions of social relations are postulated by Schutz: direct and indirect relations. As members of the larger community of interacting actors in society, people pragmatically relate to one another according to typified patterns of behavior and thought, which are deeply ingrained and taken for granted in the collective conscience—phenomenologically stated, in the natural attitude. This describes the indirect type of interaction with others in the world of contemporaries (the *pure They-orientation*), the interacting units functioning as mere ideal types to one another, not as "real people," and interpreting one another by means of objective (i.e., socially established, rather than subjective) meaning-contexts.

By contrast, in the directly experienced relation (the *We-relation*) the basic criterion for understanding the fellow participant is that there be a sharing of the same stream of consciousness or a mutual apprehension of the Other's subjective field. This involves the sharing of objective elements, namely, a common language, and typical behavior and ideas, as a fundamental prerequisite. This is essential if the Other's *stream of consciousness* is to be apprehended; the latter becomes possible if one is able to imagine that it is "flowing side by side with [one's] own."[8] As Schutz remarks, this experience is achieved "only to the extent that I directly experience [the Other] within an *actualized content-filled* We-relationship" (my emphasis) (1997: 166).

The sharing of a "common lived experience" (Schutz, 1997: 171), or an "undivided" cultural environment, which makes it possible for people in the directly experienced relation to grasp the other's subjectivity, allows us to extrapolate from this situation to the discussion of the intergroup encounter. We can gain a sense of what is in the minds of other people out there by reference to the typicality of social life. In this sense, the subjective reality of the individual is transposed to the collectivity; at the same time, the subjective constructions in the minds of individuals are generated from the materials drawn from life in the group, that is, from the group's stock-of-knowledge. The *personal ideal type*, according to Schutz (1997: 190), "is a function of the very question it seeks to answer … it is dependent upon the objective context of meaning [which symbolizes group life]." This suggests a reciprocal relation that to some extent parallels the sociological idea of *seeing the general in the particular* (Berger, 1963).

As a general pattern, members of any given society aspire to be like any other member of that society—that is, to be a generalized other, not some particular other. This consists of being perceived and related to by others in reference to his/her typical characteristics, as having to do with typical behaviors, linguistic patterns, and so on. The social existence of individuals, therefore, must ideally equate them with every other member of the wider community, rather than conferring upon them the identity of *otherness*. It is in this sense of being undistinguishable at the level of meaning, in the eyes of the society as well in their own self-image, that we can speak of the pivotal role of subjective factors in intergroup relations and of the condition of anonymity as being associated with social equality. Persons are no longer singled out as particular others: in the present analysis, as *racial others*. They become a symbol of the universal standard, or generalizability, for the community as a whole. Their typified conduct reflects that of the society. As Schutz remarked in this regard (1997: 195), "[a]nonymity may mean the generality of a typifying scheme."

In racially dichotomous social systems, and in those cases when racial hierarchies in those systems are rigidly enforced through the force of the law—the case of, for example, slavery times and the Jim Crow period in the U.S.—individuals of mixed parentage who were phenotypically close enough to members of the white dominant group to *pass* for white would have fallen into the sea of

---

[8] The notion of *being on the same page* with someone else in contemporary U.S. culture is roughly equivalent to sharing a stream of consciousness with the other person, to living in the other person's subjective meaning-context.

phenotypically undifferentiated persons making up the white population. They were perceived to be like everybody else. Their life situation, therefore, would have changed drastically. If a slave, a person in this condition would have been able to flee the plantation setting and mingle freely anywhere with the general population. During the Jim Crow era, this person would move about even more freely, without the severe physical and social constraints normally forced upon African-Americans during the period. If discovered, punishment would be swift and harsh, in both cases. Being able to "pass" meant that the public appearance of these individuals could only be expressed in the most careful, limited, and guarded of ways, through very basic typical patterns of behavior. Their linguistic typifications, given their subcultural origin (i.e., their experience of having lived under the rigidly separatist conditions of the plantation, and of Jim Crow, respectively), would have been a dead giveaway. Their newly gained freedom and equality under the auspices of anonymity—that is, of the protection afforded by ideal-typical representation as general (rather than particular) members of the community—was still precarious and short-lived, given their prior life of separation from the dominant meaning-system (cultural lifestyle) of the society.

6   Assimilation vs. Exclusion: Political Implications

As stated above, immigrants do not typically aim to remain differentiated from the new society's general population indefinitely but rather seek to become fully integrated into the new sociocultural environment. It is true that the immediate concern of these individuals is to experience structural (i.e., economic, political, educational) integration, but ultimately and ideally, the assimilative process must translate into full-scale inclusion of the newcomers in *all* areas of social life.[9] By the second generation the society, in most cases, will

---

[9] This applies in societies across the board, but in those which enforce a racially bipolar social organization, such as the U.S., a dual pattern of assimilation of incoming groups, based on the white/nonwhite distinction, has been the prevailing practice. It may be useful at this point to elaborate on the cultural experience of the *white ethnics* in the U.S. and the groups codified as nonwhite. Where minority ethnic-racial communities are concerned, formal and informal separatism, together with various forms and degrees of discrimination, has a strong psychological effect on the minority persons involved, as manifested, for instance, in problems of identity. These aspects were registered by Clark (1957: ch. 3) in research done at a time when Jim Crow arrangements were still in effect. They had to do with general feelings of inferiority, self-hatred, frustration, and humiliation—in other words, with unnecessary psychological burdens and turmoil centered on the recognition of having inferior social identity. When the minority group is no longer burdened by formally sanctioned segregation and discrimination, but remains culturally segregated, the sense of social dislocation and estrangement—of *otherness*—of its members does not entirely disappear, even when these individuals experience significant advancement in the formal sectors of social life. That is, this effect may persist independently of the political, economic, or educational placement of these individuals in the social hierarchy. Ultimately, this has a self-perpetuating effect. Insufficient cultural inclusion leads to attachment to subcultural modes of living, continuing otherness vis-à-vis the majority cultural pattern, further cultural exclusion, and so forth.

The assimilative experience and corresponding sense of identity of the white-ethnic groups, expectedly, differ in a significant way in that these individuals tend to be incorporated at all levels of the assimilative process (see also Spinasse, 2008, for a discussion of the assimilation of Germans in Brasil).

have completely absorbed them. The obstacles to assimilation associated with the first generation will have essentially disappeared, and the descendants of the newcomers will have been assimilated structurally, biologically, culturally, and psychologically.

The political implications of the assimilative process stand out more clearly in cases of pluralist (i.e., separatist), racially bipolar social systems, where the level and form of acceptance of incoming groups is strongly regulated by ascribed (racial) status. For the incoming groups classified as nonwhite full-scale inclusion into national life normally remains out of reach. They may, over time, experience varying amounts of *structural* integration (i.e., into the economic, political, and educational spheres) but are not completely absorbed at the cultural, biological, and psychological levels. As a result, these groups are forced to forge subcultural lifestyles and cultural systems, which crystallize over time and carry injurious consequences for them, namely, their existence as permanent others in the larger society and their permanent confinement to minority status and its attendant ills, both symbolic and material.

In these societies cultural separatism works as a pivotal support of white political rule. The boundary lines that separate the dominant and minority cultural models have, in recent decades, been protected at all costs *by both* the dominant and nondominant racial communities. Regarding the dominant group, this is done because of its concern with maintaining a mythologized conception of white culture as the absolute, pure standard for society and a representation of the group's political privilege. Regarding the minority community, it is invested in the preservation of its cultural uniqueness for psychological and political reasons in that its subcultural difference *vis-à-vis* the national model is not only embraced as a basis of identity but also utilized as a mechanism for maximizing its political and economic representation in the society-at-large.

Some considerations about the issue of cultural appropriation and the nature of culture may be of service here. The culture of a given society may be defined as "the total, socially acquired lifestyle of a group of people, including their patterned, repetitive ways of thinking, feeling, and acting" (Harris, 1997: 88). It operates in terms of the cohesive interrelatedness of its component traits. Some of these traits may stand out for the cohesive and intense form in which they are manifested, thus eventually leading to the emergence of what sociology and anthropology designate as national character.

Therefore, amidst all the variety—regional, religious, socioeconomic, ethnic, racial, and so on—expected to operate in any given society, something "common to life" cutting across the diverse areas and levels of daily life produces uniformity in a degree sufficiently high to distinguish the society from any other. As Perry (1949: 4–5) says, the melting pot not only dissolves the differences but unifies them into a "broth with an unmistakable flavor of its own."

The idea of cultural appropriation runs counter to the canonical views of culture outlined here. It is a function, and dysfunction, of racially bipolar social organization and the race-based naturalization of cultural identity, which is conducive to the permanent characterization of minority communities as *others*. A crucial premise of racist ideology is that the cultural traits of a group as well as the lifestyle variations across the racial parts of the population defined as white and nonwhite are a fixed, essential (i.e., biologically determined) property of these groups. This view contradicts the actual nature of culture as something fluid and dynamic, and in constant syncretic interrelation with the customs and practices of other groups. Hence, it stands in the way of cultural integration.

In the U.S., the dissemination of minority (sub)cultural expressions has been going on for decades and was operative, to a lesser extent, even during the Jim Crow period—that is, these cultural expressions entered the parameters of dominant-group life and were significantly absorbed in some instances. A case in point is the influence, over the last century, of the (West) African musical heritage (not undiluted, but mixed) on white musicians and the general public. One television documentary (*The 1990s*) suggested that during that decade, in U.S. cultural life, aspects of black culture (e.g., music, clothing styles) were adopted by the general population. This suggests that after the divisive patterns of social life during the Jim Crow era were eradicated in the early 1970s, the dominant white group shifted toward embracing and encouraging minority-group cultural features.

This may, at first glance, suggest cultural integration in true syncretic form, but in reality it merely consists of the adoption of these traits *qua minority-group* traits by the dominant group.[10] The cultural gap between the majority

---

[10] Given the naturalization of majority and minority ways of living, and the intersubjective recognition (for the population as a whole) of a quasi-metaphysical separation between the white and nonwhite parts of the population, the exchange of cultural traits between them does not conform to the model of syncretism put forward by Bastide (1971). As a rule, syncretized cultural forms would be alien, an aberration, in the separatist social order. To illustrate, when jazz music began to evolve and spread in the U.S. in the first quarter of the twentieth century, this was a highly seductive, sensually overpowering type of musical experience for the young white middle-class set of the time. It allowed for greater sexual intimacy on the dance floor, but everyone understood this to be an expression of black culture, not "American" (i.e., white) culture, which was still wedded to the more "respectable" European-American musical forms (e.g., the fox-trot, the waltz).

The strongly negative reaction on the part of the older generation of white Americans toward black musical culture was revealed in the fact that, no less than Henry Ford, the legendary industrialist, sponsored and funded a folk dance crusade, where such dance styles as the Virginia reel were cultivated. Additionally, as is well known, white musicians gradually incorporated elements of jazz into their own playing style, producing a kind of music that blended those elements with European syncopation. These syncretized musical forms became hugely popular nationwide—for example, Big Band music and swing music of the 1930s and 1940s. As jazz music found its way into the recording industry, and jazz records began to be produced and sold on a large scale (e.g., Bessie Smith's blues recordings), the music came to be known as *race records*. This underscores the status of jazz as a phenomenon outside the mainstream of American sociocultural life (i.e., outside "white civilization").

and minority parts of the population, therefore, remains largely undisturbed, to this day, which means that the phenomenon in question does not involve the merger, at the national level, of different cultural strains into a syncretically formed product, to which all members of the society have equal claim.[11] Rather, it involves the unilateral appropriation (construction) of the subjectivity of the Other. The unilateral nature of this relation is seen in the absence of full-measure interpenetration of the cultural elements involved, inasmuch as, as has been repeatedly stated here, the end of the Jim Crow system was not followed by the cultural integration of the groups involved. The distinctiveness of the minority group, which stemmed from slavery conditions first, then from 70-odd years of Jim Crow segregation, was preserved. Therefore, the subcultural nature of the minority group has been largely characterized by the practice of eschewing any cultural aspect perceived to be associated with the white dominant group.[12]

7   CULTURAL INTEGRATION AND INTERGROUP LIFE

The cornerstone of this study is the idea that, within any human community, cultural integration is the *conditio sine qua non* of mutual intelligibility among social groups. The central idea in this respect is that the greater the degree of integration of society's members into the national culture, the greater the access of everyone to the motivational basis of the behavior of everyone else. This holds especially true when it involves the interaction between the majority part of the population and subcultures.

---

[11] The idea of common ownership of cultural products within a given national community may be illustrated here with the example of Brazilian society. In principle, any member of that society is able to identify with, or claim ownership of, any aspect of the overall culture or subset of it. The cultural elements in question include things as diverse as, for example, the national dance form—the samba, a product of the mixture of European and West African musical traditions; the folk tales of Amerindian origin; the abstract paintings of the Brazilian modernists of the 1920s; the syncretized folk Catholicism, heavily imbued with West African religious influences; the *feijoada*, a dish which originated in the slave quarters of Brazilian plantations in the 1800s, and is now Brazil's national dish.

[12] In connection with the enduring effect of intergroup separatism in U.S. society, it is worth considering here the remarks by Dollard (1957: 418) who, in the 1930s, draws attention to the subcultural mode of existence for the African-American population and to the fact that "a different kind of collective conscience has been standardized in the Negro group." In 1908, the second decade of Jim Crow, Charles Francis Adams (cited in Frazier, 1957: 687) presciently addressed the deep-seated character of racial separatism in U.S. society, by stating that African-Americans would be "only partially assimilated" and would not become [culturally] absorbed. At that time, he added, the "Negro" was and would remain "an alien element in the body politic ... a foreign substance."

This section draws together the major points made so far. We have addressed the two principal modes of social relations in the Schutzian system, to wit, social relationships "between contemporaries," involving people who, as Schutz (1997: 181)says, "coexist[s] with me in time, but whom I do not experience immediately," and the closer, more intimate, face-to-face direct relation. In the one, the social actor appeals to objective meaning in order to grasp the behavior of others. In the other, subjective meaning is the primary means of apprehension of the Other.

In the indirect relation, the scheme of typical conduct that the social actor-*qua*-interpreter imputes to all other persons is assumed to apply to her/his own conduct as well. Implicit here is the assumption on the interpreter's part that: "This is what I would do if I were in this situation." This aspect of interchangeability linked to the society-wide typicality of behavior is of first importance, as explained earlier. In both types of situations the people involved are assumed to *share* the same interpretive scheme, that is, the same cultural environment.

The actor's interpretation of the behavior of others undergoes constant revision as sociocultural change occurs. For instance, over the last couple of decades the high-five gesture (in which one person slaps the upraised palm of the hand against that of another) has become ever more widespread and ingrained in U.S. culture, very much part of the repertoire of typified behaviors of the population. It is not interpreted as an overture to physical aggression, as might have been the case several decades ago, but rather as an expression of celebration, congratulation, or even a greeting.

Given the historical framework of racial inequality against which this problem must be addressed, some critical repercussions of established separatism, beyond the immediate difficulties of dominant-minority communication and the possibly frequent upsurges of tension and animosities, will be thrown into relief. The problem of identity for members of the subaltern racial community stands out significantly, insofar as the permanent imputation of *otherness* by the hegemonic racial group generates problems of self-esteem for them (feelings of inadequacy, inferiority, etc.). This often results in tendencies of self-exclusion from the national mainstream, in particular, to use the appropriate terminology, the rejection of white meaning, that is, of all that is interpreted by non-white people as pertaining to the cultural life of the white group. One aspect of it is the rejection of traditional conceptions and practices of social achievement, which has been thematized as the *ethos of nonachievement* (see, e.g., Gregory, 1992; also, Lacayo, 1989). Needless to say, this particular ramification of separatism exerts a deeply harmful effect on the subaltern group. Inevitably, it leads to further entrenchment in subcultural living and separation from national life, more social disadvantage and differentiation from the majority pattern of living, further assignment of negative meanings to minority group life, further self-exclusion, and so forth. A vicious circle of prejudice and social exclusion is set in motion.

Race-based intergroup separatism vitiates the communicative process between people from majority and minority racial groups, respectively, in both modes of social interaction. discussed. Not only does it limit the ability of members of one group to correctly interpret the meaning of the conduct of the other, by recourse to its typicality, to objective meaning (the mode of understanding of others' behavior called observational), but also, and even more cogently, in the directly experienced, less anonymous, lived relation. This is because the interpretive schemes, the relevances, typifications, and so on, that members of each group will appeal to in their quest to understand the typicality of behavior of the other group in each mode of interaction will be drawn from separate stocks-of-knowledge. This creates a gap between the majority-group and subcultural meaning-contexts. Culturally differentiated groups are more likely to fail to meet the expectations, on each other's part, of typical behavior and thought, thus paving the way for interpretive and communicative breakdown ("interactional chaos"; Weigert, 1983: 76–77; see also Weigert, 1975) and/or aggressive confrontations.

The history of social groups sustains the current ways and acting and thinking of individuals in the collectivity. In connection with this, it is fitting to consider Schutz's view (1997: 27–30) concerning the importance of the past and future circumstances of people in determining what can be taken for granted as typical about them. Put differently, these circumstances shape their cultural make-up. Concerning the stable and durable nature of cultural differences between the dominant and minority racial segments of the population, the past circumstances of these segments will obviously be different, given their historical asymmetrical power standings in the society. That being the case, the subjective life of both groups will be influenced differently by each group's history, and the maintenance of cultural separatism will prevent these two separate sets of historical circumstances from merging into a unified history of the national community as a whole. The subjective life of members of the ruling racial group will therefore continue to be influenced by a history of domination over the other group. The subjective life of members of the minority racial group will therefore continue to be influenced by a history of subordination to the other group. Again, this dual pattern, stemming from long-standing power inequality between the two groups, will endure as long as race-based power inequality and dominant/minority cultural fragmentation endure.

In contrastive perspective, cultural integration yields different results. The historical backgrounds of particular groups in the society are all treated as parts of the national history, something that is shared and identified with by *all* members of the society, something seen as belonging to all and pertaining to all—not just a separate property of some specific subcultural community. It is in this sense of universal, unqualified sharing of the national culture—its practices and ways of thinking—and the resulting undifferentiated cultural condition of the population that cultural integration may be considered as a vitally important source of social equality. The contrast here is stark in relation to intergroup relations under cultural separatism, in which the meaning-context of the other group is, by and large, a kind of *terra incognita*. Groups that have been historically driven into a subcultural lifestyle owing to the physical and symbolic constraints of legally upheld segregation have to contend daily with the divergence of meaning-contexts in a manner that parallels the experience of the Schutzian stranger (Schutz, 1944), except that in the latter case the experience was temporary and occurred *in a foreign land*.

Affairs of consciousness, more precisely the aspect of meaning, have been shown in this analysis to play a role of cardinal importance in the constitution of sociocultural life and, more specifically, in intergroup relations and the establishment of power relations between these groups. This work has drawn on Schutz's discussion of meaning and social relations in the effort to demonstrate the importance of cultural integration as a key element in race relations and equality. The meaning-contexts, or modes of thinking and perceiving, of groups lie at the foundation of human action, in that they structure the way members of society create and pursue particular patterns of coexistence with others.

REFERENCES

Bastide, R. (1971). *African civilizations in the new world*. C. Hurst.

Berger, P. L. (1963). *Invitation to sociology: A humanistic perspective*. Anchor Books.

Camara, E. (2003). Dimensões Ontológicas de Raça e Cultura em Sistemas Binários. In *Estudos de Sociologia* (pp. 71–90). UFPE.

Camara, E. (2014). Estrutura e Significado: Implicações Fenomenológicas e Politicas do Sotaque Regional Brasileiro. *Interdisciplinary Journal of Portuguese Diaspora Studies, 3*(1), 155–176.

Camara, E. (2021). *The critical phenomenology of intergroup life: Race relations in the social world*. Lexington Books.

Clark, K. B. (1957). *Prejudice and your child*. The Beacon Press.

de Queiroz, M. I. P. (1979). Principe de participation et principe de coupure. La contribution de Roger Bastide à leur définition sociologique. In *Archives de Sciences Sociales de Religion*: Editions de l'EHESS.

Dollard, J. (1957). *Caste and class in a Southern town*. Doubleday.

Dreher, J. (2011). Alfred Schutz. In G. Ritzer (Ed.), *The Wiley-Blackwell companion to major social theorists* (pp. 489–510). Wiley-Blackwell.

Ferguson, H. (2006). *Phenomenological sociology: Experience and insight in modern society*. Sage.

Franklin, J. H. (1997). Ethnicity in American life: The historical perspective. In Virginia Cyrus (Org.), *Experiencing race, class, and gender in the United States*. Mayfield Publishing Co.

Frazier, E. F. (1957). *The Negro in America*. Rinehart, and Winston.

Gates, H. L. (1997). Black London. *The New Yorker*, April 20–May 5, pp. 195–205.

Gregory, S. S. (1992). The hidden hurdle. *Time*, March 16, pp. 44–46.

Guest, K. J. (2017). *Cultural anthropology: A toolkit for a global age*. W.W. Norton.

Gurwitsch, A. (1962). The Common-Sense World as Social Reality: A Discourse on Alfred Schutz. *Social Research, 29*(1), 50–72.

Harris, M. (1997). *Culture, people, nature: An introduction to cultural anthropology* (7th ed.). Longman.

Knox, Robert. (1850). *The races of men: A fragment.* Lea and Blanchard.

Lacayo, R. (1989). Between two worlds. *Time*, March 13, pp. 58–68.

Landgrebe, L. (1940). The world as a phenomenological problem. *Philosophy and Phenomenological Research, 1*, 35–58.

Lengermann, P., & Niebrugge, J. (1995). Intersubjectivity and domination: A feminist investigation of the sociology of Alfred Schutz. *Sociological Theory, 13*(March), 25–36.

Lévy-Bruhl, L. (1910). *Les Fonctions Mentales Dans Les Societés Inférieures.* Librairies Alcan & Guillaumin Réunis.

Natanson, M. (1973). *Phenomenology and the social sciences.* Northwestern University Press.

Perry, R. B. (1949). *Characteristically American.* Alfred A. Knopf.

Schutz, A. (1944). The stranger: An essay in social psychology. *American Journal of Sociology, 49*(May), 499–507.

Schutz, A. (1957/1964). Equality and the Meaning-Structure of the Social World. In Arvid Brodersen (ed.) *Collected Papers II.* The Hague: Martinus Nijhoff.

Schutz, A. (1970a). *Reflections on the problem of relevance* (R. Zaner, Ed.). Yale University Press.

Schutz, A. (1970b). Concept and theory formation in the social sciences. In D. Emmett & A. MacIntyre (Eds.), *Sociological theory and philosophical analysis.* Macmillan.

Schutz, A. (1997). *The phenomenology of the social world* (G. Walsh & F. Lehnert, Trans.). Northwest University Press.

Schutz, A., & Luckmann, T. (1973). *The structures of the lifeworld.* Vols. I and II (R. M. Zaner & H. T. Engelhardt Jr., Trans.). Northwestern University Press.

Spinasse, K. P. (2008). Os Imigrantes Alemães e seus Descendentes no Brasil: A Língua como Fator Identitário e Inclusivo. *Revista Conexão Letras, 3*(3).

Sumner, W. G. (1906/1960). *Folkways.* Mentor Books.

Thomas, W. I. (1937). *Primitive behavior: An introduction to the social sciences.* McGraw-Hill.

Thomas, W. I., & Thomas, D. S. (1928). *The child in America.* Knopf.

Weigert, A. (1975). Alfred Schutz on a theory of motivation. *The Pacific Sociological Review, 18*(1), 83–102.

Weigert, A. (1983). *Social psychology: A sociological approach through interpretive understanding.* The University of Notre Dame Press.

Cultural Objects with or Without Cultural Difference?

Chung-Chi Yu

1 INTRODUCTION

My chapter inquires into the ambiguity of how Husserl conceives of cultural objects. On the one hand, by introducing the concept of experiential world he points out the universal structure of cultural objects; yet, on the other hand, he recognizes the aspect of cultural difference that is inherent in the concept of cultural object.

The chapter explores the significance of such ambiguity by pointing out its similarity to Husserl's own ideas about "the experience of the other" [*Fremderfahrung*]. On this basis, the chapter will evoke Waldenfels' notion of other [*das Fremde*]. Provided that "the accessibility of the originally inaccessible" is valid not only for the experience of the other person but also for the experience of cultural objects, the concept of cultural object is to be discussed in the broad framework of relation between lifeworld, homeworld, and alienworld. While the intertwining relationship between different cultures is recognized in this regard, this chapter holds that in encountering cultural objects from alien cultures the respect for the difference of cultural objects should not fall victim to the identification of the common of all cultures, as Husserl ultimately seems to do.

C.-C. Yu (✉)
National Sun Yat-sen University, Taipei, Taiwan
e-mail: ccyuster@g-mail.nsysu.edu.tw

© The Author(s), under exclusive license to Springer Nature
Switzerland AG 2023
C. Belvedere, A. Gros (eds.), *The Palgrave Handbook of Macrophenomenology and Social Theory*,
https://doi.org/10.1007/978-3-031-34712-2_11

2   I

What are cultural objects, and how does Husserl conceive of them? Obviously, they are distinguished from natural objects that exist within causal relations in nature. Cultural objects, namely, belong to the cultural dimension that human beings create. Cultural objects are historical and, most of all, spiritual, insofar as they result from the creative activities of human beings. However, cultural objects are also real objects, as they belong to material realities. They are spiritually created, yet materially based. The dual aspect of cultural objects permits us to view them in two different ways. Either we see them as realities, real things in causal connections, or we see exclusively the ideal aspect of them, treating them as ideal objects (Hua IX, pp. 400-401). Both ways of treating cultural objects are misleading, however, because the first sees only the natural side, whereas the second sees only the spiritual aspect. Cultural objects are something in-between. They are corporeal-spiritual objects [*körperlich-geistige Gegenständlichkeit*] (Hua IX, p. 111). Put differently, they comprise two layers: the "*sinnliche Unterlage*" and the "*aufgestufte Kultur-Bedeutung.*" Both the *sinnliche* and the *außersinnliche* aspects are equally essential (Hua IX, p. 404). The first component of cultural objects can be reached as a result of abstraction from the concrete cultural meaning. Cultural objects can thus become pure reality (Hua IX, p. 118). This is a result of the dismissal of their spiritual, mental aspects, that is, as long as the originally spiritual [*das Urgeistige*] is ignored. We thus see only pure physical things, the *res extensa* proposed by Descartes (Hua IX, p. 380).

Husserl suggests interpreting both layers, the *sinnliche Unterlage* and the *aufgestufte Kultur-Bedeutung*, with the help of the distinction between real physical units [*reale physische Einheit*], which are temporally individualized, and the irreal, ideal unit of significance [*irreale, ideale Einheit von Bedeutungen*] (Hua IX, p. 398). This distinction is well known since his early major work, *Logical Investigations.*

Significance can be incorporated into different material media. For example, the same mathematical theorem can be printed in different books and with different colored printouts (Hua IX: 400; 503). Similarly, a musical melody can be played by different musical instruments, be it a flute or a piano, and it can also be recorded by a recorder of whatever kind, be it analog or digital.

The irreal, ideal unit of significance can be repeated in different embodiments because it constitutes the essential, identical part of cultural objects. Yet we should not overemphasize such ideal aspects of cultural objects, because without embodiment cultural objects lose their essential characteristics as such. The real, physical aspect of cultural objects should never be sacrificed, for cultural objects are also objects existing in the spatiotemporal world in terms of causal determinations. Defined by Husserl as a mind on objects in the surrounding world [*eine Seele an umweltlichen Gegenstände*] (Hua IX, p. 229), culture is what it is only when related both to the subjective and natural aspects, which constitute the in-between of subject and object or the in-between of spirit and nature. As a consequence, cultural objects possess both *sinnlicher Leib* and *besonderer Sinn*, and they never lose their character as worldly objects [*Weltobject*] (Hua IX, p. 502).

3   II

Cultural objects result from production—and production is done for the sake of certain purposes. That is to say, cultural objects always serve some particular ends. The original meaning of cultural objects can be traced back to the activities of creative subjects, who intend the meaning and purpose of these objects and express their meaning through production or creation.[1] The users or beholders can comprehend such a meaning. Taking a weapon as an example, Husserl points out that the purpose of the weapon that is expressed by the intentionality of the producers can be captured by the warriors, for whom the weapon serves as an instrument for fighting (Hua IX, pp. 113-114; Husserl, 1977, p. 86). This example shows that cultural objects are not only meaningful to the producers but also always located in a web of social relations, that is, within a certain cultural group that serves as the background for cultural objects as products.

Besides, cultural objects, in particular the useful ones, are produced and comprehended as objects of a certain type. In accordance with a purpose-meaning [*Zwecksinn*], they serve as instruments to this end. Therefore, any object that fulfills the same purpose can be treated as a cultural object of the same type. For example, an arrow is regarded as an arrow in terms of the type "arrow"; its individuality does not play any role (Hua IX, p. 117).

As mentioned above, cultural objects have a cultural significance that is determined as an "*außersinnlicher Charakter.*" This character cannot be explained through natural properties but only through cultural sense. However, such cultural sense is always different from culture to culture, which means that the cultural significance of cultural objects cannot claim to be universally valid. Rather, it is rather restricted to its own circle. Husserl gives the following example:

> Even though Bantu people (or any people who have no "access" to our world) treat us as persons and experience us as subjects who actually or possibly have mutual understanding with them, they nevertheless do not experience us as

---

[1] In regard to the origin of cultural sense, Molly Frigid Flynn explains, "Understanding cultural objects, including words, requires, first, the recognizing the living body's fullness-of-soul, and second, noticing how its spirituality spreads to things involved in the body's movement" (Flynn, 2012, pp. 73-74). She also points out that "all cultural sense begins here. The spirit of the person, which animates the person's living body, animates also things in the world by way of the person's bodily involvement with them" (p. 73). Flynn emphasizes that cultural sense originates from the human body's engagement with cultural objects through the evocation of spirit, without necessarily producing or utilizing them. However, one may question whether the human body can engage with natural objects in the same way. If this is the case, it becomes difficult to distinguish between cultural and natural objects, resulting in a loss of the specificity of cultural sense.

Europeans, as scientists, in particular mathematician, geographers etc. or as employees, engineers, landlords, young nobles etc. – to sum up, we as what we actually are.... The Bantu people seem to "see" our "parks", our houses, churches among other things, these things are in their eyes spatial objects, and some of them seem to be characterized as buildings or gardens. However, there is difference. As regards the space-time determinations, the pure nature, there must be some commonness, nevertheless when the question is related to the reason why those buildings are constructed in that manner, relevantly, when the question is related to the aesthetic or practical "meaning", then it is beyond the comprehension of the Bantu people. (Hua IX, p. 498)[2]

There is a cultural *gestalt* [*Kulturgestalt*] in every cultural circle (Hua IX, p. 491), just like every single person is characterized by his life-gestalt [*Lebensgestalt*] (Hua IX, p. 489). The cultural world is a historical world. Cultural objects have historicity, which refers to the living sphere of a certain cultural group. The cultural world is a world in which people share some common norms of actions and styles of perceptions, which facilitate their mutual understanding. People outside of this cultural circle, however, do not share these norms and styles. Viewed by insiders, for example, Europeans, the Bantu people from Africa are outsiders; they have difficulty seeing the cultural significance of European cultural objects. The cultural significance of the cultural objects belonging to Europeans is, so to speak, limited to the Europeans.

In a word, cultural objects involve cultural difference (Hua IX, p. 497), and every cultural world is more or less enclosed in itself. As Husserl sees it, the *personale Eidetik* is the discipline that deals with the essential characteristics of every culture, which includes the stable form of intentionality prevalent in the cultural group. It studies how the lifeworld of a cultural group is constituted. According to Husserl, every particular culture is related to a certain kind of humanness [*Menschentum*], which generates a sort of noetic *a priori* [*noetisches Apriori*] in the cultural group (Hua IX, p. 500). This specific form of humanness can be transmitted from generation to generation and helps shape or substantiate the tradition of this culture. A certain sociocultural group is thus a historical unity, and this particular style of humanness develops toward a specific "personality," which lays ground for mutual communication between people of the same group. In general, the cultural objects play a pivotal role in such communication because they function as the medium of mutual understanding.

4   III

The cultural world of a certain cultural group makes up what Husserl later calls "homeworld" [*Heimwelt*], in contrast to alienworld [*Fremdwelt*] (Hua XV, pp. 214; 219; 431-432). The notion of homeworld, scattered throughout

---

[2] Similar examples are to be found in regard to the difference between Europe and China, see Hua XXXIX (p. 159).

Husserliana XV, refers to the normal lifeworld of the "homecomrades." Normality is the result of tradition, which is transmitted from generation to generation. Generality [*Generalität*] is the key notion in Husserl's descriptions of both the homeworld and the alienworld. The alienworld is thus understood as the world with which the homecomrades lack a common tradition, that is, no common forerunners through generations. Since tradition and history shape cultural characteristics, the differences between homeworld and alienworld can be viewed as differences in culture.

Now, Husserl raises the question: Can cultural differences be surpassed or overcome? Is there a common core for both the homeworld and the alienworld? (Hua IX, p. 498). Husserl seems to be optimistic by introducing the idea of the one world [*die eine Welt*][3] and suggesting there has to be a commonly recognizable core accessible to all people regardless of cultural backgrounds.

When we look at facts related to the real worlds of different personal communities, we encounter the following difficulty: Is there still an objective world along with different worlds? Let us look at the question in accordance with consciousness: Are people from different communities unable to understand each other? Do they share the same world? Is there not this same sun, star, earth, and so on, for all? When people argue with each other, no matter which culture they belong to, they become persons for each other, and they all belong to the object-world [*Objektwelt*]. For them there exists the universal world for all human beings. At the same time, as mentioned above, this world continues to exist naturally[4] (Hua IX, p. 380).

But one might wonder, what are the contents of such a common ground for all cultural worlds? Is it still a world of culture? Husserl seems to deny this by saying: "The experiential world is concrete; it is given in original perception. But if it is accessible to all people in accordance with perception, it refers to nature" (Hua IX, p. 380).

When the common ground is deprived of cultural sense, it seems to become the world of nature. But is it the world of pure nature? Does what Husserl means by nature in such a context denote nature seen through the eyes of natural scientists? Obviously, he denies that. Husserl rejects the idea that the common core is a world irrelevant to the subjects, pointing out that the nature in the lifeworld is not the nature in natural science (Hua IX, p. 401).

---

[3] According to Klaus Held's interpretation, this "one world" is constituted in the same way as the intersubjectivity illuminated in the Fifth Cartesian Meditation. Just like the other subject (alter ego) is to be recognized through his body, especially through the similarity of his body and mine, so is the forerunner of the other cultural world recognizable through basic human phenomena like birth and death. The experience of generality creates so to speak the bridge between culture and culture (Held, 1991).

[4] See Hua IX (p. 380) and Hua XV (p. 632), where Husserl says, "For all that, no matter how foreign, there is commonality, earth and heaven, day and night, stones and trees, mountain and valley, diverse animals—everything that can be grasped analogically in the most general type, albeit as strange." I take this citation from Dermot Moran (2011, p. 463-494).

What, then, is such a common core? What does Husserl refer to when he says that what is common to all possible worlds is the natural world, the world devoid of cultural sense? In this a context, Husserl brings up the natural world concept [*natürlicher Weltbegriff*], of which he says: "The natural world-concept is the structure of identity that is valid for all the people throughout all the various surrounding worlds" (Hua IX, p. 493).

It is a concrete world that can be experienced in its reality, ultimately given in original perception (Hua IX, p. 380). Two closely related concepts, the personalistic attitude [*personale Einstellung*] and the experiential world [*Erfahrungswelt*], will help clarify the natural world concept and should be elaborated next.

The personalistic attitude is the attitude that the human being assumes when dealing with things in the surrounding world. This attitude involves interest in the meaning and value of things, and in it:

> My body is […] given for me in the surrounding world as the center of the rest of the surrounding world, as a spatial thing of the surrounding world with somatic properties, in which I hold sway, and even as that by which I exercise an influence upon the rest of the surrounding world, etc. (Hua IX, p. 228; Husserl, 1977, p. 175)

This attitude is definitely different from the naturalistic attitude that exclusively has interest in pure nature, which is deprived of value and meaning. For Husserl, the surrounding world is related to the personalistic attitude, and pure nature results from the abstraction from this attitude (Hua IV, p. 185). Originally, the world is never independent of our experiences. The items we encounter are never just natural things but always involve significations beyond pure nature, not to mention the persons we encounter. As a person, I am living in the world with all these things and other persons. The sociocultural science deals with the personal subject living in his surrounding, cultural world (Hua XXVII, p. 211). In this situation, things around him are significant [*bedeutsam*] (Hua IX, p. 111; Husserl, 1977, p. 84). Husserl even notes that between the personal subject and his objects there is an intertwining relationship (Hua IX, p. 226; Husserl, 1977, p. 173).

Thus seen, the eidetic description of the personalistic attitude can provide us with an appropriate approach to understand the world that is common to all people regardless of cultural difference. Husserl calls a study of this world "the eidetic study of the world of natural experience" [*die Eidetik der natürlichen Erfahrungswelt*] (Hua IX, p. 225). Insofar as this science aims at describing the *a priori* of the experiential world, it is close to phenomenological psychology as "a most general science of the world" [*eine allgemeinste Weltwissenschaft*] (Hua IX, p. 225).

Phenomenological psychology, the universal science of the world or "the eidetic study of the world of natural experience," is to be characterized as *a priori*, eidetic, intuitive, descriptive, and intentional. In addition to that, it remains in the natural attitude instead of adopting the transcendental attitude. *A priori* implies that between subject and world there is a universal structure that is revealed through constant styles and types. Such *a priori* universal structures make up the presuppositions of daily life. Yet these presuppositions often go unnoticed. Even the subject involved does not pay attention to them. In daily life, people are preoccupied with all kinds of matters that concern their existence. One needs to step back in order to get in touch with these presuppositions and with the subject that has been constantly co-functioning. What is hinted at is none other than what Husserl means by phenomenological reduction.

Through reduction we become aware of the presuppositions of daily life and come in touch with the experiential world. As Husserl explains, "by the title 'experiential world' we mean clearly what makes up the unity of concordant total actuality which is continually reestablished in the course of our experiences" (Hua IX, p. 59; Husserl, 1977, p. 44).

The world is a world related to the subject, not just the world of pure nature, as mentioned above. Such an experiential world has a universal structure that is revealed in stable types and styles. On the one hand, the structure is related to the subject; on the other, to the world. The subject and the world are just correlated to each other.

Husserl points out further that the experiential world, with its eidetic structure, is the "all-inclusive world for natural sciences and socio-cultural sciences" (Hua IX, p. 232; Husserl, 1977, p. 178). It contains the world truth [*Weltwahrheit*] (Hua IX, p. 63; Husserl, 1977, p. 47) that constitutes the basis for all truths in factual sciences, be they natural or sociocultural. Based on the truth of this world, we can be sure about truth in scientific knowledge. The world is a domain of prescientific experience, the structures of which are reflected in other sciences (Hua IX, pp. 64, 46, 232; Husserl 197, pp. 33, 47, 178).

Thus, the experiential world is the foundation of all scientific research. The experience has it that, as human beings living in the natural attitude, people hold lots of unshakable beliefs that concern the reality and totality of the world. We accept it as firmly as possible. But that which is revealed in original experiences is for Husserl much too contaminated by the scientific culture, which is why we may find it extremely difficult to return to the original world and recognize it as such. It is for this reason that Husserl repeatedly recommends the use of the phenomenological reduction, which helps overcome such difficulties.

The investigation of cultural objects serves as a clue to the phenomenological study of the core of human experience. The meaning of cultural objects, no matter how subjective-relative it is, no matter how diversely different it is from culture to culture, remains a subject worthy of eidetic research. As Husserl argues:

No matter how clear or unclear such a science is, how valid or entirely invalid, just like all the human works, they belong to the moments of the world as the world of pure experience. For this reason, they may provide us with a point of departure in regard to the investigation into the pure experience of the world, that is to say, they lead to the description of the universal field of the spiritual culture and make us aware of the structural differentiation of the concrete contents of the experience that belongs to the experiential world, for example the subjectivity of the human being and animal, or the cultural constructs that at first sight are not in principle clearly enough articulated. (Hua IX, p. 380)

The study of cultural objects counts as the pre-stage to the study of the experiential world with the help of the natural world concept and the personalistic attitude. The personalistic attitude is the attitude that people assume in the daily lifeworld; therefore, it is very close to the natural attitude. Based on this attitude, the world is full of animations or spiritual meaning. It is not pure nature as it appears to the eyes of natural scientists. The world is a world of spiritual sense, for such attitude and cultural objects are not only treated as things with natural properties but as things full of meaning, sense, value, and so on.

Of course, due to the fact that the natural attitude, no matter how personalistic, is limited by its naive-mindedness, it is impossible for it to look inward and gain a deep insight into what has been going on. Only by way of reduction, that is, self-awareness in a phenomenological sense, will such an end be attained. The moment he gains insight into himself, he gains a brand-new understanding of his surrounding world. On this basis, he can see cultural objects in a fresh manner. Following the reduction, the world is no longer the same as it used to be, but it is not entirely different either.

5   IV

Husserl considers cultural objects to be different from culture to culture, while also seeing in them the universal structure common to all human beings. The ambiguity is quite obvious. In order to deal with this ambiguity, I would like to draw on the viewpoint of Bernhard Waldenfels, who advocates for the notion of the "Other" [*Fremdheit*]. He introduces this notion by starting with Husserl's concept of "the experience of the other" [*Fremerfahrung*], which is in itself ambiguous.

According to Waldenfels, what is essential in the discourse of Husserl's question about the Other is not "what is the other" or "how can I get access to the other." Instead, Husserl asks about the way the Other presents itself. That is to say, for Husserl, there is no such independent Other that exists objectively regardless of whether he is experienced by me or not. He insists that the other is determined by the way in which he is accessed [*die Fremdheit ist durch die Art ihrer Zugänglichkeit bestimmt*] (Waldenfels, 1990, p. 48). Besides, the Other presents itself only in a paradoxical manner: "the verifiable accessibility of what is not originally accessible" (Hua I, p. 144).

The paradoxical form of the other, "the verifiable accessibility of what is not originally accessible," is interpreted by Waldenfels as lively absence [*leibhaftige Abwesenheit*]. This idea is inspired by Merleau-Ponty's conception of the Other as the elsewhere itself instead of as staying elsewhere [*Das Fremde ist nicht einfach anderswo, sie ist das Anderswo, und zwar eine "originäre Form des Anderswo"*] (Waldenfels 1997, p. 26). The Other cannot be defined solely in a negative way; it is not just "what remains to be known." The Other is closely related to the present by way of withdrawal [*Entzug*], just like memory, which is no longer present but retains its impact on the present. Waldenfels says:

> The experiencing-the-other does not mean that there exists something inaccessible in contrast to something accessible. We see clearly from the Husserlian definition of the other that the moment someone escapes from us, it presents itself. (Waldenfels, 1997, p. 29)

An adequate understanding of the Other does not necessarily presuppose the pure "sphere of ownness" [*Eigenheitssphäre*] because we not only encounter the Other in other persons; we encounter it in us as well. There exists the Other in ourselves and in our cultures, which has to do with intersubjective Otherness [*intersubjektive Fremdheit*] and intercultural Otherness [*interkulturelle Fremdheit*], respectively. The Other in us is not hidden in dark corners; it is instead vividly present. Waldenfels uses the following examples to show this fact: my birth and my name being given. These two happenings seem to stay in the far past, the past that never comes back again; however, they are present almost at every moment of my life. What if my life were never given? What if I had not a name? I came to the world through my birth and am known through my name. But the beginning of my life and my being known through namegiving is never part of my memory, "of myself," "of my consciousness in the strict sense." I am myself, but this self is never clear to me like crystal. Waldenfels refers to the experience of looking at one's own past photo. He wonders: Can I recognize myself as myself? Is he not someone foreign to me, with whom I can hardly identify myself? (Waldenfels 1997, p. 30).

It follows that the Other does not exist somewhere beforehand; it just originates in "drawing the line." The other is thus always relative. When we draw a line, we have to stand on one side of the line, just like when we tell the difference between genders. It is impossible for us not to stand on either the male or female side. That is, we can never assume the existence of a third gender to distinguish the genders. Similarly, we are never able to stand outside any culture to compare culture (Waldenfels 1997, pp. 19-21). Our involvements are unavoidable each time we make any kind of distinction. The Other never comes by itself; there is never "the Other in itself" who waits for me to get in touch with. The Other is Other only when we draw the line between self and the Other, and I always have to assume a side to stand on.

Waldenfels treats the Other, on the one hand, as relational, such as the right and the left. Since there is never a right side in itself, there is never an Other in itself either. The Other is always established through a kind of order, just like the right or the left has no meaning without relating to some standpoint. The Other is never localized somewhere; it is instead the result of the establishment of a certain kind of order. An order, once established, will determine what belong to it and what not; anything that does not belong to this order is excluded as outside, as Other. Yet, on the other hand, Waldenfels apparently places a more fundamental significance upon the Other; it is in itself the origin of the establishing order. The Other is that which we respond to, and establishing the order can be seen as one way of responding. The latter, in return, decides what is inside and what is outside; it thus contributes to the commonly understood meaning of the Other, which is in contrast to the self. The Other, thus understood, can be described as the Other of the second order, which is distinct from the "primordial Other."

As we have already seen above, the Other is treated as the second self, to which the term "alter ego" refers. But the "primordial other" is never the second self. It is what pushes us to speak and to take action. It is also the original force to distinguish the Other from the self. In short, it cannot be viewed as belonging to any order at all. That which inspires the establishment of order is not to be put into that order in reverse. And the Other never allows itself to be put into the saying about the Other. We make mistakes sometimes when we think, "the saying about the totality is in itself the saying by the totality" (Waldenfels, 1993, p. 62). But, regrettably, the significance of the other has not been fully recognized and has been treated now and then as the second self; it is inscribed in a certain order, and its significance is just omitted. The reason for its oblivion is that the Other is not easy to recognize, as long as we do not pay enough attention. The other presents itself only in the form of calling. As Waldenfels explains: "The Other is not something determinate, it is what awaits the response – and nothing more" (Waldenfels 1997, p. 180).

The Other is that which is calling for response; even the avoiding attitude is a kind of response, and the self is defined in this context accordingly as "responding to the calling." Even though easily overlooked, the Other is detected everywhere because "the Other penetrates all our experiences" (Waldenfels 1997, p. 180).

That which inspires our speech and action cannot be fully expressed in our speech and action in return. It shows itself only in an indirect way. The attraction of the alien culture and the other gender is also similar; people can only respond to this attraction by being involved or escaping from it.

6   V

When dealing with the homeworld and the alienworld, Husserl points out that the homeworld refers to the normal lifeworld of "my fellow people." It is characterized by cognitive and behavioral norms shared by those who belong to this group. These norms are developed over generations. For Husserl, the alienworld is different from the homeworld because they have no common ancestors. Besides, since these long-standing traditions shape specific cultural characteristics for each culture, we may conclude that there is a cultural difference between homeworld and alienworld. As indicated above, Husserl believes that this cultural difference can be overcome by "the one world" [*die eine Welt*], which is seen as the common basis for all homeworlds.

Waldenfels points out that Husserl's discourse on the homeworld and alienworld is ambiguous; on the one hand, he stresses the obvious distinction between the two; but, on the other, he brings up "the one world" to abolish this differentiation. In Waldenfels' view, the consequence of this ambiguity is the oblivion of the Otherness of the alienworld. Waldenfels suggests that the relationship may be reinterpreted as an intertwining [*Verschränkung*]. He denies the existence of any independent culture and rejects the egocentric way of treating other cultures. From his perspective, this is exactly the way Husserl treats the relationship between European culture and other cultures (Waldenfels 1997, p. 150).

Contrary to Husserl, the Other is the key notion for Waldenfels in his discourse on the homeworld and alienworld. As indicated above, traditionally, the Other is viewed as the non-self, something that is different from the self or does not belong to the self. It refers to an unclear domain that contrasts with the clear domain of "I." And this unclear domain is something that waits to be recognized, overcome, or even conquered (Waldenfels 1997, pp. 59-60).

In modern Europe, beginning with Descartes, the subject has been places in the center of philosophical discourse. Regarding ethnic problems, nationalism is put in a central place. In addition, Eurocentrism is also evident in dealing with the relationship between European culture and other cultures. Under these circumstances, the distinction between self and other, homeworld and alienworld, is taken for granted. I am purely I, and the Other is purely the other. However, the relationship between the Other and I is never symmetrical. The asymmetry results from the fact that people always look the Other or other cultures from their own point of view. The Other is consequently depreciated as the non-self. It is merely treated in the negative sense.

We have seen above that, according to Waldenfels, the Other is spread all over our experiences. Experiencing-the-Other, in terms of Husserl, is just one of the examples. The relationship between homeworld and alienworld can also be seen as another typical example. Waldenfels' critical attitude toward the Husserlian discourse of experiencing-the-Other is also evident in his critical stance toward Husserl's treatment of intercultural relationships. He contends that I am full of other in myself; the self is not completely clear. Further, we see that the giving of my name, with which I identify myself, occurs without my participation. This inner Other suggests that between the self and the Other there is an intersection, which makes the interaction between me and the other possible (Waldenfels 1997, p. 156). The way Waldenfels interprets interculturality is similar to his way of interpreting intersubjectivity. The Other in the homeworld and the alienworld co-constitutes the between-worlds [*Zwischenwelten*], which contributes to the intertwining relationship between different worlds. The between-worlds also serves as the basis for mutual understanding between cultures.

On the basis of calling and response [*Anspruch-Antwort*], Waldenfels indicates a paradox in the intercultural relation: The characteristics of every culture has to be grateful for its response to the other, no matter whether this other stems from inside or outside. Waldenfels says: "The response involves listening to the voice of the other, but it is not obedience, because our response is creative rather than just repeated" (Waldenfels, 1993, p. 64).

> That which we respond to and have to respond to is not under our control, and it is not out of our free invention…. Any pure own culture (*reine Eigenkultur*) is a culture that does not respond any more; it repeats only the answer that it already has or just the variations. (Waldenfels, 1993, pp. 63-64)

Generally speaking, people used to undermine cultural difference between the self and the other (my own group and the other group) by way of "appropriating the other" [*Aneignung*] or "giving up to the other" [*Enteignung*]. The consequence is the sacrifice of other cultures. According to Waldenfels, the meaning of "inter" in the intertwining relationship of homeworld and alienworld should never be sacrificed by any "arrogant single culture" [*angemaßte Monokultur*], nor should it be sacrificed by the contrary move. The *Aneignung*, in the strict sense, is sort of sticking to the borderline between cultures, whereas the *Enteignung* means the abolishing of the borderline. They both want to escape from what Waldenfels calls the dizzy "borderline-play" [*Grenzspiel*].

Such borderline-play is the true origin of intersubjectivity and interculturality. It helps bringing about the discursive models and norms [*diskursive Mustern und Normen*] that enable communication and interaction between cultures (Waldenfels, 1990, p. 68). The original understanding of language can be taken as an example in this context. Waldenfels contends that mutual understanding between cultures through language is made possible from the outset because it is based on phonological symbolism, which is encountered from culture to culture. For example, "mal" indicates "being grand," whereas "mil" indicates "being tiny." Without this kind of original understanding of language, we can hardly explain how people from totally different cultures can begin to understand each other and why children always find their ways to the language of the adults, as well as why normal persons can communicate with psychotic patients (p. 69).

As far as the debate of cultural relativism and universalism is concerned, Waldenfels points out that they both have something in common; that is, they compare their own cultures with those of the Other. Waldenfels emphasizes that no significant comparison between cultures and life forms is possible as long as we take our own standpoints for granted. The asymmetrical attitude is almost unavoidable each time we make comparisons, just because we can hardly stand outside our own culture. The Husserlian discourse about intercultural relationships may provide us with a typical example.

How does homeworld and alienworld relate to each other for Husserl? On the one hand, he acknowledges the basic difference between them; it is therefore not unimaginable for people to encounter shock and amazement from other groups. However, Husserl, on the other hand, introduces the "fundamental ground" [*fundamentale Grundschicht*] to undermine this difference as well as the shock and amazement.

The Husserlian notion of the one world is the result of the expanding of the homeworld. Such a self-centered idea neglects the intertwining phenomena between cultures and the intersecting between-worlds. Husserl's discourse is based on the assumption that the Other is nothing but secondary to me. And regarding the communication between self and Other, it presumes the priority of the former over the latter. This priority is strengthened by the commonness proposed by me. The idea of "one world," understood as the first ground and the last horizon, fits perfectly to fulfill this role of commonness.

Waldenfels is opposed to Husserl on this point: He thinks that Husserl typically displays the attitude of *Aneignung*. The appropriation of the Other, as Waldenfels describes it, means the use of rationality as an instrument to conquer and possess the Other. In Waldenfels' understanding, it is only the Europeans who have ever assumed this attitude toward other cultures. It is not only based on ethnocentrism, which is usually visible among many cultures, but also based on logocentrism, the focal point of which is reason. Inherent to reason is the potential to equalize everything and advocate the common aspect. Nothing remains unfamiliar; that is the consequence. Although Europeans encounter others and deal with others, they seldom let the Others express themselves. This is the typical position that modern European used to hold. As long as we understand the attitude of *Aneignung* adequately, we will not be surprised why the modern Europeans were so enthusiastic about colonizing other ethnic and cultural groups. They considered themselves to be representatives of universal reason, and it is their vocation to conquer the "foreign" land [*"fremdes" Land*], no matter how it was fulfilled, through military power or a civilizing method (p. 63).

7   Conclusion

Cultural objects are something that people (either from alien or one's own group) give meaning to; they are constituted objects. For this reason, by encountering alien cultures it happens quite often that the specific meaning of that culture is not recognized.[5]

---

[5] In the essay "A Gurwitschean Model for Explaining Culture or how to use an Atlatl," Embree mentions a student who happens to encounter an artifact used by ancient Indians in North America while wandering in the wild. The student begins with little knowledge about the utensil, seeing it first as "a stick of wood less than a meter long with a small protuberance at an end" or at most "a piece of equipment of some sort from the caves." He ends up knowing the item as "a spear thrower," which is named "atlatl" by professional archeologists (Embree, 1997).

Although the interplay between familiarity and unfamiliarity is quite obvious in Husserl's discourse about cultural objects, he tends to undermine the aspect of unfamiliarity by introducing the universal structure that all human beings cannot be deprived of. Even though the problem of cultural objects does not come into the vision field of Waldenfels, when he mentions the attraction of an alien culture as an example, the problem of cultural objects does come to his attention. And based on his viewpoint, we might be able to build up a more comprehensive account of what cultural objects are all about. Let us sum up the points indicated by Waldenfels that are relevant to the problem of cultural objects.

Waldenfels emphasizes that no significant comparison between cultures and life forms is possible as long as we take our own standpoints for granted. The asymmetrical attitude is almost unavoidable each time we make comparisons, just because we can hardly stand outside our own culture. The Husserlian discourse about intercultural relationships may provide us with a typical example.

When we think we look at cultural objects from other cultures, we already presuppose our own culture as unquestionable standpoint. There is a borderline that divides what is ours and what is not. But that way we dismiss the fact that there is a determining order which is normally unquestioned and firmly accepted.

By the way, Waldenfels is opposed to Husserl, as the latter typically displays what the former calls the attitude of *Aneignung*. The appropriation of the Other, as Waldenfels describes it, means the use of rationality as an instrument to conquer and possess the Other. In Waldenfels' understanding, it is only the Europeans who have ever assumed this attitude toward other cultures. It is based not only on ethnocentrism, which is usually visible among many cultures, but also on logocentrism, the focal point of which is reason. Inherent to reason is the potential to equalize everything and advocate the common aspect. The consequence is that nothing remains unfamiliar. Put differently, although Europeans encounter Others and deal with them, they seldom let the others express themselves.

Husserl's appeal to universalism is, consequently, a movement of abstraction from cultural objects. Granted that the intentional structure of consciousness is reflected in cultural experiences, we might raise the question about the universality of natural experience that Husserl suggests. Even if we agree that encountering cultural objects—familiar or not—denotes the encountering intentional structure, it does not mean that each time we encounter cultural objects we witness the commonness of all cultural objects only because of the universal structure that lies behind. The diversity of cultural objects makes it so that, by encountering the unfamiliar ones, we witness the alien properties therein. As we come close to them and learn about their meaning, we broaden our own horizon of knowledge. Universals are not at all plain facts in cultural issues. The difference always remains as it is in the cultural dimension of human existence, which demands acceptance as well as respect.

REFERENCES

Embree, L. (1997). A Gurwitschean model for explaining culture or how to use an atlatl. In J. C. Evans & R. W. Stufflebean (Eds.), *To Work at the Foundations. Contributions to Phenomenology, vol. 25* (pp. 141–171). Springer.

Flynn, M. B. (2012). The cultural community: An Husserlian approach and reproach. *Husserl Studies, 28*(1), 25–47.

Held, K. (1991). Heimwelt, Fremdwelt, die eine Welt. In E. W. Orth (Ed.), *Perspektiven und Probleme der Husserlschen Phänomenologie* (pp. 132–162). K. Alber.

Husserl, E. (1968). In W. Biemel (Ed.), *Phänomenologische Psychologie. Vorlesungen Sommersemester 1925* (2nd ed.). Martinus Nijhoff [Hua IX].

Husserl, E. (1977). *Phenomenological Psychology: Lectures, summer semester, 1925* (J. Scanlon, Trans.). The Hague: Martinus Nijhoff.

Moran, D. (2011). Even the Papuan is a man and not a beast: Husserl on universalism and the relativity of cultures. *Journal of the History of Philosophy, 49*(4), 463–494.

Waldenfels, B. (1990). *Der Stachel des Fremden*. Suhrkamp.

Waldenfels, B. (1993). Verschränkung von Heimwelt und Lebenswelt. *Philosophische Rundschau, 40*(2), 97–108.

PART V

Phenomenology of History

Husserl's Views on Levels of History with Their Modes of Rationality, Self-Preservation, and Types of Social Organization

Roberto Walton

1   Introduction

The essay sums up Edmund Husserl's search for the grounds of the teleological relations that govern intersubjectivity and provide an example of a "progressive bringing into play" (*progressives In-Spiel-Setzen*), which has its reversal in a "regressive removal of strata" (*regressive Abschichtung*) (HuaM VIII, 187).[1] Historical development concerns "'reason' in all forms" because it shows a three-step progression with "a lower level," a "higher level," and "the highest level of rationalization" (Hua XLII, 69, 432). In this sequence, in which lower levels remain in function within higher levels, an advance is made from primal history through actual histories to rational history with corresponding modes

---

[1] References of Husserl in the text are to *Husserliana. Gesammelte Werke*, *Husserliana. Materialien*, and *Husserliana. Dokumente*, cited as Hua, HuaM, and HuaD with the indication of volume and page. See the final References. When the original text in both German and the English translation is consulted, the page number of the English translation will follow a semi-colon after the page number of the German text.

R. Walton (✉)
Facultad de Filosofía y Letras, Universidad de Buenos Aires/CONICET, Buenos Aires, Argentina

© The Author(s), under exclusive license to Springer Nature Switzerland AG 2023
C. Belvedere, A. Gros (eds.), *The Palgrave Handbook of Macrophenomenology and Social Theory*,
https://doi.org/10.1007/978-3-031-34712-2_12

of social organization in symbiotic communities, second-order communities, and the community of love along with different types of self-preservation. Thus, the development of self-preservation is placed in parallel with the development of reason. Consider this significant passage: "Levels of founded and relatively existing strata of self-preservation, and each has its own verifications, its own reiterations, coincidences, and its own modalizations, its own conflicts between validity and validity" (Hua XXXIX, 458). At the highest stage, as the "function of a universal praxis," philosophical knowledge must deal with "the possibility of 'a true self-preservation' for each and every subjectivity, both individual and social, in an infinite connection," that is, a possibility that involves "the problems of 'universal harmony,' and also those of an authentic 'mankind'" (HuaD III/6, 461).

2   PRIMAL HISTORY

The possibility of history rests on human beings living in a chain of generations, within a homeworld with its basic social sedimentation, on the ground offered by the earth, and in the midst of instinctive strives that support a development towards higher forms. Earth, primal generativity, homeworld, and instincts make up a primal history (*Urhistorie*, *Urgeschichte*) as the ground that provides the conditions of possibility for actual history. Husserl states that instincts serve to the preservation of the species and the individual in the species. They are primal impulses that guide the development of human beings by means of intentions directed to a satisfaction and render an ever-increasing adaptation. Drives to nourishment, reproduction, communalization, attraction or repulsion, reaction against those who break down harmony, and other strivings are encompassed, as a total instinct, by an "instinct-of-'self-preservation' " (" *'Selbsterhaltungs'-instinkt*") (Hua XLII, 97; see pp. 93 n., 134).

In the system of instincts, two modes contribute decisively to a development towards the highest level of history. One is the "originary instinct with an interest directed to the constitution of nature and so to objectivation" (Hua XLII, 460). It goes through all egos guiding the constitution of the world and ensuing both harmonies in all particular constitutions and the attainment of a stable and secure surrounding world that guarantees self-preservation. The other mode is "the instinct directed universally to a satisfactory life among and with others, to a life in common with them in the protection against common necessities and for the promotion of common interests in a common well-being" (Hua XLII, 134). An "instinct of love," "generative love," or "primal form of love of neighbour" (Hua XLII, 108, 512) is also included. As the distinctive traits of rational history, the universal community of truth and the universal community of love point back genetically to an origin in the instinct of objectivation that guides the constitution of things and the social instincts that strive for a community.

Self-preservation occurs first in a passive life that acquires its goals from momentary demands without having an idea of self-preservation as a conscious end. However, it motivates care for comprehensive goals and sets teleological processes in motion. Goals can also be inherited passively from the community. Social instinct is associated with a "care for life" (*Lebenssorge*) (Hua XLII, 472, 520), that is, for the how of existence, for provisions of food, and so forth. The goal of nutrition is to find means of nourishment for every day and to store provisions for the future. In a care for provision, the means of nutrition must be supplemented again and again and protected against unfavourable conditions. Care for life also includes a solicitude for the members of the whole homeworld and the incorporation of children to a family tradition and more extended traditions. Insofar as they are surrounded by a homeworld of individuals that act according to goals, children learn to understand activities directed to goals and teleological meaning of useful objects (see Hua XV, 420). Husserl refers to "[t]he family instinct or drive, the 'enjoyment' in the harmony, in the practice of family-love as fulfilment of this instinct" (Hua XLII, 512). In this realm of "abstract historicity" there is already a communalization of self-preservation that develops through a "progression in concretion" (Hua XV, 138 n.) from narrow to more embracing homeworlds that are also unities of self-preservation.[2]

There is a stagnant self-preservation of primitive people that live a limited life in a state of balance between fear and hope. Goals in the life of a family or a tribe seek to preserve life in a temporal horizon that stands under the ideal of maintaining the best possible present with no reference to a distant future. But manifold interests soon arise and lead to a state in which hope permanently surpasses fear in a life of present satisfaction and the expectation of a future with more intense satisfactions. This new type of self-preservation is linked in "a horizon of upward movement (*Horizont des Aufschwunges*)" to "open possibilities of ascending such as the increasing acquisition of goods and the creation of a cultural world as a cultural world that enriches itself continually and enhances itself by increase of value" (Hua XXIX, 39). This leads to actual history.

Instinctive intentions show at first an empty consciousness with its empty direction. These blind or undeveloped instincts do not anticipate goals in the mode of a possible fulfilment. Only when perceived in the moment of satisfaction are the goals revealed. When they cease to be concealed, instinctive goals can then be explicitly aimed at. Striving is then "directedness towards the telos anticipated in representation (*das vorstellungsmäßig antizipierte Telos*), a telos that has the character of a value" (Hua XLII, 124). Husserl speaks of an end-value with regard to which the intermediate stages of action are mediating values. Instead of blind and undeveloped, instincts are now developed or disclosed.

---

[2] This continues through actual history. One can recall here Klaus Held's views on the homeworld in ancient Greece and in the advanced civilizations of the Middle East and East Asia, where "living together in a family as the place of life-preservation has shaped traditionally the foundation of human life" (Held, 2010, p. 139).

Impulse can be inhibited both by the competition of other impulses and by obstruction in the process of its fulfilment. This can lead to a greater effort in order to overcome obstacles. In contrast to animals, human beings are supplied with a horizon of possibilities of being and nonbeing. Concordance can be attained but also possibilities that extend to deception and entail "the passage through 'modalization'" (Hua XLII, 68). Furthermore, the rationality of instincts is considered not only by regarding the structure intention/fulfilment but also by indicating the rational character of acquisitions that serve as a basis for further developments. There is an instinctive habituality that emerges from a corresponding activity and contributes to the organization of perceptive, emotional, and practical activity: "The 'rational' tradition, the 'rational' genesis, the rational 'instincts' (acquired and explainable), namely, dark anticipation, acquired habits and apperceptions that determine objectivating intending, thought, valuation and action" (Hua XV, 611).

Husserl refers to the differences between a family and other families, between a community of families as a tribe and other communities, and so forth. The division of mankind into branches within primal generativity unfolds as a basis for generativities of a higher order that always appear linked to it. This leads, as we shall see, to the level of actual history, that is, to communities with their historical traditions. This division brings forth the opposition between internal and external history. Whereas the former is related to the homeworld, the latter is related to the alien worlds and is adapted to other lines of succession for generativity. This difference between familiarity and strangeness is "a fundamental category of all historicity, which relativizes itself in many strata" (Hua VI, 320; 275).

A distinction emerges in this primal level between symbiotic communities and communities formed in view of common ends that may have a lesser or greater scope. Symbiotic communities are characterized by "a living together motivated by originary instincts, by a vague being-attracted to equals, by pleasure in the being-there of others, and missing them when they are not there" (Hua XIII, 107). Symbiosis is found in the natural care of parents for their children and the instinctive striving towards the being together of members of a family. The State can be traced back to primal generativity in the sense that there is an instinctive basis that forces a teleological orientation on human development. The "natural State" is a "State that emerges from the natural community of descent (*aus einer natürlichen Abstammungsgemeinschaft*)," and this common ancestry can lead to a "community of subordination of the will under the authority of the head of a lineage, of despots, tyrants, and so forth" (Hua XIII, 110). Thus, the State is, in part, an expression of the concrete form which is adopted by the natural organization of peoples. But this is, according to Husserl, only one of the models to conceive the formation of the State. The other model deals with an artificial State that depends on social acts as a condition that renders possible going beyond symbiotic communities. It will be considered in the following section.

In the relationship between instinctive impulse and its fulfilment, its modalization, and axiological increase from mediating values to end-values, we come across the genetic origin of rationality: " *'Reason' in instinct. The obscure reason"* (Hua XLII, 86; see Hua VI, 53, 273; 52, 338). Recall that the relationship between intention and fulfilment is linked to evidence and renders a criticism of reason possible. And also that intentionality is characterized by an aiming-at, the fulfilment or satisfaction of which lies in attainment, that is, the experience of being-by-the-goal-itself. A rough draft of these processes is outlined in instinct by the easing of tension when the target of an empty intention is reached. This makes up the teleological ground for rationality and is tied to an "instinct directed to advancement" (*Instinkt zum Fortschritt*) (Hua XLII, 134) because it shows the beginning of the rational structure in the relationship intention-fulfilment, in processes of verification, and in a first mode of apperception linked to habitualization. Intention and fulfilment do not involve a final stage because the process in which momentary intentions are fulfilled always upholds new intentions in the fulfilment. Even if it is subject to finite ends, this movement outlines what will appear in the final stage when reason is guided by an unattainable end sustained by manifold fulfilments. Referring to the link of teleology with the stage of instincts that play the role of primal protentions, Husserl writes: "*Levels of instincts, of originary drives, demands* (which at first still do not know where they are going), systematically laid one on another, pointing over themselves to a higher level. This is a *teleology*" (Hua XLII, 118). In summary, a constitutive genesis is guided by a universal instinct that unifies all particular instincts and shows a unity of development in a pathway that goes from potentiality to actuality. A distinctive trait of this development is its intersubjective character and the inclusion, according to its form, of a humanized or cultural world: "In its primal instinct each individual subject supports the whole development not as its solipsistic development, but rather as a development of mankind" (Hua XLIII/3, 176).[3]

3   A First Development of History

On the basis offered by the chain of generations in primal generativity, the establishment of enduring and encompassing ends brings forth a higher-order spiritual generativity that takes on—in new forms tied to these goals—the

---

[3] If we consider the teleological origin and goal of human development, the following claim cannot be maintained consistently: "Husserl never comes to make sociality a primitive origin of the personal dimension of subjective existence: the ego is and remains the fundamental origin of all the constitutive life up to its personal dimension" (Perreau, 2013, p. 268). That the ego is the necessary starting point for philosophical reflection does not prevent an ensuing genetical analysis from showing the emergence of the ego out of an instinctive intersubjective past and its orientation to a future ethical intersubjective community. As Husserl puts it: "If we now step over from transcendental egology, that is, from the ego thought in an abstract and solipsistic character to the human community and its world, then the existent world, which now takes on an intersubjective sense of being, extends itself in a new manner for me as ego (and then for every I)" (HuaM VIII, 165).

protentional thrust pertaining to the universal instinctive intentionality. A "breakdown of the lower reason" opens the pathway to higher levels in an "inversion of originary instincts" (Hua XLII, 440). This makes up the realm of "reason in the first sense (*Vernunft im ersten Sinne*), which lives in its natural first historicity or traditionality" (Hua XXIX, 40). It is "the natural concept of reason" or, as Husserl puts it, "the simple honest reason of natural sound human understanding" (*die biedere, ehrliche Vernunft der natürlichen, gesunden Menschenverstandes*)" (Hua XXIX, 386).

Conscious life is orientated towards coherence first in an instinctive manner and then in this further step through acts which express a decision of the will and aim at a cohesive whole. A new level in the fulfilment of empty intentions places itself over instinctive relations and is therefore superimposed on the sheer lapsing of generations. Although human beings live in some form of culture from the very beginning, they must acquire a wider acquaintance with the surrounding world and develop culture in levels of historical modes of being. Thus homeworlds become lifeworlds endowed with manifold intersubjective relations and an inheritance that supplies primal generativity with a cultural tradition. Nevertheless, in the midst of new acquisitions, primal instincts remain "permanently in force, but permanently against the background of traditions" (Hua XLII, 130).

A rational praxis emerges through the reflection on practical possibilities and impossibilities regarding projects within a care for self-preservation. A broad sense of rationality emerges in the deliberation on ends and in the establishment of a tradition of usages and methods that can be understood again by others (see Hua VI, 337; 290). This extends to the regulation of communal life and the practices of functionaries that deal with these problems. Praxis is guided by analogies that concern goals and means, actions and procedures, and so on, and can be corroborated or deceived. Here one must take into account particular modes of fulfilment, verification, and truth. Regarding the intensification or cancellation of apperceptive anticipations, Husserl characterizes the circle in which practical activities are accomplished as a realm with nontheoretical interests in verification. Practical analogies enlighten new actions and allow attempts to achieve similar goals by the use of similar means. This is to say that actions will be more or less rational according to the degree of verification and ensuing firmness of the analogies: "In practical confirmation, analogizing corroborates itself and leads to a firmer theoretical and practical apperception than in previous analogizing" (Hua XXXIX, 420). Husserl adds: "The axiological and practical confirmation consists in the pure satisfaction that legitimates the practical anticipation in its realizing fulfilment, and does not legitimate in the opposite case" (Hua XXXIX, 857). Since the orientation of praxis implies a horizon of future in which possibilities of fulfilment or cancellation coexist, modalizations occur in a similar manner to those that appear in experience. Husserl highlights similarities between the analysis of the care of life and the analysis of modalization in perception when he examines the conditions of self-preservation in practical life. "This world has its right to be, and acting within this world has in itself its practical reason, which confirms itself in general and also refutes itself in particularities" (Hua XXXIX, 418; see 857).

An example provided is that of a merchant that in danger of breakdown cries out: " 'My existence' is threatened, my self-preservation is threatened, I am falling into ruin, my existence is lost, I can preserve myself no more" (Hus XLII, 520). Confronted with this situation, the merchant can work out other manners of proceeding within his practical professional life in an open horizon of possibilities of preservation by means of changes that overcome inconsistencies. Life-concern is reflected in a hope focused on certain possibilities and is subject to confirmation or cancellation. The corroboration of what is expected amounts to success and disagreement to a downfall. The merchant's actions are subject to corrections just as further perceptions can introduce doubts, fall in negation, or restore certainty. As Husserl explains: "Care is the mode of feeling that emerges out of the modalization of activity and out of the permanent predelineation of a horizon of possible failure, in which ways of foreseeable and true success, of success subject to corrections, develop" (Hua XLII, 521). Furthermore, new modes of life-hope and life-care can be considered. Another possible profession may appear as an available means to ensure self-preservation.

Truth in practical reason is relative to a variety of horizons of anticipation. Thus relativity is not only connected with possible cancellation as a result of open and undetermined horizons but is also tied to horizons of anticipation, that is, the different situations or surrounding worlds. The meaning of experiences and actions, and the degree of assurance required by them, is determined by everyday life, so that modifications in truth depend on the change of situations: "Every truth is referred to its situations and this change is not to be named 'falsity of what was assured a moment ago as true,' but rather 'truth as that of a new situation' " (Hua XXXIX, 192). Therefore, in prescientific life, knowledge conditioned by situations and traditions provides the means to know what is true or false according to its significance for our changing practical interests. This means that "it is to be rationally decided, with regard to every truth and falsity, which are the grounds and differences relevant and irrelevant for the case" (Hua XXIX, 386). Since it runs parallel to the requirements of practical interest, verification is not theoretical. In this previous stage to scientific and philosophical rationality, truth is attached to relevancy for practical intentions.[4]

In contrast to symbiotic societies and incipient social subjectivities as a family or a tribe, actual history is the realm of social acts in which individual or first-order subjects merge into second-order subjects or higher-order personalities. Togetherness (*Miteinander*) and intermingling (*Ineinander*) of their

---

[4] Husserl deals here with what Heinrich Rombach calls the "plurality of reason" or "multiveracity of reason" (Rombach, 1987, pp. 236, 317, 430) and Bernhard Waldenfels names *dóxa* as the embodiment of a third mode of *epistéme*, besides those of science and philosophy, which is contained in different world orders that exclude each other (see Waldenfels, 1985, pp. 34–55).

acts bring forth "a unity of having-an-effect and being-subject-to-effects-one--in-another (*eine Einheit des Ineinanderhineinwirkens und -gewirktwerdens*)" (Hua XIV, 271). As the acts of a subject go over to other subjects and come back from them in a community of communication and reciprocal action, there emerge social actions characterized by the unity of a performance that follows a unique valuation and will. Husserl observes that "subjectivities constitute themselves as unities of different levels, and we also have there, but in a completely different sense, multiplicities and unities, the enduring subject of permanent convictions, and also enduring apperceptions (of the one objective world), enduring valuations, needs, volitions" (Hua XIV, 202).[5]

Relations within a social personality can be relations of coordination if all the members hold an equal rank or relations of subordination if there is a differentiation in positions of mastery and servitude. The latter relation can also be the result of an agreement between co-members in an association of coordination with a varying range and duration (see Hua XIV, 213).[6]

Many headed personalities of higher order are in a way a copy of first-order subject. Social habitualities or traditions that emerge from the sedimentation of social acts that make up a tradition are analogous to the habitualities of an ego. And to individual acts correspond the united acts of their manifold members. The centralization in the board of directors of an association or in the government of a State is similar to that of the ego as the centre of irradiation of acts. Resemblances regarding centralization can also vanish as in the case of a dance society or a linguistic community (see Hua XIV, 220, 405–406).

In this interconnection, the relevant features of individual self-preservation—endurance, change, unification by means of valuations and goals, and universal care—also have a counterpart in the manner of a large-scale projection on the personalities of higher order. The features of individual self-preservation are also regarded as belonging to social self-preservation. Individuals preserve themselves not as rigid identities in the identical unity of properties: "An ego has no possible rigid properties; it is not a unity of alteration in the sense of a physical substance. It has no substantial being in this sense. It is a unity throughout a tendency to self-preservation; it is insofar as it strives to be, and strives to be itself" (Hua XLII, 338). Self-preservation is contrasted to the permanence in the midst of alterations of what is not an ego: "I am not first and preserve myself afterwards, being is self-preservation" (Hua XV, 367 n.). There is no substantial being in the self, and a true self consists in the realization of values as part of a process of "self-shaping (*Selbstgestaltung*) directed to the ethical subject" or "self-shaping towards authenticity" (Hua XLII, 481, 484). Self-preservation is the outcome of striving towards unity, which is obtained by

---

[5] David Carr stresses the importance of this constitution of unities in a second order: "The consideration of the first-person plural or we-subject opens up a whole new description of social existence and action. The concepts of membership and participation allow us to consider experience and action from the participant's perspective. Social groups need no longer be viewed as third-person phenomena" (Carr, 2014, p. 118).

[6] See Toulemont (1962, pp. 117–123).

establishing an inner balance of constituent elements. This provides satisfaction in a level of relative stability, without which the development of the ego would be restrained. Most important among the constituent elements in the equilibrium are care, hope, reaffirmation of the positivity of life, and rationality.

The drive towards harmony is also a drive that "actualizes itself in a particular case by overcoming factual conflicts" (Hua XLII, 226). In discordance there is always a tendency to the production of new harmonies. In this continuous striving towards harmony, discordance is removed, corrections are introduced, and new choices are made because the finite moments of a continuous process undergo criticisms set off by inconsistencies. Husserl writes: "The ideal of self-preservation: the ego can only be satisfied and fortunate if it lives as an ego harmonious in itself, in every sense, and if every discordance dissolves itself in a higher harmony" (Hua XLII, 174). Self-preservation entails keeping convictions about goals and correcting them with new convictions under the control of a definite validity in a coincidence and harmony with oneself: "The ego is a practical ego, it strives towards something, an object of its will. But it stands under the law of self-preservation. It can only preserve itself as an ego, when a definite validity runs through its decisions" (Hua XLII, 367). Striving towards a unity of convictions implies remaining faithful to oneself. Everyone must consider the extent in which "*a best possible life, a life of self-faithfulness*, is to be attained, and so must project it in a general manner" (Hua XLII, 454).

Self-preservation is never the attainment of a final end. As there is no stop (*Haltepunkt*) and each moment is a passage (*Durchgang*), even speaking of self-preservation is not adequate. Husserl writes: "Not self-preservation but rather self-becoming (*Selbstwerdung*) is the goal of self-seeking (*Selbstsuche*); [...] a search of the true self, which, nevertheless in a constant search is a constant finding and further search of oneself" (Hua XLII, 286). A life that seeks self-preservation is a "*life in the previous care (Vorsorge) that becomes the universal care for the whole future life*" (Hua XLII, 426). Provisions are made beforehand for particular cares and also for possible disappointments. The ideal of a desirable whole life with a unitary style entails the habitual certainty of an assured existence, control over the surrounding world, and the possibility of structuring it, with the help of others, into a world of goods that will ensure a satisfactory life. A communalization is included in which the adjustment and unification of diverse interests is directed to self-preservation.

Husserl refers to a life of care that is not isolated but rather is a moment in a universal and connected horizon of subjects searching for agreements around common capacities and acquisitions (see Hua XLII, 521). As mentioned above, personalities of higher order are enduring, unified by values and goals, and subject to regulations. The individual will-of-self-preservation always develops "in connection with its associates in the horizon of humanity" (Hua XLII, 225). Societies, nations, and all sorts of spiritual generativities are also engaged in the preservation of themselves and their correlative worlds as well as of the individuals on which they are grounded. Husserl writes: "Life in self-preservation in different levels, containing always alien self-preservation in one's own self-preservation" (Hua XLII, 417). And he adds with regard to the striving of mankind towards a unification in harmony: "Throughout all disturbances and conflicts attainment of self-preservation, i.e., of inner balance, of satisfaction" (Hua XLII, 387).

In the development of communities, Husserl distinguishes three stages in which behaviour is regulated externally. The first stage is that of custom (*Sitte*) as a transmitted social form demanded and sanctioned only on the basis of tradition. It amounts to a regulation of behaviour as a habitual practice, that is, to "norms of behaviour purely referred to the relation between human beings as they stand next to each other" (Hua XIII, 107). With a distinct lack of ends, actions are subject to a social "ought" with its approvals and disapprovals. Custom makes up a framework of communitarian normality, of what we are accustomed to in the broadest sense, as the realm of what is adequate or decent (das *Schicksale*). This encompasses modes of personal life and forms of professional life as a convenient standard. We have been trained since childhood and then in our social dealings over and over again, and the outcome is that custom "has for whoever acts in this manner the phenomenological character of the imposed, of the demanded from outside, of what should be in the sense that deviations from it are disapproved of" (Hua XLII, 341–342).

A second stage is constituted by law (*Recht*). The same as custom it is also externally demanded, but its content shows rationality in the sense that it is fit for an end. It establishes regulating forms that are endowed with a coercive power over the members of a society. Law is distinguished from other cultural formations of human beings that deal with each other—language, literature, art—because it is characterized by a stable communitarian link that brings forth the unity of a volitional consciousness by means of duties and rights. Husserl highlights the stable condition that a legal link has for the binding of human acts as well as the limits that it sets for the will of individuals. Along with rules about what is allowed or prohibited there are rules regarding punishment for transgressions.

A further stage within custom is a sphere of virtuous custom (*tugendhafte Sitte*) that differentiates itself as morality (*Sittlichkeit*) and provides a stock of good customs. Morality shares an imposed obligation with custom and rationality according to ends with law. The "specific colouring of morality," with its virtues and moral disposition, is tied to a community in which actions are praised or disapproved by a circle of spectators or "ethical chorus" that expresses the impersonal domain of the "one" (*Man*) or "they" in the sense that one does not abandon a friend, one helps the poor, and so forth. The "one" concerns both a "descent and civilized" person and what is morally "correct" within "a community of undetermined judgment." Thus morality has a variable structuration according to the circle of spectators that determine the moral judgement. Husserl writes: "The moral 'ought' is no more than the outer clothing, so to say, of ethical virtue" (Hua XLII, 343; see 341–343). A further step will lead to truly virtuous actions that involve the passage from an external judgement to self-determination. An ethical life that presupposes an active ego as the highest level in this stratification will be the subject matter of our next section.

A central theme in the sphere of law is the State. A community of subjects constitutes through social acts this personality of a higher order "by means of law" (Hua XV, 48). In other words, "a juridical regulation of the relationship of human beings to each other is a State" (Hua XIII, 106). It is a whole of persons in which not everybody knows everybody as could happen in an association and in which there is a community of will regarding all full-citizens: "this State-will is an enduring social directionality of the will and in general a directionality for acts, which have effects in a habitual manner and are centred in an I in analogy with the individual ego" (Hua XIV, 406).

Husserl observes that the State is "a unity by means of power, of mastery (*Herrschaft*)" (Hua XV, 412) and mentions levels of mastery or dominance within an association limited to a village, an association extended to many villages, and an all-comprehensive State. Harmony is shaped in the State by norms that are imposed on human beings and fix the spheres of freedom in contrast with what is prohibited. There are functionaries in charge of the enforcement, but in a more general sense, Husserl contends that all the members of a society, from simple citizens to officials of the highest rank, have a function in the State without a reciprocal knowledge as happens within a limited association (see Hua XIV, 182). A contrast is established between the realm of application for legal norms and the sphere that is beyond their reach. It is the distinction between what is demanded by the State and what is left free by laws. For example, a trader seeks protection against the interruption of legal forms in commercial dealings with other traders and clients which he gives credit, whereas neither the purchases of daily life nor friendly help fall within lawful regulations.

Whereas the State entails a lawful regulation of reciprocal relations, the Church entails a lawful regulation of behaviour with regard to God and his divine representatives on the earth. Both coincide if the head of a State is endowed with power in the Church, and hence the latter generates a community of behaviour that intersects with that of the citizens. If human beings fail to comply with obligations imposed by God, they can be punished according to an equivalent of juridical relations (see Hua XIII, 106–107).

States show a two-sidedness because they are both natural and artificial. A natural origin of the State in the realm of primal generativity has been considered in the previous section. A further stage is attained with second-order subjectivities that establish the State as the artificial product of human activity and history. Whereas the natural aspect amounts to ethnical origin and descent, the artificial aspect goes back to an agreement or covenant for the institution of the State. Karl Schuhmann argues that a circular structure encompasses within a reciprocal dependence both the origin and the established heritage. On the one side, the emergence out of a community of ancestors, which would separate the natural State from the artificial State, is a motivation for an artificial institution of the State. A natural or previously given side is to be found in a State because it emerges in connection with a teleology that is always operating in an inter-subjective community and prepares it beforehand as a condition of possibility for actions of the will. On the other hand, the State is maintained by spontane-ous and conscious subjects, and this is the reason why a conventional character should be ascribed to it. But the orientation of the will, which would separate the artificial State from the natural State, is incorporated to the determination of the natural State due to the precedence of instinctive drives and their teleo-logical orientation, which are taken up by human will. Thus, as an institution tied to a tradition, the State depends both on a heritage that conditions its conservation (natural side) and on a reinstitution that renders its continuation possible (artificial side).[7]

Husserl stresses the shortcomings of the natural concept of reason: "Therefore, regarding real praxis, human beings do not actually come to a 'self-preservation' " (Hua XLII, 382). He says this explicitly in view of the fact that satisfaction cannot be ensured by means of an increase in the production and acquisition of goods. Furthermore, with the State we are still in a stage previous to ethics. Husserl states that factual States and their validity "are sub-ject to an 'ethical' judgment according to the absolute (purely ideal, a priori) ethical norms" (Hua XIII, 107). As we cannot be satisfied with "ethical truth as a truth tied to situations (*Situationswahrheit*)" (Hua XLII, 484 n.), the development from custom to morals demands a teleological continuation towards the inner or proper character of virtue. Thus, a search for "a new man-ner of self-preservation" (Hua XLII, 368) must be attempted.

4   Second Historicity

A "second historicity" (Hua XXIX, 41) begins with a new type of tradition in which, with an open horizon of practical possibilities, reason advances as if the horizons were infinite and every attained value were the lower level for higher levels. The establishment and re-establishment of meaning has now infinite tasks and must lead to both a community of truth and an ethical community. Furthermore, Husserl points to the transformation of philosophy into phe-nomenology as a new step within second historicity characterized by a "devel-opment into a personal autonomy and an all-encompassing autonomy for mankind" (Hua VI, 273; 338) and the emergence of a "universal phenomeno-logical reason" that "clarifies the absolute autonomy, grounds it, and estab-lishes it absolutely" (Hua XLII, 440).

Ethical life is the highest point in the striving towards self-preservation, which, in the midst of obstacles and conflicts, tends to unify personal and com-munitarian life in a universal harmony (see Hua XLII, 172 n.). In this strive, a lower self, whose goals seek mere pleasure or power, is superseded by a higher self which is endowed with a new type of freedom because, by virtue of its more elevated ends, it is freed from the hostility which limits the life of those who

---

[7] See Schuhmann (1988, pp. 90–96).

have not yet reached ethical self-consciousness. To build up the superior self as a person involves decisions in favour of spiritual values and those of the person, that is, the values of love of neighbour and love of self in their authentic form in which they are devoid of selfishness. A rational education plays a fundamental role in this development with different stages of perfection in the attainment of freedom and a universal human self-responsibility. Since it lays out the rules according to which all the other actions have to develop in favour of the harmony of the best possible mankind, ethics is the "royal science" (*königliche Wissenschaft*) (Hua XXXVII, 319).

Husserl states the following categorical imperative: "Do always the best that is attainable in the whole sphere that is subject to your rational influence!" (Hua XXVIII, 350–351). This is in the first place a formal demand that compels us in a further step to examine the horizons in which our acts take place, that is, the material values comprised within the sphere of our practical possibilities and the realization of what is most valuable. Understanding the best and outlining the sphere of rational influence run through several individual and social stages that reach their highest point in a communitarian formulation of the imperative.

Values of goals must be considered in an overview that encompasses one's whole life with its future and past horizons. This brings forth an "ethical consciousness" (*ethisches Gewissen*) (Hua XXVII, 29, 32) in which values and goals are adopted for the guidance of will along our entire life-horizon in a continuous and consistent self-shaping. This is followed by a life-decision in favour of their realization and the earnest attempt to achieve them in a faithfulness to the decision by means of subordinated momentary actions performed in particular situations. These acts are, therefore, legitimated in advance rather than by a subsequent appreciation: "In the persistence of life in good consciousness (*im guten Gewissen*) following what I should to the best of my ability and to the extent that I recognize it in particular cases, I remain faithful to myself, and in this authentic self-preservation I grow up to be an ethical human being, to be a human being of ethical certainty and force" (Hua XLII, 405).

The habitualization of acts according to the ethical consciousness gives rise to a style or "ethical disposition" (*ethische Gesinnung*) (Hua XLII, 332). The next step is "self-satisfaction" (*Selbstzufriedenheit*) understood as the outcome of the constant realization of the ethical disposition in actions that have a firm justification and generate the situation of being in peace with oneself. Husserl underlines its relationship with self-preservation: "*Satisfaction* (*Befriedigung*) is intentionality of actual '*self-preservation.*' Dissatisfaction is inhibition of self-preservation" (Hua XLII, 426). Self-satisfaction is the "core of happiness" (*Zentrum der Glückseligkeit*) (Hua XLII, 311), but this further stage also requires that what is uncontrollable by us in our health and in the surrounding world does not obstruct the achievement of our goals.

As the final stage in this development, self-satisfaction and happiness also include a "loving care" (*liebende Sorge*) or "loving solicitude" (*liebende Fürsorge*) for others (Hua XLII, 397, 513). The life of others is also a striving towards self-preservation, and in love "alien striving is (or becomes) my own striving," so that "in my true self-preservation, alien self-preservation itself is incorporated and becomes my own" (Hua XLII, 467). This means that self-preservation is generated as an answer to calls. This openness to interpellations makes criticism regarding a closed circle of self-preservation unjustified. The call of others, of a finite profession, or of love leads to "the responsive seeing-to, hearing-to" (*das antwortende Hinsehen, Hinhören*) and to "the 'responsive' behaviour" (*das 'antwortende' Verhalten*) (Hua XV, 462, 476). In the case of love, the ego "follows a 'call' ('*Ruf*'), a 'calling' ('*Berufung*'), a most intimate call that touches the deepest inwardness—the most inner center of the ego itself—and is determined to decisions of a new kind, to 'self-responsibilities,' self-justifications of a new kind" (Hua XLII, 358). Sacrifice is not excluded because Husserl contends that, as a case of authentic love of neighbour, "in the decision for sacrifice an act of life is performed" in which, even if a worldly life is forsaken, a "true life" is attained by virtue of the affirmation of "the life of mankind as a life that is absolutely demanded, magnificent, and good *in infinitum*" (Hua XLII, 439).

Other persons are also absolute subjects that I must recognize as a source of personal values, and as soon as an individual subject is given in empathy, "it is my absolute duty to promote it as this subject" (Hua XLII, 337). This means that "it is inherent to the categorical imperative of the singular subject to aspire to this superior form of community and this superior form of the individual self and *individual life as an officer of an ethical community*" (Hua XLII, 315 s.). Thus the infinite task of giving an ethical status to mankind is guided by the goal outlined by "an open horizon of social bonds of love and a community of work in which we all on average make headway and can help ourselves in the enhancement of existence" (Hua XLII, 332).

All co-subjects are included and conceived as subjects of true self-preservation, so that the well-being of others concerns each member of the community. In view of the togetherness of individuals in a community and the necessary link between individual and collective development of reason, autonomy as the distinctive trait of transcendental subjects cannot amount to individualism.[8] The entire process is directed to the cancellation and correction of disharmonies, and at the highest level amounts to the establishment of a community of love as "the uppermost ideal of an 'authentic existence' of the individual and of mankind in the form of an 'authentic' existence of the community" (Hua XLII, 428). The teleological advance to this ideal will be a theme of our next section. At this point we reach the field of truly rational praxis aimed at the harmonious valuable being of the community of subjects. Husserl spells out the larger aim and purpose of his ethical investigations as follows:

> From this emerges the *Idea of a personal communitarian intersubjective praxis*, not directed to the world in order to 'dominate' it, to take advantage of it, but

---

[8] See Toulemont (1962, p. 154).

rather directed to mankind—that is, to all of us in community—in order to educate it as an absolute mankind (namely, in a transcendental manner in the direction to an absolute transcendental subjectivity). (Hua XLII, 438)

Advancing towards a higher level of self-preservation requires a close interpenetration of universal self-responsibility and self-reflection (*Selbstbesinnung*)
beyond a looser link in the lower levels. This kind of meditation shows the relative condition of achievements and the possibility of progress. The reason is
that it is tied to a self-criticism that depends on the establishment of the best
possible for the moment and the further consciousness that, as the most desirable at a particular time, what has been considered best can be surpassed. This
movement is driven forward, according to Husserl, because rational human
beings unfold a "disposition to reason" (*Vernunftanlage*) that is "installed"
(*angelegt*) in them and already emerges in "previous levels of truth and being"
with a "previous certainty of the end" (Hua XLII, 443–444). Husserl has in
mind a total self-responsibility that includes all the range of particular ends and
pathways for their attainment and is not restricted to one's own ends but
encompasses the whole communitarian life.

5   A Rational Community

Schuhmann argues that Husserl has a negative view on the function of the
State in the sense that no instruments are outlined in order to ensure the ethical ends of mankind. The role of the State would be to counteract all what
prevents achieving this objective.[9] Nevertheless, if rights and duties are set out
within an overreaching teleological rationality, and existing States are subject
to an ethical judgement, there is more in the State than a coercive force. It is
equally possible to articulate a positive function if custom, on the one hand,
provides an impulse, and, on the other, ethical norms spread downwards
through the legal sphere and furnish ideas that contribute to the organization
of a new order. It is arguable that Husserl suggests this permeation when he
points to a two-level approach to order and draws attention to a motivating
force for an advance from a legal sphere to an ethical realm: "The order of will
by means of power and laws of power (legislation). Another order of will: that
of the harmony of will" (Hua XLII, 512). If we look more closely to motivations for will in the sphere of law, we see that an impulse to a higher order can
be contained in its fitness to an end and in the fact that "law is—even if not
totally, but rather in a changing scope—precisely at the same time, content of
a good custom (*Gehalt der guten Sitte*)" (Hua XLII, 341). This means that the
State may have a share in bringing about the teleological movement that

[9] See Schuhmann (1988, pp. 116–118).

advances from custom through law to a culmination in virtuous custom and ethics.[10]

Husserl's 1923 articles on "Renewal" begins as follows: "Renewal is the general calling of our troubled present, [...]. Therefore, we say: *something new must happen*; it must happen within us and through us" (Hua XXVII, 3 s.). This amounts to a reinstitution of reason and philosophy as the strict science which was first established by Socrates and Plato in an attempt to elucidate an objective world as contrasted to the relative worlds of pre-philosophical epoch. The practical side of this reinstitution includes the foundation of a rational community, that is, "the idea of people and State organized from purely ethical sources" (Hua XIII, 107) by means of an " 'ethical' politics" (Hua XV, 380). This means that a transcendental universal intersubjectivity should live in harmony according to an ideal style of value and operate accordingly. Husserl writes: "The absolute universe of transcendental subjects organizes itself in an absolute State, in an absolute personality of a higher order, creates for itself a 'governing' personality" (Hua XLII, 223).[11] In a brief outline, a rational community presupposes an essential structure of man, a teleology of reason, and heroism in the fight against contingency.

Regulation by habitualization—typical of the natural sound human understanding—is surmounted because self-preservation at its highest point is linked to "the universal essential form of transcendental total-subjectivity," which was "pre-ontologically formed" (*vorontologisch geformte*) in the sense of being latent in the lower stages of development and now provides rational will with its "explicit goal" and so outlines "the horizon of authentic humanity" (Hua XV, 378–382). As an eidetic form is marked out for mankind, it is also emphasized that the world "*must be essentially like that,*" and this amounts to an obligation of fulfilling the "*conditions of possibility of a harmonious value-being as a field of human rational praxis*" (Hua XLII, 333). In an equivalent approach to these problems, Husserl distinguishes in the realm of self-reflection a "cosmological world-reflection" (*kosmologische Weltbesinnung*) and an "axiological-practical world-reflection" (*axiologisch-praktische Weltbesinnung*). The former investigation sets aside the "concrete person in a life and striving for self-preservation" (Hua XLII, 516) in order to examine the world merely according to its being and being-so. It is a theory of factually existing human beings.

---

[10] Husserl indicates a directionality for a legal order when, in a letter to Arnold Metzger (4. IX.1919) with reference to the latter's article on "the phenomenology of revolution," he expresses his understanding of a "radical disposition (*radikale Gesinnung*) which is firmly decided not to look at and conduct life as a commercial business under the two continuing headings of 'should' and 'having' (in which 'should' expresses nothing but the demands of 'having'), and is the deadly enemy of all 'capitalism', of all definite valuation and hence senseless accumulation of 'having' and correlatively of all egoistic valuation of persons" (HuaD III/4, 407).

[11] Husserl writes: "Scientists and scientifically educated persons live in the certainty that they are called to the reformation of the whole human life, and also of political life, and as soon as the new spiritual attitude shows practically its superiority (*Überlegenheit*), political leaders are henceforth naturally philosophically educated" (Hua XXIX, 14).

But a theoretical attitude can also pay attention to values and goals, and then it becomes "a *theoretical doctrine of possible human beings and a possible mankind*" and can be characterized as an eidetic science "*of the possibility, of the conditions that render possible practically a human true self-preservation*, of a life that is to be ruled by volition with the goal of a lasting satisfaction" (Hua XLII, 519). This is to say that theoretical interest is undertaken "in the service of a unitary and comprehensive interest in 'happiness' or of a universal life-will, a will of self-preservation, directed to a universal harmony, amidst the overcoming of occurring discordances" (Hua XLII, 518).

Husserl contends that mankind should not consider universal science as an arbitrary cultural product but rather "as its *organ for a universal practical self-examination*, and draw from it norms that, in the life of chance and hindrances, can nevertheless lead to upper levels" (Hua XLII, 489). He criticizes "men of facts" who "carefully exclude all valuative positions, all questions of the reason or unreason of their human subject matter and its cultural configurations" (Hua VI, 4; 6). This criticism of naturalism is a dominant theme in the Vienna Lecture about "Philosophy and the Crisis of European Humanity," held in May 1935 (see Hua VI, 314–348; 269–299). The naturalization of conscience leads to its analysis in a form analogous to the world of external experience, through processes which turn subjectivity into a set of objective data. As Pierre Trotignon points out in *Le coeur de la raison*, naturalism with its elimination of the difference between the concept of person and the concept of natural object lies at the foundation of the practices of totalitarianism, since "everything is solved in the exterminating immanence of the mechanical."[12]

Teleology is another fundamental feature in the foundation of a rational community. It is the consequence of a development set forth under the guidance of the eidetic form of a rational mankind and directed to its throughout realization. In a normative use, theoretical truths regarding the eidetic structure provide will with explicit goals. Consequently, Husserl highlights "*the possibility of a universal teleology, the volitional source (Willensquelle) of which lies in human being itself*" (Hua XLII, 478). This goal is postulated as the idea of the true and full rationality in its manifold manifestation as theoretical, emotional, and practical in a community of truth and love (see Hua XXVIII, 228; VI, 275–276; 341). As we have seen, Husserl describes a sequence of steps in the course of a personal and social-historical development. Each step in the process is a relative stage, but this does not prevent an absolute goal from being the final aim in an endless endeavour. A clear definition of the goal involves an explication of horizons, a critical evaluation of the disclosed possibilities in self-reflection, the assessment of a possible progress with regard to an increase of value, and the extrapolation of an ideal goal to which this development moves forward.

As regards the projection of goals, we see that, in the development of teleology, after finite goals with no conscious general ends as the satisfaction of

---

[12] Trotignon (1986, p. 282).

hunger, and finite goals within general ends as the development of a particular training in order to have success a profession, we finally arrive at full-fledged universal goals that are tied to infinite ideas. To the extent that there is "an infinite horizon of tasks" centred around the ideas of reason, there emerges "a revolutionizing in historicity, which is now the history of the cutting-off of finite mankind to development as it becomes mankind with infinite tasks" (Hua VI, 324; 279).

Since teleology is open to modalizations and crises, contingency is a third main feature. The development of infinite tasks can be affected by dispersion in particular ends, concealment under trends that contradict them, or obstacles such as natural disasters, social misfortunes, and evil acts. All this entails the danger of a life devoid of purposes and meaning and deprived of an active self-preservation. Nevertheless, contingencies can play a positive role because they are means for the development of our freedom. They have the function of granting dignity and justification to our life insofar as they become a motivation for a more encompassing reason, and we enclose them within a realm of rationality. Under negative conditions, hope can be maintained in the possibility of building a future life by means of one's own actions. This shows the difference between human beings that live in a loss of hope and life in the positive situation of a permanent concern about the modes in which it can be fulfilled in a will to live.

Hence human beings live in a state of permanent tension between finitude and infinitude, factuality and ideas, non-reason and reason, or destiny and freedom. Thus there emerges the question of the possibility of living among contingencies: "How can men live without having solved the antinomy between the demand for the configuration of the world and the inability to account for destiny?" (Hua XLII, 422). The answer is to be found in the practice of the "heroism of persistence despite accumulated misfortunes" (Hua XLII, 325). Let us recall the end of the Vienna Lecture in which two possibilities are outlined as the outcome for the crisis of European existence, namely, "the downfall of Europe in its estrangement from its own rational sense of life, its fall into the hostility towards the spirit and into barbarity; or the rebirth of Europe from the spirit of philosophy through a heroism of reason that overcomes naturalism once and for all" (Hua VI, 347–348; 299). The proposed final goals do not warrant an actual factual realization but depend on the stance taken by individuals in view of their attainment. This is an essential possibility that should be saved as such: "Consequently, the active life of a community, of the whole mankind, can adopt—even if this has not happened in any previous historical reality—the unitary figure of practical reason, that of an 'ethical' life" (Hua XXVII, 22).

These three features of a rational community—essence, teleology, and contingency—must be borne in mind in their interconnection. The possibilities outlined by an axiological-practical world-reflection are put into practice by a teleological will, but obstacles stand in the pathway of accomplishments. In other words, rational teleology expresses a philosophical demand, the development of which is exposed to the irrational difficulties that rational subjects are faced with. Husserl makes an appeal for a rationalization of irrationality: "*Mankind hovers between rationality and irrationality.* Everything rational has its horizons of irrationality. But irrationality is itself a structure of the rationality apprehended with a broader scope (*eine Gestalt der weiter gefassten Rationalität*)" (Hua XLII, 489). A favourable attitude towards an all-inclusive rationality attains, in the case of future unfortunate circumstances, the value of an example both for oneself and for others. Furthermore, when confronted with unexpected events, mankind should not be overwhelmed by them because support can be found in the chain of generations. Husserl also holds that the thought of death loses the negative connotation of a lack of value if we consider ourselves participants "in a mankind that endlessly continues to preserve itself (*in einer sich endlos forterhaltenden Menschheit*), that can socialize itself freely and raise itself to an ethical sociality" (Hua XLII, 317). Regarding insertion in a generative link, Husserl stresses the attainment of a positive outcome in the course of extended periods: "Practical possibilities to be actualized fruitfully despite contingency are in general there and are probable horizons of distant effect" (Hua XLII, 325).

REFERENCES

Carr, D. (2014). *Experience and history. Phenomenological perspectives on the historical world*. Oxford University Press.

Held, K. (2010). *Phänomenologie der politischen Welt*. Peter Lang.

Husserl, E. (1962). *Die Krisis der europäischen Wissenschaften und die transzendentale Phänomenologie* (W. Biemel, Ed.). *Husserliana* VI. Martinus Nijhoff. English Edition: 1970. *The crisis of European science and transcendental phenomenology*. Translated by D. Carr. Evanston: Northwestern University Press. Cited as Hua VI.

Husserl, E. (1973a). *Zur Phänomenologie der Intersubjektivität. Texte aus dem Nachlass. Erster Teil: 1905–1920* (I. Kern, Ed.). *Husserliana* XIV. Martinus Nijhoff. Cited as Hua XIII.

Husserl, E. (1973b). *Zur Phänomenologie der Intersubjektivität. Texte aus dem Nachlass. Zweiter Teil: 1921–1928* (I. Kern, Ed.). *Husserliana* XIV. Martinus Nijhoff. Cited as Hua XIV.

Husserl, E. (1973c). *Zur Phänomenologie der Intersubjektivität. Texte aus dem Nachlass. Dritter Teil: 1929–1935* (I. Kern, Ed.). *Husserliana* XV. Martinus Nijhoff. Cited as Hua XV.

Husserl, E. (1988). *Vorlesungen über Ethik und Wertlehre 1908–1914* (U. Melle, Ed.). *Husserliana* XXVIII. Kluwer Academic Publishers. Cited as Hua XXVIII.

Husserl, E. (1989). *Aufsätze und Vorträge (1922–1937). Mit ergänzenden Texten* (T. Nenon and H. R. Sepp, Eds.). *Husserliana* XXVII. Kluwer Academic Publishers. Cited as Hua XXVII.

Husserl, E. (1993). *Die Krisis der europäischen Wissenschaften und die transzendentale Phänomenologie. Ergänzungsband aus den Nachlass 1934–1937* (R. N. Smid, Ed.). *Husserliana* XXIX. Kluwer Academic Publishers. Cited as Hua XXIX.

Husserl, E. (1994). *Briefwechsel* (K. Schuhmann and E. Schuhmann, Eds.). *Husserliana-Dokumente* III, vols. 6–10. Kluwer Academic Publishers. Cited as HuaD III with the indication of volume.

Husserl, E. (2004). *Einleitung in die Ethik. Vorlesungen Sommersemester 1920/1924* (H. Peucker, Ed.). *Husserliana* XXXVII. Kluwer Academic Publishers. Cited as Hua XXXVII.

Husserl, E. (2006). *Späte texte über die Zeitkonstitution (1929–1934). Die C-Manuskripte* (D. Lohmar, Ed.). *Husserliana-Materialien* VIII. Springer. Cited as HuaM VIII.

Husserl, E. (2008). *Die Lebenswelt. Auslegungen der vorgegebenen Welt und ihrer Konstitution. Texte aus dem Nachlass (1916–1937)* (R. Sowa, Ed.). Husserliana XXXIX. Springer. Cited as Hua XXXIX.

Husserl, E. (2013). *Grenzprobleme der Phänomenologie. Analysen des Unbewusstseins und der Instinkte. Metaphysik. Späte Ethik. Texte aus dem Nachlass (1908–1937)* (R. Sowa & T. Vongehr, Eds.). *Husserliana* XLII. Springer. Cited as Hua XLII.

Husserl, E. (2020). *Studien zur Struktur des Bewusstseins. Teilband III. Wille und Handlung. Texte aus dem Nachlass (1902–1934)* (U. Melle & T. Vongehr, Eds.). *Husserliana* XLIII. Springer. Cited as Hua XLIII/3.

Perreau, L. (2013). *Le monde social selon Husserl* (*Phaenomenologica*) (Vol. 209). Springer.

Rombach, H. (1987). *Strukturanthropologie, „Der menschliche Mensch".* Karl Alber.

Schuhmann, K. (1988). *Husserls Staatsphilosophie.* Karl Alber.

Toulemont, R. (1962). *L'essence de la societé selon Husserl.* Presses universitaires de France.

Trotignon, P. (1986). *Le coeur de la raison. Husserl et la crise du monde moderne* (p. 282). Fayard.

Waldenfels, B. (1985). *In den Netzen der Lebenswelt.* Suhrkamp.

History as Macro-phenomenon: Heidegger and Gadamer

George Bondor

1   INTRODUCTION

Discussing history as a macro-phenomenon, from a perspective that can be called macro-phenomenology, raises two important difficulties. First, phenomenology has been perceived as ahistorical or even anti-historical. The origins of this perception can be found in Husserl's critical remarks on the historical character of phenomena, the consideration of which could not satisfy the claim of universality of the eidetic analysis. The return to the things themselves implied, at the same time, overcoming the analysis that was typical of the history of philosophy but also of the cultural sciences of the spirit (Husserl, 1965). Heidegger (1992–93, p. 176) recalls the ahistorical tendency of Husserlian phenomenology. In his early lectures and courses, as well as in *Being and Time*, he makes a *historical turn* that is also a *hermeneutical turn*, continued by Gadamer and Ricoeur.

This is where the second difficulty comes in. Phenomenology begins as a micro-phenomenology. Both Husserl and Heidegger (the latter during his phenomenological decade) understand the phenomenological method as a description or an interpretation of the original givenness, that is, of what is

Translated by Mariana Constantinescu

G. Bondor (✉)
"Alexandru Ioan Cuza" University of Iasi, Iași, Romania
e-mail: bondor@uaic.ro

shown in the immanence of the ego, respectively of *Dasein*. The efficiency of this approach is based on the radicality of the phenomenological reduction and on the theory of intentionality. Criticizing the reflexivity-based foundation of Husserlian phenomenology, Heidegger tries to consider history in several ways: the historicity of facts (of phenomena), but also the historical (and thus hermeneutic) situation of the researcher, as well as the historicity of the language in which the philosophical research is carried out.[1] These three elements that he introduces into the phenomenological analysis can be seen, at the same time, as strategies to question the claim of Husserlian phenomenology to immediately and intuitively access the original givenness. If we accept that the entry of history into phenomenology can be equated with its *hermeneutic turn*, it is because Heidegger, followed by Gadamer and Ricoeur, nuanced the claim to the immediate knowledge of phenomenology, limiting it by appealing to a few structures of mediation, about which one can argue that they are marks of hermeneutic rationality.

However, this text will be limited to the so-called hermeneutic turn of phenomenology and will be restricted to the thinking of Heidegger and Gadamer. Beyond comparisons, polemics, or critical receptions, it is more important to explore the ways in which in early phenomenology, a micro-phenomenology par excellence, historical phenomena, and concepts can be interpreted as outsets to a macro-phenomenology and, at the same time, as a critique of inauthenticity and alienation.

In his phenomenological decade, and generally before *Kehre*, Heidegger was a faithful follower of micro-phenomenology. Phenomenological analysis and interpretation pertain to a first-person philosophy. Even now trying to find hermeneutical alternatives to the presupposition of the epistemological centrality of the subject, established by modern thought, Heidegger still preserved the centrality of *Dasein*. Moreover, in *Being and Time*, this centrality was ontologically formalized as *Jemeinigkeit*, by which the orientation of the entire existential analytics toward *my* own *Dasein*, therefore toward the first-person *Dasein*, was defined. And then, how is it possible to talk about a macro-phenomenon if any phenomenon is given to the ego in the first person, being therefore by definition a micro-phenomenon?

Even if *Dasein* is the only being that can give meaning and that can pose the question of meaning, Being is neither a property of *Dasein* nor a representation or concept invented by it. Already with the question of Being, a phenomenon that is not available to *Dasein* is investigated. We could say that being is a macro-phenomenon itself. At the same time, the exploration of the unavailable character of *Dasein* itself takes place by identifying a set of problems,

---

[1] For the translation of Heidegger's concept of *Geschichtlichkeit*, rendered by John Macquarrie and Edward Robinson as "historicality," I prefer the term "historicity," as translated by Joan Stambaugh (cf. Heidegger, 1996) and as it appears in the translation of Gadamer's major work by Joel Weinsheimer and Donald G. Marshall (cf. Gadamer, 2004, cited TM). For the rest of the terminology in *Being and Time*, I will use John Macquarrie and Edward Robinson's translation (cf. Heidegger, 1962, cited BT).

phenomena, and concepts that illustrate this inner limit of it: thrownness, situatedness, facticity, Being-in-the-world, wholeness.

Of all of Dasein's existentials, historicity—along with Being-in-the-world—is probably closest to the status of a macro-phenomenon. But the path to the analysis of this phenomenon goes through the investigation of numerous problems, phenomena, and structures, which have both a methodological and an existential meaning. Starting from historicity, an *a priori* structure of *Dasein*, the existential foundation of universal history also becomes possible, that is, of that history in which the individual is a part and which he describes as a historical narrative. This triad made up of factical history, the ego as a historical being, and historiology, with their correlations, represents the phenomenal field of passages and bridges between a micro-phenomenology and a macro-phenomenology. The understanding of these correlations deserves to be analyzed in exactly this place of maximum tension between a classical phenomenological analysis—which strictly respects the theses of intentionality and reduction, therefore the description and analysis in the first person—and the phenomenological description of an integrative and complex structure such as history, with its many phenomenal aspects.

2   The Hermeneutic Turn of Phenomenology? Or the Phenomenological Turn of Hermeneutics?

The mentioned philosophical tension can be better captured if we deepen the so-called *hermeneutic turn of phenomenology* but also what we could call *the phenomenological turn of hermeneutics*. In other words, the entry of history into the field of interest of phenomenology is not opposed but complementary to the call that hermeneutics makes to the phenomenological method, in its traditional, pre-Heideggerian sense, as a method of historical *Geisteswissenschaften*. Let us state the idea in even more radical terms.[2] In its beginnings, phenomenology sought eidetic universality, but it was deprived of history; on the contrary, hermeneutics was already using history as the defining element of all its research, but it was in search of objectivity and universality. The interweaving of the two research programs, having such different styles, is most likely due to a philosophical contingency. Both Husserl and Heidegger entered a fruitful dispute with Dilthey, whose philosophy represents a synthesis between the entire previous history of hermeneutics, the transcendental problem of Kantian philosophy, and the Hegelian philosophy of objective

---

[2] The importance that phenomenology continues to have within current philosophy makes most researchers think of the relationship with hermeneutics from the perspective of the history of phenomenology, which is why, as we have said, a *hermeneutic turn* is often invoked, and the project that thus arises is called *hermeneutic phenomenology*. However, hermeneutics has a much older history, and the same theoretical encounter is also important from the perspective of this discipline. In hermeneutics, the problem of history was already at the center of research, and the adoption of the phenomenological method represents a turning point in the history of this discipline, a moment emphasized by the main histories of hermeneutics (Gadamer, Grondin, Greisch, etc.).

spirit.[3] I am inclined to think of this encounter as a success of both, and not as their failure. The encounter between the claims to universality of phenomenology and hermeneutics was made possible precisely by thematizing the phenomenon of history. But the universality that they both sought is not the one they each possessed prior to their encounter. If they initially started from the epistemological formulation of the idea of universality, which is contained both in the Husserlian premise of reflexivity, and in the claim of hermeneutics to philosophically thematize the objectivity of understanding, the two end up undertaking a common project precisely because they turn toward ontology.

The relationship between phenomenology and hermeneutics therefore starts from a major tension, which Husserl and Heidegger expressed differently. The way Heidegger resolves this tension paves the way for Gadamer's hermeneutic ontology, which was elaborated starting from the method of phenomenology but also for Ricoeur's ontology. Moreover, Ricoeur eminently describes the relationship between phenomenology and hermeneutics: "hermeneutics is built on the basis of phenomenology," but, on the other hand, "phenomenology is not able to establish itself without a hermeneutical presupposition" (Ricoeur, 1975, p. 85, 1986, p. 40).

It is often noted that, in *Philosophy as a Rigorous Science*, Husserl quotes Dilthey's warning about the tension between historical consciousness and rational systems of concepts (Husserl, 1965, p. 125). For Husserl, evidence is achieved ahistorically. In both *Ideen* and *Philosophy as a Rigorous Science*, the historical sciences of the spirit (history, the sciences of civilization, sociology, etc.) are subject to phenomenological reduction. As a social reality, the spirit is a transcendent, mundane object, just like nature. That is why both historians and natural science researchers deal with mundane facts (physical or mental) which are conceived from within the prejudices of the so-called natural attitude. By applying the phenomenological reduction, the historical spirit becomes a layer of the world constituted in the immanence of the ego. Of course, in a figurative sense, the ego has its own "history" by virtue of the original synthesis of temporality: "The ego constitutes himself for himself in, so to speak, the unity of a 'history'" (Husserl, 1982, p. 75). Each process of consciousness has its own "history" because its genesis is temporal. In the context of transcendental idealism in *Cartesian Meditations*, the matter of the "meaning" of history is part of the ethical-religious problems or, strictly speaking, of the metaphysical problems, "but stated in the realm where everything that can have a possible

---

[3] Heidegger is, however, tempted to partially save him from at least one of these sources, showing that Dilthey is not at all influenced by "dogmatic Kantianism" (Heidegger, 1979, GA 20, p. 20).

sense for us must be stated" (1982, p. 156), namely in the monadic sphere of the constitution of the ego and in that of the constitution of intersubjectivity.[4]

In a late text, Heidegger accepted that his path of thought can be understood starting from hermeneutical premises, which explain both the continuity and the coherence of an entire array of problems (1975, p. 95 sq., p. 122 sq.). Although they are used to criticize the epistemological (reflexive) positioning of Husserlian phenomenology (cf., e.g., von Hermann, 2001, p. 143), these concepts and issues are not taken as such from Dilthey. On the contrary, his attempt to ground the human sciences in the concept of life and in *Lebenszusammenhang* is considered to be insufficient.

3   HISTORICAL CONCEPTS IN HEIDEGGER'S EARLY LECTURES

Let us recall some landmarks from Heidegger's early courses. In his *Habilitation* work on Duns Scotus, he takes on the task of reconciling history and temporality, on the one hand, with the immutability and claim for validity that characterize "logic," on the other. The objective value of the categories should therefore be grounded in the life of consciousness, which is historical and temporal. The only firm ground from which the philosophical exercise must spring is the historicity of the "living spirit," later called the "facticity of existence." The "living spirit," an expression taken from Dilthey and used in his first lectures to denote the human being is, essentially, a historical spirit (see Vattimo, 1985, pp. 13–15; Pöggeler, 1990, pp. 19–22).

The encounter with Dilthey's hermeneutics played an important role in shaping Heidegger's early thought. It was particularly the discovery of the factical-historical character of the concept of life that led him to nuance the claim of Husserlian phenomenology to be a philosophy devoid of any prejudice. Factical life cannot be completely free of prejudice, Heidegger shows in the lecture *Einführung in die phänomenologische Forschung*, from 1923/24 (Heidegger, 1994a, GA 17, p. 2). Heidegger had already shown, in his review of Jaspers, *Anmerkungen zu Karl Jaspers "Psychologie der Weltanschauungen"* (Heidegger, 2004a, GA 9, pp. 1–44), that "thinking without presuppositions can itself be achieved only in a self-critique that is historically oriented in a

---

[4]With *Krisis*, Husserl reorients the transcendental approach through a "teleological-historical reflection" that gives phenomenology a critical dimension. Historical reflection is necessary to highlight the "intentional origins" guiding what inquirers deem knowable, possible, and conceivable, that is, constellations of concepts, principles, and "depth problems" which organize our lifeworld and exercises a hidden normative pull on our knowledge (Husserl, 1970). This critical going back to the depth problems must be, on the other hand, a teleological one, since the community of consciousnesses must have not only a past, but also a future, a *telos*, a common task, so a regulative idea which, for Husserl, is that of progress toward theoretical freedom. Following in the footsteps of Ricoeur, we can therefore affirm that already in Husserl phenomenology is realized as hermeneutics. For the presence of hermeneutics since Husserlian writings belonging to transcendental idealism, see also Luft (2011). According to other commentators, Husserl's reflections would belong to a critical philosophy of history, which must be distinguished from the speculative philosophy of history (see Casement, 1988, pp. 229–240).

factical manner." However, Dilthey's concept of life, as well as Husserl's concept of self, has an objectual character, of mere presence. As Heidegger points out in the lecture *Phänomenologische Interpretationen zu Aristoteles. Einführung in die phänomenologische Forschung*, life has two tendencies (Heidegger, 1994b, WS 1921/1922, GA 61). When oriented toward itself and understood as such, life shows itself as a context of significance (*Bedeutsamkeitszusammenhang*). On the contrary, when it is oriented toward "objectivation" ("*Objectivierung*") or reification (*Verdinglichung*), life is actually its opposite, an "*Entlebung*." The theme is found in several places, of which a special place is given to the understanding of life as *tentatio* (*Versuchung*) and as care, seen as a struggle against losing oneself in the world (*Augustinus und der Neuplatonismus*, SS 1921, in Heidegger, 2011, GA 60).

From his very first lectures, Heidegger attaches great importance to Dilthey's concept of life-nexus (*Lebenszusammenhang*). In his lecture *Die Idee der Philosophie und das Weltanschauungsproblem* (KNS 1919), he shows that life is historical and must be conceived as a whole, and not as a sum of component parts (Heidegger, 1987, GA 56/57, p. 117). In turn, living is neither an object nor a process, but an event (*Ereignis*) (1987, p. 75). Identified with an original pre-theoretical science, that is, with phenomenology, philosophy is meant to free pre-theoretical life from the self-estrangement to which that orientation of life which is guided by theoretical reflection leads (Heidegger, 1993b, GA 58). Philosophy is thus a comprehensive interpretation of pre-theoretical life (*verstehende Auslegung des vor-theoretischen Lebens*), which has a factical and historical character. This idea also appears in the lecture *Grundprobleme der Phänomenologie* (WS 1919/1920, in Heidegger, 1993b, GA 58), where the fundamental categories of factical-historical life are analyzed, philosophy being defined as experience (*Erfahrung*), that is, an "original science of factical life itself" (*Ursprungswissenschaft des fakitschen Lebens an sich*). The analysis of the formal structure of experience is also at the center of the lecture *Einleitung in die Phänomenologie der Religion* (WS 1920/1921, in Heidegger, 2011, GA 60), in which it is stated that philosophical research must always start from everyday experience.[5]

The concepts and issues analyzed in his early courses outline a field for the thematization of historical phenomena and of the structure that will be called historicity (*Geschichtlichkeit*). Already in his course *Ontologie (Hermeneutik der Faktizität)*, in 1923, the concepts of "life" and "living spirit" denote "*Dasein* itself," which is totally permeated by its factical situation (Heidegger, 1988, GA 63, p. 7, 1999, p. 5). The entire research is called *hermeneutics*, designating "the unified manner of the engaging, approaching, accessing, interrogating, and explicating of facticity" (Heidegger, 1988, GA 63, p. 9, 1999, p. 6). Through it, *Dasein* gains access to itself: both to its own alienation (its falling) and to its authentic self-understanding. Therefore, hermeneutics plays the role of an "awakening" from the state of alienation to which it is currently abandoned

[5] For the concept of experience, see David Carr (2014).

and, at the same time, of a "wakefulness" (*Wachsein*) for itself (Heidegger, 1988, GA 63, pp. 15–16, 1999, p. 12). This is why hermeneutics[6] has the character of a *Destruktion*: the solidified interpretations (*Ausgelegtheiten*) that have become dominant, leading *Dasein* outside itself, must be subjected to destruction; it is therefore necessary that, through a *destructive return* (*im abbauenden Rückgang*), we access the original sources of the interpretation itself (cf. also Heidegger, 2003, p. 34).

Heidegger names history and philosophy as ways of interpretation of *Dasein*. Through their mediation, *Dasein* tries to understand itself. In history, it objectivates itself as "has-been" (*Gewesenes*) and in philosophy as "always-being-in-such-a-manner" (*Immersosein*). The two ways of objectivation of *Dasein* are mentioned in order to be subjected to critique and then overcome. Historical consciousness and philosophy are nothing but ways in which *Dasein* understands itself through today's current interpretation. Equating the ideal of the objectivity of historical knowledge with the distance between the subject and the object, historical consciousness fails to fully elaborate the possibility of having a knowledge in which the presuppositions of the researcher of history do not pre-determine the direction of his research, including in the sense of uncritical acceptance of current ideologies. However, according to Heidegger, it is this particular effort that is suspicious, placing the entire historiology in the sphere of *Dasein*'s inauthentic relation to its own past. In this context, Heidegger suggests that it is necessary to understand "the total fact of man" (Heidegger, 1988, GA 63, p. 56, 1999, p. 44), but not through the ready-made interpretation of today, which leaves *Dasein* with the impression that it holds its own past, but also the present and even the future of *Dasein*. This is where destruction comes in, which is necessary to free *Dasein* not only from current interpretations but also from the temptation to think it is available to its own self.

4   DESTRUCTION AND UNDERSTANDING, BETWEEN
PHENOMENOLOGY AND HERMENEUTICS

For Heidegger, destruction is not the refusal of tradition or its annihilation, but a historical critique through which it is possible to verify the original meanings of metaphysical concepts. Understood as destruction, the hermeneutics of facticity, therefore, has an emancipatory intention (Grondin, 1993, p. 144). Its purpose is to recover the living elements of tradition. Historicity is the essential determination of *Dasein* that makes it, explicitly or only implicitly, be its own past. In other words, *Dasein* is captured not only by the world in which it already exists but also by the tradition to which it belongs. "This tradition keeps it from providing its own guidance, whether in inquiring or in choosing" (Heidegger, 1993a, SZ, p. 21, 1962, BT, pp. 42–43). The impression given by some lectures, as well as the 1924 conference *Der Begriff der Zeit* (Heidegger, 2004b, GA 64, p. 114), is that the concept of tradition

---

[6] For other clarifications regarding the hermeneutics of facticity, see also Grondin (2003b, pp. 60–67) and Kisiel (1993).

designates the situation of *Dasein* under the influence of *das Man*.[7] It therefore seems to be assigned to the sphere of inauthenticity: tradition hides rather than shows, it blocks the access to origins, and it contributes to oblivion and removes the need to return to sources. It conveys only a first instance, global, and domineering interpretation of *Dasein*, which blocks it from genuine access to itself (Heidegger, 1993a, SZ, p. 21).

Then, the task of destruction is presented, namely the weakening of the rigid, solidified tradition, a fact that would make it possible to explicitly resume the question about the meaning of Being. The past, as it becomes present through the history of ontology, is interrogated and interpreted in order to clarify the present situation of ontology. However, ontology has always envisaged Being as presence. This, for Heidegger, is the most important "constant" of the metaphysical approach. Thus, hermeneutics can achieve its task of making factical existence visible, beyond the concepts of metaphysics, only through destruction and as interpretation (*Auslegung*).[8] Dasein undertakes the care toward how the facticity of its existence is fulfilled every time. Being under the modality of interpretation every moment, *Dasein* is an *ens hermeneuticum*, and the access to its facticity is also a hermeneutic one (Grondin, 2003a, pp. 48–49). This fact is proven by the enumeration of the four meanings of hermeneutics, in § 7 of *Being and Time* (Heidegger, 1993a, SZ, p. 37).

Ontically, *Dasein* is always within a certain understanding of being (Heidegger, 1993a, SZ, p. 12), which accompanies every relation to being. We do not know where it comes from within us, but only that it is somehow given to us. This *Faktum*, the facticity of *Dasein*, is the starting point of Heideggerian hermeneutics. Characterized by Being-in-the-world, *Dasein* is situated in already given possibilities of understanding, without it being their "constitutive" origin itself, like in Husserlian phenomenology. This is the state of thrownness (*Geworfenheit*), which expresses the fact of the past (*Gewesenheit*) which *Dasein* carries. Thrownness signifies a "facticity of its being delivered over" (*Faktizität der Überantwortung*) (Heidegger, 1993a, SZ, p. 135): *Dasein* has to exist within those possibilities to which it has been delivered over, and thus it is never available to itself (Grondin, 1994, p. 70). The connection with the topic of history is obvious. Thrownness (*Geworfenheit*) refers to having been (*Gewesenheit*), which is an ontological structure of *Dasein*. In so far as it is, *Dasein* is something that has been thrown. Care is grounded in *Gewesenheit*, not in *Vergangenheit*, and only therefore can *Dasein* exist as something thrown. *Dasein* "always is indeed as already having *been*." It is situated precisely because it is a thrown Fact. "The primary existential meaning of facticity lies in the character of having been" (Heidegger, 1993a, SZ, p. 328, 1962, p. 376).

[7] Both in his 1923 course and in *Being and Time*, Heidegger also resorts to a destruction of the everyday way of being. On the concepts of *Durchschnittlichkeit* and *das Man*, as well as on the neutral character of the everyday relative to authentic and inauthentic existence, see Haar (1994, pp. 61–67).

[8] "Hermeneutik ist Destruktion" (Heidegger, 1988, GA 63, p. 105). The terms Heidegger uses are *Abbau* and *Destruktion*.

Dasein understands according to the possibilities toward which it projects itself, by virtue of its fore-structure, made of *Vorhabe, Vorsicht,* and *Vorgriff*. Through this fore-structure, Heidegger redefines the idea of the hermeneutic circle, which has been defined as the circularity between the part and the whole in the history of hermeneutics. But given the thrownness, *Dasein* is not the master of its projections, of the possibilities toward which it is projected, nor of the structure of understanding. On the contrary, it exists every moment in an elementary complementarity of projection and thrownness, which qualifies it as a "thrown project" (*geworfener Entwurf*): "it projects itself upon possibilities into which it has been thrown" (Heidegger, 1993a, SZ, p. 284, 1962, BT, p. 330), and not toward others, which it would tailor as it pleased. The complementarity between *Geworfenheit* and *Entwurf* actually indicates the complementarity between past and future, between what is already given to *Dasein* and its freedom. In Heidegger, understanding becomes an *ontological* concept, upon which the methods of the *Geisteswissenschaften*, which Dilthey called explanation and comprehension, are based (1993a, SZ, p. 143, p. 336). If hermeneutics was regional in its history, now it raises the claim to *universality*, being rooted in the existence of *Dasein*: more precisely, it becomes a descriptive "repetition" of the existentiality of understanding.

5   HERMENEUTIC CIRCULARITY: LIFE AND HISTORY

In his lecture *History of the concept of time: Prolegomena*, Heidegger had already shown that phenomenology is neither systematic nor historiographical, but it grants access to an original sphere located before the traditional division into systematic knowledge and historical knowledge. This is the sphere of pre-theoretical life, which is historical and factical, and which must interpret itself as it is, and not as a mere object. Self-interpretation is a hermeneutics, Heidegger shows, that is, a phenomenology that moves away from the theoretical-reflexive character of the Husserlian approach, but also from the prejudice of traditional hermeneutics, according to which, in the sciences of the spirit, understanding could be objective if the researcher is located at a distance from the researched object, somehow managing to access the life context of the era in which the research object (text, work of art, historical fact, etc.) was created. Dilthey took the definition of understanding through the part-whole relationship from Romantic hermeneutics, and his concept of *Lebenszusammenhang*—usually translated by life-nexus, but also by connectedness of life or context of life—must be understood starting from this Romantic figure of the hermeneutic circle.

The part-whole relation is at the heart of Romantic hermeneutics. In his courses on hermeneutics, Schleiermacher (1978, p. 2, 1995, p. 77) starts from the idea that "every discourse has a two-part reference, to the whole language and to the entire thought of its creator." There is a close interdependence between the two: language modifies the spirit, and the latter shapes the language. According to Schleiermacher, the task of hermeneutics is understanding, defined as the inversion (*Umkehrung*) of the act of giving speeches, which is nothing but the externalization of thought. Therefore, hermeneutics aims at the reconstruction (*Nachkonstruieren*) of the thought from which a discourse arose. Both language and thought are indeterminate totalities that acquire determinations. Language, a whole of possibilities, becomes something determined when the individual uses it. The infinite, then, becomes finite. Each author makes his own "cut" into the field of language, making a more or less conscious selection. Therefore, the understanding of the linguistic side of the discourse, which Schleiermacher calls grammatical interpretation, can only take place if the whole of the language in which the author writes is reconstructed. The same is true of the psychological side of interpretation. The ideas expressed in a speech spring from the whole of the author's thinking, which is a whole of possibilities, some of which are actualized, becoming determined ideas. Just as language is "something infinite," so is human thought constantly changing, which is why the task of hermeneutics is infinite.

Conceiving the relationship between speech and language, and between speech and thought, as a relationship between part and whole, Schleiermacher talks about the circularity of understanding. The part cannot be understood unless the whole in which it is contained is reconstructed, and the whole can only be understood by understanding the parts that compose it. However, the idea of the circularity of understanding can be misleading. It can make us believe that understanding entails a kind of hermeneutic closure, a movement within a circle from which one cannot get out. In fact, understanding is neither static nor closed. It involves moving from one part-whole circle to another, a kind of cumulative understanding, one that advances progressively and increases continually. A figure that better expresses this idea is the spiral: understanding is the deepening of the meaning by passing from the initial context to another, more comprehensive one, in the light of which the understanding from the initial context is corrected, and the process can continue, drawing an open spiral (cf. Jung, 2001, pp. 65–66). In Schleiermacher, psychological interpretation is dependent on the idea that the understanding of a foreign life occurs through transposition into the interiority of the other, called divination (or empathy). In addition, through comparison with the interiority of the other, a better self-understanding is, in fact, achieved.

Both methods—empathy and comparison—were taken up by Dilthey. Empathy becomes a re-experience (*Nachfühlen*) for Dilthey, being necessary in order to know from the inside the lived experience (*Erlebnis*) from which a written expression (*Ausdruck*) arose. Lived experience, the individual unit of life, must be understood in relation to the entire course of life (*Lebensverlauf*): "The course of a life consists of parts, of lived experiences that are inwardly connected with each other" (Dilthey, 1965, p. 195, 2002, p. 217). Life has a structural character, having a permanent relationship with its parts, which are lived experiences: "It is only because life itself is a structural nexus in which lived experiences stand in experienceable relations that the connectedness of life is given to us" (ibid.). In Dilthey, the concept of *Lebenszusammenhang* has a metaphysical (and at the same time epistemological) character, and not a transcendental-phenomenological one, like the Husserlian *Lebenswelt*, with which it has sometimes been compared (Makkreel, 1982). But it is, above all, hermeneutic (in the sense of the methodological hermeneutics that is characteristic of Romanticism and Dilthey), especially due to the part-whole hermeneutic circularity, which is involved both in the relationship between life, lived experiences, and expressions, and in the hermeneutic relationship between life, re-experiencing, and understanding, as a method of *Geisteswissenschaften*.

Prior to Romantic hermeneutics, it was not well acknowledged that, in order to understand an author, it was necessary to understand his era. Dilthey clearly shows that any author (and any individual in general) carries with him the spirit of his age, which can be understood through the knowledge of biography and autobiography. This is a principle of historicism (Boeckh, Droysen, Dilthey, etc.). In Dilthey, Romantic sources merge with Hegelian ones: reconstructing the spiritual whole of the era is equivalent to understanding the objective spirit (morals, law, family, etc.). The projects of critical philosophy of history, as Raymond Aron (1950) calls the theories of Dilthey, Rickert, Simmel, and Weber, are based on a Hegelian presupposition regarding the relationship between the individual and history but taken up again through the Kantian problem of critical philosophy. But it is precisely this purpose of hermeneutics, that is, the reconstruction of the historical spirit starting from its expressions, which had the claim of objectivity because it believed in the possibility of overcoming, through empathy, the distance between the interpreter and the author's era, that actually started from the assumption of the existence of this distance, which was a temporal distance, as Gadamer called it, and at the same time an epistemic distance between the subject and the object.

6   The Integrality of Dasein: New Meanings of the Hermeneutic Circle

Taking Yorck's side, instead of Dilthey's, Heidegger revolutionizes the traditional discipline called hermeneutics, whose radical transformation represents a *phenomenological turn* or, in other words, an *ontological turn*. Heidegger's confrontation with Dilthey's concept of *Lebenszusammenhang* is not in the least accidental. For in this concept, we already find both the idea of the whole of life and that of the coherence (or structure) of life. However, Heidegger will show that the question of *Lebenszusammenhang* is a misleading one, its destruction revealing that its origin lies in the idea of inauthentic historicity (1993a, SZ, p. 387). The critique of Dilthey's concept of life-nexus was a good starting point for Heidegger, because this was, in fact, the vulgar concept of history. The concept of *Lebenszusammenhang* lacks an ontological foundation. Understood as a sequence of experiences in time, it belongs to the entities within-time-ness, being placed in the area of what is ready-to-hand and present-at-hand. Therefore, as Heidegger shows, the idea of historicity should not be founded upon the concepts of life, living, and life-nexus, but on temporality.

The three-dimensional hierarchization of temporal modes gives an order in which historicity finds a precise place: the original temporality is positioned under the orientation of the future, historicity has a special relationship with the past, and within-time-ness is the orientation toward the present. The unity of temporality, which resides in the unity of the three temporal ecstasies, reiterates, on another level, the totality (*Ganzheit*) of *Dasein* which is sought from the beginning and which is foreshadowed by Being-in-the-world, and then it is described as care. At the same time, the unity of the three temporal ecstasies corresponds to the unity of the three aspects that define the constitution of *Dasein*: existentiality, facticity, and falling. This correspondence clearly indicates that the interest in the past requires the elaboration of both the facticity and the historicity of *Dasein*, a fact that has been intuited and developed by Heidegger since his early lectures. His constant concern within existential analytics is also to highlight the coherence of *Dasein*'s existential structures. Through the analysis of historicity, the two aspects that Heidegger wanted to unite, namely history and systematicity, are synthesized to the greatest extent. But totality cannot consist neither in the temporal sequence of experiences nor in the internal consciousness of time, nor in the sum of existential structures, but it resides in *Dasein*'s relationship with the future. *Dasein* shows itself in its authentic existential project as an anticipation of death. Historicity and historiology are thus rooted in the future as *Zukommenlassen*. At the same time, as Jean Greisch also shows, the analysis of the past and of historicity is necessary because, together with the issue of *Dasein*'s self-projection toward its ultimate possibility, death, there is a risk of forgetting that Dasein is at the same time something that has been thrown (Greisch, 1994, p. 364). This risk is avoided through the question posed by Heidegger in § 74: "we must ask whence, in general, *Dasein* can draw those possibilities upon which it factically projects itself" (1993a, SZ, p. 383, 1962, BT, p. 434).

The four meanings of the concept of history, mentioned by Heidegger in § 73, already not only circumscribe the sphere of interest of the problem of history but also indicate the way in which the "phenomenological construction" of historicity must start from the analysis of the historical character of equipments of the past. With this problem, Heidegger seeks an existential foundation for the problems left unsolved, since they were treated as self-evident, and which we meet both in Dilthey's hermeneutics and in the epistemological approach to history (Simmel, Rickert).

1. The first is the idea that the past does not stop exerting its effects upon the present, which will lead Gadamer to the concept of "consciousness of being affected by history."
2. The notion of *historical reality* could not be defined without conceiving the beings of the past starting from their way of being in the world of *Dasein* which has-been-there (*dagewesen*), but also without understanding

that their historical character is given by the *Dasein* of now, which recognizes them as expressions of the possibilities of the then world which are passed on to it, which it inherits, which it can undertake, turning them into its own possibilities, toward which it projects itself. In short, this is the answer to the above question. The existential relation to its own past is the historical primordial element, which belongs to *Dasein*, and which it can invest in equipments (the secondary historical element). The historical character of the equipments, which Heidegger calls world history (*Weltgeschichte*), will also establish the current notion (as well as the Hegelian one) of "universal history," without being identical to it.

3. What is passed on is not a "repository" that we must keep intact, to bequeath to the next generation but "possibilities." This inheritance can only be undertaken by *Dasein* in resoluteness, that is, in the face of its own death.

4. Dasein's relation to its own existential possibilities—and especially to its ultimate possibility, mortality, inherited and nevertheless chosen—is designated by Heidegger using the term fate (*Schicksal*). If fate is Dasein's primordial historizing (*Geschehen*), its historizing is a co-historizing (*Mitgeschehen*) because of its Being-with-Others (*Mitsein*). This destiny (*Geschick*), which is more than the simple sum of individual fates, defines, according to Heidegger, "the historizing of the community, of a people" (1993a, SZ, p. 384, 1962, BT, p. 436).

What we have here is an existential foundation of history, of individual fate, and of collective destiny, and thus the intersection between these two, but also the concept of generation, found in Dilthey, which is quoted in this context: "Our fates have already been guided in advance, in our Being with one another in the same world and in our resoluteness for definite possibilities. Only in communicating and in struggling does the power of destiny become free. Dasein's fateful destiny in and with its 'generation' goes to make up the full authentic historizing of Dasein" (Heidegger, 1993a, SZ, pp. 384–5, 1962, BT, p. 436). The use of Dilthey's concept of "generation" in quotation marks indicates, very likely, that this concept cannot provide an ontological foundation, but it remains an ontic concept (cf. also 1993a, SZ, § 6). At the same time, it seems to be placed on the same level with Jaspers' concept of "worldview" (*Weltanschauung*). Of course, Dasein takes on self-interpretations and interpretations of the world that belong to its generation and the worldview of its age. This was precisely the theory of understanding of traditional hermeneutics, elaborated by Schleiermacher and developed by Dilthey, and which, as we have shown, is illustrated by the figure of the part-whole hermeneutic circle. For Heidegger, however, the unconscious takeover of the generation's and epoch's worldview amounts to an inauthentic way of being, derived from the inauthentic historicity of Dasein. However, the quotation marks may indicate that the term generation should be conceived in all its indeterminacy. The generation can be a source of inauthentic self-understanding if its data takes over Dasein. On the contrary, the generation can even be the concrete structure, where individual fate and collective destiny meet, the factical place where the authenticity of the individual Dasein and the authenticity of the community determine, through their unity, the authentic historizing of Dasein.[9]

How can the identification of the authentic occurrence of Dasein as the *interweaving of individual fate and collective destiny* be seen as an intersection between micro-phenomenology and macro-phenomenology? First of all, the matter must be understood in the classical terms of phenomenology. The existential structures that indicate Dasein's possibility of being with others, to be part of a communal destiny and therefore to share an interpretation of the world with its generation and era, are conceived by Heidegger as conditions of possibility of Dasein, having a transcendental-phenomenological character. They inevitably belong to a first-person phenomenology. But at the same time, through their exploration, Heidegger identifies the inner limits of Dasein: (1) the fact that it is not transparent to itself but is factically involved in situations that make it fallen, therefore inauthentic; (2) the fact that it projects itself toward possibilities that are chosen by it, but also inherited (by virtue of historicity); (3) the fact that its projection toward the ultimate possibility, its own death, is achieved through a state of authentic resolution, designated by Heidegger as the "primordial historizing of Dasein"; and (4) although resoluteness is an individual action of Dasein, the ultimate possibility for which this resolution is activated is already given to Dasein by virtue of its thrownness (*Geworfenheit*). Thus, even Dasein's purely individual moods and actions, such as anxiety, taking over the possibilities, authentic repetition, and struggling, which come to it from the future of its mortality, can be activated by it only because, in a sense, they are already given to it as its possibilities. (5) The intersection between fate and destiny, which describes the historicity of Dasein, actually restates, within the framework of the problem of history, the fact that Dasein is a unity between *Geworfenheit* and *Entwurf*, but at the same time the fact that it is characterized by facticity.

As we have shown, the problem of the unity of Dasein, which is pursued throughout all existential analytics, is distinguished here from Dilthey's very concept of *Lebenszusammenhang*. For Dilthey, this concept referred to the whole of the individual's life (the whole to which each particular experience must be related), but the understanding of the objectifications (expressions, externalizations) of life was only possible if the whole of life was put in relation to the whole of the era, of the culture, with the vision of the world that defines it. However, this way of conceiving the relationship of the individual with the whole of life and culture is tied to inauthenticity. Heidegger's reply starts from another totality besides life, age, and culture, namely from Being-in-the-world. At the starting point of existential analytics, this existential structure unitarily

---

[9] An additional argument for this interpretation is the fact that, in *Kasseler Vorträge*, the concept of generation is linked to the structure of *Miteinandersein* (Heidegger, 1992–93, pp. 174–175).

captures Dasein, even if undifferentiated in its structures. By virtue of this structure, Dasein is always factically involved in relations with things in the environment (*Umwelt*).

The consequences of the emphasis on everydayness (*Alltäglichkeit*) are important. (a) First of all, the pre-theoretical familiarity that Dasein has with the things of the *Umwelt* and with the environment as such, as a unit prior to any theory, is thus highlighted. (b) Second, the phenomenological (and ontological) analysis of this familiarity is claimed to be prior to the epistemological subject-object relationship. Precisely for this reason, the ontological analysis of history does not start from historical objects as such but from the significance of equipments that the beings of the past have in the environment of the Dasein that was, a world that it opened in the past. c) In its everyday actions, Dasein does have a familiarity not only with things in its *Umwelt* but also with other people, whom it meets in the world it shares with them (*Mitwelt*) due to its existential structure called Being-with (*Mitsein*) and its underlying structures (*Mitdasein, Miteinandersein*).

However, this precise analysis is continued by the thematization of collective destiny (*Geschick*). Moreover, the way in which Dasein simultaneously has (intentional) relations with equipments in the *Umwelt* and with the other Dasein in the *Mitwelt* has repercussions on the understanding of historicity as primordial historizing, conceived as a unity between fate and destiny. Last but not least, the authenticity of these relationships depends precisely on the possibility for Dasein to understand itself in its wholeness. As we have seen, totality—and at the same time authenticity—is gained through Dasein's resoluteness, thus through the temporalization of the future in the mood of anxiety. So, Dasein also transfers the authenticity it gained by projecting it toward its future, to its relationship with the past and the present. The authentic meaning of the past derives from Dasein's relationship with itself (care), in its own world (*Selbstwelt*), more precisely from its relationship with its authentic future (anxiety). The authentic past comes from the future: "The character of 'having been' arises from the future" (Heidegger, 1993a, SZ, p. 326, 1962, BT, pp. 373–4). Thus, the extension (*Ausdehnung*) between birth and death, a notion by which Heidegger rethinks Dilthey's notion of *Lebenszusammenhang*, does not refer to a quantitative wholeness but, we could say, to a qualitative one, existentially founded in Dasein's anticipation of death, therefore in the temporalizing of the future.

What exactly can be called, in this case, a historical object? Objects are "historical" not because they belong to a past world, but because the Dasein of now has access (by virtue of its disclosedness, therefore, of truth) to the world of the Dasein that was, to its environment (*Umwelt*), and thus it has access to the things with which that Dasein was then in a relationship of everyday familiarity (being preoccupied with them). Heidegger necessarily extends the analysis of equipments to an analysis of the relations that the Dasein that was had, in the with-world (*Mitwelt*), with other Dasein, reports designated as solicitude (*Fürsorge*). The analysis of this *Mitwelt* from the past influences the ontology of historicity by elaborating the concept of destiny, which describes, as we can recall, "the historizing of the community, of a people" (Heidegger, 1993a, SZ, p. 384, 1962, BT, p. 436). This could be Heidegger's reply to the problem of understanding the era and the culture, as solved by Dilthey. The concept of *Volk* seems assigned to an authentic way of being. Although the sources of this term are unclear, and its use has also been interpreted in a political note, it seems to play the role of a formal correspondent of *das Man* but in the note of authenticity. Thus, it designates "a community of authenticity," that is, "the authentic community of individuals prepared to take upon themselves the responsibility for choice in light of the finitude of existence" (Barash, 2003, p. 169). The primary meaning of the term is that of a transcendental-phenomenological structure, as is its inauthentic counterpart, *das Man*. However, as Ricoeur (1985, p. 112) shows, the fact of transferring the theme of being toward death to the community sphere is devoid of any caution, representing the source of misunderstandings of this possible political philosophy with tragic and heroic accents.

7   HISTORY AS A MACRO-PHENOMENON: FROM THE INAUTHENTIC TO THE AUTHENTIC

At first glance, the concept of world history (*Weltgeschichte*) can only denote an inauthentic mode, as it is derived from the temporal mode of the present, which exerts a constant pressure on Dasein to understand itself starting from the mode of being of presence-at-hand and from the impersonal *das Man*. However, this term must probably also be understood in its indeterminacy: when Dasein is taken over by the things in its present world, the world history is inauthentic; on the contrary, it is authentic when Dasein gains its authenticity from the temporalization of the future. Even the Hegelian meaning of the term, "the invincible progression of the consciousness of freedom," does not have its ontological sources in the temporality of finite Dasein but rather expresses the becoming of cultures and nations. However, becoming can express the mode of being of the world but not of history. An important consequence is Heidegger's critique of the traditional distinction between nature and history, a distinction shared by hermeneutics and historicism, and equally accepted by Dilthey and Yorck. A true ontological grounding of history (and of the sciences of the spirit) must go beyond the distinction between nature and history (or between nature and culture). Things are not in themselves natural or historical but become so by virtue of the temporal meaning that Dasein gives to them. "These entities within-the-world *are* historically as such" (Heidegger, 1993a, SZ, pp. 388–9, 1962, BT, p. 440). Through its historicity, Dasein gives entities within-the-world a historical character, just as it gives them an involvement (*Bewandtnis*) and significance (*Bedeutsamkeit*). The cohesion of the environment, made possible by the structures called involvement and significance, is now deepened due to the temporality and historicity of Dasein. The equipment of the past comes to be a historical object today, and the action of an individual from the past comes to be considered a historical event today. The ontologization of history actually blurs traditional historiology's emphasis on objects and actions, shifting the focus to possibilities. The equipment, respectively the action of the past, signified something in the world of Dasein at that time, which Dasein projected itself toward certain possibilities of its own. The Dasein of now encounters past actions and past objects (turned ruins, monuments, etc.) as inherited possibilities, which it can choose, undertake, and toward which it can project itself. A possibility becomes *mine* to the extent that I assume it through resolution, self-repetition, and explicit transmission. Therefore, the repetition of a possibility from the past is not equivalent to a passeist attitude but to the response now given to that possibility. Through the resolution of now, Dasein revokes the bad influence of the past on the present (Greisch, 1994, p. 366). But we might say, it also revokes the bad influence of the present. Thus, the most radical possibility that it can assume by inheriting it is its own finitude. It comes to *Dasein* from both its past and its future. The authenticity thus gained, paired with the authenticity of the community, is also transferred to the past, which can only be authentically understood in this manner.

History, Heidegger shows, must be understood as a "recurrence" of the possible when it is rooted in authentic historicity (1993a, SZ, pp. 391–2). If viewed exclusively from the perspective of the present (1993a, SZ, § 75; GA 65, pp. 129–135), history ends up being dominated by the museal attitude, which historiology theorizes through the notions of document, archive, and trace. The consequence on how to conceive the historiology is obvious. Historical understanding is not only a method that is specific to certain sciences, a procedure stipulated within a set of sciences (of the spirit). Even its desired objectivity, meant to satisfy the claim to general validity (*Allgemeingültigkeit*), cannot be procedurally constituted within the historical sciences of the spirit. That is why Heidegger considers that the tendency of historiology "to place unique 'individual' events into a series, or whether it also has 'laws' as its objects, is one that is radically mistaken" (1993a, SZ, p. 395, 1962, BT, p. 447).

The meaning of this critique of historiology is strictly phenomenological, more precisely a phenomenological-hermeneutic one. The tendency of the sciences of the spirit (as they were thematized by Dilthey) to rely on universally valid truths (eras, cultures, worldviews, generations, objective understanding, cohesion of life, series of events, norms, historical laws, etc.) is rooted in Dasein's inauthentic way of being, which is a theoretical and impersonal way of being. Apparently, the phenomenological ontology of history analyzes history—and all the phenomena through which it is interpreted—more as a micro-phenomenon than as a macro-phenomenon. It is true that the "macro" features of history, by which it is commonly defined, are rooted in individual Dasein. The authentic work of the historian derives from the existential meaning of history, that is, from authentic historicity, which is nothing but the repetition of authentic possibilities of existence (Heidegger, 1993a, SZ, p. 396, 1962, BT, p. 448). Historical facts cannot be repeated, no matter how much traditional historiology tries to discover laws and meanings of history, which ensure a minimum repeatability of phenomena, as is found in natural sciences. However, Heidegger puts into play the *existential* repetition of possibilities, even if they are individual ones. We can conclude from this that the repeatability of possibilities is a mark of the fact that history is a macro-phenomenon.

Early phenomenology claims a phenomenality that gravitates around the subject, thus a micro-phenomenology. But it is no less true that precisely the exploration of Dasein's historical character reveals the limits of its individuality. The discovery of its limits restores the scenario of hermeneutic circularity between part and whole, but on two totally different levels: authentic and inauthentic. The misunderstood integrality of human existence, which Heidegger analyzes at length, amounts to the loss of self through its capture by vast historical totalities. On the contrary, the positive wholeness of man is only earned individually, by understanding his own limits, which are given to him by his very historicity. Thus, we could argue that history is a macro-phenomenon because it represents an inner limit of Dasein, a criterion of self-criticism, of the "judgment" of the present (cf. Greisch, 1994, p. 378), and implicitly a criterion of selection that the historian makes regarding past facts that deserve to become objects of study of historiology (Heidegger, 1993a, SZ, p. 395, 1962, BT, p. 447).

In his works after *Kehre*, Heidegger puts to work a destructive hermeneutics of the history of metaphysics, which continues the hermeneutics of facticity and the hermeneutics of Dasein (Grondin, 2003a, pp. 50–51, 2003b, pp. 71–73). It aims to uncover the hidden presuppositions of the history (or "destiny") of metaphysics, that is, of the history of the understanding of Being. The problem of history therefore remains a hermeneutic theme, without the relationship between the type of phenomenality developed in the so-called *seingeschichtliches Denken* and the phenomenological method being clear.

8   BELONGING AND FACTICITY: GADAMER

Gadamer's philosophy is avowedly hermeneutics, as it investigates the phenomenon of understanding, which is the fundamental human way of being. Thus conceived, understanding seems to denote intentionality itself. Gadamer's analyses do not fit into the old epistemological problem of hermeneutics, but his fundamental question is thus: what happens to us when we understand? Hermeneutics, therefore, investigates the conditions for the possibility of understanding (Gadamer, 1999b [GW2], p. 438, 2004, TM, p. XXVI). Thus, understanding is interrogated as the basis—environment, element, universe— in which our existence and, implicitly but secondarily, all knowledge is rooted. Constituted as a *Geschehen* (event, process, historizing), understanding carries us with it without knowing where it comes from within us. It is, therefore, unavailable to us while also being the element within which we live and which mediates any possible relationship with others (Grondin, 1999, p. 37). Gadamer analyzes understanding in relation to the facticity of human being. The freedom of the relationship with the human being cannot go beyond his situation. In Heideggerian terms, understanding has as an insurmountable limit the thrownness (*die Geworfenheit*), that is, the past, which limits from the very beginning the projection toward possibilities: "Dasein that projects itself on its own potentiality-for-being has always already 'been'. This is the meaning of the existential of 'thrownness' " (Gadamer, 1999a, WM, p. 268, 2004, TM, p. 254). The consequence is that it must be deepened in the context of "understanding the historical tradition." The phenomenon that, thus, emerges is belonging (*die Zugehörigkeit*) to tradition, which is inscribed in the historically finite structure of Dasein as originally as the projecting toward future possibilities (Gadamer, 1999a, WM, p. 266). This is why understanding is not seen as a set of rules; "rather, being situated within an event of tradition, a process of handing down, is a prior condition of understanding" (Gadamer, 1999a, WM, p. 314, 2004, TM, p. 308). In this event of tradition (*Überlieferungsgeschehen*) we find the central concept of Heideggerian analysis, that of *Geschehen* (translated by "historizing" in the *Sein und Zeit* translation), but its application to the concept of tradition suggests removing this term from the sphere of the inauthentic, where Heidegger mostly placed it. In the context of this idea, it has been said that understanding is conditioned by the finitude of man (Grondin, 1999, p. 120). At the same time, it has been shown that the term *belonging*, indicating radical finitude, achieves the junction between metaphysics and hermeneutics (Gadamer, 1999a, WM, pp. 462–3; Greisch, 1993, pp. 430–433).

Gadamer, like Heidegger, criticizes the nineteenth-century historical school (Ranke, Droysen), for explaining individual historical phenomena through their wider context (the epoch or even universal history). The hidden vice of this mode of explanation is that, although it takes into consideration the historical character of the events, it does not take into account the historicity of the historian. The antecedence of the historical tradition to the historical present is not thematized at all within this school (Gadamer, 1999a, WM, p. 201). But as Gadamer shows, the conscience of the historian is also formed by virtue of his belonging to historical tradition. His historical consciousness should not be separated from his life. Still in congruence with Heidegger, Gadamer distinguishes himself from Dilthey, whom he considers a simple successor of Romantic historicism but also of Cartesian "positivism," from which he inherits the ideal of an ultimate foundation. Thus, historical consciousness operates an apparent elevation above the flow of history, having the illusion that its study will thus gain a maximum degree of objectivity. This illusion is based on the idea that historical consciousness is also a way to self-knowledge (Gadamer, 1999a, WM, p. 239). Gadamer sees an expression of the modern philosophy of consciousness in this assumption; he opposes to it the concept of *wirkungsgeschichtliches Bewußtsein*, by which he tries to give historical consciousness an ontological meaning; it is "inevitably more *being* than consciousness" (Gadamer, 1976, p. 38, 1999b [GW2], p. 247).

Belonging to a tradition is thematized by Gadamer through the figure of the "hermeneutic circle." It expresses the fore-structure of understanding, any meaning being previously targeted by the prejudices (*Vorurteile*) that constitute our historical reality (1999a, WM, p. 281). Gadamer, however, accompanies this Heideggerian idea with the classic motif of the circularity between part and whole, which is present in ancient rhetoric and which he invokes to express the subject's belonging to a wider instance (tradition) within the scope of which understanding is achieved, as a permanent mediation between past and present (1999a, WM, p. 295). But if Heidegger saw anticipations of meaning as coming from the future, Gadamer sees them as coming from the past.[10] This idea can be read as a reply to Heidegger (Grondin, 1999, p. 126). Also bringing to attention the model of understanding texts, Gadamer notes that, by discussing the *als* structure of interpretation, with its *Vorhabe*, *Vorsicht*, and *Vorgriff* moments, Heidegger wanted to indicate that anticipations of meaning must become conscious and controllable to us, so that they may truly be conditions of possibility of right understanding, instead of mere subjective prejudices which prevent it (Gadamer, 1999a, WM, p. 274).

The antecedence of prejudices is not epistemological but transcendental-phenomenological. The transcendental side of Gadamerian philosophy must be invoked with caution, because Gadamer reproached to Heidegger the fact that existential analytics focuses too much on the transcendental structures of *Dasein* (1999a, WM, p. 260 sq.), to the detriment of the facticity of these structures, which was much more highlighted in the early Heideggerian project of the hermeneutics of facticity. We can conclude from this that Gadamer does not want to offer a systematics of some transcendental structures (such as existential analytics) but tries to emphasize the facticity of these structures, the concrete way in which they are at work in one history or another. Too much transcendentalism means too little facticity. Perhaps for this reason, Gadamer prefers the—apparently modest—term of prejudices, which are unconscious to us; they are not at our disposal, nor can we distinguish *a priori* between productive and erroneous prejudices (Gadamer, 1999a, WM, p. 301; Gadamer, 1997, p. 285). "The historicity of our existence entails that prejudices, in the literal sense of the word, constitute the initial directedness of our whole ability to experience" (Gadamer, 1976, p. 9, 1999b [GW2], p. 224).

The critical problem of hermeneutics—that of the legitimacy of prejudices—receives an answer through the concept of temporal distance, a hermeneutic filter which has the function of bringing the past closer to the present rather

[10] This specification appears in a reply to Karl-Otto Apel, "Regulatory Ideas or Truth-Happening?: An Attempt to Answer the Question of the Conditions of the Possibility of valid Understanding," in: Lewis Edwin Hahn (ed.), *The Philosophy of Hans-Georg Gadamer*, Chicago and La Salle, Illinois, Open Court Publishing Company, 1997, pp. 67–94. The quoted statement is on p. 95 ("Reply to Karl-Otto Apel", pp. 95–97), and Apel's statement that provoked it is on p. 68.

than to create distance.[11] However, we have a complex solution instead, through the issues of the hermeneutic circle and dialogue (Grondin, 1999, p. 136). At stake is a "state of vigilance" (*Wachheit*) toward the controlled achievement of the fusion of horizons through the very movement of tradition, a task that falls to the "historically effected consciousness" (Gadamer, 1999a, WM, p. 312, 2004, TM, p. 306; Grondin, 1999, p. 144). By this latter concept, Gadamer considers the awareness of the hermeneutic situation in relation to the tradition to which we belong, a situation that cannot, however, become perfectly transparent to us (1999a, WM, p. 307, 2004, TM, p. 301).

By inserting the "substantial" phenomenon of tradition into the fact of understanding, the latter can be thought of as a play between the strangeness (*Fremdheit*) and the familiarity (*Vertrautheit*) of tradition toward us (Gadamer, 1999a, WM, p. 300, 2004, TM, p. 295). The Heideggerian terminology intersects with a Hegelian one here: the occurrence of tradition in any understanding is conceived according to the model of the presence of substantiality in any subjectivity (Gadamer, 1999a, WM, p. 307, 2004, TM, p. 301). At stake is the issue of the limitation of individual consciousness by a larger subject—here, *wirkungsgeschichtliches Bewußtsein*—which was probably constructed after the Hegelian concept of objective spirit (Grondin, 1994, p. 59; Fruchon, 1994). Several elements express the same issue here. For example, the fundamental historicity of human existence, in other words our involvement in various histories at every moment, treated through the concept of *Wirkungsgeschichte*, indicates in another way that being is prior to consciousness. The hermeneutic concept of prejudice is rooted in this very phenomenon. Furthermore, the idea that "in fact history does not belong to us; we belong to it" is developed by referring to the great historical realities—family, society, the state, etc.—prior to individual experiences and self-consciousness (Gadamer 1999a, WM, p. 221, p. 281, p. 307, 2004, TM, p. 213, p. 278). Here, Gadamer approaches the demands of a critical analysis of the social structure, but mostly due to the Hegelian foundation of his hermeneutics, which turns against Dilthey's historicism, rather than due to the phenomenological method. The concept of *Wirkungsgeschichte* expresses the anteriority of the macro-phenomenon of history: "Understanding is, essentially, a historically effected event" (Gadamer, 1999a, WM, p. 305, 2004, TM, p. 299). It has been said that this term can be seen as a hermeneutical counterpart of the Heideggerian notion of *Seinsgeschichte*, as it expresses not only a linear continuity between past and present, but also diversion, deviation, denial, and forgetting (Teichert, 1991, pp. 112–115). Gadamer also explicitly states that he used the concept of "consciousness of being affected by history" in connection with the concept of hermeneutics in *Sein und Zeit* but drawing inspiration from the Heideggerian concept of "destiny of being" (*Seinsgeschick*): "Unlike a known history, there

---

[11] Beginning with the fifth edition of the work, revised for inclusion in the *Gesammelte Werke*, Gadamer adds a note designed to soften the initial claim, showing that distance—and not just temporal distance—fulfills this hermeneutic task (1999a, WM, p. 304, note 228).

remains a superordinate destiny which limits our possibilities of thinking and of understanding" (Gadamer, 1999c, GW 3, pp. 346–347). From a hermeneutic point of view, the subject can no longer be seen as the master of meaning. We understand to the extent that, steeped in the tradition to which we belong, we succeed in applying meaning to our own hermeneutical situation. Unlike Romantic hermeneutics, which in Schleiermacher's version was a project of "reconstruction of meaning," Gadamer's hermeneutics presupposes a productive behavior determined by the necessity of the application operation (*Anwendung*) (Grondin, 1993, pp. 176–177). Using the concept of application, Gadamer recovers something of the projective side of understanding, so important in Heideggerian existential analysis, but which *Truth and Method* seemed to forget.

The relationship between tradition and language has its origins in the reflections of Wilhelm von Humboldt and Heidegger. Man's relationship with the world appears to be linguistically mediated. The methodological reflection on truth depends on the fact that "we are necessarily caught within the limits of our hermeneutic situation when we ask about truth" (Gadamer, 1999b [GW2], p. 51). Belonging to a tradition is an element of truth itself (Gadamer, 1999b [GW2], p. 41). Gadamer takes up a Heideggerian theme here, stating that the reflection on one's own conditioning does not impinge on the scientificity of historical analysis. On the contrary, it is precisely the awareness of where we stand that must be considered as the sign of historiology's scientificity: "who we ourselves are and what we can hear from the past" (Gadamer, 1999b [GW2], p. 40). Gadamer shows that the hermeneutic situation is an interrogative one since every statement must be seen as an answer to a question. Discovering the interrogative layer behind the statements involves breaking the leveling sphere of everyday preconceptions, which according to Heidegger was the task of phenomenological destruction. Its purpose is for us to appropriate our history, just as it is part of us. Now, history is part of us precisely to the extent that we belong to history. Man is characterized by historicity, which is an elementary determination of his being. However, historicity is the sign of human finitude. Here, finitude is no longer the future possibility of man, but his insertion in history, truth, and language. Language itself "has its own historicity." Moreover, truth "has its own temporality and historicity." Truth is only possible while addressed, in question and answer, and in agreement on the thing itself (Gadamer, 1999b [GW2], pp. 55–56). The truth, therefore, does not belong to the isolated subject, for no man can access the whole truth. However, as Gadamer says, the whole truth can encompass both participants in the dialogue. It comes from beyond the subject, highlighting its finitude. Its discovery fully defines the hermeneutic experience. Thus, history, language, and truth can be viewed as macro-phenomena.

If we judge Gadamer's philosophy in relation to Heidegger's thought—a relation that Gadamer himself interprets—we notice that his hermeneutic ontology mainly investigates the "passive side" of man's way of being. In this resides his constant concern to bring out not only the existential structure of historicity, but even the concrete side of this structure in the concrete historical traditions in which it is always found. The co-originating character of thrownness (*Geworfenheit*) and project (*Entwurf*), declaratively assumed, does not seem perfectly covered by Gadamerian analyses. Being thrown into the world and into history (and not least the fact of being thrown into a language), an idea translated by the notion of belonging (*Zugehörigkeit*), is a constant concern of these investigations, while the project character of understanding does not receive an explicit elaboration. The disparity between the two is obvious. Although Gadamer refers to the Heideggerian analysis of the horizon of the future and of authenticity, this is not the focus of his main work. Perhaps only the concept of *subtilitas applicandi* makes up for the fading of the explicit analysis of the future and the projection toward possibilities. Within the perimeter of this philosophy, radical novelty seems to be impossible, as is the experience of something completely different, from the stranger from another tradition to the complete Other. The universal that ontology must make interpret is traced here in its "flight" toward the concrete, in its mixture with factical history. What seems like a step back could also be a step forward.

Heideggerian phenomenology claims acts of heroism, the power to experience finitude and anxiety, the revolutionary act of self-transcendence, the perseverance of the operation of reduction and destruction, the fight against concealment, illusion, and obscuration in order to access the Being of Dasein and, last but not least, the power to recognize powerlessness, the fact that we are unavailable to ourselves. Gadamerian hermeneutics blurs the heroic side, preferring instead the calm of practical wisdom (*phronesis*) and the recognition of our place in our own tradition. Small inner revolutions take place, but they no longer radically separate authenticity from inauthenticity, nor do they require the activation of radical moods. However, the critical dimension of Gadamerian philosophy resides in the commitment to the analysis of the concrete wholes in which man is involved.

REFERENCES

Aron, R. (1950). *La Philosophie Critique de l'Histoire. Essai sur une théorie allemande de l'histoire* (2nd ed.). Vrin.

Barash, J. A. (2003). *Martin Heidegger and the problem of historical meaning* (2nd revised and expanded ed.). Fordham University Press.

Carr, D. (2014). *Experience and history: Phenomenological perspectives on the historical world*. Oxford University Press.

Casement, W. (1988). Husserl and the philosophy of history. *History and Theory, 27*(3), 229–240.

Dilthey, W. (1965). *Der Aufbau der geschichtlichen Welt in den Geisteswissenschaften*. In *Gesammelte Schriften* (VII. Band, 4. Auflage). Teubner & Göttingen: Vandenhoek u. Ruprecht.

Dilthey, W. (2002). *The foundation of the historical world in the human sciences*. In R. Makkreel & F. Rodi (Eds.), *Selected works* (Vol. 3). Princeton University Press.

Fruchon, P. (1994). *L'herméneutique de Gadamer. Platonisme et modernité, tradition et interprétation.* Les Éditions du Cerf.

Gadamer, H.-G. (1976). *Philosophical hermeneutics* (D. E. Ling, Trans.). University of California Press.

Gadamer, H.-G. (1997). Dialogischer Rückblick auf das gesammelte Werk und dessen Wirkungsgeschichte. In J. Grondin (hrsg.), *Gadamer-Lesebuch.* J.C.B. Mohr (Paul Siebeck).

Gadamer, H.-G. (1999a). *Wahrheit und Methode.* In *Gesammelte Werke* (Band 1). J.C.B. Mohr (Paul Siebeck). [cited as WM]

Gadamer, H.-G. (1999b). *Gesammelte Werke* (Band 2). J.C.B. Mohr (Paul Siebeck). [cited as GW2]

Gadamer, H.-G. (1999c). *Gesammelte Werke* (Band 3). J.C.B. Mohr (Paul Siebeck). [cited as GW3]

Gadamer, H.-G. (2004). *Truth and method* (2nd revised ed.). Translation revised by J. Weinsheimer & D. G. Marshall. Continuum. [cited as TM]

Greisch, J. (1993). Herméneutique et métaphysique. In *Philosophie* (Institut Catholique de Paris, Faculté de Philosophie), 15 (*Comprendre et interpréter. Le paradigme herméneutique de la raison*). Beauchesne.

Greisch, J. (1994). *Ontologie et temporalité. Esquisse d'une interprétation intégrale de Sein und Zeit.* PUF.

Grondin, J. (1993). *L'universalité de l'herméneutique.* PUF.

Grondin, J. (1994). *Hermeneutische Wahrheit? Zum Wahrheitsbegriff Hans-Georg Gadamers* (2. Auflage). Beltz Athenäum Verlag.

Grondin, J. (1999). *Introduction à Hans-Georg Gadamer.* Les Éditions du Cerf.

Grondin, J. (2003a). Stichwort: Hermeneutik. Selbstauslegung und Seinsverstehen. In D. Thomae (Ed.), *Heidegger-Handbuch: Leben – Werk – Wirkung* (pp. 47–51). Verlag J.B. Metzler.

Grondin, J. (2003b). Le passage de l'herméneutique de Heidegger à celle de Gadamer. In *Le tournant herméneutique de la phénoménologie.* PUF.

Haar, M. (1994). *La fracture de l'histoire. Douze essais sur Heidegger.* Éditions Jérôme Million.

Heidegger, M. (1962). *Being and time* (J. Macquarrie & E. Robinson, Trans.). Blackwell. [cited as BT]

Heidegger, M. (1975). Aus einer Gespräch von der Sprache. In *Unterwegs zur Sprache* (5. Auflage). Neske.

Heidegger, M. (1979). Prolegomena zur Geschichte des Zeitbegriffs. In *Gesamtausgabe* (Band 20). Vittorio Klostermann. [cited as GA 20]

Heidegger, M. (1987). Die Idee der Philosophie und das Weltanschauungsproblem (KNS 1919). In *Gesamtausgabe* (Band 56/57). Vittorio Klostermann. [cited as GA 56/57]

Heidegger, M. (1988). Ontologie (Hermeneutik der Faktizität). In *Gesamtausgabe* (Band 63). Vittorio Klostermann. [cited as GA 63]

Heidegger, M. (1992–93). Wilhelm Diltheys Forschungsarbeit und der Kampf um eine historische Weltanschauung. *Dilthey-Jahrbuch* 8, pp. 143-177.

Heidegger, M. (1993a). *Sein und Zeit* (17. Auflage). Max Niemeyer. [cited as SZ]

Heidegger, M. (1993b). *Grundprobleme der Phänomenologie* (WS 1919/1920). In *Gesamtausgabe* (Band 58). Klostermann. [cited as GA 58]

Heidegger, M. (1994a). "Einführung in die phänomenologische Forschung" (WS 1923/24). In Gesamtausgabe (Band 17, 2). Klostermann. [cited as GA 17, 2]

Heidegger, M. (1994b). Phänomenologische Interpretationen zu Aristoteles. Einführung in die phänomenologische Forschung. In *Gesamtausgabe* (Band 61, 2., durchgesehene Auflage). Klostermann. [cited as GA 61]

Heidegger, M. (1996). *Being and time* (J. Stambaugh, Trans.). State University of New York Press.

Heidegger, M. (1999). *Ontology—The hermeneutics of facticity* (J. van Buren, Trans.). Indiana University Press.

Heidegger, M. (2003). Phänomenologische Interpretationen zu Aristoteles, Ausarbeitung für die Marburger und die Göttinger Philosophische Fakultät (1922). Hrsg. von Günter Neumann. Philipp Reclam jun.

Heidegger, M. (2004a). Anmerkungen zu Karl Jaspers 'Psychologie der Weltanschauungen'. In *Gesamtausgabe* (Band 9, 3. Auflage). Klostermann. [cited as GA 9]

Heidegger, M. (2004b). *Der Begriff der Zeit (Vortrag 1924)*. In *Gesamtausgabe* (Band 64). Klostermann. [cited as GA 64]

Heidegger, M. (2011). *Gesamtausgabe* (Band 60, 2., überarbeitete ed.). Klostermann. [cited as GA 60]

Hermann, F.-W. von. (2001). Heideggers Grundlegung der Hermeneutik. In A. Gethmann-Siefert & E. Weisser-Lohmann (Hrsg.), *Kultur−Kunst−Öffentlichkeit. Philosophische Perspektiven auf praktische Probleme*, Festschrift für Otto Pöggeler zum 70. Geburtstag. Wilhelm Fink Verlag.

Husserl, E. (1965). *Philosophy as rigorous science*. In Q. Lauer (Trans.), *Phenomenology and the crisis of philosophy* (pp. 71–147). Harper & Row.

Husserl, E. (1970). *The crisis of European sciences and transcendental phenomenology* (D. Carr, Trans.). Northwestern University Press.

Husserl, E. (1982). *Cartesian meditations. An introduction to phenomenology* (D. Cairns, Trans., 7th impression). Martinus Nijhoff Publishers.

Jung, M. (2001). *Hermeneutik zur Einführung*. Junius Verlag.

Kisiel, T. J. (1993). *The genesis of Heidegger's Being and Time*. University of California Press.

Luft, S. (2011). *Subjectivity and lifeworld in transcendental phenomenology*. Northwestern University Press.

Makkreel, R. A. (1982). Husserl, Dilthey and the relation of the life-world to history. *Research in Phenomenology, XII*, 39–58.

Pöggeler, O. (1990). *Der Denkweg Martin Heideggers* (3. erweiterte Auflage). Neske.

Ricoeur, P. (1975). Phenomenology and hermeneutics. *Noûs, 9*(1), 85–102.

Ricoeur, P. (1985). *Temps et récit*, Tome III: *Le temps raconté*. Seuil.

Ricoeur, P. (1986). *Du texte à l'action. Essais d'herméneutique II*. Seuil.

Schleiermacher, F. D. E. (1978). The hermeneutics: Outline of the 1819 lectures (J. Wojcik & R. Haas, Trans.). *New Literary History, 10*(1), Literary Hermeneutics, 1–16.

Schleiermacher, F. D. E. (1995). *Hermeneutik und Kritik*. Herausgegeben und eingeleitet von Manfred Frank (6. Aufl). Suhrkamp.

Teichert, D. (1991). *Erfahrung, Erinnerung, Erkenntnis. Untersuchungen zum Wahrheitsbegriff der Hermeneutik Gadamers*. Verlag J.B. Metzler.

Vattimo, G. (1985). *Introduction à Heidegger* (J. Rolland, Trad.). Les Éditions du Cerf.

Dialectics and Contingency: Merleau-Ponty and the Historical Network

Graciela Ralón and Maximiliano Cladakis

1   INTRODUCTION

The present work aims at elucidating the way in which Merleau-Ponty under-stands history from a dialectical perspective, whereby contingency is not por-trayed as an error, but rather as one of its constitutive elements. Our goal is to show that the phenomenological interpretation of history can contribute to a wider understanding of social, political and economic phenomena, without con-fining these to a closed sphere that ossifies the dynamism of the historical pro-cess. Our first step is to try and explore the two pillars upon which the very logic of history rests: on the one hand, we find that the events—be they of a political, social or historical nature—are endowed with a human significance that permits the integration of different aspects into "a single history"; on the other hand, we have the idea that the moments of this logic do not follow each other with-out sequence but are directed toward an end. However, although the events form a single text, they are not rigorously connected with each other, since there is always "play in the system" and, moreover, the dialectic of history can

G. Ralón (✉)
Escuela de Humanidades, Universidad Nacional de San Martín (UNSAM), Buenos Aires, Argentina
e-mail: gralon@unsam.edu.ar

M. Cladakis
Universidad Nacional de San Martín (UNSAM)/National Council for Technical and Scientific Research of Argentina (CONICET), Escuela de Humanidades, Buenos Aires, Argentina

267

C. Belvedere, A. Gros (eds.), *The Palgrave Handbook of Macrophenomenology and Social Theory*,
https://doi.org/10.1007/978-3-031-34712-2_14

deviate at any given stage to become an unpredictable adventure. In the words of Merleau-Ponty, the contingency of history "means that even if the diverse orders of events form a single intelligible text, they are nonetheless not rigorously bound together, that there is a certain amount of free play in the system" (Merleau-Ponty, 1968, p. 89).

The interpretation of history that we are aiming for does not give up on rationality but attempts to reconfigure and expand the teleological reading undertaken by Husserl. Guided by his philosophical presentiment, that is, by "the expression of a vital presentiment which arises through unprejudiced reflection" (Husserl, 1970, p. 276), our aim is to understand history as the unfolding of sense and its development toward an ideal pole that is always provisional. The historical field irradiates in different directions but does not determine beforehand which of these are more relevant than others. In other words, the contingency of the historical field provides us with signals, but these signals are not the postulates of mathematical formulation. Consequently, the ambiguity of history can be perfectly understood, but the said understanding does not imply its reconfiguration into an absolute translucency; instead, what we have is a partial understanding whereby opacities cannot be excluded. Hence, the dialectic of history is imperfect and always open, thereby distancing itself from deterministic models that are considered to be manifestations of a "bad dialectic." The dialectic of history understands itself not as what *constitutes* the totality, but as that which is *situated* in the totality. The totality in which the dialectic unfolds is not a closed but an open whole where the various interactions with the world take place as part of an originary contingency which cannot be exorcised by a formal understanding. The mystery of history is the mystery of our existence in the world, where the question concerning the significance of events is connected with the unpredictability of historical becoming.

The understanding of history as the "advent of sense" and, more specifically, the consideration of its rational structure are two points that we shall address in the next section of this work as we introduce the Husserlian perspective on history. Let us be clear from the outset that our reading takes place within the framework of phenomenology, but although we recognize that Husserl has given us the basic tools to think about history in philosophical terms, the interpretation that we provide here distances itself from the transcendental edge that underlies Husserlian phenomenology, insofar as our main objective consists in presenting the discussion about the philosophy of history in accordance with the notion of a "rationality in contingency."

2   History and Sense

If, in order to gain a better perspective on the problem, we consider one of the pillars upon which the logic of history lies, a pillar we shall try to delineate in the present work (i.e., that the events, regardless of their nature, have a human significance which enables them to be incorporated into a single story), then Husserl's interpretation seems paradigmatic to us. In a study entitled, "Husserl and the Sense of History," Paul Ricoeur argues that the reflection about history offered by the German phenomenologist seems closely tied to the crisis undergone by humanity, a crisis which "calls for a reaffirmation of a task, but a task which by its structure is a task for everyone, a task which develops a history" (Ricoeur 1967, p. 151). Thus, the crisis concerning the sense (or nonsense) of existence presents itself as a question that, when considered from within the bounds of history, becomes "a question both of history and *in* history" (p. 151).

Now, from Husserl's own perspective, philosophical reflection about history exhibits a kind of teleology, that is, a rational structure which delineates a historical trajectory. Moreover, the reflection about history is *indirect* insofar as it does not concern events taken as extra parts but, on the contrary, focuses on history as the "advent" (*avénement*) of sense.

From the opening lines of "The Vienne Lecture," Husserl insists on the close relationship existing between the philosophy of history and teleology:

> I shall venture the attempt to find new interest in the frequently treated theme of the European crisis by developing the philosophical-historical idea (or the teleological sense) of European humanity. As I exhibit, in the process, the essential function that philosophy and its branches, our sciences, have to exercise within that sense, the European crisis will also receive a new elucidation. (Husserl, 1970, p. 269)

The notion of crisis is introduced by Husserl as a means to reflect about history and, in particular, about the history of philosophy, all the way from its originary inception to its final, though always provisional, consummation. To shed light on this crisis entails reorienting oneself through a kind of philosophical existence that concerns not only the theoretical order (i.e., the free self-givenness of norms on the basis of a pure reason that orientates itself in accordance with infinite goals) but also the ethical order. This means that "man should be changed ethically [but that] the whole human surrounding world, the political and social existence of mankind, must be fashioned anew through free reason, through the insights of a universal philosophy" (Husserl, 1970, p. 8).

In his later writings, Husserl warns us with an even greater sense of urgency about the need to refound both science and philosophy by rendering explicit the dangers associated with the threats of the modern age. In The Vienna Lecture entitled "Philosophy and the Crisis of European Humanity," he characterizes philosophy and science as the essence of the West. The idea of the West—but also of Europe—does not necessarily coincide with precise geopolitical limits. In fact, Husserl (1970) speaks of a spiritual structure of Europe (*die geistige Gestalt Europas*), by which he means a teleological experience of history presenting itself as "(...) the developmental beginning of a new human epoch – the epoch of mankind which now seeks to live, and only can live, in the free shaping of its existence, its historical life, through ideas of reason, through infinite tasks" (p. 319).

Thus, we are not faced with a Eurocentric conception of history, not at least in the traditional sense, but rather with an understanding of historicity in universal terms. In the progression from latent reason to manifest reason, a given crisis can be decomposed as consisting of three moments. Firstly, it presupposes the aforementioned rational condition, with the three aspects that constitute its origin. Secondly, it entails a distancing from that same origin as well as from the teleology contained within itself (i.e., the inauthentic reinstitution of the originary institution through distancing or forgetting). Thirdly, the crisis is overcome when the motivation embedded within the tradition, besides promoting the realization of a final sense implicated in the initial institution, leads to the recovery of those lost initial goals. As Roberto Walton (2016) points out, what takes place is a "(…) transformation of human existence through scientific and philosophical culture, guided by infinite goals" (p. 110). Husserl, therefore, uncovers the emergence of a new epoch of humanity in which freedom, reason and historicity are articulated as integral features of its identity.

In this regard, the German philosopher situates the emergence of Western humanity within a specific time and place: Greece in the seventh and sixth centuries BC. What originates in ancient Greece is "(…) a common cultural spirit [which,] drawing all of humanity under its spell, is thus an advancing transformation in the form of a new [type of] historical development" (Husserl, 1970, p. 277). The coming into being of Greek philosophy is the most salient features associated with the becoming of the West. With the advent of philosophy, rationality is configured under the guise of a *telos* that propels the unfolding of history. In Husserl's view an intrinsic bond between philosophy and history is thus consolidated, and the latter is understood as the universal becoming of reason.

It is important to note from the start the contrast between rationality as it emerges from the Greek world and the interpretation of it that was introduced in the Renaissance. While, on the one hand, we have a comprehensive form of rationality which involves, and endows with significance, the different dimensions of human existence, with the emergence of modern science, by contrast, rationality is reduced to the mathematical *ratio* and science to a process of homogenization and quantification:

> Rationality, in that high and genuine sense of which alone we are speaking, the primordial Greek sense which in the classical period of Greek philosophy had become an ideal, still requires, to be sure, much clarification through self-reflection; but it is called in its mature form to guide [our] development. On the other hand we readily admit (and German Idealism preceded us long ago in this insight) that the stage of development of *ratio* represented by the rationalism of the Age of Enlightenment was a mistake, though certainly an understandable one. (Husserl, 1970, p. 290)

Merleau-Ponty points out that, for Husserl, rationality is the only conceivable path, since the alternative is simply chaos. Against the threat of an "anonymous adversity," the solution is to promote knowledge and action. In the study entitled "The Philosopher and Sociology," the French phenomenologist highlights the following with great emphasis:

> To be human at all is essentially to be a human being in a socially and generatively united civilization; and if man is a rational being *(animal rationale)*, it is only insofar as his whole civilization is a rational civilization, that is, one with a latent orientation toward reason or one openly oriented toward the entelechy which has come to itself, become manifest to itself, and which now of necessity consciously directs human becoming. (Husserl, 1970, p. 15)

Merleau-Ponty adopts three essential principles from Husserl when it comes to thinking about history. First, there is an overlap between the question of history and the question concerning its significance. The problematic of history cannot be reduced to an assemblage of facts, but always involves the very meaning of human experience. Second, the French philosopher revisits the issue of the rationality of history, conceived as a form of non-scientific understanding. The reduction of reason to the mathematical *ratio* is such that it can no longer make sense of the fundamental questions surrounding human existence. Third, the relationship between the event and history becomes essential to the author of *The Phenomenology of Perception*. The event necessitates a resumption and a reconfiguration of sense. As Gloria Serban points out, this is already present in Husserl's thought. The historical event is an event of sense, that is, an event which recovers the dual process consisting of an advent and a conservation of sense. The event, therefore, institutes a tradition. However, tradition should not be mistaken with ossification. This is precisely the great danger that haunts the entire tradition. From this perspective, the tradition creates a double movement comprising the forgetting and the reactivation of sense. The enlargement of the tradition does not amount to a grand synthesis, but rather to a movement where the loss and the forgetting of sense are fused with its own recovery. In fact, the new is possible through "a resumption which is loss, not totalization, and which for that reason is able to open another development of knowledge" (Merleau-Ponty, 2010:59)

3   The Dialectical Unfolding of History

In this section, we would like to emphasize that the Hegelian project, understood as a comprehensive approach to history, occupies a central place especially in the phenomenological interpretations of Ricoeur and Merleau-Ponty, as we will see. In *Modern French Philosophy*, Vincent Descombes notes that beginning in the 1930s, an unusual interest in Hegel's work was awakened in the French philosophical milieu. According to Descombes, this was due to two main factors: on the one hand, a renewed interest in Marxism motivated by the success of the Russian Revolution and, on the other hand, the courses on the *Phenomenology of the Spirit* taught by Alexandre Kojève in that same decade.

Descombes remarks that at the time the French academic environment was dominated by the different currents of Neo-Kantianism and, in this sense, it is worth pointing out that the generation of intellectuals that emerged during those years would soon grow critical of its predecessors.

As Sartre himself writes in 1961:

> The horror of dialectic was such that Hegel himself was unknown to us. Of course, they allowed us to read Marx; they even advised us to read him; one had to know him in order to refute him. But without the Hegelian tradition, without Marxist teachers, without any planned program of study, without the instruments of thought, our generation, like the preceding ones and like that which followed, was wholly ignorant of historical materialism. (Sartre, 1985, p. 26)

Sartre's words validate Descombes' assertion. Hegel was not a studied author back then and the next generation would soon become interested in his thinking, which they would link closely to that of Marx. This link between Hegel and Marx was partly the result of Lenin's directive that in order to understand Marx one had to understand Hegel first and partly a byproduct of the kind of Hegelian Marxism popularized by the first Lukács. In this context, the concept of "dialectics" soon became a central notion for the new generation of French thinkers.

Furthermore, Descombes notices the radical change undergone by French philosophy as concerns the appreciation of dialectics:

> Before 1930 it was understood pejoratively; for a neo-Kantian the dialectic was the 'logic of appearances', whereas for a Bergsonian it could engender nothing but a purely verbal philosophy. After 1930, on the contrary, the word was almost always used in a eulogistic sense. It was now thought proper to transcend 'analytical reason' (the Kantian *Verstand*) or again 'mechanism', by means of the dialectic. (Descombes, 1980, p. 10)

Without a doubt, the connection between Hegel and Marx is one of the points that attracted French postwar philosophers the most. Against the prevailing Neo-Kantianism of the French Academy, Hegelian philosophy presented itself as a situated form of thought. The notion of dialectic became reconfigured through an inseparable bond tying it to history's own development. As Merleau-Ponty points out in "The War Has Taken Place," the occupation of France marked the discovery of history in all its devastating power by the French intelligentsia. On the other hand, the ideas of negativity and struggle presented themselves as key elements for a philosophy that tries to understand itself against the background of its own time. At some point, especially after the reception of the *Phenomenology of the Spirit*, Hegel became the philosopher who encouraged the reading of history in philosophical terms.

In this sense, it is worth mentioning the article by Jean-Nöel Cueille (2000), "The Depth of the Negative: Merleau-Ponty Versus Hegel's Dialectic," in which the author argues that Merleau-Ponty views the Hegelian phenomenology as an antecedent of the kind of genetic phenomenology that he himself endorses. The Merleau-Pontyian genetic phenomenology and the Hegelian phenomenology would share the fundamental task of thinking the ambiguity that is constitutive of human beings with respect to their social and natural environment, that is, within a framework that is not exhausted by the viewpoint of reflective knowledge, but rather embedded in the depths of the originary ontological structures upon which knowledge itself lies.

Several of Merleau-Ponty's arguments support Cueille's argument. In "Philosophy and Non-philosophy Since Hegel," Merleau-Ponty connects Hegel's thought with a decisive concept from Husserlian phenomenology: the notion of "one-in-the-other" (*Ineinander*). "Consciousness, the true progress of knowledge, does not consist in the external comparison of the two terms, but in the 'mutual encroachment' [*Ineinander*] of object-knowledge, noeses-noemata…" (Merleau-Ponty 1996, p. 301). Merleau-Ponty thinks that, in Hegel's philosophy, consciousness is bound with the object—that its transformation leads in turn to a transformation of the object and vice versa. This gives Merleau-Ponty an opportunity to establish a rapport between Hegel's thought, certain aspects of Husserlian genetic phenomenology and his own brand of phenomenology.

As for the relevance of the dialectic, in his course devoted to dialectical philosophy, Merleau-Ponty looks very closely at the three definitions of the term that also appear in his course on the history of philosophy: a thought of opposites, a "subjective" thought and a circular thought. In the first instance, a fundamental element of the dialectic rests upon Hegel's famous formula, that is, the negation of the negation. This is an "operative contradiction" in which negation does not only introduce a new term in order to cancel the initial positive meaning but simultaneously destroys and reconstructs the positive. Secondly, the dialectic portrays an inquisitive attitude, so that being does not remain inert in itself but "makes it appear before someone as the response to an interrogation" (Merleau-Ponty 1996, p. 80). Thirdly, the dialectic presents itself as a circular thought. This circularity does not mean that the opposing terms are to be included within an all-encompassing whole. Instead, the activity of questioning without end entails a dialectic without synthesis which is not contrarian to the idea of an overcoming that summons together, while simultaneously excluding, the possibility of phases in a hierarchical order, with a third term taking on a new position that is superimposed as an antithetical moment.

At this point, it is worth noting that, in *The Visible and the Invisible*, Merleau-Ponty finds it necessary to make a distinction between a good and a bad dialectic. Bad dialectics is an alternative form of thought which consists in applying the logic of the understanding to the movement of things and, in this way, attempts to reconstruct being through thetic thought, that is, by a group of statements leading to the confinement of the human being into a realm of dilemmas that have no solution. By contrast, a good dialectic consists in positing a medium where the movement of things and the initiatives of human beings somehow intersect. A hyperdialectic or good dialectic, Merleau-Ponty says, is a thought that "is capable of reaching the truth because it envisages without restriction the plurality of relationships and what has been called ambiguity" (Merleau-Ponty, 1968, p. 94). Differently put, a hyperdialectic is a thought that assumes not only the ambiguous situations resulting from the plurality of relationships in which things are implicated but also the inexhaustible modalities of expression as well as the multiplicity of dimensions which are exhibited by the very being that nourishes and sustains them. It is, therefore, a thought capable of incorporating the contingency of events, which are no longer regarded as a defect or weakness over the course of history but, quite to the contrary, as the very condition of its significance.

4   Rationality, Total Mediation and the End of History

The relationship between Husserl and Hegel is simultaneously one of nearness and one of distance. In the previous two sections, we highlighted the adoption by French phenomenology in general, Merleau-Ponty in particular, of several arguments put forth by these two philosophers. However, Merleau-Ponty's philosophical preoccupation with history is also articulated in terms of a critical distancing with respect to some of the arguments developed by Husserl and Hegel. In his text "Should We Renounce to Hegel?" Ricoeur argues that, to a significant extent, the criticisms directed at Hegel are an "expression of our incredulity" (Ricoeur, 1988, p. 193) vis-à-vis the idea that reason "governs the world, and that world history is therefore a rational process" (Ricoeur, 1988, p. 194). Indeed, the distancing from Hegel's philosophy, according to Ricoeur, finds its most profound expression in the lack of conviction concerning the subjugation of history by reason.

This lack of faith in the creed of reason, its immanence in history, forms the basis of historical experience as such:

> Indeed, contemporary, far from filling this lack in the philosophy of right, has accentuated it, in the twentieth century. We have seen the heritages it tried to integrate in terms of one guiding idea come undone. Eurocentrism died with political suicide of Europe in the First World War, with the ideological rending produced by the October Revolution and with the withdrawal of Europe from the world scene, along with the fact of decolonization and the unequal – and probably antagonistic – development that opposes the industrialized nations to the rest of the world. (Ricoeur, 1988, p. 204)

Ricoeur's words are edifying. The faith in a rational unfolding of history, the idea of an ultimate reconciliation of history, and the notion of a universal Spirit all break down as a result of history's own unfolding. In this precise sense, something similar occurs to the various postulates derived from Husserl's understanding of history. Above all, the notion of a transition from latent reason to manifest reason becomes relativized by a phenomenological-hermeneutic inquiry into the meaning of history.

The distance with respect to Hegel is simultaneously a relative distance with regard to Husserl. Judith Revel (2017) claims that the aforementioned "The War Has Taken Place" is Merleau-Ponty's crucial texts because, although it was written after the defeat of Nazi Germany, the experience of the war came to define the exercise of philosophy as the acquisition of a reflective gaze toward life itself, so that human beings assumed their own situation as well as the concrete gestures, and relationships among them, in such a way that these became instituted as the proper ground of philosophical thinking. The possibility of creating "a theory of history" is based, according to Revel, on the fact that the logic of history is not teleological (it does not admit a final synthesis) and, consequently, the dialectic turns out to be an open process (it discards the very possibility of lineal and mechanical causality).

In a way, the experience of war, occupation, ethnic persecution and concentration camps broke with the optimism associated with a teleological and rational unfolding of history. Merleau-Ponty warns us, on the one hand, that the historical event cannot be fully explained, that all we can do is indicate the motivations that delineate a possible history. On the other hand, human beings interact with one another against a background of historicity that they themselves have not chosen but which, in a sense, assigns various roles that transcend them, modifying the significance of their individual actions. Differently put, the movement of history evidences that contingency is not tantamount to a dark destiny or inscrutable fatality; there is no evil force or malign genius pushing human life toward chaos because each of our actions, by virtue of taking into consideration all other actions, recovers them and reorients them toward a universal aim: "The human world is an open or unfinished system and the same radical contingency which threatens it with discord also rescues it from the inevitability of disorder and prevents us from despairing of it..." (Merleau-Ponty, 1969, p. 188).

Already in the *Phenomenology of Perception*, Merleau-Ponty (1945) states: "The true Waterloo resides neither in what Fabrice, nor the Emperor, nor the historian sees, it is not a determinable object, it is what comes about on the fringes of all perspectives, and on which they are all erected" (p. 363). Class and nation, for instance, are events that burst into the living history of people. And yet, their characterization is always provisional and ambivalent and never manages to exhaust the significance of what they seek to define:

> The historian and the philosopher are in search of an objective definition of class or nation: is the nation based on common language or on conceptions of life; is class based on income statistics or on its place in the process of production? It is well known that none of these criteria enables us to decide whether an individual belongs to a nation or a class. (Merleau-Ponty 1945, p. 303)

As for the idea of a final reconciliation or synthesis of history, in *Adventures of the Dialectic* Merleau-Ponty addresses the question by focusing, above all, on the practical/political consequences of adopting the idea of a consummation of history. Although our object of discussion is not Hegelian philosophy but its Marxist rendering, it is not difficult to appreciate how these issues are mutually intertwined. This articulation between the theme of revolution and the "end of history" takes place in the context of an understanding of the dialectic according to which the said notion is presented as a progressive unfolding that advances from an inferior to a superior stage of development. With respect to the historical-political sphere, it determines in a mechanistic manner that "state production will of itself put forth its socialist and communist consequences, and one will see humanism and the dialectic bloom and flower, while the State fades away" (Merleau-Ponty, 1973, p. 96).

From this perspective, each contradiction is overcome in a new stage of development that will engender, in turn, a new contradiction and so on until a final synthesis is reached from which no further contradictions can emerge. The Revolution would be that final synthesis that cancels all existing contradictions and, consequently, also marks the effective consummation of the dialectic in its historical unfolding.

As Miryan D'Revault (2001) points out, what Merleau-Ponty does not accept is the transmutation of history into an "idol." The idolatry of history manifests itself, according to the author, in the guise of an object moved by pre-established laws. If we pay close attention to certain key texts from the period, it becomes apparent how the dialectic is portrayed as a process that mechanically determines both the natural and the human worlds. From this standpoint, history becomes an object that unfolds according to laws intrinsic to its own development. Hence, there is a teleological significance to history that, even if it presents itself as dialectical, in truth presupposes a mechanicism. In accordance with this understanding of history, human beings are the result of its inherent movement. By contrast, Merleau-Ponty tries to desacralize history: it is no longer something external to us, but on the contrary, it constitutes "a strange object, an object which is ourselves" (Merleau-Ponty, 1973, p. 20). Precisely, the strangeness of this object makes it impossible for it to be conceived of from an objectivist perspective. History is not an object that faces a subject; history is us and we are it.

For Merleau-Ponty, history is neither an "idol" nor the mere product of pure actions conducted by human beings in an absolutely unconditional manner; instead, history is the "medium" where human existence unfolds. The dogmatic constitution of the dialectic-history-revolution triad results in the annihilation of the said medium and, in this regard, the idea of the proletariat as a universal class turns out to be crucial. Its triumph—the ceasing of power through the Revolution—would result in the end of all historical contradictions as well as in the realization of the dialectic. Accordingly, history itself is responsible for singling, in its dialectical trajectory, the one class which must fulfill its definitive consummation, insofar as "it will be the last of all classes, the suppression of all classes and of itself as a class" (Merleau-Ponty, 1973, p. 210).

5   A Dialectic Open to the Event

However, this is not to say that history is not rational, but rather that its rationality is always provisional. The historical event is irreducible to a cause-and-effect type of explanation. On the contrary, from the moment that the event surges up, it defies all explanation; it is an overflowing that exceeds all reduction and, in this sense, it is also an integral experience around which particular actions, as well as unexpected, anonymous and collective forces, tend to converge. It is the task of the historian to try to establish causal connections among these phenomena in order to explicate the event. However, such a task amounts to a second-order abstraction. The historian does not experience the event directly but tries to find rationality in it. This is not to say that Merleau-Ponty negates the value of the task before us. Rather, the point is that the significance of the event surpasses any reduction and, as a result, the task of the historian turns out to be infinite.

Merleau-Ponty's reflections about history go hand in hand with his reflections about the event and its contingent nature. Here, it is worth highlighting the remarks made by Ricoeur, namely, that "the event is our master" (Ricoeur, 2008, p. 166). The significance of the event, manifested in this phrase, extends in two complementary directions. First of all, we should note that it is closely tied to the critique of the idea of a self-constitution of consciousness. Against the modern interpretation of consciousness as a constitution that is autonomous both from itself and from the world, the sovereignty of the event stresses the passive dimension of our existence. Accordingly, the French philosopher asserts that "we exist because we are seized by those events that happen to us" (Ricoeur, 2008, p. 167). For Ricoeur, there is an unassailable relationship between our concrete existence in the world and the event. In this sense, there is a tight bond between us and the event through which our passivity is disclosed, since the event is not the result of our spontaneity, but simply *happens to us*. The event constitutes us; we do not constitute it.

On the other hand, the centrality of the event implies a reinterpretation of history according to which the latter cannot be reduced to a mechanistic model. The event gives itself in the form of an instituting power that provides meaning to a plurality of experiences. Moreover, the event inaugurates a new significance that reconfigures history and, in this sense, it is possible to appreciate how history is not reducible to the sum of free actions by human agents.

Ricoeur's reflections blend in well with Merleau-Ponty's own meditations about history. In his *Notes on Passivity*, dedicated to the subject of dreaming, the unconscious and memory, Merleau-Ponty introduces the notion of a "wild history" in order to make the point that the said history is well beyond both "objective" history and the particular histories of individual lives:

Here, too, the bi-directional genesis of the given to us, and also of us to the given (we only conceive history prior to us as a sector of our history). Or rather, not two opposed movements (the objective history we create, and our *Sinngebung* creating objective history…What is given is their intersection, the articulation of these perspectives on each other…Thus to awaken wild history (beyond "objective" history, which does not concern consciousnesses, and beyond history as an appendage of my personal adventure…we, like the humans of the past, have only open significations and situations whose sense is in genesis. (Merleau-Ponty 2003, pp. 133–134)

According to this view, the event emerges from within a field encircled by horizons: on the one hand, that of the instituted and, on the other, that of the multiple possibilities engendered by the event itself. Hence, as Merleau-Ponty reminds us, every institution displays a double aspect: "*Endstiftung* at the same time as *Urstiftung*. That is what sedimentation is: trace of the forgotten and thereby a call to thought which depends on itself and goes farther" (Merleau-Ponty 2003, pp. 58–59). There is a double movement from the past to the future and from the future to the past: "*Urstiftung* and forgetfulness join back up with themselves in a way different from Hegel's conservation and overcoming" (Merleau-Ponty, 2002, pp. 81–82). In this sense, the dialectic entails precarious totalizations that are never complete and must be reorganized at any given juncture.

Now, the contingency of the event does not entail an abandonment of the dialectic. Here, Merleau-Ponty contrasts the dialectic with the idea of the "end of history." In *Adventures of the Dialectic*, he explicitly states: "What then is obsolete is not the dialectic but the pretension of terminating it in an end of history" (Merleau-Ponty, 1973, p. 206). Merleau-Ponty differentiates the dialectic from the idea of the "end of history" and at the same time stresses the forfeiture of the latter while affirming the validity of the former. In sharp contrast with mechanistic conceptions of the dialectic, he puts forth a radically different interpretation. He speaks of a dialectic that stays "in its place," in what amounts to an attempt to establish the limits and possibilities of the dialectic, which in turn implies a reinterpretation of what a dialectic entails. For Merleau-Ponty, the dialectic is the opposite of any dogmatic position insofar as it discovers in each element a partial truth but does not impose itself as an absolute truth. However, this understanding of the dialectic has led certain authors to conclude that Merleau-Ponty understands by "dialectic" something bearing little or no resemblance to the traditional notion. Sartre himself claims that Merleau-Ponty discreetly adopts "a method which takes the form of a decapitated dialectic" (Sartre 1965, p. 60).

Nevertheless, Merleau-Ponty understands very well that a dialectic that does not impose itself *qua* absolute truth permits a situated form of thinking which does not reduce the world to a process of thesis, antithesis and synthesis. Such a dialectics does not require that the world conform to pre-established categories because it is a form of thought that rests on an openness to the world. In connection with the latter point, the relationship that Merleau-Ponty proposes between "dialectic" and "totality" is crucial. Faced with the idea of the dialectic as a structure serving to articulate reality, Merleau-Ponty argues, "It is a thought which does not constitute the whole but which is situated in it. (…) It is incomplete so long as it does not pass into other perspectives and into the perspectives of others" (Merleau-Ponty, 1973, p. 203). In this sense, the dialectic is not the expression of a previously constituted totality, nor is it the realization of the said totality, but instead can be found in everything that there is and everything that remains, much like history, always unfinished.

If the dogmatic conception of dialectics contains at its core the idea of necessity, Merleau-Ponty conceives of the dialectic as a thought of openness to contingency. History, as a result, is not excluded from the demand to be incorporated into an already given intellectual scheme. On the contrary, history recovers all its richness, a richness articulated with ambiguity and paradox. In this sense, the Merleau-Pontyian dialectic is one full of ambiguity and paradox, since it does not consist in the overcoming/elimination of contradictions. In the Merleau-Pontyian dialectic, contradictions are not overcome in subsequent syntheses, but there is a sense of circularity that cannot be curtailed by the idea of a mechanical process.

Ricoeur raises the following question: "can we still claim to think about history and the time of history?" (Ricoeur, 1988, p. 207). He does so after having abandoned the idea of total mediation that the philosopher is supposed to uncover. Alternatively, he proposes the following:

> But another way remains, that of an open-ended, incomplete, imperfect mediation, namely, the network of interweaving perspectives of the expectation of the future, the reception of the past, and the experience of the present, with no *Aufhebung into* a totality where reason in history and its reality would coincide. (Ricoeur, 1988, p. 207)

To give up the idea of a total synthesis of history is not tantamount to giving up our thinking about history. On the contrary, this abandonment opens up the possibility of a thought open to history and its contingent character. The dialectic that abandons the gist of a total mediation of history calls for an assumption of the finitude associated with philosophical consciousness whereby the significance of historical becoming maintains a certain opacity that can never be completely brought to presence.

6   Conclusion

The problematization of history turns out to be fundamental for Merleau-Ponty. The arguments developed by the French philosopher concerning dialectics integrate contingency into a non-dogmatic plexus in which the latter cannot and should not be exorcised. Separated from the idea of a grand synthesis or total mediation, the dialectic is instituted as a thought of openness to contingency, a thought which unfolds within the totality, making room for the tensions and oppositions of the historical world but without canceling them out. Instead, the point is to make sense of them as the different facets that constitute our collective life. From this perspective, contingency does not amount to a problem for history in the sense of the "possibilities of error" associated with scientific thought; instead, it is the very medium in which history itself can be realized.

In this sense, history presents us with the medium in which human existence is inscribed. This inscription entails a double play through which we are simultaneously shaped by history and become the makers of history. The opening of thought to ambiguity turns out to be extremely invigorating for an understanding of the historical unfolding of human life. At issue is an overcoming both of the reduction of history to a series of unconnected, random events and of a mechanistic teleological model of history as such.

On this last point, it is worth emphasizing the importance of Merleau-Ponty's thesis that "all events are a type of historical event." This statement suggests that we can elucidate the profound significance of the relation between the meaning of the event and that of history. Although, on the one hand, the event entails the institution of a new field of sense, this cannot be reduced to an explosion irrupting from nowhere. The event that inscribes itself in the historical network reopens and reclaims a received inheritance: the tradition or the instituted. In this sense, the articulation between the event and history seals off the movement of the tradition by avoiding the dangers of ossification that Husserl warned us about. The tradition is, at the same time, conservation and transformation of significance.

Bibliography

Cueille, J. (2000). La profondeur du négatif: Merleau-Ponty face à la dialectique de Hegel. In *Chiasmi International. Publication trilingue autour de la pensée de Merleau-Ponty,* Nro. 2, Vrin, Paris.

Descombes, V. (1980). *Modern French Philosophy,* Trans. L. Scott-Fox and. J. M. Harding. New York: Cambridge University Press.

Husserl, E. (1970). *The Crisis of European Sciences and Transcendental Phenomenology.* Trans: David Carr, : Northwestern University Press.

Merleau-Ponty, M. (1968). *The Visible and the Invisible,* Trans. Alphonso Lingis. Evanston: Northwestern University Press.

Merleau-Ponty, M. (1969). *Humanism and Terror. An Essay on the Communist Problem,* Trans: John O'Neill, Boston, Beacon Press.

Merleau-Ponty, M. (1973). *Adventures of the Dialectic,* Trans: Joseph Bien, Evanston: Northwestern University Press.

Merleau-Ponty, M. (2002). *Husserl at the Limits of Phenomenology,* Trans: Leonard Lawlor, : Northwestern University Press.

Merleau-Ponty, M. (2010). *Institution and Passivity. Course Notes from the Collège de rance (1954-1955),* Trans: Leonard Lawlor, Evanston: Northwestern University Press.

Revel, J. (2017). Historie sédimentée, historie ouverte: un autre chiasme? *Alter,* *25*, 115–134.

Ricoeur, P. (1988). *Time and Narrative. Vol. III*, Trans: Kathleen Blamey and David Pellauer, : The University Chicago Press.

Ricoeur, P. (2008). *Fe y filosofía*. Prometeo.

Sartre, J. P. (1985). *Critique de la Raison dialectique. Tome I. Théorie des ensemblee pratiques*. Gallimard.

Walton, R. (2016). Niveles de la teleología y la historia en la fenomenología de Husserl. Enrahonar. *An International Journal of Theoretical and Practical Reason,* *57*, 100–120.

PART VI

Collective Personalities and Agency

Supra-personal Agency: A Husserlian Approach to the Problem of Individual Responsibility in Relation to Collective Agency and Social Normativity

Esteban Marín-Ávila

1   Introduction

In this chapter, I wish to discuss Edmund Husserl's idea that groups can appear as persons to which it is possible attribute actions, as well as to elaborate on the idea that the individuals that belong to them can be held responsible for such actions. I will argue that the phenomenon of collective agency is related to a kind of social group, called by Husserl "personality of higher order" [*Personalität höherer Ordnung*], that involves a particular kind of normativity. The normativity that follows from collective agency need not be evident for the individuals that are subject to it. However, I will suggest that our practical intentions and actions as members of groups and, in general, as social beings, can only be rational if we are willing and able to reflect on this normativity and the valuings beneath it.

E. Marín-Ávila (✉)
Universidad Michoacana de San Nicolás de Hidalgo, Morelia, Mexico
e-mail: esteban.marin@umich.mx

2   THE TWO LEVELS OF HUSSERL'S THEORY
OF INTERSUBJECTIVITY

It is important to keep in mind that Husserl raises the question of the constitution of other Egos at a radically fundamental level. For him, the problem of the constitution of objective time and space, and with it, of a world that has the meaning of being a real one, cannot be addressed without raising the question of what it means to perceive other subjects or, in other words, of what is involved in perceiving Others. It is therefore important to be aware of Husserl's distinction between the constitution of mere intersubjectivity and social intersubjectivity. As Caminada has pointed out, Husserl's theory of intersubjectivity "does not presuppose non-social individuals that can commit themselves to become social" (Caminada, 2016, p. 286) but accounts for the constitution of personal life and social groups as based on a pre-reflective communality or intersubjectivity.

In works like *Cartesian Meditations* and *Ideas* II, Husserl developed a theory of the passive, associative constitution of other subjects through pairing [*Paarung*].[1] We could call it his "basic theory of empathy." That this is not a theory of communication can be appreciated by consulting most of the texts where Husserl wrote about social acts, since he consistently insists that they presuppose some form of givenness of Others through empathy. This is clearly stated in the *Cartesian Meditations*, for at the end of the Fifth he writes:

> The *constitution of humanity*, or of that community which belongs to the full essence of humanity, does not end with what has been considered up to now. On the basis, however, of community in the last sense acquired, it is easy to understand the possibility of *acts of the Ego that reach into the other Ego through the medium of appresentative experience of someone else* and, indeed, the possibility of *specifically personal acts of the Ego* that have the character of acts of mine directed to you [*Ich-Du-Akte*], the character of *social acts*, by means of which all human personal communication is established. To study these acts carefully in their different forms and, starting from there, to make the essence of all *sociality* transcendentally understandable is an important task. With communalization proper, *social communalization*, there become constituted within the Objective world, as spiritual Objectivities of a peculiar kind, the various types of social communities with their possible hierarchical order—, among them the pre-eminent types that have the character of *"personalities of a higher order."* (Husserl, 1960, pp. 131–132)

Husserl distinguishes thus at least two important levels of communalization or intersubjectivity: (1) a level that is constituted by merely being aware of other Egos, and (2) another level, called "communalization proper" and "social communalization", that can only be constituted through what he calls "acts of mine directed to you" or "social acts" [*soziale Akte*], of which the more basic

---

[1] For a reading of this theory in the context of contemporary debates in cognitive sciences, see Vincini (2020).

ones are communications. For Husserl, communication as a social act presup-poses a non-social communalization, that is, a non-social reciprocal orienta-tion, a non-social constitution of a common world. His theory of collectivities must be understood precisely as pertaining to a higher level of intersubjectivity, that is, to social intersubjectivity.

Perhaps the most common and widespread objection to Husserl's theory of the constitution of sociality concerns the collectivities that he called "personali-ties of higher order" [*Personalitäten höherer Ordnung*], a concept that is related to a thread of possible phenomenological inquiry into the social reality that has not been sufficiently developed yet.

While several phenomenologists and social scientists (see Schutz, 1967, pp. 199–200, and 1970, pp. 38–39; Luckmann, 1992; Schuhmann, 1988; and Carr, 1987, pp. 267–280) have been right to point out, against what they believe to be the position of Husserl, that actions are always performances of individual persons, in the following lines I hope to be able to show that attrib-uting agency to a collectivity is more than a metaphor. No doubt Husserl would agree in stating that consciousness can only be attributed to individuals. However, he claims that to be a member of a personality of higher order implies acting as functionary of a collective agent.[2] To explain the possibility of collec-tive agency and personalities of higher order it is not necessary to assume that there is a collective mind or consciousness beyond that of the individual ones. Collective agency can rather be explained by describing how individuals per-form actions that only make sense for them because they are synthetized, or intertwined, with the actions of other individuals. Collectivities do not have conscious experiences, but the conscious experiences of the individuals can be intertwined with the conscious experiences of other individuals in such a way that they attribute their own actions both to them, as individuals that contrib-ute to a collective will, and to the group itself that is constituted by this collec-tive will.

3   Husserlian Remarks on Communication, Social Acts, and the Constitution of the Social World

Husserl's remarks on the constitution of social intersubjectivity, personalities of higher order, and social normativity are intimately related to the concept of social act. It is important to mention that the theory of social acts to which Husserl alludes in several of his works was not only developed by him but also by two of his closest students: Edith Stein (1922, 1925) and Adolf Reinach (1988). While Stein wrote about different social entities and personalities of higher order—including the State—Reinach came to analyze social acts in the

---

[2] This point is missing in Salice's (2022) didactic and schematic account of personalities of higher order and normativity. In my view, Salice fails to acknowledge important differences between the approaches of Husserl and Searle by insisting in that social normativity is entirely different from other forms of normativity and involves desire-independent reasons for action.

context of the problem of the foundations of civil law and arrived at conclusions that closely resemble those of Austin (1962) and Searle (2010) regarding speech acts.[3]

The first thing that is convenient to say about Husserl's concept of "social acts" is that it includes communications [*Mitteilungen*] and other acts that necessarily involve communication, such as issuing an order, making a request, and the like.

However, in several texts, Husserl suggests that communications are a particular instance of the broader phenomenon of expression. And it is worth noting that the phenomenon of expression also comprises the mere bodily appearance of any Self before Others, which is always in this sense a gesture. As in most of his writings on empathy, in *Ideas* II Husserl claims that, when we perceive another Self, we perceive a unity of a given present body [*Körper*] and an appresented corporal lived experience [*Leib*] that animates it—a life that is co-present, but as something merely indicated and that can never be given in original presence. Significantly, to this he adds there that the unity body and lived experience is analogous to that of the body of a word and its meaning. Following this idea, Husserl suggests that much in the same way as, when we read or listen, words are synthesized in higher unities of meaning and corporal appearance (visual or auditory signs), such as sentences and phrases, so too when we spend time observing other Selves, we perceive their corporal appearances as synthetized in progressively higher, more complex unities of meaningful behavior that imply several corporal appearances (Husserl, 1973b, pp. 236–247).

The suggestion of an analogy between the givenness of other Selves as *Leibkörper* (animated physical bodies) and words is further developed by Husserl in several writings of the 1930s (See Husserl, 1973c, pp. 79–90, 657–659, 663–665). In one of them, he explores an interesting and phenomenologically sound idea that can be further developed to fill some of the missing links between his theories of basic empathy and social intersubjectivity. He states that while bodies are expressions of the existence of persons, words express communications directed to other persons.

> For those who see, listen, or speak, *words* are 'expressions' [*Ausdrücke*], *bodies* are expressions. The former are expressions for communications directed to other humans, the latter are expressions of the existence [*Dasein*] of persons. The word-expression puts humans as addressed in what is expressed, and not only as speakers. The first and more simple expression is that of the bodily appearance [*leiblichen Aussehens*] as human body, which presupposes naturally someone who 'sees' and understands [it]. (Husserl, 1973c, pp. 664–665)

[3] On social acts and Husserl's account of the constitution of sociality, cf. Crespo and Ferrer (2016), Perreau (2013), Marín Ávila (2018a) and Sacrini (2022).

In so far as Others are perceived through their concordant behavior, the bodies that express their existence appear in a dynamic way, in movement (Husserl, 1973a, pp. 143–145). However, their bodies also express a relation with the worldly context to which they belong: "In any case, the surrounding world is always the full world of corporal things [*Körperwelt*] to which all expressions belong together" (Husserl, 1973c, p. 664). The body that expresses the existence of a person is always a thing in the context of a surrounding world and not something that relates to it in a second moment. It is important to keep this in mind when thinking of the relationship between corporality, communicative acts, and language.

I think that with the odd claim that word-expressions—and more broadly, the social acts which he identifies as communications [*Mitteilungen*] or communicative acts—"express humans as addressed," Husserl means that word-expressions make apparent to whoever grasps them the fact that they are intentionally directed to an addressee. Accordingly, in the manuscripts of 1921 that are known as *Gemeingeist I*, Husserl characterizes communication as the will [*Wille*] or impulsive striving [*triebhaftes Streben*] to determine or move spiritually the Other to strive or to have the will to come to know something (Husserl, 1973b, pp. 168–169). He provides several examples of this, some of which do not involve language, and distinguishes between several cases that differ in complexity: a "speaker" merely pointing with her finger or with a stick to something that she and her addressee are perceiving together; describing and highlighting aspects of what they are perceiving together; communicating about something that can only be remembered or that is not present in general; speaking to someone who is not present, and so on (Husserl, 1973b, p. 168).

What I wish to stress here is that Husserl describes communication as a will or as a striving that seeks to move the will of Others, and that, if it is successful, constitutes a community of will [*Willensgemeinschaft*] (Husserl, 1973b, p. 169).[4] As we will see later, the fact that the practical intentions of a plurality of persons constitute a community or nexus of will is compatible with domination and asymmetries between them. However, communication, the basis of all sociality, is already a collective endeavor in the sense that it implies the synthesis of volitive living experiences of at least two different persons.

When a communication takes place, the "speaker" lives in the volitive living experience of expressing something to another person, which implies that she wants her addressee to want to grasp this expression. The "listener," on the other hand, lives in the volitive living experience of wanting to grasp the expression that the "speaker" addressed to her. This idea is more clearly developed in another manuscript written a decade later:

---

[4] It is worth noting that Husserl's account of communication is consistent with the research of scientists like Michael Tomasello (2008) that claim that collective intentionality, and particularly joint attention, is the basis of human language.

At the basis of all sociality lies (first in the originality of the actually produced social activity) the actual nexus of the communicative community, the mere community of addressing [*Anreden*] and picking up the address [*Aufnehmen der Anrede*], or more clearly, of 'speaking to' and 'listening to'. [...] The communication is as such taken over, picked up. My willing to communicate, that is, my act with its meaning content, goes into the apresented Other when he undertakes the activity of appropriation, the listening that penetrates in him.

To explain how this communication develops from the mere bodily appearance of the Other, Husserl adds:

—in understanding the Other as listener, what is shown comes from the external gestures of the Other. These gestures 'express' in the first sense the listening-to. From this first apresentative expression another communicative expression is developed when the Other also says, 'I understand', reacts—for example—politely at the address with a 'please', etc. (Husserl, 1973c, pp. 475–476)

A few lines after, we find a further description of the volitive intertwinement that makes Husserl characterize the states of affairs constituted by communication precisely as a community:

Not only do I perform acts and not only do I come to be understood by the Other as performing acts, but the execution of my act motivates in him a certain co-execution, acts of picking up the communication, of going into the purpose of the communication. In the address and the picking up of the address, the Other and I come to a first unification. I am not only for me, and the other is not only in front of me as an Other, but the Other is my You, and by speaking, listening, and replying, we form a We that is unified, communalized, in a peculiar way. (Husserl, 1973c, p. 476)

The fact that communication involves a basic kind of volitive communalization is particularly relevant for the topic of this chapter because it explains why Husserl thought that other more complex sorts of social acts made it possible to constitute personalities of higher order, a concept that scandalized not only Schutz (1967, pp. 199–200, 1970, pp. 38–39), but other thinkers that were even more deeply acquainted with Husserl's writings on intersubjectivity and had access to his *Nachlass*, like Karl Schuhmann (1988).

According to Husserl, communications make possible other more complex social acts in which the addressee is determined or moved not only to acknowledge something but also to perform an action in her surrounding world. Thus, after describing communication in *Gemeingeist I*, Husserl adds:

Until now we have been dealing with the mere communication of facts; a certain community of will and a certain understanding is present here. But there is another *practical understanding in strict sense, a practical community of will*, namely, the case where in the status of the contact, the You is determined not only to get to know something, but to perform another action, for example, an exterior action that has an impact in the physical or spiritual surrounding world. (Husserl, 1973b, p. 169)

In contrast with his student Reinach (1988), Husserl was more concerned with describing how different kinds of associations—families, States, gangs of thieves, households, and so on—can be constituted through these more complex social acts than with the different forms that the acts themselves could assume, like that of promises, orders, requests, declarations, and acting in representation. But precisely because of this focus, the observations of Husserl shed light on collective agency and on the practical logic that underlies the normativity that comes together with belonging to groups that can be considered agents, that is, to personalities of higher order.

In the text from which the last quotation is taken, Husserl merely mentions as examples of different forms of social acts those of ordering, making a request and making a pact [*Vereinbarung*]. To my knowledge, he didn't describe them more exhaustively elsewhere, except from certain brief remarks (see Husserl, 1973d, pp. 98–110). He merely characterizes the order as the act of communicating a will with the purpose that such communication would be a medium for an Other to fulfill this will under coercive or menacing circumstances. The act of making a request is described as that of communicating a wish with the hope that this would be a medium for another person to fulfill it. Contracting takes place when someone commits to fulfill the desire of someone else under the condition that she will in turn commit to fulfill a desire of her own (Husserl, 1973b, pp. 169–170).

4   Personalities of Higher Order

Social acts that determine their addressees to perform actions, what we could anachronically call "performative acts," make it possible to constitute groups that have a more unified volitive structure than that of those constituted through mere communication. While the communities born of mere communication—be it a relatively ephemerous interaction or an historical, generational one—are communities of persons affecting one another, *Wirkungsgemeinschaften*, more complex social acts, such as issuing orders, or making requests or pacts, render possible the constitution of associations [*Verbände*] and of personalities of higher order (Husserl, 1973b, p. 201).

When considering Husserl's writings on this topic, it is important to keep in mind that such associations are constituted by several individuals that do something together and that the former are persons in the sense that what is done by these individuals can only be explained as the practical intentional object of the group itself: its goal or set of goals. In this sense, the association of individuals, and not the individuals separately, is constituted as the agent of whatever is done through the communalized will of their members. To say it shortly, these associations are persons in as far as they manifest themselves as agents.

The question is then how we come to perceive the acts of several different individual persons as parts of a unified act whose agent is a personality of higher order. According to Husserl, personalities of higher order can be given or become manifest to the persons who are members of them. When I do something together with other persons, I am aware of my doing as a doing of the group: as *our* doing. However, outsiders can also perceive personalities of higher order empathically based on their own experience as members of other groups of this kind (Husserl, 1960, pp. 132–136, 1973b, pp. 180–184, 200–204).

Husserl observed that individuals become members of personalities of higher order by engaging in social acts, and by doing so, they become aware of themselves and of their counterparts as subjects that strive to realize the same goals. He pointed out that they are aware of themselves in this way not as theoretical or doxical intentional objects but as practical ones (Husserl, 1973b, p. 171). In other words, this awareness is not a representation. This means that to engage in social acts involves making oneself objective [*gegenständlich*] as an agent and to be determined intersubjectively as having an identity as such an agent, that is, as having a public identity.

These observations are related to another important idea: that when someone does something together with other persons, and consequently, becomes member of a personality of higher order, she also becomes a subject determined by the collective practical intention of the group in a particular way for which Husserl uses the term "function" (Husserl, 1973c, pp. 200–201, 1973d, p. 104, 108; Cf. Jacobs, 2010, 2016). Notice in passing that this concept of "function" resembles that of "role," which was picked up by Schutz from Talcott Parsons and Edward Shils (Schutz, 1964, p. 232, 269) and inherited by Thomas Luckmann's and Peter Berger's social constructivism (Luckmann & Berger, 1991). In other words, each of the members of the association is aware of herself as being an agent in the mode of a functionary of the will of a collective agent and is thus determined as member of a We.

Even when it is common for real personalities of higher order to have complex and sometimes rather contradictory sets of goals, to think of examples that pursue relatively simple goals seems to make easier to single out structural traits that belong to all of them.

In different texts, Husserl explores basic and in different respects extreme types of personalities of higher order and the corresponding identities of their members. For example, he explores the structure of possible groups of this kind which—according to him—can be born from mere instinctual strivings, like families composed by fathers, mothers, and offspring that have different functions in relation to the goal of taking care and supporting each other (Husserl, 1973b, pp. 180–181); or associations that involve extreme forms of domination, such as a master slave relationship, in which the function of the master is that of commanding and the function of the slave is that of obeying (Husserl, 1973b, pp. 181–182). In the following section I will come back to these two examples and make some critical remarks in relation to them. Other examples of personalities of higher order discussed by Husserl include a nation-State, which involves different kinds of functionaries that range from regular citizens to members of the government, or the yet-to-be-realized universal personality of higher order composed by all human beings, which he identified with the name of "humanity." As it is well known, Husserl thought that the philosopher is a special kind of functionary of the humanity, implying that the identity of the philosopher is inseparable from the striving to bring about such community (Husserl, 1988b, pp. 3–94).

As I will try to show in the next section, to think of identities and their associated roles in terms of "functions" involves more than mere choice in the terminology. It suggests that they are based on nexuses of volition, which involve value assumptions. With this, it becomes possible to focus on some of the sources of the normativity that come together with these identities and roles and, more broadly, with the constitution of the social dimension of reality.[5]

5   Personal Identities, Functions, and Normativity

Husserl's account of the constitution of sociality comes together with crucial remarks related with what, following Sophie Loidolt, could be called a form of "imperative normativity" (Loidolt, 2019). To differentiate it from other forms of imperative normativity that are also experienced as a call or a demand, I will use the expression "social normativity."[6] As we will see, social normativity is essentially related with the fact that we can act together with other persons and constitute personalities of higher order.

To begin to address this topic, I wish to stress two points that follow from the exposition of the last section:

(1) To be a member of a personality of higher order implies having an identity as a functionary of it. For instance, the identity of being a member of a particular university and belonging to it in the mode of a teacher, student, administrative worker, and so on. (2) This identity is inseparable from the particular way in which one contributes or is expected to contribute to fulfill the goal of the association. In as far as in this respect the practical development of the member is subject to criticism, her identity as member of the association is subject to criticism as well.[7] The teacher that does not contribute to what is

---

[5] This kind of approach does not seem beforehand incompatible with Schutz's account of the kind of normativity that issues from roles and their relation to "typifications of interaction patterns which are socially approved ways of solving typical problems" (Schutz, 1964, p. 269). However, it sheds a new light as to how and why these typifications are socially approved by different groups.

[6] For a panoramic view of different forms of normativity in Husserl, see Loidolt (2009).

[7] In this chapter I am leaving aside the problem of belonging to a group by decree. One can also come to belong to a group by decree [*Bestimmung*], a social act that was examined by Reinach in a way that resembles Searle's analyses on declarations (See Reinach, 1988; Searle, 2010). A decree can be effective in as far as there is a promise to accept the authority of individual or collective person that issues it. This means behaving according to what whoever issues the decree says that should be (Reinach, 1988). Anything can be incorporated to a personal association by decree, even objects. However, only persons that take part in the doings of the group can be considered responsible for the doings of the group itself and subject to the kind of criticism that I am describing here.

expected from her according to the purpose of the university, for instance, teaching courses and tutoring students, is a bad teacher even when she might be an excellent learner or researcher.[8] Allow me to elaborate on this point and to introduce in relation to it the problem of the normativity that is inherent to all personalities of higher order.

Husserl's basic insight in relation to social normativity is that, when acting together with other persons, to fail to fulfill or to poorly fulfill one's part amounts to frustrate the efforts of the partners of that collective action. Consequently, the awareness that one has a duty to other members of the group to which one belongs comes from the fact that deviation from this function gives them motives to make a criticism and thereafter to issue a demand or a claim. One of the passages where Husserl explains this more clearly is centered in the example of a personality of higher order with the form of a family. Even though the example is problematic when considering that Husserl suggests that the particular kind of family that he has in mind is born out of an instinctive, natural basis, it might still be a good example once we question this assumption and consider such kind of family as a socio-historical institution, in this case, one shaped by a patriarchal system:

> We see that in the communities of families that develop naturally, the first thing is the naturally naïve care of the mother for the children, that of the man for the mother as partner and as mother of the children, etc.
>
> The omission of such natural care due to distraction, momentary egoism, irrationality, etc., leads to the *criticism* and then to the *personal demand* [*Aufforderung*], to the order, for example. *The ought [Sollen] develops*: the "he must", and on the part of who experiences and accepts the imposition [*Zumutung*], the "I ought". [...] *Each member of the family is a responsible subject*, a subject which has an I-ought inside this generality [of the total action] which is determined in the particular cases. [...] The term *function* alludes to the way the subjects are practically determined, and precisely under the point of view of a particular goal which is in the service of an encompassing goal of the complete social association—in this case, the family. [...] In the family, the father has the function of 'head of the family', the woman, that of wife and mother, etc. The step toward the expressions *duty* and *ought* is evoked through the negative: the deviation disturbs the concordance of the will [*Willenseinstimmigkeit*] and is a condition for the reaction of censure. (Husserl, 1973b, pp. 180–181)

One can criticize this example on the basis that to attribute a common will to communities where oppression occurs hides raw coercion and complex power relationships and structures. However, my point is that basic forms coercion and power relationships can be explained by describing the imposition of concordances of will, the imposition of forms of collaboration. That Husserl does not idealize this concordance of will as something morally good is clear in the same text a few lines later, when he observes that the functions and obligations

---

[8] These two points are illustrated with great clarity in Jacobs (2010).

that come with belonging to personalities of higher order can be based on a voluntary act of contracting but also imposed by force as in the extreme case of the association between master and slave (Husserl, 1973b, pp. 181–182). An especially important implication of this is that to fail to comply with what one "ought" to do amounts to breaking or disturbing the personal relationship that comes together with the concordance of will.

> The slave that escapes is no longer really a slave (abstracting from the law, that is out of play here). A rebellion of slaves breaks the master-slave-relation. Violence, the defeat of the uprising, reproduces it, and the expression is accurate in so far as the new relationship is known [*bewusst*] as a continuation of the old one. The slave acknowledges the ought, and also the ought retrospectively for the time in which he had broken it. (Husserl, 1973b, pp. 181–182)

It can already be seen that Husserl's insights into the grounds of this normativity in communities that involve nexuses of will—that is, collective goals—makes it possible to provide explanations that point to the practical logics and dynamics that underlie such phenomena (see Jacobs, 2010). To move forward in this direction, it is possible to inquire the following: Why would the concordance of will ground normative claims? Why breaking a concordance of will and frustrating collective efforts would motivate such a criticism and consequently the consciousness of an ought?

To address these questions, we must go back to Husserl's basic insight into the presuppositions of normative claims, which is that they always involve valuings. In *Logical Investigations*, he writes that:

> each normative proposition presupposes a certain sort of valuation or approval through which the concept of a 'good' or 'bad' (a value or a disvalue) arises in connection with a certain class of objects: in conformity with this, objects divide into good and bad ones. To be able to pass the normative judgment 'A soldier should be brave', I must have some conception of a good soldier. (Husserl, 2001, p. 35)

Because of this, the normative proposition:

> 'A soldier should be brave' rather means that only a brave soldier is a good soldier, which implies (since the predicates 'good' and 'bad' divide up the extension of the concept 'soldier') that a soldier who is not brave is a 'bad' soldier. *Since* the value-judgment holds, everyone is entitled to demand of a soldier that he should be brave. (Husserl, 2001, p. 34)

This account is developed and nuanced later in Husserl's lessons on formal ethics, in which he advanced a normative theory of the formal conditions under which an action can be rational, as well as a theory of practical normativity (Husserl, 1988a). At that point he adds that there is a subjective dimension of values that is not comparable to what happens with doxical determinations because a value can only be said to be valid for a given subject in view of her context. Therefore, objective judgments of value must refer to the concerned subjects and their circumstances, and duties are relative to the capabilities of those who are said to have them (Husserl, 1988a, p. 89, 149; cf. Marín Ávila, 2018b). However, the idea that normativity is grounded in value assumptions is maintained intact there and further developed in his lessons on ethics of 1920–1924 (Husserl, 2004).

If the concordances of will that are inherent to personalities of higher order ground normative claims, this is due to the fact that these willings, the goals of the associations, are valuable for the persons who issue the criticisms. If these criticisms and the following duties are also accepted by the criticized functionaries, this means that the latter also value such concordances of will, be it in themselves, or derivatively as related to other things that hold value for them.[9]

It follows from the above that oppressive personalities of higher order ground normative claims based on different values for those who obtain benefits and those who suffer from them. For instance, if someone subjugated accepts a duty before her oppressor, this might imply that she values something that is under threat. The menace of a punishment gives to the concordance of will of such social relationship a derivative value for someone who would not value it by itself. The oppressed person must comply with her duties before the oppressor, for otherwise something valuable for her would be at risk. Because she values the menaced thing, she experiences the normative call to comply. For instance, in traditional families where women are subjugated, important motives to collaborate and to accept their duties are related with systemic and interpersonal economic factors, such as limited access to the work market, or related to social disciplinary measures that are systemically applied to women who transgress the traditional order (Pateman, 1988; Fraser, 2014; Segato, 2010). In extreme historical forms of subjugation, obedience is motivated by threats against life and physical integrity. If the master's motive to constitute a personality of higher order with the slave is using her work and ultimately her life for the former's benefit, the reasons for the slave to comply are related with the conservation of her life or the life of her family, as well as with preserving their physical integrity. Obviously, personalities of higher order and the concordances of will involved in them need not be born out of agreements. They are often originated by social interactions—social acts like orders, prescriptions, requests, or promises—that create interpersonal states of affairs.

Nevertheless, there are also cases where oppressed people in a personality of higher order comply with their duties as functionaries allegedly for the same reasons as their oppressors. Ideology can assume in this case the form of concealment of an unfavorable situation for the oppressed that was created by the oppressor. Domination can be established by creating situations in which it is convenient for the oppressed to comply, and this might come together with concealment of the fact that these situations were created by the oppressors. A

---

[9] On derivative values, see Husserl (1988a, pp. 70–71).

phenomenological analysis of the practical logic that underlies a personality of higher order and of the differentiated valuings that motivate the members of it to collaborate, and thus to continue to belong to it, can throw light into forms of domination that are based on depriving some members of goods to which they would otherwise have access,[10] as well as on creating undesirable situations if they do not collaborate and thus belong to this groups (Tilly, 2005).

6 Collective Agency and Personal Responsibility

Personalities of higher order are agents because there are actions that can be attributed to them. The individuals that contribute to these actions perform them precisely as members or functionaries of the group. A member of a sport team or a family is aware that the match was won or lost by the team, or that the family as a whole took care of its members. This point has been stressed by several thinkers, including John Searle, who relies in the Wilfrid Sellars' concept of "we-intention" (Searle, 2010). The awareness that the author of a given action is not an I, but a We, comes together with having the practical intention to do things to achieve goals that can only be achieved if other persons do other things. The central point here is that the will of a personality of higher order, what is done by it, is not identical with a course of actions undertook by any of its members.

Even in personalities of higher order that involve extreme forms of domination, what is done by the group cannot be explained as the fulfillment of the volition of one of its members. It might be the case that the slave complies with all the demands of the master, with all the resolves—or empty practical intentions—that the master dictates as orders addressed to her. In that case, the doings of the slave are not entirely her own, for their sense is to fulfill the resolutions of the master, what the master wants. Thus, these doings cannot be explained unless we consider the resolutions of the master that they fulfill. All the same, the resolutions of the master are not entirely her own, for they cannot be understood if we do not consider the doings of the slave and what the slave can do. The resolutions of the master are meant to be fulfilled through the actions of the slave.

But to acknowledge that some actions can only be attributed to personalities of higher order, and not to individuals, does not mean that the individuals that belong to such associations are not responsible for those actions. They are responsible as collaborators of the personalities of higher order: as functionaries. In so far as they belong to the group by doing different things, they also bear different responsibilities for what is collectively done.

Individual responsibility in collective actions performed by a personality of higher order can be appreciated in as far as the concordance of will of the group, its collective nexus of will, is accurately described. To do this, it is useful

---

[10] An instance of this case, among others, would be the historical phenomena that Marx called "primitive accumulation" (see Marx, 1992; Federici, 2004).

to rely on the phenomenological distinction, traced by Husserl, between empty practical intentions—like resolves and decisions—and fulfilling practical intentions—actions (Husserl, 1988a, 2004). A practical intention can be described, following Husserl, as the consciousness that something will be or will exist as a consequence of having intended it, that is, as a consequence of being conscious of it in a particular way which can be precisely characterized as a practical positing consciousness. An empty practical intention is the positing consciousness of something that will come to be or exist as a consequence of future actions (Husserl, 1988a, pp. 103–111).

For instance, if I take the resolution to go hiking next weekend, then this resolution is different from a mere belief. It is the practical positing of an action. As such, it will be fulfilled by the several actions that fulfill the goal of "having gone hiking," actions that are a consequence of such resolution. If I have doubts concerning what should I do the weekend, if should go hiking or stay at home to finish a manuscript, then I can give a practical answer to this practical question in the form of deciding. According to Husserl's terminology, a decision is an empty practical intention that can be characterized as a practical answer to a practical question (Husserl, 1988a, p. 119).

The contribution that an individual makes to the doings of a personality of higher order can thus have the form of empty volitions that shape its collective nexus of will, like making decisions or taking resolutions by issuing orders, or it can have the form of actions that fulfill empty volitions of those members that decide and resolve. Of course, a given individual can contribute in both ways by making decisions or taking resolutions on behalf of the group, and at the same time doing things and complying with instructions that express decisions made by other members, or by acting on behalf of the group according to her own resolutions, as a representative of it.

Let us consider two controversial examples that might be illustrative because of the reprehensible character of some the goals that they pursue: an informal community police that becomes corrupt and turns to criminal activity, and a criminal family.

There are some members of personalities of higher order that take resolutions and make decisions that institute or renew the group's goals. The motives of these members to belong to the personal association include the value that they place on these goals, since they resolved or decided precisely that these goals should be pursued. For instance, the leader of a community police might decide to cease to patrol certain neighborhoods to facilitate illegal activities in those areas in exchange for bribes. A member of a family that runs a business might decide to involve the business in illegal activities, like selling goods that she has stolen. In these examples, we might assume that the policeman and the family member place some value in pursuing such criminal activities.

Let's suppose that there are other members of these personalities of higher order that do not make relevant decisions regarding the goals of the groups. An officer of a community police might do her job of patrolling the zones to which she is assigned and responding to emergency calls of the community without even being aware that the personal association is corrupt because it serves criminal goals. Or she might know it and still do the job that she is asked to do without deciding anything regarding the goals of the personal association herself. Similar examples can be constructed, mutatis mutandis, for the case of children or other members of a family that work at the criminal business run by it but do not make decisions. They might be exploited to sell the stolen goods at the counter without having decided the kind of business in which the family is involved or even knowing it.

According to what we argued before, the activities of a personality of higher order—in our examples, giving protection to criminals in exchange for bribes, or stealing and selling stolen goods—can be attributed to the group as such. I think it could also be said that these activities can be attributed to *all* the members of the group. They belong to it precisely as functionaries that collaborate in the doings of the group itself. Knowingly or unknowingly, all the members of the community police and all the participants in the family business are engaged in aiding criminal activities and in stealing and selling stolen goods, respectively. These things are done by all of them. However, the meaning of the doings of the personal association is embedded in a different context for each member because the motivations to do it, and, therefore, to belong to the group, are different. Moreover, as we have seen, the motives to collaborate and thus belong to a group of this sort can include all forms of coercion.

Because they can be held responsible for any of their doings, individuals that are members of personalities of higher order can also be held responsible for their actions as functionaries of such groups. However, the decisions or actions of a member of a personal association can only be meaningful for her if she knows what she is doing, what the group does, and what are her motives to come to belong or to continue to belong to it. If a member of the criminal family does not know that when she picks up some of the goods of the business she is stealing, or that the family business consists in the described criminal activities, then attributing her responsibility for the doings of the group faces the same challenges as attributing her responsibility for any other thing that she might do without knowing. If she does not know why she belongs to the group, that is, why she collaborates—out of love for her relatives, fear of retaliations if she does not comply, or sheer personal interest—then she is in a similar situation as when she acts blindly as an individual. She could be accused of remaining deliberately and conveniently blind because this serves her self-interest, but that is another question.

In addition to those cases related with ignorance of one's actions, the group doings, and the motives to collaborate and to belong to it, there are other cases where individual responsibility in the doings of a personal association should be nuanced or even ruled out.

On the one hand, a functionary of a personality of higher order can be coerced to contribute to fulfill its goals. We have already encountered an extreme example of this sort set by Husserl: the community of master and slave. Let us suppose that masters motivate slaves to work for them by threatening their lives, as well as those of their family members, if they do not comply. To build on the example, we could imagine a scenario where the duties of the slaves include helping the masters to discipline, capture, buy, and sell other slaves. The goal of this personality of higher order could be thus described as making economical profits for the master by disciplining, capturing, buying, and selling slaves. Are the slaves that collaborate in the activities of disciplining, capturing, buying, or selling other slaves responsible for these doings? There are many gray areas in between, but in as far as these activities are completely coerced, the slaves are evidently not responsible for the doings of the pro-slavery group.

On the other hand, a personal association can pursue contradictory goals. An example of this is a community police that is partially corrupt. An officer might do her job, as it is defined by the goal of serving the community and by the official rules of the corporation, even when she knows that her boss and some other colleagues are corrupt and serve criminal goals. She might still collaborate with the corrupt members of the personality of higher order in relation to common goals—after all, her function as member of the group demands her to do it—but not in the criminal ones. One could say that this difference in the conception of the goals that they pursue when they collaborate splits the personal association in two subgroups: a subgroup of corrupt members and another subgroup of "clean" ones. For a "clean" member, knowing that a member is corrupt is a motive not to collaborate with her, and vice versa, because collaborating with a member of the other group would prevent the goal of her subgroup to be fulfilled. Each of these subgroups could be considered a personality of higher order, even though both groups are members of another greater personality of higher order that includes both: the community police that provides security and other services to the community while also exploiting and attacking it in alliance with criminal groups. The contradictory set of goals of the real community police, which is partially corrupt, can be the object of dispute by its members. They might do many things, issue orders and prescriptions, make requests, comply with orders or deliberately ignore them, and so on, with the purpose of making their goals prevail against the goals of other subgroups, or of changing them altogether for new ones. There are many possible forms of shaping the concordance of will of a personality of higher order through actions and empty practical intentions expressed as social acts.

Is the officer that is not corrupt—who acts according to the formally declared goals of the community police—responsible for the criminal doings of the police group as a whole? If we suppose that she is aware of these criminal doings and that she is not coerced to collaborate, to answer this question we would have to inquire into her motives for collaborating and thus consenting to the doings of the community police as a whole. She might consider, for instance, that having a partially corrupt community police is better for the population than not having any police at all, or that the only way in which the community can have good police is if honest people join it and make sure that the goals of providing services to the population prevail over the criminal ones. However, it could be the case that she considers that having such corrupt police is worse for the community than not having any police at all and that the group is beyond the possibility of renewal. In that case, even when she is not corrupt, her collaboration with the group might be ethically reprehensible insofar as the doings of the group are also her own doings.

Still, in many cases the members of a personality of higher order are not fully aware of the doings of the group. To this extent, the doings of the group can be considered independent of those of its members. Modern bureaucratic organizations can be extreme and increasingly common examples of this situation. According to Arendt, totalitarian bureaucratic rule is characterized by having an onion-layered structure where militants or functionaries of one hierarchical level are kept less informed about the organization than those above (Arendt, 1976, pp. 392–418). This allows for what she identifies as a rule of nobody that can become an extreme form of tyranny (Arendt, 1976, p. 213, 245, 1998, p. 40, 45). According to the theory of personalities of higher order that I have introduced here, bureaucracy as the rule of nobody can be described as a situation where many of the individuals that contribute to a collective will are artificially deprived of the possibility of gaining insight into it. Such situation is fostered by concealing the goals of the group to its functionaries, which include both officials of the government and plain citizens. As Arendt saw, this form of rule is ethically problematic, and precisely for this reason the conditions that make it possible should be carefully examined.

What problems are posed by living in a world in which we increasingly ignore what we do as members of higher-order personalities of all sorts? These groups include the public or private institutions in which we work, the small and large communities to which we belong—including virtual ones—but also the states of which we are citizens or residents of their territory, for we collaborate with them at the very least by complying with different sorts of regulations. As societies become more complex, the knowledge of the doings of their multiple personalities of higher order with their subgroups become more diffuse and difficult to know.

I wish to conclude by pointing out that, from a phenomenological point of view, the problem of undertaking actions or in general positing practical intentions without being aware of their meaning—that is, without evidence or intuition—is a core ethical problem. According to Husserl, a person can only act rationally if she reflects into her motives for doing what she does and determines that it is something that she must do (Husserl, 1988a, 2004). In this sense, the analysis of supra-personal forms of agency shows that to act rationally it is not enough to be able and willing to reflect on the obscure subsoil of our instinctive and passive motivations (Husserl, 1952), but also on the obscure horizon of the collective actions in which we are engaged and the social norms that are imposed on us as a consequence of belonging to groups and having identities as functionaries of them.

REFERENCES

Arendt, H. (1976). *The origins of totalitarianism*. A Harvest Book—Harcourt, Inc.

Arendt, H. (1998). *The human condition*. The University of Chicago Press.

Austin, J. L. (1962). *How to do things with words*. Oxford University Press.

Caminada, E. (2016). Husserl on groupings: Social ontology and phenomenology of we-intentionality. In T. Szanto & D. Moran (Eds.), *Phenomenology of sociality: Discovering the 'we', Vol. 3* (pp. 281–295). Routledge.

Carr, D. (1987). *Interpreting Husserl. Critical and comparative studies* (Phaenomenologica 106). Martinus Nijhoff.

Crespo, M., & Ferrer, U. (2016). *Die Person im Kontext von Moral und Sozialität. Studien zur frühen phänomenologischen Ethik*. Verlag Traugott Bautz GmbH.

Federici, S. (2004). *Caliban and the witch. Women, the body, and primitive accumulation*. Autonomedia.

Fraser, N. (2014). Behind Marx's hidden abode. *New Left Review, 84*, 55–72.

Husserl, E. (1952). *Husserliana IV. Ideen zur einer reinen Phänomenologie und phänomenologischen Philosophie. Zweites Buch: Phänomenologische Untersuchungen zur Konstitution* (M. Biemel, Ed.). Martinus Nijhoff.

Husserl, E. (1960). *Cartesian meditations: An introduction to phenomenology* (D. Cairns, Trans.). Martinus Nijhoff.

Husserl, E. (1973a). Cartesianische Meditationen. In S. Strasser (Ed.), *Husserliana I. Cartesianische Meditationen und Pariser Vorträge* (pp. 41–186). Martinus Nijhoff.

Husserl, E. (1973b). *Husserliana XIV. Zur Phänomenologie der Intersubjektivität. Texte aus dem Nachlass. Zweiter Teil. 1921–28* (I. Kern, Ed.). Martinus Nijhoff.

Husserl, E. (1973c). *Husserliana XV. Zur Phänomenologie der Intersubjektivität. Texte aus dem Nachlass. Dritter Teil. 1929–35* (I. Kern, Ed.). Martinus Nijhoff.

Husserl, E. (1973d). *Husserliana XIII. Zur Phänomenologie der Intersubjektivität. Texte aus dem Nachlass. Erster Teil. 1905–1920* (I. Kern, Ed.). Martinus Nijhoff.

Husserl, E. (1988a). *Husserliana XXVIII. Vorlesungen über Ethik und Wertlehre. 1908–1914* (U. Melle, Ed.). Kluwer Academic Publishers.

Husserl, E. (1988b). *Husserliana XXVII. Aufsätze und Vorträge* (T. Nenon & H. R. Sepp, Eds.). Martinus Nijhoff.

Husserl, E. (2001). *Logical investigations. Volume 1* (J. N. Findlay, Trans.). Routledge.

Husserl, E. (2004). *Husserliana XXXVII. Einleitung in die Ethik. Vorlesungen Sommersemester 1920 und 1924* (H. Peucker, Ed.). Kluwer Academic Publishers.

Jacobs, H. (2010). Towards a phenomenological account of personal identity. In C. Lerna, H. Jacobs, & F. Mattens (Eds.), *Philosophy, phenomenology, sciences: Essays in commemoration of Edmund Husserl* (Phaenomenologica, vol. 200) (pp. 333–361). Springer.

Jacobs, H. (2016). Socialization, reflection, and personhood. In S. Rinofner-Kreidl & H. Wiltsche (Eds.), *Analytic and continental philosophy: Methods and perspectives* (pp. 323–335). Walter de Gruyter.

Loidolt, S. (2009). *Anspruch und Rechtfertigung: Eine Theorie des rechtlichen Denkens im Anschluss and die Phenomenologie Edmund Husserls*. Springer.

Loidolt, S. (2019). Experience and normativity: The phenomenological approach. In A. Cimino & C. Leijenhorst (Eds.), *Phenomenology and experience: New perspectives*. Brill.

Luckmann, T. (1992). *Theorie des sozialen Handelns*. De Gruyter.

Luckmann, T., & Berger, P. (1991). *The social construction of reality*. Penguin Books.

Marín Ávila, E. (2018a). Sobre la racionalidad del deber social. Reflexiones sobre el deber social con base en observaciones de Edmund Husserl y Adolf Reinach. In M. Crespo (Ed.), *Filosofía trascendental, Fenomenología y Derecho natural*. Olms.

Marín Ávila, E. (2018b). On axiological and practical objectivity. Do Husserl's considerations about objectivity on the axiological and practical realms demand a phenomenological account of dialogue? In I. Quepons & R. Parker (Eds.), *The new yearbook for phenomenology and phenomenological philosophy. Volume XVI. Phenomenology of emotions* (pp. 212–230). Routledge.

Marx, K. (1992). *Capital Volume 1* (B. Fowkes, Trans). Penguin Group.

Pateman, C. (1988). *The sexual contract*. Stanford University Press.

Perreau, L. (2013). *Le monde social selon Husserl* (Phaenomenologica 219). Springer.

Reinach, A. (1988). Die apriorischen Grundlagen des bürgerlichen Rechtes (1913). In K. Schuhmann & B. Smith (Eds.), *Sämtliche Werke. Textkritische Ausgabe 1. Werke* (pp. 141–278). Philosophia Verlag.

Sacrini, M. (2022). *Socialidade e cultura em Husserl*. Editora Phi.

Salice, A. (2022). Husserl on shared intentionality and normativity. *Continental Philosophy Review*. https://doi.org/10.1007/s11007-022-09593-w

Schuhmann, K. (1988). *Husserls Staatsphilosophie*. Verlag Karl Alber.

Schutz, A. (1964). Equality and the meaning structure of the world. In A. Brodersen (Ed.), *Collected papers II. Studies in social theory* (pp. 227–273). Martinus Nijhoff.

Schutz, A. (1967). *The phenomenology of the social world*. Northwestern University Press.

Schutz, A. (1970). Edmund Husserl's *Ideas*, Volume II. In I. Schutz (Ed.), *Collected papers III. Studies in phenomenological philosophy* (pp. 15–39). Martinus Nijhoff.

Searle, J. (2010). *Making the social world. The structure of human civilization*. Oxford University Press.

Segato, R. (2010). *Las estructuras elementales de la violencia*. Prometeo.

Stein, E. (1922). Beiträge zur philosophischen Begründung der Psychologie und der Gesteswissenschaften. *Jahrbuch für Philosophie und phänomenologische Forschung* 5.

Stein, E. (1925). Eine Untersuching über die Staat. *Jahrbuch für Philosophie und phänomenologische Forschung* 7.

Tilly, C. (2005). *Trust and rule*. Cambridge University Press.

Tomasello, M. (2008). *Origins of human communication* (Jean Nicod Lectures). MIT Press.

Vincini, S. (2020). The pairing account of infant direct social perception. *Journal of Consciousness Studies, 27*(1–2), 173–205.

Edmund Husserl and Alfred Schutz on Collective Personalities

Rosana Déborah Motta

1   INTRODUCTION

Alfred Schutz is considered one of the keenest readers of Edmund Husserl's work and, at the same time, the founder of social phenomenology. His interest in phenomenology arose after Felix Kaufmann's recommendation to study Husserl's work, where he would be able to find solid arguments to reveal how subjects constitute the world given to consciousness. Many of the concepts used by Husserl, such as meaning [*Sinn*], experience [*Erfahrung*], and the life-world [*Lebenswelt*], are central to Schutz's approach and paved the way for the development of social phenomenology. In the following paragraphs, we will explore the nature of Schutz's approach and why he chose to adopt a phenomenological perspective. Specifically, we will examine the foundational operation that Schutz developed, which ultimately led to the creation of social phenomenology.

Part of this foundational maneuver was to deliver a deadly blow to the naturalistic explanations of the social, which, from Comte onward, tried to explain the basic constitutive elements of sociality by applying tools that belonged to the natural-scientific method. Phenomenology could lead to the foundation of a science of the essence of the social that can reach an exhaustive comprehension of social facts and their clarification; that is, a social science that reduces social phenomena to the state of immediate data and investigates them in their

R. D. Motta (✉)
Universidad de Buenos Aires, Buenos Aires, Argentina
e-mail: rmotta@sociales.uba.ar

C. Belvedere, A. Gros (eds.), *The Palgrave Handbook of Macrophenomenology and Social Theory*,
https://doi.org/10.1007/978-3-031-34712-2_16

essence (Hussel, 1989b). To achieve this goal, it was necessary, of course, to return to the essential facts of the life of consciousness, which can only be accomplished by means of transcendental constitutive analysis.

Schutz considered the egological way to be preparatory and was concerned about the "phantom" of solipsism. For this reason, he based himself on the exact parallelism suggested by Husserl between the transcendental ego and the empirical ego and chose to transfer the structures of the transcendental consciousness to the mundane consciousness. This is mainly due to the fact that Schutz believed that Husserl was not familiar with the concrete problems of the social sciences, and this fact is evident in the criticisms he made of transcendental intersubjectivity. The strongest of these criticisms comes after his reading of *Cartesian Meditations* (Schutz, 1966, pp. 51–91), topic which we deal with in another work (Motta, 2007). Here, we will focus on the criticism of the same problematic made by Schutz after his reading of *Ideas II*, and we will basically focus on the way in which he analyzes the concept of community or personal units of a higher order, and the place that Husserl assigns to communication in constituting the region of the spirit [*Geist*]. Let us start from the opposition described by Husserl between a personalistic and a naturalistic attitude.

2   CLARIFICATION OF THE OPPOSITION BETWEEN THE NATURALISTIC AND THE PERSONALISTIC ATTITUDE: THE CONSTITUTION OF THE PERSONAL WORLD

Husserl arrives at the description of the region of the social once the distinction between naturalistic and personalistic attitude is made. The former differs from the latter because it is rooted in nature; that is, it shares the essence-thing [*Ding*] as a body in the sense of the physical-natural object. The soul, on the other hand, can only be grasped as being injected into the body. This way, the physical acquires aesthesiological and spiritual dimensions that drive the body's abilities and volitions. The natural scientist can analyze the location and description of these movements by examining the physical thing as a "real animal."

Unlike the natural scientist, the pure psychologist can analyze the soul without reference to the natural world. The region of spirit cannot be located in the spatial sense of the material thing. Husserl argues that the soul is not next to the body or "in" the body, meaning that it does not occupy "the place" of the material thing as part of the "*res extensa*" in a Cartesian sense.

In the same way, the soul is not part of objective, natural time, that is, of the time of the world. The soul or pure consciousness "is a genuine temporal field, a field of 'phenomenological' time [...] and this must not be confused with objective time" (Husserl, 1989a, p. 188). However, there is a possibility for the soul to apprehend natural time and, through it, achieve a perfect matching with inner time.

And yet, Husserl states that this game of oppositions becomes visible once the consequent reduction has been applied, revealing that the naturalistic attitude is not the only possible one. The phenomenological reduction makes it possible, among other things, to analyze nature in the realm of the essential correlation between what is constituted and what is constituting. Therefore, it is only from this starting point that we can differentiate the mental states that belong to the acts in which man is conscious of himself, others, and the reality of the world around him. These acts are connected in the development of actions—of the individual personality—and in the use of things that surround him, which are not just mere material objects.

Things that we encounter in our surrounding world [*Umwelt*] are intended for personal use and are distinct from material things in that they are understood as things for myself. It is through this understanding that the ego relates to the contents of the environment that stand out, such as useful things, singular persons, or formations of personal units of a higher order, that is, communities. When the ego reflects on the connections that bind the relationships between egos, and on its own volitional direction toward a shared world, a different attitude emerges, one that is distinct from the naturalistic attitude, yet completely natural. This means that when we consider our world, we do not perceive it in the same way as a biologist with a scientific purpose; rather, our concern is primarily practical.

To live as a person means to live in social relationships of mutual knowledge and to simultaneously live in a surrounding world that is experienced meaningfully. Through the act of giving meaning, the surrounding world becomes a world for myself. Thus, the person is only truly a person as long as he or she is subject to his or her surrounding world. This necessary correlation between the ego and its world can be accordingly found in a higher order of collective subjectivity. "[T]o each person belongs his surrounding world, while at the same time a plurality of persons in communication with one another has a common surrounding world" (Husserl, 1989a, p. 195).

Despite this, the primary bond that enables other forms of connection to occur is established by the motivation that the personal ego has with things. Unlike the causal relationship that a physical body has with material things, this particular relationship is based on the experience of things and their being "thought or in some other way intended and posited, things as such, intentional objects of personal consciousness" (p. 199). As Husserl states, the noematic units have a motivating force from which the ego gives itself, "gives up" to its own experience. Therefore, we could say that the personal attitude or motivational attitude is the practical attitude: "that is, what we always have here is the active or passive ego and indeed in the proper intrinsic sense" (p. 199).

It is now time to consider the existence of a higher order of constitution, which involves describing the shared performance of personal egos as they are volitionally directed toward the surrounding world.

3   THE PERSON WITH OTHER PERSONS: THE CONSTITUTION
     OF THE SPIRITUAL WORLD

We find ourselves with others moving toward a common surrounding world [*Mitumwelt*] and, since we are personal subjects with volitional capacities like them, we are personal subjects and not mere things in a natural sense. Whoever treats personal subjects as mere things "is precisely blind to the spiritual sphere" (Husserl, 1989a, p. 201). And that is why our analysis will put aside any discovery of the natural region and its corresponding science.

To begin with, we have Husserl's description of how others are given to us in presence. According to him, the other emerges as a counter-subject [*Gegensubjekt*] by the simple fact of understanding his or her practical existence directed to the common objectivities of which "our" surrounding world is made. We find ourselves in a personal conglomerate, in an intentional intertwining of our life, understanding this common world of us simultaneously and also approaching it comprehensively.

In these acts, relationships are determined in a new sense, that is, intertwining them with each other. This intertwining is based on the motivating force, which, as explained above while referring to things of the physical world, is also a binding force for other people. At a higher level, and through addressing each other and in the execution of intentional acts that are meant for mutual understanding, relationships of intra-understanding are built. They establish mutual relations between the egos and, at the same time, an inherent relationship between them and the surrounding world. From here, the communicative world is shaped by unfolding acts of mutual comprehension and of intra-comprehension.

By essence, the communicative world is related to people who are in it and in front of it. People in this environment are not given to each other as objects, but as correlative subjects, as companions. And for this reason, mutual relations of a social order are built. Sociality arises from communicative acts that are specifically social. In these acts, the ego addresses the others and embraces them, and, in turn, the others turn to the ego in "acts of discrepancy or consonance."

It is necessary to note that the idea of a personal subject in this theory actually stretches from the singular subject to social conglomerates of subjects. And thus, "this world for me, then as a personal subject, is at the same time an intersubjective world [...] as a world of common objects, common values, common uses, common actions and achievement, cultural objects, in short, a common surrounding world" (Drummond, 1996, p. 244). Husserl points out that through this communication of subjects with each other, personal units of higher order are formed in a correlative way; units that are associations of subjects with their environment and in communication with each other. Taking these associations as a point of departure, and moving to a further degree of progress, one arrives at the idea of the whole social subjectivities, which are actually or potentially present and in mutual communication, and one also arrives in the end at the notion of the world of the spirit. The world of the spirit is thus formed by all the social subjects at their lower or higher level, which are in actual or partly actual and partly potential communication with each other. This world evokes a phenomenon of action and communication between beings who live in a common surrounding world, possibly sharing objective or subjective situations, which are worldly experiential (Iribarne, 1985). The world of the spirit is the realm of interconnected spiritual subjects, communities, and objects that exist as a reality for the spirit. In other words, it is a reality that is imbued with meaning and significance, but is also open to acquiring new meanings and interpretations at any given time.

4   SCHUTZ'S CRITICAL READING OF *IDEAS II*

In 1934, Husserl informed Schutz that he had decided not to publish the second volume of *Ideas II* because he believed that he had not yet found a satisfactory solution to the problem of intersubjectivity, which he thought he had solved in the *Cartesian Meditations* of 1932 (Schutz, 1966, p. 17). However, in his review of the 1952 work, Schutz notices that the topics dealt with in the second volume of the *Ideas* are of decisive importance for the foundation of the social sciences (p. 18).

Accordingly, in a letter sent to Gurwitsch in 1952, the sociologist expressed his excitement at reading *Ideas II*, as he found much of what Husserl said to be very similar to his own thoughts (Grathoff, 1989, p. 152). Schutz's focus was mainly on the Husserlian concepts of the body and its expressions, the socio-spatial juxtaposition of personal subjects, and the concept of interchangeability of points of view.

Despite the fortunate concurrences, Schutz finds serious problems in the ontological gradation of the levels of the world of the spirit, that is to say, the distinction between founding and founded levels in their constitution. The first difficulty that Schutz detects is the lack of clarity in Husserl's explanation of how egos access a common knowledge in relation to their environment, shaping this way the communicative experience, even though a "we" experience is not occurring. Conversely, Schutz argues that communication presupposes a "knowledgeable" community from the outset, meaning that a common environment and social relationship must be present prior to any communicative act. Thus, it is not possible to deduce the common environment and social relationship solely from the idea of communication, since every communicative act or expressive movement, such as a visual or acoustic sign, actually requires the foundation of an external process—a common environment that belongs to us (Schutz, 1966, p. 38). This confusion of planes is not intentional but arises when Husserl thinks about the personal ego revealing itself meaningfully and through its expressions, as well as taking an attitude toward others who, in turn, interpret the indications of the other body by addressing the surrounding world in relation to their communicative acts, and vice versa.

In contrast to Husserl's view, Schutz proposes that the reciprocal attitude, or the pure "we relationship," is the foundational level of sociality, from which all concrete social relations arise. According to Schutz, communication presupposes a pre-existing common environment and social relationship, which cannot be deduced from the act of communication itself. Therefore, the reciprocal attitude, which allows for communication, is already the fundamental form of any social relationship, and cannot be derived from communication (p. 38). According to Schutz, communication requires a prior "mutual tuning-in relationship" founded on the world of everyday life, which is the ground for all practical purposes and the only imminent reality. The world of everyday life is a common ground made up of a body of knowledge at hand that is articulated by the addition of experiences or their intentional correlates and is mediated by a specific biographical situation. In this sense, every experience can be examined with reference to its sedimentation history, where its fundamental significance is revealed. Thus, reflection finds its evidence only in the process of resorting to its original founding experience in the world of life (Schutz, 1967, pp. 133–139).

The second problem for Schutz is at a higher level of the process, namely, in the constitution of personal units of higher order which, as Husserl states, arise from communication between personal subjects who communicate with each other and with their world around them. According to Husserl, these personal units of higher order form a common environment, albeit without subjects, which he calls the community of spirits. This community of spirits has a counterpart in the world of objects that are meaningful to the spirit.

Schutz finds it unclear how a community without subjects, such as the one proposed by Husserl, can exist, given that the life-world is primarily given to subjects as their personal world and as a world of significant culture, which historical subjects contribute to creating. Schutz believes that Husserl's use of inappropriate metaphors to explain the passage of notions of subjectivity, person, communication, and the surrounding world to higher levels is unnecessary for clarifying the concept of a social person. In other words, social communities cannot be regarded as personalities of a higher order, and it is absurd to find in them traits revealed by the analysis of individual persons. Husserl committed the fallacy of hypostatizing abstract concepts and attributing them a personal existence.

In short, the challenges in clarifying the essence of the social cannot be resolved through transcendental phenomenology's constitutive analysis, as it cannot shed light on the constructions produced by a thought situated at the level of the life-world and the social sciences. A constitutive phenomenology of the natural attitude is required, which, unlike transcendental phenomenology, aims to address these issues at the level of everyday intersubjectivity by elucidating its specific methods.

As Carlos Belvedere puts it, "Schutz's interest in the constitutive analysis of the natural attitude lies in the constitutional analysis made in the social sciences and not in the general issue of constitution. Consequently, what has been said so far should be interpreted only as preliminary observation to an inquiry into the original constitution of the structures of social reality, since Schutz's ultimate intention is to account for the constitution of social relations with their different degrees of concreteness and specificity" (Belvedere, 2012, p. 55).

Lastly, Schutz questions whether Husserlian social theory has its roots in the programs of Hegel, Durkheim, or the Wundt school. According to the Austrian sociologist, the theories of Simmel, Weber, or Scheler are closer to the spirit of phenomenology insofar as they reduce sociality to the simple fact of subjects finding themselves in a common and shared world, which aligns with the original conception of phenomenology.

5   Conclusions

As we have already pointed out, Schutz considers that the foundation of the social sciences will not be found in the theory of constitution with transcendental roots, and hence not in transcendental phenomenology, but rather in the constitutive phenomenology of the natural attitude. Although Schutz acknowledges the importance of Husserl's work for the social sciences, he points out the insufficiency of transcendental phenomenology to solve, on the one hand, the problem of the constitution of transcendental subjectivity within the reduced egological sphere and, on the other hand, the constitution of "societies as subjectivities of a higher order, the nature of which can only be described as eidetic" (Schutz, 1967, p. 149).

Following Schutz, the priority of the communal is found in the attentive description of the natural attitude, which, as we have stated at the beginning of this chapter, is different from the naturalistic attitude, and which Husserl has endorsed through a phenomenological reduction to the communal natural stratum.

And yet, after this brief conclusion, should we not ask ourselves again why we choose phenomenology, and what the competence of its analysis in the realm of the social sciences is? An answer to such a question could be found in the way Schutz conceived sociology, that is, as a science that produces second-degree constructs derived from those that take place in everyday life.

Schutz believed that phenomenology was a valuable method for enriching social analysis, particularly in interpretive sociology, as it focuses on experienced reality. However, he also emphasized the importance of addressing the problematic of intersubjectivity as a fundamental ontological category of human existence, a precondition for any immediate existence in the life-world. For Schutz, recognizing the co-experiencing of the world could only be achieved through the shared cultural constructs and communication between the Other and the self, through which common descriptions of the shared world are exchanged. Through these exchanges, we seek agreement on what the world is. As a result, the constitution of the objective world is an intersubjective achievement based on the connection of the subjects who take part in the communicative encounter. This means that the richness of the phenomenological analysis lies mainly in the exegesis of the problem of the *Lebenswelt*, which clarifies the essence of the social. Schutz argues that this analysis is intended to become a philosophical anthropology, for the concept of the life-world is the basis of meaning for all sciences—the social sciences, the natural sciences, and philosophy. All reflection must therefore be endorsed by the original founding experience in the life-world, leaving us the endless task of thought, which is to make intelligible the intentional constitution of contributing subjectivity in reference to it, that is, its basis of meaning.

References

Belvedere, C. (2012). Sobre la constitución del orden social. Lineamientos para una ontología social fenomenológica. In C. Belvedere (Ed.), *La constitución de lo social. Aportes para el diálogo entre sociología y fenomenología* (pp. 53–73). Universidad Nacional de General Sarmiento.

Drummond, J. (1996). The "spiritual" world: The person, the social and the communal. In T. Nenon & L. Embree (Eds.), *Issues in Husserl's ideas II* (pp. 57–68). Kluwer Academic Publishers.

Grathoff, R. (1989). *Philosophers in exile: The correspondence of Alfred Schutz and Aron Gurtwitsch, 1939–1959*. Indiana University Press.

Husserl, E. (1989a). *Ideas pertaining to a pure phenomenology and to a phenomenological philosophy. second book: Studies in the phenomenology of constitution*. Kluwer Academic Publishers.

Husserl, E. (1989b). Philosophy as a rigorous science. In *Phenomenology and the crisis of philosophy* (pp. 9–24). The Academy Library Harper & Row.

Iribarne, J. (1985). La fenomenología como monadología. *Escritos de Filosofía, 15–16*(Año VIII), 71–82.

Motta, R. (2007). La recepción schutziana de la V Meditación Cartesiana de Husserl. In *Jornadas de Jóvenes Investigadores*. IIGG, Universidad de Buenos Aires.

Schutz, A. (1966). *Studies in phenomenological philosophy. Collected papers III.* Martinus Nijhoff.

Schutz, A. (1967). *The problem of social reality. Collected papers I.* Martinus Nijhoff.

The Place of Imagination in the Sociology of Action: An Essay Drawing from Schutz

Javier Cristiano

1 PRESENTATION AND FRAMING OF THE PROBLEM

This chapter intends to establish some systematic connections between action theory and imagination, a task we undertake from within Schutz's work, for several reasons. First, Schutz is the only author, along with G. H. Mead,[1] who in the tradition of theoretical sociology has incorporated a concept of imagination at the very heart of an explicit theory of action. Second, because of the vastness of the philosophical setting in which Schutz situates the problem. Husserl's phenomenology, and indirectly its continuators,[2] offers an almost inexhaustible setting for pursuing such an investigation. Third, because of Schutz's conceptual precision and sensitivity to detail, which have no equivalent in contemporary social theory and which are, for our purposes, particularly necessary. Fourth, and on a different register, it seems important to us to contribute to the revitalization of a work that has often been read with unfounded

---

[1] See specifically Mead (1972: 337-346). For an analysis of creativity in Mead's work, see Joas (1985).

[2] For an advanced and up-to-date introduction to Husserl's work see San Martín (2008). For an overview of post-Husserlian phenomenology, see Waldenfels (1997).

J. Cristiano (✉)
Universidad Nacional de Córdoba (1UNC), Córdoba, Argentina

C. Belvedere, A. Gros (eds.), *The Palgrave Handbook of Macrophenomenology and Social Theory*,
https://doi.org/10.1007/978-3-031-34712-2_17

prejudices[3] and whose stature and complexity contrast with the uninspired horizon of current sociology.

What we are about to undertake, however, is not a reading and systematization of Schutz's work but an attempt at a complementary elaboration. As we shall see in the next section, Schutz analyzed the link that interests us in a partial way, but this does not imply that the task cannot be completed drawing from his work and the resources it provides. We therefore offer a tentative attempt at continuity, the results of which we hope will also be of interest from other perspectives for theories both of the imagination and of action. Our first step (Sect. 2) will be to establish how imagination appears in Schutz's proposal, setting the limits of its treatment and the course of our further investigation. Sections 3 and 4 offer the results of that investigation and constitute the core of our work. Section 5 attempts to draw consequences from this study for the treatment of the classical structure/action problem, which can be reopened, we argue, from this perspective. The final considerations place the discussion in the broader perspective of future research.

Like in every study of this kind, there is a background of motivations here, which are independent of the work to be read, but which it is important to make explicit. We are interested in the concept of imagination because we suppose that it may be useful in the reconstruction of action theory from a critical perspective. This simply means that for a conception of social theory attentive to its political reflexivity, action theory is a strategic point and especially the way in which "agential" capacity is thematized. In this respect, it can be argued that the sociology of action has connected with the problems of critique in three basic ways. One is by highlighting from theory those aspects of action that allow for expectations of a different social order. Habermas' communicative capacity or Honneth's response to moral grievance can be taken as examples. The second is by showing the effective social conditions that limit the deployment of this capacity, as Marxism has classically done and, for example, as P. Bourdieu does. The third is by focusing on the activity of those actors or groups that in specific historical situations embody critique, as Marxism also did with the proletariat, and more recently feminism or postcolonial studies have done.

In our opinion, the concept of imagination can play an important role in the first of these levels. This intuition is grounded on significant works such as those of Castoriadis, Marcuse, Benjamin, Sartre, and Bloch,[4] which are situated in a field closer to social philosophy and have had little or no connection with

---

[3] The vitality of the Schutzian tradition is testified by the revival of the publication of the *Collected Papers* (volumes V and VI have been published in 2011 and 2012 respectively), as well as by the publication since 2009 of the annual issues of the *Schutzian Research* (http://www.zetabooks. com/schutzian-research-2.html). The work of Belvedere has been decisive in dismantling the prejudices and misunderstandings cast over Schutz's work not by its pedagogical popularization but by the most prominent social theorists. See Belvedere (2010: 41-62) and Belvedere (2004).

[4] Castoriadis (2005), Marcuse (1974: 140-158), Benjamin (2005: 465-466), Sartre (1986: 179-194), Bloch (1986: 85-132).

the sociology of action. Hence, the interest in building bridges between a concept as philosophically vast as imagination[5] and a specific but key issue in sociological theory, such as the theory of action. This study, which draws from a work far removed from the spirit of critical theory,[6] points in this general direction.

2 Imagination in the *Collected Papers*

We begin our journey by presenting the way in which the question of imagination appears in Schutz's work. Specifically, it does so in two moments (Butnaru, 2009: 207-212): in the analysis of the nature of action and in the analysis of the way in which consciousness constitutes the meaning of "the real."

i) Schutz deals with the first of these problems in the framework of his critical discussion of Weber's methodology, to which he imputes a lack of precision in his primary category of the "meaning of social action." In his detailed discussion of this matter, which he carries out assisted by Husserl (Schutz, 1967: 53-57) he asks about the nature of the experience that accompanies the action, answering that what is essential to that experience is a particular form of orientation toward the future, consisting in the fact that the future is what one wants to realize with the action. Every experience is future oriented, in the sense that it is accompanied by protentions that connect the present experience with immediately following experiences. What distinguishes action is that these protentions take the form of projections or "anticipatory expectations," referring to the future state of affairs that the actor intends to produce.

All action implies in this sense a "project," not in the sense of a conscious and lucid plan but in the sense of a teleology. And it is at this point that imagination appears for the first time. Also drawing from Husserl (Schutz, 1962: 145), Schutz speaks specifically of "phantasy" to refer to the capacity of consciousness to anticipate future action as if it were an act already performed. He

---

[5] An intellectual history of the concept can be found in Lapoujade (1988). For a more analytical approach see Warnock (1976) and, for a pre-modern philosophical perspective, Ferraris (1999). Although not exclusively focused on imagination, the impressive work of Steiner (2001) is highly recommended. Without pretending to offer here an elaboration of the concept, it seems necessary to clarify that at least two major meanings converge in it. The first is epistemological and refers to imagination as a function in the production of all knowledge, from perception to the most complex theoretical abstractions. In all these processes imagination, as the capacity to produce image beyond sensory information, is an essential faculty. The Kantian definition of imagination as a bridge between sensibility and understanding is an example in this regard (Warnock, 1976). The second meaning emphasizes not so much knowledge as creation; it alludes to the production of images not only beyond the senses but also beyond "the real" or what is conceived as "reality." Sartre spoke about this plane of imagination as "the great irrealizing function of consciousness" (Sartre, 1986: 5) and Castoriadis, perhaps the author who took this analysis further, of imagination as an incessant power of novelty creation (Castoriadis, 2005). In asserting that imagination can be an important concept for critical theory we fundamentally consider this second level, which of course has multiple and complex relations with the first one.

[6] For the links between phenomenology and critical theory see Wolff (1978: 509-515).

uses an expression from scholastic grammar (*modo futuro exacti*) to indicate the time of this complex operation, in which what has not yet happened appears as past.

Every meaningful action therefore implies a project, and every project is a fantasy; every action, therefore, includes a component of imagination. But what kind of imagination? Not the kind of imagination we have in mind when we use the word, namely an imagination associated with ideas of "creation" or "invention." Schutz calls this phenomenon "phantasy" in the sense that it is something non-real, and more specifically not yet real, but not in the sense that it is an "invention" or a "novelty." This is, we argue, the first limit that can be crossed in his proposal, analyzing concretely when and how this fantasy can also be *creative* or *inventive*. This is the subject of the next section.

Why Schutz concentrates on this meaning of fantasy is clear when we recognize his priorities. Schutz starts from a conception of action whose center is in the world of daily life, the scene of most of our actions governed by a "pragmatic motive." This leads him to emphasize the routine character of action plans, which he describes as "recipes" that inertially connect motives, means, and ends. At the same time, the fantasy that accompanies projects is a "realistic" fantasy, as it is limited by what Schutz calls "practicability." Unlike "free" phantasy, projective phantasy implies the will to realize the project and must therefore adhere to the limits imposed by "the real." Both of these things—routine inertia and realism—give projective phantasy a bounded character with respect to the sense that "phantasy" or "imagination" has in its usual meaning and also in the broader technical meaning given to it by Husserl.[7]

ii) The second area in which imagination appears is that of the meaning of "real." What Schutz argues is that there is not one reality but many, in the sense that there are different realms of meaning to which we attribute "accents of reality." The world of theater, for example, is "real" while I am caught up in the drama, and the same is true of the scientific world while I am writing an academic paper. However, one of these realities is the "paramount" one, namely the world of everyday life. We are in it most of the time, and we always return to it. It is the world in which we act, the world whose reality we share with others, and above all the world whose facticity imposes itself on our action.

This is the framework in which the second concept of imagination appears, this time as one of these multiple realities. It is the "world of fantasies" (*Phantesiewelt*) to which art, daydreams, stories, and possibly mythology belong, and which derives its characteristics precisely from its contrast with everyday life: in it we do not act but we fantasize, now in a strict and possibly "creative" sense. The more or less "creative" or "inventive" dimension is

---

[7] According to Marc Richir (Richir, 2010), Husserl hardly referred to the matter in his best known works, but the publication, only in 1980, of volume XXIII of *Husserliana*, offers an explicit treatment of it that Husserl elaborated as a draft in 1904–1905. We do not know whether Schutz knew about these unpublished works; we do know that he does not mention them, in spite of which, and following Richir's exposition, they seem to be compatible with what Schutz later on analyzes as the "world of fantasies" (see point ii).

variable (we can always repeat the same reverie), but there is substantially "creation" in the sense of the fabrication of a parallel world essentially distinct from the "real" world.

What is missing in this second area, and what we will try to elaborate, is nothing less than its connection with action. Here too, for reasons internal to his work, Schutz stresses the praxeologically innocuous character of this "world of fantasies," describing it, for example, as "a causally inefficacious shadow" (Schutz, 1967: 94), and always insisting on its differences with the world of everyday life, which is the world of action. It is clear, however, and Schutz himself acknowledges this on various occasions, that the world of fantasies has sociological significance only insofar as it is connected to action. We will then try to elaborate this connection in Sect. 4.

We point out, in summary, two gaps in Schutz's analysis: the fantasy that accompanies all action is a realistic and routine fantasy, which does not generally have a creative and inventive character but which may occasionally have one. Fantasy in its full sense, free and creative fantasy, is an activity of consciousness to which we are destined precisely when we do not act. The challenge therefore is to connect action with creative imagination and creative imagination (the world of fantasies) with action.

3   Imagination in the Constitution of Action Projects

In this section, we undertake the first of these tasks. We will propose five levels of insertion of "creative" imagination in action. First, there are circumstances, analyzed by Schutz, in which the routines of action are questioned; we will argue that at such moments imagination can intervene in action not only as anticipatory fantasizing but also as the invention of new projects. Second, the "realistic" character of projects becomes less strict and the consideration of their practicability more flexible in long-term projects, where imagination can have more space. Third, the understanding of the actions of others, a constitutive process of intersubjectivity, requires, in particular circumstances susceptible of analysis, the presence of invention and creativity. Fourth, the creation of new projects has particular characteristics, also amenable to phenomenological analysis, in that it takes place collectively and not individually. Fifth, the actors have different inclinations toward creative fantasy, "dispositions" that can also be analyzed drawing on some of Schutz's notions.

Breaks with Routine and the Nature of "New" Projects

In the world of everyday life we proceed in a routine way, in the sense that we participate in a "natural attitude" in which things and events are self-evident to us. What we once learned in a "polythetic" way (in successive steps that needed our attention) becomes a "monothetic" structure into which our attention no longer penetrates. However, unreflective inertia is broken in circumstances that can be encompassed in the idea of "problematic situations" (Schutz &

Luckmann, 1974: 8-15), where there is a "failure of connection" between what is presented to us and our schemas of interpretation. This is an example Schutz takes from the skeptical philosopher Carneades (Schutz & Luckmann, 1974: 182): the coiled rope I see in the corner of a poorly illuminated room *could* be a snake or in another example from Schutz: this animal in front of me appears to be a dog, but it does not have the characteristics of any breed I know.

This type of operation refers to knowledge about the world; our action in the world is guided as we have seen by a specific type of polythetic structure, which Schutz calls "recipe knowledge," which consists essentially of projects converted into habit, either strictly repeated (as in motor skills) or with a margin of variation (as in the application of the knowledge of a trade).

There are, however, two types of circumstances in which the appeal to recipes becomes problematic: (i) when the actor sets out to do something that as such he has never done before and (ii) when he sets out to achieve a state of affairs for which he knows of no suitable "means." For example, the actor sets out to enter the world of political activism, something he has never done before and about which he has only vague assumptions (i); the actor needs to convince a large number of anonymous people to collaborate with a personal cause of his, which has been unexpectedly imposed on him (he needs to raise money to pay for an operation) (ii). We hypothesize that in circumstances such as these the merely anticipatory fantasy, which characterizes all action, can turn into inventive phantasy or creative imagination. It may, but it does not necessarily occur (and whether it does or does not depend on factors that we will discuss in part 3.5).

How does imagination operate, and what does it actually do in these circumstances? Schutz's writings offer a variety of resources in this respect, some of which are listed below, without claiming to be exhaustive.

First, there is a process that can be described as the intensification of conjecture. The imagination comes to fill in the gaps of the unknown, postulating things, events, or circumstances that respond hypothetically to the question of "how it must be" in the world I am venturing into. Schutz stresses on several occasions that the social world presents itself to us in concentric circles ranging from the fully known to the entirely unknown, passing through zones of intermediate familiarity (Schutz, 1962: 14). When we set out to act in a realm of little or no familiarity, we have to imagine that world in a way that is different from the usual projective fantasy. The process may have different degrees of "awareness" and self-evidence, at one end of which is conscious imaginative conjecture and at the other mere tacit intuition.

Secondly, in these cases, more or less reflexive processes of exploration of the "social stock of knowledge" are also set in motion. This notion is introduced by Schutz to refer to the accumulation of knowledge that an actor has as a result of his social milieu and his particular biographical inscription in it (Schutz, 1967: 77). In many contexts (Schutz & Luckmann, 1974: 105) he adds the expression "at hand" (stock of knowledge "at hand") to indicate its availability for practical purposes. It can be postulated that, when imagination is set in motion, it includes (or takes the form of) an exploration and active use of that "stock," an exploration and active use that is at rest in "normal" circumstances. I will have to look for experiences and information I do not generally have in mind about what it is to be politically engaged or what the spheres in which it occurs are like; for example, I will bring to mind conversations I once had with activists, or scenes from a film on the subject, or an experience of mine which, although not activist, was one of group organizing.

Schutz's third concept that contributes to this analysis is that of "typification."[8] It is also taken from Husserl (Schutz, 1967: 148-149) and refers to the selection and abstraction involved in all knowledge. By saying that what I have in front of me appears to be a dog, but does not belong to any known breed, I am bringing into play a type (dog) and several subtypes (Doberman, Pinscher). Every type implies a selection of relevant traits and has been constituted at some point in time according to pragmatic criteria of importance. It therefore includes, still following Schutz-Husserl, both a sphere of determination (the recurrent features of the thing or situation) and a relatively indeterminate "horizon": I know what a dog is, but there is an infinite variation within its possible materializations.

The idea of a "new project" can be clarified in several respects by this concept. Firstly, novelty can consist in the combination of "types" that remained isolated. For example, when I relate the type "sports meeting" to the type "political group," which I have incorporated in my readings or in my forays into cinema. Secondly, the presence of new situations initiates a process that Schutz described under the title "re-explication of the horizons" (Schutz & Luckmann, 1974: 12), which involves making explicit that implicit horizon of indeterminacy, "loading" new components into the type, and thus expanding its content. Third, the imagination can directly create new types when it comes to encompass a reality under a new category.

The concept of "type" is, as can be seen, very broad, both in the importance of what it encompasses (dog/political activism) and in its extension (physical object/complex social institution). The importance of the analysis becomes clear if we underline that, for Schutz, knowledge of social reality is always typical, since the actions, the actors, and also the causal relations that we recognize in the world are typical. We will return to these questions below when we analyze how they operate not only in the formulation of new projects but also in the understanding of the projects and actions of others (point 3.3).

What has been said does not of course exhaust neither the phenomenology of "new" projects nor the nature of the operations involved in their formulation. It does, however, give the idea of project-creating imagination a more precise and concrete meaning than it usually has, even in philosophical analyses of the problem of imagination. We shall return to this too in the conclusions.

---

[8] The cited article by Butnaru provides an extensive analysis of the relationship between typification and fantasy (Butnaru, 2009: 203-207).

Displacing the Limits of Practicability: The Long Term

We advanced in Sect. 2 a second aspect in which projective fantasizing is limited as an exercise of imagination: it is a "realistic" fantasizing, since the will to carry out the project imposes plans adjusted to the conditions of the real. The hypothesis we are going to propose now is that this realism is less rigid in long-term projects, which opens up a tendentially greater space for imagination. We are talking about imagination, at this point, as an activity of consciousness that displaces the limits of what is experienced as real, one of the key aspects of the concept's history, including its Husserlian version.[9]

Let us recall at the outset that all action is based on a project in which the act is represented as already accomplished. One of the reasons why Schutz adopts this conception is that it allows us to establish the limits of the action, that is, when the action can be said to begin and end (Schutz, 1967: 62-63).[10] When I see a person hitting a log with his ax I can describe what he is doing by saying exactly that (he hits a log with an ax), but I can also say *he is preparing firewood, he is doing his day's work, or he is protecting himself from the cold*. Each of these descriptions implies a different attribution of meaning, and each refers to a different action project. This means that the phenomenon "action" has a very large variation in terms of temporal scale, and hence Schutz introduces the typical ideal notions of "day-plan" and "life-plan" (Schutz & Luckmann, 1974: 57-58) to indicate that each actor harbors a multiplicity of projects, which intermingle in complex ways and promote short-time actions (answering the phone/preparing for tomorrow's class) alongside long-time actions (becoming a specialist in a discipline).

On any of these scales, however, a project is such to the extent that it aims at its realization or, as Schutz says, to the extent that it includes a voluntary "fiat" that postulates it as a possible action and not a mere "fantasy." Every project is therefore tied to an assumption of "practicability," which is what we colloquially describe as "realism": the experience that what I am projecting is realizable in this world as I know it. In fact, in analyzing the basis of that practicability (Schutz, 1962: 74-77), Schutz argues that it is based on two sets of experiences: that of the "presupposed world" (things I take for granted as reliable knowledge) and that of my biographically determined situation (experiences I have of my situation according to the particular here and now in which I formulate the project).

The question we are interested in posing in this regard is the following: under what conditions can this "realistic" attachment of the project be less

---

[9] The world of *Phantasia* is "another world, radically separated from the world of the current present" (Husserl, *Husserliana* Vol. XXIII, quoted by Richir, 2010: 424).

[10] This difficult problem (when an action begins and ends) is largely ignored by sociological action theory. Giddens can be considered an exception drawing from the tradition that, after Schutz, made more progress toward determining the problem: analytic philosophy. It is one of Schutz's many merits that he expressly raised it in his first book in 1932, well before the Anglo-Saxon developments of the mid-century.

strict? More precisely, when is the reality on whose belief the project is based a reality whose borders with the non-real can be considered more open? Our thesis is that a key variable in this respect is the time span of the project, and that the more long term it is the more blurred the boundary of realism is, in three concrete senses: (i) the distant act to be performed tends to be more diffuse in its contours and in its nature; (ii) the "presupposed world" is more liable to doubt, ambiguity, and ambivalence; (iii) between the biographically determined situation in which the project is represented and the situation in which the act will be concretized, there is a temporal distance that flexibilizes what can be considered attainable or unattainable by the action.

Let us take the example of a very long-term project, such as that of a young person who orients his career and working life toward an economically prosperous retirement. As in all projects, we have here a representation of the act to be carried out, but in this case it is a particularly indeterminate and vague representation, essentially because the "I" to which the project refers is a different "I" from the current "I" that formulates it. We could even say that the man I represent to myself as the "subject" of my future act has the approximate form of another one with whom I identify. This distance, which we might call "identity" distance, is maintained even if we assume an actor who projects in the long term in great detail.

Secondly (ii), what the world will be then, when my act has already been accomplished, is also more open and indeterminate than the world I presuppose when I project in the short term. There are two notions that Schutz takes from Husserl that are important in this regard. Schutz argues that in formulating action plans we set in motion two idealizations (in the sense of two tacit assumptions) which he calls "so and so" and "I can do it again." The first one refers to the assumption that the world will continue to be the way it is, and the second one refers to the assumption that the results I have obtained with my actions on other occasions can be repeated in the future. It seems clear that if there is a context in which these idealizations may be subject to doubt, it is in the long term.

The third sense (iii) refers to the biographical situation in which I formulate the project and how it differs from what my situation will be when it is realized. It is from the biographical situation that I establish two distinctions (Schutz & Luckmann, 1974: 38-41): between what is spatially and temporally within my reach and what is not, and between the part of the social world that I can modify with my action and that which is imposed on me or is independent of what I do. In our example, it is clear that both limits are more likely to be modified to the extent that I project further in time: today I can play sports that I may not be able to play when I retire; when I retire I may have time to learn a skill that I cannot learn today; the financial system on which my project depends may impose modifications of different kinds on me.

The example we have chosen is clear but has the disadvantage of being only individual and perhaps somewhat trivial from a sociological point of view. We can search for other examples to realize the importance of this discussion. Let us think, for example, of an actor who projects in the long term the realization of political and social values (equality), where he also brings into play an acting self, a knowledge of the social world, and an idea of what is accessible and what is not accessible to his action. In this case, we have a much more complex phenomenology, in which the importance of imagination also becomes clearer. If this actor affirms, for example, that socialism, in the long term, is achievable, he is not posing a utopia in the ordinary sense of impossibility: he is aiming at concrete actions in the immediate context that are involved in the long-term project. At this point, a whole series of questions that have occupied philosophers of the imagination (see note 4) converge with the problems of the sociology of action. We only intend to leave this great field of research open, by simply stating that the notion of the long-term project is of vital importance to it.

The Understanding of the Action of Others as an Activity of the Imagination

The next two aspects are a continuation of the first one (3.1). In this case, the question is that, in addition to using the imagination to formulate new projects, we use it to interpret other person's projects as new ones. In this way we touch on the array of problems linked to the "understanding of the meaning of action," which occupied Schutz throughout his life (Schutz, 1967: 97-118; Schutz, 1962: 34-46) and on which, from other perspectives, the problems of the imagination have been projected.[11] Needless to say, we do not intend to cover it in its entirety but only in what we have just enunciated: the place of the imagination in the grasping of other people's projects as "creative" projects.

Let us begin by clarifying what "understanding the action of others" means. In Schutz's view, it means knowing what is going on in their mind at the time of their action. This grasping is not direct, for I have access to the subjectivity of another person only through his body, which offers itself to me as a "field of expression" of his experiences (Schutz, 1967: 20-25; 100). What I grasp, moreover, is not just any mental state, but concretely the project that defines the action of the other. To understand is, in this sense, to attribute projects, an activity in whose complex structure Schutz also emphasizes the role of imagination, but again in a restricted sense: we imagine ourselves doing what the other is doing.

In the natural attitude, all this happens in the same spontaneous way that we described in our own projects: we use a store of knowledge, we follow Husserl's idealizations, and so on. The circumstance that interests us is one in which the evidence of understanding becomes problematic, for it is there that imagination can play a more important role than usual. Formally, this occurs at the

---

[11] See, for example, the way in which imagination appears in Max Weber's extensive review of the methodological discussions of his time (Weber, 1975). In a very different context the topic was also addressed by Hannah Arendt (see Heuer, 2005).

confluence of two circumstances: (i) when the action of another person is meaningful to me in some sense, and (ii) when it appears to me as strange, atypical, or not immediately comprehensible. In this circumstance, our analysis on the creation of new projects (Sect. 3.1) can be taken up again, since what we are doing is creating a project, although it is not our own. Briefly, here too we face a process of intensification of conjectures. We see, for example, someone working with logs but doing something unfamiliar to us, which we do not immediately understand. We conjecture that he is playing, that he is producing a work of art, that he is trying out options for making something, and that he is trying to get our attention. At the same time, we rehearse a reflexive return to our own stock of knowledge. We have once seen someone doing something similar, but we are not fully aware of it now. We have never seen anyone making a work of art of this particular kind, but we know some artists and have seen them at work. In all this, we bring into play various typifications, which in Schutz's vocabulary are "personal" types and "courses of action" (Schutz, 1967:187). Our stock of knowledge is populated by types of persons such as the artist, the worker, or the joker, each associated with typical courses of action (artists often do things that are indecipherable at first). Just as when I work out my own creative projects, I combine these types there, re-explain their horizons, and eventually come to produce new types.

Of course, there is in all this an essential difference, and that is that it is not me who is planning to act, but I am interpreting the ongoing action of others. This circumstance implies many displacements in such an analysis. The most important element, we argue, is the fact that the way in which we motivationally link ourselves to action is different: it is not the will to produce a state of affairs in the world with my action that mobilizes myself but the will to give meaning to the action of others. It is a will that, at another level of analysis, is linked to my own action projects because it has a pragmatic motivation.

The examples we have proposed correspond to one level of understanding, which is that of direct interaction with an immediately present alter. Schutz has elaborated a scheme of the structure of our social experience in which this direct relation is only one aspect. Outside and beyond our experience there is a set of spheres of sociability in which the other is not a concrete human being but a diffuse one whom I know in increasing degrees of typicality and anonymity. Schutz divides them into contemporaries (the others who share the same time of my life, but with whom I have no direct contact: the unknown mail clerk who will take my letter out of the mailbox and carry it to its destination), predecessors (those who preceded me in time in my society, and with whom direct contact is now impossible), and successors (those who will come after me, with whom direct contact is impossible, and whose actions are indeterminate).

In these "indirect" worlds, the role of the imagination is different and more ambiguous in its meaning. Being only weakly dependent on my sensorial here and now, imagination is on the one hand more important, since it is presented to us almost exclusively as an "image," but on the other hand, it is the subject of strict typification, which simplifies and condenses it for practical purposes. I have never been, and possibly never will be, face-to-face with members of the business class; this class, and the unknown individuals who compose it, is represented to me as personal types and stabilized course-of-action types, all of which is sufficient for my practical purposes. It is, therefore, a world potentially very permeable to the imagination, for almost everything in it is "image," but it is also a still and "resolved" world insofar as its distance from my here and now does not generally demand anything else. We touch here on a subject of singular importance, not for the imagination/action link but for the imagination/society link. Authors such as Castoriadis have pushed the analysis of this aspect of imagination to its limits, arguing that the social consists essentially of an "imaginary institution" (Castoriadis, 2005) whose precarious rootedness in the rational and the real is the Archimedean point of all order. If our analysis is correct, the understanding of the distant other is an essential aspect of this more general phenomenon.

The Collective Production of New Projects

As in the previous point, we transfer the analysis of Sect. 3.1 to a different sphere, in this case the imagination of a group. We propose to analyze what happens when imagination is put at the service of the constitution of new projects in instances of social interaction. Here again we touch on a much broader field of problems, namely that of "collective action." To the best of our knowledge, the elaboration of a phenomenology of collective action is a largely unfinished task, and in any case, it is clear that Schutz's work contains only a few hints in this regard.[12] It is thus a broad and significant topic, of which we address only one aspect.

Social interaction can be described as a process in which an ego and an alter ego mutually influence each other's actions (Schutz, 1962: 22-26). In its simplest form, such as the question/answer exchange, an actor (ego) asks a question that becomes the motive for the alter ego's action (the answer). More precisely, ego elaborates a project whose purpose is obtaining information; this project, once executed, becomes the motive of an alter ego's project (offering the requested information), which materializes as a response. In the process, what we have said about the formulation of projects applies: that projects are based on a stock of knowledge, on typifications, on idealizations, and so on. When the interaction is not face-to-face, the typification is also more rigid, and the actions are more rigidly defined.

The situation that interests us is one in which the interaction is carried out in order to achieve not consecutively linked goals but a common goal. More precisely, it is a situation in which the common goal does not admit a routine response but requires a "creative" response. In other words, when ego and

---

[12] The essay on the interaction between musicians in an orchestra is important in this respect: Schutz (1976: 159-178).

alter ego interact to produce together a new action project. What happens in this situation can be described by applying our results from Sect. 3.1, with the important difference that the constitution of the project in this case leaves the internal forum and becomes a matter of public deliberation.

First we have processes of conjectural intensification, in which ego and alter bring their respective knowledge pools into play in order to fill gaps in the unknown, just as ego does on an individual level. This process can be described as an "addition" of elements, in the sense that the alter pool includes contents that are foreign to the ego pool, and vice versa. You have faced a problem or a situation similar to this one, which I have not; your explanation of that experience can be combined with different previous experiences of mine, from which nuances and connections can emerge that are new to both of us. Second, we explore together in a reflexive way our respective bodies of knowledge, broadening or re-signifying them. Thirdly, we find together, each in our own stock of knowledge, and in the body of knowledge we share, new horizons for our typifications, new combinations of types, and novel types themselves. The essential point, and we stress it again, is that all these processes, similar to those occurring at the individual level, are now mediated by an instance of publicity, which implies objectification and which converts the internal (my stock) into external (our stock).

Now, we are assuming a situation in which three conditions are present: (i) only two people interact; (ii) they interact in dialogue; (iii) they interact in cooperation, in the sense that they contribute equally to an equally shared goal. The variation of these assumptions opens up a wide field of research, of which some elements can be sketched. With regard to (i), if there are not two but several creative actors, a more complex circulation of influences over motives can be postulated (e.g., one speaking ego sets in motion the motivations of multiple alters). At the same time, there will be in such cases a diversity of stocks of knowledge, which will imply wider and more varied processes of revision and "addition."

All this makes creation a more indeterminate process as the amount of participants increases, at least other things being equal (ceteris paribus). As for (ii), a non-dialogical process of collective creation is perfectly possible, as Schutz himself suggests in his aforementioned analysis of musical activity and as some subsequent analyses inspired by Schutz have shown (Figueroa-Dreher, 2016). In addition to bringing into play a common stock of knowledge, without which no creation is possible, in these non-dialogical interactions other sign systems are activated, such as those of bodily expression or musical notation. Schutz proposed a theory of symbolism that we will deal with later (infra, 4.2) but from which we can advance the thesis that all signification requires the process of consciousness that Husserl called "apresentation." The collective creation of new projects outside of linguistic interactions can therefore be investigated as a complex play of apresentations. As for (iii), the intended state of affairs may not be the same for all participants or may not be equally important for all. Relationships between participants may not necessarily be egalitarian and may involve power relations, differentiated institutional ranks, and so on. All this has an impact on the mode and results of collective creation.

Finally, the imaginative constitution of collective projects is one thing, but their execution is another. What should properly be called "collective action" is the execution of what is planned collectively, while it is possible to speak of "creative" collective action in cases where what is invented as a group is put into practice as a group. The distance between one thing and the other also implies important variants: all or some of those who participated in planning can act together, and they can of course modify along the way, collectively or not, what was planned as a group.

What has been said is enough to establish the hypothesis that creative imagination is a process with idiosyncratic characteristics when we move from the individual to the collective, since it is neither limited to a direct translation nor the mere complexification of what happens on the individual level: it includes qualitatively different elements. At this point, we also leave open the question of the relevance of methodological individualism, defended by Schutz in his first work (Schutz, 1972: 34) although by no means consubstantial with a phenomenological approach to the social world.

Imagination as a Function of Systems of Relevance

We leave to the end the question that ordinary sociological sensibility would first ask: what explains why an actor imagines more or less, whether he imagines in one way or another, and whether he does it more or less habitually. This question has its analytical framework in the structure/action link, which we will address at the end. In this section, we limit ourselves to one of its aspects, which is the different dispositions to imagination that actors may have as a result of social and biographical conditions. We will clarify this idea by referring to a specific concept of Schutz, namely relevance (Schutz, 2011: 93-133; Schutz & Luckmann, 1974: 182-229).

With the term "relevance" Schutz refers to the fact that the world is always presented to us in a gradation of more or less important elements. My interest in books makes the book stall at the fair more significant to me than the craft or clothes stalls, but it also makes me pay attention to the detail of a library when watching a film or pay attention to what my occasional companion in the bus is reading. Schutz distinguishes three levels of relevance, which are (i) that of the subject (what we pay attention to), (ii) that of interpretation (what schema of interpretation we select to give meaning to the subject), and that of motivation (iii) (which of our motivations are relevant to action). The first, which he calls "thematic relevance," refers to the direction of our consciousness in relation to objects and states of affairs in the world. It can be a spontaneous direction, as in the example of the books, but it can also be imposed, if something goes out of the familiar course and is presented to us as a "forced" requirement (the snake-rope in the example of Carneades). "Interpretative relevance" (ii) refers to the fragment of our stock of knowledge that we activate to interpret the subject, again spontaneously (in the library of the film I notice books that are in my area of interest) or imposed (what I need to know about this animal is whether it bites). "Motivational relevance" (iii) refers to an important distinction proposed by Schutz between "in-order-to" and "because" motives (Schutz, 1962: 70). The former refer to the future state of affairs that I want to achieve with my action, to the plans and projects that determine it. The latter ("because" motives) are the previous experiences that condition the project. For example, a thief's motive-for is to get hold of the victim's money; his motive-because refers to the past experiences that have turned him into a thief (socialization experiences). "Motivational significance" refers both to what types of motives are more relevant and to the direction each one takes in terms of its content.

Our thesis is that these three levels have concrete links with the greater or lesser inclination toward imaginative activities. In terms of thematic relevance (i), it is clear that an actor may have "the imaginary" as a predominant object of attention, as is the case for people with artistic or creative inclinations in general. In technical terms, this means that the "world of fantasies" as a "finite provinces of meaning" has "relevance" for that actor and motivates part of his or her action. Whether it does so to a greater or lesser extent depends on its hierarchy of relevance, which is neither unique nor exclusive. As for interpretative relevance (ii), one can postulate the general idea of a creative use of the stock of knowledge, the development of which really exceeds our possibilities, but which in any case could be enriched by contributions from a phenomenology of aesthetic experience. In his examples, Schutz emphasizes above all the idea of a framing of issues on the basis of typifications, orienting the analysis to predominantly cognitive problems. The use of the stock of knowledge to give perceptual depth to the world and the connection of themes with elements of the stock of knowledge which are not intended for them in principle are aspects of the use of the stock of knowledge oriented toward the creative imagination. With regard to motivational relevance (iii), we have already spoken at length about the formulation of "new" projects, which in the framework we have just introduced would correspond to the "reasons for" action. The notion of "because" motives suggests the idea of an inclination toward the formulation of creative projects, which has been formed in the course of socialization and which indicates a particular disposition of the actor. In our opinion, the notion of "because motives" has a rare generality in Schutz's proposal,[13] which links it in very broad strokes to "past experiences" of the actor and even connects it to the psychoanalytic concept of the "unconscious" (Schutz, 1974e: 88). This breadth has advantages for our analysis, as the field of investigation it leaves open is truly immense. The reference to the subconscious, for example, makes it possible to introduce into the analysis the psychoanalytic thematization of fantasy as the domain of the pleasure principle over the reality principle (Laplanche & Pontalis, 1973).

---

[13] It is rare because of its importance and the rigor that generally characterizes Schutz's writing.

All this refers to individual actors and their systems of relevance. We will see later that these systems are fundamentally social since they have emerged collectively and have become fixed in common institutions. What has been said for the individual level is therefore valid for the collective level, so that it can be argued that there are social orders with a greater or lesser inclination toward imaginative activity and that this occurs at the thematic, interpretative, and motivational levels. The Weberian description of rationalization speaks of a society in which the cognitive control of the world displaces the enchantment of magic; the theses developed by Fromm or Marcuse speak of a displacement of the pleasure principle by the reality principle; many critical arguments deal with the technical and mercantile subjugation of art: these and other similar theses project the problem of dispositions onto a macro and structural dimension. We will return to them in Sect. 5.

4   The Imaginary as a Finite Province of Meaning

We now turn to the second field of the imagination in Schutz's work: that of the "world of fantasies" which corresponds to art, reveries, and fiction in general. We propose here three connections with the theory of action. First, although it is a world analytically alien to action, it becomes action when fantasy is the object of communication. Second, that communication involves processes of symbolization, which clarify the nature of imagination as a process of consciousness. Third, the world of fantasies intervenes in the formation of the identity of the acting self. In contrast to the previous point, we face the difficulty that the texts in which Schutz deals with these issues have a more provisional and tentative form than others (Schutz, 1962: 234-240; 340-347; Schutz, 1976: 135-178). There is therefore more interpretative interference on our part and more possibility of distance from his work in the development we propose.

The Communicative Action of Fantasies

At the beginning we mentioned the general features of the theory of the "finite realms of meaning," which we will now consider in more detail in order to clarify the sense in which to fantasize is not to act, and in order to try, from there, to reconnect fantasy with the theory of action.

We said that for Schutz there is not one but multiple realities, which are such in the sense that when we attend to them the rest of the world is bracketed. When I am reading a novel or a philosophical work, or when a child plays, we give these phenomena an "accent of reality," which literally makes rest of the world fade away. In this, all realms of meaning are equal, but there is one that is "paramount" in two respects: it is one that I take for granted that others share with me, and it is one that sets limits to my action. When I read a novel on the bus, I know that the reality I am experiencing is not shared by the other passenger; when I stop reading and look out the window, I do assume that what I see is as unquestionable for the other as it is for me. Moreover, I believe that neither he nor I can decide about it arbitrarily: we are in one part of the journey and not in another; we need time to get to the next town; and if one of us wants to take the other's seat, we have to ask him to do so.

The defining features of the "fantasies world" emerge from the contrast with those of this "fundamental" reality.[14] In the world of fantasies we do not have to control the environment and are therefore free with respect to its imperatives. The intersubjective common time becomes a private time that we can manipulate at will, the inter-objective common space ceases to rule as in the ordinary world, and so do the guidelines that limit our relationship with others. This freedom is organized by the social stock of knowledge, typifications, language, and culture, but it is "freedom" in the sense that it has no logically insurmountable constraints, except those that determine what is conceivable (I can imagine a centaur, but not an irregular decahedron[15]) and those of the internal consciousness of time (my stream of consciousness is irreversible even in the most daring fantasy).

These precisions help to clarify the sense in which imagining, according to Schutz, is different from acting. In his analysis of the concept of "action" (Schutz, 1962: 209-212; 67-68; Schutz & Luckmann, 1974: 3-8) he strives, as we have seen, to give this category the precision that it generally lacks. He argues that what gives unity to action is the project, but he also argues that we can only speak of action when there is an execution, that is, when what is projected is physically manifested. The difference between doing and mere thinking lies in the material insertion of the action in the world, whether through the body or through products. If there is action, and not mere thinking, there is incorporation into common time and space, which is precisely the realm of determinations. The world of fantasies, therefore, is a world alien to action in the sense that if we act we lose the freedom we have in fantasy. To put it more simply, acting is not reducible to thinking.

However, this does not mean that fantasy does not influence action. We identify two statements by Schutz that invite us to elaborate this link as a complement to his proposal. The first one refers to the category of "enclave," which he introduces in a footnote (Schutz, 1962: 233-234, note 20) and which he defines as the interference of elements from one sphere of meaning in another (e.g., in a project I take elements from the scientific world). The world

---

[14] Schutz specifically speaks of "the various worlds of phantasms," a "heterogeneous" set that includes "realms of day-dreams, of play, of fiction, of fairy-tales, of myths, of jokes" (Schutz, 1962: 234). He also considers that "philosophy has not worked upon the problem of the specific constitution of each of these innumerable provinces of our imaginative life" (*Ibid*.). And he presents his description of the world of fantasies as a provisional enumeration of "some" of its features (*Ibid*.). All this illustrates what has been said about the tentative character of his proposal in this regard, as well as about the need, which as far as we know has not yet been fulfilled, to continue this analysis in a more systematic way.

[15] This differentiation refers to Husserl's distinction between "predicates of existence" and "predicates of reality": a centaur contradicts predicates of existence; a decahedron contradicts predicates of reality, in the sense that besides being non-existent it is impossible to conceive.

of fantasies can be interpreted from there as a dynamizer of the stock of knowledge used in the action, which opens up a wide field of analysis, at the social level and at the individual level. The novel I was reading on the bus represents a fictional world, but the plan I executed when I arrived took some inspiration from it. There is a part of the world I do not know directly; among the sources of my ideas about it is the world of fantasies (the little I know about Egypt I learned from cinema). The world of fantasies can be interpreted, in a broader sociological perspective, as a collective reservoir of images, experiences, information, and assumptions, which on the one hand are based on the social heritage and on the other hand participate in its renewal. They may do so to a greater or lesser extent and in empirically varied ways, depending on the role that society assigns to fantasy. The important thing is that from this perspective, the imaginary world has an impact on action, through its influence on the stock of knowledge.

However, for fantasy to influence in this way, it is necessary for it to transcend the private world, and this is what the second statement refers to. Schutz also mentions that we can fantasize alone but also in a group (Schutz & Luckmann, 1974: 32), which implies that fantasy can be the subject of interaction, and therefore of action. We claim that this idea can be translated in terms of a *communicative action of fantasies*, an action that is such in the strict Schutzian sense, as it includes a project and an execution. The project would be the creation of a fictitious world and its communication to others; the execution is the act of externalization of what has been created and of materialization of the communication. The importance of this type of action lies in the fact that it connects two finite realms of meaning: the world of fantasies and the world of everyday life.

There remains one last aspect to consider, which is the possibility of elaborating the action/fantasy link beyond Schutz's concept of action. This link is not farfetched because in the distinctions he elaborates to specify the concept, a notion of "conduct" appears (Schutz, 1962: 211), whose boundaries are not precise but include the absence of a plan (he defines action as a behavior in which there is a project, which implies that not in all of them there is one) and the distinction between manifest and "latent" behavior (which suggests the idea of thought as tacit behavior). For methodological reasons he addresses exclusively meaningful action as we have defined it, but this part of his argument we just mentioned indicates that he did not think that the reality of action is exhausted in it. We, therefore, leave formulated the hypothesis of a different connection between action and fantasy in those other dimensions of action that go beyond meaningful action.[16]

[16] This point is particularly delicate and would justify an ad hoc investigation. In his work of 1932, Schutz draws on the Bergsonian distinction between a reflexive level of consciousness, in which it turns on itself by halting and compartmentalizing its flow, and the level of *duree* or "pure duration," in which it presents itself as a perpetually creative flow, without neither form nor repetition. The description of that primary level as a level with those characteristics, and the explicit connection Bergson makes between *duree* and creation, suggests the hypothesis of a different access to the problem of creative imagination by the theory of action. Schutz (1967: 45-53); Bergson (1944: 3-17).

Symbolism as the Stuff of Imagination

For communication to take place something in the world has to be interpreted as an expression of something else, that is, it has to be a "sign" or "symbol." In his extensive essay on "Symbol, Reality and Society," and later in the drafts edited by T. Luckmann (Schutz, 1962: 287-386; Schutz & Luckmann, 1989: 277-286), Schutz elaborated the basis of a semiotics theory that complements and takes the theory of finite realms of meaning to a new terrain. The development of that theory is rudimentary, but it suggests important derivations for our topic. The key point is that the "matter" of which fantasy is made would be, according to this analysis, semiotic, in the concrete sense that we elaborate below.

The starting point is again Husserl, this time in his notion of "apperception" or "analogical perception" (Schutz, 1962: 294-295). For Schutz, all semiotic processes set in motion a mechanism of consciousness that consists of presenting something absent through something present, as happens, for example, when we know the back of an object without needing to see it. Apperceptive processes are many and link different phenomena (the seen with the unseen, but also the present with memory, or memory with fantasy); signs and symbols are a special case, in which these relations are stabilized and become repetitive.

Signs are of crucial importance for the theory of action, because it is through them that actors can transcend their immediate here and now. In Schutz's terms, there is a "world within actual reach" (Schutz, 1962: 326-329), determined by my spatial and temporal coordinates, from which a "transcendent" world extends that escapes my sphere of direct experience and which we can only apprehend through signs and symbols.

From there, Schutz elaborates a gradation of "sign relations" according to whether the "transcendence" involved is more or less far reaching. At the most primary level he places "marks," which refer to a world that is not present to me now but which was present to me before and will be present to me later (e.g., the marks I make in a book). On the next level are the "indications," which connect a present experience with phenomena that I know are associated with it, but which are not here and now (that smoke refers to fire, which I am not seeing). At the next level, he places "signs," which connect the present with a very special absence: other people's minds. The "inside" of other people is never immediately accessible to me but through mediations (body, object) that are valid as "signs." "Symbols" are the highest degree, and what they make "present" are abstract realities whose existence is exclusively symbolic. From what someone does I can represent his mind, which is something different from representation. A poem, a logical or mathematical demonstration, or a novel, exist only as representation. In Jaspers' language, which Schutz adopts here, it is "an image for something that is not accessible in any other way" and which "exists for us merely in so far as it exists in the image" (Schutz, 1962: 332).

The "symbol," in short, is the way in which we access everything that not only transcends our present here and now but also transcends any possible here and now. The realms of meaning that escape the "world of everyday life" have this property, and the "world of fantasies" clearly has it. Art, fiction, play, and myth can only come to our experience in symbolic terms and can, therefore, be said to be made of symbols. In this sense we claim that the "stuff" of fantasy is semiotic, which has at least two important consequences for our discussion.

First, to say that fantasy is made of symbols opens the door to a strictly semiotic analysis of the imagination. Schutz takes some steps in that direction but without systematic pretension. He argues, for example, that each member of the "apresentational pair" is offered to consciousness not in isolation but in relation to others, which allows for a complex nuanced analysis of signification. He also says that the symbol is an apresentational form "of a higher order" because it is based on the simpler forms of marks, indications, and signs. He refers to the impossibility of fully translating a symbolic meaning into a linguistic one. He proposes concrete illustrations of symbolism in the fields of poetry and science. He even suggests the anthropological thesis of universal apresentational references rooted in the human condition.[17] These indications, simply sketched out, build quite clear bridges with much more systematic developments in the specialized studies of sign and discourse, before Schutz, but above all after him.[18] There is nothing, in principle, to prevent us from using this collection of concepts and instruments to clarify imaginative processes in semiotic terms and to do so not only for their theoretical precision but also for their empirical analysis. To mention just a few examples, structuralist analyses of story structures (Greimas, Barthes), analyses of fiction and verisimilitude as a discursive strategy (Todorov), or studies on the logic of images and the imaginary (Durand, Wunenburger).

The second implication has to do with society itself conceived as an object of imagination. For society, too, when it transcends the level of the immediately present other, is accessible to us exclusively through symbols. In close contact, we have an acting other whose mind we can represent to us by means of "signs"; beyond that, when the object is institutions or values, or when we conceive of phenomena such as the history or destiny of a community, we can only proceed by means of symbolization. The fact that the same is true of imaginary objects suggests the hypothesis of an encounter between the presentation of the social and the world of fantasies, with the latter having an impact on the former. The notion of utopia can be considered as the pure form of this

[17] Schutz (1962). See pages 298-299; 331; 345-347; 332, respectively, for each of the mentioned points.

[18] We have in mind the extensive development of "semiotics" since the 1960s, especially in France.

encounter, the variants of which are, of course, wider. We have reached by another route the considerations we made regarding long-term projects (3.2) and regarding the indirect experience of the social as imaginary matter (3.3).

Imagination and Constitution of the Acting Self

This last point can be considered as an aspect of the first one (4.1), but it is briefly dealt with separately because of its importance for the theory of action. If the "world of fantasies" can influence the constitution of the stock of knowledge, it also affects the actor's representation of himself, which depends on this stock and his particular "biographical inscription." In the first place, this concerns the typifications of persons and courses of action, of which, as we have seen, the stock of knowledge offers a repertoire. This stock also involves processes of self-typification (Schutz, 1962: 19), which are characteristic of social interaction: when I put my letter in the letterbox, I am not only assuming typical employees with typical tasks, but I am conceiving myself as a typical user. To the extent that the world of fantasies can participate in the generation and stabilization of types, its influence in self-typing can also be sustained. Moreover, it can be thought that its influence is greater when the action is less habitual (I have to do something that I do not usually do, so in my search I turn to the world of fantasies). To be sure, there are social contexts of greater and lesser dependence on self-typing with respect to fantasy.

Our experience of ourselves is in any case not limited to self-typification but encompasses the complex of phenomena we call "identity," in which a potentially important presence of the world of fantasies can also be postulated. This terrain has been little explored by Schutz, but it is clear that his theory of action presupposes a reference to the self that acts as a relatively constant self. In the shaping of this self-image, a variety of phenomena come together, among which the world of fantasies has at least a place.

5   IMAGINATION AS CAPACITY: ACTION, IMAGINATION, AND SOCIAL STRUCTURE

We have reached this point with an important collection of distinctions on the action/imagination link. We have said little, however, about the consequences of all this and, more precisely, about the social impact of action when it is moved by, or brings into play, the imagination. This problem encompasses nothing less than of the problem of the action/structure link, which is beyond our scope here and requires resources that Schutz's work does not provide.[19]

---

[19] It has been common to criticize Schutz for his disinterest in "structural" issues. The following analysis shows that, although it was not indeed a central issue for him, it is possible to elaborate from his perspective an idea of "structure." It is true, however, that we should transcend the abstract and philosophically grounded level at which he situates his work in order to reach a more detailed conceptualization in this regard.

We want to approach it anyway, even if only schematically, from what Schutz contributes and from the results we have obtained so far, because even with these limitations, important clarifications are possible.

The Structural Dimension in Schutz

We have to face the problem that Schutz does not offer an explicit concept of "social structure."[20] We believe we are faithful, both to the resonances of that concept and to the spirit of Schutz's work, if we affirm that "the structural" in his proposal would include the following elements:

(i) Every social actor must rely on the existence of an objective context of meaning (Schutz, 1962: 27), which is social in the sense that it is the anonymous accumulated product of generations and in the sense that it has empirical priority over what the actor himself can produce.[21]

- At the most general level this context of meaning is composed of typifications, which organize the world as a cognitive mesh that the actor incorporates in his socialization. The typifying means par excellence is language, although not all types are expressed as words and although language is more than a set of typifications.

- Typifications have their origin in "pragmatic motivations," which are not the same in every society and culture. We have already seen (in 3.1) that anything can be a "type," in the sense that any collection of traits can give rise to a category (animal, dog, x breed of dog, big or small dog, working or pet dog). Beneath the structure of types there are thus "problem relevances" (Schutz, 1976: 235), things that a society and a culture establish as relevant for reasons that are ultimately "practical." There are also different "domains of significances," which may be more or less depending on empirical contexts, and may or may not be related to each other, in turn in more or less systematic ways. The "social distribution" of these significances is not necessarily homogeneous and may manifest itself differently in different groups within the same society.

- Typifications and significations support a configuration of social roles and functions, which transform the concrete actions of concrete human beings into typical activities associated with typical roles and typical motivations. The process includes the self-typing discussed in 4.3, which in turn involves the configuration of the actor's motivational structure according to the roles he or she plays.

- At the most general level the domains of significations and typifications are organized in a "relative natural conception of the word" (Schutz, 1962: 348),

---

[20] The concept of "structure," however, is central to his work, as his posthumous work edited by T. Luckmann indicates right from the title. On the "structuralist" character of Schutz's work, see Belvedere (2010: 123-155).

[21] It has empirical but not logical priority. From a phenomenological point of view, all meaning has its origin in an individual consciousness, even if the temporal and spatial location of that origin is impossible to establish.

a notion Schutz takes from Max Scheler and which alludes to a culture's broader definitions of its place in the cosmos.

(ii) In addition to this "objective context of meaning," the social structure implies relations of power, which Schutz thematizes by means of two notions that we have not yet used: "acting on others" and "action on which one acts" (Schutz, 1967: 147). The former refers to action whose project consists in influencing the experiences of others in order to influence their motivation and, thus, their action. The "action acted upon" is, conversely, that in which the "motive because" is the previous action of another person. The schema refers both to the direct social relationship and to mediated relationships with non-present others, both present, past, and future (contemporaries, successors, and predecessors). I can in this sense be influenced by the action of my ancestors and influence that of my successors; I engage with my contemporaries in a variety of relations of influence, mutual or unidirectional, symmetrical or not, through various "means."

(iii) Finally, the "paramount" reality of everyday life has, in addition to these social limits, spatial and temporal ones, the extent of which depends on the state of social technologies and their accessibility to the actor. It is technical readiness in a broad sense that fixes the exact scopes of what is temporally and spatially possible for an actor at a given moment—although the experience of some limit has a universal character.

Obviously, the three elements are intertwined, and obviously they are very abstract in the formulation that can be made from Schutz. He does not present them as factors in a theory of structure, nor does he make any precise judgments about their hierarchical ordering. They are sufficient, however, to formulate some hypotheses about the role of imagination in the permanence and change of these factors.

Imagination and Structural Change

(i) In the first part of our analysis we established that imagination is involved in the production of new projects, especially in problematic circumstances that break with routines (Sect. 3.1). The existence of new projects implies the execution of new actions, which can have an impact on each of the elements we have just mentioned. Whether or not it does so depends on empirical variables, but from a logical point of view, it can be said that new actions are an enabling factor for structural change. We use this expression, "enabling factor," because it is not a necessary or sufficient condition. It is not a necessary condition because structural change can arise from a different combination of the same actions, as some analyses of rational choice theory have shown in another context.[22] It is not a sufficient condition because novel actions may contribute to the continuity of the structure rather than to its change, as shown by many critical analyses of capitalism as an innovation-dependent system. The existence

---

[22] For example, some cases of "counter-finality" analyzed by Elster, 1978: 106-122.

of novel actions, which from Schutz's point of view requires novel projects, must then be understood as a potentially influential factor in structural change, and this at all the levels we have just distinguished:

- As far as typifications are concerned, we have already seen that the re-exploration of horizons and the elaboration of new types are part of the very phenomenology of new projects. To the extent that these modifications become institutionalized and acquire existence as part of the social heritage, they will also represent changes in the structure, more or less important according to the type or field of types in question.

- As far as the systems of relevances are concerned, everything seems to indicate that Schutz did maintain, on this point, a certain hierarchical relevance of the "relevances with respect to the problem" in relation to the other elements of the structure. He transfers the "pragmatic" component that characterizes individual action to society and culture in general, in the sense that the objective contexts of meaning have their origin in the "relevances" of a society. If this is correct, it can be said that new projects that bring essential relevance into play are also of strategic importance for structural change.

- The same applies to the structure of types and functions, except that it is not a question of meanings but of actions and relations, of "executions" in the sense already mentioned. Schutz, it must be said at this point, introduced these notions in the framework of his frequentation of American sociology, forced by his exile[23] and always a little tense with respect to his initial phenomenological program. Even so, the presence of these expressions invites us to transfer to his references Parsons' elaboration of a sophisticated grammar in which the modification of the structure of roles admits various explorations (e.g., roles are hierarchically organized; there are "integrative" or "coordinating" roles, which fulfill functions of allocation of rewards and distribution of scarce goods; and the structure of roles depends on the organization of the cathexis of the psychic system—Parsons & Shills, 1962).

(ii) The place of new projects in contexts of interaction in which power relations are at stake deserves separate attention. As we have seen, what we are dealing with here is the project of one actor to influence the experiences of another, from which his projects, and hence his actions, emerge. The novelty of the projects can be seen here as a function of the effectiveness of this influence, which has structural implications if the interactions are institutionalized. This applies in both directions of the flow of power (exercise of power/resistance to power).

(iii) All of the above refers to an individual actor, according to the logic that Schutz himself proposes in his analysis. It seems obvious that this is all the more true when it comes to new projects created and implemented collectively (3.4), on the assumption that for structural change the action of the many is more important than that of the few. In this sense, everything we have said about the

---

[23] Schutz, born in Vienna in 1859, had to leave Austria as a result of the Nazi invasion. After a temporary stay in Paris, he went into permanent exile in New York in mid-1939.

phenomenology of the collective creation of projects is valid for projects that affect types, significances, and structural relations of power.

(iv) Along the same lines, the analysis of the link between action/imagination/structure can and must include the phenomenon of reflection and action voluntarily oriented toward transforming the structure. In the previous quick sketches, we have implicitly assumed that the actors in question implement new projects with motivations unrelated to structural change, which in any case comes about as an unintended or unintentional consequence. A deliberate decision to project structural change is also a possibility, the probabilities of which are variable depending also on empirical factors. What is at issue here is structural change as a new project, individual or collective, which touches on a key point of the link between imagination and social change as an aspect of political action.

(v) The consideration of the structure as a system of roles and functions also suggests the hypothesis of social roles more or less inclined to imaginative activity, with which we can return to our analysis of "because motives" and "motivational" relevances (point 3.5). There we put forward the idea that the "because motives" of some actors may be more inclined to the creation of new projects, which we can now connect to socialization into such roles. The existence of such roles has several consequences for the analysis of the action/structure link. On one level, it is a socially controlled incitement to imagination, as is the case, for example, with "creative" roles, which has structural reproduction effects rather than transformation effects. On another level, one can think of the implications of the actions performed within the framework of these roles on other roles or on the wider structure of typifications and relevances, in which case novelty can indeed become structural novelty. A distinction can also be postulated between open and closed creative roles, depending on whether or not the incitement to creation is subordinated to an institutionally established objective. In art, at least in certain forms of artistic activity, novelty is valid in itself, while in the creative professions it is valid as a means to another end.

(vi) The "relative natural conception of the word," which is as we have seen the most general level of the structure, can also be considered more open or more closed to imaginative activity. We already advanced this point in Sect. 3.e and in Sect. 4.2, in reference to symbolism as the "stuff" of the imagination. Actors have a capacity to imagine that can be described phenomenologically as the result of various operations of consciousness (typification, analogical apperception), but whether these operations are carried out, whether they are carried out more or less frequently, and whether they are carried out with one "content" or another depends on an environment of social meanings that are those of a certain epoch and a culture. In this context, the hypothesis of natural-relative worldviews that are more or less permeable to the imagination can be put forward, both in reference to the projective imagination (Sect. 3) and to the fantastic imagination (4). The Weberian thesis of Western rationalization, later taken up by the Frankfurt School, offers an important illustration of a culture in whose worldview the retreat of myth (Adorno & Horkheimer, 2002), the reduction of art to technical and mercantile principles (Benjamin, 1989), or the exhaustion of utopian energies (Habermas, 1986) describes structural conditions that stifle the unfolding of the imagination. Castoriadis' call for a "project of autonomy" (Castoriadis, 2005:101-114) responds to the same diagnosis with the ideal of a society that promotes imagination as reflexive critique and constant openness to novelty. These discourses, strongly charged with normative content, are sufficiently indicative of the implications of the distinction raised and support our initial consideration of the subject's link to critical theory.

(vii) Finally, we have alluded several times to society as the very object of imaginative activity. For Schutz the social is first and foremost another person present here and now, but it is also a variety of absent others that extend in time and space beyond my own coordinates. In that "transcendent" world the imagination occupies an essential place in terms of the image of something absent but also, as we try to argue, as the object itself of the creative imagination. There is here a profound connection between imagination and possible social worlds, which has been picked up from many perspectives and which has, with respect to the action/structural change link, also a fundamental importance, which can be synthesized as follows: the imaginary, as a function of consciousness that strains the limits of the real, contributes to establishing not only what the social world is but also what it can become.

We note that these statements are only sketches for possible hypotheses; they are sufficiently interesting, however, to indicate a direction of research that should transcend Schutz, seeking its complement in a more systematic notion of "structure."

6   Concluding Remarks

Our work has consisted in differentiating levels at which imagination has relevance for action theory. In each case, we have used Schutz's concepts to elaborate our own analyses, but we have not been exhaustive, neither in our use of the work, nor of course in relation to its sources. We believe, therefore, that we have left ample space for further research, and we believe that such spaces can be approached from other perspectives, not just phenomenological ones.

The main overall achievement we claim to have reached consists in situating the imagination in the sociology of action without falling into the extremes of annulling it, reducing it to social forces, or on the contrary, exalting it as if it were an extra-worldly power. Both risks are present, and to notice this it is enough to look at the way in which the questions of imagination and creation are dealt with in social science, and the way in which the defenders of imagination tend to approach it in fields such as aesthetics or artistic reflection. Regardless of the accuracy of our analyses, they start from the assumption that a sociological perspective on the subject should seek to locate imagination in the actual functioning of action, offering nuances that account for that functioning as accurately and as unbiasedly as possible.

We close with two considerations regarding methodological issues. The first is that, while we insist that our analyses are compatible with Schutz's approach, this is less evident with regard to his conception of empirical science. Especially in his early works, he defended a strongly Weberian-inspired idea of science in close proximity to economics, where typical ideal modeling is the guiding principle and where there is even a preference for rational ideal types (Schutz, 1967: 239-241; Schutz, 1976: 81-88). Although the issue would merit special treatment, it seems clear that an emphasis on imagination is difficult to reconcile with such a model of science. However, the phenomenology of the social that Schutz proposes, and from which we have centrally drawn, is logically independent of such assumptions.

The second consideration concerns our own analysis and the way we have proceeded. Since we have attempted to continue Schutz's work, we have done phenomenology, but given the implications this has in philosophical terms, we are obliged to acknowledge that ours has been a basic phenomenology, alien to the training that authentic reflexive analysis requires. In this aspect too, the panorama must remain open to further enquiry.

REFERENCES

Adorno, T., & Horkheimer, M. (2002). *Dialectic of Enlightenment*. Stanford University Press.

Belvedere, C. (2004). "Intención e intencionalidad en las críticas de la teoría social a Alfred Schutz." En De Ípola, E. (Coord.). *El eterno retorno. Acción y sistema en la teoría social contemporánea.* : Biblos.

Belvedere, C. (2010). *Problemas de fenomenología social. A propósito de Alfred Schutz, las ciencias sociales y las cosas mismas.* Prometeo.

Benjamin, W. (1989). "La obra de arte en la época de su reproductibilidad técnica." En *Discursos interrumpidos I.* : Taurus

Benjamin, W. (2005). *El libro de los pasajes.* Akal.

Bergson, H. (1944). *Creative Evolution.* Random House.

Bloch, E. (1986). *The Principle of Hope* (Vol. I). MIT Press.

Butnaru, D. (2009). Tipification and Phantasia: News Possibilities for an Ontology of the Lebenswelt. *Schutzian Research, 1,* 1.

Castoriadis, C. (2005). *The Imaginary Institution of Society.* Polity Press.

Elster, J. (1978). *Logic and Society.* John Wiley and Sons.

Ferraris, J. (1999). *La imaginación.* Visor.

Figueroa-Dreher, S. (2016). *Improvisieren. Material, Interaktion, Haltung und Musik aus soziologischer Perspektive.* Wiesbaden, Springer VS.

Habermas, J. (1986). The new obscurity: the crisis of the welfare state and the exhaustion of the utopian energies. *Philosophy and Social Criticism, 11,* 2.

Heuer, W. (2005). "«La imaginación es el prerrequisito del comprender» (Arendt): sobre el puente entre pensamiento y el juzgamiento." *Cuadernos de Ética e Filosofía Política,* n° 7.

Joas, H. (1985). *George Herbert Mead: A Contemporary Reexamination of His Thoutht.* Polity Press.

Laplanche, J., & Pontalis, J.-B. (1973). *The Languaje of Psycho Analisys.* Hoggard Press.

Lapoujade, M. (1988). *Filosofía de la imaginación.* Siglo XXI.

Marcuse, H. (1974). *Eros and Civilization.* Beacon Press.

Mead, G. H. (1972). *Mind, Self and Society.* Chicago and London, The University of Chicago Press.

Parsons, T., & Shills, E. (1962). *Toward at General Theory of Action.* Harvard University Press.

Richir, M (2010) "Imaginación y *Phantasia* en Husserl." *Eikasia,* Año VI, Vol. 34.

San Martín, J. (2008). *La fenomenología de Husserl como utopía de la razón.* Biblioteca Nueva.

Sartre, J. P. (1986). *The Imaginary.* Routledge Taylor & Francis.

Schutz, A. (1962). *Collected Papers I. The problem of Social Reality.* The Hague, Martinus Nijhoff.

Schutz, A. (1967). *The Phenomenology of the Social World.* Northwestern University Press.

Schutz, A. (1976). *Collected Papers II. Studies in Social Theory.* The Hague, Martinus Nijhoff.

Schutz, A. (2011). *Collected Papers V. Phenomenology and the Social Sciences.* New York, Springer.

Schutz, A., & Luckmann, T. (1974). *The Structures of the life-world.* Heineman.

Schutz, A., & Luckmann, T. (1989). *The Structures of the Life-World, Vol. II.* Northwestern University Press.

Steiner, G. (2001). *Grammars of Creation.* Faber.

Waldenfels, B. (1997). *De Husserl a Derrida. Introducción a la fenomenología.* Paidós.

Warnock, M. (1976). *Imagination.* University of California Press.

Weber, M. (1975). *Roscher and Knies: the logical problems of Historical Economics.* Free Press.

Wolf, K. (1978). Phenomenology and Sociology. In T. Bottomore & R. Nisbet (Eds.), *A History of Sociological Analysis.* Basic Books.

PART VII

Phenomenology of Digitalization

The (Dis-)Entanglement of Knowledge and Experience in a Datafied Life-World

Nicolai Ruh

We are living in a datafied world. This means that more and more aspects of the world are being captured, quantified, and analyzed by digitally networked technologies (Couldry & Mejias, 2019, p. 3). Currently, we can observe the *convergence of (at least) three key technologies*: the Internet of Things (IoT), Big Data (the possibility to store and process vast amounts of data over a long period of time), as well as the rise of artificial intelligence (AI).[1] These

[1] There are also other key developments in the digital sphere that have an essential impact on how we experience and gain knowledge about the world. Virtual Reality (VR) applications like the metaverse or Augmented Reality (AR) would be obvious examples. IoT, Big Data, and AI technologies are used in various areas of application (medical image recognition, automated transportation, etc.). With the release of ChatGPT in November 2022, the impact of artificial intelligence on the life-world has reached a new degree of visibility. This is because technologies based on generative artificial intelligence are used and experienced as interaction partners by which knowledge about the world is accessed and recomposed according to idiosyncratic principles. This chapter was written before the broad public release of these generative AI technologies. It focuses on AI-based technologies that generate knowledge about human behavior based on the data traces that people unwittingly leave behind when interacting with networked objects and digital content. These technologies of dataficaton are less visible than ChatGPT and the like. However, they make up a large part of digital knowledge production and have a mediated impact on how we experience the world, ourselves, and our fellow human beings. Therefore, the statements and arguments of this article remain valid in the light of these new developments in the field of artificial intelligence.

N. Ruh (✉)
Lucerne University of Applied Sciences and Arts, Lucerne, Switzerland
e-mail: nicolai.ruh@hslu.ch

C. Belvedere, A. Gros (eds.), *The Palgrave Handbook of Macrophenomenology and Social Theory*,
https://doi.org/10.1007/978-3-031-34712-2_18

343

technologies are constantly working autonomously underneath the surface of our everyday experience. However, they take the technical traces of our everyday activities as "raw data" to produce knowledge about our behavior that is used to categorize, influence, and predict our actions (compare Beer, 2019; Gitelman, 2013; Zuboff, 2019; van Dijck, 2014). Examples of technologies of datafication range from recommender systems as used in marketing and political campaigning (compare Bucher, 2018; Burkell & Regan, 2019) to AI-based behavioral analytics software that is applied in law enforcement (compare Tayebi & Glasser, 2016) or in human resource management (compare Eubanks, 2019).

How these technologies work and how this classification takes place "exceed[s] the phenomenological horizon of human subjects" (Hong, 2020, p. 30) and therefore eludes direct phenomenological analysis. In this chapter, I argue that although these technologies operate underneath the level of our perception, they do shape our experiences of the life-world, ourselves, and others. Inaccessible to our cognitive apparatus these technologies reorganize a semiotic referral system that increasingly co-shapes our orientation in the world.

The goal of my chapter is to discuss a conceptual framework that allows us to bring in line (inter-)subjective experiences in a datafied life-world with their structural conditional contexts. I, therefore, choose a phenomenologically grounded sociology of knowledge approach. Alfred Schutz's and Thomas Luckmann's formalizations of the "Structures of the Life-World" (Schutz & Luckmann, 1974, 1989) allow me to trace the structural conditions that inform our cognitive coordinate system which guides our orientation in a life-world that is increasingly mediated by networked technologies.

In *part one* I argue that knowledge about the social world as part of the life-world is grounded in (inter-)subjective experiences of humans who perceive each other in different degrees of mediacy. I follow Shanyang Zhao's observation that the "here and now" increasingly loses its excellent position as the zero-point for our orientation in the world. Social media platforms like Facebook, Instagram, and YouTube extent our interactive appropriation of the life-world. Consequently, our experiences of the life-world are increasingly shaped by interactions with physically distant others who Zhao classifies as "consociated contemporaries" (Zhao, 2004).

In *part two* I outline that datafication technologies alter the *opacity structure of the life-world*. The omnipresent technological infrastructure ubiquitously senses, processes, and interprets the technical residuals we unconsciously leave behind when interacting with networked objects and people in our everyday life. It does so according to semiotic principles we cannot comprehend with the help of the cognitive coordinate system that guides our orientation in the world. This process of knowledge generation detaches the technical residuals of our actions from their initial contexts of meaning. It alters our temporal and spatial positionedness in the life-world as well as our relatedness to others, and it co-shapes our experience of ourselves and our surrounding world. Algorithmic recommendations, for example, open gateways to specific segments of reality.

They confront us with products, ideas, and social encounters we would otherwise not have had access to. But they also put resistance to our actions and have an exclusionary dimension (compare boyd & Crawford, 2012; Davis et al., 2021).

In *part three* I discuss in how far Schutz' and Luckmann's semiology can help us understand the process of how we meaningfully integrate the results of algorithmic knowledge production into our experience of the life-world. I argue that datafication technologies establish a semiotic referral system underneath the layer of our perception. They take the technical residuals we unconsciously leave behind when interacting with networked objects as "indications" (*Anzeichen*) for our behavior and our motivation. Then they place mnemotic orientation points into our everyday life-world that share structural similarities with "marks" (*Merkzeichen*). We use these "appresentative vehicles" to integrate elements of the life-world into our experience that transgress our immediate perception. I contest that the cognitive landmarks set by AI-based systems restructure the temporal and spatial conditions under which we experience the world and others.

I conclude that these considerations can help us better understand the formation of large-scale social phenomena like the emergence of the "society of singularities" (Reckwitz, 2020) or "echo chambers" (Rosa, 2019).

1   PART 1: THE EVERYDAY LIFE-WORLD EXPERIENCE AS THE POINT OF DEPARTURE FOR OUR KNOWLEDGE ABOUT THE SOCIAL WORLD

Alfred Schutz is the founder of a phenomenologically grounded sociology of knowledge. According to this school of thought, every social phenomenon—from the everyday mundane to the spheres of science and politics—is ultimately grounded in the *intersubjective experience of a commonly shared life-world*. According to Schutz and Luckmann, the everyday life-world—the "paramount reality" (*ausgezeichnete Wirklichkeit*)—is the unquestioned point of departure from which we act into and experience the world.[2] At the basis of all knowledge about the life-world is the subjective experience of the individual actor—the ego agens—in the temporal and spatial immediacy of the "here and now." It is through specific unquestioned assumptions that we take it for granted that

---

[2] Schutz and Luckmann borrowed the concept of the "paramount reality" from US-American pragmatist William James. Whereas James used this concept to describe the persuasive reality structure of objects that are physically graspable and manipulable by our actions, Schutz and Luckmann extent the idea of the paramount reality to all elements of the world that we unquestioningly perceive as naturally given and manipulable by our actions. This can include elements of the life-world that are not immediately available to us but that act back on us and that can—in principle—be manipulated by our actions. The limits of the "manipulative zone" are determined by the technologies available to a given society (see Schutz & Luckmann, 1974, 5 ff.).

there are other people out there who share similar experiences and motives for actions as we do (Schutz & Luckmann, 1989, 3ff.).[3]

We access the world outside of our immediate experience, such as the minds of other people and their motives for actions through specific means that Schutz and Luckmann call "indications, marks, signs, and symbols" (Schutz & Luckmann, 1989, p. 131). However, we never gain direct access to the ontological structure of the objects of the life-world or to the "subjectively intended meaning" of the actions of our fellowmen (see Schutz, 1997, 226 ff.). We can only approximate the "adequacy of meaning" (*Sinnadäquanz*) of the elements of an intersubjectively shared life-world, and the means for that is interpreting the meaning that other humans have already attached to them. This means that all knowledge about the social world "begins with the premise that the meaning of any object in the lifeworld is intersubjectively constituted through human interaction" (Zhao, 2007, p. 141).

According to Berger and Luckmann, role expectations, social institutions, and worldviews are sedimentations of collectively shared "stocks of knowledge" that are constantly being perpetuated and mutated by the members of a given society in a dialectical process of internalization and objectivation (Berger & Luckmann, [1966] 1991). The hot substrate of these sedimentations of knowledge, however, is the "lived experience" (*Erlebnis*) of the individual (Schutz & Luckmann, 1989, p. 3).

In short, according to this phenomenologically grounded sociological approach knowledge about the social world as part of the life-world is:

1. Aligned to self-knowledge and *experience* (*introspection* and *observation*)
2. Internalized and externalized through interactions with others in *different degrees of mediacy* and therefore *intersubjective*
3. Embedded into and shaped by a specific *temporal and spatial structure* of the life-world
4. Embedded into a specific *motivational structure* that guides our actions and those of others
5. *Ambiguous*, since it is perspective knowledge that is interpreted against the background of *different contexts of meaning*

The social world presents itself to me in its meaningfulness (*Sinnhaftigkeit*) in different degrees of temporal and spatial mediacy. The "here and now" is the zero-point for my orientation in the world. According to Schutz and Luckmann this "primary zone of operation" (*unmittelbare Wirkzone*) has an excellent status for testing reality. It is the "here and now" where I can experience the world and other human beings in the greatest "fullness of their symptoms" (*Symptomfülle*) (Schutz & Luckmann, 1974, 252 ff.). I can also immediately

---

[3] Schutz and Luckmann refer to these unquestioned assumptions as the "interchangeability of standpoints" as well as the "congruency of relevance systems" that entails the "general thesis of the reciprocity of perspectives and motives" (compare Schutz & Luckmann, 1974, 59 ff.).

test the results of my actions. But even in the closest proximity of the "here and now" I do not get immediate access to the experience of other human beings and their motivations. I must interpret their behavior and their facial expressions as well as their body language to come close to the meaning-adequacy of what they are doing; however, I can still misinterpret their behavior.[4]

According to Schutz, we use specific generalizations and idealizations to extrapolate our own experiences to those of other human beings. In the "natural attitude" (*natürliche Einstellung*), we bracket out ontological questions about the problem of intersubjectivity. We take it for granted that our counterpart experiences a shared situation in a more or less similar way than we do ("general thesis of the reciprocity of perspectives"). We also assume that her motives are reasonable in the sense that they are guided by a specific *motivational structure* that we share and can comprehend ("general thesis of the reciprocity of motives").[5] Based on previous experience we know that the social world has a specific *temporal and spatial structure* that transgresses the "here and now" and that augments but also limits our sphere of influence. I know that I can do specific things when I change places and I know I can come back to where I started (idealization of the "I can do it again") (compare Schutz & Luckmann, 1974, p. 55). This hints to a continuity structure that informs our perception of the life-world (idealization of the "and so forth and so on") (ibid.). We know that our behavior and that of others is informed by events that took place in the past ("because-motives"), and other actions are aimed to achieve a desired outcome in the future ("in-order-to motives"). We are also aware of the fact that some behavior is informed by intrinsic interests ("motivated relevances") and other behavior is the result of external circumstances that limit our options for action ("imposed relevances") (ibid., 182 ff.).

It is important to sketch out these cognitive structures that guide our orientation in an intersubjectively shared life-world, because they fundamentally differ from the way AI-based systems "make sense"[6] of human behavior. I will highlight the impact of data-based knowledge generation on our experience of the life-world in part three.

But for now, it is important to highlight, how digitally networked information and communication technologies alter our positionedness in the world and our relatedness to other human beings. Our life-world transcends our "primary

---

[4] For example, I can interpret the blinking of the eye of my friend as a meaningful gesture, whereas for her it is an involuntary reflex.

[5] See Footnote 3.

[6] AI systems do not make sense of the behavior of human beings, because they are unable to comprehend what they are doing since they do not have a conscious mind that is able to perceive the world based on experiences. However, we will see that these machines process the technical residuals of our actions. They do this either based on pre-assumptions about the social world that their developers have inscribed into them (supervised learning) or they generate their own world models (deep learning). The technical data is processed as indications for our actions in the world, and the result of the data-processing is thrown back into our world of experience.

zone of operation"[7] in various dimensions: time, space, the social world, and other provinces of meaning that have a completely different reality structure (dreams, the sphere of fantasy, religion, etc.). In the following we will focus on the interrelated transcendencies of space, time, and the social world.

As we already noted, for Schutz and Luckmann, the "here and now" is the zero-point of our coordinate system in the world. It is from this immediate sphere that we estimate the temporal and spatial scope and impact of our actions, and that we project our actions, either based on motives that are grounded in the past (because-motives) or on future attainabilities (in-order-to motives). In addition to these temporal and spatial transcendencies the social world is characterized by various degrees of anonymity to other human beings. Schutz draws the distinction between "consociates" (Mitmenschen) and "contemporaries" (Zeitgenossen) (Schutz & Luckmann, 1974, 59 ff.). The *realm of consociates* refers to interpersonal relationships based on reoccurring face-to-face encounters. In these "we-relationships" we share a specific re-attainable physical proximity with others, and with *intimate fellows* we also share the temporal simultaneity of "growing old together." The human beings that we never met or had direct personal encounters with but coexist with us during the same time fall in the *realm of contemporaries* (ibid.).[8]

What is of importance here is that the differing degree of temporal and spatial proximity to our fellowmen is accompanied by a differing degree of mediacy to his experience and therefore to the subjectively intended meaning of his actions. The more time we spend with someone in reoccurring face-to-face encounters, the better we know how to put into context and interpret her gestures, facials expressions, and the motivations behind her actions. The more mediate the interaction is, the less symptoms we have at our disposal from which we can draw conclusions about her intentions as well as the context of meaning her actions are embedded in.

This is of specific importance in the digital age, where more and more social interaction takes place over the internet. According to Shanyang Zhao online communication brought along a new type of fellowmen: the *consociated contemporary*. These are other humans that we have never met in person but with whom we spend a lot of time online in chat rooms and social networks (Zhao, 2004). Zhao argues that this time spent together and the biographical information we gather and put into context compensate to a certain degree for

---

[7] Schutz and Luckmann distinguish between the "primary zone of operation" and "the secondary zone of operation." Both are part of what they call, in accordance with George Herbert Mead, the "manipulative zone." The primary zone, however, describes the objects that we can manipulate and experience within our immediate reach, whereas the objects in our secondary zone of operation lie outside our immediate reach and are only manipulable by means of technical mediation (compare Schutz & Luckmann, 1974, 42 ff).

[8] It should be noted that Schutz conceived of these categories not as a binary juxtaposition but rather as a continuum, since people that we have direct contact with can fade into the realm of contemporaries and people we have never met can enter our intimate sphere (ibid.).

the lack of immediately observable symptoms that give us clues on how to interpret the actions of others.

2   PART 2: THE OPACITY STRUCTURE OF A DATAFIED LIFE-WORLD AND THE DETACHMENT OF KNOWLEDGE FROM EXPERIENCE

However, I argue that the paradigm of datafication makes problematic the interpretation of technically mediated clues that give us insights into how the social world is structured beyond the sphere of our immediate "here and now." I contest that the surveying, mapping, and influencing of the world through datafication technologies change the opacity structure of the life-world (compare Ruh, 2021a, 2021b, 91 ff. and 104 ff.). The ubiquitous tracking of our lives by globally dispersed third parties and the correlation of this technical data with the data traces of millions other people unbeknownst to us create a second, imperceptible layer of the life-world. Within this virtual layer, which is temporally and spatially detached from our immediate experience, AI systems create knowledge about our behavior and our motivational structure according to semiotic principles that are incomprehensible to us.

For us to get a glimpse into this imperceptible but omnipresent layer of the life-world as well as into its idiosyncratic principles of knowledge generation, we must bear in mind the convergence of three digital key technologies: The Internet of Things (IoT), Big Data, and the role of AI-based systems of knowledge generation.

With the Internet of Things we constantly interact with more and more objects (smart phones, smart TVs, wearables, smart cars, etc.) that are connected over the internet and that permanently exchange data about us among each other and with third parties unbeknownst to us (compare Peter et al., 2020). Big Data—the usage of cloud servers and cloud computing—allows the storage and processing of vast amounts of data over a long period of time (compare Mayer-Schonberger & Cukier, 2013). AI-based systems of (un-)supervised machine-learning and deep learning detect pattern within these huge troves of data (compare Goodfellow et al., 2016; Nandi & Pal, 2022). The way this generation of pattern takes place fundamentally exceeds our cognitive capacities (compare Hong, 2020). This form of knowledge generation is based on the abstraction of phenomena (people, objects, as well as their characteristics and their interrelatedness) into a complex array of technical data (Kitchin, 2014). Dodge and Kitchin point out that it would be more correct to speak of "capta" (*Latin capere*—*"to take"*) as the atoms of data generation because data are more accurately speaking the output of the selection and harvest "from the sum of all potential data" (Kitchin & Dodge, 2011). Consequently, digital data are not the result of a simple mapping between something given in the world of experience and its technical abstraction. Rather, data are the product of a selective abstraction process that is often guided by the making of pragmatic choices of what is technically available that can be turned into information about something (Hong, 2020, p. 94).[9] Since the production of data involves the making of contingent choices, Lisa Gitelman and others point out that the term "raw data" is an oxymoron (compare Gitelman, 2013).

The methods by which AI systems generate patterns out of vast amounts of structured or unstructured data are mostly a combination of supervised and unsupervised machine learning (compare Nandi & Pal, 2022). With supervised learning, the AI system receives preselected and structured training data as an input (e.g., images of faces that people assigned to specific psychological states) and learns on this basis to recognize pattern in vast data troves. AI systems based on deep learning and neuronal networks, however, develop their own "world models" by building more complex concepts out of simpler ones (e.g., pixels → edges → corners and contours → object parts → objects) (compare Goodfellow et al., 2016, p. 6). Especially deep learning systems can develop a high degree of complexity that makes it impossible even for their developers to reconstruct the process of how exactly a certain output came into being. That is why these AI systems are often described as epistemic "black boxes" (compare Lee & Björklund Larsen, 2019; Trites, 2019; Reviglio & Agosti, 2020).

What is of concern to us here is that the process of knowledge generation is detached from human experience, and the same goes for the vast amount of structured and unstructured data that is the source for this knowledge generation. To understand the impact of these technologies on the opacity structure of the life-world one must take a closer look at the scope and quality of the produced knowledge. Rob Kitchin provides an ontological assessment of the nature of Big Data (Kitchin, 2014). According to him and others (e.g., Mayer-Schonberger & Cukier, 2013) knowledge generated out of Big Data strives for (at least) four characteristics. It aims to be:

1. *Exhaustive* in that it not only captures a representative sample of a population but the population as a whole (N = all)
2. Fine-grained in *resolution* because it allows to uniquely identify individuals via MAC addresses, E-Mail- and social media accounts, and so on, and to assign them with detailed attributes (e.g., age, gender, purchase habits, when and where an individual communicated with whom over what device, etc.) (N = 1)
3. *Relational* in nature because it allows data to be correlated over different datasets and sources
4. *Flexible* in that it is expandable in its scalability with the effect that the accuracy of its output increases with the amount of input it receives (Kitchin, 2014)

[9] In "The Data Revolution" Rob Kitchin gives a detailed account over the various types of structured and unstructured data that AI systems sift through and create patterns out of metadata, geo-location data, MAC addresses, images, chat messages, purchases, XML-tagged web pages, and so on (Kitchin, 2014).

What that means for the opacity structure of the life-world is that we are living in a world where an omnipresent technological infrastructure is permanently (re)establishing contexts of meaning between ourselves, others, as well as objects and events in the world that are fundamentally inaccessible by our cognitive orientation system. When we listen to a specific song on our music streaming service at a specific time in a specific place, then the algorithms put us in touch with the music of other listeners who share similar attributes that the algorithms assign to us and them. So-called context-aware recommender systems use complex context-related information that can include thousands of parameters to embed their targeted product recommendation in a specific context of meaning. For example, they correlate geolocation data and body data from smartwatches to find out if we are listening to certain types of music while jogging or driving a car (compare Adomavicius et al., 2011).

This means that we become the bearer of attributes that the AI system assigns to us based on the technical capta that it can uniquely identify as belonging to us. According to researchers at Spotify, "personalization is based on contextual features describing what the system knows about the user, their context, and the item" they engage with (McInerney et al., 2018, p. 32). The results of these metrics are not based on sociological considerations of what constitutes a particular attribute. They are the outcome of a "practical priority" of what is measurable and available as technical data (see Hong, 2020, p. 94). To optimize the output of the system it is not at all the focus of their developers to get to know and intersubjectively understand the context of meaning in which I listen to a particular song. For them it is sufficient to formalize and readjust the parameters that lead to a desired output. It is often a trial-and-error game in fine-tuning the parameters of an AI system to achieve a desired outcome on the side of the user. In a whitepaper the researchers at Spotify describe the problem of "filter bubble pathologies" (McInerney et al., 2018, p. 31) as the result of ignoring specific parameters when optimizing recommendations. Overlooking one parameter could lead the AI to guide users into a filter bubble, where they are only confronted with too similar content (ibid.).

This tweaking of the technological architecture to influence the experience and behavior of the user to generate a specific output follows a cybernetic understanding of the social world (compare Wiener, 1954). The interplay of technical readjustment and user feedback is called "collaborative filtering," where the user gives either "implicit" or "explicit feedback" (compare Beel et al., 2015). Implicit feedback refers to indications of users' behavior that the user generates unconsciously when interacting with content (e.g., by buying products, listening to a song, or watching a video). Explicit feedback refers to ratings and "likes" consciously placed by users to show her (dis-)approval (ibid.). When setting incentive structures, assumptions from psychological behavioral economics also come into play to "nudge" the user toward a desired behavior (compare Thaler & Sunstein, 2008).

The takeaway here is that we are increasingly acting in a world where the results of our actions are spatially and temporally detached from the contexts of meaning that our actions are embedded in. Unbeknownst to us, the technical infrastructure permanently recontexualizes the technical residuals of our actions with that of others and establishes a virtual link between us and other elements of the life-world outside of our immediate reach, be them other human beings, aesthetic content, products, or ideas. This putting into relation between us and other elements of the life-world takes place according to semiotic logics that are inaccessible to us. However, this virtual dimension alters our experience of the life-world. The decisions made by algorithms can open up gateways to social encounters or they can bring me in touch with elements of the life-world that I would not have encountered otherwise. The datafication of the life-world therefore has an *epistemic as well as a performative dimension* (compare Raley, 2013).

I argue that although the semiotic processes that relate us to other elements of the life-world are intangible with our cognitive coordinate system, we must nevertheless meaningfully reconcile their output with our experience of the life-world. In the following I will show how Schutz's semiology can help us better understand the dialectic of knowledge production and experience in a datafied world.

3   Part 3: The Reintegration of Algorithmic Knowledge into the Experience of the Life-World

In order to be able to explain how this reintegration of technical knowledge into our experience of the life-world takes place, we must take a brief look at the cognitive mechanism of "appresentation" as well as *indications, marks,* and *signs* as vehicles to bridge the transcendencies of the life-world. We will then see how the datafication paradigm restructures the temporal and spatial dimensions of the life-world and competes with these cognitive orientation guides.

According to Schutz and Luckmann we orient ourselves in the world beyond our immediate sensitive reach with the help of specific "vehicles" that allow us to bring to our experience elements of the life-world that we cannot directly perceive with our senses. These vehicles that allow us to bridge the transcendencies of space, time, and the social world are called "indications, marks and signs"[10] (Schutz & Luckmann, 1989, 131 ff.).

The cognitive mechanism by which we can bring into our experience elements of the life-world that transgress our immediate sensitive experience is called "appresentation." It is "a performance of consciousness that is essential to the life-world experience" because without this mechanism, "a person would

---

[10] In addition to these three vehicles there exists a fourth category: "symbols." Symbols allow us to bring to our experience non-everyday realities like the sphere of religion or the nation. I will neglect this form of appresentational vehicle because we only want to focus on the transcendencies of the everyday life-world (space, time, and the consciousness of others) and exclude non-everyday realities from our considerations.

remain to a considerable extent caught within the limits of the flux of actual experience" and be unable to orient herself in space and time as well as in the social world (ibid., p. 132). Appresentation is an active "performance of consciousness" that allows us to use a "present datum of perception" to bring to our experience "something at present not given." This might be objects of the life-world we can bring into our reach when we change our physical position but also elements that are fundamentally inaccessible for us like the consciousness and experience of other human beings. The appresentive mode of "paring and the analogous meaning-transference that occurs in it" is based on a "passive synthesis of association." However, it differs from simple association in that it establishes an "associative union." This union is characterized by the fact that the vehicles of appresentation (indications, marks, signs) dissolve behind the appresented meaning. The appresenting vehicle and the appresented meaning are "so fused that they stand within the functional community of one perception, which simultaneously presents and appresents" (ibid., p. 133). This is, for example, the case when we read the word "tree" and instantly visualize the physical object of a tree. Schutz and Luckmann point out that the principles behind that fusion do not necessarily have to be understood by us:

> [T]he confirmation of appresentative relations in later experiences is not necessarily dependent on one's ability to explain the nature of this relation, which can be obscure just as well as transparent. So it is also without essential significance whether the appresentative relation was originally established step by step, like a logical argument, or as it were automatically, in a single attentive grasp. (ibid., p. 137)

This observation is of importance for our further considerations. We will see that datafication technologies place orientation points into the life-world that allow us to overcome the transcendencies of the "here and now" as well as the transcendencies to the minds of other people. However, the semiotic referral system according to which these technologies put into relation technical data traces with events in the life-world (be they mental activities or material events) is inaccessible by our cognitive coordinate system. I argue that the pre-reflexive mode of mental coupling allows us to integrate the output provided by AI systems as coherent and meaningful elements of the life-world experience.

It must be noted that the pre-reflexive instantaneous coupling that takes place in the cognitive mechanism of appresentation is *derived either from my subjective experience* (indications, marks) or *from intersubjective knowledge that is based in the communal experience of the life-world* that I share with others (signs).

Indications (Anzeichen) give me information about what is outside my immediate reach: smoke coming from the other side of the hill points to a fire that I cannot immediately see (Schutz & Luckmann, 1989, 135ff.). When I see a lightning, I can assume to hear thunder within seconds. Smoke and thunder are examples for indications that occur naturally in the life-world. These events are naturally related to each other in time or space and are accessible to our experience. Corporal expressions of other human beings represent a special type of indication. They appresent elements of the life-world that I, in principle, cannot directly access: the experience and the consciousness of others. Based on my own experience, however, I can assume that some facial expressions hint to the experience of fear and others to that of joy. Schutz and Luckmann point out that they were tempted to classify corporal expressions as a "sign" (*Zeichen*)—a category of appresentative vehicles they reserved for semiotics that are explicitly directed toward communication (ibid., 141. ff.). However, bodily expressions cover a broader field of meaning than that which is consciously aimed at intersubjective interpretation.

They also entail signals that I involuntarily send out into the world and that can be interpreted by others as clues to my motivations or to my inner psychological state (ibid., 135 ff.). My blinking of an eye, for example, can be interpreted by my colleague as an indication of me lying about something or as an expression of nervousness, even though it might only be a grain of sand that made my eye blink. Whereas the appresentative pairings of natural indications like smoke and thunder are rather unequivocal, indications that hint to the subjective experience or inner motivation of an alter ego are much more ambiguous and open to misinterpretation.[11] The more context information we have, the more likely it is that we interpret an indication that hints to another humans' experience or motivation correctly.

What is of importance here is that we are constantly sending out clues that others pre-cognitively take as an indication for our mood or our motivation. This is even more true in a datafied life-world, where everything we do is constantly sensored by an omnipresent technological infrastructure. In the age of artificial intelligence however, the paring of the indication and that what is being indicated is not established by a human observer who matches his observations with his own motivational structure and his tacit knowledge about the world. Here, the semiotic mapping of a technical event with something that happens in the life-world and that can be ascribed to a human being that has a motivational structure is accomplished by AI-based algorithmic systems.

Depending on the type of AI (supervised learning, unsupervised learning, neuronal networks), this mapping process is to a varying degree informed by sedimentations of knowledge that stem from intersubjective experience. This is the case, for example, with specific types of face-recognition software that are based on supervised models of machine learning. Here, human observers feed the AI model with presorted images of human faces that they have previously assigned to certain states of mind (compare Kortli et al., 2020). The AI model

---

[11] This does not mean that natural indications cannot be misinterpreted. A loud noise that I interpret as thunder can also indicate a fighter jet breaking the sound barrier. But understanding the subjectively intended meaning of an alter ego's actions is way more context dependent. The more context information I have that I can match with my experiences and my own relevance system, the closer I can get to the subjectively intended meaning of the action of others.

uses these images as training data and matches them with an enormous amount of input data to improve its matching accuracy. However, the AI system does not get mediated access to the motivational structure of the people on the pictures. It only matches data points that for the human observer in their totality resemble the visual appearance of faces that express a certain mood (compare Goodfellow et al., p. 6). This means that knowledge that is ultimately grounded in the experience of a human observer gets detached from a cognitive frame of interpretation and transferred into a context of technical knowledge construction. According to this heuristic, the benchmark for successful classification does not lie in the approximation of a subjective experience via the interpretative mapping of an indication (facial expression) and an emotional state (fear, anger, etc.). Rather, the AI system learns to optimize the matching criteria for classifying technical data via vast amounts of training data. These heuristic principles are then applied to concrete situations in the life-world.

Let's take as an example the situation of a job interview, which is recorded in the first stage of a selection process and evaluated by an AI system for problematic behavior. In this case, the interpretation of corporal expressions is detached from the concrete context of meaning of the situation. The knowledge of what a nervous or angry face looks like is written into the algorithm. However, the algorithm does not know the specific context of meaning, such as why the applicant makes a tense face in her video presentation. Maybe she is dealing with a personal trauma or has a specific mimic as a default. But even if the AI system had this contextual knowledge, it would not be able to empathize with the situation because it has no consciousness. Since it makes decisions according to statistical and probabilistic criteria as well as the principle of large numbers, it would not be able to understand the individual case in a meaningful way and to match the motivational structure of the applicant with its own. However, the AI system is also not prone to emotional short-circuiting.

We stated above that the rationale for an appresentative pairing must not need to be (inter-)subjectively rationalizable. For our case this means that the corporal expression of the applicant could trigger an unconscious emotional response on the side of the human HR person. She could unwittingly be reminded of a person she had negative experiences with in the past and project these experiences on the applicant.

An experienced HR expert, however, would be aware of these mnemotic processes and distance herself from her own emotions. She is aware of the requirements and expectation framework of the situation and would consciously block out feelings that would guide her actions in another context of meaning. At the same time, she would benefit from her professional experience. In a personal job interview she would match the corporal expressions of the applicant with a variety of other observations and with her intuition, which in turn is based on experiential knowledge. She could so approach the meaning behind the applicant's behavior via targeted but also discreet inquiries.

This example only scratches the surface of the complexity behind the entanglement of (inter)subjective stocks of knowledge and their context-specific actualization that takes place when we interpret indications like the corporal expressions of others. The example of AI-based filtering processes also shows how these technologies decouple a decision-making process that was until recently based on (inter-)subjective experience from this contextual framework. No matter how complex these framework conditions may be, they are still intersubjectively comprehensible since we have tacit knowledge about the motivational structure that informs our experience and actions and we are able to extrapolate that knowledge to others.

As we have seen above, the principles according to which AI systems establish a semiotic connection between a technical event and something that we retrospectively experience and interpret as a meaningful fact of the life-world qualitatively differ from and are not accessible by the structures of relevance that guide our everyday life-world experience. A striking example for this is face-recognition software police units in the US use to compare suspects' photos to mugshots and driver's license images. As it turns out these technologies often discriminate against people with darker skin. This discrimination however is not—or at least not only—caused by racist prejudices that are inscribed into the algorithm by the developers but also because the software has technical problems with correctly identifying people with darker skin.[12]

This example shows two things: *firstly*, these technologies establish semiotic relations according to idiosyncratic logics that qualitatively differ from how humans make sense of the world. *Secondly*, although the racial bias was a result of technical idiosyncrasies, the classifications the software produces can cause effects in the life-world that are then interpreted against the background of intersubjectively shared stocks of knowledge. In this case the output produced by the software caused the police officers to reproduce stereotypes against people with dark skin. This means that the technical idiosyncrasies were meaningfully integrated into the life-world experience and showed effect in the "paramount reality" of the respective individuals.

Contrary to the previous example of the job interview, the discriminatory software caused the initiation of a social interaction, between the police officer and an alleged criminal. In the first example, the software filtered out the applicant before she was able to present herself in the next round in front of a human jury. Both examples illustrate that AI-based decision systems that operate on knowledge which is decoupled from human experience can act as gatekeepers for initiating social relationships. In both cases a dialectical relation between the production of knowledge that is detached from experience and its experiential outcome becomes apparent.

So far, we focused on indications as appresentative vehicles. We have stated that the way AI systems produce knowledge about the world outside our

---

[12] See "Racial Discrimination in Face Recognition Technology," online available under: https://sitn.hms.harvard.edu/flash/2020/racial-discrimination-in-face-recognition-technology/ (May 2022).

immediate experience differs substantially from our approaches to bring to our experience elements of the life-world that are beyond our immediate reach. In the previous section we stated that datafication practices also fundamentally restructure our temporal and spatial positionedness in the world. The Internet of Things senses everything we do, Big Data makes it possible that every micro-event of what we are doing is stored over long periods of time, and AI systems allow physically distant third parties to analyze our past and present behavior for the purpose of predictive analytics and micro-targeting.

I argue that Schutz' and Luckmann's semiology can help us understand how these principles of knowledge production effect our mnemotic orientation in the life-world. For this we must take a closer look at another type of appresentative vehicle they refer to as *marks (Merkzeichen)*. Marks are mnemotic tools that I consciously use to give orientation to my future self, for example, when I highlight specific paragraphs in a text. Marks can be seen as a subjective cognitive bridge between the past, the present, and the future. They allow me to focus on something that I in the past declared to be of importance, and it allows me to send a message to my future self. I set marks in specific contexts of meaning that are not necessarily accessible to others. Although marks are rather arbitrary subjective mnemotic devices they can be interpreted as such by an observer if she has enough context information. Schutz and Luckmann exemplify this with a knotted handkerchief that I find lying on the street, a knotted handkerchief that falls out of my friend's trousers, and a knotted handkerchief that falls out of my friend's trousers from whom I know that he often forgets his wife's birthday. With this context knowledge I will most likely interpret the knotted handkerchief as an indication for my friend's mark. This background knowledge that I share with my friend with whom I spend a lot of time in communal face-to-face interactions not only allows me to identify the knotted handkerchief as a mark. It also allows me to reconstruct the context of meaning against which the knotted handkerchief functions as a mark (Schutz & Luckmann, 1989, 137 f.).

In a datafied life-world the technological infrastructure constantly places mnemotic orientation points in my "manipulatory zone" based on the technical residuals of my actions and those of others that self-learning algorithms classify as an indication for my motivational structure. This is, for example, the case with recommender systems used by dating services, E-commerce, or streaming platforms. Dating platforms show me people in my physical proximity that I might be interested to meet because of shared interests or choices I made in the past. E-commerce platforms suggest me products based on topics that I searched for on the internet or because of products that other people bought who also bought the same products that I have bought in the past. YouTube offers me a customized range of content based on my watching habits over the last years that its algorithms match with the watching habits of millions of other users worldwide.

I suggest that these orientation points share structural similarities with marks in that they build mnemotic bridges between the past, the present, and the future. However, they reverse the semiotic relationship between indications and marks: recommender systems often do not interpret my technical traces as marks that were consciously set by myself.[13] Rather, they take the data traces that I and others unconsciously leave behind over a long period of time in different contexts of meaning as an indication of my motivational structure in order to place recommendations for possible partners, products, music, and worldviews that I might be interested in. Although the working principles of these recommender systems are not comprehensible for me, the output they generate can be quite convincing and cause complex mnemotic chain reactions that influence my temporal orientation and inform my actions.

What is of interest to us is two things:

1. The semiotic heuristics according to which objectified knowledge about my motivational structure is produced by the underlying technical infrastructure
2. The way I subjectively incorporate the results of this technical knowledge production into my experience of the life-world

We have stated above that the technological infrastructure does not have mediated access to my motivational structure in the way other humans—be they close friends or passing acquaintances—have. Big Data–based AI systems do not interpret my actions against the background of a shared "system of relevance" (compare Schutz & Luckmann, 1974, 182 ff.) that they refine through intersubjective knowledge production and constant face-to-face interaction. These systems produce objectified knowledge about the social world by finding, extracting, and correlating patterns in vast amounts of technical data that they ascribe to populations of different granularity. In this sense, what we perceive as personalized data is actually the result of technical pattern recognition within large data sets. These data troves entail data that can be ascribed to my past and present behavior but also to the present and past behavior of millions of other people. It is the correlation of the mapping of my personal data over a longer period of time with that of others who share a similar but slightly different digital footprint that results in what is called "personalized data" (compare McInerney et al., 2018). What YouTube's recommender system offers me is a statistical relationship of choices that is informed by choices I made in the past but also by the choices made by others. Predictive behavioral analytics is the result of statistically overlaying the behavior

---

[13] Here a distinction must be made between "implicit" and "explicit feedback" mechanisms. As we have seen, some recommender systems also use explicit "likes" and ratings consciously given by the user as criteria to optimize their output. These consciously placed semiotic devices can function as marks. On Spotify, for example, I can assign "hearts" to songs to then integrate them later into my playlist. Here the possibility of assigning hearts to content is a feature that on the one hand allows me to consciously place orientation points for myself but on the other hand serves the platform to gain more information about my motivational structure to optimize its output (compare McInerney et al., 2018).

of a large number of other people who have a similar digital footprint to mine (compare McCarthy et al., 2019). The choices they made in the past are choices that I—with a certain probabilistic likelihood—might want to make in the present or the future. These statistical connections that AI systems establish between myself and others exceed my phenomenological horizon. However, in the life-world experience I interpret the offerings made by recommendation systems as something that is meaningfully related to my current situation or to my biography, as something that is temporally connected to my personal situation. This is due to the fact that I interpret the elements of the life-world according to the structural conditions of my cognitive apparatus that guide my orientation within the life-world. Even if I am a developer of AI systems, I will most likely blend out my knowledge of how these systems operate in my everyday experience and tend to accept their output as something meaningfully related to my experience. I suggest that the immediate mediacy of the cognitive pairing that takes place in the mental process of appresentation plays a huge part in this meaningful integration of technological knowledge production.

But it is not only the statistically established bond with others that transgresses my phenomenological horizon. It is also Big Data's capacity to store every micro-event of my behavior that exceeds my mnemotic abilities. My search engine "knows" what I searched for on the day and the minute five years ago and can confront me with its savant knowledge about my life. This entanglement between the creation of objective knowledge about my behavior that is detached from my experience and the knowledge that is created about the behavior of others confronts me in the life-world as something that has the mnemotic quality of marks. This confrontation can trigger appresentative chain reactions.

My music streaming service, for example, can provide me with a mixtape of my youth that it created by correlating my exact listening habits of the last years with those of other users with whom I share a similar demographic background (age, gender, etc.). The mixtape is likely to contain songs that I haven't heard in years but that throw me back into my youth. This can unleash a mnemotic chain reaction like that described by Marcel Proust in "In Search of Lost Time," where the taste and smell of a sweet cookie soaked in lime blossom tea catapults the author back to his youth and evokes various detailed and vivid biographic episodes in his mind's eye (compare Proust, 1913–1927).

This example hints to a dialectic conditional relationship between technical knowledge production and experience in a datafied life-world. It is quite likely that the listener will continue searching for songs that he heard in his youth after having had this biographic flashback. These choices then again will trigger the algorithm and refine its recommendations. Sometimes the technical infrastructure also gives us linguistic clues as to how certain recommendations came about. Although the algorithms include an incomprehensible variety of parameters in the analysis of user behavior, AI researchers at Spotify have found that describing to the user why she is confronted with specific content helps for the acceptance of "explainable recommendations" (McInerney et al., 2018). In

Schutz and Luckmann's semiology language is the prime example for *signs* (Zeichen)—appresentative vehicles that are directed toward intersubjective communication (Schutz & Luckmann, 1989, 138 ff.). What takes place here can be described as the transfer of technical indications for user behavior into intersubjectively comprehensible signs with mark-like qualities. Knowing that Spotify provides me specific content because "other people who liked this artist also like that artist" allows me to plausibilize the choices made by algorithms, and it also allows me to experience a form of kinship with the content that connects me with other people.

These appresentative vehicles can guide my attention to political or aesthetic content and get me in touch with people worldwide with whom I consolidate a particular worldview or an aesthetic taste over a longer period of time. Depending on the type of social interaction that is initiated by algorithms, these people (e.g., influencers and their followers) can become my consociated contemporaries with whom I build up an intimate reciprocal relationship by growing old together and sharing biographical information.

In this sense, datafied knowledge production can lead to the genesis of subcultural communities that would not have existed otherwise. These communities are then solidified and consolidated through personal communication and the sharing of intersubjective experiences. This has effects on the experience of the everyday life-world. I can get to know and befriend people all over the world with outlandish interests whom I would never meet in the physical proximity of my hometown. This can lead to the consolidation of belief systems or aesthetic tastes that are only shared within this particular community but not by the people with whom I interact with in my everyday life (compare Kozyreva et al., 2020, 109 ff.). This may be accompanied by experiences of alienation from the consociates and fellowmen in my physical environment. Changing media usage behavior away from traditional mass media toward data-driven social media contributes to the formation of insular communities who share exotic interpretations of reality (ibid.). The emergence and consolidation of conspiracy myths in the wake of the COVID pandemic is a prime example of how AI-powered recommender systems can help consolidate ideological echo chambers (ibid., 120 ff.). In this case, the experience of physical isolation over a longer period of time most likely had a reinforcing effect, because the individuals in question could not align their interpretations of reality with significant others to the extent that would have been possible under non-pandemic circumstances.

However, this is not to say that this dialectic relation of datafied knowledge production and experience must inevitably lead to closed worldviews. The algorithms do not force us into feedback loops in a deterministic manner. We are constantly interacting with the technological infrastructure that is sensing our behavior and refining its output depending on the complexity of our input data. When the machine output is too coarse, we often perceive that as an experience of incongruity. It is not rarely that we perceive the suggestions made by recommender systems as being at odds with our actual motivations or interests. In this case, the pre-reflexive coupling between the mark-like landmark and another element of the life-world is interrupted, and our attention is redirected to the technological infrastructure. We then experience that the algorithms made choices for us that are incongruent with our system of relevance. Sometimes the technological idiosyncrasies shine through in the choices made by an algorithm. Big Data has a way more detailed knowledge about what I did when and where than I have. However, it does not have access to my system of relevance. It does not know why I searched for something on the internet. It does not know whether my actions were driven by intrinsic or extrinsic motivations. Did I search for a particular drug because I have the flu or out of medical curiosity? Do I watch YouTube content on conspiracy theories because I feel emotionally drawn to these simplified interpretations of reality or because I look at them from the theoretical attitude of a social scientist?

In these cases it becomes obvious that AI systems do not have access to my system of relevance and that they operate according to idiosyncratic logics that are not accessible by the logics of my cognitive apparatus in the natural attitude under the "pragmatic motive".[14] The algorithm does not approach the subjectively intended meaning of my actions by interpreting a single situation against the background of an intersubjectively shared structure of relevance that it refined over a longer time span by "growing old" together with me like a friend who knows me in and out. The algorithm is caught in a particular temporal logic that projects the past into the present and the future in a probabilistic manner (compare Hong, 2020, p. 110). Regression analysis as a common method in machine learning, for example, extrapolates regularities in the data structure into the future for predictive analysis (compare McCarthy et al., 2019, p. 12). The more data the self-learning algorithm has as an input the more likely it will come up with the right predictions. If my present behavior deviates from the prediction it will adjust its parameters accordingly to come up with more precise suggestions in the future.

This means that, although the algorithm accompanies me all the time, it does not grow old together with me like a friend who experiences the evolution of my motivational structure in reciprocity with his own. Although the algorithm adopts to my present behavior it cannot let go of the past and "judges" everything I do against the background of the behavior of my former self. A friend with whom I grew old with knows that the motivational structure of my sixteen year old self deviates from the one of my forty year old self. Although we might talk about our common childhood memories and although we experience a continuity in the basic character of the other, we know of the biographic fractions that formed the identity of the other and we have broad context knowledge to make sense of the others' actions.

---

[14] According to Schutz our everyday actions are guided by a "pragmatic motive". In order to achieve our practical goal, we bracket out ontological questions about the "So-Sein" of the world (Schutz & Luckmann, 1974, 8 ff.).

AI recommender systems however have the tendency to keep me in a biographic loop. Consequently, I must actively break out of the algorithmic pattern to confront myself with something new. If I only listen to the music I listened to as a teenager, then my music streaming service will tend to keep me in a nostalgic loop. However, if I actively feed the algorithm with complex input, then the resulting output becomes diversified as well.

4   OUTLOOK: TENDENCIES OF SINGULARIZATION AND THE EMERGENCE OF ECHO CHAMBERS

I might experience the resulting offerings of the algorithms as a feature of distinction that separates me from others and that provides my self-perception with an aura of singularity. Andreas Reckwitz points out that late modern "societies of singularities" are characterized by the valorization of the singular and the devaluation of the average. Singularity however cannot be achieved by one distinctive feature of one's lifestyle. It is a complex and sophisticated assemblage of interests and aesthetic choices that are not unique in themselves but are perceived as singular in their totality (compare Reckwitz, 2020). In that the technological infrastructure takes every micro-event of my behavior as an input and condensates this input into a tailored output in the form of mark-like landmarks that guide my attention to putatively singular aesthetic impressions, it plays an important role in the formation of the experience of a singular self. Below the life-world experience, however, the social structure of the society of singularities can be depicted as a fine-meshed social network in which the distinction efforts show up as network nodes of different size. Taking a closer look at the dialectic between knowledge production and experience in a datafied life-world can contribute to a better understanding of the constitutive conditions and dynamics of differentiation within a society of singularities as well as of the emergence of new forms of classism that come along with it.

The perspective I have sketched here starts from a dialectic relationship between subject and world-between subjective experience and objectified knowledge. It, therefore, can also contribute to a "sociology of human relationships to the world" as outlined by Hartmut Rosa (2019, 2020). Rosa's phenomenologically grounded approach of critical sociology poses the question of the conditions of the possibility for a successful relationship to the world. To avoid anthropological fallacies about the nature of man, Rosa assumes a reciprocal conditional relationship between subject and world in that "both sides—subject and world—are first formed, shaped, and in fact constituted in and through their mutual relatedness" and that subjects "do not stand opposite to the world, but rather find themselves already *in a world* with which they are interconnected or interwoven" (Rosa, 2019, 53). It is therefore not only the "subject's attitude toward, outlooks on, and relatedness to the world" that determine the conditions of a satisfying relationship with the world but also "what constitutes and is knowable as world" that functions as a "co-variable." For Rosa, the good life is the "result of the relationship to the world defined by the establishment and maintenance of stable *axes of resonance* that allow subjects to feel themselves *sustained* or even *secured* in a responsive, accommodating world" (Rosa, 2019, 49). Resonance, therefore, is the antonym to alienation. A resonant relationship between subject and world entails four characteristics:

1. I am *affected* by the elements of the life-world that I encounter, be them other persons, ideas, or aesthetic experiences. They must "move" or "touch" me, or "speak" to me in one way or another; otherwise I experience them as "mute" and not related to myself.
2. I experience myself as *self-effective* in the encounter with the elements of the life-world. This means they must trigger an emotional response in me, and at the same time I must experience my response as having an effect on them.
3. I experience this mutual affection as an *adaptive transformation* of myself and the elements of the world that I encounter. This is the case, for example, when I not only read but also process a book. After my reading I feel that I have undergone a transformation. I am not the same person as before. But at the same time, the book, person, piece of music appears to me as something different than before the encounter.
4. Experiences of resonance are characterized by *uncontrollability (Unverfügbarkeit)*. This means that I can neither force myself to be affected by the world, nor can I force the world to be affected by my actions. The elements of the world speak with their own voice. I cannot impose my will on them or bring them under my control. Therefore, resonance is not a permanent state that can be established and maintained forcefully (Rosa, 2020, 31 ff.).

This last aspect—the unruliness and self-will of the world—is central for an understanding of the conditional possibilities for the establishment of stable axes of resonance. Rosa devoted an entire book on the uncontrollability of the world (compare Rosa, 2020). He observes that late modern societies are characterized by manic efforts to bring into reach and make controllable every single last aspect of the world. The scientific means for that is objectifying the elements of the world to make them quantifiable and therefore calculable. The empirical juxtaposition of the observing subject and the world as its objects lets the world become a "point of aggression," something that must be controlled. Rosa argues that, ironically, these efforts of objectifying the world to make them more controllable would lead to the world becoming ever more uncontrollable (ibid.).

Technologies of datafication also make visible and objectifiable aspects of the life-world that before escaped our grasp (compare Couldry & Mejias,

2019). According to Sun-ha Hong the paradigm of datafication alters the benchmarks of what counts as legitimate knowledge about the world. The efforts to objectify knowledge about the human body (e.g., through fitness wearables) or the world are guided by the idea of "epistemic purity" and the promise of a "raw and untampered representation of empirical reality, on which basis human bodies and social problems might also be cleansed of complexity and uncertainty" (Hong, 2020, p. 8).

For him, what drives data-led thinking is the "desire for saturating the horizon, for complete capture of the world of possibilities through technology" (ibid., p. 55). This objectivation of knowledge about ourselves and the world— the detachment of knowledge from experience—would encourage a "distributed kind of phenomenology, where we actively feel that what we know, what we see and what we feel is not quite "our own"" (ibid.).

One might now be hastily led to characterize this experience of externalization as an experience of alienation. Here the question is whether this other, which confronts us as objectified knowledge about the world and about us, has something to say, whether it speaks with its own voice and makes something resonate in us—in short, whether it carries within itself the conditions of the possibility of a resonant relation to the world. Can we integrate this objectified knowledge into our experience of ourselves and the world as something meaningful that has a transformative effect on us and that lets us experience ourselves as self-effective. Here, a distinction probably must be made from application area to application area. In the quote above, Hong has in mind a self-quantifier community that uses its objectified body data as an incentive for self-improvement. In this case, it is quite conceivable that self-measurement is also accompanied by an experience of self-efficacy and adaptive transformation: I experience a correlation between my physical efforts, the changing of the objective data about my body, as well as my experience of my body over time. This can certainly go hand in hand with experiences of mutual transformation between myself and the objectified knowledge about myself.

My reflections focused on the dialectical relationship between the production and experience of behavioral knowledge in a datafied world. As we have seen this process is characterized by:

1. A technical objectification of my motivational structure via the statistical correlation of my data traces with those of others over longer time periods.
2. The internalization of the results of this objectivations by myself and others.

Step one takes place underneath the level of my experience and is characterized by an idiosyncratic process of semiotic alignment of technical data with behavioral information about myself and others that qualitatively differs from how I make sense of the world according to my structures of relevance. This process thus contains a moment of self-will and unruliness that eludes my grasp.

The second step is characterized by a channeling of the access possibilities to sections of the world. As we have seen in the example of recommender systems, the technical infrastructure puts me in relation with others who seem to have the same or similar interests as I do. It also puts me in relation with objects of the world that according to the AI's own logic are likely to be meaningful to me. As we have seen, we must in turn integrate these points of orientation meaningfully into our experience of the world and interpret them in a sign-like manner against the background of our system of relevance. Here the question arises whether we experience these contents of the world that recommender systems confront us with as something we get affected and irritated by. According to Rosa the aspect of irritation is of specific importance for resonant experiences with the world. That the world contents speak to me with their own voice is the necessary condition for me to be able to incorporate them in a process of mutual transformation. If I only get confronted with worldviews that are too similar to my own, I might get affected by them, but I will not get in resonance with them. The result is the emergence of "echo chambers" that Rosa exemplifies with National Socialism's longing for "pseudo-resonance": the urge to dissolve oneself in a Volksgemeinschaft that builds a demarcation line toward a world that is experienced as cold and mute (Rosa, 2019, 283).

Here the question arises, whether and in how far recommender systems contribute to the emergence of echo chambers. One could argue that if recommender systems know me well enough, they can guide me into echo chambers. However, as stated above, even if these systems are designed to only confront me with people and content of my liking, they still operate according to idiosyncratic logics that are fundamentally incongruent with my system of relevance. However, I can experience their output as meaningful, and their temporal logics of projecting my past and present behavior into the future might cause mnemotic feedback loops. Nevertheless, we are not at the mercy of the algorithms' decisions and can expand our horizon of experience through our active behavior. If we are actively engaged with the world and looking for new content, then recommender systems can help us expand our horizon and confront us with irritating new perspectives. Aside from our media usage behavior it plays an important role to which extend we interact with people with divergent worldviews in our physical everyday reality and how we emotionally address these views (with interest, indifference, or repulsion). For these reasons, one-sided technology-deterministic or pessimistic conclusions must be avoided. Nevertheless, the question remains whether these technologies could be specifically designed to make resonance experiences more likely, for example, by the algorithm suggesting world content that specifically irritates me.

References

Adomavicius, G., Mobasher, B., Ricci, F., & Tuzhilin, A. (2011, Fall). Context-aware recommender systems. *AI Magazine*, 67–80.

Beel, J., Gipp, B., Langer, S., & Breitinger, C. (2015). Research paper recommender systems: A literary review. *International Journal on Digital Libraries, 17*(4), 305–338.

Beer, D. (2019). *The data gaze: Capitalism, power, and perception*. SAGE Publications.

Berger, P. L., & Luckmann, T. ([1966] 1991). *The social construction of reality: A treatise in the sociology of knowledge*. Penguin Books.

boyd, d., & Crawford, K. (2012). Critical questions for big data: Provocations for a cultural, technological, and scholarly phenomenon. *Information, Communication & Society, 15*(5), 662–679.

Bucher, T. (2018). *If...then. Algorithmic power and politics*. Oxford University Press.

Burkell, J., & Regan, P. M. (2019). Voter preferences, voter manipulation, voter analytics: Policy options for less surveillance and more autonomy. *Internet Policy Review. Journal on Internet Regulation, 8*(4), 1–24.

Couldry, N., & Mejias, U. A. (2019). Datafication. *Internet Policy Review. Journal on Internet Regulation, 8*(4), 1–10.

Davis, J. L., Williams, A., & Young, M. W. (2021, July–December). Algorithmic reparation. *Big Data & Society*, 1–12.

Eubanks, B. (2019). *Artificial intelligence for HR: Use AI to support and develop a successful workforce*. Kogan Page.

Gitelman, L. (Pub.). (2013). *'Raw data' is an oxymoron*. MIT Press.

Goodfellow, I., Bengio, Y., & Courville, A. (2016). *Deep learning*. MIT Press.

Hong, S.-h. (2020). *Technologies of speculation: The limits of knowledge in a data-driven society*. New York University Press.

Kitchin, R. (2014). *The data revolution: Big data, open data, data infrastructures and their consequences*. SAGE.

Kitchin, R., & Dodge, M. (2011). *Code/space: Software and everyday life*. MIT Press.

Kortli, Y., Jridi, M., Al Falou, A., & Atri, M. (2020). Face recognition systems: A survey. *Sensors, 20*, 342. https://doi.org/10.3390/s20020342

Kozyreva, A., Lewandowsky, S., & Hertwig, R. (2020). Citizens versus the internet: Confronting digital challenges with cognitive tools. *Association for Psychological Science, 21*(3), 103–156.

Lee, F., & Björklund Larsen, L. (2019). How should we theorize algorithms? Five ideal types in analyzing algorithmic normativities. *Big Data & Society*, 1–6.

Mayer-Schonberger, V., & Cukier, K. (2013). *Big data: A revolution that will transform how we live, work, and think*. Houghton Mifflin Harcourt.

McCarthy, R. V., McCarthy, M. M., Ceccuchi, W., & Halawi, L. (2019). *Applying predictive analytics. Finding value in data*. Springer.

McInerney, J., Lacker, B., Hansen, S., Higley, K., Bouchard, H., Gruson, A., & Mehrotra, R. (2018). Explore, exploit, and explain: Explainable recommendations with bandits. *Twelfth ACM Conference on Recommender Systems (RecSys'18)*, Vancouver, BC, Canada. ACM, New York, NY, USA, 9pp. https://doi.org/10.1145/3240323.3240354

Nandi, A., & Pal, A. K. (2022). *Interpreting machine learning models. Learn model interpretability and explainability methods*. Apress.

Peter, D., Alavi, A. H., Javadi, B., & Fernandes, S. L. (Pub.). (2020). *The cognitive approach in cloud computing and Internet of Things technologies for surveillance tracking systems*. Academic Press.

Proust, M. (1913–1927). *À la recherche du temps perdu*. Grasset and Gallimard; *In search of lost time* (C. K. Scott Moncrieff, Trans.). Modern Library, 1992.

Raley, R. (2013). Dataveillance and countervailance. In L. Gitelman (Pub.), *'Raw data' is an oxymoron* (pp. 121–145). MIT Press.

Reckwitz, A. (2020). *The society of singularities*. Polity.

Reviglio, U., & Agosti, C. (2020). Thinking outside the black-box: The case for "algorithmic sovereignty" in social media. *Social Media + Society*, 1–12.

Rosa, H. (2019). *Resonance*. Polity Press.

Rosa, H. (2020). *The uncontrollability of the world*. Polity Press.

Ruh, N. (2021a). 'The universe believes in encryption'—Implementing math into the ontological layer of the digitally augmented life-world. In J. Dreher (Pub.), *Mathesis Universalis—Die aktuelle Relevanz der 'Strukturen der Lebenswelt'*. Springer VS.

Ruh, N. (2021b). *"Trust the math—Encryption is your friend"*. *Zum Umgang mit ontologischer Unsicherheit in einer digitalisierten Lebenswelt*. Springer VS.

Schutz, A. ([1932] 1997). *The phenomenology of the social world*. Northwestern University Press.

Schutz, A., & Luckmann, T. (1974). *The structures of the life-world Volume I*. Heinemann Educational Books.

Schutz, A., & Luckmann, T. (1989). *The structures of the life-world Volume II*. Northwestern University Press.

Tayebi, M. A., & Glasser, U. (2016). *Social network analysis in predictive policing: Concepts, models and methods*. Springer International Publishing AG.

Thaler, R. H., & Sunstein, C. R. (2008). *Nudge: Improving decisions about health, wealth, and happiness*. Yale University Press.

Trites, A. (2019). Black box ethics: How algorithmic decision-making is changing how we view society and people: Advocating for the right for explanation and the right to be forgotten in Canada. *Global Media Journal, 11*(2), 18–30.

van Dijck, J. (2014). Datafication, dataism and dataveillance. Big data between scientific paradigm and ideology. *Surveillance & Society, 12*(2), 197–208.

Wiener, N. (1954). *The human use of human beings: Cybernetics and society*. Houghton Mifflin.

Zhao, S. (2004). Consociated contemporaries as an emergent realm of the lifeworld: Extending Schutz's phenomenological analysis to cyberspace. *Human Studies, 27*, 91–105.

Zhao, S. (2007). Internet and the lifeworld: Updating Schutz's theory of mutual knowledge. *Information Technology & People, 20*(2), 140–160.

Zuboff, S. (2019). *The age of surveillance capitalism: The fight for a human future at the new frontier of power*. Public Affairs.

The "Waste Land" of the Digitalized Life-World: Alfred Schutz's Contribution to a Theory of Digitalized Societies

Charlotte Nell

1 INTRODUCTION

Like only a few other "process terms" (Joas, 2017, p. 356), "digitalization" is one of the most frequently used diagnostic concepts in the social sciences, intended to capture the societal transformations of the twenty-first century (Seeliger & Sevignani, 2021, p. 10; Lievrouw & Loader, 2020). The indicated structural change seems fundamental as it affects diverse social realms: Digitalization, understood as the process of re-presenting features of reality into a "discrete-numerical system" (Nassehi, 2019, p. 34), and on this basis into symbols or images, is not only rampant within the societal subsystems of economy, politics or education; moreover, it can be considered as a motor of social change in general. Hence, digitalization is frequently considered as a "macro-process."[1] Nonetheless, digitalization also initiates changes in the

[1] A macro perspective on digitalization analyzes "how the structures and processes of the digital network are changing" (Neuberger, 2017, p. 120).

C. Nell (✉)
Friedrich-Schiller-Universität Jena, Jena, Germany
e-mail: charlotte.nell@uni-jena.de

© The Author(s), under exclusive license to Springer Nature
Switzerland AG 2023
C. Belvedere, A. Gros (eds.), *The Palgrave Handbook of
Macrophenomenology and Social Theory*,
https://doi.org/10.1007/978-3-031-34712-2_19

life-worldly experiences of actors, transforming the ways people meet, work, exercise or enjoy themselves—phenomena that are typically identified with a "micro" perspective in the social sciences (Blau, 1987).[2]

Focusing on digitalization as a structuring process that has imposed transformations on the social world, in this chapter I will show how the work of the Austrian sociologist Alfred Schutz offers substantial contributions to a theory of (digitalized) late-modern societies. This at first may seem an unusual undertaking, as Schutz is seldom considered as a macro thinker (Belvedere & Gros, 2019). Rather, he re-presents a common point of reference for micro-analyses of "virtual worlds," such as the emerging realities of video chats, videogames, or social networks (see Osler, 2021; Berger, 2020; Hardesty & Sheredos, 2019; Ollinaho, 2018; Liberati, 2017). Nonetheless, in this chapter I will demonstrate how Schutz provides (at least) three building blocks for sketching out the structure of the social world under the conditions of digitalization. As a result, it can be argued that his approach draws upon both micro and macro perspectives in a systematic manner.

For this, I will proceed in four steps. First (1), I will discuss some contemporary social theoretical approaches to the study of digitalization, namely, practice theory, Science and Technology Studies (STS) and System Theory, to show how Schutz's insistence on the crucial relevance of the foundational role of the subjective point of view for social research contributes to developing a "non-conflationist" social theory of digitalization. Second (2) I will use his account of "multiple realities" and his theory of "signs and symbols" to describe the specific microstructure of digitalized phenomena. Third (3), I will sketch Schutz's contribution to the transformation of the *structures of the social world* initiated by digitalization. (4) Finally, I will discuss Schutz's contribution to a macro-oriented theory of digitalized societies. Ultimately, I follow a twofold objective: By showing how Schutz re-presents a classic for a theory of virtuality, I also aim to demonstrate how his work can be of use for a theory of digitalized (late-)modern societies and hence for an analysis of macro processes.

2   DIGITALIZATION AS AN ISSUE FOR SOCIAL THEORY

The "digital revolution" has rekindled the question of how sociality can be conceptualized. Scholars have increasingly taken up the task of demonstrating how conventional social theory[3] operates with an unacknowledged *face-to-face* archetype as the micro foundation of social theory that serves as a "point zero"

---

[2] Peter Blau draws the line as follows: "Microsociology and macrosociology involve contrasting theoretical perspectives on social life (…) The units of analysis are different—individuals in the first case and populations in the second—and so are the concepts and variables—attributes of human beings in microsociology, emergent properties of population structures in macrosociology" (Blau, 1987, p.71).

[3] Building on Lindemann, I understand social theory as the fundamental "assumptions" about the constitution of "the social" (Lindemann, 2009, p. 15). In contrast, "theory of society" refers to concrete sociohistorical analyses of specific societal formations, for example, "capitalist," "modern," or "digitalized" ones.

from which sociality emerges (Knorr Cetina, 2009; Suchman, 2008, p. 150; Latour, 2005, p. 61). Prominently, Karin Knorr-Cetina has made a significant contribution to the critique of the face-to-face *topos* in social theory, particularly in her examination of Erving Goffman's concept of the "social situation." Knorr-Cetina contends that Goffman's framework inadequately assumes physical co-presence as a necessary condition for social interaction (Knorr Cetina, 2009, p. 62). The *face-to-face topos*, however, is not only present in Goffman's work but also in other classic social theorists, for example, in Georg Simmel's concept of "reciprocity" (Simmel et al., 2009 [1908], p. 571), G.H. Mead's description of the "conversation of gestures" (Mead, 1967 [1934], p. 50), or Alfred Schutz's concept of the "We-relationship" (Schutz, 1972 [1932], p. 157). In all these approaches, the basic unit of the social emerges in situations that are constitutively bound to a *body-to-body* starting point, implying the physical *and* temporal co-presence of human actors. Consequently, traditional social theories seem insufficient in providing a comprehensive account of interactions that do not seem to rely on *body-to-body* communication as their starting point, as, for example, e-mail and online chats, which, however, are increasingly pertinent in the contemporary digital era (Giddens, 1990, p. 39).

Knorr Cetina, in contrast, revises the bodily face-to-face foundation of sociality in favor of a "new global interactionism" (Knorr Cetina, 2009, p. 63), replacing Goffman's "territorial copresence" (Goffman, 1981, p. 84) with the concept of "response presence" (Knorr Cetina, 2009, p. 63) as the constitutive condition for the emergence of social interaction. Rather than tying the emergence of social interactions to the physical space, she proposes the term "synthetic situation" as an analytical category "in which we find ourselves in one another's [...] response presence, *without needing to be in one another's physical a presence*" (Knorr Cetina, 2009, p. 69, my emphasis). According to this view, not the physical-territorial *presence* but the *mutually shared attention* between two actors constitutes social encounters. Knorr Cetina's approach has proven fruitful in the analysis of virtual realms, updating a social theory of encounters and interactions under the conditions of a globalized world (see Knoblauch, 2017, p. 369; Preda, 2008, p. 905).

3   Beyond the Face-to-Face Archetype: Three Social Theoretical Approaches to a Study of Digitalization

Generally speaking, three social theoretical approaches can be differentiated in the literature on digitalization: (1) The interdisciplinary approach of "Science and Technology Studies" (STS) that emerged as a critical reflection on the field of science in the mid-1960s (Edge, 1995, p. 4) and of which Karin Knorr Cetina can be considered an important spokeswoman; (2) the tradition of System Theory as especially established by Niklas Luhmann, who has reformulated social theory starting from "communication" as its basic unit (Reckwitz, 2002, p. 248); and (3) practice theory (Schatzki et al., 2001). Before I outline the commonalities between these three social theoretical paradigms, I will briefly sketch the main characteristics of each of them and how they diverge from the conventional face-to-face *topos* in social theory:[4]

(1) As already stated, Knorr Cetina's work can be considered a significant milestone in the field of STS that seeks to uncover the agency of "non-human actants" and their share in the (re-)production of the social (Latour, 2005, p. 10; Callon, 1995, p. 53; Knorr Cetina, 1995, p. 140f.). In STS, the concept of agency is characterized by the delegation and distribution of actions among both human and non-human "actants." These actants work collaboratively in a network of "translation" (Callon, 1995, p. 52). The approach analyzes the *in-* and *trans-situ* fabrication of the social as a product of the collaboration of different actants that work together in specific *constellations* or *networks* (Gertenbach & Laux, 2019, p. 32). Accordingly, it draws upon a "flat" concept of agency as established by Bruno Latour in his "Actor-Network-Theoretical"-approach ("ANT") in which different entities, for example, computers and humans, cooperate within a network to collaboratively establish communication and interaction (Latour, 2005, p. 61; Callon & Latour, 1992, p. 353). STS hence tends to operate with a suspension of the subjective experience of (human) actors (Callon, 1995, p. 58). STS's focus on how interaction is mediated, achieved, and accounted for through shared agency and "distributed cognition" (Giere, 2008, p. 261) nonetheless constitutes a fruitful contribution to digitalization studies.

(2) System Theory as coined by Bielefeld sociologist Niklas Luhmann represents the second approach that starts with a criticism of the implicit and inadequate human-centered focus of conventional "old European" social theory (Luhmann, 1995, 21, 2012, p. 5). In this regard, it parallels STS's rejection of attributing an extraordinary agential position to human actors. Luhmann develops a theory of "social systems," in which systems are neither constituted by actors nor by actions, but by "communicative operations" as the result of a "three-part selection process" (Luhmann, 1995, p. 140) of information, utterance, and understanding. In this sense, he proposes to analyze the social as distinct from "psychic systems" and hence also from human intentions, motives, or experiences (Luhmann, 1995, p. 109; Greshoff, 1999, p. 33f.). His approach analytically decouples communicative operations from physical co-presence (Luhmann, 1995, p. 4, 42). Adopting this perspective, digitalized and non-digitalized (inter-)actions, such as online chats and face-to-face conversations, seem "functionally equivalent" as operations of social systems (Held, 2019, p. 162f.; Heintz, 2014, p. 236; Werron,

---

[4] Even though STS and practice theories are closely connected, and Knorr Cetina is also a co-author of the "practice turn" (Schatzki et al., 2001), I think the most significant discrepancy lies in the "ontological monism" of practice theory versus the "ontological pluralism" of Actor-Network-Theory (ANT).

2016, p. 260).[5] Ultimately, System Theory builds on the assumption that the subjective point of view is inaccessible to observation, thus disqualifying as a research object for sociology in general (Luhmann, 1995, p. 179; Knoblauch, 2008, p. 67).

(3) Lastly, "practice theories" in the legacy of Pierre Bourdieu, Anthony Giddens, or Andreas Reckwitz have become a common point of reference in the study of digitalization (Reckwitz, 2017, p. 225; Laube, 2016; Stock, 2011). Drawing upon a "flat social ontology" (Schatzki, 2016, p. 33), practice theories operate with the analytical perspective of a "decentration of human minds" for an analysis of the social in favor of a *relational* perspective (Reckwitz, 2002, p. 259; Schäfer, 2016, p. 13). Building on the works of Marx, Wittgenstein, and/or Heidegger, among others, practice theories start from the assumption that *practices* are the basic unit of sociality (Stock, 2011, p.10), contrasting conventional action-oriented approaches. Moreover, practice theories highlight the contextuality and embeddedness of routinized practices in cultural orders of knowledge and artifacts (Reckwitz, 2016, p.173; Schäfer, 2016, p.14). While in this regard practice theories show a close affinity to STS approaches (Schäfer, 2016, p. 147), they do not entirely adopt the "symmetric anthropology" in the sense of Latour (Prinz, 2016, p. 183). On the contrary, they show an elevated sensitivity toward the *embodiment* of the social as well as to the materiality and affectivity of subjectivities (Schäfer, 2016, p. 16; Reckwitz, 2016). Accordingly, practice theories are interested in the process of how specific subjectivities as carriers of embodied knowledge are brought about and actualized in digital practices. For this purpose, the subject is usually analyzed as a product of practices (Archer, 2009, pp. 3–4; Reckwitz & Rosa, 2021, p. 172).

Starting from "networks," "communications," or "practices" as the basic unit of the social, the theories depart from the face-to-face *topos* of conventional social theories, which demonstrably makes them suitable with the study of digitalized socialites. Furthermore, all three approaches present an attempt to overcome the classical "micro-macro" duality in social theory by proposing a basic unit in which structural as well as agentic processes are believed to be synthesized (Schäfer, 2016, p. 11; Callon, 1995, p. 60; Luhmann, 1995, p. 393). The logics of the different micro and macro processes are collapsed into one category, for example, those of "practice" or "communication" (see Archer, 2009, p. 82). To bridge this binary divide, the subjective experience is expelled from the analytical framework altogether. Precisely the departure from face-to-face experience as the starting point of the analysis of sociality allows these theories to turn to digitalized phenomena such as "computer networks" (Knorr Cetina, 1995, p. 145).

---

[5] The most prominent applications of Luhmann's theory to digitalization on the level of theory of society can be found in Armin Nassehi's (2019) and Dirk Baecker's (2017) approaches.

However, at the same time, the baby is thrown out with the bathwater. In all three approaches, the category of subjective experience is factored out: Actors are reduced to mere "carriers" of communication or practices (Archer, 2009, p. 245; Reckwitz, 2002, p. 256) and *experience*—for example, the experienced difference between meeting someone face-to-face or on screen—is neglected. Also, the subjective point of view of actors is analytically suspended; therefore, digitalized interactions appear qualitatively indistinguishable from their non-digitalized counterparts. Accordingly, an analysis of the specific qualities and phenomenality of digitalization is dismissed. Digitalization appears just as a continuation of other practices of communication, while from an analytical perspective its specific qualities remain intangible. Yet, the fundamental transformations of the actor's world-relations, captured in concepts such as "space-time-compression" (Harvey, 1989, p. 147) or the "acceleration of the tempo of life" (Rosa, 2013, p. 78), point to an analysis of the subjective point of view and hence a "non-conflationist"[6] methodological framework.

In contrast, Alfred Schutz's phenomenologically founded social theory offers a framework that allows for a close description of precisely these transformations starting with the analysis of experience from the first-person perspective (Dreher, 2021, p. 353; Eberle & Srubar, 2010; Eberle, 1999). In this respect, I argue that Schutz offers a starting point for "non-conflationist" theorizing that can be fruitfully extended to a theory of digitalization. This is due to two reasons: (a) His methodological position allows for an adequate description of the experience and specific phenomenality of digitalized phenomena on a micro-level. Furthermore, (b) on a macro-oriented level, his work offers a heuristic to describe the transformation of the structure of the social world imposed by digitalization. In the next sections, I systematically sketch Schutz's contribution to a theory of digitalization, starting with his methodological claims for a phenomenologically based inquiry of the social.

4   SCHUTZ'S INSISTENCE ON THE IMPORTANCE OF THE SUBJECTIVE POINT OF VIEW FOR AN ADEQUATE STUDY OF THE SOCIAL

Schutz's project of providing a systematic foundation for the social sciences has its prominent point of departure in Max Weber's conception of the social sciences as a discipline that is concerned with the interpretation of the meaning

[6] Margret Archer criticizes conventional social theories for suffering from "analytical conflation." She argues that most social theories tend to neglect the qualities of either the structural level ("upward-conflation"), the agentic level ("downward-conflation"), or both in the definition of one through the other ("central-conflation," Archer, 2009, p. 87). In contrast, Archer proposes an "analytical dualism" in which a duality between agency and structure is sustained (p. 245). Even though she does not discuss Luhmann's System Theory, she argues that "the bottom line [for downward-conflation] is always that actors may be indispensable for energizing the social system (no people: no society) but it is not they whose actions give it direction by shaping structural properties" (p. 81).

(*Verstehen*) of social action (Weber, 1978, p. 7; Schutz, 1972, p. 25; Eberle & Srubar, 2010, p. 17). More specifically, Schutz aims to clarify Weber's program, especially his conceptualization of "meaning." For this, Schutz turns to the phenomenological method established by Edmund Husserl to formalize the general processes by which actors sort their everyday experiences and navigate the social world (Schutz & Luckmann, 1974, p. 3; Schutz, 1972, pp. 12–13). Schutz aims to excavate the different layers of how meaning is constituted and understood and he commences this endeavor with a thorough examination of the structures of the experience of the *everyday* world (Schutz, 1962, p. 3; Eberle, 2012, p. 282).[7] For Schutz, the subjective point of view, however, is not only the point of departure of a descriptive analysis of the social, but it also functions as an ethical vanishing point in his work (Barber, 1991; Gros, 2020; Eberle, 1999, p. 82). Schutz's methodological stance hence seems beneficial to both, an adequate description and a modest evaluation of digitalization.

To start with the former, Schutz argues in a Husserlian manner that the structure of the social world can only be analyzed adequately by starting from the actors' point of view (Schutz, 2011, pp. 21, 25; Schutz & Luckmann, 1974, p. 3). As posited in his "postulate of subjective interpretation," "[s]uch an analysis refers by necessity to the *subjective point of view*, namely, to the interpretation of the action and its settings in terms of the actor" (Schutz, 1962, p. 34, m. e.). Without a close and precise analysis of the subjective point of view, the analysis of the *meaningful* constitution of the social world remains intangible as Schutz argues (Schutz, 1976, p. 16). Accordingly, the decisive task of the social sciences lies precisely in uncovering and specifying the processes by which meaning is constituted and attributed to action. Schutz understands the issue of "dealing with subjective phenomena in objective terms" (Schutz, 2011, p. 26) as *the* methodological task for the social sciences.

Furthermore, while Schutz seems to reject strong normative claims and adopts a Weberian position of "social scientific value neutrality" (Barber, 1991, p. 137), he not only explicitly contributes to *research ethical* considerations by identifying and evaluating specific standards for appropriate and reasonable social inquiry (Schutz, 1962, p. 43; Eberle, 1999, p. 72). Moreover, as Michael Barber argues, an implicit ethical vanishing point can be found in Schutz's work, centering around the normative claim of the adequate recognition of "the subjective viewpoint" (Barber, 1991, p. 135). In fact, Schutz argues that a violation of the "subjective viewpoint" in objectification is the root of discrimination, constituting a "moral wrongness" (Schutz, 1976, p. 228), not of not being identical to a self-description but because of not being "*sensitive* to the subjective viewpoint of the Other" (Barber, 1991, p. 135). This "criticism of the 'reification' of the other" (Gros, 2020, p. 16; Eberle, 1999, p. 82)

---

[7] Ultimately, Schutz's work reveals different layers of meaning, namely, (a) the meaning actors attribute to their own action, (b) the meaning that is attributed to an action by a fellow actor, and (c) the meaning attributed by a scientific observer (Eberle, 1999; Schutz, 1962, p. 24).

hence seems to serve as an ethical principle for Schutz's methodological considerations, which perhaps can be observed best in his "postulate of adequacy" (Schutz, 1962, p. 44), where he articulates that "safeguarding the subjective point of view is the only, but a sufficient, guarantee that social reality will not be replaced by a fictional non-existing world constructed by some scientific observer" (Schutz, 2011, p. 34). For Schutz, the subjective point of view serves as a "last point of reference" (Eberle, 1999, p. 82) which should prevent the social scientist from making the mistake of scientific reification.

Ultimately, Schutz's insistence on the subjective point of view as both the ineluctable methodological starting point of an inquiry of the social and an ethical vanishing point has inspired a broad theoretical tradition. I argue that it also proves fruitful for a study of digitalization, a phenomenon which is primarily analyzed through the lens of social theories that, as I have shown, tend to suspend the subjective point of view from their methodological framework.[8] In fact, his theoretical perspective is useful on at least three different levels: (a) His analysis begins by examining the fundamental structures of experience, allowing for a comprehensive understanding of the processes that underlie the formation of meaning in the (digitalized) everyday world. Additionally, (b) Schutz theoretical perspective facilitates an assessment of the transformation of social structures as they evolve in the course of digitalization. (c) Lastly, in his critique of reification he also offers a modest ethical yardstick for evaluating such transformations (Gros, 2020). In the following, I will start by outlining his contributions to a "micro"-analysis of digitalized experience.

5   SCHUTZ'S *MULTIPLE REALITIES* AS A CLASSIC FOR THE STUDY OF DIGITALIZATION

In his essay "On multiple realities" (Schutz, 1962 [1945]), Schutz provides an extensive set of tools for a description of realities of any kind that emerge in human experience. His theory is frequently consulted by scholars studying digitalized "virtual" phenomena, for example, the augmented realities of Smartphone Apps (Liberati, 2017), the immersive reality of videogames (Hardesty & Sheredos, 2019; Hardesty, 2016), or the simulative reality of video calls (Osler, 2021; Berger, 2020; Friesen, 2014). In a nutshell, Schutz offers a heuristic to describe, compare, and ultimately distinguish different realities or, more precisely, "provinces of meaning" (Schutz, 1962, p. 32).

In summary, Schutz addresses the classic sociological problem of the character of reality by recapitulating the mundane everyday experience of actors from their subjective point of view (Schutz, 1962, p. 257). He states that

---

[8] It is important to note that Schutz's work is not restricted to an analysis of subjective experience. He argues against a position that tries to reduce social emergence and hence all social phenomena to the effects of individual actions (Endreß, 2006, p. 69). This becomes evident in his analysis of the "we-relationship," "social groups" (Schutz, 1976), and institutional orders (Belvedere & Gros, 2019).

reality *in toto* exists in plural as it consists of different spheres of reality, such as dreams, play, or fantasy (Schutz, 1962, p. 234), and, most importantly, the "paramount reality" of the intersubjectively shared world of working (p. 233). Furthermore, Schutz insists that all these spheres carry a specific "accent of reality" defining their quality of realness (p. 230). Against this background, virtual, fantasy, or dream objects move onto the horizon of the analysis of the structure of the social world as "provinces of meaning" in which actors make meaningful experiences (p. 230). Consequently, reality is not an objectively ascertainable entity but, strictly following the phenomenological tradition, a *mode of relation* (p. 207; Schutz & Luckmann, 1974, p. 21) that is characterized by a "specific cognitive style" (Schutz, 1962, p. 230). (Multiple) realities, therefore, do not simply exist "out there" but are always dependent on the attitudes and the socio-cultural meanings actors (pre-reflexively) attribute to them (Schutz & Luckman, 1974, p. 5).

Schutz seems to turn to the Husserlian method of "eidetic reduction" (Schutz, 1962, p. 115) to excavate the specific structures of the provinces. More precisely, Schutz formalizes six different features to describe and classify realities of *any* kind: Taking the "paramount reality" of the world of working as the archetype of experience, he finds that all realities are characterized by a specific (1) tension of consciousness, (2) an *epoché*, (3) a form of spontaneity, (4) a form of self-experience, (5) a form of sociality, and (6) a time perspective (p. 230).[9] Importantly, Schutz argues that the intersubjectively shared everyday "world of working" builds the ground on which all other provinces are rooted and evaluated, which is why he assigns it the highest relevance: "The world of working in daily life is the archetype of our experience of reality. All the other provinces of meaning may be considered as its *modifications*" (p. 233. my emphasis).

In turn, all experiences made in other realities, including their specific socialities, are derivations of the *intersubjective* paramount reality that Schutz ideal-typically identifies with the "face-to-face" archetype. Here, he argues, the other is perceived in "vivid present" (p. 252). This vivid presence resembles Knorr Cetina's concept of "response presence" as it is not strictly bound to a spatio-temporal community. However, Schutz introduces a gradient to this concept, contending that while the experience of the other is not constitutively tied to spatial co-presence, it is nevertheless "fullest" at "its maximum" under such circumstances:

---

[9] The everyday world is characterized by the following features: (1) it is experienced in the wide-awake state (Schutz, 1962, p. 254); (2) in it, the doubt about the existence of the world is suspended (p. 229); (3) people are related to it in the specific action type of "working" (p. 215); (4) it is characterized by a specific form of self-experience whereby the self is split into an "I" (totality of the I) and "Me" (role-taker); and (5) it presupposes the undoubtedly intersubjective structure of the everyday and (6) the specific time structure of the intersection of the inner sense of time and the cosmic time as a "vivid presence" (p. 231).

It is clear that the extension of this field, even if communication occurs in vivid present, may vary considerably. It will reach its maximum if there exists between the partners community not only of time but also of space, that is, in the case of what sociologists call a face-to-face relation. (p. 220).

Accordingly, in Schutz's framework the ideal-typical intersubjective experience is modeled after the face-to-face archetype (p. 315). In *Multiple Realities*, he in fact provides a "horizontal" theory of differentiation distinguishing different "provinces" of meaning, for example, of fantasy, play, or science, that impose their own logic of spontaneity and experience (Schutz, 1962, p. 339). However, he does not assume that the different realities are experienced in the same way but in fact he argues that the experiences of the intersubjective realm, particularly of face-to-face interactions within the "world of working" are perceived as the most complete and significant. Hence, Schutz also offers a "vertical" theory of relevancies that shows in the straticfication of the different realms of experiences. Starting from the corporeal[10] subjective point of view of the everyday actor, Schutz's theory of multiple realities therefore contributes to a more nuanced social theoretical understanding of virtual phenomena: Firstly, in pointing to the "realness" of *virtual* experiences and, secondly, in highlighting the specific differences of the various experienced digitalized phenomenalities.

6   A Schutzian Analysis of the "Digitalized Presence" of Virtual Objects

Schutz provides a conceptual toolkit to analytically disentangle the different digital provinces of meaning: While playing videogames takes place in a specific "play world" (Schutz, 1962, p. 232), talking to my cousin on Skype may as well be considered as an "extension" of the everyday world (Dreher, 2021; Berger, 2020; Zhao, 2006). Although Schutz stresses that we do make experiences in different provinces of meaning in which we also meet others, for example, others we dream of or we imagine, he distances himself from a "postmodern" position in which no difference can be made between an "original" or real object and its replicas (Lyotard, 1984, p. 4). For Schutz as we have seen, the intersubjective everyday world builds the basis for all other provinces of meaning. The everyday world hence constitutes the "paramount reality" that makes it possible to differentiate between the "real" and the "quasi-real" in reflection (Schutz, 1962, p. 233).

Yet, does the experience of digitalized phenomena necessarily imply a "province of meaning" of its own? I argue that the specific structure of digitalized phenomena holds the possibility of both, the "immersion" into other

[10] Schutz understands the body as "the center '0' of a system of coordinates which determines certain dimensions of orientation in the surrounding field and the distances and perspectives of the objects therein" (Schutz, 1962, p. 307).

provinces and of a "simulation" of the everyday world, which is experienced as an extension thereof, for example, in video calls or online chats. As Gerd Sebald argues, digitalization constitutes a specific technique of the everyday world that, just like language or music, is characterized by (1) its pragmatic-instrumental "in-order-to" orientation, (2) its technical capacity of mediatization and translation, (3) a perceived quasi-alterity of digitalized objects, and (4) a "world-constituting" power, "capable of generating different forms of aesthetic, playful, or even discursive experience." (Sebald, 2021, pp. 394–396). Accordingly, what constitutes the specific virtual experience is not necessarily that it constitutes a disinct "province of meaning" but the predominant experience of digitalized re-presentations where others are re-presented as numbers, signs, or images, resulting in in an *indirect* form of re-presentation.

Husserl refers to these experiences with his concept of "signitive" or "pictoral consciousness" (HUA 19/646), where an absent object is intended through the re-presentation—*Vergegenwärtigung*—of another object, such as a sign or image (HUA 19/646).[11] The intended object is not present but re-presented indirectly through less and emptier symptoms (HUA 19/605). Through the process of digitalized mediatization, an absent object seems to be intended indirectly through the re-presentation of another digitalized object, that is, a sign or an image, for example, the expression of love through a heart emoji in text messages (Dreher, 2021, p. 361). Thus, the intended object is not "present," but instead, a digitized symbol re-presents and denotes an "absent" object indirectly with less and emptier symptoms (Schutz, 1962, p. 255; HUA 19/646). Accordingly, digitalized phenomena also seem to carry an inherent ambiguity, as they presuppose a continuous mediation between this mode of sign or image consciousness and the mode of perception (see Wiesing, 2018, p. 112).

Schutz's theory of signs based upon Husserl's perceptual theory of "appresentation" is hence relevant to clarify the specificities of digitalized experiences (Schutz, 1962, p. 294). Appresentation, in general, is a process always operative in perception, for example, when I perceive the other person and yet appresent their motives, history, intentions, and even the "back of their heads." Signitive appresentation, however, according to Schutz, "'wakens' or 'calls forth' the appresented element, it being immaterial whether one or the other is a perception, a recollection, a fantasm, or a fictum" (p. 297). Schutz understands signs and symbols as referring to "something other than itself" (p. 294). Signitive re-presentations of an object in the everyday world thus refer to the re-presentation of another object that is immaterial or at least not "vividly present." The re-presentation in this sense is indirect. This is also manifested in the different temporality that for example digitalized re-presentations show in

---

[11] Dan Zahavi concisely summarizes Husserl's concept as follows: "As Husserl states, all types of Ver-gegenwärtigung (re-presentation) are derivative acts that point back to an actual Gegenwärtigung (presentation) in which the object is given directly, originally, and ideally" (Zahavi, 2009, p. 29, my translation).

comparison to their non-digitalized "signifier": The profile picture I see of my friend on Whatsapp does not show signs of aging or exhaustion, and I can repeat my sister's audio-message endlessly (see Sebald, 2021, p. 388). In this sense, the digitalized re-presentation constitutes a "mathematical object" representing and simulating a sensual present one (Schutz, 1962, p. 298). Moreover, the digitalized re-presentation shows a "quasi"-vividness and richness of symptoms. For example, the "happy emoji" my friend sends me on Whatsapp is a picture of a yellow circle that I perceive sensorially. I tend to take the emoji as an indication of her feelings, as a "symptom" through which I apprehend the mood of my friend (p. 295). However, the accent of reality that one attributes to the digitalized re-presentations is an "as-if" accent differing from "seeing" her happiness "directly." Furthermore, the digitalized re-presentation needs "to be fulfilled by original experience" (p. 125): The image sent to me of my friend's dog on Whatsapp is passively coupled with my recollection of the real dog and hence serves as a re-presentation of the dog right now. However, the image of the dog is experienced differently from the dog's "full vividness" I perceive when it sits in front of me. The digitalized re-presentations in this sense show a "quasi"-vividness and richness of symptoms. Even if the video-re-presentation on a display changes and moves, the particularity of the experience remains one of pictorial or signitive consciousness (Schutz, 1962, p. 298).

On the other hand, while the dog and my sister seem to reside in the same province of the "world of working," seeing Enton on *Pokémon Go* on my phone immerses me into a different province of meaning, namely, the province of meaning of play (Schutz, 1962, p. 232). In this example, Enton in fact represents a specific order of appresentation that Schutz refers to as a "symbol." Symbols are experienced in the everyday world, yet they transcend the everyday world, referring to other "realities" or "provinces of meaning." While Enton symbolizes the world of play, the heart I sent to my brother transcends me and my brother's perspective pointing to the social relationship of sibling love (Schutz, 1962, p. 362). While symbols also function based on apprehension, they are more specific as they "are the means to communicate our experiences of other transcendent realities" (Dreher, 2003, p. 153). The digitalized re-presentation is characterized by signitive or pictorial consciousness, which denotes a distinction between the re-presentation in front of me, such as a video of puppies, and the intended object itself, such as the actual presence of puppies. The signs are intended as indirect manifestations, symptoms, or indication of the other, seemingly offering a "window" to look into their or other worlds (Wiesing, 2018, p. 99). Since the medium is however usually perceived as "transparent," for example, a smartphone displaying a photo, and the experience governed by a "relative irrelevance of the vehicle" (Schutz, 1962, p. 303), the complex structure of the underlying apprehension coupling and scheme is only revealed in the analysis in the tradition of Schutz. Moreover, while my sister seems to reside in the same province of the "world of working," when I see Enton on *Pokémon Go* on my phone, this immerses me into a different province of meaning, that is, the province of meaning of play (Schutz, 1962, p. 298). In this sense, Schutz's work seems fruitful for describing the experience of different virtual phenomena on a micro-level. Nonetheless, I will show how in his description of the "structures of the social world," Schutz alludes to macro-oriented mechanisms as well.

7   Schutz's Cartography of the Social World

In his analysis of the structures of the social world, Alfred Schutz demonstrates that the experience of not meeting everyone alive in person is not exclusive to modernity or even digitalization. Starting from the subjective point of view of the mundane everyday person (Schutz, 1962, 1972), he analyzes the social world within the brackets of the "natural attitude" (Schutz, 1972, p. 44, 69) in precisely the way in which it is experienced pre-reflexively, showing that it is from the outset a social, intersubjectively shared one that is inhabited by others who are not always physically present (p. 159). Schutz argues that the experience of others varies along the fundamental axis of time and space (p. 181). To be more specific, he classifies different "regions of the social world" (p. 105) that unfold around the "face-to-face" archetype of shared time and space, which constitutes the "point zero" and thus the center of the map of the social.

Schutz differentiates between four distinct spatio-temporal regions inhib-ited by different socialites, namely, (1) the "world of directly experienced social reality" (the *Umwelt*) "inhabited" by our consociates; (2) the "more distant worlds of contemporaries" (*Mitwelt*) surrounding the former; (3) the world of our "predecessors" (*Vorwelt*); and (4) that of our successors (*Folgewelt*) (p. 30). All four regions involve specific modes of experience; for example, we can expe-rience our predecessors in the re-presentation of a memory while we have immediate experiences of our consociates, who we perceive in their vivid pres-ence (p. 208). Schutz furthermore argues that the different regions also imply different orders of relevance: Those who share our same time and space, our consociates, tend to be at the center of our life-world (Schutz & Luckmann, 1974, p. 167). This world of "consociates" is ideal-typically structured by face-to-face relations, in which the *alter ego* appears in the "here and now" (see Berger & Luckmann, 1991, p. 36). In contrast, those who do not share the same space with us and who hence live in the "world of contemporaries," appear only within "potential reach" as they are only predictively experience-able through re-presentation.

Schutz uses the heuristic dichotomy between *Umwelt* and *Mitwelt* as two analytical poles to systematize the different possibilities of actualization and concretization of social relationships along the gradient of spatio-temporal co-presence. He emphasizes that the perception of another person as "fullest" is primarily associated with the ideal-typical face-to-face encounter, in which the other person is experienced in "vivid presence" (Schutz, 1972, p. 178). In contrast, the co-temporal relationship, while serving as the analytical counter-part to the face-to-face-archetype, only provides an indirect experience of a non-vivid, typified, and even solidified re-presentation of the other person (p. 197). While the former opens the possibility of a "we-relationship" (p. 183), the spatial absence implies a typified experience and rather inhibits the perception of the individuality and uniqueness of the other person (p. 185).

8   THE STRUCTURAL TRANSFORMATION OF THE REGIONS OF THE DIGITALIZED SOCIAL WORLD

Schutz discusses the possibility of close, intimate social "we-relationships" as an elementary component of the "mundane" everyday-(inter-)actions that occupy the central position in the life-world. Yet, he highlights the importance of another type for the structure of the (modern) social world: The typified, functional, and anonymous role-bound encounter of strangers in (semi-)public and institutional spaces (Schutz, 1972, p. 202; Schutz & Luckmann, 1974, p. 73), which seems to re-present the prototype of sociality in accelerated, urban, and "modern" societies (Gros, 2021). Here, not the "thou-orientation" of the we-relationships but the typified "they-orientation" is prevalent (Schutz, 1972, p. 183). Schutz thinks of such interactions, for example, between a postal clerk and a customer, as usually taking place in *spatial* co-presence (Schutz, 1972, p. 197). In *digital* societies, however, communication is not predominantly mediated by anonymous-functional encounters between role-takers but through the "digitalized" transmission of information, that is, by the logistics of mail operated by automates.

In fact, in digitalized societies the experience of spatially absent contemporaries who communicate through e-mail, for example, friends who live on different continents, seems to have become a mundane matter. A process that Anthony Giddens aptly subsumes under the concept of "disembeddedness" as he states that:

> The advent of modernity increasingly tears space away from place by fostering relations between "absent" others, locationally distant from any given situation of *face-to-face* interaction. That is to say, locales are thoroughly penetrated by and shaped in terms of social influences quite distant from them. (Giddens, 1990, p. 18f.)

As Giddens argues, the everyday environmental presence of the spatially and physically absent "contemporaries" who are mediated by digitalized re-presentation has shifted from being an exception to a regularity of the digitalized social world. In view of this, scholars have recently called for a fundamental revision of Schutz's cartography of the social (Zhao, 2006; Ollinaho, 2018; Dreher, 2021). Most prominently, Shanyang Zhao argues that the process of digitalization has given rise to a *new* region of the social world: Bordering between the "now and here" region of the *Umwelt*, and the "there and then" region of the *Mitwelt*, the region of the "now and there" (Zhao, 2006, p. 465) has emerged, inhabited by "consociated contemporaries"

(p. 464). The intersubjective interaction with them resembles the environmental face-to-face relationships (p. 466), blurring the lines between the "world within immediate" and "potential reach" (Ruh, 2021, p. 407). In the digitalized social world, the region of the *Umwelt* and that of the *Mitwelt* seem to have merged inseparably, extending the formerly "pragmatic orientation" that for Schutz characterizes the natural attitude of the mundane everyday social world (Schutz, 1962, p. 240) to spatially absents (Dreher, 2021, p. 354).

9   The Reconfiguration of the Digitalized Life-World

Nevertheless, even under the conditions of digitalization, others do not suddenly "materialize" in front of us. Rather, they become present through digitalized re-presentations: When I e-mail my work colleagues, *FaceTime* with my Torontonian family, and watch music videos of Wilco on *YouTube*, I experience others as *signitive* "representations." The digital re-presentation of others who appear within my "actual reach"—the radius of people with whom I can interact directly—expands to include those with whom I may not have had face-to-face contact, but with whom I can interact digitally and who subsequently shape my everyday life (see Berger, 2020, p. 17; Ollinaho, 2018; Zhao, 2006).

Digitalized communication allows for a direct impact on others, even when they "reside outside our physically accessible manipulative zone" (Dreher, 2021, p. 356), perhaps most drastically illustrated by modern drone warfare (see Malaviya, 2020). Moreover, also the rules and assumptions governing the experience of the everyday world that Schutz has excavated thoroughly seem to extend to the virtual realm: The pre-reflexive assumptions[12] that facilitate the reciprocal interactions of actors in the everyday world, starting from the observation that "in daily life, I take it for granted that intelligent fellow-men exist" (Schutz, 1962, p. 11), seem to be operative within the digitalized world as well (Ruh, 2021, p. 405). The governing principles of the everyday world, as the general thesis of the alter ego, seem to remain unaltered. Furthermore, also principles of "trustful interaction" derived from the face-to-face archetype of non-digitalized communication are still considered relevant (Ruh, 2021, p. 405). Accordingly, it can be argued that the digitalized everyday world is experienced as an integrated part of the everyday world, which, in this sense, seems extended to fit the world of "contemporary consociates" (Dreher, 2021, p. 355; Zhao, 2006, p. 460).

Nonetheless, within the context of Schutz's "*Umwelt/Mitwelt*" distinction, which serves as the ideal-typical poles of the social world, a notable disparity in experiential quality emerges depending on whether I chat with a person in physical proximity or through a digital interface. Schutz in fact discusses this liminal case using the example of the telephone:

---

[12] Furthermore, the common sense thinking of the daily life is based upon two "idealizations" that constitute the "general thesis" (Schutz, 1962, p. 12).

[I]magine a face-to-face conversation, followed by a telephone call, followed by an exchange of letters, and finally messages exchanged through a third party. Here too we have a gradual progression from the world of immediately experienced social reality to the world of contemporaries. In both examples the total number of the other person's reactions open to my observation is progressively diminished until it reaches a minimum point. It is clear, then, that the world of contemporaries is itself a variant function of the face-to-face situation. (Schutz, 1972, p. 177)

Schutz observes a "decreasing vividness" in the experience of another person bound to their mode of presence (p. 177), starting from the assumption that the face-to-face interaction opens up the possibility of the richest experience of the other. Schutz's assumption is that the experience I have of another person on the phone is "emptier" (p. 58) than the one I have when we meet face-to-face, where I can almost immediately sense their sorrows, see their worries, etc.

Furthermore, also the taken-for-granted assumptions governing such interactions seem slightly modified: While in the everyday world, the "*epoché* of the natural attitude" suspends the doubt in the reality of the world (Schutz, 1962, p. 233), and "it is only on special occasions, if at all, that a serious doubt arises" (p. XXVI), similar governing rules seem to serve as a yardstick in the virtual world. However, these principles do not simply expand or generalize:

When we send an e-mail or a text message to a friend, we take for granted that the modalities of our communication are somewhat similar to a face-to-face encounter: we assume that the recipient of our communication is actually the person we intend him or her to be. (Ruh, 2021, p. 405)

Accordingly, the *digitalized epoché* of the "virtual attitude" entails a suspension of the doubt of the non-identity of re-presented sign and the appresented signifier. For instance, I assume that the picture I see on a dating platform represents the picture of a real person. In this sense, the "virtual attitude" seems to operate on the complex assumption that "people act as if they and their digitalized representations were identical." As discussed above, the digitalized presence seems to oscillate between the mode of signitive or image consciousness and the mode of perception and it is because of the *indirect* re-presentation that the "as-if reality" is "wakened" (Schutz, 1962, p. 238) that in experience manifests itself in a higher notion of doubt and "ontological insecurity" (Ruh, 2021, p. 404).

Moreover, the experience of the other through re-presentation also exhibits a higher degree of typification, abstraction, and standardization (Schutz, 1962, p. 323). In this sense, the everyday world of digitalized societies seems to a higher degree permeated by *typified* encounters. Schutz discusses the implications of the increased typification in the pragmatic everyday attitude in his concept of the "they-orientation" (p. 202). He observes that in the increasingly anonymized (modern) world, the "thou-orientation" is successively replaced by a "they-orientation" (p. 202). Assessing this transformation, he states: "An element of doubt enters into every such relationship [...] I am not therefore apprehended by my partner in the They-relationship as a real living person" (p. 202).

This rise of doubt seems amplified in digitalized societies. The "emptier" experiences of others as re-presentations explain not only the "notion of doubt" that people experience online but also the emergence of new types of "negative" socialites (Illouz, 2018, p. 329) and digital phenomena such as "ghosting," "catfishing," or "hate speech." From a Schutzian perspective, these phenomena can be analyzed as a form of disregard of another person, yet not because of the ill will of a person but as a structural dynamic that occurs because of the *mode* of digital re-presentation that accentuates the typicality of a person: He is just another profile on *Tinder*, rather than a singular person present to me in their vividness. To emphasize, in a study on ghosting, an interviewee reported: "I don't owe the other person an explanation given that I did not meet this person face-to-face" (Timmermans et al., 2021, p. 792). What is indicated here is that the relevance of the face-to-face archetype of the everyday world yet seems persistent, as people who are not met face-to-face are considered less relevant. Against this background, the digitalized social world does not simply seem extended but fundamentally reconfigured.

10   Conclusion: The "Waste Land" of the Digitalized Late-Modern Life-World[13]

Digitalization seems to have fundamentally transformed the structure of the social world as people increasingly perceive digitalized re-presentations that either simulate "consociate others" or serve as an immersion into other provinces of meaning. Moreover, also a tendency toward an increasing "typification," "ontological insecurity," and "communicative intransparency" seems detectable (Ruh, 2021; Illouz, 2018, p. 68). Ruh notes that for the digitalized social "mathematics functions as a basic reality test that creates an isolated sphere of clarity and provability" (Ruh, 2021, p. 411). As the world is increasingly pervaded by "mathematical objects" intended to provide orientation (*Google Maps, Wikipedia*) and practical and technical domination over the world (weather apps, timers, tracking), the province of meaning of the exact, positivistic sciences seems to have become increasingly relevant for orientation in the everyday world. In this sense, the pressures imposed by the self-evident and self-referential digitalized mechanisms, rooted in the "mathematical idealization" of an objective, causal, and naturalistic model of the world (Husserl, 1996, §9), seem to yield "imposed relevances beyond our control" (Schutz,

---

[13] Schutz discusses T.S. Eliot's famous poem "Waste Land" in his lecture on Eliot's Theory of Culture in 1950, outlining the modern "sterility of a society without faith" (Schutz, 2011, p. 275).

1976, p. 129), invoking pressures of quantification and (self)-optimization (King et al. 2021, p. 151), while at the same time they offer a seemingly valid "reality test" warranting an "ontological security" for the digitalized sphere in moments of doubt (Ruh, 2021, p. 414). Actors increasingly seem to turn to the delocalized "positive" and "*technical* knowledge" of scientifically modeled abstractions of experiences that "can be dissected into isolated facts, rules, instructions, or maxims" (Großheim, 2010, p. 55) and hence easily quantified, compared, and digitalized, readily accessible on Google, Wikipedia, Reddit, etc., in order to acquire orientation. The imposed relevancies of the scientific province of meaning amplified through digitalization hence tend to disqualify lived experience as a source for orientational knowledge. Furthermore, technical knowledge seems to serve as legitimate knowledge used to ratify and evaluate the reality and validity of experiences—for example, people googling whether they are sick or weigh too much. Ultimately, the cause of the experienced "shrinkage" or "compression" of time and space (Rosa, 2013, p. 72) may not solely originate from the digital expansion of the "world within reach" but also conceivably in the homogenization of diverse experiences and leveling of multitudes of meaning, which result from the "colonization" of the finite province of meaning of the positive sciences (i.e., a translation into data, numbers, or causalities). Thus, the process of digitalization appears to transform the once-diverse "multiple realities" into a homogenized, digitalized "modern wasteland."

References

Archer, M. S. (2009). *Realist social theory. The morphogenetic approach.* Cambridge University Press.

Baecker, D. (2017). Wie verändert die Digitalisierung unser Denken und unseren Umgang mit der Welt? In R. Gläß & B. Leukert (Eds.), *Handel 4.0* (pp. 3–24). Springer.

Barber, M. (1991). The ethics behind the absence of ethics in Alfred Schutz's thought. *Human Studies, 2/3*(14), 129–140.

Belvedere, C., & Gros, A. (2019). The phenomenology of social institutions in the Schutzian tradition. *Schutzian Research, 11*, 43–74.

Berger, P. L., & Luckmann, T. (1991). *The social construction of reality. A treatise in the sociology of knowledge.* Penguin.

Berger, V. (2020). Phenomenology of online spaces: Interpreting late modern spatialities. *Human Studies, 43*, 603–626.

Blau, P. M. (1987). Contrasting theoretical perspectives. In J. C. Alexander, B. Giesen, R. Münch, & N. J. Smelser (Eds.), *The micro-macro link* (pp. 71–85). University of California Press.

Callon, M. (1995). Four models for the dynamics of science. In S. Jasanoff (Ed.), *Handbook of science and technology studies* (pp. 29–63). SAGE Publications, Inc.

Callon, M., & Latour, B. (1992). Don't throw the baby out with the bath school! A reply to Collins and Yearley. In A. Pickering (Ed.), *Science as practice and culture* (pp. 343–368). Univ. of Chicago Press.

Dreher, J. (2021). Überlegungen zu einer Phänomenologie der digitalen Welt. In J. Dreher (Ed.), *Mathesis universalis—Die aktuelle Relevanz der „Strukturen der Lebenswelt"* (pp. 349–370). Springer Fachmedien Wiesbaden.

Dreher, J. (2003). The symbol and the theory of the life-world: "The transcendences of the life-world and their overcoming by signs and symbols". *Human Studies, 26*(2), 141–163.

Eberle, T. S., & Srubar, I. (2010). Einleitung. In A. Schütz, T. S. Eberle, M. Walter, & R. Grathoff (Eds.), *Zur Methodologie der Sozialwissenschaften* (pp. 9–44) (Alfred-Schütz-Werkausgabe/hrsg. von Richard Grathoff, Bd. 4). UVK Verl.-Ges.

Eberle, T. S. (1999). Die methodologische Grundlegung der interpretativen Sozialforschung durch die phänomenologische Lebensweltanalyse von Alfred Schütz. *Österreichische Zeitschrift für Soziologie, 24*(4), 65–90.

Eberle, T. S. (2012). Phenomenological life-world analysis and ethnomethodology's program. *Human Studies, 35*(2), 279–304.

Edge, D. (1995). Reinventing the wheel. In S. Jasanoff (Ed.), *Handbook of science and technology studies* (pp. 3–23). SAGE Publications, Inc.

Endreß, M. (2006). *Alfred Schütz* (Klassiker der Wissenssoziologie) (Vol. 3). UVK.

Friesen, N. (2014). Telepresence and tele-absence: a phenomenology of the (in)visible alien online. *Phenomenology & Practice, 8*(1), 17–31.

Gertenbach, L., & Laux, H. (2019). *Zur Aktualität von Bruno Latour*. Springer Fachmedien Wiesbaden.

Giddens, A. (1990). *The consequences of modernity*. Repr. Polity Press (67).

Giere, R. N. (2008). Cognitive studies of science and technology. In E. J. Hackett (Ed.), *The handbook of science and technology studies* (pp. 259–278). MIT Press.

Goffman, E. (1981). *Forms of talk*. University of Pennsylvania Press.

Greshoff, R. (1999). *Die theoretischen Konzeptionen des Sozialen von Max Weber und Niklas Luhmann im Vergleich*. VS Springer.

Gros, A. (2021). Die Beschleunigung der Lebenswelt: Alfred Schütz' Beiträge zu einer Phänomenologie der spätmodernen Weltbeziehung. In J. Dreher (Ed.), *Mathesis universalis—Die aktuelle Relevanz der „Strukturen der Lebenswelt"* (pp. 291–316). Springer Fachmedien Wiesbaden.

Gros, A. (2020). The reification of the other as a social pathology. *Schutzian Research, 12*, 13–44.

Großheim, M. (2010). Von der Maigret-Kultur zur Sherlock Holmes-Kultur. Oder: Der phänomenologische Situationsbegriff als Grundlage einer Kulturkritik. In M. Großheim (Ed.), *Phänomenologie und Kulturkritik. Über die Grenzen der Quantifizierung* (Neue Phänomenologie) (Vol. 15, pp. 52–84). Orig.-Ausg, Alber.

Hardesty, R. A. (2016). Living-into, living: A Schutzian account of the player/character relationship. *Glimpse, 17*, 27–34.

Hardesty, R. A., & Sheredos, B. (2019). Being together, worlds apart: A virtual-worldly phenomenology. *Human Studies, 42*(3), 343–370.

Harvey, D. (1989). *The condition of postmodernity. An enquiry into the origins of cultural change*. 1. publ. Blackwell.

Heintz, B. (2014). *Die Unverzichtbarkeit von Anwesenheit. Zur weltgesellschaftlichen Bedeutung globaler Interaktionssysteme/Personal encounters. The indispensability of face-to-face interaction at the global level*. De Gruyter.

Held, T. (2019). Face to Face Sozio-interaktive Potentiale der Videotelefonie. *Journal für Medienlinguistik, 2*(2), 157–194.

Husserl, E. (1996). *Die Krisis der europäischen Wissenschaften und die transzendentale Phänomenologie. Eine Einleitung in die phänomenologische Philosophie* (Philosophische Bibliothek, Vol. 292, 3. Aufl). Meiner.

Illouz, E. (2018). *Warum Liebe endet: Eine Soziologie negativer Beziehungen.* Suhrkamp.

Joas, H. (2017). *Die Macht des Heiligen. Eine Alternative zur Geschichte von der Entzauberung* (2. Auflage ed.). Suhrkamp.

King, V., & Gerisch, B., & Rosa, H. (Eds.). (2021). *Lost in perfection. Zur Optimierung von Gesellschaft und Psyche.* Suhrkamp.

Knoblauch, H. (2008). Sinnformen und Wissenstypen Soziologie des Wissens und der Kommunikation. In H. Willems (Ed.), *Lehr(er)buch Soziologie* (pp. 131–147). VS Verlag für Sozialwissenschaften.

Knoblauch, H. (2017). *Die kommunikative Konstruktion der Wirklichkeit.* Springer Fachmedien.

Knorr Cetina, K. (1995). Laboratory studies. The cultural approach to the study of science. In S. Jasanoff (Ed.), *Handbook of science and technology studies* (pp. 140–166). SAGE Publications, Inc.

Knorr Cetina, K. (2009). The synthetic situation: Interactionism for a global world. *Symbolic Interaction, 32*(1), 61–87.

Latour, B. (2005). *Reassembling the social. An introduction to actor-network-theory.* 1. publ. Oxford University Press.

Laube, S. (2016). Goffman mediatisieren. Über das Zusammenspiel von Vorder- und Hinterbühnein digitalisierten Praktiken. In H. Schäfer (Ed.), *Praxistheorie. Ein soziologisches Forschungsprogramm* (pp. 285–300). transcript (Sozialtheorie).

Liberati, N. (2017). Phenomenology, pokémon go, and other augmented reality games a study of a life among digital objects. *Human Studies, 41*(2), 211–232.

Lievrouw, L. A., & Loader, B. D. (2020). *Routledge handbook of digital media and communication.* Routledge.

Lindemann, G. (2009). *Das Soziale von seinen Grenzen her denken* (1. Auflage ed.). Velbrück Wissenschaft.

Luhmann, N. (1995). *Social systems. Unter Mitarbeit von Eva M. Knodt.* Stanford University Press.

Luhmann, N. (2012): *Theory of society* (Vol. 1). Unter Mitarbeit von Rhodes Barrett. Stanford University Press.

Lyotard, J. F. (1984). *The postmodern condition. A report on knowledge* (Vol. 10). University of Minnesota Press.

Malaviya, S. (2020). Digitising the virtual. Movement and relations in drone warfare. *Millennium, 49*, 80–104.

Mead, G. H. (2013). *Mind, self, and society.* University of Chicago Press.

Nassehi, A. (2019). *Muster. Theorie der digitalen Gesellschaft.* C.H. Beck.

Neuberger, C. (2017). Soziale Medien und Journalismus. In J.-H. Schmidt & M. Taddicken (Eds.), *Handbuch soziale Medien* (pp. 101–127). Springer VS.

Ollinaho, O. I. (2018). Virtualization of the life-world. *Human Studies, 41*(2), 193–209.

Osler, L. (2021). Taking empathy online. *Inquiry (United Kingdom),* 1–37. https://www.tandfonline.com/doi/citedby/10.1080/0020174X.2021.1899045?scroll=top&needAccess=true&role=tab&aria-labelledby=cit

Preda, A. (2008). STS and social studies of finance. In E. J. Hackett (Ed.), *The handbook of science and technology studies* (pp. 901–920). MIT Press.

Prinz, S. (2016). Dispositive und Dinggestalten. Poststrukturalistische und phänomenologische Grundlagen einer Praxistheorie des Sehens. In H. Schäfer (Ed.),

Praxistheorie. Ein soziologisches Forschungsprogramm (pp. 181–198). transcript (Sozialtheorie).

Reckwitz, A. (2002). Toward a theory of social practices a development in culturalist theorizing. *European Journal of Social Theory, 5*(2), 243–263.

Reckwitz, A. (2016). Praktiken und ihre Affekte. In H. Schäfer (Ed.), *Praxistheorie. Ein soziologisches Forschungsprogramm* (pp. 163–180). transcript (Sozialtheorie).

Reckwitz, A. (2017). *Die Gesellschaft der Singularitäten. Zum Strukturwandel der Moderne.* Suhrkamp.

Reckwitz, A. & Rosa, H. (2021). Spätmoderne in der Krise. Was leistet die Gesellschaftstheorie? Suhrkamp.

Rosa, H. (2013). *Social acceleration. A new theory of modernity* (Vol. 148). Columbia University Press.

Ruh, N. (2021). "The Universe Believes in Encryption"—Implementing math into the ontological layer of the digitally augmented life-world. In J. Dreher (Ed.), *Mathesis universalis—Die aktuelle Relevanz der „Strukturen der Lebenswelt"* (pp. 399–426). Springer Fachmedien Wiesbaden.

Schäfer, H. (2016). *Praxistheorie. Ein soziologisches Forschungsprogramm.* transcript.

Schatzki, T. R., Knorr-Cetina, K., & Savigny, E. von. (2001). *The practice turn in contemporary theory.* Routledge (44).

Schatzki, T. R. (2016). Praxistheorie als flache Ontologie. In H. Schäfer (Ed.), *Praxistheorie. Ein soziologisches Forschungsprogramm* (pp. 29–44). transcript (Sozialtheorie).

Schutz, A. (1962). *Collected papers. Volume I: The problem of social reality* (M. Natanson, Ed.). Martinus Nijhoff (I).

Schutz, A. (1972). *The phenomenology of the social world* (1st paperback ed.). Northwestern University Press (Northwestern University Studies in Phenomenology & Existential Philosophy).

Schutz, A. (1976). *Collected papers II. Studies in social theory* (Phaenomenologica Ser, vol. 15). Ebook (A. Brodersen, F. Kersten und A. Schimmelpenninck, Ed.). Springer.

Schutz, A. (2011). *Collected papers V phenomenology and the social sciences* (L. Embree, Ed.). Springer.

Schutz, A., & Luckmann, T. (1974). *The structures of life-world.* Heinemann.

Sebald, G. (2021). Software als Mathesis universalis der Lebenswelt? Zur begrifflichen Fassung der softwareförmigen Technisierung der Lebenswelt. In J. Dreher (Ed.), *Mathesis universalis—Die aktuelle Relevanz der „Strukturen der Lebenswelt"* (pp. 385–398). Springer Fachmedien Wiesbaden.

Seeliger, M., Sevignani, S. (Eds.) (2021). *Ein neuer Strukturwandel der Öffentlichkeit?* Nomos Verlagsgesellschaft. 1. Auflage. Leviathan, Sonderband 37. Baden-Baden: Nomos.

Simmel, G., Blasi, A. J., Jacobs, A. K.; Kanjirathinkal, M. J. (Eds.) (2009). *Sociology. Inquiries into the construction of social forms* (K. H. Wolff, Ed.). Brill.

Stock, J. (2011). Eine Maschine wird Mensch? Von der Notwendigkeit, Technik als integralen Bestandteil sozialer Praktiken zu akzeptieren—Ein Theorie-Report. Working Paper TUTS-WP-2-2011. Technical University Technology Studies.

Suchman, L. (2008). Feminist STS and the Sciences of the Artificial. In E. J. Hackett (Ed.), *The handbook of science and technology studies* (pp. 139–163). MIT Press.

Timmermans, E., Hermans, A.-M., & Opree, S. J. (2021). Gone with the wind: Exploring mobile daters' ghosting experiences. *Journal of Social and Personal Relationships, 38*(2), 783–801.

Weber, M. (1978). *Max Weber: Selections in translation* (v. W. G. Runciman, Ed.). Cambridge University Press.

Werron, T. (2016). Gleichzeitigkeit unter Abwesenden Zu Globalisierungseffekten elektrischer Telekommunikationstechnologien/Simultaneity across distance. On globalization effects of telecommunication technologies. In B. Heintz & H. Tyrell (Eds.), *Interaktion—Organisation—Gesellschaft revisited: Anwendungen, Erweiterungen* (pp. 251–270). Alternativen. De Gruyter.

Wiesing, L. (2018). *Artifizielle Präsenz. Studien zur Philosophie des Bildes* (5 Auflage). Suhrkamp.

Zahavi, D. (2009). *Husserls Phänomenologie.* Deutsche Ü. Mohr Siebeck: UTB.

Zhao, S. (2006). Everyday life: Toward a new analytic stance in sociology. *Sociological Inquiry, 76*(4), 458–474.

PART VIII

Social Classes and Sociomaterial Structures

Doing Phenomenology on Social Classes: Theoretical and Methodological Challenges and Possibilities

Mercedes Krause

Within the field of class analysis, quantitative and qualitative lines of research can be identified, each of them having their own interests and traditions. Statistical analysis, on the one hand, focuses on the transformation and reproduction of class structure, occupational structure, the basis of social class recruitment, monogamy/heterogamy, life conditions, and the possibilities of intra- and intergenerational mobility in relation to the economic-social development model of that space and time. Qualitative research, on the other hand, analyzes the historical and everyday constitution of social classes and class relations, the effective ways in which actors define and practice their class membership, their culture, their political struggles, their life strategies and lifestyles, among others.

Mercedes Krause holds a PhD in Social Sciences from the University of Buenos Aires (UBA), Argentina. She is a researcher at Instituto de Investigaciones Gino Germani (IIGG-UBA) and at Centro de Estudios de Estado y Sociedad (CEDES). She is also Assistant Professor of Research Methods. Her areas of interest include social phenomenology, class analysis, intersectionality and health inequalities.

M. Krause (✉)
Faculty of Social Sciences, Instituto de Investigaciones Gino Germani, University of Buenos Aires, Buenos Aires, Argentina

Centro de Estudios de Estado y Sociedad, Buenos Aires, Argentina

Although quantitative research does transcend the actual occupants of different class positions, cultural and meaning dimensions must always be defined with reference to specific families and subjects, along with their practices and concrete ways of life. Therefore, quantitative research is usually associated with macro-sociology and qualitative research is related to the micro-sociological study of social classes. This schematization can prove very useful in order to organize the field of class analysis and locate oneself within it.

However, is this link necessarily right? At first glance, this seems to imply an antinomy between two major research paradigms, which is typically associated with the fundamental polarization between structure-agent and a certain scale of phenomena of concern.

The aim of this chapter is to show what social phenomenology can offer to the study of social classes, not only in comparison to quantitative research but also as a distinctive approach within qualitative research which attends to the motivations and (inter-)subjective elaborations of the actors involved in macro-social phenomena. Social classes constitute real entities whose origin lies in a system of economic production which is based on exploitation and domination (Wright, 2015). However, social relations and groups are objectified and made effective along with their symbolic worlds (Dreher, 2012, p. 111). In order to understand their reproduction and sustainability over time, it is advisable to address the study of how their objectivity is legitimized and reaffirmed in everyday life, that is, how social classes are lived. This is a fertile ground for social phenomenology.

I will illustrate this theoretical-methodological proposal by referring to my own PhD research (Krause, 2016), which is found along the line of analysis that reinstates the role of social classes—and cultural class differences—as a basic form of social inequality (Crompton et al., 2000; Wright, 2015). Moreover, the research I have carried out links the constitution of meanings and everyday practices to the construction of social relations of inequality, so as to particularly address the study of how social class is experienced in the everyday life of families living in the Metropolitan Area of Buenos Aires between 2009 and 2015 and having trajectories of reproduction within the same social class.

Choosing social phenomenology as a relevant approach to class analysis can provide us with a new outlook on a problem that has been extensively studied from other perspectives. But, it also entails a dual challenge. On the one hand, it involves an important theoretical articulation, considering the fact that the issues of social classes and class culture have been scarcely dealt with by the phenomenological tradition. On the other hand, it poses the methodological challenge of conducting empirical research from a phenomenological perspective, bearing in mind that—with the exception of the health sciences—this approach has mainly been developed through theoretical research. Back in 1945, Schutz himself acknowledged that social scientists considered phenomenology to be some sort of metaphysics that disregarded empirical facts and was rendered inaccessible because of its language (Schutz, 2003a,

p. 111). Consequently, those of us interested in empirical social research from a phenomenological perspective have not only to become acquainted with broader philosophical issues and their ontological and epistemological assumptions but also to endure a rather hostile atmosphere for sociologists trying to explore empirical forms of research within a context of heated theoretical and methodological discussions regarding what is—and what is not—phenomenology[1].

Within phenomenological scholarship, there seems to be no consensus on "the best way to practice, use and apply phenomenology in a non-philosophical context" (Zahavi, 2020. p. 1). This poses a challenge in terms of uncertainty and controversy which makes this field difficult for social science novices to access (Finlay, 2012, p. 17).

In the following sections of this chapter, I will first relate the social phenomenology of Alfred Schutz and his successors to class analysis. Next, I will review some challenges and possibilities regarding the use and practice of social phenomenology in empirical research. Then, I will proceed to identify the class analysis dimensions on which social phenomenological approach could shed light. Finally, I will synthesize my position by arguing that these guidelines do not necessarily represent a micro-social analysis.

1   Phenomenology and Social Classes

The phenomenological perspective is rooted in the work of Edmund Husserl, who believed that logical systems had somehow flattened our understanding of human life and caused a crisis in the sciences. The science of phenomena arises when Husserl advocates a return to the things themselves and shows that lifeworld is the ground of all concepts, including those belonging to the most abstract and formalized sciences (Belvedere, 2012, p. 109).

Thus, phenomenology concerns "the degree of 'fit' between the world and our concepts about the world" (Breiger, 1995, p. 117). It focuses on the intersection between consciousness and the world—or, rather, between thought and what is being thought of—on the assumption that neither of these entities can be understood separately (Belvedere, 2012; Giorgi, 1994; Zahavi, 2020).

Phenomenology deals with the world *as-it-is-experienced* by the different social actors, considering aspects that are implicit and that are given to us as part of our perception of the world in which we live (Bevan, 2014, p. 136). The concept of lifeworld [*Lebenswelt*] emphasizes precisely that social reality should not be conceived as something fixed and external but rather as a world of experiences lived through the individual's corporeality as the zero-point of orientation. Phenomenology draws our attention to one's normal and effortless

---

[1] See, for example, the contributions published in successive volumes of *Qualitative Health Research* (2017, 2018 and 2019).

way of being-in-the-world and argues that, in our natural attitude, reality is taken for granted.

Since 1900 phenomenology has spread from Germany to the rest of the world and has migrated from philosophy into "more than twenty" disciplines (Embree, 2007, p. 12). It has become an approach that contains multiple perspectives within: realist, constitutive, existential, hermeneutic and culture phenomenology, among others. Social phenomenology—also called worldly phenomenology—is the closest version to sociology and was developed by Alfred Schutz and his successors, in dialogue with the hegemonic structural functionalism of the time (Eberle, 2014).

In contrast to Husserl's phenomenology, social phenomenology does not delve into transcendental or pure (i.e., ontologically neutral) consciousness but rather into the phenomena of mundane intersubjectivity (Dreher, 2012, p. 117). For Schutz, therefore, natural attitude should not be "disconnected" from reflective activity but rather become the primary object of study (Motta, 2018, p. 132). Social phenomenology seeks to deal, concisely, with the (inter-) subjective perspective of actors in their everyday life, that is, in their natural attitude (Schutz, 2003a). It enables us to find the *essence* [*Wesen*] of the lived experiences shared by the members of a society or social group (Patton, 2001) by addressing people's socio-cultural a priori—their stock of knowledge, typifications and relevance structures—and by describing how, in different historical periods and in different situations, different things are taken for granted (Motta, 2018, p. 130).

Thus, Schutz's phenomenology constitutes a stream within phenomenology that places greater emphasis on the intersubjective and socio-cultural nature of the lifeworld and on the temporal and spatial aspects of experience and social relations giving rise to common beliefs, attitudes and forms of behavior. Schutz relates this social inheritance of meaningful typifications to Scheler's concept of *relative natural view of the world* [*relativ natürliche Weltanschauung*] and Sumner's *folkways* (Schutz, 2003a, p. 43).

Schutz furthermore highlights the importance of the biographically determined situation and the systems of relevance for the definition of one's own perspective on the social world (Schutz, 2003a). In this regard, individuals do not perceive all aspects of reality, but "only apprehend and interpret the aspects of reality that appear as relevant in a specific context, to a specific goal, from a specific biographical situation" (Santos & Susin, 2021, p. 53).

This is how the coordination between experience, knowledge and action, and—ultimately—the meaningful construction of reality is regulated (Dreher, 2012, p. 107). That is to say that individuals define their circumstances, typify their problems at hand, choose solutions and take different courses of action on the basis of what they consider significant or *relevant*. And this applies to both day-to-day plans and long-term life courses.

However, all these fundamental conditions for the life of the individuals are not presented to them as objective data to be confronted. Rather, they are selected and passed on to them as social recipes or typical patterns of action:

individuals also learn why it is worthwhile to make an effort in their lives, according to what their situations impose. Within these limits, they learn what can be endured and what is "unbearable" (Schutz & Luckmann, 2001, p. 108). This interpretative work assumes that individuals have at their disposal relevances and typifications, whose role is precisely to "naturalize" or harmonize ways of life (Santos, 2016. p. 234).

So the question is not how individuals in isolation make sense of their experiences and act in the world but how individuals *in community* make sense of their experiences and organize their lives in order to make the world intelligible and robust. Common-sense knowledge is cultural and intersubjective, considering that both the stock of knowledge at hand and the typifications and systems of relevance are constituted intersubjectively (Schutz & Luckmann, 2001) and within a specific social structure (Berger & Luckmann, 2008). It is a social construct which is updated in each individual in a particular way, mainly through socialization and language, but whose origin is mostly social and is passed onto them by their friends, parents, teachers and their teachers' teachers (Schutz, 2003a, p. 44). Thus, the stock of knowledge and the typifications of a given social group are influenced by power structures that condition their experiences at their foundations (Dreher, 2014a).

The world of everyday life—the *paramount reality*—is marked by experiences that transcend it and is not restricted to practical events in which individuals have been directly involved (Santos, 2010). Schutz extends the concept of the lifeworld by including other spheres of extraordinary reality and the social world. These cannot be transported directly into the *world of working* [*Wirkwelt*], but they can guide concrete actions (Dreher, 2014b) and provide a scheme of reference for interpreting the world, the people and the courses of action: what is at hand and what is not.

This also presupposes coercitive aspects of social life (such as socioeconomic status, social classes and political domination) which impose certain relevances on individuals and create, through different generations, their own forms of socialization (Motta, 2018, p. 130). It could be thought that the social structure conditioning the biographically determined situation of the individual and defining typical contexts of experiences and acts, along with possibilities of social interaction, is somehow implicit in Schutz's definition of the lifeworld.

In this vein, although social phenomenology does embrace the notion of stratification, its contributions to the study of social inequalities have been rare. Schutz barely mentions the concepts of status and social classes in his work (Schutz, 2011). He identifies race, geopolitical structure, political power relations and the conditions of economic production as material factors [*Realfaktoren*] to which a certain inherited legacy of interpretations [*Idealfaktoren*] is associated and points out that the latter can also modify social reality and direct the management of material factors (Schutz, 2003b, p. 230).

We can also find some passages dealing with the relations between workers and bourgeoisie in the work of Merleau-Ponty (1975), and a line of feminist research developed mainly from the works of Simone de Beauvoir and Edith

Stein (Fisher & Embree, 2000; Kruks, 2014; Young, 1980). Nonetheless, social phenomenology has been generally criticized for not dealing with objective structures of inequality. Contemporary social theory, in particular, has deliberately reduced the lifeworld to a plexus of symbolic products, placing social phenomenology within the subjectivist pole (Belvedere, 2012). In recent years, however, the "objectivist Schutz" (López, 2014) has received renewed attention.

The current stage of development of the phenomenological tradition could be characterized by empirical work and reflexive analysis of generations, social classes, gender and ethnicity among other dimensions of the lifeworld that have been scarcely explored (Embree, 2007). Within this framework, we can find conceptual contributions regarding not only the relations between phenomenology, Marxism and gender studies (Abercrombie, 1982; Ahmed, 2019; Embree, 2007; Sallach, 1973) but also the constitution of subjective experiences of social inequality (Banega, 2014; Dreher, 2014b; López, 2016). Empirical contributions include Charlesworth's (2000) description of working-class life in Rotherham, Britain, within a context of deindustrialization and poverty. Santos (2010) and Santos and Susin (2021) analyze experiences of inequality, violence and delinquency from the perspective of incarcerated adolescents and adult women living in slums [*favelas*] in Rio de Janeiro, Brazil. The research work that I have carried out seeks to understand how the intersubjective family order contributes to sustaining and legitimizing macro-social structures of inequality in terms of social classes, genders and generations.

2   Doing Phenomenology

Lifeworld theory provides a precise and unique conceptual framework for the analysis of actors' subjectivity (Eberle, 2014, p. 200). As such, it has influenced the development of qualitative methodologies for empirical social sciences (Dreher, 2012). However, classical phenomenology was never concerned with developing its own methods for phenomenologically oriented empirical research. Some authors have pointed out this pending issue and criticized the fact that phenomenological debates tend to focus on technical, conceptual and philosophical arguments disregarding attention to practical application (Bevan, 2014; van Manen, 2019). Among the different issues to be faced in the design and practice of an empirical phenomenology, there are some that I have chosen to discuss and will be presented below.

Philosophical, Theoretical or Methodological Approach

One of the first challenges lies in finding the status of phenomenology within the research design. Taylor and Bodgan (1987, p. 15) associate phenomenology with all sorts of qualitative research, considering it—just like positivism for quantitative research—the origin of the paradigm. Other authors see it as the intellectual root from which some qualitative perspectives stem, such is the case of grounded theory, symbolic interactionism, ethnomethodology and discourse analysis (Tesch, 2013, p. 27). Others regard it as a theoretical orientation with specific epistemological and methodological concerns (Creswell, 2007; Patton, 2001) or as just a method (Eberle, 2014). In fact, some phenomenological postulates have become generalized and are nowadays common ground for qualitative studies, such as the search for understanding participants' perspective or the concern with human experiences and meanings (Daher et al., 2017, pp. 1–2; Patton, 2001; van Manen, 2017a, p. 775).

How, then, can proper phenomenological studies be distinguished from general qualitative research? According to Patton (2001, p. 104), the specificity of phenomenological research can be found by looking at its foundational question: what is the meaning, structure and essence of the lived experience of this phenomenon for this group of people? Examples of phenomenological questions in empirical research include: How do parents of adolescents with terminal cancer perceive time and parenthood (Hayout & Krulik, 1999)? What is it like for women to do physical activity in public spaces (Allen-Collinson, 2011)? What does it mean to live with cerebral palsy (Høffding & Martiny, 2016)? How do expanding families (with young children and youths) experience their social class and the reproduction of social classes in their everyday lives (Krause, 2016)? What is it like for a school-aged child to live with a ventricular assist device (van Manen, 2017b)? What are the motivations and meaningful configurations of those interacting in a Social Community and Solidarity Economy market (Laborda, 2020)?

What Counts as Phenomenology

In close relation to the previous point, there are several studies including phenomenology as a keyword, or at least mentioning it in a rhetorical form, but certainly without a clear sense of how such a positioning can guide and shape the research question. In this regard, Patton (2001, p. 107) distinguishes between a properly phenomenological study—which focuses on what and how a phenomenon is experienced—and a more general phenomenological perspective—which highlights the importance of first-person perspectives on the social world. Similarly, Zahavi (2019, p. 901) stresses the difference between phenomenology and phenomenality—the qualitative character of experience.

Revisiting Wertz, Finlay (2012, p. 9) posits that it is perhaps best to recognize research which does not fully embrace the phenomenological project as phenomenologically inspired or phenomenologically oriented, and to reserve the definition of phenomenological research only for that which describes *the things in their appearing* and focuses on lived experiences and apply the reductions[2]. Similarly, for Giorgi (1997), the basic phenomenological reduction

---

[2] The *epoché* or *eidetic* reduction consists of "the 'bracketing' of the assumptions of the natural attitude upon which we regularly rely in everyday life" (Eberle, 2014, p. 186). The *transcendental reduction* or *phenomenological reduction* constitutes a second step in search of the essence of phenomena, in which we suspend not only our previous judgment on the phenomenon but also the very existence of the phenomenon (Eberle, 2014, p. 186).

"is the minimum condition necessary to claim phenomenological status for one's research" (p. 204). For van Manen (2017a, p. 777), genuine phenomenological research must practice *epoché* and phenomenological reduction. In this discussion, doubts regarding the limits of the field arise: "How deeply rooted in phenomenological philosophy must qualitative research be in order to qualify as phenomenological?" (Zahavi, 2020, pp. 1–2). Is it absolutely necessary to use Husserlian techniques such as *eidetic variation* or phenomenological reduction (Finlay, 2012, p. 18)?[3]

Basically, applying phenomenology in qualitative research depends on the possibility of relying on phenomenological philosophy, while avoiding the adoption of—on the one hand—a much too superficial understanding of phenomenology and—on the other hand—a much too philosophical, complicated and impractical version of it. Counterintuitively, some of the most recognized attempts to make the practice of phenomenology accessible outside the field of philosophy, such as Smith's Interpretative Phenomenological Analysis (IPA) or van Manen's phenomenology of practice, have been heavily criticized "for not being well-integrated with phenomenological philosophy" (Høffding & Martiny, 2016, p. 2).

As part of the aforementioned debate published in *Qualitative Health Research*, it has been argued that IPA is not phenomenology (van Manen, 2017a, 2018) or that it is albeit "in the most superficial sense of the term" (Zahavi, 2020, p. 2)—a statement to which Smith (2018) replied that neither van Manen nor anyone else should have the power to arbitrate what counts as phenomenology and what does not, considering that "phenomenology is such a complex and multifaceted entity" (p. 1957).

By taking phenomenology as a conceptual framework to be brought into play in the design of empirical research, we could probably circumvent these prescriptive definitions regarding the basic conditions for using phenomenology as a method. Following Zahavi (2020, p. 8; 2021), neither *epoché* nor phenomenological reduction is necessary to do empirical research.[4] These are fundamental concepts of Husserl's, although they are subjected to his transcendental phenomenology. For Zahavi (2019), "to conduct phenomenologically informed qualitative research is not merely a question of being open-minded and interested in first-person experience. It is very much also about adopting and employing a comprehensive theoretical framework concerning the subject's relation to himself or herself, to the world, and to others" (p. 906).

---

[3] The *eidetic variation* or *free imaginative variation* is another method developed by Husserl for phenomenological analysis. Its objective is to identify the *eidos*, the invariant properties of the phenomenon, by imagining its possible forms or variations (Eberle, 2014, p. 185).

[4] Following Giorgi (1994, p. 212), part of the controversy surrounding the *epoché* in empirical research lies in how its scope is interpreted. For him it should not be thought of in ideal terms, such as bracketing everything given to consciousness in a more or less permanent way, but only in relation to the research question and as a temporary attitude, limited to the analytical stage of the research process.

Within this framework, it would be most productive to start from the research problem itself and think: What phenomenology concepts are meaningful for this topic of interest? How can they provide us with deeper levels of understanding of the research phenomenon? What are the most appropriate techniques to address this consistently? In my work, the phenomenological scaffolding is given by the Schutzian conceptual framework summarized above regarding how power structures condition lifeworld experiences and the question of how social classes are lived in the everyday life of people who share the same social, spatial and temporal horizon. Likewise, by analyzing families with young children and youths and by focusing on the reproduction of class culture, I have thematically dealt with the *We-relationship*, the constitution of the *self*, and the expectations and projections for the future.

Pre-reflexive or Reflexive Experiences and How to Access Them

The focus of the analysis on pre-reflexive or reflexive experiences has also been part of the debate on what counts as phenomenology. According to van Manen (2017a), this has been one of the most common misconceptions regarding the basic criteria to be met by phenomenological research. For him the definition of phenomenology should be restricted to "the study of the primal, lived, pre-reflective, pre-predicative meaning of an experience" (p. 776).

In response, both Smith (2018, p. 1956) and Zahavi (2019) have argued that both types of experience are legitimate parts of phenomenological analysis. In the words of Zahavi (2019), "an important part of the phenomenological work is to understand the transition between our pre-reflective and pre-conceptual grasp of the world and our subsequent conceptualization of and judgment about it" (p. 904). The everyday is something instantaneous, immediate and simply lived, as much as something accumulated, reflected upon and critically evaluated (Jacobsen, 2009, p. 15). Phenomenology is concerned with purely practical experiences as well as with the positionality of the actor (Embree, 2011).

In addition, we could also discuss who has accessibility to lived experiences. Some authors have argued that it is convenient to live experiences as directly as possible and then try to become aware of them. Many others defend the possibility of doing a second-person phenomenology in which we can go around the social world and talk to people who are actually doing and experiencing phenomena in their everyday life. This is where qualitative methods have the most to contribute; "as soon as one ventures into fields informed by empirical analysis and especially those that target experiences that are not available to one's own first-person perspective, the phenomenological interview becomes relevant" (Høffding & Martiny, 2016, p. 23). In philosophical phenomenology, reflexive analysis is done by the philosopher in some sort of isolation and through phenomenological writing, "whereas in phenomenological research initial reflection is by the person who has undergone a particular experience, and this reflection is a primary interpretation" (Bevan, 2014, p. 137).

Therefore, in order to understand the perspective of the actors and their experiences of the lifeworld, the most common and recommendable thing to do is to conduct in-depth interviews with people who have directly experienced the phenomenon of interest (Adams & van Manen, 2017; Bevan, 2014; Creswell, 2007; Høffding & Martiny, 2016; Kvale, 2007; Moustakas, 1994; Patton, 2001; Santos & Susin, 2021)[5]. Interviews allow having access to the most important and significant elements of subjective interpretation, that is, systems of typifications and relevances and the stock of knowledge (Santos, 2010), and exploring how people make sense of their experiences and their ways of being-in-the-world. Interviews can be a means to adopt another origin of coordinates for the orientation of lifeworld phenomena (Schutz, 2003a, p. 141).

If phenomenological research is characterized by the exploration of how people make sense of experience and transform it into consciousness—both individually and collectively—methodologically speaking, it is necessary to capture and describe in depth how phenomena are experienced in the natural attitude: how they are perceived, described, felt, judged, remembered, made sense of and talked about with others (Patton, 2001, p. 104). It is assumed that "there is an essence or essences to shared experience" (Patton, 2001, p. 106) and that in order to recognize this, it is paramount to obtain rich, experiential descriptions of how the phenomenon is experienced and to avoid collecting vague explanations, generalizations and abstract definitions (Høffding & Martiny, 2016; van Manen, 1990, p. 64).

Several authors have recommended asking broad, general questions at the beginning of the interview (Giorgi, 1997; Moustakas, 1994; Zahavi, 2020, p. 6). These allow interviewees to deploy their own systems of relevance and expose their concerns, rather than imposing those of the researcher (Santos, 2010; Santos & Susin, 2021; van Manen, 2017b). Others have focused on how to handle the questioning process according to a phenomenological structure, for example, by gathering a textural description of the experience and then advancing into a more structural description of the contexts or situations that have influenced the experience (Creswell, 2007; Moustakas, 1994), or conducting the interview respecting the three domains of phenomenological reduction: contextualization (eliciting the lifeworld in natural attitude), apprehending the phenomenon (modes of appearing in natural attitude) and later clarifying the phenomenon (meaning through imaginative variation) (Bevan, 2014). These recommendations provide us with information regarding a model.

---

[5] Different branches of phenomenology assume different features and interests when applying empirical research. Hermeneutic phenomenology is likely to include documentary analysis, and existential phenomenology relies to a greater extent on observation and participation.

However, research practice is often more complex. As Zahavi (2019) highlights, "What if the participants who are being interviewed and who are requested to provide rich descriptions of, say, what it is like to live with depression or chronic obstructive pulmonary disease, are only able to offer very coarse and superficial descriptions?" (p. 6). Additional suggestions may include conducting more than a single interview or using clarifying questions (Bevan, 2014; Creswell, 2007; Høffding & Martiny, 2016; Kvale, 2007; Moustakas, 1994). Regardless of the enquiry strategy, it is always important to provide the interviewees with enough time and a trusting atmosphere, bringing their attention to their lived experiences so that they can find the words to retell them (Zahavi, 2020, p. 6).

It is also important to consider who we will be interviewing, what their expectations or demands are and how we will access them—all aspects that need to be considered every time we carry out research. The art of interviewing is learnt while doing so: "there is no right or 'sure fire' way to elicit lived experience descriptions, because each phenomenon demands its own line of inquiry, and different individuals often require different prompts" (Adams & van Manen, 2017, p. 786).

3   Phenomenological Dimensions of Class Analysis

Addressing How Social Class Is Lived

Quantitative studies of social classes use the occupational distributions of a population as a descriptive model of social structure. Because class positions are closely linked to exploitation and economic resource management, by means of social structure we can measure their impact on a wide range of social issues such as education, health and household economy, among others. Compared to most quantitative studies, qualitative approaches allow us to open the "black box" of tables and learn about these social processes through their members' perspectives. Compared to other qualitative approaches, one of the most distinctive features of phenomenological research is that it gives us the possibility to understand social classes in terms of lived experiences. Researching the lifeworld of the members of different social classes is equivalent to studying how the world presents itself as reasonable and meaningful in their consciousness and how it is filtered by their very position in the social structure.

The phenomenological perspective, additionally, provides us with a greater epistemological foundation for producing scientific knowledge through an (inter-)subjective, biased, common-sense perspective on the world (Creswell, 2007; Dreher, 2012; Giorgi, 1994; Zahavi, 2019). Building on Husserl's concern regarding "how objectivities of different kinds, from the prescientific ones to those of the highest scientific dignity, are constituted by consciousness" (Zahavi, 2019, p. 903), we might ask, for example, how social classes are experienced in everyday life in terms of the feelings and the sense of trust that their existence creates in their members; how class advantages are created, recreated and changed on a daily basis; how behaviors and patterns of values, practices and future expectations that contribute to the reproduction of social classes are configured in every household.

At this point the *how* something is experienced becomes more relevant than *what* is experienced (Høffding & Martiny, 2016). Other kinds of qualitative research designs (such as ethnography or oral history) would put an emphasis on the factual information reported. We could, for example, research on class lifestyles by addressing where middle-class families live, what schools their kids attend, what activities they share, etc. Following a phenomenological perspective, I have decided to not focus on these aspects but on how the interviewees assume their social positions and reflect upon themselves and their environment, how they typify themselves by differentiating themselves from others, how they project themselves into the future, how their decisions relate to their stock of knowledge and biographical situations, and how they act in accordance with this definition of their situation.

In this regard, I was interested in not only what they do concerning their health, education and household economics but also how their practices make sense to them. Studies which focus on facts, conversely, would probably not reach the same understanding of social classes, their practices and ways of living. Schutz formulates it as follows: "phenomenology does not study the objects themselves, but is interested in their *meaning*" (Schutz, 2003a, p.123). *Relevance* has been identified as the most important phenomenological problem in lifeworld research because it involves asking how we make sense of objects and events around us, and how we perceive, know, recognize and act in everyday life. Consequently, the basic foundation for action is not to be found in the objective life conditions of individuals but in how they interpret them (Santos, 2010, p. 159).

My results have shown that middle-class and working-class experiences are different in terms of the living conditions, the needs and the constraints that their members have faced along their trajectories. The use of family trees as an analytical tool and as an information production tool has allowed me to compare their family trajectories across three or more generations and to visualize what resources these are based on according to social class (e.g., jobs, educational credentials and health coverage, among others).

However, it is not just their experiences that are different but also the different ways in which they interpret them. Through the stories that accompanied the creation of their family trees, I could also see that concepts like "crisis" and "study"—and other elements that appear as relevant in both social classes—do not have the same meaning in both social contexts. Therefore, the analysis focused on the interpretation that the subjects have of their own reality, their trajectories and their social practices, and on the comprehension of how the things they do in their everyday life have a much broader meaning.

What it means to be there on a daily basis, in a home of a certain social class with children and young people who must be socialized in an inherited and shared culture, did not interest me so much in terms of what these families do but rather in terms of what is *relevant* to them in the context of their upbringing and their social reproduction. I was interested, for example, in these middle-class parents' accounts of the discussions that they have (or do not have) with their children at mealtimes, or in the accounts of how they help their kids do their homework, or how they decided together which extracurricular activities to keep doing or quit when they were under stress. All these aspects came up as issues of *relevance* for middle-class parents. They were concerned with their children developing critical reasoning and forming their own (class) "judgment" [*criterio*], which will later translate into different forms of value such as the ability to defend arguments and choose interests of their own, or to ask for additional help or information whenever they consider it necessary. These are experiences so deeply entangled with common-sense that they will have crucial consequences on how children conceive themselves and others and what socio-structural opportunities and constraints they are willing to face in their adolescence and adulthood (Lareau, 2015).

I also asked the interviewees how they thought that families from other social classes—with either more or less resources available—acted. I encouraged them to compare their current everyday lives with the type of life they had when they were teenagers in their parents' house and also to confront it with the plans they had for their future when they were teenagers. These questions were very productive triggers in my approach to the way social classes are experienced in everyday life while addressing their variations.

It should be noted here again that, in asking such questions, my intention was not to make factual claims about other social classes or to find out whether they actually do what they say they do, for example, how often they have debates and do research with their children, or whether or not the plans they had when they were teenagers were exactly the same as they describe them in the present. What really interested me, instead, was to understand how participants, in relation to significant others, make sense of a certain way of being-in-the-world, specific to their social class; that is to say, their perception of how other families or social classes live was important only in terms of meaning.

This focus on the reproduction of class culture in everyday family life allowed me to analyze social classes as an intersubjective phenomenon—not as a finished entity but as a realization of meaning, always ongoing, (re)produced through everyday conversations and interactions, and grounded in the lifeworld. This did not imply a voluntarist positioning or a disregard for the objective structures of inequality in which people and their social relations are embedded. Relevance, typifications and other forms of common-sense knowledge were framed in material processes and social relations of production and reproduction.

Giving Credit to Actors' Interpretations and Narratives

From this perspective, interviewees are seen as real and active interpreters of everything they face in life. It is assumed that they will try to find meaning in their experiences (Bevan, 2014, p. 136). They will especially try to understand the disturbances or unexpected events of their reality as they know it and as it is taken for granted. If one of the pillars of Schutz's social phenomenology is Husserl's philosophy, we can think of Weber's interpretive sociology [*verstehende Soziologie*] as being the other (Gros, 2018, p. 28), and therefore, interpretation by the actor is a fundamental part of phenomenological analysis.

Schutz (1993) problematizes the Weberian concepts of subjective meaning, social action and ideal type in order to endow the program of interpretive sociology with more heuristic support and epistemological validity (Krause, 2013). Within the common-sense experience of everyday life, sensible behavior is not assumed to be rational but reasonable action, "within an unquestioned and undetermined frame of constructs of typicalities of the setting, the motives, the means and ends, the courses of action and personalities involved and taken for granted" (Schutz, 2003a, p. 59).

It is the social sciences that must construct rational models of reasonable behavior (Schutz, 2003a, p. 68). And for this, "the details, biases, errors, and prejudices that we carry with us in everyday life are exactly what have to be understood" (Giorgi, 1997, p. 243). Biographical and lifeworld narratives make it possible to retrieve such elements of (inter-)subjective interpretation, because they are not so much social science methods as actors' methods of knowing and making their world understandable (Schutz, 2003a).

It is advisable sometimes to encourage participants to recall vividness and describe specific situations, incidents or anecdotes in detail (van Manen, 2017c: 810), "as it was the first time" (van Manen, 1990, p. 65). This strategy would be especially useful if there was a specific event that took the interviewee out of his or her natural attitude and shifted his or her attention to a reflective awareness. When it comes to health issues, it is frequent to enquire about such disruptive experiences, where the taken for granted becomes the focus of awareness, and actors spontaneously and actively engage in making sense of what is happening (Smith, 2018, pp. 1955–1957), by means of questions such as Do you remember when you first found out that you were ill? What was it like? How did your body react? Did you have any doubts? What was it like to tell others?

Class culture—like our bodily skills—is taken for granted when it works well. It can remain in the background of our actions as something on which we can rely. Following Schutz, a group's culture—its *relative natural view of the world*—constitutes a set of socially approved knowledge and behavior patterns, mostly transmitted intergenerationally and routinely as special versions of the in-group (here, of the social class). Such a schema of orientation, interpretation and action is *naturalized* and, therefore, taken for granted until further notice (Gros, 2018, p. 31). It is what enables the members of an in-group to relate to each other among peers and to orient themselves without difficulty in familiar surroundings, "as if at home" (Schutz, 2003b, p. 232).

Social mobility processes—like illnesses or disabilities—can change that and bring into question what was previously taken for granted. As de Gaulejac

(2013) describes, declassifications can entail numerous conflicts regarding oneself, ascendants and peers. Temporary regressions in living conditions in times of economic or family crises may also require changes in routines and special attention focused on the present. Macro-social crises—including the COVID-19 pandemic—confront us with an unprecedented scenario, dissolving our trust in the social prescriptions and typifications that we used to know and take for granted, including the value of currency. We could also think of big life choices—for example, becoming parents or school choices—as moments that entail a different attention to the ordinary. At these moments of decision-making, we act according to a distant future horizon and visualize images about who we would like to become in order to guide our present (Hitlin & Elder Jr, 2007).

Asking interviewees about all these extraordinary circumstances may be another way of empirically addressing not only what is involved in the reproduction of the lifeworld of different social classes but also how the stock of knowledge functions pragmatically—until further notice—and how aspirations are adjusted to possibilities in contextualized conditions.

The Performative and Sociohistorical Dimension of Meaning: Class Practices as Culturally Saturated Processes

To understand the complex field of meaning and motivation implicit in class practices, we must focus on meaning [*Sinn*]. Schutz (1993) draws on Husserl in order to define meaning as "a certain way of looking at an aspect of an experience that belongs to us" (p. 71). That is, since in the stream of consciousness, experiences extend uninterruptedly and organically, the actor must stop to think reflectively about a past—or imagined as past—experience in order to define it as a discrete experience, with its own beginning and end and, therefore, with meaning. In this way, we only have access to subjective meanings as objectified constructs, albeit momentarily (Harrington, 2000, p. 734). Meaning constitution is an operation of intentionality (Schutz, 1993, p. 82) that is permeated culturally and historically by the interpretative schemes of a particular Here and Now from which we can single out an experience, select some aspects of it—among many others—and typify it.

This notion of meaning by Schutz does not refer to the purely semantic character of the term (Daher et al., 2017). It presents an explicit pragmatic component, "since the individual is considered from the point of view of action, or imminent action" (Santos, 2010, p. 137). By giving a meaning to something we do not only define it but also establish a position toward this phenomenon (Daher et al., 2017). When actors interpret the things that they are confronted with (people, ideas, events and even structural constraints), they assume their position in the world and, in doing so, they set their course of action (Santos, 2010, p. 140). This is based on *in-order-to motives* and *because motives* acquired and processed by the actor in a contextualized manner, within the framework of their biographically determined situation, their stock of knowledge at hand, their previous experiences and plans, and their systems of relevance.

In analyzing the practices of healthcare, education and household economics of different social classes, I have assumed that these are fundamental issues for social reproduction, that they have a great impact on people's quality of life and that they are interwoven with class relations as they involve the appropriation (or not) of structural opportunities (Sautu, 2016). But, above all, I have taken them as "culturally saturated processes" (Markus & Kitayama, 2003, p 6). They imply a commitment of actors to a certain class culture and a realization of meaning.

The accounts of their daily practices not only describe them but also affect these experiences, organize them, give them a certain naturalness and, therefore, contribute to the reproduction of a certain social order. The interviews show that families fight for the ways of life that they consider desirable and justify the differences they may have as regards Others. There is this idea that one is one and the other is the Other. We can thus see how the objectivity of social classes is (inter-)subjectively endorsed, legitimized and reaffirmed in everyday family life through a set of common-sense typifications that guide our everyday practices.

Understanding How Social Classes Affect Its Members' Being-in-the-World

The intentional, spatial, temporal and social structure of the lifeworld is indeed invariant but is the concrete content of that structure which is the object of empirical analysis (Eberle, 2014, pp. 187–188) and can provide us with an understanding of how social classes affect their members. This strategy of investigating the four existential axes on which the experience is based (i.e., the fundamental structure of the lifeworld) is suggested by van Manen (1990) and endorsed by Zahavi (2020, p. 5) as a very useful proposal for the practice of phenomenology. In relation to social classes, we could think of them as axes along which social stratification is filtered.

One first existential axis refers to "the phenomenological fact that we are always bodily in the world" (van Manen, 1990, p. 103). Social classes mainly affect the body by means of its use in work processes but also influence food and taste, physical activities and abilities, clothing, care, and so on. However, phenomenology recovers the psychophysical unity of individuals in order to emphasize that we are not *object bodies* [*Körper*] but above all living and *lived bodies* [*Leib*]. In the perception of one's own body and intercorporeality, multiple orientations are possible (Legrand, 2007). In this regard, we could qualitatively investigate how the social structure is lived through the body; how our body experiences vary between groups or social classes, in interactions between classes; and how they serve to justify structural inequalities.

On the axis of temporality, a distinction is also made between objective and subjective time in order to show that our awareness of time—how we feel the passage of time—depends on the context, for example, when we wait, when we work, when we enjoy ourselves, when we are sick or healthy, young or old. In terms of class analysis, we could also address the different time horizons that frame class practices, such as money uses, schooling or healthcare processes. In carrying out this research, I have found that the perception of time horizon is a response to social situations and conditions for action. Although middle-class families see money mainly as a means of stability and long-term investment, in working-class families its everyday use is described in detail, as a household and short-term currency, which also harbors family negotiations and conflicts, regarding its administration.

Their educational decisions and practices are also permeated by different temporalities. The middle-class families interviewed, take for granted the different steps that their children will take from a very early age in order to reach higher levels of education, whereas some working-class families are not even sure whether or not their kids will complete the current school year. Moreover, the time dimension in the process of diagnosis and treatment of illnesses, and the perception of the health risk involved in that lapse of time, also differ between social classes. These results show that although future projections serve to stabilize the world as intelligible and guide present actions, they also imply that there are resources and steps needed to achieve aspirations which are not always available. Drawing on Hitlin and Kirkpatrick Johnson (2015), we could possibly claim that different time horizons in different social classes reflect the knowledge they have about their structural constraints and opportunities.

On the axis of relationality or lived human relations, we could address the typifications of social positions and the criteria that we use to direct our attention to others: who we think is similar to us and who is not; who deserves our respect or does not; what is a family and how far my family extends; what is friendship and who my friends are; with whom I am interested in sharing my lifeworld and who is—on the contrary—totally anonymous to me. We could say that this relates to the most subjectively visible and typical aspects of social classes, to "the consciousness of group affiliation and differentiation" (Weber, 1964, p. 692). The latter translates into practices of sociability, tastes, orientations and values shared by the in-group, as well as into the use of stigmatizing categories when referring to Others, the denial of their experiences and subjective points of view, and the imposition of one's own relevances.

Resuming my research, middle-class families see welfare benefits for low-income sectors of society as "ill-gotten money" that is easily "blown" by those who live in "shanty towns." These people are looked down on for suffering different health problems, including malnutrition, getting medical treatment in "disgusting" public hospitals and studying in "appalling" school buildings. In turn, working-class families oppose the hegemonic discourses of the middle-class. They claim to use money from welfare programs for their children, mainly to buy food. They choose public schools that are "really good" and "clean" and avoid private schools because they are "looked down on" or "feel discriminated against" in them. Their bad experiences in different healthcare sub-sectors are attributed to "shitty doctors" who treat them "like cattle" and "won't even look you in the face." Such typifications of the Other imply not only alienation and anonymity but also power relations of one class over the other, which are not only symbolic but also material and are based on production and domination endorsed by these typifications.

The axis of spatiality or lived space deals with the different ways of inhabiting spaces inside and outside the home. Spatiality thus can account for how we perceive distances and feel the experience of either living in a certain neighborhood or walking through it; how structural, environmental, socioeconomic and housing inequalities are experienced in a given area; how different social classes take or do not take over public spaces; how class practices happen in specific environments (e.g., studying or reading in a room with a specific table, light, silence, etc.), among others.

4   CONCLUSION

Conley (2008) argues that the paradox of social classes is that at the very moment we start measuring them, we start losing them. Social classes are a complex phenomenon, impossible to characterize empirically in a comprehensive manner.

In the analysis of social classes, each research tradition becomes more or less useful depending on the different aspects that we decide to address in our attempt to gain thorough understanding of social structure. As in any other field, researchers engaged in the study of social classes should evaluate their methodological choices and theoretical positions considering what it is that they expect to understand.

Throughout this chapter I have listed a number of issues that are compatible with a phenomenological analysis of social classes—not wishing to be exhaustive but inspiring—and I have illustrated some of them by resorting to my own research. I also hope to have provided elements that will favor the adoption of a phenomenological approach when carrying out empirical research and will foster greater confidence and awareness of its implications. In the following, I will summarize my position regarding the reasons why I suggest that this path should be taken.

First, when we are interested in maintaining a critical realist position at the ontological level, "which admits to a reality independent of consciousness (while accepting knowledge of this can only come through study of consciousness)" (Finlay, 2012, p. 30). The social reality to be investigated consists of whatever presents itself to consciousness and should therefore not be restricted to a small-scale sociology. On the contrary, as Giorgi (1994, p. 192) argues, one of the aspects that make phenomenology attractive is its *comprehensiveness*, both in terms of the phenomena to be investigated and in terms of the theoretical abstraction it can achieve with regard to them. Phenomenology seeks to understand phenomena as wholes (Daher et al.,

2017, p. 10) subsuming and interrelating their most concrete forms. It allows us to address social classes as wholes as opposed to problems confined to one domain (e.g., education, economics, health) and to articulate multiple everyday practices as part of the lifeworld of different social classes. That is, how a set of everyday practices come together to create this coherent experience of the world that different social classes have.

A phenomenological approach also has the advantage of being an analysis on the everyday, but not from a subjectivist, micro-social and spontaneous perspective. As I argued above, social phenomenology takes into account the notions of social constructions, inherited stocks of knowledge and experiences, and social stratification and power.

Second, social phenomenology does not only consider social structure and other macro-social dimensions of inequality. Above all, it is interested in revealing how these are experienced as part of the lifeworld. It enhances our sensitivity with regard to the diversity of experiences and the freedom to interpret them. It allows us to think through the problematic of meaning by showing how the (inter-)subjective constitutes, provides continuity to and changes the objective by means of those activities which—through routine, values and norms, as well as power relations—ontologically constitute the lifeworld. Social phenomenology does not aim at moving away from objectivity but rather understanding it. Social classes, as well as gender and other social dimensions of inequality, are considered part of our everyday experiences in a real social world, above abstract entities of sociological theory.

Third, qualitative interviews serve to address (inter-)subjective meanings; get to know significant aspects of human existence that we have not experienced firsthand; and—ultimately—understand possible ways of living in contextualized conditions and their differences between social classes. In other words, phenomenological research can challenge our assumptions, broaden our horizon of meaning and provide us with a broader understanding of socio-culturally specific lifeworlds.

In closing, researchers involved in social phenomenology embark on a quest to understand the essence of the lived experiences of social groups in their everyday lives. In this chapter I have argued that the study of such experiences must take into account the multiple processes of inequality that run through people's lives, accompanying them in every social interaction. From a phenomenological perspective on social classes, I have been interested in the reproduction of social relations of inequality within the family sphere, just the way it appears in the consciousness of its members, and with the attention it is paid in their everyday lives.

By understanding this symbolic dimension of the reproduction of social inequalities, it would also be possible to study how these interpretations of common-sense and social actions can be modified, and to become aware of when and under what conditions the relations of meaning that sustain the social structure as we know it can be overturned, so that social change can then take place.

Acknowledgments This chapter was written within the framework of the PRII R20-42 project "Phenomenology and intersectionality: theoretical-methodological challenges to address social inequalities," funded by the Institutional Research Recognition Program of the Faculty of Social Sciences, University of Buenos Aires. I would like to express my deepest gratitude to its members—Narela M. Benegas, Joaquín Balbi, Nicolás Rosinke, Sofía Robiolio Bose, Tomás Giri, Rocío Salgueiro and Anabel Abatedaga—for their time and dedication to fruitful discussions which I have tried to capture in this chapter. I am also indebted to Ruth Sautu and Betina Freidin, as this chapter reflects the result of many years of training in the field of class analysis and social inequalities in everyday life.

REFERENCES

Abercrombie, N. (1982). *Clase, estructura y conocimiento*. Península.

Adams, C., & van Manen, M. A. (2017). Teaching phenomenological research and writing. *Qualitative Health Research, 27*(6), 780–791. https://doi.org/10.1177/1049732317698960

Ahmed, S. (2019). *Fenomenología Queer: orientaciones, objetos, otros*. Colectivo Sudakuir.

Allen-Collinson, J. (2011). Running Embodiment, Power and Vulnerability: Notes Toward a Feminist Phenomenology of Female Running. In E. Kennedy & P. Markula (Eds.), *Women and exercise: the body, health and consumerism* (pp. 280–298). Routledge.

Banega, H. M. (2014). Stock of Knowledge as Determined by Class Position: A Marxist Phenomenology? *Schutzian Research, 6*, 47–60. https://doi.org/10.5840/schutz201464

Belvedere, C. (2012). *El discurso del dualismo en la Teoría Social Contemporánea: Una crítica fenomenológica*. Eudeba.

Berger, P., & Luckmann, T. (2008). *La construcción social de la realidad*. Amorrortu.

Bevan, M. T. (2014). A method of phenomenological interviewing. *Qualitative health research, 24*(1), 136–144. https://doi.org/10.1177/1049732313519710

Breiger, R. L. (1995). Social Structure and the Phenomenology of Attainment. *Annual Review of Sociology, 21*, 115–136. https://doi.org/10.1146/annurev.so.21.080195.000555

Charlesworth, S. J. (2000). *A phenomenology of working class experience*. Cambridge University Press.

Conley, D. (2008). Reading Class Between the Lines (of This Volume): A Reflection on Why We Should Stick to Folk Concepts of Social Class. In A. Lareau & D. Conley (Eds.), *Social class: How does it work?* (pp. 366–374). Russell Sage Foundation.

Creswell, J. W. (2007). *Qualitative inquiry and research design: Choosing among five approaches*. SAGE.

Crompton, R., Devine, F., Savage, M., & Scott, J. (2000). *Renewing Class Analysis*. Blackwell.

Daher, M., Carré, D., Jaramillo, A., Olivares, H., & Tomicic, A. (2017). Experience and meaning in qualitative research: A conceptual review and a methodological device proposal. *Forum: Qualitative Social Research, 18*(3), 62–85.

Dreher, J. (2012). Fenomenología: Alfred Schütz y Thomas Luckmann. In E. de la Garza Toledo, & G. Leyva (Coords.), *Tratado de metodología de las ciencias sociales: perspectivas actuales* (pp. 96-133). FCE/UAM-Iztapalapa.

Dreher, J. (2014a). Fenomenología del poder. In J. Dreher, & D. G. López (Comps.), *Fenomenología del poder* (pp. 21-36). USTA.

Dreher, J. (2014b). Mundo de la vida, constitución de desigualdades sociales y jerarquías de poder simbólicas. In J. Dreher, & D. G. López (Comps.), *Fenomenología del poder* (pp. 111-128). USTA.

Eberle, T. S. (2014). Phenomenology as a Research Method. In U. Flick (Ed.), *The SAGE Handbook of Qualitative Data Analysis* (pp. 184–202). SAGE.

Embree, L. (2007). *Fenomenología continuada: Contribuciones al análisis reflexivo de la cultura*. Morelia/Red Utopía.

Embree, L. (2011). *Reflective Analysis: A First Introduction into Phenomenological Investigation*. Zeta Books.

Finlay, L. (2012). Debating phenomenological methods. In N. Friesen, C. Henriksson, & T. Saevi (Eds.), *Hermeneutic Phenomenology in Education: Method and Practice* (pp. 17–37). SensePublishers Rotterdam.

Fisher, L., & Embree, L. (Eds.). (2000). *Feminist phenomenology*. Springer.

de Gaulejac, V. (2013). *Neurosis de clase: Trayectoria social y conflictos de identidad*. Del Nuevo Extremo.

Giorgi, A. (1994). A phenomenological perspective on certain qualitative research methods. *Journal of Phenomenological Psychology, 25*(2), 190–220. https://doi.org/10.1163/156916294X00034

Giorgi, A. (1997). The theory, practice, and evaluation of the phenomenological method as a qualitative research procedure. *Journal of phenomenological psychology, 28*(2), 235–260. https://doi.org/10.1163/156916297X00103

Gros, A. (2018). ¿Saben los cientistas sociales qué es el "mundo de la vida"? Retornando a la "protofundación" de Edmund Husserl y a la "retoma" de Alfred Schutz. *Diferencias, 4*(7), 15–35.

Harrington, A. (2000). Alfred Schutz and the 'Objectifying Attitude'. *Sociology, 34*, 727–740. https://doi.org/10.1017/S0038038500000444

Hayout, I., & Krulik, T. (1999). A test of parenthood: dilemmas of parents of terminally ill adolescents. *Cancer Nursing, 22*(1), 71–79. https://doi.org/10.1097/00002820-199902000-00013

Hitlin, S., & Elder, G. H., Jr. (2007). Time, self, and the curiously abstract concept of agency. *Sociological Theory, 25*(2), 170–191. https://doi.org/10.1111/j.1467-9558.2007.00303.x

Hitlin, S., & Kirkpatrick Johnson, M. (2015). Reconceptualizing agency within the life course: The power of looking ahead. *American Journal of Sociology, 120*(5), 1429–1472. https://doi.org/10.1086/681216

Høffding, S., & Martiny, K. (2016). Framing a phenomenological interview: what, why and how. *Phenomenology and the Cognitive Sciences, 15*(4), 539–564. https://doi.org/10.1007/s11097-015-9433-z

Jacobsen, M. H. (2009). Introduction: The Everyday. An Introduction to an Introduction. In M. H. Jacobsen (Ed.), *Encountering the Everyday: An Introduction to the Sociologies of the Unnoticed* (pp. 1–42). Palgrave Macmillan.

Krause, M. (2013). Sentido común y clase social: una fundamentación fenomenológica. *Astrolabio, 10*, 5–29.

Krause, M. (2016). *Prácticas cotidianas en el cuidado de la salud, la educación y la economía doméstica: Un análisis del mundo de la vida en familias de clase media y clase trabajadora del Área Metropolitana de Buenos Aires a comienzos del siglo XXI*

(Tesis de Doctorado), Facultad de Ciencias Sociales, Universidad de Buenos Aires, Buenos Aires.

Kruks, S. (2014). Women's 'Lived Experience': Feminism and Phenomenology from Simone de Beauvoir to the Present. En M. Evans, C. Hemmings, M. Henry, H. Johnstone, S. Madhok, A. Plomien, & S. Wearing (Eds.), *The SAGE handbook of feminist theory* (pp. 75-92). SAGE.

Kvale, S. (2007). *Doing Interviews.* SAGE.

Laborda, V. D. C. (2020). *Del anonimato a la empatía. Configuraciones significativas que circulan en los mercados solidarios de la Ciudad de Buenos Aires* (Tesis de Maestría), Universidad Nacional de Tres de Febrero, Buenos Aires.

Lareau, A. (2015). Cultural Knowledge and Social Inequality. *American Sociological Review, 80*(1), 1–27. https://doi.org/10.1177/0003122414565814

Legrand, D. (2007). Subjectivity and the body: introducing basic forms of self-consciousness. *Conscious Cogn, 16*(3), 577–582. https://doi.org/10.1016/j.concog.2007.06.011

López, D. G. (2014). El "Schutz objetivista": Aportes de las reflexiones schutzianas al problema del orden social. In J. Dreher, & D. G. López (Comps.), *Fenomenología del poder* (pp. 65-86). USTA.

López, D. G. (2016). La experiencia subjetiva de la desigualdad en la vida cotidiana: Contribuciones de la sociología fenomenológica de Alfred Schutz. *Trabajo y sociedad, 27*, 221–232.

van Manen, M. (1990). *Researching Lived Experience: Human Science for an Action Sensitive Pedagogy.* SUNY.

van Manen, M. (2017a). But is it phenomenology? *Qualitative Health Research, 27*(6), 775–779. https://doi.org/10.1177/1049732317699570

van Manen, M. A. (2017b). The ventricular assist device in the life of the child: A phenomenological pediatric study. *Qualitative Health Research, 27*(6), 792–804. https://doi.org/10.1177/1049732317700853

van Manen, M. (2017c). Phenomenology in its original sense. *Qualitative health research, 27*(6), 810–825. https://doi.org/10.1177/1049732317699381

van Manen, M. (2018). Rebuttal rejoinder: Present IPA for what it is—Interpretative psychological analysis. *Qualitative health research, 28*(12), 1959–1968. https://doi.org/10.1177/1049732318795474

Markus, H. R., & Kitayama, S. (2003). Models of agency: Sociocultural diversity in the construction of action. In V. Murphy-Berman & J. J. Berman (Eds.), *Cross-cultural Differences in Perspectives on the Self. Vol. 49 of the Nebraska Symposium on Motivation.* University of Nebraska Press.

Merleau-Ponty, M. (1975). *Fenomenología de la percepción.* Península.

Motta, R. D. (2018). Sociología fenomenológica y fenomenología social. Conversaciones con Carlos Belvedere. *Diferencias, 4*(7), 126–136.

Moustakas, C. (1994). *Phenomenological research methods.* SAGE.

Patton, M. Q. (2001). *Qualitative Research & Evaluation Methods.* SAGE.

Sallach, D. (1973). Class Consciousness and the Everyday World in the Work of Marx & Schutz. *Critical Sociology, 3*(27), 27–37. https://doi.org/10.1177/089692057300300403

Santos, H. (2010). Adolescents and experiences with violence: making sense of subjective interpretations of life-world. *VIBRANT-Vibrant Virtual Brazilian Anthropology, 7*(2), 135–165.

Santos, H. (2016). Biography and Action: A Schutzian Perspective to Life-world. *Società Mutamento Politica, 6*(12), 231–243. https://doi.org/10.13128/SMP-17856

Santos, H., & Susin, P. (2021). Relevance and Biographical Experience in Urban Social Research. *Schutzian Research, 13,* 51–75. https://doi.org/10.5840/schutz2021134

Sautu, R. (2016). *Economía, clases sociales y estilos de vida.* Lumiere.

Schutz, A. (1993). *La comprensión significativa del mundo social: Introducción a la sociología comprensiva.* Paidós.

Schutz, A. (2003a). *El problema de la realidad social: Escritos I.* Amorrortu.

Schutz, A. (2003b). *Estudios sobre teoría social: Escritos II.* Amorrortu.

Schutz, A. (2011). T. S. Eliot's Theory of Culture. In L. Embree (Ed.), *Collected Papers V. Phenomenology and the Social Sciences* (pp. 275–289). Springer.

Schutz, A., & Luckmann, T. (2001). *Las estructuras del mundo de la vida.* Amorrortu.

Smith, J. A. (2018). "Yes it is phenomenological": A reply to Max Van Manen's critique of interpretative phenomenological analysis. *Qualitative Health Research, 28*(12), 1955–1958. https://doi.org/10.1177/1049732318799577

Taylor, S. J., & Bogdan, R. (1987). *Introducción a los métodos cualitativos de investigación: La búsqueda de significados.* Paidós.

Tesch, R. (2013). *Qualitative research: Analysis types and software.* Routledge.

Van Manen, M. (2019). Rebuttal: Doing phenomenology on the things. *Qualitative Health Research, 29*(6), 908–925. https://doi.org/10.1177/1049732319827293

Weber, M. (1964). *Economía y Sociedad.* FCE.

Wright, E. O. (2015). *Understanding class.* Verso books.

Young, I. M. (1980). Throwing like a girl: A phenomenology of feminine body comportment motility and spatiality. *Human Studies, 3*(1), 137–156. https://doi.org/10.1007/BF02331805

Zahavi, D. (2019). Getting it quite wrong: Van Manen and Smith on phenomenology. *Qualitative Health Research, 29*(6), 900–907. https://doi.org/10.1177/1049732318817547

Zahavi, D. (2020). The practice of phenomenology: The case of Max van Manen. *Nurs Philos, 21*(2), e12276. https://doi.org/10.1111/nup.12276

Zahavi, D. (2021). Applied phenomenology: Why it is safe to ignore the epoché. *Continental Philosophy Review, 54*(2), 259–273. https://doi.org/10.1007/s11007-019-09463-y

Depragmatized Knowledge and Sociomaterial Structures: Illustration from Economics as a Province of Special Knowledge

Ossi I. Ollinaho

1 Introduction

This chapter outlines a general view on how knowledge, as conceptualized by Alfred Schütz (Schutz, 1962; Schutz & Luckmann, 1973) and his students (Berger & Luckmann, 1966), relates to the ongoing process of (re)producing sociomaterial structures. The aim is to explicate how higher forms of knowledge, particularly depragmatized knowledge created within provinces of special knowledge, are used to bring about societal structures as part of which people act in their everyday. Doing this, the chapter bridges the pragmatically motivated everyday activities transpiring within and as part of the sociomaterial structures and the theoretical underpinnings of these structures within the Schutzian framework.

While Schutz's main focus was at the micro level of intersubjective cognitive processes, he also provided tools for understanding the creation of sociomaterial structures with higher forms of knowledge, particularly in the last section of the *Structures of the Life-World, Volume 1* (Schutz & Luckmann, 1973, p. 241–331). However, depragmatized knowledge in which that entire book culminates, has not been taken on in the subsequent literature. While the importance of higher forms of knowledge has been highlighted by Luckmann (1983) and Marx's argument about the relationship between 'pure theory' and

O. I. Ollinaho (✉)
University of Helsinki, Helsinki, Finland

C. Belvedere, A. Gros (eds.), *The Palgrave Handbook of Macrophenomenology and Social Theory*,
https://doi.org/10.1007/978-3-031-34712-2_21

economic surplus is acknowledged (Berger & Luckmann, 1966), explicit focus on the concept of depragmatized knowledge in the Schutzian framework is close to nonexistent (cf. Ollinaho, 2014, 2012, 2023; Ollinaho & Pajunen, 2019). Depragmatized knowledge refers to knowledge created within provinces of special knowledge that lacks an explicit connection with the immediate act-contexts of the life-world so that there are no obvious pragmatic criteria to differentiate between 'correct' and 'false' knowledges (Schutz & Luckmann, 1973). Depragmatized knowledge has been proliferating with the specialization of societies to the extent that virtually all knowledges in the social sciences and in the natural sciences are to a considerable degree depragmatized.

It seems that the depragmatized type of knowledge and the pragmatic nature of human activity have remained as largely separate streams of thought in social phenomenology. To my knowledge, Schutz did not elaborate on higher forms of knowledge being used to bring about social and material structures, and neither has subsequent scholarship. But why it is important to explain a social phenomenological account of social structures? Taking seriously what Schutz writes about the natural attitude within which people predominantly pragmatically act upon their imminent social and biophysical world, which they take for granted most of the time, means that the sociomaterial structures as part of which people act, effectively organize and order these activities, albeit not deterministically. The contemporary sociomaterial structures, prominently those related to money (Hornborg, 2019; Mellor, 2019; Nelson, 2022), are organizing and ordering human activities to accelerate in a dead-end, so to say. This has alarmed many and sustainability has also become a key motivator for academics facing the multifaceted contemporary predicament inherent in the normal workings of industrial production (Rudel et al., 2011) within capitalist hegemony. However, mainstream solutions rely on ever more economic growth and are prominently crafted by the neoclassical orthodoxy of economics (Gills & Morgan, 2021; Hickel, 2020; Keen, 2020).

Taking the case of economics, this chapter illustrates the condition of highly specialized contemporary societies in which to a large extent depragmatized knowledges are routinely applied and have societal consequences and relevance, regardless of their correctness. The implications of understanding the functioning of the provinces of special knowledge as social practices where depragmatized knowledge are applied urge, among other things, to relocate the struggle for sustainability. Since providing ever more data of the destructive consequences of human activities is ineffective (Ollinaho, 2016), the focus of sustainability efforts ought to be shifted toward the very practices within which applications of depragmatized knowledge help bringing about sociomaterial structures that organize and order these very human activities. While the former is a question of having more environmental sciences and communications, the latter is prominently a question of power relations and conceptual struggles within and between different provinces of special knowledge, particularly that of economics, which holds a special position as the principal science advocating economic and monetary issues that have become pivotal to the contemporary realities virtually everywhere.

The rest of this chapter is structured as follows. I will first conceptualize social and material structures of the life-world according to Schutz's work complementing it with practice theoretical concepts. I will then address the concepts of specialization of knowledge and depragmatized knowledge with an attempt to conceptualize how they are used to bring about sociomaterial structures. Then, I will illustrate these concepts with a preliminary case study of the province of special knowledge of economics. To conclude, I will discuss the implications of this chapter.

2   SOCIAL AND MATERIAL STRUCTURES

The main interest of social phenomenology has been to describe the subjective- and intersubjective-level processes of dealing with and gearing into social reality, rather than describing how the historically unfolding sociomaterial contexts and structures of that social reality are maintained and modified with the use of higher forms of knowledge. While Schutz (1962) and Berger and Luckmann (1966) do take much time to elaborate on how social institutions can be initiated in theory at a micro level (i.e., between two people and their offspring), little effort has been put to theorizing the contemporary realities in which specialized knowledge dominates the crafting of social structures. Schutzian framework, however, offers adequate tools for the conceptual endeavor to understand how social structures, "temporally persistent and (usually) macro-level institutions and social relations" (Gunderson, 2021, p. 745) are brought about. According to Schutz (1962), we have an eminently pragmatic interest in our reality, and this reality exhibits both material (or natural) and social constrains or structures offering resistance to our activities, thereby directing our daily life semi-automatically in a pragmatic manner. This is of course only so far as we live in the 'natural attitude', which Schutz sees as the "fundamental attitude of normal adult" (Schutz & Luckmann, 1973, pp. 21–22) in which people suspend the doubt of the reality. It is worth here to take a lengthy quote from Schutz to explicate how he conceptualizes the way people gear into their paramount realities:

> "The individual living in the world always experiences himself as being within a certain situation which he has to define. ... the concept of a situation to be defined contains two principal components: The one originates from the ontological structure of the pregiven world. ... The other component which makes it possible to define certain elements by singling them out of the ontologically pregiven structure of the world originates from the actual biographical state of the individual, a state which includes his stock of knowledge in its actual articulation" (Schutz, 1970, p. 122).

This chapter begins its analysis with this dichotomy of subjective knowledge and the 'ontological component' of the intersubjective reality "imposed on us by the natural and social world" (Schutz & Luckmann, 1973, p. 17), which can be thought of as a province of reality that cannot be wished away (Berger & Luckmann, 1966). Schutz wrote that the paramount reality is "a world of well circumscribed objects with definite qualities, objects among which we move, which resist us and upon which we may act" (1962, p. 208). These objects "offer resistance to our acts which we have either to overcome or to which we have to yield" as we through our "bodily movements—kinaesthetic, locomotive, operative—gear, so to speak, into the world, modifying or changing its objects and their mutual relationships" (Schutz, 1962, p. 208, 209). But the biophysical sphere is not the only sphere that constrains us; people "work not only upon inanimate things but also upon [their] fellow-men, induced by them to act and inducing them to react" (Schutz, 1962, p. 218). Schutz used the term "constraint" rarely, but when he did, he wrote that socialization and social circumstances impose constraints on our gearing into the social reality (Schutz & Luckmann, 1973, p. 184). When we are socialized into a particular social reality, it imposes us with social force that constraints our activities. Berger and Luckmann wrote:

> The institutions, as historical and objective facticities, confront the individual as undeniable facts. The institutions are there, external to him, persistent in their reality, whether he likes it or not. He cannot wish them away. They resist his attempts to change or evade them. They have coercive power over him, both in themselves, by the sheer force of their facticity, and through the control mechanisms that are usually attached to the most important of them. (Berger & Luckmann, 1966, p. 76)

The term structure is in frequent use in Schutz's texts and its referents are typically linked to the subjective actor; for instance, he wrote that "the social scientist confronts a reality whose structure originates in subjective common-sense constructs and typifications" (Schutz, 1964, p. 21). Structures for Schutz, so to say, have their root locus in the actor. Even the notion of environment "would have to start from the face-to-face relation as a basic structure of the world of daily life" (1962, p. 221). When writing about structures, Schutz was clear, however, in that "the earth is its universal spatial structure that embraces the spatial environments of each of us" (1962, p. 222) and that "a particular historical social structure has governed a particular chain of typical communicative processes" (Schutz & Luckmann, 1989, p. 155). So even though Schutz typically refers to cognitive-level processes by using the term 'structure', he also acknowledged them as broader social and material macro-level issues. While in this chapter, I distinguish between the material and the social dimensions for analytical reasons, they are always intrinsically bundled in our realities. For this, I refer to these structures as *sociomaterial* structures, which also encompass virtual realms (Ollinaho, 2018).

Social as Activity

In the view advanced here, the social and the material come together in act-contexts structured by historically unfolding and typically deeply ingrained patterns of human activity: institutionalized social practices. According to Schatzki, social practice is "a temporally unfolding and spatially dispersed nexus of doings and sayings" (Schatzki, 1996, p. 89). For Schatzki, social practice is a sweeping concept that embraces two overall dimensions: activity and organization. Human activity, so to speak, hangs together in particular bundles. Our subjective knowledge and relevance, based on which we interpret and act upon phenomena, originate from our experiences in actual life situations (Leontyev, 1977; Schutz, 1962), that is, activities of various sorts. They are constituted as part of social practices and are therefore from the outset dependent on social reality. The collectivity of the social world and the material, biophysical surroundings in which such social interaction takes place co-constitute the root momentum for activity, so to say. It could be said that social structures are made of activity and material structures are encountered in activity.

It can be seen that tools, equipment or material artifacts mediate activity within social practices (Miettinen et al., 2012), and broader material arrangements, such as infrastructures, connect different practices (Shove et al., 2015). Practices always consume and transform matter-energy through metabolic processes, not only 'endosomatic' metabolism of the human bodies but also, and today much larger, 'exosomatic' metabolism of matter and energy flows that equipment and infrastructures entail (Giampietro & Mayumi, 2001). Materiality cannot be meaningfully detached from the social practices that use and transform; in social theory, materiality ought to be understood relationally, that is, in relation to social practices (Ollinaho & Arponen, 2020). Accordingly, some materiality that practices involve remains essentially unchanged within any particular act of reproduction while some materiality is transformed within such acts of reproduction. I have labeled such relational types of matter as stuck and loose matter, respectively (Ollinaho, 2014).

The practice lens implies seeing the social world as constituted by practices, and "practice is best understood as a kind of institution" (Lounsbury & Crumley, 2007, p. 995–996). Berger and Luckmann (1966) claimed that institutions exist only in connection the recurrent realization of the social drama, which people play out as particular role-holders. Institutions entail processes of sedimentation intersubjective meanings that are recurrently reactivated within practices (Belvedere & Gros, 2019). Practices and institutions involve recurrent activities and, hence, habitualization (Berger & Luckmann, 1966) and "repetition of the same" (Schatzki, 2002, p. 9), even though, obviously, "no act can be performed twice in exactly the same manner" (Meyer & Höllerer, 2014, p. 1329). If "notions of recurrence, typification, solidified patterns, and relative durability are at the core of what institutions are" (Meyer & Höllerer, 2014, p. 1329), sociomaterial structures are essentially social practices that role-holders carry through their recurrent patterned activities that are mediated by technologies and embedded in infrastructures. Crucially, institutional practices are patterned through roles; "roles make it possible for institutions to exist, ever again, as a real presence in the experience of living individuals" (Berger & Luckmann, 1966, p. 92). In this way, roles are linked to institutions, which latter is the key to understand societies qua "agglomerations of institutions" (Berger & Luckmann, 1966, p. 73).

3   DEPRAGMATIZED KNOWLEDGE

In this section, my aim is to clarify how the so-called higher forms of knowledge are created and how they may become progressively separated from their immediate act-contexts. We begin with the basics of knowledge, as conceptualized by Schutz. Accordingly, knowledge is structured in (at least) three ways: as (1) subjective and social knowledge; as (2) general and special knowledge and as (3) "solutions to socially relevant problems" (Schutz & Luckmann, 1973, p. 294), which all are dependent on the particular social reality. Even though the subjective acquisition of knowledge is the origins of all knowledge, most of subjective knowledge "as a preorganized stock of problems, with the means for their solution, procedural rules and the like" (Schutz, 1964, p. 121) is "derived from elements of the social stock of knowledge" (Schutz & Luckmann, 1973, p. 262). Social stocks of knowledge are created when subjectively acquired knowledge becomes accepted and embodied as objectivated as "products of human activity that are available both to their producers and to other men as elements of a common world" (Berger & Luckmann, 1966, p. 49). In other words, through objectivation, subjective processes are accepted and embodied "in the objects and events of the everyday life-world" (Schutz & Luckmann, 1973, p. 264).

When so objectivated, subjectively acquired experiences become "idealized, anonymized, typified, if they enter into the stock of knowledge" (Schutz & Luckmann, 1973, p. 122). The constitution of these objectivations—that idealize, anonymize and typify subjectively acquired knowledge—into complex social stocks of knowledge requires a system of signs: "The typifying medium *par excellence* by which socially derived knowledge is transmitted is the vocabulary and the syntax of everyday language. The vernacular of everyday life is primarily a language of named things and events" (Schutz, 1962, p. 14 emphasis in original). The second basic knowledge structure presupposes that people within a particular society have distinct roles (they may have various roles at the same time) and knowledges. The possibility of separating knowledge from action begins with the creation of provinces of special knowledge: "The separation of elements of knowledge into 'autonomous' provinces of meaning and their institutional specialization" (Schutz & Luckmann, 1973, p. 316).

Provinces of Special Knowledge and Social Roles

While "generally relevant knowledge is routinely transmitted to 'everyone,' knowledge relevant for specific social roles is routinely transmitted only to the 'role-holder' concerned" (Schutz & Luckmann, 1973, p. 299). Specialization and segmentation of common stock knowledge depend on "the degree of division of labour, with the concomitant differentiation of institutions" (Berger & Luckmann, 1966, p. 98). Particular provinces of special knowledge are characterized by certain systematizations of knowledge that are pertinent and accessible only to particular social role-holders and indeed only through initiation to such special knowledge one may become such role-holder. Furthermore, "the specialists become administrators of the sectors of the stock of knowledge that have been socially assigned to them" (Berger & Luckmann, 1966, p. 95). In the contemporary world, "the acquisition of special knowledge necessarily becomes more and more a 'career'" (Schutz & Luckmann, 1973, p. 314). I will again use a lengthy quote to picture how specialization is conceptualized:

> Through progressive partitioning and 'specialization,' the various provinces of special knowledge gain a certain, albeit limited, 'autonomy.' The various provinces of special knowledge become progressively further 'removed' from general knowledge. The distance between 'laymen' and 'experts' becomes greater. On the one hand, relatively involved, more or less tedious, meaningful presuppositions (learning sequences) come to precede the acquisition of special knowledge. On the other hand, even the transmission of special knowledge depends increasingly on role-specific prerequisites. (Schutz & Luckmann, 1973, p. 314)

According to Berger and Luckmann, analyzing social roles "reveals the mediations between the macroscopic universes of meaning objectivated in a society and the ways by which these universes are subjectively real to individuals" (Berger & Luckmann, 1966, p. 96). Roles also make possible for different persons to have different realities, as pictured by Benita Luckmann through her concept of small life-worlds (Luckmann, 1970). Roles make visible the social distribution of knowledge. Schutz sees the inequality of the distribution of knowledge as a fundamental category of social life that "deserves to be made the central theme of a sociology of knowledge which is aware of its true task" (Schutz, 1970, p. 121). The inequality of social distribution of knowledge entails unequal access to expert positions created in different provinces of special knowledge but also stratification between these provinces (Schutz & Luckmann, 1973).

Provinces of special knowledge can be seen as entailing entire professions (Abbott, 1988); in addition to the population of experts themselves, this includes academic and other educational spheres that provide initiation to these provinces as well as a variety of professional associations. Having completed their initiation to particular special knowledge, experts then either continue advancing within the academic or educational sphere of the province or, most often, find their place in the society. Most typically, this means being employed within an organization, a governmental, non-governmental or business organization or then creating their own organization or self-employment. Therefore, provinces of special knowledge ought to be seen as constituted by the practices of academic institutions and the labor of experts scattered around the organizational realm of a particular society and, increasingly, the entire globe. However, professional associations also have their role in such provinces (Greenwood et al., 2002) attempting typically to maintain the profession's coherence and often keep experts updated with the 'advances' made in the kernel of the province. Provinces of special knowledge gradually evolve, not only due to 'advances' in their academic spheres but largely through inter- and intraprovisional competition and collaboration that can take various forms (Abbott, 1988; Comeau-Vallée & Langley, 2020).

Higher Forms of Knowledge

Specialization and differentiated social roles need not imply depragmatization but rather conceal "within itself the possibility for progressive 'depragmatization' and 'theoretization'" (Schutz & Luckmann, 1973, p. 316). Schutz was very clear in that it should not be seen as evident that such depragmatization may take place: "Detachment of theoretical areas of knowledge from lifeworldly act-contexts the progressive de-pragmatization, is a highly specific social-historical process" (Schutz & Luckmann, 1973, p. 303). Only in a particular societal circumstance such a process, in which higher forms of knowledge are created, may be initiated: "Knowledge which is connected with specific social roles, which is borne by these roles, and whose further transmission is part of the range of tasks that belong to them, can be freed from the immediate context of acts involved in the concrete solutions to problems: it can become the Object of reflection" (Schutz & Luckmann, 1973, p. 302).

A presupposition in freeing knowledge from the pragmatics of everyday life is a society organized in a way that individuals can concentrate on their particular roles in the society not directly concerned with subsistence. The availability of an economic surplus, as Berger and Luckmann write, "makes possible certain individuals or groups to engage in specialized activities not directly concerned with subsistence" (Berger & Luckmann, 1966, p. 98-99). They write that this requirement for economic surplus was first noted by Marx. It is the pragmatic autonomy of particular social groups from their immediate act-contexts that affords the creation of higher forms of knowledge. Such groups can create 'pure theory' or purely ideal systems of knowledge that are not directly linked with mastering their situation at hand or, indeed, any 'here and now' pragmatic activity-situation. In other words, a sufficiently high degree of autonomy is the condition for the development of "systems of explicit elements of knowledge on a higher level of 'ideality'" (Schutz & Luckmann, 1973, p. 284).

Higher forms of knowledge are always objectivated as systems of signs and to an important degree idealized and anonymized; most typically such symbolic repository is the language of everyday life. Even if higher forms of knowledge also have their origins in the subjective acquisition of knowledge just as all knowledge is, going back to such origins is virtually impossible because of the typically long and often inaccessible historical development of these systems of signs. Their origins in the subjective acquisition and subsequent objectivations may date back generations. However, it is important to note that such systems are only "*relatively* independent of 'place and time'" (Schutz & Luckmann, 1973, emphasis in original). It ought to be clear that the "further removed the transmitting is from the acquisition, and the more detached the transmitted knowledge is from the stratifications of immediate lifeworldly experience", Schutz and Luckmann write, "the more the transmitted knowledge evades an everyday, pragmatic reconsideration by the one taking over the knowledge" (Schutz & Luckmann, 1973, p. 282).

Autonomy of Provinces of Knowledges

Even though higher forms of knowledge gain autonomy from any particular imminent 'here and now' act-contexts, objectivations of knowledge remain always somehow linked to the pragmatic life-world. It ought to be seen that the "anchoring of even extensively systematized provinces of knowledge in the social structure stipulates, to begin with, that knowledge is detached only incompletely from the immediate act-context and the necessities of its use in concrete situations" (Schutz & Luckmann, 1973, p. 303). It is obvious that the continuation of the institutions requires the recurrent activities of people as particular carriers of social roles; the carriers of these social roles must somehow and to some degree have access to the economic surplus in its different forms. Thus, even though particularly the academic spheres of the provinces of special knowledge have gained autonomy from the direct experiences and relevance of the general populations (Schutz & Luckmann, 1973), they have not become autonomous fields of activity *per se*. Instead, they increasingly have to follow and respond to certain assessments that have typically been designed in administrative sciences, economics and related fields—and indeed, these same provinces have also become obliged to follow these same assessments (e.g., Münch, 2014).

It has long been noted that the academic spheres of the provinces of special knowledge are under tight control and they have to justify themselves by producing more than others do in order to stay in business, that is, secure funding, which is necessary (yet not sufficient alone) for their survival within academic capitalism (Hackett, 1990). The conventional *raison d'être* of academic disciplines can be seen to be tightly linked to their claimed ability to benefit the society at hand, particularly its ruling class, which has been argued to have changed due to transnational practices and capital entering to the world of universities (Kauppinen, 2012). However, as written, provinces of special knowledge are not confined to academic institutions. Most experts in any province of special knowledge embody the province within various non-academic positions and roles as part of the myriad organizational practices.

It seems that what is commonly experienced as relevant is no longer the problem for provinces of special knowledges to solve (if it ever was), but instead to recurrently solve the (unresolvable) riddle of becoming ever more productive (in a rather abstract way)—or at least provide an edifice justifying such claims in order to secure funding. It is argued that such development has further pushed many provinces of special knowledge away from the commonsensical. As Schutz and Luckmann (1973) argue, ever more depragmatized specialized knowledge is produced, 'consequences' and 'applications' of which percolate and become transformed and assimilated in general knowledge. However, the relationship between general and special knowledge is not reciprocal, exactly because special knowledge percolates opaquely down to the general knowledge through its applications and consequences in a way of constructing and legitimizing sociomaterial structures as part of which and upon which people act in their everyday. The "the dialectic between social reality and individual existence in history" is further blocked through such applications rendering the social reality opaque (Berger & Luckmann, 1966, p. 209).

Rivalry Between Provinces of Knowledge

The institutional configuration of provinces of special knowledge produces experts of various types each role carrying with it a "socially defined appendage of knowledge" (Berger & Luckmann, 1966, p. 96). But the practices of these experts and provinces of knowledge they constitute also entail conflicts with each other "in a struggle for a 'power monopoly'" (Schutz & Luckmann, 1973, p. 315). Perhaps the main trophy in this rivalry that Abbott (1988) calls interprofessional competition is the centrality with regard to the operation of the society at large. With such, here labeled as interprovincial competition, I refer to the quest over who ends up providing grand narratives or frameworks for interpreting events, processes and relevance in the society, but also to the prominence of attracting resource flows (gaining prominent chunks of the societal economic surplus), thus enabling the further consolidation of the domination over other provinces of knowledge. Professions aim to gain and maintain their prominence through various types of methods, part of which is an attempt to keep the experts spread out in the society tightly connected and united, for instance, through professional associations (Greenwood et al., 2002). It is also important to maintain "control of knowledge and its application", which means, as Abbott writes, "dominating outsiders who attack that control" (Abbott, 1988, p. 2).

Groups of experts or professions may have conflicts between them that may be articulated in various forms in the empirical realities. Competition may take place over central subject positions in the societal communicative practices such as media and furthermore over knowledges that end up routinely passed on through education and institutional setting more broadly. However, rivalry between different provinces of knowledge is not one that attempts to dissolve others, but such that aims to make the other subservient to it. Certainly, there is also collaboration between different provinces (Comeau-Vallée & Langley, 2020). It is clear that medicine does not attempt to undo, say, engineering or administrative science or *vice versa*. Rather, provinces of knowledge have their particular roles in the societal operation and their knowledges and practices are interlinked a manifold of ways. Yet, they all compete over the same societal resources, that is, people and material resources, such as the workforce and government funding. There is also an ontological struggle between different provinces of knowledge. While the so-called hard sciences rely on exact methodologies and assume epistemologically positivist worldviews, particularly critical social sciences aspire to spread a view that "human world also has an 'inside', that it is a world of individual subjects, of persons" (Luckmann, 2008, p. 280).

Certainly, such rivalry is most typically a question of everyday practices in which different role-holders routinely depend on their identity and knowledge as an expert of a particular field when attempting to impose their interpretation and associated applications on the reality over the interpretations of others. But there are also more conscious strategic activities, also typically highly institutionalized, through which experts in leading roles in the provinces of special knowledges have explicit objectives to advance the interests of their profession. Professions or groups of experts, Schutz and Luckmann argue, "form one of the institutional catalysts of power concentration" (Schutz & Luckmann, 1973, p. 315). It is argued that one such a prominent process of power concentration has taken place in *economics* as the provider of knowledge used to diagnose socially relevant problems and provide solutions to them.

4 Province of Special Knowledge of Economics

Even though the main objective of this chapter is to provide conceptual clarification of depragmatized knowledges and their role in bringing about sociomaterial structures, I find it important to root the conceptual view through some empirical considerations. I will illustrate the conceptual view with a glimpse into economics as a province of special knowledge. Money and economic affairs have become part of the everyday life-worlds also through their role in the media, as economic news have become part of the routinely transmitted core of television (Boydstun et al., 2018). Economy has become the main concern in societies as so many things depend—impinge—upon it. It can be noted from the outset that economics and economists have gained entrance to the dominant positions in institutions that control the creation of money, such as central banks, ministries of finance as well as commercial banks and other financial institutions (Nelson, 2022). When linking such prominent positions with a trivial observation that money has become indispensable for a decent life in virtually any society today (Mellor, 2019; Ollinaho & Arponen, 2020), it can be said that the province of special knowledge of economics has become one of the most prominent provinces of special knowledge, if not *the* most prominent.

Intra-provincial Struggles

However, provinces of special knowledge are rarely unified within. There may be intense struggles within particular provinces. So, even though the neoclassical branch of economics is the singular hegemonic paradigm within economics and has been for a good while, it has continuously been challenged by heterodox economists not aligned with the mainstream conceptions (e.g., Gills & Morgan, 2021; Hudson, 2016; Keen, 2011). Indeed, orthodox knowledge within the province of economics is under constant challenge and alternatives such as ecological economics and feminist economics have been gaining ground within economics (Berik & Kongar, 2021; Hanaček et al., 2020). Mainstream experts quite naturally fight back with an attempt to maintain their centrality in providing the lenses for interpreting the world as well as holding on to the central subject positions and resource flows, but the exacerbating anomalies such as the environmental predicament and inequalities that the current orthodoxy fails to address adequately make such defensive practices more difficult.

Some particular knowledge-related issues over which such struggle within economics takes place are the right ends and means of development (and what development means), the relationship between economic growth and wellbeing, the essence of and control over money and debt, and issues of gender and race. But there are also world systemic questions over capital accumulation, the nature of economics and economic affairs, the nature of global trade and investment, the relationship between the so-called Global North and the Global South. Even though it claims differently, neoclassical economics is a thoroughly political frame that grants agency to markets and their famous invisible hand, thereby naturalizing and mystifying even the most predatory and destructive relations between groups (or classes) of people, organizations and nations as natural laws of economics. Assumptions matter. For instance, by ignoring the phenomenon of rentier income, the current economics orthodoxy calls for a limitless growth of the extractivist rentier class (Hudson, 2016); by ignoring the debt-nature of money, it allows the continuous drain of wealth from the Global South to the Global North and the maintenance of the scarcity of money (Hickel et al., 2021; Järvensivu, 2016); by downplaying the gravity of the climate change, it allows the continuation of the exponential economic growth (Keen, 2020).

Problems and Solutions

It may be seen that provinces of special knowledge make two general types of claims: they observe and justify what are relevant social problems to be solved and they provide the (theoretical) means to resolve such problems. Certainly, the province of special knowledge that diagnoses a problem need not be the same province that provides solutions to it. Provinces of special knowledge do not directly voice these problems to the societal discourses, but through knowledge embodied in role-holders (experts) and through media of various kinds.

As written, the provinces of special knowledge contain entire professions, members of which work are scattered in a range of organizations in a society. Through their labor, typically salaried work, people initiated into a particular province of special knowledge apply their knowledge routinely in their duties. Many of the applications ought to be seen as being done through such mechanism, rather than through the direct application of academic knowledge. This is important with regard to how particular elements of special knowledge may endure even under possible Kuhnian paradigmatic scientific revolutions (Kuhn, 1962) in the academic spheres of the provinces. Professional associations have a pertinent role not only in organizing professions but also in inflicting changes in institutions (Greenwood et al., 2002).

Another distinct type of mechanism through which special knowledges become applied is the media. Problems that are relevant—or at least that have some relevancy—for 'everyone' are typically debated (also) in public arenas. In such political debates, several special knowledges are applied. Even though experts are already routinely listened to, such as in newspapers, and experts of various types also write to them directly, mostly such texts are written by journalists—who, of course, are experts as well. Regardless of this, the essential issue is that there is a medium through which knowledge created in provinces of special knowledge typically goes through when it is applied to yield a solution to a particular societal problem. In other words, experts need a loudspeaker, which in general can be referred to as the media. While the media is certainly fragmented and not unified in its stances—in terms of what kind of knowledge is applied within—it can be seen that provinces of special knowledge provide the mass media content with which it creates relevant social problems "which require 'solutions', which generate 'problems', which require 'solutions'", and so on (Luhmann, 2000, p. 78). Such a view of legitimate problems calling for solutions (Berger & Luckmann, 1966; Schutz, 1962) is termed as a prognosis presupposing diagnostics in the framing literature (Benford & Snow, 2000).

Applying Expert Knowledge

In organizations of various types, experts initiated into special knowledges come together, and distinct types of special knowledges are co-applied to particular problems, so to say. It ought to be seen that economics (in the form of pragmatic considerations and constraints related to issues such as feasibility, profit and growth) is virtually always present in such co-applying. Economics departments and business schools produce economics experts who apply the knowledge they have been inculcated with in virtually all types of organizations. Everything is always calculated in terms of money; economists, controllers, accountants and the like routinely impose monetary frames to activities of any sort within basically any type of organization. Therein they help to induce decisions, policies and assessments typically in line with assumptions underlying neoclassical economics and objectives of endless accelerating economic growth, quest for limitless profits, reduction of labor costs, thrive for productivity and competitive advantages, and so on. It ought to be seen that in this way, economics perfuses much of organized human activities, particularly at work within organizations. It ought to be noted that applying specialized knowledge of economics is not a neutral issue, and therefore, it is not the same as mathematics or calculating the physical strength of buildings. Instead, it always entails assumptions, values, ethical issues and claims that, in addition to being inherently political, are also largely depragmatized knowledge. Therefore, applying economics in distinct instances should be taken to the fore as political acts, rather than as being mere matter of course.

If journalists constitute the profession that works as a medium through which special knowledge comes to be installed in public discourses, economics as a profession (as a province of special knowledge) works as a pragmatic gatekeeper for increasingly extensive parts of life, particularly the sphere of work. Money certainly penetrates non-working spheres of everyday life as well. It works as the increasingly exclusive pragmatic means through which necessities and luxuries alike are acquired. It is a trivial contemporary observation that decent life in any late modern society requires money. Practices of getting income, typically salaried work, but far from confined to it, ought to be seen "the kernel of the contemporary life-world ... which presupposes life outside work as well as structures and delimits activities at all levels of the economy" (Ollinaho & Arponen, 2020, p. 10). Knowledge related to monetary issues in non-work everyday life need not be exact, but most typically simple applications suffice for daily purchases. For larger acquisitions, such as real estate, experts are routinely relied on. But everyday knowledge could better be seen as being part of calculus, not economics in its social scientific sense.

Issues at Stake with Economic Knowledges

In general terms, economics as province of special knowledge brings about sociomaterial structures by applying its conceptual knowledge to a particular legitimate (definitive and accepted) societal problem, such as poverty, climate change or lack of wellbeing, growth or development. The current economics orthodoxy proposes solutions to problems through sets of policies such as continuous exponential economic growth, austerity solutions for debt crises or carbon markets to mitigate greenhouse emissions. It ought to be seen that central provinces of special knowledge are those pertinent social locations that craft these societal problems in the first place, and that such problems are interpretations that are dependent on different assumptions about human activities and affairs. For instance, linking economic growth to wellbeing requires at least assuming that material wealth is a source of wellbeing, irrespective of how much and what type of material wealth there is or how it is distributed. Taken further, one needs to assume that any increases in economic activity eventually end up in bringing more wealth to everyone. There is even a so-called trickle-down effect according to which even policies such as tax cuts for the rich

DEPRAGMATIZED KNOWLEDGE AND SOCIOMATERIAL STRUCTURES...   431

benefit everyone eventually. While such an effect contrasts with the empirical observation of the suck-up of wealth to the top of the societal pyramids at the times of rentier economics (Greenwood & Holt, 2010; Hudson, 2016), this does not stop its use in justifying economic policies.

Applications of special knowledge in economics have pertinent societal consequences. The orthodoxy of economics appears to be closely linked with the ideology of neoliberalism: "Neoclassical economics played the role of a meta-ideology as it legitimized, mathematically and 'scientifically', neoliberal ideology and deregulation" (Bresser-Pereira, 2010, p. 1). By first successfully arguing for the need for endlessly increased material wellbeing, economics orthodoxy provides basic (yet interrelated) means such as growth, deregulation, productivity and markets. How these are then understood and conceptualized determines how they are being advanced at the policy level and put into practice through various laws and within organizations. If growth is not qualified, any source will be used to attempt to increase economic activity and in the recent neoliberal history, this has taken place through expanding the field of economic activity as well as deregulating this field at the expense of democratic decision-making (Teivainen, 2012). Deregulation has taken the means of removing capital controls in global terms, prying open previously public or non-commercial fields of activity such as healthcare and education (Hudson, 2016).

What is at stake at the societal level regarding mere monetary issues is the way how and by whom money is created, what kind of money is created, how much it is created, how it is distributed and made accessible to different social classes, how expensive it is to borrow money, what happens when it is not paid, and so on. Economics also entails other, more diverse societal questions such as employment (for instance, determining the desired [or optimal] level of unemployment); regulation of economic activities; relationships between different sectors of the economy, between different economies, and between imports and exports; the size of the government budget; determining adequate level of national debt; and so on. Typically, such societal questions are not confined within the province of special knowledge of economics but entail applying knowledges created in other provinces as well. However, as written, it ought to be seen that knowledges in economics are applied to provide the paramount framework within which other knowledges must limit or at least position themselves.

5   So What? (With Regard to Schutzian Framework)

Through 'progress', societies have become increasingly specialized so that the share of specialized knowledge has increased up to a point at which all individuals are dependent upon it; one can hardly survive anymore with only general knowledge without the help of experts, an observation that was already trivial half a century ago (Schutz & Luckmann, 1973). We may be aware that we are dependent on the applications of special knowledge crafted in engineering in the form of energy and other infrastructures. We are satisfied (i.e., we can continue our activities routinely) when our mobile phone works and know that we do not have to know how it works ourselves. But we may not be that aware of the nature of applying social sciences knowledge, particularly in the province of special knowledge of economics, as addressed in this chapter. Such applications appear as matters of course in a similar way as in the hard sciences, even though economics is a 'soft science' imbued with politics.

Schutzian scholars have emphasized the pragmatic and the pre-theoretical knowledge: "theoretical knowledge is only a small and by no means the most important part of what passes for knowledge in a society" (Berger & Luckmann, 1966, p. 83). This chapter has emphasized that the use of higher forms of (increasingly depragmatized) knowledge is a pertinent issue in the contemporary realities and can link the pragmatic and theoretical spheres of social activity. This does not refer to people today being more theoretical in their everyday life than before, but instead to that specialized knowledge is used to craft sociomaterial structures as part of which people gear into pragmatically. The phenomena of applying depragmatized knowledge in the societal discourses, thereby creating problems and justifying solutions to solve them, as well as within organizations by experts working within, are massively important with regard to understanding the functioning and the ongoing creation of social realities.

The problem of applying to an important extent depragmatized knowledge to inform and guide policy decisions is that such knowledge need not to be correct in any meaningful way, but it suffices for it to be used. As Berger and Luckmann wrote, we ought to concern ourselves with "whatever passes for 'knowledge' in a society, regardless of the ultimate validity or invalidity (by whatever criteria) of such 'knowledge'" (Berger & Luckmann, 1966, p. 15). Schutz and Luckmann explicated that for the pre-symbolic level, typically embodied, knowledge "pragmatic criterion for the differentiation between 'correct' and 'false' knowledge can be set up as obvious" (Schutz & Luckmann, 1973, p. 283). They claimed that a certain anonymization, typification and idealization of such subjective knowledge always take place when subjectively acquired knowledge is objectivated and in parallel, the life-worldly criterion for the correctness of knowledge gets dissolved. However, for knowledge created in provinces of special knowledge, which is detached from any imminent act-contexts, the criterion for judging the correctness of knowledge is nowhere at sight. As Simmel wrote, "existence rests on a thousand premises which the single individual cannot trace and verify to their roots at all, but must take on faith" (Simmel, 1950, p. 313).

Our contemporary societies are filled with abstract knowledge, which can only be adequately grasped when initiated to that particular (niche of) province of special knowledge from which such knowledge has originated. While the origins of commonly relevant knowledge are opaque to people, this is perhaps even more so for the specialized knowledge that forms complex chains of arguments based on assumptions often derived centuries ago. However, since the mere academic spheres of various provinces of special knowledge have grown to become massive fields of thousands of scholars, it is increasingly difficult for even experts to grasp their field of special knowledge. While in general, institutions exist only through the reiterated 'programmed' and typically routine performances of living role-holders, they exist as an external reality so that "the individual cannot understand them by introspection" (Berger & Luckmann, 1966, p. 78). This further means that questioning the structures of that social reality becomes ever more difficult, since it is impossible to ground (Toulmin, 2003) such problematization on pragmatic criterion of any 'here and now'. It seems that it is difficult to disrupt whatever depragmatized knowledge that is routinely passed on, since the knowledge is not unambiguously linked with empirical realities and is always based on assumptions of various types.

Schutz has been seen as a rather apolitical scholar and this may be read from quotes such as: "It is entirely irrelevant for a description of a world taken for granted by a particular society whether the socially approved and derived knowledge is indeed true knowledge" (Schutz, 1962, p. 348). The above statement may well be taken as true with regard to disinterested observed of the social world (Schutz, 1962). However, if we are even slightly concerned about the massive social and ecological impacts of the use of depragmatized knowledge routinely applied within the province of special knowledge of economics, there is a dire obligation to become interested in both the truthfulness and the consequences of this particular province of special knowledge. The depragmatized knowledge of the current economics orthodoxy needs to be widely contested. We need to check the social predicament regarding the increasing mental "mal-being" (as contrasted with wellbeing) and environmental predicament that have arisen largely because of the continuous thrive for endless exponential growth imposed routinely by experts initiated in mainstream economics in the ever more extractivist global economy (Chagnon et al., 2022). It ought to be seen that this struggle is not one taking place confined to the province of special knowledge of economics but one that entails an interprovincial contestation mainly between social sciences experts, but also social movements of various types.

6   Conclusions and Discussion

This chapter began with an explanation of how the social is made of activity and is historically contingent. That is, it tends to follow a path paved in the past. The paving of the path means that in the past, social and material constrains are and have been created that organize and order social activities into particular formation and direction. How are such pathways of the social realm created and paved? In essence, I have argued that in today's societies, this path-paving makes use of and requires higher forms of knowledge, which is increasingly depragmatized. Certainly, the path is not forged only with knowledge, but power structures, particularly the control of the central subject positions (at the global-level UN organizations, dominant governments [particularly the

US], large corporations, the media), are inherent in this. Provinces of special knowledge as conceptualized by Schutz are important social assemblages through which such higher forms of knowledge are not only created and applied but those provinces compete for the prominence as suppliers of knowledge to the society as well as for economic surplus.

This chapter conceptualized the role of special knowledge of economics in designing and justifying sociomaterial structures at different levels of society. Sociomaterial structures can be conceptualized as a confluence of social practices that role-holders carry through their recurrent patterned activities and technologies and infrastructures that are encountered in such activities. In brief, at the societal level, legitimate problems such as employment, growth and productivity are used to justify solutions such as deregulation and competition. At the organizational level, legitimate problems such as feasibility, profitability and growth are routinely used to justify 'solutions' such as productivity, economies of scale and cost reductions. In the non-working everyday life, the application of economics is typically so simple that little other than elementary level mathematics is used in daily tasks. It could be seen that the lower in the nested system or institutionalized practices (Holm, 1995; Ollinaho, 2023) we look, the more economics becomes mere calculus. And *vice versa*: the higher in this nested system we analyze, particularly at the world system level (Frank & Gills, 1993), the more economics entails political issues that the scientific edifice of neoclassical economics thrives to depoliticize.

The daily material constraints or structures such as the urban infrastructure, food production and the Internet are increasingly artificial or human-made, since the 'natural' environment constituted by all the other species has been pushed to the margins of societies. In other words, it is not so much the climatic conditions or the other-than-humans that determine the material constraints for the everyday in the urban areas, but the built environment, such as houses, roads, energy system, etc. For their part, the constraints that are characteristically social are social practices as part of which people act in their daily life. While provinces of special knowledge provide justifications for creating and maintaining such sociomaterial structures, it should be clear that "the chain of transmission *can* be interrupted for certain elements of knowledge and even for whole provinces of knowledge" (Schutz & Luckmann, 1973, p. 297, emphasis added). It should be seen that this is extremely difficult.

As depragmatized knowledge is not imminently linked to any 'here and now' act-context, such knowledge can be most adequately disrupted through symbolic means: through questioning and problematizing its assumptions and the way how such knowledge was derived in the first place (Ollinaho & Pajunen, 2019). However, even though the assumptions on which entire theories are built would not be waterproof, which is the case of neoclassical economics (e.g., Hudson, 2016; Keen, 2011), it is not straightforward to end up dismantling such theories. Certainly, anomalies such as the great financial crisis, that was not anticipated by any neoclassical economist and still cannot be explained within its frames, can be of help when attempting to dethrone the current economics orthodoxy. However, due to the detachment from empirical contexts, the occupation of the major subject positions in public discourse arenas and, perhaps most pertinently, the entire population of experts initiated in neoclassical economics will ensure that it is extremely difficult to dethrone it. Due to the routine application by populations of economists at work, economic growth, a major item of knowledge in the toolbox of mainstream economics, incessantly surfaces in government policies and in the UN's goals for sustainable development (Kreinin & Aigner, 2022). Thereby it constitutes a frame of relevance, contextual background and a set of constraints for other policies and practices. However, it should not be difficult to understand that sustainability in a finite planet is incommensurate with economic growth *ad infinitum*.

To illustrate what continuous economic growth means, let us think of 3% annual growth of the world economy. Such a rate of growth means doubling the economy in about 20 years. In 2100, the size of the economy would be around 10 times bigger, in 2200 around 200 times bigger and in 2300 nearly *4000* times bigger than today. Given the impossibility of decoupling growth from material throughput (Hanaček et al., 2020; Hickel, 2020; Kallis, 2020), such exponential growth is a mere impossibility in the longer term. Even attempts to pursue ever-accelerating patterns of growth are destructive both with regard to the social realm as well as to the planetary environment (Chagnon et al., 2022; Gills & Morgan, 2021; Hickel, 2020; Krausmann et al., 2018), as growth requires the continuous cheapening of raw materials and labor (Patel & Moore, 2017). The degrowth literature has proliferated in the past decade, taking to the fore and questioning the established patterns of continuous economic growth, the very root of the destructive path we are steadfastly advancing.

While the relationship of the work of Schutz and Austrian school of economics has been a focus of phenomenological analysis (López, 2016; Pietrykowski, 1996) and there are some phenomenological accounts of economics (e.g., Ailon, 2020; Knudsen, 2004), economic growth and even capitalism remain largely neglected in social phenomenology and there would be much to cover in theorizing phenomenological political economy. Indeed, Schutzian research could benefit from focusing on economic activities also because they are "fundamental requirements for social institutions to exist and reproduce themselves and, further, the dynamics of capitalism deeply impact social relations and consciousness" (Gunderson et al., 2020, p. 47). Also, as money has become indispensable for decent life in contemporary societies, practices of incomegetting have acquired centrality as structurers of everyday life and therefore established as prominent mediators of human-nature metabolism (Ollinaho & Arponen, 2020). Enlightening social practices linked with money and relevances they impose to life-worlds through phenomenological scrutiny would be important not only with regard to everyday practices but also and perhaps principally in terms of national and global structures that end up imposing social and material constraints to everyone in business-as-usual futures (Ollinaho, 2023). While this chapter focused on explaining the depragmatized nature of knowledge used to create social structures in more general terms, it also aimed to point to some relevant directions phenomenological research could advance in order to contribute to sustainability transitions.

References

Abbott, A. (1988). *The System of Professions: An Essay on the Division of Expert Labor.* University of Chicago Press.

Ailon, G. (2020). The Phenomenology of Homo Economicus. *Sociological Theory, 38*(1), 36–50. https://doi.org/10.1177/0735275120904981

Belvedere, C., & Gros, A. (2019). The Phenomenology of Social Institutions in the Schutzian Tradition. *Schutzian Research, 11,* 43–74. https://doi.org/10.5840/schutz2019113

Benford, R. D., & Snow, D. A. (2000). Framing Processes and Social Movements: An Overview and Assessment. *Annual Review of Sociology, 26*(1), 611–639. https://doi.org/10.1146/annurev.soc.26.1.611

Berger, P., & Luckmann, T. (1966). *The Social Construction of Reality: A Treatise in the Sociology of Knowledge.* Doubleday.

Berik, G., & Kongar, E. (Eds.). (2021). *The Routledge handbook of feminist economics.* Routledge.

Boydstun, A. E., Highton, B., & Linn, S. (2018). Assessing the Relationship between Economic News Coverage and Mass Economic Attitudes. *Political Research Quarterly, 71*(4), 989–1000. https://doi.org/10.1177/1065912918775248

Bresser-Pereira, L. C. (2010). The global financial crisis, neoclassical economics, and the neoliberal years of capitalism. *Revue de La Régulation, 7*(1). https://doi.org/10.4000/regulation.7729

Chagnon, C. W., Durante, F., Gills, B. K., Hagolani-Albov, S. E., Hokkanen, S., Kangasluoma, S. M. J., Konttinen, H., Kröger, M., LaFleur, W., Ollinaho, O., & Vuola, M. P. S. (2022). From extractivism to global extractivism: The evolution of an organizing concept. *The Journal of Peasant Studies, 1–33.* https://doi.org/10.1080/03066150.2022.2069015

Comeau-Vallée, M., & Langley, A. (2020). The Interplay of Inter- and Intraprofessional Boundary Work in Multidisciplinary Teams. *Organization Studies, 41*(12), 1649–1672. https://doi.org/10.1177/0170840619848020

Frank, A. G., & Gills, B. (Eds.). (1993). *The World System: Five hundred years or five thousand?* Routledge.

Giampietro, M., & Mayumi, K. (2001). Multiple-Scale Integrated Assessment of Societal Metabolism: Introducing the Approach. *Population and Environment, 22*(2), 109–153.

Gills, B., & Morgan, J. (2021). Teaching climate complacency: Mainstream economics textbooks and the need for transformation in economics education. *Globalizations, 18*(7), 1189–1205. https://doi.org/10.1080/14747731.2020.1808413

Greenwood, D. T., & Holt, R. P. F. (2010). Growth, Inequality and Negative Trickle Down. *Journal of Economic Issues, 44*(2), 403–410. https://doi.org/10.2753/JEI0021-3624440212

Greenwood, R., Suddaby, R., & Hinings, C. R. (2002). Theorizing Change: The Role of Professional Associations in the Transformation of Institutionalized Fields. *Academy of Management Journal, 45*(1), 58–80.

Gunderson, R. (2021). How Do Social Structures Become Taken for Granted? *Social Reproduction in Calm and Crisis Human Studies, 44*(4), 741–762. https://doi.org/10.1007/s10746-021-09592-5

Gunderson, R., Stuart, D., & Houser, M. (2020). A political-economic theory of relevance: Explaining climate change inaction. *Journal for the Theory of Social Behaviour, 50*(1), 42–63.

Hackett, E. J. (1990). Science as a Vocation in the 1990s: The Changing Organizational Culture of Academic Science. *The Journal of Higher Education, 61*(3), 241. https://doi.org/10.2307/1982130

Hanaček, K., Roy, B., Avila, S., & Kallis, G. (2020). Ecological economics and degrowth: Proposing a future research agenda from the margins. *Ecological Economics, 169*, 106495. https://doi.org/10.1016/j.ecolecon.2019.106495

Hickel, J. (2020). *Less is More: How Degrowth Will Save the World*. William Heineman.

Hickel, J., Sullivan, D., & Zoomkawala, H. (2021). Plunder in the Post-Colonial Era: Quantifying Drain from the Global South Through Unequal Exchange, 1960–2018. *New Political Economy, 26*(6), 1030–1047. https://doi.org/10.1080/1356346 7.2021.1899153

Holm, P. (1995). The Dynamics of Institutionalization: Transformation Processes in Norwegian Fisheries. *Administrative Science Quarterly, 40*(3), 398–422.

Hornborg, A. (2019). The Money–Energy–Technology Complex and Ecological Marxism: Rethinking the Concept of "Use-value" to Extend Our Understanding of Unequal Exchange, Part 1. *Capitalism Nature Socialism, 30*(3), 27–39.

Hudson, M. (2016). *Killing the Host: How financial parasites and debt bondage destroy the global economy*. Counterpunch Books.

Järvensivu, P. (2016). *Rajattomasti rahaa niukkuudessa*. Like Kustannus.

Kallis, G. (2020). *The case for degrowth*. Polity Press.

Kauppinen, I. (2012). Towards transnational academic capitalism. *Higher Education, 64*(4), 543–556. https://doi.org/10.1007/s10734-012-9511-x

Keen, S. (2011). *Debunking Economics – Revised, Expanded and Integrated Edition: The Naked Emperor Dethroned?* Zed Books.

Keen, S. (2020). The appallingly bad neoclassical economics of climate change. *Globalizations, 1–29*. https://doi.org/10.1080/14747731.2020.1807856

Knudsen, C. (2004). Alfred schutz, Austrian Economists and the Knowledge Problem. *Rationality and Society, 16*(1), 45–89. https://doi.org/10.1177/1043463104036622

Krausmann, F., Lauk, C., Haas, W., & Wiedenhofer, D. (2018). From resource extraction to outflows of wastes and emissions: The socioeconomic metabolism of the global economy, 1900–2015. *Global Environmental Change, 52*, 131–140. https://doi.org/10.1016/j.gloenvcha.2018.07.003

Kreinin, H., & Aigner, E. (2022). From "Decent work and economic growth" to "Sustainable work and economic degrowth": A new framework for SDG 8. *Empirica, 49*, 281–311. https://doi.org/10.1007/s10663-021-09526-5

Kuhn, T. S. (1962). *The Structure of Scientific Revolutions (4th edition)*. University of Chicago Press.

Leontyev, A. N. (1977). Activity and consciousness. In *Philosophy in the USSR: Problems of Dialectical Materialism* (pp. 180–202). Progress Publishers.

López, D. G. (2016). The epistemic claim to the life-world: Alfred Schutz and the debates of the austrian school of economics. *The Review of Austrian Economics, 29*(2), 177–203. https://doi.org/10.1007/s11138-014-0280-x

Lounsbury, M., & Crumley, E. T. (2007). New Practice Creation: An Institutional Perspective on Innovation. *Organization Studies, 28*(7), 993–1012. https://doi.org/10.1177/0170840607078111

Luckmann, B. (1970). The Small Life-Worlds of Modern Man. *Social Research, 37*(4), 580–596.

Luckmann, T. (2008). On Social Interaction and the Communicative Construction of Personal Identity. *Knowledge and Reality. Organization Studies, 29*(2), 277–290. https://doi.org/10.1177/0170840607087260

Luhmann, N. (2000). *The reality of the mass media*. Stanford University Press.

Mellor, M. (2019). *Money: Myths, truths and alternatives*. Policy Press.

Meyer, R. E., & Höllerer, M. A. (2014). Does Institutional Theory Need Redirecting?: Does Institutional Theory Need Redirecting? *Journal of Management Studies, 51*(7), 1221–1233. https://doi.org/10.1111/joms.12089

Miettinen, R., Paavola, S., & Pohjola, P. (2012). From Habituality to Change: Contribution of Activity Theory and Pragmatism to Practice Theories: From Habituality to Change. *Journal for the Theory of Social Behaviour, 42*(3), 345–360. https://doi.org/10.1111/j.1468-5914.2012.00495.x

Münch, R. (2014). *Academic Capitalism: Universities in the Global Struggle for Excellence*. Routledge.

Nelson, A. (2022). *Beyond Money: A Postcapitalist Strategy*. Pluto Press.

Ollinaho, O. I. (2012). *Origins of institutional change: Brazilian alcohol fuel program between 1975 and 2000* [Doctoral dissertation]. Aalto University.

Ollinaho, O. I. (2014). Institutions and Cumulative Change. *SSRN Electronic Journal*. https://doi.org/10.2139/ssrn.3303103

Ollinaho, O. I. (2016). Environmental destruction as (objectively) uneventful and (subjectively) irrelevant. *Environmental Sociology, 2*(1), 53–63. https://doi.org/10.1080/23251042.2015.1114207

Ollinaho, O. I. (2018). Virtualization of the life-world. *Human Studies, 41*(2), 193–209. https://doi.org/10.1007/s10746-017-9455-3

Ollinaho, O. I. (2023). What is 'business as usual'? *Towards a Theory of Cumulative Sociomaterial Change Globalizations, 20*(4), 611–627. https://doi.org/10.1080/14747731.2022.2142013

Ollinaho, O. I., & Arponen, V. P. J. (2020). Incomegetting and Environmental Degradation. *Sustainability, 12*(10), 4007. https://doi.org/10.3390/su12104007

Ollinaho, O. I., & Pajunen, K. T. (2019). A Cognitive-Material Approach to Institutional Disruptions: The Case of the Brazilian Ethanol Program. *SSRN Electronic Journal*. https://doi.org/10.2139/ssrn.3365699

Patel, R., & Moore, J. W. (2017). *A History of the World in Seven Cheap Things: A Guide to Capitalism, Nature, and the Future of the Planet*. University of California Press. https://doi.org/10.1525/9780520966376

Pietrykowski, B. A. (1996). Alfred Schutz and the Economists. *History of Political Economy, 28*(2), 219–244. https://doi.org/10.1215/00182702-28-2-219

Rudel, T. K., Roberts, J. T., & Carmin, J. (2011). Political Economy of the Environment. *Annual Review of Sociology, 37*(1), 221–238. https://doi.org/10.1146/annurev.soc.012809.102639

Schatzki, T. R. (1996). *Social Practices: A Wittgensteinian Approach to Human Activity and the Social*. Cambridge University Press.

Schatzki, T. R. (2002). *The site of the social: A philosophical account of the constitution of social life and change*. Pennsylvania State University Press.

Schutz, A. (1962). *Collected papers I: The Problem of Social Reality*. Martinus Nijhoff.

Schutz, A. (1964). *Collected papers II: Studies in Social Theory*. Martinus Nijhoff.

Schutz, A. (1970). *Collected papers III: Studies in Phenomenological Philosophy.* Martinus Nijhoff.

Schutz, A., & Luckmann, T. (1973). *The Structures of the Life-World, vol 1.* Northwestern University Press.

Schutz, A., & Luckmann, T. (1989). *The Structures of the Life-World, vol 2.* Northwestern University Press.

Shove, E., Watson, M., & Spurling, N. (2015). Conceptualizing connections: Energy demand, infrastructures and social practices. *European Journal of Social Theory, 18*(3), 274–287. https://doi.org/10.1177/1368431015579964

Simmel, G. (1950). *The Sociology of Georg Simmel.* Free Press.

Teivainen, T. (2012). Overcoming Economism. *Review (Fernand Braudel Center), 25*(3), 317–342.

Toulmin, S. E. (2003). *The Uses of Argument, Updated Edition.* Cambridge University Press.

Index[1]

[1] Note: Page numbers followed by 'n' refer to notes.

Printed in the United States
by Baker & Taylor Publisher Services